Twentieth-Century Short Story Explication

An Index to the Third Edition and Its Five Supplements 1961–1991

WARREN S. WALKER
Horn Professor Emeritus of English
Texas Tech University
and
BARBARA K. WALKER
Curator, Archive of Turkish Oral Narrative
Texas Tech University

THE SHOE STRING PRESS
1992

First published 1992 by The Shoe String Press, Inc.,
Hamden, Connecticut 06514

The paper in this book meets the guidelines for permanence and durability of the Committee on Production Guidelines for Book Longevity of the Council on Library Resources. ∞

Printed in the United States of America

Library of Congress Cataloging-in-Publication Data

Walker, Warren S.
Twentieth-century short story explication : an index
to the third edition and its five supplements, 1961–1991
Warren S. Walker and Barbara K. Walker.
p. cm.
1. Walker, Warren S. Twentieth-century short story explication.
2. Short story—Indexes.
I. Walker, Barbara K. II. Title.
Z5917.S5W332 1992
[PN3373] 91-9856 016.8093′ 1—dc20
ISBN 0-208-02320-8 (alk. paper)

For Frances Rutter
godmother of
Twentieth-Century Short Story Explication

PREFACE

This Index is intended to facilitate the use of the volumes (twelve) of *Twentieth-Century Short Story Explication* that appeared between 1961 and 1991 and that cover explications through 1988. It lists in one or two lines all of the citations compiled during thirty years for any given short story. Inasmuch as the Third Edition was cumulative, the present index refers to only six volumes, the Third Edition (1977) and its five Supplements (1980, 1984, 1987, 1989, and 1991). The Third Edition is shown as **3 ed.** (boldface), and the Supplements are simply numbered **1, 2, 3, 4, 5** (boldface). The page numbers follow each volume in arabic numerals.

Example:

"Daisy Miller." **3 ed.** 355–56; **1.** 100; **2.** 152; **3.** 201; **4.** 137–38; **5.** 161.

For all volumes of *Twentieth-Century Short Story Explication* we have been guided by the definition of *short story* provided in the Wilson Company's *Short Story Index*: "A brief narrative of not more than 150 average-sized pages." By *explication* we suggest simply interpretation or explanation of the meaning of a story, including observations on theme, symbol, language, and sometimes structure. This excludes from the bibliography what are essentially studies of sources, biographical data, and background materials. Occasionally there are explicatory passages cited in works otherwise devoted to such external considerations. All page numbers in the regular volumes refer strictly to interpretive passages, not to the longer works in which they occur.

Whatever the original languages of the stories themselves, the explications are here limited to those published in the major languages of Western Europe. Although these parameters may seem unduly restrictive, the fact of the matter is that they encompass the vast majority of critical studies of the genre. The growing numbers of competent Indian writers, for example, are far more frequently discussed in English than they are in Hindi, Bengali, or Tamil. Similarly, despite the emphasis on indigenous languages among African states that were once colonies, their major literary journals are usually printed in French or in English.

Over the past three decades 16,691 stories by 2,304 authors worldwide have, to our knowledge, been explicated in major Western languages. Not surprisingly, some storytellers have received much more critical attention than others. This may be largely the result of the quantity or the quality of their artistic production. For the sheer number of their stories receiving one or more interpretations, here are the top twenty authors:

Author	*Number of Stories Explicated*
Rudyard Kipling	142
Anton Chekhov	134
Joyce Carol Oates	123
Henry James	115
William Faulkner	100
Donald Barthelme	93
John Updike	91
Ivan Bunin	90
Nikolai Leskov	90
Guy de Maupassant	89
Ray Bradbury	89
Sarah Orne Jewett	84

Frank O'Connor	84
Katherine Mansfield	80
Julio Cortázar	76
Isaac Bashevis Singer	76
Isaac Babel	75
Mary Lavin	75
F. Scott Fitzgerald	74
Alice Munro	74

But the masterpieces of the genre may well be those individual stories whose narrative cunning, thematic complexity, and tonal subtlety have repeatedly challenged the insight of readers. The top twenty stories receiving the greatest number of explications are predominantly by authors whose names do not appear in the above listing. Only Faulkner and James appear on both lists.

Story	*Author*	*Number of Explications*
"Heart of Darkness"	Joseph Conrad	359
"Billy Budd"	Herman Melville	252
"The Turn of the Screw"	Henry James	219
"The Stranger"	Albert Camus	192
"Bartleby the Scrivener"	Herman Melville	185
"Benito Cereno"	Herman Melville	170
"The Bear"	William Faulkner	165
"The Fall of the House of Usher"	Edgar Allan Poe	165
"The Dead"	James Joyce	154
"Young Goodman Brown"	Nathaniel Hawthorne	146
"Metamorphosis"	Franz Kafka	141
"The Secret Sharer"	Joseph Conrad	136
"Death in Venice"	Thomas Mann	135
"The Fall"	Albert Camus	125
"My Kinsman, Major Molineux"	Nathaniel Hawthorne	125
"The Old Man and the Sea"	Ernest Hemingway	122
"The Beast in the Jungle"	Henry James	114
"Notes from Underground"	Fyodor Dostoevsky	109
"Rappaccini's Daughter"	Nathaniel Hawthorne	103
"The Open Boat"	Stephen Crane	88

Although this volume was constructed entirely from materials within *T-CSSE* itself, we are constantly aware of the help that made the whole series possible. We are indebted to the editors and contributors of such journals as *PMLA, Modern Fiction Studies, Studies in Short Fiction,* and *Journal of Modern Literature*. Our thanks are also due to many other hands, especially those of Amy Chang, Carol Roberts, and Delia Arteaga of the Interlibrary Loan Department of Texas Tech University.

Warren S. Walker
Barbara K. Walker
Texas Tech University

KHWAJA AHMAD ABBAS

"Seven Hindustani." **4.** 1.
"The Umbrella." **4.** 1.

LEE K. ABBOTT

"Time and Fear and Somehow Love." **5.** 1.

PARK ABBOTT

"Last Laugh." **2.** 1.

SUFI 'ABD ALLAH

"The Empty Seat." **3.** 1.
"A Girl's School." **3.** 1.
"I Am a Murderess." **3.** 1.
"I Chose My Husband." **3.** 1.

YAHYA TAHER ABDULLAH

"Granddad Hasan." **5.** 1.

ABE KŌBŌ

"Red Cocoon." **5.** 1.
"Stick." **5.** 1.

ROBERT ABERNATHY

"Hostage of Tomorrow." **1.** 1.

WALTER ABISH

"Crossing the Great Void." **4.** 1.
"The English Garden." **3.** 1.
"In So Many Words." **3.** 1.
"The Second Leg." **5.** 1.
"This Is Not a Film This Is a Precise Act of Disbelief." **3.** 1; **5.** 1.

PETER ABRAHAMS

"The Virgin." **2.** 1.

SHOLEM YANKEV ABRAMOVITSH [pseudonym MENDELE MOKHER SEFORIM]

"Burned-Out Beggars." **3.** 1.
"Secret Thunder." **3.** 1.
"Shem and Japhet on the Train." **3.** 1.

THOMAS ABRAMS

"And When I Die Be Sure to Let Me Know." **1.** 1.

CHINUA ACHEBE

"Akueke." **1.** 1; **2.** 1.
"Beginning of the End" [originally "The Old Order in Conflict with the New"]. **3.** 1.
"Civil Peace." **1.** 1; **2.** 1.
"Dead Man's Path." **1.** 1; **2.** 1; **3.** 1.
"Girls at War." **1.** 1; **2.** 1.
"In a Village Church." **3.** 1.
"The Madman." **1.** 1; **2.** 1; **3.** 2.
"Marriage Is a Private Affair." **1.** 1; **2.** 1.
"The Sacrificial Egg." **3 ed.** 1; **1.** 1; **2.** 1.
"Uncle Ben's Choice." **1.** 1; **2.** 1.
"Vengeful Creditor." **1.** 1; **2.** 1; **3.** 2.
"The Voter." **1.** 1.

ALICE ADAMS

"Barcelona." **5.** 1.
"Roses, Rhododendron." **4.** 1.
"The Swastika on Our Door." **5.** 1.
"To See You Again." **4.** 1.

BILL ADAMS

"God Rest You Merry, Gentlemen." **3.** 2; **5.** 1.

EDWARD C. L. ADAMS

"The Animal Court." **5.** 2.
"Big Charleston." **5.** 2.
"The Big Swamp of the Congaree." **5.** 2.
"A Damn Nigger." **5.** 2.
"A Freshet on the Congaree." **5.** 2.
"Jonas." **5.** 2.
"Thirteen Years." **5.** 2.
"Tournament in Heaven." **5.** 2.

FRANCIS ADAMS

"The Hut by the Tanks." **4.** 1.

ALEKSANDER ADMIRALSKII

"The Genius." **3.** 2.

ADALET AĞAOĞLU

"Come On, Let's Go." **5.** 2.

JAMES AGEE

"Bound for the Promised Land." **1.** 2.
"Boys Will Be Brutes." **1.** 2.
"Death in the Desert." **1.** 2.

"Dedication Day." **1.** 2.
"Dream Sequence." **2.** 1.
"The House." **1.** 2.
"The Morning Watch." **3 ed.** 1; **1.** 2; **2.** 2.
"A Mother's Tale." **3 ed.** 1; **1.** 2; **3.** 2.
"1928 Story." **3 ed.** 1.
"Six Days at Sea." **3 ed.** 1.
"They That Sow in Sorrow Shall Reap." **1.** 2.
"The Waiting." **3 ed.** 1; **2.** 2.
"A Walk Before Mass." **3 ed.** 1; **1.** 2.
"Wall." **1.** 2.

SHMUEL [SHAY] YOSEF AGNON [SHMUEL YOSEF CZACZKES]

"Agunot." **3 ed.** 1; **1.** 2; **4.** 1.
"And the Crooked Shall Be Made Straight." **3 ed.** 1.
"Another Face" [same as "A Different Face"]. **3 ed.** 2; **2.** 2; **4.** 1; **5.** 2.
"Another Talit" [same as "A Different Talit"]. **3 ed.** 2; **4.** 1.
"The Ascent of the Soul." **3 ed.** 1.
"Ascents and Descents." **3 ed.** 2.
"At Hemdat's." **3 ed.** 2.
"At the Death of Tsadik." **3 ed.** 2.
"At the Entrance of the Day." **3 ed.** 2.
"The Banished One." **3 ed.** 2.
"Beneath the Tree." **3 ed.** 2.
"The Betrothal Oath" [same as "The Betrothed"]. **3 ed.** 2; **3.** 2.
"The Black Canopy." **4.** 1.
"The Candles." **3 ed.** 2.
"The Covering of the Blood." **3.** 2.
"The Dead Child." **3 ed.** 2.
"The Doctor and His Divorcée" [same as "The Doctor's Divorce"]. **3 ed.** 2; **4.** 1.
"The Document." **3 ed.** 2.
"Edo and Enam" [same as "Iddo and Aynam"]. **3 ed.** 2; **1.** 2; **2.** 2; **3.** 2; **4.** 1.
"Eternal Peace." **3 ed.** 2.
"The Face and the Image." **3 ed.** 2; **2.** 2; **3.** 2; **4.** 2.
"Fathers and Sons." **3 ed.** 3.
"Fernheim." **3 ed.** 3.
"The First Kiss." **4.** 2.
"Forevermore." **3 ed.** 3; **4.** 2.
"Friendship." **3 ed.** 3; **4.** 2.
"From Dwelling to Dwelling." **3 ed.** 3.
"From Heaven." **3 ed.** 3.
"The Garment." **3 ed.** 3.
"Hemdat." **3 ed.** 3.
"The Hill of Sand." **4.** 2.
"The Home" [same as "The House"]. **3 ed.** 3; **1.** 2.
"Honoring Father." **3 ed.** 3.
"In the Forest and in the City." **3 ed.** 3.
"In the Heart of the Seas." **3 ed.** 3; **3.** 2.
"In the Noontide of Her Day" [same as "In the Prime of Her Days"]. **3 ed.** 3; **4.** 2.
"The Kerchief." **3 ed.** 3; **4.** 2.
"The Kidnappers." **3 ed.** 3.
"Kipurim." **3 ed.** 3.
"Knots." **3 ed.** 3.
"The Lady and the Pedlar." **4.** 2.
"The Last Bus." **3 ed.** 4; **1.** 2; **4.** 2.
"Lawlessness." **3 ed.** 4.
"The Legend of the Scribe" [same as "The Scribe"]. **3 ed.** 4; **3.** 3; **4.** 2.
"The Letter." **3 ed.** 4; **1.** 2; **4.** 2.
"Like David They Fashioned Themselves Musical Instruments." **3 ed.** 4.
"Linen Man." **5.** 2.
"Metamorphosis." **3 ed.** 4.
"Miriam's Well." **3 ed.** 4; **4.** 2.
"The Month of Tishre." **3 ed.** 4.
"Nights." **3 ed.** 4.
"Offerings for the Dead." **3 ed.** 4.
"On One Rock." **3 ed.** 4.
"On the Road." **3 ed.** 4.
"On the Tora." **3 ed.** 4.
"One Night." **3 ed.** 4.
"The Orchestra." **3 ed.** 4; **4.** 2.
"Ovadia the Cripple" [same as "Ovadia the Lame"]. **3 ed.** 4; **4.** 2.
"The Paths of Righteousness." **3 ed.** 4.
"The Sense of Smell." **3 ed.** 5.
"Sheepfolds." **3 ed.** 5.
"The Sign." **5.** 2.
"The Soil of Erets Yisrael." **3 ed.** 5.
"The Song That Was Sung." **3 ed.** 5; **4.** 2.
"The Tale of a Goat." **3 ed.** 5.
"Tehilah." **3 ed.** 5.
"Thus Far." **3 ed.** 5.
"To Father's House." **3 ed.** 5.
"To the Doctor." **3 ed.** 5; **4.** 2.
"Twofold." **3 ed.** 5.
"A Whole Loaf." **3 ed.** 5; **1.** 2; **4.** 2.
"With Our Youth and with Our Aged." **3 ed.** 5.

DEMETRIO AGUILERA-MALTA

"The *Cholo*'s Vengeance." **3.** 3.

JOSÉ AGUSTÍN

"Cual es la onda." **5.** 2.

AGYEYA [whole name]

"Gangrene." **2.** 2.

LARS AHLIN

"Coming Home to Be Nice." **1.** 3.
"No Eyes Await Me." **1.** 3.
"Squeezed." **1.** 3.
"The Wonderful Nightgown." **1.** 3.

IQBAR AHMAD [AHMED]

"The Grandmother." **3 ed.** 5.
"The Kumbh Fair." **4.** 3.
"Time to Go." **3 ed.** 5.

KASSIM AHMAD

"A Common Story." **4.** 3.

AI WU

"In the Mountain Gorge." **4.** 3.
"A Lesson in Life." **4.** 3.

ILSE AICHINGER

"The Bound Man." **3 ed.** 6.
"Eliza, Eliza." **3 ed.** 6; **5.** 3.
"Ghost Ship." **3.** 3.
"Spiegelgeschichte." **3 ed.** 6.
"Wo ich wohne." **2.** 3.

ROBERT AICKMAN

"Compulsory Games." **4.** 3.
"The Fetch." **4.** 3.
"The Stain." **4.** 3.

AMA ATA AIDOO

"Certain Winds from the South." **2.** 2.
"Everything Counts." **3 ed.** 6; **2.** 2.
"For Whom Things Did Not Change." **2.** 2.
"A Gift from Somewhere." **3 ed.** 6; **2.** 3.
"In the Cutting of a Drink." **3 ed.** 6; **2.** 3.
"Last of the Proud Ones." **2.** 3.
"The Late Bud." **2.** 3.
"The Message." **2.** 3.
"No Sweetness Here." **3 ed.** 6; **2.** 3.
"Something To Talk About on the Way to the Funeral." **3 ed.** 6; **2.** 3.
"Two Sisters." **3 ed.** 6; **2.** 3.

CONRAD AIKEN

"The Dark City." **3 ed.** 6; **2.** 3.
"Impulse." **3 ed.** 6; **1.** 3.
"The Last Visit." **2.** 3.
"Life Isn't a Short Story." **3 ed.** 7; **2.** 3.
"Mr. Arcularis." **3 ed.** 7; **3.** 3.
"No, No, Go Not to Lethe." **3 ed.** 7.
"The Professor's Escape." **3 ed.** 7.
"Round by Round." **2.** 3.
"Silent Snow, Secret Snow." **3 ed.** 7; **2.** 3; **3.** 3; **5.** 3.
"Spider, Spider." **3 ed.** 7; **2.** 4.
"Strange Moonlight." **3 ed.** 7–8; **2.** 4; **3.** 3.
"Thistledown." **2.** 4.
"Your Obituary, Well Written." **2.** 4.

CHINGIZ AITMATOV

"Farewell, Gul'sary!" **2.** 4.
"The Rivals." **3.** 3.
"Spotted Dog by the Sea's Edge" [same as "Skewbald Dog Running at the Edge of the Sea"]. **2.** 4; **3.** 3.

AJÑEYA [SACCIDANANDA HIRANAND VATSYAYAN]

"Cursed." **5.** 3.
"Hili-bon's Ducks." **5.** 3.
"Home Abandoned." **5.** 3.
"An Incident in the Naga Mountains." **5.** 3.
"Letterbox." **5.** 3.
"Links." **5.** 3.
"Major Chaudhri's Return." **5.** 3.
"A Meeting." **5.** 3.
"More Important Than Reason." **5.** 3.
"Muslims Are Brothers." **5.** 3.
"The Pagoda Tree." **5.** 3.
"Providing a Refuge." **5.** 3.
"Revenge." **5.** 4.
"Shadow." **5.** 4.
"There the Gods Live." **5.** 4.
"The Traitor." **5.** 4.
"Unblemished." **5.** 4.
"The Words of a Cell." **5.** 4.

VASILY PAVLOVICH AKSENOV [VASILY AKSYONOV]

"Colleagues." **4.** 3.
"Halfway to the Moon." **3 ed.** 8; **2.** 4; **3.** 3; **4.** 3.
"It's Time" [same as "It's Time, My Friend, It's Time"]. **3 ed.** 8; **4.** 3.
"Little Whale." **3 ed.** 8.
"Local Troublemaker Abramashvili" [same as "The Local Hooligan Abramashvili"]. **2.** 4; **4.** 4.
"The Odd-Ball." **3 ed.** 8; **2.** 4.
"Oranges from Morocco." **3 ed.** 8; **2.** 4; **4.** 4.
"The Overloaded Packing-Barrels" [same as "The Overstocked Tare of Barrels"]. **2.** 4.
"Papa, What Does It Spell?" **3 ed.** 8; **2.** 4; **4.** 4.
"Parachuting." **4.** 4.
"Paved Roads." **2.** 4.
"Rendezvous." **2.** 4.
"The Steel Bird." **2.** 5.
"The Strange One." **2.** 5.
"A Ticket to the Stars." **2.** 5; **4.** 4.
"Victory." **3 ed.** 8; **2.** 5; **4.** 4.
"The Village of Sviyazhsk." **4.** 4.

AKUTAGAWA RYŪNOSUKE

"Autumn." **5.** 4.
"The Ball." **3.** 4.
"A Clod of Earth [Soil]." **3.** 4; **5.** 4.
"Cogwheels." **2.** 5; **5.** 4.
"Creative Frenzy." **5.** 4.
"Death of a Convert." **5.** 4.
"Death of a Martyr." **3.** 4.
"Death Register." **3.** 4.
"Dialogue in Darkness." **5.** 4.
"The Early Life of Daidōji Shinsuke." **3.** 4.
"The Fires." **1.** 3.
"The Flatcar." **5.** 4.
"The Garden." **5.** 4.
"Genkaku's Villa" [same as "The House of Genkaku"]. **3.** 4; **5.** 4.
"The Handkerchief." **2.** 5; **3.** 4.
"The Hell Screen" [same as "The Horrors of Hell"]. **2.** 5; **4.** 4; **5.** 4.
"In a Grove." **2.** 5; **3.** 4; **5.** 5.
"Kappa." **2.** 5; **5.** 5.
"Kesa and Morito." **5.** 5.
"The Life of a Fool." **5.** 5.
"A Life Spent at Frivolous Writing." **3.** 4.
"The Mirage." **5.** 5.
"Momotaro." **5.** 5.
"The Nose." **4.** 4; **5.** 5.
"One Day of the Year's End." **5.** 5.
"Rashōmon." **3.** 4; **4.** 4; **5.** 5.
"The Spider's Thread." **3 ed.** 8; **3.** 4; **5.** 5.
"Tobacco and the Devil." **2.** 5.
"Ways of the Philippes." **1.** 3.

PEDRO ANTONIO DE ALARCÓN

"The Comendadora." **2.** 5.
"Death's Friend." **2.** 5.
"The Foreigner." **2.** 5.
"The French Sympathizer." **2.** 5.
"Moors and Christians." **2.** 5.
"The Nail." **2.** 5; **5.** 5.
"The Six Veils." **2.** 6.
"The Tall Woman." **2.** 6.
"The Wooden Cross." **2.** 6.

LEOPOLDO ALAS [pseudonym CLARÍN] (See CLARÍN)

BOZORG [BUZURG] ALAVI

"The Bride of a Thousand Husbands." **3.** 5.
"Dance of Death." **3.** 5.
"Expectation." **3.** 5.
"General Amnesty." **3.** 5.
"The Lead Soldier." **3.** 5.
"Pestle." **3.** 5.
"The Portmanteau." **3.** 5.
"The Sacrifice." **3.** 5.
"The Story of My Room." **3.** 5.
"The Thresher." **3.** 5.

GEORGE ALBEE

"Fame Takes the J Car." **3 ed.** 8.

A. ALBERTS

"The Car and the Nuns." **3.** 5.
"Chase." **3.** 5.
"Green." **3.** 5.

SALIM AL-BUSTANI

"A Shot from No Shooter" [same as "A Bolt from the Blue"]. **4.** 4.

LOUISA MAY ALCOTT

"The Abbot's Ghost; or, Maurice Trehearne's Temptation." **3.** 6.
"Behind a Mask; or, A Woman's Power." **3.** 6; **4.** 5.
"The Children's Joke." **3.** 6.
"Cupid and Chow-Chow." **3.** 6; **4.** 5; **5.** 5.
"A Curious Call." **3.** 6.
"Dandelion." **3.** 6.
"Fancy's Friend." **3.** 6.
"The Fate of the Forest." **5.** 5.
"An Hour." **3.** 6; **5.** 5.
"Love and Self Love." **4.** 5.
"M. L." **5.** 6.
"The Marble Woman." **5.** 6.
"Marjorie's Three Gifts." **3.** 6.
"The Moss People." **3.** 6.
"Mountain Laurel and Maiden Hair." **5.** 6.
"My Contraband" [same as "My Brothers"]. **3.** 6; **5.** 6.
"Pauline's Passion and Punishment." **3.** 6; **4.** 5; **5.** 6.
"Roses and Forget-Me-Nots." **3.** 6.
"Shadow-Children." **3.** 6.
"Taming a Tartar." **5.** 6.
"Tessa's Surprises." **3.** 7.
"Transcendental Wild Oats." **5.** 6.
"V. V.; or, Plots and Counterplots." **3.** 7.

MARK ALDANOV

"For Thee the Best." **3 ed.** 8.
"Punch Vodka." **3 ed.** 8.
"The Tenth Symphony." **3 ed.** 8.

IGNACIO ALDECOA

"Amadís." **1.** 3; **2.** 6.
"The Apprentice Conductor." **2.** 6.
"An Artist Called Pheasant." **2.** 6.
"At the 400 Kilometer Mark." **1.** 3; **2.** 6.
"Ballad of the River Manzanares." **2.** 6; **5.** 6.
"Benito the Libelist." **2.** 6.
"Bird of Paradise." **2.** 6.
"The Birds of Baden Baden." **2.** 6.
"The Bus at 7:40." **2.** 6.
"A Buzzard Has Made Its Nest in the Café." **2.** 6.
"The Eye of Silence." **2.** 6.
"The Folk from Andin Lane." **2.** 6.
"The Heart and Other Bitter Fruits." **2.** 6.
"The Humble Life of Sebastián Zafra." **2.** 6.
"The Market." **2.** 7.
"The Owl's Hoot." **2.** 7.
"The Picador's Mount." **2.** 7.
"Saint Eulalia of Steel." **1.** 3; **2.** 7.
"Solar del Paraíso." **1.** 3.
"Young Sánchez." **2.** 7.

BRIAN W. ALDISS

"An Appearance of Life." **3.** 7.
"Backwater." **5.** 6.
"Brothers of the Head." **5.** 6.
"The Circulation of the Blood." **3.** 7.
"Creatures of Apogee." **5.** 6.
"Dumb Show." **1.** 4.
"The Failed Man" [same as "Ahead"]. **1.** 4.
"Hothouse." **5.** 6.
"Last Orders." **5.** 6.
"Man in His Time." **3.** 7.
"The Saliva Tree." **2.** 7; **3.** 7.
"Segregation." **3.** 7.
"The Source." **3.** 7.
"T." **3.** 7.
"The Worm That Flies." **3.** 7.

THOMAS BAILEY ALDRICH

"For Bravery on the Field of Battle." **3 ed.** 9.
"Mlle. Olympe Zabriske." **3.** 7.
"Marjorie Daw." **3 ed.** 9; **2.** 7.
"Shaw's Folly." **3 ed.** 9.

CIRO ALEGRÍA

"Calixto Garmendia." **5.** 6.
"The Mother." **3 ed.** 9; **5.** 7.
"Muerte de cabo Cheo López." **3 ed.** 9.
"A Piece of Quartz." **3 ed.** 9; **5.** 7.
"The Stone and the Cross" [same as "The Stone Offering"]. **3 ed.** 9; **5.** 7.

FERNANDO ALEGRÍA

"A qué lado de la cortina?" **1.** 4.
"El lazo." **1.** 4.
"El poeta que se volvió gusano." **1.** 4.

SHOLEM ALEICHEM [SHOLOM RABINOWITZ]

"Another Page from the Song of Songs." **4.** 5.
"An Aytzeh." **4.** 5.
"Bandits." **4.** 5.
"Boaz the Teacher." **4.** 5.
"The Bubble Burst." **4.** 5.
"Chava." **4.** 5.
"Cnards." **4.** 5.
"Competitions." **4.** 5.
"The Dreydl." **4.** 5.
"Dreyfus in Kasrilevke." **3 ed.** 9; **2.** 7.
"An Easy Fast." **4.** 5.
"The Enchanted Tailor." **1.** 4.
"The Fiddler." **1.** 4.
"Final Pages from the Song of Songs." **4.** 5.
"Geese." **3.** 7.
"Get Thee Out." **4.** 6.
"Gitl Purishkevitch." **4.** 6.
"The Great Panic of the Little People." **4.** 6.
"Gymnasia." **1.** 4.
"Happy New Year." **3.** 7.
"Hodel." **4.** 6.
"Home for Passover." **1.** 4.
"A Hundred and One." **3.** 8.
"The Inheritors." **4.** 6.
"It Doesn't Pay to Do Favors." **4.** 6.
"The Little Pot." **1.** 4; **4.** 6.
"The Lottery Ticket." **4.** 6.
"Methuselah, a Jewish Horse." **4.** 6.
"Modern Children." **4.** 6.
"Mottel." **4.** 6.
"My First Love Affair." **4.** 6.
"On Account of a Hat." **1.** 4; **3.** 8.
"A Page from the Song of Songs." **4.** 6.
"The Passover Expropriation." **4.** 6.
"The Passover Guest." **4.** 6.
"The Penknife." **1.** 4; **3.** 8; **4.** 6.
"Pity for Living Creatures." **4.** 6.
"The Purim Feast." **1.** 4; **4.** 7.
"Shprintze." **4.** 7.
"Station Baranovich." **4.** 7; **5.** 7.
"Summer Romances." **4.** 7.
"Tales of a Thousand and One Nights." **3.** 8.
"The Tenth Man." **4.** 7.
"Tevye Goes to Palestine." **4.** 7.
"Tevye Reads the Psalms." **4.** 7.
"Tevye the Dairyman." **3.** 8.
"Tevye Wins a Fortune." **4.** 7.
"Three Little Heads." **4.** 7.
"Three Widows." **3.** 8.
"Two Shalachmones." **4.** 7.
"Visiting with King Ahasuerus." **4.** 7.
"A Wedding Without Musicians." **3.** 8.

SIDNEY ALEXANDER

"Part of the Act." **3 ed.** 9.
"The White Boat." **3 ed.** 9.

WILLIAM ALEXANDER

"The Authentic History of Peter Grundie." **4.** 7.

NELSON ALGREN

"A Bottle of Milk for Mother." **3 ed.** 9; **1.** 4.
"The Captain Has Bad Dreams." **1.** 5.
"The Captain Is Impaled." **1.** 5.
"Depend on Aunt Elly." **1.** 5.
"The Face on the Barroom Floor." **1.** 5.
"How the Devil Came Down Division Street." **3 ed.** 9; **1.** 5.
"So Help Me." **1.** 5.

AHMED ALI

"Our Lance." **3 ed.** 10.

SABAHATTIN ALI

"Geese." **2.** 7.
"Hasanboğuldu." **2.** 7.
"The Ox Cart." **2.** 7.
"Voice." **2.** 7.

EDWARD AL-KHARRAT

"Inside the Wall." **5.** 7.

GLENN ALLAN

"Boysi's Yaller Cha'iot." **3 ed.** 10.

GRANT ALLEN [CHARLES GRANT BLAIRFINDIE ALLEN]

"The Child of the Phalanstery." **3.** 8.

MARIAN ALLEN

"Ah Foo, the Fortune Teller." **2.** 8.

WOODY ALLEN

"The Kugelmass Episode." **3.** 8; **5.** 7.

CARL JONAS LOVE ALMQVIST

"The Palace." **1.** 5.
"Skällnora Mill." **1.** 5.
"The Urn." **1.** 5.

CONCHA ALÓS

"La coraza." **5.** 7.
"Cosmos." **5.** 7.
"El legroso." **5.** 7.
"Mariposas." **5.** 7.
"La otra bestia." **5.** 7.

JOÃO ALPHONSUS

"Sardanapalus." **3.** 8.
"Skyrockets in the Distance." **2.** 8.

GHADAH AL-SAMMAN

"A Crime of Honour." **3.** 8.
"The Crossing." **3.** 8.
"The Crow and the Two Time Zones." **3.** 9.
"The Fear of Other Birds." **3.** 9.
"The Great Danube." **3.** 9.
"A Gypsy Without a Haven." **3.** 9.
"The Meowing." **3.** 9.
"Oh! Damascus." **3.** 9.
"The Sixth Finger." **3.** 9.
"That Summer's Fire." **3.** 9.
"The Thread of Red Pebbles." **3.** 9.
"The Virgin of Beirut." **3.** 9.
"The Widow of Joy." **3.** 9.
"A Wounded Serpent." **3.** 9.

PETER ALTENBERG

"A Letter from Africa." **4.** 7.

FUAD AL-TIKIRLI

"The Other Face." **5.** 8.

GUSTAVO ALVAREZ GARDEAZÁBAL

"La boba y el Buda." **2.** 8.

CORRADO ALVARO

"Dorothea." **3 ed.** 10.

PAUL ALVERDES

"Kilian." **3 ed.** 10.
"Die letzte Pein." **3 ed.** 10.

JORGE AMADO

"A Carnaval Story." **4.** 7.
"The Deaths and the Victory of Rosalinda." **4.** 8.
"How Porciúncula the Mulatto Got the Corpse Off His Back." **3.** 9; **4.** 8.
"The Two Deaths of Quincas Wateryell." **1.** 5.

YEHUDA AMIHAI [AMICHAI]

"The Battle for the Hill." **3 ed.** 10.

KINGSLEY AMIS

"All the Blood Within Me." **2.** 8.
"Dear Illusion." **2.** 8.
"I Spy Strangers." **2.** 8; **4.** 8.
"Moral Fibre." **2.** 8.

ENRIQUE AMORIM

"Oxcart Stop." **3.** 9.

MULK RAJ ANAND

"The Barber's Trade Union." **3 ed.** 10.
"Birth." **3 ed.** 10; **4.** 8.
"The Bridegroom." **3 ed.** 10.
"The Cobbler and the Machine." **3 ed.** 10.
"A Cock and Bull Story." **3 ed.** 11.
"The Conqueror." **3 ed.** 11.
"A Dark Night." **3 ed.** 11.
"Death of a Lady." **3 ed.** 11.
"Eagles and Pigeons." **3 ed.** 11.
"The Elixir of Life." **3 ed.** 11.
"The Gold Watch." **3 ed.** 11.
"A Kashmir Idyll." **3 ed.** 11; **4.** 8.
"The Lost Child." **3 ed.** 11.
"Lullaby." **4.** 8.
"The Maharaja and the Tortoise." **3 ed.** 11.
"The Man Who Loved Monkeys More Than Human Beings." **3 ed.** 11.
"A Pair of Mustachios." **3 ed.** 11.
"Power of Darkness." **3 ed.** 11.
"The Price of Bananas." **3 ed.** 11.
"The Priest and the Pigeons." **3 ed.** 11.
"The Prodigal Son." **3 ed.** 11.

"The Reflections on the Golden Bed." **3 ed.** 12.
"A Rumor." **3 ed.** 12.
"The Silver Bangles." **3 ed.** 12; **4.** 8.
"The Thief." **3 ed.** 12; **4.** 8.
"Torrents of Wrath." **3 ed.** 12.
"The Tractor and the Corn Goddess." **3 ed.** 12; **4.** 8.
"A True Story." **3 ed.** 12.
"A Village Idyll." **4.** 8.

RUDOLFO ANAYA

"The Silence of the Llano." **5.** 8.
"El Velorio." **5.** 8.

BENNY ANDERSEN

"The Bouncer." **3.** 10.
"The Break-Up." **3.** 10.
"Distinctive Mark." **3.** 10.
"The Drowning." **3.** 10.
"The Family Friend." **3.** 10.
"Fat Olsen." **3.** 10.
"A Happy Person." **3.** 10.
"The Hot-Water Bottle." **3.** 10.
"Ice-Floes in the Baltic." **3.** 10.
"In the Course of Last Year." **3.** 10.
"The Intercom." **3.** 10.
"It Must Be Possible." **3.** 10.
"Kill Those Bantam Chickens." **3.** 10.
"The Matches." **3.** 10.
"The Pants." **3.** 10.
"The Passage." **3.** 10.
"The Pillows." **3.** 10.
"The Shoes." **3.** 11.
"The Telephone Call." **3.** 11.
"Ulla and Søren." **3.** 11.

HANS CHRISTIAN ANDERSEN

"The Red Shoes." **3 ed.** 12.
"The Shadow." **3 ed.** 12; **5.** 8.
"The Snow Queen." **5.** 8.

TRYGGVE ANDERSEN

"Anne Catherine Bühring." **4.** 8.
"Captain Tebetmann's Daughter." **4.** 8.
"The Dead Man." **4.** 8.
"East Among the Skerries." **4.** 8.
"The Golden Revenge." **4.** 9.
"The Great Success." **4.** 9.
"Gullik Hauksveen." **4.** 9.
"In Difficult Waters." **4.** 9.
"The Journey Home." **4.** 9.
"The Last Nights." **4.** 9.
"The Night Watch." **4.** 9.
"Old People." **4.** 9.
"The Story About the Major." **4.** 9.

POUL ANDERSON

"Call Me Joe." **3.** 11; **5.** 8.
"Captive of the Centaurianess." **5.** 8.
"Duel on Syrtis." **5.** 8.
"The Faun." **3.** 11.
"Goat Song." **3.** 11.
"Kyrie." **3.** 11.
"License." **3.** 11.
"The Longest Voyage." **3.** 11.
"The Queen of Air and Darkness." **3.** 11; **4.** 9.
"Sam Hall." **2.** 8; **4.** 9.
"Sister Planet." **5.** 8.

POUL ANDERSON and F. N. WALDROP

"Tomorrow's Children." **3.** 11.

SHERWOOD ANDERSON

"Adventure." **3 ed.** 12; **1.** 5; **2.** 8.
"Almost." **3 ed.** 12.
"Another Wife." **3.** 11.
"An Awakening." **3 ed.** 13; **4.** 9.
"The Book of the Grotesque." **3 ed.** 13; **1.** 5; **2.** 8; **5.** 8.
"Brother Death." **3 ed.** 13; **1.** 6; **3.** 11; **5.** 8.
"A Chicago Hamlet." **3 ed.** 13; **4.** 9.
"The Contract." **3 ed.** 13.
"Daughters." **3.** 12; **4.** 9.
"Death." **3 ed.** 13; **1.** 6; **2.** 9.
"Death in the Woods." **3 ed.** 13–14; **1.** 6; **2.** 9; **3.** 12; **4.** 10; **5.** 9.
"Departure." **3 ed.** 14; **2.** 9.
"Drink." **3 ed.** 14; **2.** 9.
"The Egg." **3 ed.** 14–15; **1.** 6; **2.** 9; **3.** 12; **4.** 10.
"The Flood." **3 ed.** 15; **4.** 10.
"Godliness." **3 ed.** 15; **1.** 6; **2.** 9.
"Hands." **3 ed.** 15; **2.** 9; **3.** 12; **4.** 10; **5.** 9.
"I Want to Know Why." **3 ed.** 15–16; **1.** 6; **2.** 9; **3.** 12; **4.** 10.
"I'm a Fool." **3 ed.** 16; **1.** 6; **2.** 9; **4.** 10; **5.** 9.

"In a Strange Town." **3.** 12.
"Loneliness." **3 ed.** 16–17; **1.** 6; **2.** 9; **4.** 10.
"A Man of Ideas." **3 ed.** 17; **2.** 9.
"The Man Who Became a Woman." **3 ed.** 17; **1.** 6; **2.** 10; **3.** 12; **4.** 10; **5.** 9.
"Mother." **3 ed.** 17; **2.** 10; **4.** 10; **5.** 9.
"The New Englander." **3 ed.** 17; **1.** 6; **2.** 10.
"Nice Girl." **3 ed.** 17.
"Out of Nowhere into Nothing." **3 ed.** 17.
"Paper Pills." **3 ed.** 17–18; **1.** 6; **2.** 10; **4.** 10; **5.** 9.
"The Philosopher." **3 ed.** 18; **4.** 10; **5.** 9.
"Queer." **3 ed.** 18; **2.** 10; **4.** 10.
"The Rabbit Pen." **5.** 9.
"Respectability." **3 ed.** 18; **2.** 10; **4.** 10.
"Responsibility." **3 ed.** 18.
"The Return." **3 ed.** 18.
"The Sad Horn-Blowers." **3 ed.** 18; **4.** 11.
"Seeds." **3 ed.** 18; **4.** 11; **5.** 9.
"Sophistication." **3 ed.** 18–19; **2.** 10; **3.** 12; **4.** 11.
"The Strength of God." **1.** 6; **3.** 12; **4.** 11.
"Surrender." **3 ed.** 19; **2.** 10.
"Tandy." **3 ed.** 19; **1.** 6; **5.** 9.
"The Teacher." **3 ed.** 19; **4.** 11.
"There She Is—She Is Taking Her Bath." **3.** 12.
"The Thinker." **3 ed.** 19; **4.** 11.
"The Triumph of the Modern." **3 ed.** 19.
"Unlighted Lamps." **3 ed.** 19; **1.** 7; **2.** 10.
"The Untold Lie." **3 ed.** 19–20; **2.** 10.
"Unused." **3 ed.** 20; **1.** 7.

ENRIQUE ANDERSON IMBERT

"Blackout in New York." **2.** 10.
"The Determinist Goblins." **2.** 10.
"The General Makes a Fine Corpse." **2.** 10.
"The Ghost." **2.** 10.
"My Cousin May." **2.** 11.
"The Queen of the Forest." **2.** 11.

MARÍO RAUL DE MORAIS ANDRADE

"The Christmas Turkey." **3.** 12.

STEFAN ANDRES

"Hagia Moné." **3 ed.** 20.
"Die unglaubwürdige Reise des Knaben." **3 ed.** 20.
"Die Vermummten." **3 ed.** 20.
"Wir sind Utopia." **3 ed.** 20.

HORACE T. ANDREWS

"The Cricket Pro of Halethorpe." **3.** 13.

LEONID ANDREYEV

"The Abyss." **3 ed.** 20.
"At the Window." **3 ed.** 20.
"Ben-Tobith." **3 ed.** 20.
"Christians." **3 ed.** 20.
"The Curse of the Beast." **3 ed.** 20.
"Darkness." **3 ed.** 20.
"Deception." **3 ed.** 20.
"The Festival." **3 ed.** 20.
"The Foreigner." **3 ed.** 21.
"The Governor." **3 ed.** 21.
"Grand Slam." **3 ed.** 21.
"In Springtime." **3 ed.** 21.
"In the Fog." **3 ed.** 21.
"Judas Iscariot." **3 ed.** 21.
"Laughter." **3 ed.** 21.
"Lazarus." **3 ed.** 21.
"The Life of Vasili Fiveisky." **3 ed.** 21.
"Little Angel." **3 ed.** 21.
"The Marseillaise." **3 ed.** 21.
"My Memoirs" [same as "My Notes"]. **3 ed.** 21.
"On the River." **3 ed.** 21.
"Once There Lived." **3 ed.** 21.
"Peter at the Dacha." **3 ed.** 21.
"The Red Laugh." **3 ed.** 21.
"The Seven Who Were Hanged." **3 ed.** 21–22.
"Silence." **3 ed.** 22.
"The Story of Sergei Petrovich." **3 ed.** 22.
"The Thief." **3 ed.** 22.
"Thought." **3 ed.** 22.
"Thus It Was." **3 ed.** 22.
"Vania." **3 ed.** 22.
"The Wall." **3 ed.** 22.

IVO ANDRIĆ

"Alipasha." **2.** 11.
"Baron Dorn." **2.** 11.
"Bonvalpasha." **2.** 11.
"Ex Ponto." **4.** 11.
"Lives." **2.** 11.
"Loves." **2.** 11.
"The Slave Girl." **2.** 11.
"A Story." **2.** 11.

ANONYMOUS

"Azakia: A Canadian Story." **4.** 11.
"The Captain of Banditti: A True Story." **1.** 7.
"The Counterfeiters." **4.** 11.
"Ellen Linn, the Needlewoman." **4.** 11.
"Narrative of the Unpardonable Sin." **4.** 11.
"The Story of Constantius and Pulchera." **4.** 11.
"The Three Homes: A Tale of the Cotton Spinners." **4.** 11.

S. ANSKY [S. Z. RAPPAPORT]

"The Tower of Rome." **4.** 11.

MICHAEL ANTHONY

"Enchanted Alley." **3.** 13.

RENOS APOSTOLIDIS

"The John of My Life." **5.** 9.

A. APPELFELD

"After the Wedding." **3.** 13.
"Along the Shore." **3.** 13.
"Changing the Watch." **3.** 13.
"The Cold Heights." **3.** 13.
"Cold Spring." **3.** 13.
"The Escape." **3.** 13.
"The Expulsion." **3.** 13.
"The Inn." **3.** 13.
"Known." **3 ed.** 22.
"The Last Cover." **3 ed.** 22.
"The Merchant Bartfuss." **3.** 13.
"On the Ground Floor." **3 ed.** 22.
"Regina." **3.** 13.
"Reparation." **3 ed.** 22.
"To the Isle of St. George." **5.** 10.

MAX APPLE

"Eskimo Love." **5.** 10.
"Free Agents." **3.** 13.
"Pizza Time." **5.** 10.
"Small Island Republics." **5.** 10.
"Vegetable Love." **3.** 14; **5.** 10.

DEMETRIO AQUILERA MALTA

"En cholo que se vengó." **5.** 10.

ARAHATA KANSON

"The Escapists." **3.** 14.

FRANCISCO ARCELLANA

"Benediction." **5.** 10.
"Christmas Gift." **5.** 10.
"The Flowers of May." **5.** 10.
"The Mats." **5.** 10.
"Thy Kingdom Come." **5.** 10.
"The Wing of Madness." **5.** 11.
"The Yellow Shawl." **3.** 14.

HUMBERTO ARENAL

"El caballero Charles." **5.** 10.

REINALDO ARENAS

"El hijo y la madre." **5.** 11.

RAFAEL ARÉVALO MARTÍNEZ

"Bewitched." **2.** 11.
"The Colombian Troubadour." **2.** 11; **5.** 11.
"La Farnecina." **2.** 11.
"Galatea." **5.** 11.
"Las glándulas endocrinas." **5.** 11.
"The Man Who Looked Like a Horse." **2.** 11; **5.** 11.
"Sexual Complexity." **2.** 11.
"The Sign of the Sphinx." **2.** 11; **5.** 11.
"The Wild Beasts of the Tropics." **2.** 12.

GUILLERMO ARGUEDAS

"Quico." **5.** 11.

JOSÉ MARÍA ARGUEDAS

"The Agony of Rasu-Ñiti." **4.** 12; **5.** 11.
"Los escoleros." **2.** 12; **4.** 12; **5.** 11.
"Orovilca." **5.** 11.
"Puppy Love." **3.** 14.
"Warma Kuyay." **2.** 12.
"Water." **2.** 12.

ANTONIO ARGÜELLO

"Yo y la negra histérico-musical." **5.** 11.

MANUEL ARGÜELLO MORA

"Margarita." **5.** 12.

RONALD FRANCIS ARIAS

"The Castle." **4.** 12.
"Chinches." **4.** 12.
"A House on the Island." **4.** 12.
"The Interview." **4.** 12.
"The Mago." **4.** 12.
"A Story Machine." **4.** 12.
"The Wetback." **4.** 12.

ARISHIMA TAKEO

"The Death of Osue." **3.** 14.
"The Laboratory." **3.** 14.

MICHAEL ARLEN

"Ace of Cads." **3 ed.** 22.
"The Ancient Sin." **3 ed.** 22.
"The Black Archangel." **3 ed.** 22.
"The Cavalier of the Streets." **3 ed.** 23.
"Consuelo." **3 ed.** 23.
"Farewell, These Charming People." **3 ed.** 23.
"Gay Falson." **3 ed.** 23.
"The Gentleman from America." **3 ed.** 23.
"The Luck of Captain Fortune." **3 ed.** 23.
"The Prince of the Jews." **3 ed.** 23.
"The Romance of Iris Poole." **3 ed.** 23.
"Salute the Cavalier." **3 ed.** 23.
"The Smell in the Library." **3 ed.** 23.

AYI KWEl ARMAH

"An African Fable." **4.** 12; **5.** 12.
"Asemka." **4.** 12.
"Contact." **4.** 12.
"The Offal Kind." **4.** 12.
"Yaw Manu's Charm." **4.** 13.

DAVID ARNASON

"Sylvie." **4.** 13.

[LUDWIG] ACHIM VON ARNIM

"The Heirs." **3 ed.** 23.
"Isabella von Ägypten." **3.** 14.
"Juvenis." **3 ed.** 23.
"Liturgy." **3 ed.** 23.
"Die Majoratsherren." **3.** 14; **5.** 12.
"The Matchmaker." **3 ed.** 23; **3.** 14.
"Mistris Lee." **3 ed.** 23; **3.** 14.
"Der Tolle Invalide auf dem Fort Ratonneau." **3 ed.** 23–24; **3.** 14.

HARRIETTE ARNOW

"The Hunters." **3 ed.** 24.
"Marigolds and Mules." **3 ed.** 24.
"A Mess of Pork." **3 ed.** 24.
"Washerwoman's Day." **3 ed.** 24.

JUAN JOSÉ ARREOLA

"Baby H. P." **3.** 15.
"The Bird Spider." **3.** 15.
"The Convert." **3.** 15.
"Corrido." **3.** 15.
"The Crow Catcher." **3.** 15.
"The Disciple." **3.** 15.
"Flash." **3.** 15.
"The Fraud." **3.** 15.
"He Did Good While He Lived." **3.** 15.
"In Memoriam." **3.** 15.
"The News." **3.** 15.
"Parable of the Exchange." **3.** 15.
"*Parturient Montes.*" **3.** 15.
"Paul." **3.** 15.
"The Prodigious Milligram." **3.** 15.
"The Silence of God." **3.** 16.
"El soñado." **3.** 16.
"The Switchman." **3 ed.** 24; **1.** 7; **2.** 12; **3.** 16; **5.** 12.
"A Tamed Woman." **3.** 16.
"Topos." **3.** 16.
"You and I." **3.** 16.

IGNACIO ARRIOLA HARO

"Cuarto menguante." **5.** 12.

SHOLEM ASCH

"In a Carnival Night." **3.** 16.
"Kola Street." **2.** 12; **3.** 16.
"A Quiet Garden Spot." **2.** 12.
"Reb Shlome Nagid." **3.** 16.
"Sanctification of the Name." **2.** 12; **3.** 16.
"The Village." **3.** 16.
"The Witch of Castile." **3.** 16.

ISAAC ASIMOV

"Anniversary." **3 ed.** 24; **3.** 16.
"Author! Author!" **3 ed.** 24.
"Belief." **3 ed.** 24.
"The Bicentennial Man." **2.** 12; **3.** 17; **4.** 13.
"The Black Friar of the Flame." **3 ed.** 24; **3.** 17.

"Blind Alley." **3 ed.** 24.
"Breeds There a Man . . . ?" **3 ed.** 24; **4.** 13.
"The Callistan Menace." **3 ed.** 24.
"The Dead Past." **3 ed.** 24; **3.** 17.
"Death Sentence." **3 ed.** 24.
"Dreaming Is a Private Thing." **3 ed.** 25; **3.** 17; **5.** 12.
"A Dust of Death." **3.** 17.
"The Dying Night." **3 ed.** 25; **1.** 7.
"Each an Explorer." **3 ed.** 25; **3.** 17.
"The Encyclopedists" [originally "Foundation"]. **3 ed.** 25; **3.** 17.
"Escape." **3 ed.** 25; **1.** 7; **3.** 17.
"Evidence." **3 ed.** 25; **3.** 17.
"The Evitable Conflict." **3 ed.** 25; **1.** 7; **3.** 17; **4.** 13; **5.** 12.
"The Feeling of Power." **3 ed.** 25.
"Feminine Intuition." **2.** 12; **3.** 17.
"Founding Father." **3.** 17.
"Franchise." **1.** 7.
"Galley Slave." **3 ed.** 25; **3.** 17.
"The General" [originally "Dead Hand"]. **3 ed.** 25; **3.** 17.
"Green Patches." **3 ed.** 25.
"Homo Sol." **3 ed.** 25.
"Hostess." **3 ed.** 25; **3.** 18.
"Ideas Die Hard." **3 ed.** 25.
"I'm in Marsport Without Hilda." **3 ed.** 25.
"The Immortal Bard." **3 ed.** 25.
"In a Good Cause." **3 ed.** 25; **3.** 18.
"The Key." **3 ed.** 25.
"The Last Question." **3 ed.** 26; **3.** 18.
"Liar!" **3 ed.** 26; **3.** 18; **5.** 13.
"The Life and Times of Multivac." **2.** 12; **3.** 18.
"Little Lost Robot." **3.** 18.
"Marooned Off Vesta." **3 ed.** 26; **3.** 18.
"The Martian Way." **3 ed.** 26; **3.** 18.
"The Mayors" [originally "Bridle and Saddle"]. **3 ed.** 26; **3.** 18.
"The Merchant Princes" [originally "The Wedge"]. **3 ed.** 26; **3.** 18.
"Mirror Image." **3.** 18.
"The Monkey's Finger." **3 ed.** 26.
"Mother Earth." **3 ed.** 26; **3.** 18.
"The Mule." **3 ed.** 26; **3.** 18.
"Nightfall." **3 ed.** 26; **1.** 7; **2.** 13; **3.** 18–19; **5.** 13.
"Not Final!" **3 ed.** 26.
"Obituary." **3 ed.** 26.
"Profession." **3.** 19.
"The Psychohistorians." **3.** 19.
"The Red Queen's Race." **3 ed.** 26.
"Risk." **1.** 7.
"Robbie" [originally "Strange Playfellow"]. **1.** 7; **3.** 19.
"Runaround." **1.** 7; **3.** 19.
"Satisfaction Guaranteed." **3 ed.** 26; **1.** 8; **3.** 19.
"Search by Mule" [originally "Now You See It . . ."]. **3.** 19.
"Search by the Fountain" [originally ". . . And Now You Don't"]. **3.** 19.
"Someday." **3.** 19.
"Strangers in Paradise." **3.** 19.
"Sucker Bait." **3 ed.** 26; **3.** 19.
"The Talking Stone." **3 ed.** 26.
"The Tercentenary Incident." **3.** 19.
"That Thou Art Mindful of Him." **3.** 19.
"The Traders" [originally "The Big and the Little"]. **3.** 19.
"Trends." **3 ed.** 26; **5.** 13.
"The Ugly Little Boy" [originally "Lastborn"]. **3 ed.** 26; **3.** 19.
"The Up-to-Date Sorcerer." **3 ed.** 27.
"Victory Unintentional." **3 ed.** 27.
"What Is This Thing Called Love?" **3 ed.** 27.

VIKTOR ASTAF'EV

"The King of the Fish." **2.** 13.

MIGUEL ANGEL ASTURIAS

"The Crystal Mask." **3 ed.** 27.
"Juanantes, the Man Who Was Chained." **3 ed.** 27.
"The Legend of the Singing Tablets." **3 ed.** 27.
"The Legend of the Tattooed Woman." **3.** 20.
"The Looking Glass of Lida Sal." **3 ed.** 27.
"Quincaju." **3 ed.** 27.
"Torotumbo." **3 ed.** 27.

GERTRUDE ATHERTON

"The Bell in the Fog." **4.** 13.
"The Dead and the Countess." **4.** 13.
"Death and the Woman." **4.** 13.
"The Eternal Now." **4.** 13.
"The Striding Place." **4.** 13.

EDWIN V. ATKINSON

"A Study in Ochre." **2.** 13.

PERCY ATKINSON

"Votes for Men." **1.** 8.

A. A. ATTANASIO

"Interface." **3.** 20.

MARGARET ATWOOD

"Betty." **5.** 13.
"Bluebeard's Egg." **5.** 13.
"Dancing Girls." **2.** 13; **5.** 13.
"Giving Birth." **2.** 13; **3.** 20; **5.** 13.
"The Grave of the Famous Poet." **5.** 13.
"The Hair Jewellery." **2.** 13; **5.** 13.
"Hurricane." **5.** 13.
"The Lives of Poets." **2.** 13; **5.** 13.
"Loulou; or, The Domestic Life of the Language." **5.** 13.
"The Man from Mars." **2.** 13; **3.** 20; **4.** 13; **5.** 13.
"Polarities." **2.** 13; **3.** 20; **5.** 13–14.
"Rape Fantasies." **2.** 13; **3.** 20; **4.** 13; **5.** 14.
"The Resplendent Quetzal." **2.** 13; **4.** 14; **5.** 14.
"Scarlet Ibis." **5.** 14.
"Significant Moments in the Life of My Mother." **5.** 14.
"The Sin Eater." **5.** 14.
"Spring Song of the Frogs." **5.** 14.
"Training." **5.** 14.
"A Travel Piece." **2.** 13; **5.** 14.
"Uglypuss." **5.** 14.
"Under Glass." **2.** 13; **5.** 14.
"Unearthing Suite." **5.** 14.
"The War in the Bathroom." **2.** 13; **3.** 20; **5.** 14.
"When It Happens." **5.** 14–15.

MAX AUB

"Juan Luis Cisniega." **5.** 15.

NAPOLÉON AUBIN

"My Voyage to the Moon." **5.** 15.

LOUIS AUCHINCLOSS

"The Arbiter." **5.** 15.
"The Covenant." **5.** 15.
"The Diplomat." **5.** 15.
"The Fall." **5.** 15.
"In the Beauty of the Lilies Christ Was Born Across the Sea." **5.** 15.
"The Martyr." **5.** 15.
"The Penultimate Puritan." **5.** 15.
"The Triplets." **5.** 15.

MARY HUNTER AUSTIN

"The Bandit's Prayer." **3 ed.** 27; **2.** 14.
"The Conversion of Ah Lew Sing." **2.** 14.
"The Politeness of Cuesta La Plata." **2.** 14.

WILLIAM AUSTIN

"The Man with the Clocks." **4.** 14.
"Martha Gardner, or Moral Reaction." **5.** 15.
"Peter Rugg, the Missing Man." **3 ed.** 27; **2.** 14; **4.** 14.

ARCADII AVERCHENCO

"The Young Man Who Flew Past." **3 ed.** 27.

MARTIN AVERY

"Five-Cent Photograph." **3.** 20.
"Santa's Village." **4.** 14.

RENÉ AVILÉS FABILA

"The Perfect Triangle." **3.** 20.

FRANCISCO AYALA

"El ángel de Bernini, mi ángel." **5.** 16.
"Un *quid pro quo,* o *Who Is Who.*" **4.** 14.

MARCEL AYMÉ

"Les Boeufs." **3 ed.** 28.
"Les Bottes de sept lieues." **2.** 14.
"La Canne." **2.** 14.
"La Carte." **2.** 14.
"Le Chien." **3 ed.** 28.
"La Clé sous le paillasson." **2.** 14.
"Les Clochards." **2.** 14.
"Les Cygnes." **3 ed.** 28.
"Dermuche." **2.** 14.
"Deux victimes." **2.** 14.
"En arriète." **2.** 14.
"En attendant." **2.** 14.
"La Fabrique." **2.** 15.

"Fiançailles." **2.** 15.
"L'Huissier." **2.** 15.
"L'Individu." **2.** 15.
"Josse." **2.** 15.
"Légende poldève." **2.** 15.
"Le Loup." **2.** 15.
"Le Mauvais Jars." **3 ed.** 28.
"Le Passe-muraille." **2.** 15.
"Rechute." **2.** 15.
"Samson." **2.** 15.
"Traversée de Paris." **2.** 15.
"La Vamp et le Normalien." **2.** 15.
"Le Vin de Paris." **2.** 15.

CHINGIZ AYTMATOV

"The Early Cranes." **5.** 16.

AZORÍN [JOSÉ MARTÍNEZ RUIZ]

"The Closed House." **2.** 15.
"The Clouds." **2.** 15.
"Don Quixote, Vanquished." **2.** 16.
"The Good Judge." **2.** 16.
"El secreto oriental." **1.** 8; **5.** 16.
"El topacio." **1.** 8; **5.** 16.

MARIANO AZUELA

"Domitilo Aspires to Congress." **5.** 16.
"Flies." **5.** 16.

SAMIRA AZZAM

"Because He Loved Them." **5.** 16.
"Bread of Sacrifice." **5.** 16.
"Cries of Joy." **5.** 16.
"The Feast Day from the Western Window." **5.** 16.
"Hajj Muhammad Sold His Hajj." **5.** 16.
"On the Road to Solomon's Pools." **5.** 17.
"Palestinian." **5.** 17.

ISAAC [EMMANUILOVICH] BABEL

"After the Battle." **3 ed.** 28; **4.** 14.
"Alfonka Bida." **5.** 17.
"Argamak." **3 ed.** 28; **4.** 14.
"Awakening." **3 ed.** 28; **4.** 14.
"Bagrat Ogly and the Eyes of His Bull." **3 ed.** 28.
"Berestechko." **4.** 14.
"Childhood at Grandmother's." **3 ed.** 28; **4.** 14.
"The Church at Novograd." **3 ed.** 28; **4.** 14; **5.** 17.
"Crossing into Poland" [same as "Crossing the Zbrucz"]. **3 ed.** 28; **4.** 14–15; **5.** 17.
"Dante Street." **3 ed.** 28; **4.** 15.
"The Death of Dolgushov." **3 ed.** 29; **4.** 15.
"The Deserter." **4.** 15.
"Di Grasso." **3 ed.** 29; **2.** 16; **4.** 15; **5.** 17.
"The End of St. Hypathius." **3 ed.** 29; **4.** 15.
"The End of the Old Folks." **4.** 15.
"Evening." **3 ed.** 29.
"The Father." **3 ed.** 29; **3.** 20; **4.** 15.
"First Love." **3 ed.** 29; **4.** 15.
"Froim Grach." **3 ed.** 29; **4.** 15.
"Gapa Guzhva." **3 ed.** 29; **4.** 15.
"Gedali." **3 ed.** 29; **4.** 15; **5.** 17.
"Grishchuk." **3 ed.** 29.
"Guy de Maupassant." **3 ed.** 29; **3.** 21; **4.** 15.
"How It Was Done in Odessa." **3 ed.** 29–30; **4.** 15.
"Ilia Isaacovich and Margarita Prokofievna." **3 ed.** 30.
"In St. Valentine's Church" [same as "St. Valentine's Church"]. **3 ed.** 30.
"In the Basement." **3 ed.** 30; **4.** 15.
"An Inquiry." **3 ed.** 30.
"Inspiration." **3 ed.** 30.
"Italian Sunshine." **3.** 21; **5.** 17.
"Ivan-da-Marya." **4.** 15.
"The Journey." **3 ed.** 30.
"Justice in Parentheses." **3.** 21.
"Karl-Yankel." **3 ed.** 30; **1.** 8; **4.** 15.
"The King." **3 ed.** 30; **4.** 16.
"The Kiss." **3 ed.** 30; **4.** 16.
"Kolyvushka." **3 ed.** 30; **4.** 16; **5.** 17.
"A Letter." **3 ed.** 30; **4.** 16.
"The Life and Adventures of Marvey Pavlichenko." **4.** 16.
"Line and Color." **3 ed.** 30; **3.** 21; **4.** 16.
"Ljubka the Cossack." **3 ed.** 30; **4.** 16.
"Mama, Rimma, and Alla." **3 ed.** 30; **4.** 16.
"My First Goose." **3 ed.** 31; **2.** 16; **3.** 21; **4.** 16; **5.** 17.
"My First Literary Fee." **3 ed.** 31; **4.** 16.
"Odessa." **4.** 16.
"Oil." **3 ed.** 31.
"Old Shloime." **3 ed.** 31.
"Pan Apolek." **3 ed.** 31; **3.** 21; **4.** 16; **5.** 17.
"Prischepa's Vengeance." **3 ed.** 31.
"The Public Library." **4.** 16.

"The Quaker." **3 ed.** 31.
"The Rabbi." **3 ed.** 31; **5.** 17.
"The Rabbi's Son." **3 ed.** 31; **4.** 16–17; **5.** 18.
"The Remount Officer." **3 ed.** 31.
"The Road." **4.** 17.
"The Road to Brody" [same as "The Road"]. **3 ed.** 31.
"St. Valentine's Church." **3 ed.** 31.
"Salt." **3 ed.** 31.
"Sashka the Christ." **3 ed.** 31; **4.** 17.
"Shabos Nahamu." **3 ed.** 31.
"The Sin of Jesus." **3 ed.** 32; **4.** 17.
"Squadron Commander Trunov" [originally "There Were Ten"]. **3 ed.** 32; **4.** 17.
"The *S. S. Cow-Wheat.*" **3 ed.** 32.
"The Story of a Horse." **3 ed.** 32.
"The Story of a Woman." **3 ed.** 32.
"The Story of My Dovecote." **3 ed.** 32; **4.** 17.
"Sulak." **3 ed.** 32.
"Sunset." **3 ed.** 32.
"There Were Nine of Them" [retitled "Squadron Commander Trunov"]. **3 ed.** 32; **4.** 17.
"Through the Fanlight." **4.** 17.
"Treason." **4.** 17.
"The Trial." **3 ed.** 32; **4.** 17.
"With Old Man Makhno." **3 ed.** 32; **4.** 17.
"You Were Taken in, Captain" [same as "You Were Too Trusting, Captain"]. **3 ed.** 32; **4.** 17.
"Zamoste." **4.** 17.

INGEBORG BACHMANN

"Alles." **3 ed.** 32.
"Das dreissigste." **3 ed.** 32.
"Jugend in einer österreichischen Stadt." **3.** 21.
"A Place of Coincidences." **3.** 21.
"A Step Toward Gomorrah." **2.** 16; **3.** 21; **4.** 17; **5.** 18.
"Unter Mördern und Irren." **3.** 21.
"Ein Wildermuth." **3 ed.** 32.

MURRAY BAIL

"The Drover's Wife." **5.** 18.

RAY STANNARD BAKER [DAVID GRAYSON]

"Pippins." **5.** 18.

W. BAKER-EVANS

"The Children." **5.** 18.

VLADLEN BAKHNOV

"How the Sun Went Out." **4.** 18.

ANDREI BALABUKHA

"Appendix." **4.** 18.

YA'QUB BALBUL

"Sa'ida." **3.** 21.

JAMES BALDWIN

"Come Out of the Wilderness." **1.** 8; **2.** 16.
"Exodus." **3 ed.** 33; **2.** 16.
"Going to Meet the Man." **3 ed.** 33; **1.** 8; **2.** 16; **3.** 22; **5.** 18.
"The Man Child." **1.** 8; **2.** 16; **5.** 18.
"The Outing." **3 ed.** 33; **2.** 16; **5.** 18.
"Previous Condition." **3 ed.** 33; **1.** 8; **5.** 18.
"The Rockpile." **2.** 16.
"Sonny's Blues." **3 ed.** 33; **1.** 9; **2.** 16–17; **3.** 22; **4.** 18; **5.** 18–19.
"This Morning, This Evening, So Soon." **3 ed.** 33; **1.** 9; **2.** 17; **5.** 19.

LILIA BALISNOS

"The Box." **5.** 19.

JURGI LABRAIL BALIT

"A Man with Two Wives." **4.** 18.

BETTY T. BALKE

"Apostle to Alpha." **1.** 9.

CLIFFORD BALL

"Duar the Accused." **3.** 22.

J. G. BALLARD

"The Assassination Weapon." **3.** 22.
"The Day of Forever." **3.** 22.
"The Drowned Giant." **1.** 9; **3.** 22.

"The Garden of Time." **3.** 22.
"Having a Wonderful Time." **3.** 22.
"The Impossible Man." **3 ed.** 33.
"Low-Flying Aircraft." **3.** 22.
"The Overloaded Man." **2.** 17.
"The Question of Re-entry." **3.** 22.
"The Subliminal Man." **2.** 17.
"The Terminal Beach." **3 ed.** 33; **3.** 22.
"The Time-Tombs." **3.** 23.
"The Ultimate City." **4.** 18.
"The Venus Hunters." **3.** 23.
"The Voices of Time." **3 ed.** 34; **3.** 23.

EDWIN BALMER

"The Private Bank Puzzle." **3.** 23.

JOSÉ BALZA

"Un libro de Rodolfo Iliackwood."

HONORÉ DE BALZAC

"The Abandoned Woman." **2.** 17.
"Adieu." **3 ed.** 34; **1.** 9.
"Brother in Arms." **3 ed.** 35.
"Christ in Flanders." **3 ed.** 34; **1.** 9;
"Colonel Chabert." **3 ed.** 34.
"A Commission in Lunacy." **3 ed.** 34.
"The Conscript." **3 ed.** 34.
"The Duchess of Langeais." **3 ed.** 34.
"An Episode Under the Terror." **3 ed.** 34; **4.** 18.
"Facino Cane." **3.** 23.
"Gambara." **3 ed.** 34; **1.** 9; **5.** 19.
"Gaudissart." **3 ed.** 34.
"The Girl with the Golden Eyes." **5.** 19.
"Gobseck." **3 ed.** 35; **1.** 9; **2.** 17; **5.** 19.
"La Grande Bretèche." **3 ed.** 35; **3.** 23.
"La Grenadière." **3 ed.** 35.
"The House of the Cat and the Racket." **3 ed.** 35; **2.** 17; **5.** 19.
"The Initiate." **3 ed.** 35.
"Involuntary Comedians." **3 ed.** 35.
"Louis Lambert." **3 ed.** 35; **1.** 9; **2.** 17; **4.** 18.
"Madame Firmiani." **3 ed.** 35.
"Les Marana." **3 ed.** 35.
"Massimilla Doni." **3 ed.** 35.
"Master Cornelius." **3 ed.** 35.
"Melmoth Converted." **3 ed.** 35.
"The Message." **3 ed.** 36; **4.** 18.
"A Passion in the Desert." **3 ed.** 36; **1.** 10; **2.** 17.
"The Provincial Muse." **3 ed.** 36.
"The Purse." **3 ed.** 36.
"The Red Inn." **3 ed.** 36.
"The Secrets of the Princess Cadignan." **2.** 17.
"The Succubus." **4.** 18; **5.** 19.
"An Unknown Masterpiece." **3 ed.** 36.
"Venial Sin." **4.** 19.
"El Verdugo." **3 ed.** 36.
"The Vicar of Tours." **3 ed.** 36.

TONI CADE BAMBARA

"Broken Field Running." **3.** 23.
"A Girl's Story." **4.** 19.
"Gorilla, My Love." **3.** 23; **4.** 19.
"The Hammer Man." **3.** 23; **4.** 19; **5.** 19.
"Happy Birthday." **3.** 23; **4.** 19.
"The Johnson Girls." **4.** 19.
"The Lesson." **3.** 23; **4.** 19; **5.** 19.
"Maggie of the Green Bottles." **3.** 24; **4.** 19; **5.** 19.
"Medley." **3.** 24.
"Mississippi Ham Rider." **4.** 19; **5.** 19.
"My Man Bovanne." **2.** 18; **3.** 24; **4.** 19; **5.** 20.
"The Organizer's Wife." **4.** 19.
"Raymond's Run." **3.** 24; **4.** 19; **5.** 20.
"The Sea Birds Are Still Alive." **3.** 24.
"The Survivor." **3.** 24.
"Sweet Town." **3.** 24; **4.** 19; **5.** 20.
"A Tender Man." **3.** 24.
"Witchbird." **4.** 20.

TARASHANKAR BANERJEE

"Boatman Tarini." **3 ed.** 37.

JOHN BANIN

"The Roman Merchant." **3.** 24.

RUSSELL BANKS

"Searching for Survivors (I)." **3.** 24.
"Searching for Survivors (II)." **3.** 24.

KHANATA BANNUDA

"Fire and Choice." **3.** 24.

IMAMU AMIRI BARAKA [formerly LE ROI JONES]

"The Alternative." **1.** 10; **2.** 18; **5.** 20.
"Answers in Progress." **2.** 18; **5.** 20.
"Blank." **5.** 20.

"A Chase (Alighieri's Dream)." **3 ed.** 37; **1.** 10; **2.** 18.
"The Death of Horatio Alger." **1.** 10; **2.** 18.
"Going Down Slow." **1.** 10; **2.** 18.
"Heroes Are Gang Leaders." **3 ed.** 37; **1.** 10; **2.** 18; **5.** 20.
"The Largest Ocean in the World." **2.** 18.
"No Body No Place." **2.** 18.
"Round Trip." **1.** 10.
"Salute." **1.** 10; **2.** 18.
"The Screamers." **1.** 10; **2.** 18.
"Suppose Sorrow Was a Time Machine." **1.** 10.
"Uncle Tom's Cabin: Alternate Ending." **1.** 10; **2.** 18; **3.** 25.
"Unfinished." **2.** 18.
"Words." **1.** 10.

N. BARANSKAYA

"Just Another Week." **2.** 19.

EVGENII BARATYNSKY

"Persten." **3.** 25.

JULES-AMÉDÉE BARBEY D'AUREVILLY

"A un dîner d'athées." **1.** 11; **2.** 19; **3.** 25.
"Le bonheur dans le crime." **3 ed.** 37; **1.** 11.
"Le cachet d'onyx." **3 ed.** 37.
"Le Dessous de cartes d'une partie de whist." **1.** 11; **3.** 25; **5.** 20.
"Lea." **3 ed.** 37.
"Le plus bel amour de Don Juan." **3 ed.** 37; **1.** 11.
"Le Rideau cramoisi." **1.** 11; **3.** 25.
"A Woman's Vengeance." **1.** 11; **3.** 25.

BERNARDO M. BARCEBAL

"Ma'am Weds a Farmer." **5.** 20.

RUBÉN BAREIRO SAGUIER

"Diente por diente." **5.** 20.

A[UDREY] L[ILIAN] BARKER

"Domini." **4.** 20.
"Here Comes a Candle." **4.** 20.
"The Iconoclasts." **4.** 20.

MARJORIE BARNARD

"Dry Spell." **3 ed.** 37.
"The Persimmon Tree." **3 ed.** 37.
"The Woman Who Did the Right Thing." **3 ed.** 37.

ARTHUR K. BARNES

"Hothouse Planet." **3.** 25.
"Siren Satellite." **3.** 25.

DJUNA BARNES

"Aller et Retour." **1.** 11; **4.** 20.
"The Beauty." **4.** 20.
"A Boy Asks a Question of a Lady." **1.** 11.
"Cassation" [originally "A Little Girl Tells a Story to a Lady"]. **1.** 11; **2.** 19; **4.** 20.
"The Coward." **4.** 20.
"The Doctors" [originally "Katrina Silverstaff"]. **1.** 11.
"Dusie." **1.** 11.
"Go Down, Matthews." **2.** 19.
"The Grande Malade" [originally "The Little Girl Continues"]. **1.** 11; **4.** 20.
"Indian Summer." **1.** 11.
"The Jest of Jests." **4.** 20.
"Mother." **1.** 11.
"The Nigger." **1.** 12.
"A Night Among the Horses." **1.** 12; **4.** 20.
"No-Man's Mare." **1.** 12.
"The Passion." **1.** 12; **4.** 20.
"The Perfect Murder." **1.** 12.
"The Rabbit." **1.** 12; **4.** 20.
"Spillway" [originally "Beyond the End"]. **1.** 12; **4.** 20.
"The Valet." **4.** 20.

MARGARET AYER BARNES

"Arms and the Boy." **3 ed.** 37.
"The Dinner Party." **3 ed.** 37.
"Feather Beds." **3 ed.** 38.
"Perpetual Care." **3 ed.** 38.

PIO BAROJA

"The Bakers." **2.** 19.

HÉCTOR BARRERA

"El Judas." **5.** 20.

RAYMOND BARRIO

"The Campesinos." **2.** 19.

EDUARDO BARRIOS

"Antipathy." **3 ed.** 38; **5.** 21.
"Pages of a Poor Devil." **3 ed.** 38.

JOHN BARTH

"Ambrose His Mark." **3 ed.** 38; **1.** 12; **2.** 19; **4.** 21; **5.** 21.
"Anonymiad." **3 ed.** 38; **1.** 12; **3.** 25; **4.** 21; **5.** 21.
"Autobiography: A Self-Recorded Fiction." **1.** 12; **3.** 25.
"Bellerophoniad. **3 ed.** 38; **1.** 12; **2.** 19; **3.** 26; **4.** 21; **5.** 21.
"Chimera." **2.** 20.
"Dunyazadiad." **3 ed.** 38; **1.** 12; **2.** 20; **3.** 26; **4.** 21; **5.** 21.
"Echo." **3 ed.** 38; **1.** 12; **2.** 20; **3.** 26; **5.** 21.
"Life-Story." **1.** 13; **2.** 20; **3.** 26; **4.** 21; **5.** 21.
"Lost in the Funhouse." **3 ed.** 38; **1.** 13; **2.** 20; **3.** 26; **4.** 21; **5.** 21.
"Menelaiad." **3 ed.** 38; **1.** 13; **2.** 20; **3.** 26; **4.** 21; **5.** 21.
"Night-Sea Journey." **3 ed.** 38–39; **1.** 13; **2.** 20; **3.** 26; **4.** 21; **5.** 21.
"Perseid." **3 ed.** 39; **1.** 13; **2.** 20–21; **3.** 26; **4.** 21; **5.** 22.
"Petition." **3 ed.** 39; **5.** 22.
"Title." **2.** 21.
"Water Message." **3 ed.** 39; **2.** 21; **4.** 21; **5.** 22.

DONALD BARTHELME

"The Abduction from the Seraglio." **2.** 21; **4.** 22.
"Alice." **2.** 21.
"And Now Let's Hear It for the Ed Sullivan Show." **2.** 21.
"The Apology." **2.** 21.
"At the End of the Mechanical Age." **2.** 21; **3.** 26.
"At the Tolstoy Museum." **1.** 13; **2.** 21; **3.** 26.
"The Balloon." **3 ed.** 39; **2.** 21; **3.** 27; **4.** 22; **5.** 22.
"Basil from Her Garden." **5.** 22.
"Belief." **2.** 21.
"The Big Broadcast of 1938." **2.** 21.
"Bone Bubbles." **2.** 21.
"Bunny Image, Loss of: The Case of Bitsy S." **2.** 22.
"The Catechist." **2.** 22.
"City Life." **3 ed.** 39; **1.** 13; **2.** 22; **3.** 27.
"A City of Churches." **2.** 22; **4.** 22.
"Concerning the Body Guard." **2.** 22.
"Cortés and Montezuma." **2.** 22.
"The Crisis." **2.** 22.
"Daumier." **1.** 13; **2.** 22; **3.** 27.
"The Death of Edward Lear." **2.** 22; **3.** 27; **4.** 22.
"The Dolt." **2.** 22; **3.** 27; **4.** 22.
"Down the Line with the Annual." **2.** 22.
"The Dragon." **2.** 22.
"The Educational Experience." **2.** 22.
"The Emerald." **5.** 22.
"Engineer-Private Paul Klee Misplaces an Aircraft Between Milbertshofen and Cambrai, March 1916." **2.** 22; **3.** 27.
"The Explanation." **2.** 22.
"The Falling Dog." **4.** 22.
"A Film." **2.** 22; **3.** 27.
"The Flight of Pigeons from the Palace." **2.** 23.
"Florence Green in 81." **2.** 23.
"For I'm the Boy Whose Only Joy Is Loving You." **2.** 23.
"Game." **3 ed.** 39; **2.** 23.
"Games Are the Enemies of Beauty, Truth, and Sleep, Amanda Said." **3.** 27.
"The Genius." **2.** 23.
"The Glass Mountain." **1.** 13; **2.** 23.
"Heliotrope." **2.** 23.
"An Hesitation on the Bank of the Delaware." **2.** 23.
"Hiding Man." **3.** 27.
"How I Write My Songs." **4.** 22.
"I Bought a Little City." **2.** 23.
"The Indian Uprising." **3 ed.** 39; **2.** 23; **3.** 27; **4.** 22; **5.** 22.
"Kierkegaard Unfair to Schlegel." **2.** 23; **3.** 27; **4.** 22.
"The King of Jazz." **2.** 23.
"L'Lapse." **2.** 23.
"The Leap." **2.** 23; **5.** 22.
"Marie, Marie, Hold on Tight." **2.** 23.
"Me and Miss Mandible." **3 ed.** 39; **2.** 24; **3.** 27; **5.** 22.
"A Nation of Wheels." **2.** 24.
"The New Member." **2.** 24.

"The New Music." **2.** 24.
"On Angels." **3 ed.** 39; **2.** 24.
"Our Work and Why We Do It." **2.** 24.
"The Palace." **2.** 24.
"Paraguay." **2.** 24; **3.** 27.
"The Party." **3 ed.** 39; **2.** 24.
"Perpetua." **2.** 24.
"The Phantom of the Opera's Friend." **2.** 24; **3.** 27; **4.** 22.
"The Photographs." **2.** 24.
"The Piano Player." **2.** 24.
"A Picture History of the War." **2.** 24; **3.** 27.
"The Police Band." **2.** 24.
"The Policemen's Ball." **1.** 13; **2.** 24.
"Porcupines at the University." **2.** 25; **3.** 28.
"The President." **2.** 25; **5.** 22.
"The Question Party." **2.** 25.
"Rebecca." **2.** 25.
"The Reference." **2.** 25.
"Report." **2.** 25; **3.** 28.
"Robert Kennedy Saved from Drowning." **3 ed.** 39; **1.** 14; **2.** 25; **3.** 28; **4.** 22.
"The Royal Treatment." **2.** 25.
"The Sandman." **1.** 14; **2.** 25; **3.** 28; **4.** 22.
"The School." **2.** 25; **3.** 28.
"See the Moon?" **2.** 25; **3.** 28.
"Sentence." **2.** 25.
"The Sergeant." **2.** 25.
"A Shower of Gold." **2.** 25; **3.** 28; **4.** 22; **5.** 22.
"Snap Snap." **2.** 25.
"Some of Us Had Been Threatening Our Friend Colby." **2.** 26; **3.** 28; **5.** 22.
"Subpoena." **2.** 26.
"Swallowing." **2.** 26.
"The Teaching of Don B.: A Yankee Way of Knowing." **2.** 26.
"The Temptation of St. Anthony." **2.** 26; **3.** 28.
"That Cosmopolitan Girl." **2.** 26.
"This Newspaper Here." **2.** 26.
"To London and Rome." **2.** 26.
"Up, Aloft in the Air." **2.** 26.
"The Viennese Opera Ball." **2.** 26; **3.** 28.
"Views of My Father Weeping." **3 ed.** 39–40; **2.** 26; **3.** 28; **4.** 22–23.
"What to Do Next." **2.** 26.
"The Wound." **2.** 26.
"The Young Visitors." **2.** 26.
"The Zombies." **2.** 26.

VAIKOM MUHAMMAD BASHEER

"Birthday." **3 ed.** 40.

GIORGIO BASSANI

"Ai tempi della Resistenza." **4.** 23.
"Apologo (No. 1)." **4.** 23.
"Una corsa ad Abbazia." **4.** 23.
"Cuoio grasso." **4.** 23.
"Una Lapide in via Mazzini." **4.** 23.
"Lida Mantovani." **4.** 23.
"La necessità è il velo di Dio." **4.** 23.
"Una notte del '43." **4.** 23.
"L'odore del fieno" [originally "Il muro di cinta"]. **4.** 23.
"La paseggiata prima di cena." **4.** 23.
"Pelandra." **4.** 23.
"La ragazza dei fucili." **4.** 23.
"Ravenna." **4.** 23.
"Le scarpe da tennis." **4.** 23.
"Un topo nel formaggio." **4.** 23.
"Gli ultimi anni di Clelia Trotti." **4.** 24.

HAMILTON BASSO

"The Age of Fable." **2.** 26.
"The Broken Horn." **2.** 27.
"The Edge of the Wilderness." **2.** 27.
"Fabulous Man." **2.** 27.
"I Can't Dance." **2.** 27.
"A Kind of a Special Gift." **2.** 27.
"King Rail." **2.** 27.
"Me and the Babe." **2.** 27.
"Rain on Aspidistra." **2.** 27.
"The Wild Turkey." **2.** 27.

ADAH F. BATELLE

"The Sacking of Grubbville." **2.** 27.

H. E. BATES

"Alexander." **3.** 28.
"The Bride Comes to Evenford." **4.** 24.
"The Bridge." **3.** 28.
"Charlotte Esmond." **3.** 28.
"Colonel Julian." **3.** 29.
"The Cowslip." **3.** 29.
"The Cruise of the *Breadwinner.*" **2.** 27; **4.** 24.
"Death of a Huntsman." **2.** 27.
"The Easter Blessing." **3.** 29.
"Elaine." **3.** 29.

"The Flag." **4.** 24.
"The Frontier." **3.** 29.
"The Gleaner." **2.** 27.
"Harvest." **3.** 29.
"The Holiday." **3.** 29.
"The Kimono." **3.** 29.
"Love in a Wych Elm." **3.** 29.
"The Major of Hussars." **4.** 24.
"The Mill." **3.** 29.
"The Mower." **3.** 29.
"Now Sleeps the Crimson Petal." **3.** 29.
"The Old Eternal." **3.** 29.
"The Ox." **3.** 29.
"The Place Where Shady Lay." **4.** 24.
"The Small Portion." **3 ed.** 40.
"Something Short and Sweet." **3.** 29.
"The Station." **3.** 29.
"The Watercress Girl." **3.** 30.
"The Waterfall." **4.** 24.
"The Wedding Party." **3.** 30.
"Where the Cloud Breaks." **3.** 30.

HARRY BATES

"Farewell to the Master." **2.** 27.

HARRY BATES and DESMOND WINTER HALL

"A Scientist Rises." **5.** 23.

CHARLES BAUDELAIRE

"La Fanfarlo." **3 ed.** 40; **1.** 14; **4.** 24; **5.** 23.

BLANCHE EDITH BAUGHAN

"Pipi on the Prowl." **3 ed.** 40.

BARBARA BAYNTON

"Billy Skywokie." **5.** 23.
"Bush Church." **5.** 23.
"The Chosen Vessel." **3 ed.** 40.
"A Dreamer." **5.** 23.

HERVÉ BAZIN

"The Thousand-Franc Note." **3 ed.** 40.

PETER BEAGLE

"Come Lady Death." **5.** 23.
"Lila the Werewolf." **5.** 23.
"My Daughter's Name Is Sarah." **5.** 23.
"Telephone Call." **5.** 23.
"Thirty-Day Stretch." **5.** 23.

ANN BEATTIE

"The Burning House." **4.** 24; **5.** 23.
"The Cinderella Waltz." **4.** 24.
"A Clever-Kid Story." **3.** 30; **4.** 24.
"Colorado." **4.** 24.
"Desire." **4.** 24.
"Dwarf House." **3.** 30; **4.** 25.
"Fancy Flight." **4.** 25.
"Friends." **4.** 25.
"Gravity." **5.** 23.
"Imagined Scenes." **4.** 25.
"In the White Night." **5.** 24.
"It's Just Another Day in Big Bear City, California." **4.** 25.
"Jacklightning." **4.** 25.
"Janus." **5.** 24.
"The Lawn Party." **4.** 25.
"Learning to Fall." **4.** 25.
"The Lifeguard." **4.** 25.
"Marshall's Dog." **4.** 25.
"Octascope." **2.** 28; **4.** 25.
"The Parking Lot." **4.** 25.
"Playback." **4.** 25.
"Running Dreams." **4.** 25.
"Shifting." **2.** 28.
"Snakes' Shoes." **4.** 25.
"Vermont." **4.** 25.
"A Vintage Thunderbird." **4.** 26.
"Waiting." **3.** 30; **4.** 26; **5.** 24.
"Winter: 1978." **4.** 26.
"Wolf Dreams." **4.** 26.

CHARLES BEAUMONT

"Blood Brother." **3.** 30.

SIMONE DE BEAUVOIR

"The Age of Discretion." **5.** 24.
"Anne." **5.** 24.
"Chantal." **5.** 24.
"Lisa." **5.** 24.
"Marcelle." **5.** 24.
"Marguerite." **5.** 24.
"Monologue." **5.** 24.
"A Very Easy Death." **5.** 24.
"The Woman Destroyed." **5.** 24.

LOUIS BECHE

"The Awful Duel on Utuana." **3 ed.** 41.
"A Basket of Breadfruit." **3 ed.** 41.
"A Blackbirding Incident." **3 ed.** 41.
"The Chilean Bluejacket." **3 ed.** 41.
"A Dead Loss." **3 ed.** 41.
"The Fate of the *Alida*." **3 ed.** 41.
"'Frank' the Trader." **3 ed.** 41.
"Lufton's Guest." **3 ed.** 41.
"Luliban of the Pool." **3 ed.** 41.
"The Man Who Knew Everything." **3 ed.** 41.
"Nerida, the Maid of Suwarrow." **3 ed.** 41.
"Ninia." **3 ed.** 41.
"Saunders and the Devil Fish." **3 ed.** 41.
"A Tale of a Mask." **3 ed.** 41.
"The Trader's Wife." **3 ed.** 41.
"Yorke the Adventurer." **3 ed.** 41.

WARREN BECK

"Detour in the Dark." **3 ed.** 42.

SAMUEL BECKETT

"Afar a Bird." **3.** 30.
"All Strange Away." **5.** 24.
"Assumption." **3 ed.** 42; **1.** 14; **3.** 30; **4.** 26.
"The Calmative." **3 ed.** 42; **1.** 14; **2.** 28; **3.** 30; **4.** 26; **5.** 25.
"A Case in a Thousand." **3 ed.** 42; **3.** 30; **4.** 26.
"Dante and the Lobster." **3 ed.** 42; **1.** 14; **2.** 28; **4.** 26.
"Ding Dong." **3 ed.** 42; **2.** 28.
"Draff." **3 ed.** 42.
"Echo's Bones." **3.** 30.
"The End." **3 ed.** 42; **1.** 14; **2.** 28; **3.** 30; **4.** 26.
"Enough." **3 ed.** 42; **1.** 15; **2.** 28; **3.** 31; **4.** 26; **5.** 25.
"The Expelled." **3 ed.** 42; **1.** 15; **2.** 28.
"Fingal." **3 ed.** 42; **2.** 28.
"First Love." **1.** 15; **2.** 28; **3.** 31; **4.** 26; **5.** 25.
"For to End Yet Again." **2.** 28.
"From an Abandoned Work." **3 ed.** 42; **2.** 28.
"He Is Barehead." **5.** 25.
"Horn Came Always." **2.** 29.
"How It Is." **3 ed.** 43; **1.** 15; **3.** 31; **4.** 26; **5.** 25.
"Imagination Dead Imagine." **3 ed.** 43; **1.** 15; **3.** 31; **4.** 26; **5.** 25.
"Lessness" [same as "Without"]. **3 ed.** 43; **1.** 15; **3.** 31.
"The Lost Ones." **3 ed.** 43; **1.** 15; **3.** 31; **5.** 25.
"Love and Lethe." **3 ed.** 43.
"Old Earth." **4.** 26; **5.** 25.
"Ping." **3 ed.** 43; **1.** 15; **3.** 31; **4.** 26.
"Premier Amour." **3 ed.** 43.
"Residue." **3 ed.** 43.
"Still." **3.** 31; **4.** 27.
"Texts for Nothing." **3 ed.** 43.
"Walking On." **3 ed.** 43.
"A Wet Night." **3 ed.** 43; **1.** 15.
"What a Misfortune." **3 ed.** 43.
"Yellow." **3 ed.** 43.

WILLIAM BECKFORD

"The Vision" [originally "Long Story"]. **3.** 31.

GUSTAVO ADOLFO BÉCQUER

"Los ojos verdes." **3.** 31; **5.** 25.

RAJINDAR SINGH BEDI

"Lajwanti." **3 ed.** 44.

MAX BEERBOHM

"The Crime." **5.** 25.
"The Dreadful Dragon of Hay Hill." **3 ed.** 44.
"Enoch Soames." **2.** 29.
"Hilary Maltby and Stephen Braxton." **3 ed.** 44.
"Yai and the Moon." **3 ed.** 44.

SAMAD BEHRANGI

"The Bald Pigeon Keeper." **3.** 31.
"The Little Black Fish." **3.** 32.
"One Peach—A Thousand Peaches." **3.** 32.
"Twenty-Four Restless Hours." **3.** 32.

EMILIO BELAVAL

"Nuestra Cruz Menchaca." **5.** 25.

MARY BELL

"Sing Kee's China-Lily." **2.** 29; **3.** 32.

SAUL BELLOW

"Address by Gooley MacDowell to the Hasbeens Club of Chicago." **3 ed.** 44.
"Cousins." **4.** 27; **5.** 25.
"Dora." **5.** 26.
"A Father-to-Be." **3 ed.** 44; **1.** 15; **2.** 29; **3.** 32; **5.** 26.
"The Gonzaga Manuscript." **3 ed.** 44; **1.** 15; **5.** 26.
"Him with His Foot in His Mouth." **4.** 27; **5.** 26.
"Leaving the Yellow House." **3 ed.** 44; **1.** 16; **2.** 29; **3.** 32; **5.** 26.
"Looking for Mr. Green." **3 ed.** 44–45; **1.** 16; **2.** 29; **3.** 32; **4.** 27.
"The Mexican General." **2.** 29; **3.** 32; **5.** 26.
"Mosby's Memoirs." **1.** 16; **2.** 29; **3.** 32; **4.** 27; **5.** 26.
"The Old System." **3 ed.** 45; **3.** 32; **5.** 26.
"Seize the Day." **3 ed.** 45–46; **1.** 16; **2.** 29; **3.** 32–33; **4.** 27; **5.** 26.
"A Sermon by Dr. Pep." **3 ed.** 46; **1.** 16; **3.** 33.
"A Silver Dish." **4.** 27; **5.** 26–27.
"The Trip to Galena." **3 ed.** 46; **3.** 33.
"Two Morning Monologues." **3.** 33.
"What Kind of Day Did You Have?" **4.** 27; **5.** 27.

ANDREI BELY [BORIS NIKOLAEVICH]

"Adam." **2.** 30.
"The Baptized Chinese." **1.** 16.
"The Bush." **2.** 30.
"A Luminous Fairy Tale." **2.** 30.
"A Man." **2.** 30.
"The Mountain Princess." **2.** 30.
"We Await His Return." **2.** 30.
"The Yogi." **2.** 30.

NATHANIEL BENCHLEY

"Deck the Halls." **3 ed.** 47.

HANS BENDER

"Die Wölfe kommen zurück." **3.** 33.

MARIO BENEDETTI

"As Always." **3 ed.** 47.
"El cambiazo." **1.** 30.
"The Iriate Family." **3 ed.** 47.
"The Rest Is Jungle." **3 ed.** 47.
"Twilight Zone." **3 ed.** 47.

VÜS'AT O. BENER

"The Homecoming." **1.** 16.

JUAN BENET

"Afterwards." **3.** 33.
"Baalbec: A Stain." **2.** 30; **3.** 33.
"Catalysis." **2.** 30; **3.** 33.
"De legos." **2.** 30.
"Después." **2.** 30.
"Duel." **2.** 30; **3.** 33.
"Evil of Parity." **3.** 33.
"Final Nights of a Damp Winter." **3.** 33.
"From Far Away." **3.** 33.
"Garet." **3.** 34.
"An Incomplete Line." **3.** 34; **5.** 27.
"It Was Ruined." **3.** 34.
"Mourning." **3.** 34.
"Numa: A Legend." **3.** 34.
"Obiter Dictum." **3.** 34.
"Por los suelos." **4.** 27.
"Reichenau." **2.** 30; **3.** 34.
"Seemingly Empty Hours." **3.** 34.
"Sub rosa." **3.** 34.
"Syllabus." **2.** 31; **3.** 34.
"TLB." **2.** 31; **3.** 34.
"A Tomb." **3.** 34.
"Viator." **3.** 34.
"The Way It Used to Be." **3.** 34.
"You Will Never Get Anywhere." **3.** 34.

STEPHEN VINCENT BENÉT

"The Angel Was a Yankee." **4.** 27.
"As It Was in the Beginning." **3 ed.** 47.
"The Bishop's Beggar." **3 ed.** 47.
"By the Waters of Babylon." **3 ed.** 47; **1.** 16; **3.** 35.
"A Death in the Country." **3 ed.** 47.
"The Devil and Daniel Webster." **3 ed.** 47; **4.** 28.
"Doc Mellhorn and the Pearly Gates." **4.** 28.
"Freedom's a Hard-Bought Thing." **3 ed.** 48.
"The Gold Dress." **4.** 28.
"Into Egypt." **3 ed.** 48.
"Jacob and the Indians." **3 ed.** 48.
"Johnny Pye and the Fool-Killer." **3 ed.** 48; **4.** 28.

"The King of the Cats." **4.** 28.
"The Land Where There Is No Death." **4.** 28.
"The Last of the Legions." **3 ed.** 48.
"The Minister's Books." **4.** 28.
"O'Halloran's Luck." **4.** 28.
"The Prodigal Children." **3 ed.** 48.
"Sea Serpent." **4.** 28.
"Too Early Spring." **3 ed.** 48.
"A Tooth for Paul Revere." **4.** 28.
"William Riley and the Fates." **4.** 28.

GREGORY BENFORD

"And the Sea Like a Mirror." **4.** 28.
"Deeper Than the Darkness." **4.** 28.
"In Alien Flesh." **5.** 27.

ANTONIO BENÍTEZ ROJO

"El escudo de hojas secas." **1.** 16.
"Estatuas sepultadas." **1.** 17.
"Primer balcon." **1.** 17.
"La tierra y el cielo." **1.** 17.

GOTTFRIED BENN

"Gehirne." **3 ed.** 48.

YITZHAK BEN NERO

"Nicole." **5.** 27.

ARNOLD BENNETT

"The Artist's Model." **3.** 35.
"The Death of Simon Fuge." **3 ed.** 48; **3.** 35; **5.** 27.
"Matador of the Five Towns." **3 ed.** 48.
"The Muscovy Ducks." **3 ed.** 48.
"The Woman Who Stole Everything." **3 ed.** 48.

EDWARD FREDERIC BENSON

"Naboth's Vineyard." **4.** 28.
"Pirates." **4.** 28.

SALLY BENSON

"The Overcoat." **3 ed.** 48.

STELLA BENSON

"The Desert Island." **3.** 35.
"A Dream." **3.** 35.
"Hope Against Hope." **3.** 35.
"Story Coldly Told." **3 ed.** 49; **3.** 35.
"Submarine." **3.** 35.

OLES BERDNYK

"The Journey into the Antiworld." **3.** 35.

M. J. BERDYCZEWSKI

"The Lonely." **2.** 31.
"My Enemy." **2.** 31.
"Partners." **2.** 31.
"The Qaddish and Two Far Away." **2.** 31.
"The Two." **2.** 31.
"Two Josephs." **2.** 31.

DAVID BERGELSON

"The Revolution and the Zussmans." **3 ed.** 49.

WERNER BERGENGRUEN

"Die drei Falken." **3 ed.** 49.
"Die Feuerprobe." **3 ed.** 49.
"Das Feuerzeichen." **3 ed.** 49.
"Der spanische Rosenstrock." **3 ed.** 49.
"Die Wunderbare Schreibmaschine." **3 ed.** 49.

HALMAR BERGMAN

"Sardanapal." **1.** 17.

ISAAC DOV BERKOWITZ

"At the Table." **3 ed.** 49.
"A Barbarian." **3 ed.** 49.
"The Chauffeur." **3 ed.** 49.
"Cucumbers." **3 ed.** 49.
"Cut Off." **3 ed.** 49.
"Faivke's Judgment Day." **3 ed.** 50.
"Grandchild." **3 ed.** 50.
"Guests." **3 ed.** 50.
"Moshkele Pig." **3 ed.** 50.
"Severed." **3 ed.** 50.
"The Uprooted." **3 ed.** 50.
"Yom Kippur Eve." **3 ed.** 50.

THOMAS BERNHARD

"Die Verrückte Magdalena." **3.** 35.

HERMAN BERNSTEIN

"A Ghetto Romance." **5.** 27.

GINA BERRIAULT

"The Stone Boy." **2.** 31.

JOHN BERRY

"New Shoes." **3 ed.** 50.

JOHN BERRYMAN

"The Imaginary Jew." **3 ed.** 50.

ALFRED BESTER

"Adam and No Eve." **3.** 36.
"The Biped, Reegan." **3.** 36.
"The Broken Axiom." **3.** 36.
"Disappearing Art." **3.** 36.
"Fondly Fahrenheit." **3.** 36.
"The Four-Hour Fugue." **3.** 36.
"Hell Is Forever." **3.** 36.
"Hobson's Choice." **3.** 36.
"Life for Sale." **3.** 36.
"The Men Who Murdered Mohammed." **3.** 36.
"Oddy and Id." **3.** 36.
"Of Time and Third Avenue." **3.** 36.
"Out of This World." **3.** 36.
"The Pi-Man." **3.** 36.
"The Push of a Finger." **1.** 17.
"The Roller Coaster." **3.** 36.
"Something Up There Likes Me." **3.** 37.
"The Starcomber." **3.** 37.
"They Don't Make Life Like They Used To." **3.** 37.
"Time Is the Traitor." **3.** 37.
"The Unseen Blushes." **3.** 37.
"Voyage to Nowhere." **3.** 37.

ALEXANDER BESTUZHEV-MARLINSKY [ALEXANDER BESTUZHEV]

"Ammalat-Bek." **4.** 29.
"The Cuirassier." **3 ed.** 50.
"Eisen Castle." **4.** 29.
"An Evening at a Bivouac." **3 ed.** 50; **4.** 29.
"The Frigate *Hope*." **3 ed.** 50.
"Neuhausen Castle." **4.** 29.
"The Reval Tournament." **4.** 29.
"Roman and Olga." **3.** 37.
"A Second Evening at a Bivouac." **3 ed.** 50.
"The Terrible Divination." **3 ed.** 50.
"The Test." **3 ed.** 51; **4.** 29.
"The Traitor." **3 ed.** 51.
"Wenden Castle." **4.** 29.

DORIS BETTS

"The Astronaut." **3.** 37.
"Beasts of the Southern Wild." **1.** 17.
"Clarissa and the Depths." **3 ed.** 51.
"The Dead Mule." **2.** 31.
"The Mandarin." **3.** 37.
"The Sympathetic Visitor." **1.** 17.
"The Ugliest Pilgrim." **1.** 17; **3.** 37.
"The Very Old Are Beautiful." **3.** 37.

GEOFFREY BEWLEY

"Passage from India." **4.** 29.

DHARM VIR BHARATI

"The Son of Hirnakush." **3.** 37.

BHABANI BHATTACHARYA

"Attainment." **3 ed.** 51.
"Bird's Feather." **3 ed.** 51.
"The Faltering Pendulum." **3 ed.** 51.
"Steel Hawk." **3 ed.** 51.

AMBROSE BIERCE

"The Affair at Coulter's Notch." **3 ed.** 51.
"An Affair of Outposts." **3 ed.** 51; **3.** 38.
"A Baby Tramp." **3 ed.** 51; **3.** 38; **5.** 27.
"The Boarded Window." **1.** 17; **2.** 31.
"A Bottomless Grave." **3.** 38.
"Charles Ashmore's Trail." **3.** 38.
"Chickamauga." **3 ed.** 51; **3.** 38; **5.** 27.
"The Coup de Grâce." **3 ed.** 51; **3.** 38.
"The Damned Thing." **3 ed.** 52; **3.** 38; **4.** 29.
"The Death of Halpin Frayser." **3 ed.** 52; **3.** 38; **4.** 29.
"The Eyes of the Panther." **3.** 38.
"The Famous Gilson Bequest." **3 ed.** 52; **3.** 38; **4.** 29.
"George Thurston." **3 ed.** 52.
"Haïta the Shepherd." **3 ed.** 52; **3.** 38.
"The Haunted Valley." **2.** 31.
"A Horseman in the Sky." **3 ed.** 52; **1.** 17.
"A Jug of Sirup [sic]." **3.** 38.
"Jupiter Doke, Brigadier General." **3 ed.** 52; **3.** 38.
"Killed at Resaca." **3 ed.** 52.

"The Man and the Snake." **3 ed.** 52; **3.** 38.
"Mr. Masthead, Journalist." **3.** 39.
"The Mocking-Bird." **3 ed.** 52; **3.** 39.
"The Moonlit Road." **3 ed.** 52; **3.** 39.
"Moxon's Master." **3 ed.** 52; **3.** 39; **4.** 29; **5.** 28.
"My Favorite Murder." **3 ed.** 52; **3.** 39.
"The Night-Doings at 'Dead-Man's'." **3.** 39.
"An Occurrence at Owl Creek Bridge." **3 ed.** 53; **1.** 17; **2.** 32; **3.** 39; **4.** 29–30; **5.** 28.
"Oil of Dog." **3 ed.** 53.
"One Kind of Officer." **3 ed.** 53.
"One of the Missing." **3 ed.** 53; **2.** 32; **3.** 39.
"One Officer, One Man." **3 ed.** 53; **3.** 39.
"Parker Adderson, Philosopher." **3 ed.** 53; **2.** 32; **3.** 39.
"A Son of the Gods." **3 ed.** 53; **3.** 39.
"The Story of a Conscience." **3 ed.** 54; **3.** 39.
"A Tough Tussle." **3 ed.** 54; **3.** 39.
"A Watcher by the Dead." **3 ed.** 54.

EANDO BINDER [BINDER BROTHERS]

"Rope Trick." **3.** 40.

RUDOLF BINDING

"Angelucia." **3 ed.** 54.
"Der Opfergang." **3 ed.** 54.
"Unsterblichkeit." **3 ed.** 54.
"Die Waffenbrüder." **3 ed.** 54.
"Der Wingulf." **3 ed.** 54.

HAROLD BINDLOSS

"The Two Priests of Konnoto." **3 ed.** 54.

ADOLFO BIOY CASARES

"The Child of His Friend." **3 ed.** 94.
"Cómo perdí la vista." **4.** 30.
"The Feast of the Monster." **3 ed.** 94.
"Mosca y Arañas." **5.** 28.
"El otro laberinto." **3.** 40.
"La trama celeste." **5.** 28.

JOHN PEALE BISHOP

"The Cellar." **3 ed.** 54.
"The Corpse in the House." **3 ed.** 54.
"The Fireplace." **3 ed.** 54.
"If Only." **3 ed.** 55.
"A Man Who Thought." **3 ed.** 55.
"Many Thousands Gone." **3 ed.** 55.
"Porphirio." **3 ed.** 55.
"Resurrection." **3 ed.** 55.
"Toadstools Are Poison." **3 ed.** 55.
"Young Death and Desire." **3 ed.** 55.

MICHAEL BISHOP

"Blooded on Arachne." **5.** 28.
"Death and Designation Among the Asadi." **3.** 40.
"Dogs' Lives." **5.** 28.

ANDREI [GEORGIEVICH] BITOV [sometimes BITUV]

"Country Place." **2.** 32.
"The Departing Monakhov." **4.** 30.
"Journey to a Childhood Friend." **2.** 32.
"Penelopa." **2.** 32.

JEROME BIXBY

"It's a *Good* Life." **5.** 28.

ALGERNON BLACKWOOD

"Ancient Sorceries." **3 ed.** 55.
"The Damned." **3 ed.** 55; **4.** 30.
"The Listener." **2.** 32.
"The Man Whom the Trees Loved." **4.** 30.
"The Pikestaffe Case." **4.** 30.
"A Psychical Invasion." **2.** 32.
"Secret Worship." **2.** 32.
"The Transfer." **2.** 32.
"The Willows." **3 ed.** 55; **2.** 32; **5.** 28.

CLARK BLAISE

"Among the Dead." **3.** 40.
"The Bridge." **3.** 40.
"Broward Dowdy." **3.** 40.
"A Class of New Canadians." **3.** 40.
"Extractions and Constructions." **3.** 40.
"Eyes." **3.** 40.
"The Fabulous Eddie Brewster." **3.** 40.
"Going to India." **3.** 40.
"Grids and Doglegs." **3.** 40.
"He Raises Me Up." **3.** 41.
"How I Became a Jew." **3.** 41.
"I'm Dreaming of Rocket Richard." **3.** 41.
"The March." **3.** 41.

"A North American Education." **3.** 41; **4.** 30.
"Notes Beyond a History." **3.** 41; **4.** 30.
"Relief." **3.** 41.
"The Salesman's Son Grows Older." **3.** 41; **4.** 30; **5.** 29.
"The Seizure." **3.** 41.
"Snow People." **3.** 41.
"The Street." **3.** 41.
"Words for a Winter." **3.** 41.

WILLIAM H. BLAKE

"A Tale of the Grand Jardin." **5.** 29.

TOMÁS BLANCO

"Los aguinaldos del Infante: Glosa de Epifania." **5.** 29.
"Cultura: Tres pasos y un encuentro." **5.** 29.
"La Dragontea: Cuento de Semana Santa." **5.** 29.

VICENTE BLASCO IBÁÑEZ

"The Last Lion." **5.** 29.

RUDOLFS BLAUMANIS

"Frost in Spring." **3 ed.** 55.
"Thunderstorm." **3 ed.** 55.
"Week." **3 ed.** 56.

MEIR BLINKIN

"Card Game." **3.** 41.
"Family Life: A Chapter." **3.** 41.

JAMES BLISH

"Against the Stone Beasts." **5.** 29.
"Beanstalk." **3.** 41.
"Beep." **3.** 42; **5.** 29.
"Bindlestiff." **5.** 29.
"Citadel of Thought." **5.** 29.
"The City That Was the World." **5.** 29.
"Common Time." **3 ed.** 56; **3.** 42; **5.** 30.
"Darkside Crossing." **5.** 30.
"A Dusk of Idols." **3.** 42; **5.** 30.
"First Strike." **5.** 30.
"Get Out of My Sky." **5.** 30.
"A Hero's Life" [revised as "A Style in Treason"]. **3.** 42.
"Let the Finder Beware." **3.** 42; **5.** 30.
"Mistake Inside." **5.** 30.
"More Light." **5.** 30.
"No Jokes on Mars." **5.** 30.
"Okie." **5.** 30.
"Our Binary Brothers." **5.** 30.
"Sargasso of Lost Cities." **5.** 30.
"Seeding Program." **5.** 30.
"Skysign." **5.** 30.
"Statistician's Day." **5.** 30.
"Surface Tension." **3 ed.** 56; **5.** 30.
"Testament of Andros." **3.** 42.
"There Shall Be No Darkness." **3.** 42; **5.** 30.
"The Thing in the Attic." **5.** 31.
"This Earth of Hours." **5.** 31.
"To Pay the Piper." **5.** 31.
"Tomb Tapper." **3.** 42; **5.** 31.
"Watershed." **5.** 31.
"We All Die Naked." **3.** 42; **5.** 31.
"A Work of Art" [originally "Art-Work"]. **3 ed.** 56; **3.** 42.
"The Writing of the Rat." **5.** 31.

JAMES BLISH and JUDITH ANN BLISH

"Getting Along." **5.** 31.

JAMES BLISH and VIRGINIA KIDD

"On the Wall of the Lodge." **3.** 42.

JAMES BLISH and DAMON KNIGHT

"The Weakness of RVOG." **5.** 31.

ROBERT BLOCH

"The Cloak." **4.** 31.
"The Dark Isle." **4.** 31.
"The Feast in the Abbey." **4.** 31.
"Iron Mask." **4.** 31.
"The Shadow from the Steeple." **4.** 31.
"The Shambler from the Stars." **4.** 31.
"Slave of the Flames." **4.** 31.
"Terror in Cut-Throat Cove." **4.** 31.
"That Hell-Bound Train." **4.** 31.
"Yours Truly, Jack the Ripper." **4.** 31.

RUDOLPH BLOCK

"End of the Task." **1.** 18.

ESTHER B. BOCK

"Ah Choo." **3.** 42.

JAIME TORRES BODET

"Antonio Arnoux." **3 ed.** 56.
"The Birth of Venus." **3 ed.** 56.
"Close-up of Mr. Lehar." **3 ed.** 56.
"Paralysis." **3 ed.** 56.
"To Live Again." **3 ed.** 56.

LOUISE BOGAN

"Dove and Serpent." **3.** 42; **4.** 31.
"Journey Around My Room." **3.** 42; **4.** 31.
"Keramik." **3.** 43; **4.** 31.
"Letdown." **3.** 43.
"The Long Walk." **3.** 43.
"Sabbatical Summer." **3.** 43.
"The Short Life of Emily." **4.** 31.
"Summer Day." **3.** 43.
"Whatever It Is." **3.** 43.
"With Mirrors." **3.** 43.
"Zest." **3.** 43.

HEINRICH BÖLL

"Action Will Be Taken." **3.** 43.
"The Adventure." **3.** 43.
"Arise, Please Arise." **5.** 31.
"At the Bridge." **3.** 43.
"The Balek Scales." **3 ed.** 56; **3.** 43; **5.** 31.
"The Black Sheep." **3.** 43.
"The Bread of Spring." **3 ed.** 56; **2.** 32.
"Business Is Business." **3.** 43; **5.** 31.
"Candles for the Madonna." **3.** 43.
"Christmas Every Day." **3 ed.** 56.
"Daniel the Just." **5.** 32.
"The Death of Elsa Baskoleit." **3 ed.** 57; **3.** 43; **5.** 32.
"The Discarder." **5.** 32.
"Dr. Murke's Collected Silences." **3 ed.** 57; **1.** 18; **3.** 43; **5.** 32.
"Epilogue to Stifter's *Nachsommer.*" **2.** 33; **3.** 44.
"The Foragers." **5.** 32.
"Hauptstädtisches Journal." **3.** 44.
"The Immortal Theodora." **3.** 44.
"In the Land of the Rujuks." **3.** 44.
"In the Valley of the Thundering Hooves." **3 ed.** 57; **5.** 32.
"Like a Bad Dream." **4.** 32; **5.** 32.
"The Man with the Knives." **3 ed.** 57; **3.** 44; **5.** 32.
"Mate with the Long Hair." **5.** 32.
"Mein teures Bein." **3.** 44.
"The Message." **5.** 32.
"My Sad Face" [same as "My Melancholy Face"]. **3.** 44; **5.** 32.
"The News." **3.** 44.
"No Tears for Schmeck." **3.** 44.
"Not Just at Christmas Time." **3 ed.** 57; **3.** 44; **5.** 32.
"On the Hook." **5.** 32.
"Our Good Old Renée." **3.** 44.
"Over the Bridge." **3 ed.** 57.
"Resignation." **3.** 44.
"Reunion in the Avenue." **5.** 32.
"Reunion with Drüng." **3.** 44; **5.** 33.
"Something Is Going to Happen." **5.** 33.
"Stopover in X." **3.** 44.
"That Time in Odessa." **5.** 33.
"The Train Was on Time." **3 ed.** 57.
"Traveler, If You Go to the Spa" [same as "Traveler, You Will Come to a Spa"]. **3 ed.** 57; **2.** 33; **3.** 44; **5.** 33.
"Unexpected Guest." **3.** 45.
"We Broommakers." **3.** 45.
"When War Broke Out." **5.** 33.
"Zimpren Railroad Station." **5.** 33.

MARÍA LUISA BOMBAL

"The New Islands." **3.** 45.
"The Tree." **3 ed.** 57; **3.** 45; **5.** 33.

NAPOLEON BONAPARTE

"Le Masque prophète." **5.** 33.

NELSON BOND

"The Cunning of the Beast." **3.** 45.
"The Priestess Who Rebelled." **5.** 33.

MARITA BONNER

"High Stepper." **5.** 34.
"On the Altar." **5.** 34.
"One True Love." **5.** 34.
"Reap It as You Sow." **5.** 34.

SHERWOOD BONNER [KATHERINE S. B. McDOWELL]

"The Case of Eliza Bleylock." **1.** 18.
"Coming Home to Roost." **1.** 18.
"The Gentlemen of Sarsar." **3 ed.** 57; **1.** 18.
"Hieronymus Pop and the Baby." **1.** 18.

"In Aunt Mely's Cabin." **1.** 18.
"Lame Jerry." **3 ed.** 57; **1.** 18.
"On the Nine Mile." **1.** 18.
"The Revolution in the Life of Mr. Balingall." **1.** 18.
"Sister Weeden's Prayer." **1.** 18.
"The Valcours." **1.** 18.
"The Volcanic Interlude." **1.** 18.

ARNA W. BONTEMPS

"Boy Blue." **3 ed.** 57.
"The Cure." **3 ed.** 58.
"Let the Church Roll On." **3 ed.** 58.
"A Summer Tragedy." **3 ed.** 58; **1.** 18; **2.** 33.
"3 Pennies for Luck." **3 ed.** 58.

WOLFGANG BORCHERT

"At Night Rats Go to Sleep, After All." **3 ed.** 58; **2.** 33.
"Billbrook." **3 ed.** 58; **2.** 33.
"Bread." **2.** 33.
"Coffee Is Indefinable." **2.** 33.
"The Crow Flies Home at Night." **2.** 33.
"The Dandelion." **2.** 33.
"Down the Long, Long Street." **3 ed.** 58; **2.** 33.
"The Giraffe." **2.** 33.
"Jesus Won't Do His Part Any More." **2.** 33.
"The Kitchen Clock." **3 ed.** 58; **2.** 33.
"Maybe She Has a Pink Blouse." **2.** 34.
"My Pale Brother." **3 ed.** 58; **2.** 34.
"Stay a While, Giraffe." **2.** 34.
"A Sunday Morning." **2.** 34.
"The Three Dark Kings." **3 ed.** 58; **2.** 34.
"Voices Are There—in the Air, in the Night." **2.** 34.

PÉTRUS BOREL

"Dina, la belle Juive." **3 ed.** 58.
"Don Andréa Vesalius l'anatomiste." **3 ed.** 58.
"Passereau l'écolier." **3 ed.** 58.

JOHAN BORGEN

"Chance." **1.** 19.
"Honeysuckle Vine." **1.** 19.
"Legend." **1.** 19.
"Morning on Montparnasse." **1.** 19.
"Night and Day 1." **1.** 19.
"Ocean in Winter." **1.** 19.
"She Willed It." **1.** 19.
"Star Song." **1.** 19.
"Trustworthy and Dutiful." **1.** 19.

JORGE LUIS BORGES

"Abenjacán the Bojarí, Dead in His Labyrinth" [same as "Ibn-Hakkan al-Bokhari . . ."]. **3 ed.** 59; **1.** 19; **3.** 45; **4.** 32; **5.** 34.
"The Aleph." **3 ed.** 59; **1.** 19; **2.** 34; **3.** 45; **4.** 32; **5.** 34.
"The Approach to Almotásim." **3 ed.** 59; **2.** 34; **3.** 45; **5.** 34.
"Averroes' Search." **3 ed.** 59; **1.** 20; **2.** 34; **3.** 45; **5.** 34.
"The Babylonian Lottery." **3 ed.** 59–60; **1.**20; **2.** 34; **3.** 46; **4.** 32; **5.** 34.
"Biography of Tadeo Isidoro Cruz (1829-1874)" [same as "The Life of . . ."]. **3 ed.** 60; **1.** 20; **2.** 34, 37; **4.** 34; **5.** 36.
"The Book of Sand." **2.** 35.
"Borges and I." **2.** 35; **4.** 32.
"The Bribe." **2.** 35.
"Brodie's Report" [same as "Dr. Brodie's Report"]. **1.** 20; **2.** 35.
"The Challenge." **2.** 35.
"The Child of His Friend." **3 ed.** 60.
"The Circular Ruins." **3 ed.** 60; **1.** 20; **2.** 35; **3.** 46; **5.** 34.
"El condenado." **5.** 35.
"The Congress." **3 ed.** 60; **4.** 32; **5.** 35.
"The Cult of the Phoenix" [same as "The Sect of Phoenix"]. **3 ed.** 61; **2.** 38.
"The Dead Man." **3 ed.** 61; **1.** 20; **2.** 35; **5.** 35.
"Death and the Compass." **3 ed.** 61; **1.** 20; **2.** 35; **3.** 46; **4.** 32; **5.** 35.
"Deutsches Requiem." **3 ed.** 61; **1.** 20; **2.** 35; **3.** 46; **4.** 33; **5.** 35.
"The Dreadful Redeemer Lazarus Morell." **3 ed.** 62; **1.** 20; **3.** 46.
"The Duel." **3 ed.** 61; **2.** 35.
"The Elder Lady." **3 ed.** 61.
"Emma Zunz." **3 ed.** 61–62; **1.** 20; **2.** 36; **3.** 46; **4.** 33; **5.** 35.
"The Encounter." **1.** 20; **4.** 33.
"The End." **3 ed.** 62; **1.** 20; **2.** 36.
"The End of the Duel." **2.** 36; **3.** 46; **4.** 33; **5.** 35.

"The Enigma of Edward Fitzgerald." **1.** 20.
"Everything and Nothing." **2.** 36; **4.** 33.
"Examination of the Work of Herbert Quain." **3 ed.** 62; **1.** 20; **2.** 36; **3.** 46; **5.** 35.
"The Feast of the Monster." **3 ed.** 62.
"Funes the Memorious." **3 ed.** 62; **1.** 21; **2.** 36; **3.** 46; **4.** 33; **5.** 35.
"The Garden of Forking Paths." **3 ed.** 62; **1.** 21; **2.** 36; **3.** 47; **4.** 33; **5.** 36.
"The God's Script" [same as "The Writing of the Lord"]. **3 ed.** 62–63; **2.** 36; **3.** 47; **4.** 33.
"The Gospel According to Mark." **3 ed.** 63; **2.** 36; **3.** 47; **5.** 36.
"Guayaquil." **3 ed.** 63; **1.** 21; **2.** 36.
"Horse." **2.** 37.
"The House of Asterion." **3 ed.** 63; **1.** 21; **2.** 37; **4.** 33.
"The Immortal." **3 ed.** 63; **2.** 37; **3.** 47; **5.** 36.
"The Improbable Impostor Tom Castro." **1.** 21.
"The Intruder." **3 ed.** 63; **2.** 37.
"Juan Muraña." **3 ed.** 64; **1.** 21; **4.** 33; **5.** 36.
"The Library of Babel." **3 ed.** 64; **1.** 21; **2.** 37; **3.** 47; **4.** 34.
"The Maker." **3 ed.** 64; **1.** 21; **5.** 36.
"The Man at the Pink Corner." **3 ed.** 64; **2.** 37; **3.** 47.
"The Man on the Threshold." **3 ed.** 64; **2.** 37; **4.** 34.
"The Masked Dyer, Hakim of Merv." **5.** 36.
"The Meeting." **2.** 37.
"The Mirror and the Mask." **2.** 37.
"The Other." **1.** 21; **2.** 37; **5.** 36.
"The Other Death." **3 ed.** 64; **1.** 21; **2.** 38; **3.** 47; **5.** 36.
"Pierre Menard, Author of *Quixote*." **3 ed.** 64; **1.** 21; **2.** 38; **3.** 47; **4.** 34; **5.** 37.
"The Restitution of the Key." **3 ed.** 64.
"The Secret Miracle." **3 ed.** 65; **1.** 21; **2.** 38; **3.** 47; **4.** 34; **5.** 37.
"The Sect of Thirty." **1.** 21; **2.** 38.
"The Shape of the Sword" [same as "The Form of the Sword"]. **3 ed.** 65; **1.** 21; **2.** 36, 38; **5.** 37.
"The Sorcerer Postponed." **1.** 21.
"The South." **3 ed.** 65; **1.** 22; **2.** 38; **3.** 48; **5.** 37.
"The Story of Rosendo Juárez" [earlier titled "Hombre de la esquina rosada" and "Political Legend"]. **3 ed.** 63; **1.** 22; **2.** 38; **5.** 37.
"Story of the Warrior and the Captive." **2.** 38.
"Streetcorner Man." **2.** 39.
"Theme of the Traitor and the Hero." **3 ed.** 65; **1.** 22; **2.** 39; **4.** 34; **5.** 37.
"The Theologians." **3 ed.** 65; **1.** 22; **2.** 39; **5.** 37.
"Three Versions of Judas." **3 ed.** 65; **1.** 22; **2.** 39.
"Tlön, Uqbar, Orbis Tertius." **3 ed.** 65–66; **1.** 22; **2.** 39; **3.** 48; **4.** 34; **5.** 37.
"The Two Kings and Their Two Labyrinths." **2.** 39.
"The Uncivil Master of Ceremonies Kotsuké no Suké." **5.** 37.
"The Unworthy One." **3 ed.** 66; **5.** 37.
"Utopia of a Tired Man." **1.** 22; **2.** 39.
"The Wait." **3 ed.** 66; **2.** 39; **3.** 48.
"The Watcher." **2.** 39.
"The Widow Ching, Pirate." **3 ed.** 66; **5.** 38.
"The Zahir." **3 ed.** 66; **1.** 22; **2.** 39; **3.** 48; **4.** 34; **5.** 38.

TADEUSZ BOROWSKI

"Auschwitz, Our Home (A Letter)." **3.** 48.
"A Day at Harmenz." **3.** 48.
"The People Who Walked On." **3.** 48.
"This Way for the Gas, Ladies and Gentlemen." **3.** 48.

F. VAN DEN BOSCH

"Disponent Andersson." **3.** 49.
"House of Rain." **3.** 49.
"Nom-de-Guerre." **3.** 49.

JUAN BOSCH

"In a Hut." **5.** 38.
"Luis Pie." **4.** 34.
"Two Dollars' Worth of Water." **3.** 49.
"The Woman." **4.** 34; **5.** 38.

HERMAN CHARLES BOSMAN

"Dopper." **5.** 38.
"Kafir." **3 ed.** 66.
"Mafeking Road." **5.** 38.
"The Rooinek." **3 ed.** 66.

ANTHONY BOUCHER

"Balaam." **3.** 49.
"The Quest for St. Aquin." **3.** 49.

JEAN LOUIS BOUQUET

"Assirata, or The Enchanted Mirror." **2.** 40.

ELIZABETH BOWEN

"Ann Lee's." **3.** 49; **4.** 34.
"Breakfast." **3 ed.** 66; **3.** 49.
"The Cat Jumps." **3 ed.** 67; **4.** 35; **5.** 38.
"The Cheery Soul." **4.** 35.
"Coming Home." **1.** 22.
"The Dancing Mistress." **3 ed.** 67.
"Dead Mabelle." **3 ed.** 67; **5.** 38.
"The Demon Lover." **3 ed.** 67; **1.** 22; **2.** 40; **3.** 49; **4.** 35; **5.** 38.
"The Disinherited." **3 ed.** 67; **4.** 35.
"The Easter Egg Party." **3 ed.** 67.
"Foothold." **3 ed.** 67.
"The Good Girl." **3 ed.** 67.
"Green Holly." **4.** 35.
"The Happy Autumn Fields." **3 ed.** 67; **1.** 22; **2.** 40; **3.** 49; **4.** 35.
"Her Table Spread." **3 ed.** 67; **2.** 40; **4.** 35.
"Human Habitation." **5.** 38.
"I Hear You Say So." **3.** 49.
"In the Square." **3 ed.** 67.
"The Inherited Clock." **3 ed.** 68; **4.** 35.
"Ivy Gripped the Steps." **3 ed.** 68; **2.** 40; **4.** 35.
"Joining Charles." **4.** 35.
"The Jungle." **3 ed.** 68.
"Little Girl's Room." **3 ed.** 68; **4.** 35.
"Look at All Those Roses." **2.** 40; **5.** 39.
"A Love Story." **3 ed.** 68.
"Making Arrangements." **1.** 22.
"The Man of the Family." **3 ed.** 68.
"Maria." **3.** 49; **4.** 35.
"Mrs. Moysey." **3 ed.** 68.
"Mysterious Kôr." **3 ed.** 68; **1.** 22; **2.** 40; **3.** 50; **4.** 35; **5.** 39.
"Pink May." **4.** 35.
"Queer Heart." **3 ed.** 68.
"Shoes: An International Episode." **3 ed.** 68.
"Songs My Father Sang Me." **4.** 35.
"Summer Night." **3 ed.** 68; **1.** 22; **3.** 50; **4.** 36.
"Tears, Idle Tears." **3 ed.** 68; **5.** 39.
"Telling." **3 ed.** 68.
"The Tommy Crans." **2.** 40.
"A Walk in the Woods." **1.** 23.
"Woodby, John." **1.** 23.
"The Working Party." **3 ed.** 68.

JANE BOWLES

"Camp Cataract." **2.** 40; **5.** 39.
"Plain Pleasures." **2.** 40.
"A Stick of Green Candy." **2.** 40; **5.** 39.

PAUL BOWLES

"Allal." **4.** 36.
"At Paso Rojo." **3.** 50; **5.** 39.
"By the Waters." **3 ed.** 69; **3.** 50.
"Call at Corazón." **3.** 50; **5.** 39.
"The Circular Valley." **4.** 36.
"The Delicate Prey." **3 ed.** 69; **2.** 40; **3.** 50; **5.** 39.
"The Dismissal." **4.** 36.
"A Distant Episode." **3 ed.** 69; **3.** 50; **5.** 39.
"Doña Faustina." **4.** 36.
"The Echo." **3.** 50; **5.** 39.
"The Eye." **4.** 36.
"Fqih." **4.** 36.
"A Friend of the World." **3 ed.** 69; **4.** 36.
"The Frozen Fields." **3.** 50; **4.** 36; **5.** 39.
"The Garden." **4.** 36; **5.** 39.
"He of the Assembly." **3 ed.** 69; **5.** 39.
"Here to Learn." **4.** 36; **5.** 39.
"The Hours after Noon." **3 ed.** 69; **4.** 36; **5.** 39–40.
"How Many Midnights." **3.** 50; **5.** 40.
"The Hyena." **3.** 50; **4.** 36; **5.** 40.
"If I Should Open My Mouth." **4.** 36; **5.** 40.
"Istikhar, Anaya, Medagan and the Medaganat." **4.** 36.
"Kitty." **4.** 37; **5.** 40.
"The Little House." **4.** 37.
"Pages from Cold Point." **3 ed.** 69; **3.** 50; **5.** 40.
"Pastor Dowe at Tacaté." **3.** 50; **5.** 40.
"Reminders of Bouselham." **4.** 37.
"The Scorpion." **4.** 37.
"The Story of Lahcen and Idir" [originally "Merkala Beach"]. **3 ed.** 69; **4.** 37.
"The Successor." **4.** 37.
"Tapiama." **3.** 50; **4.** 37.
"Tea on the Mountain." **3 ed.** 69; **5.** 40.

"Things Gone and Things Still Here." **4.** 37.
"A Thousand Days of Mokhtar." **3.** 51.
"The Time of Friendship." **3 ed.** 69; **3.** 51; **4.** 37; **5.** 40.
"Under the Sky." **3 ed.** 69; **3.** 51.
"The Wind of Beni Midar." **3 ed.** 69; **4.** 37.
"You Are Not I." **5.** 40.
"You Have Left Your Lotus Pods on the Bus." **5.** 40.

HJALMAR HJORTH BOYESEN

"Asathor's Vengeance." **2.** 41.
"A Dangerous Virtue." **2.** 41.
"A Disastrous Partnership." **2.** 41.
"A Good-for-Nothing." **4.** 37.
"The Horns of a Dilemma." **2.** 41.
"A Norse Emigrant." **2.** 41.
"Queen Titania." **2.** 41.
"A Story of a Blue Vein." **2.** 41.
"The Story of an Outcast." **2.** 41.
"Swart Among the Buckeyes." **2.** 41.
"Truls, the Nameless." **2.** 41.

KAY BOYLE

"Army of Occupation." **5.** 40.
"Art Colony." **3 ed.** 69.
"The Astronomer's Wife." **3 ed.** 69; **5.** 40.
"Begin Again." **4.** 37.
"Big Fiddle." **4.** 37.
"Black Boy." **4.** 37.
"The Bridegroom's Body." **3 ed.** 69; **4.** 37.
"The Canals of Mars." **4.** 38.
"Count Lothar's Heart." **3 ed.** 69.
"The Crazy Hunter." **3 ed.** 70; **4.** 38.
"Decision" [originally "Passport to Doom"]. **4.** 38.
"Defeat." **4.** 38.
"Effigy of War." **3 ed.** 70.
"Episode in the Life of an Ancestor." **4.** 38; **5.** 40.
"Evening at Home." **3 ed.** 70.
"The First Lover." **4.** 38.
"Frankfurt in Our Blood." **4.** 38.
"French Harvest." **4.** 38.
"I Can't Get Drunk." **4.** 38.
"Keep Your Pity." **3 ed.** 70.
"Kroy Wren." **3.** 51.
"The Lost." **5.** 41.
"Luck for the Road." **3 ed.** 70.
"Madame Tout Petite." **4.** 38.
"Maiden, Maiden." **4.** 38.
"Major Alshuster." **4.** 38.
"Major Engagement in Paris." **4.** 38.
"Men." **4.** 38.
"Natives Don't Cry." **3 ed.** 70.
"On the Run." **4.** 38; **5.** 41.
"One of Ours." **3 ed.** 70.
"Polar Bears and Others." **4.** 38.
"Portrait." **4.** 38.
"Rest Cure." **3 ed.** 70; **1.** 23; **4.** 39.
"Seeing the Sights of San Francisco." **4.** 39.
"Spring Morning." **4.** 39.
"Summer." **4.** 39.
"They Weren't Going to Die." **3 ed.** 70; **4.** 39.
"This They Took with Them." **4.** 39.
"Three Little Men." **4.** 39.
"Vacation-Time." **4.** 39.
"Wedding Day." **4.** 39; **5.** 41.
"The White Horses of Vienna." **3 ed.** 70; **3.** 51; **4.** 39.
"Winter Night." **3 ed.** 70; **4.** 39.

PATRICK BOYLE

"At Night All Cats Are Grey." **3 ed.** 70.
"Meles Vulgaris." **3 ed.** 70.

T. CORAGHESSAN BOYLE

"Descent of Man." **5.** 41.
"A Women's Restaurant." **4.** 39.

LEIGH BRACKETT

"All the Colors of the Rainbow." **3.** 51.
"The Beast-Jewel of Mars." **4.** 39.
"Enchantress of Venus." **3.** 51.
"Mars Minus Bisha." **4.** 39.
"Purple Priestess of the Mad Moon." **4.** 39.
"The Road to Sinharat." **4.** 40.
"The Tweener." **3.** 51.

LEIGH BRACKETT and RAY BRADBURY

"Lorelei of the Red Mist." **4.** 40.

MALCOLM BRADBURY

"A Goodbye for Evadne Winterbottom." **4.** 40.

RAY BRADBURY

"And So Died Riabouchinska." **1.** 23.
"And the Moon Be Still As Bright." **2.** 41.
"And the Rock Cried Out." **2.** 41.
"The Anthem Sprinters." **1.** 23.
"August 2026: Then Will Come Soft Rains." **5.** 41.
"August 2002: Night Meeting." **4.** 40.
"The Beggar on O'Connell Bridge." **1.** 23.
"Boys, Raise Giant Mushrooms in *Your* Cellar!" **3.** 51.
"The Cistern." **1.** 23; **4.** 40.
"The Concrete Mixer." **1.** 23.
"The Crowd." **1.** 23.
"Dark They Were and Golden Eyed." **1.** 23; **2.** 41; **3.** 51.
"Death and the Maiden." **1.** 23.
"Downwind from Gettysburg." **3.** 51.
"The Dwarf." **1.** 23.
"The Earth Men." **2.** 41.
"Embroidery." **3.** 51.
"The Emissary." **1.** 23.
"The Exiles." **1.** 23.
"Fever Dream." **1.** 23; **3.** 51.
"The Fire Balloons." **3 ed.** 70; **2.** 41–42.
"The Fireman." **2.** 42.
"The Flying Machine." **3.** 52.
"G. B. S.—Mark V." **2.** 42; **3.** 52.
"The Garbage Collector." **3.** 52.
"The Golden Apples of the Sun." **1.** 24; **4.** 40.
"The Great Wide World Over There." **1.** 24.
"Hail and Farewell." **3.** 52.
"The Highway." **3.** 52.
"Homecoming." **3.** 52.
"I See You Never." **3 ed.** 71.
"I Sing the Body Electric." **1.** 24.
"Icarus Montgolfier." **1.** 24.
"The Illustrated Man." **1.** 24.
"Invisible Boy." **1.** 24.
"Jack-in-the-Box." **1.** 24; **2.** 42; **3.** 52; **5.** 41.
"The Jar." **3.** 52.
"The Lake." **1.** 24.
"The Long Years." **2.** 42.
"The Lost City of Mars." **2.** 42; **3.** 52.
"The Machineries of Joy." **1.** 24.
"The Man in the Rorschach Shirt." **3 ed.** 71.
"The Man Upstairs." **1.** 24; **2.** 42; **3.** 52.
"Marionettes, Inc." **3.** 52.
"The Martian." **2.** 42.
"A Medicine for Melancholy." **1.** 24.
"The Million-Year Picnic." **3.** 52.
"The Miracles of Jamie." **2.** 42.
"The Musicians." **2.** 42.
"The Next in Line." **2.** 42; **3.** 52.
"The Night." **5.** 41.
"Night Call Collect." **1.** 24.
"Night Meeting." **1.** 24; **2.** 42.
"No Particular Night or Morning." **1.** 24; **3.** 52.
"The October Game." **5.** 41.
"The Off Season." **2.** 42; **3.** 52.
"The One Who Waits." **3 ed.** 71; **3.** 52.
"The Other Foot." **2.** 42.
"The Pedestrian." **3.** 53.
"Perhaps We Are Going Away." **3.** 53.
"Pillar of Fire." **1.** 24.
"Powerhouse." **1.** 24.
"The Rocket Man." **1.** 24.
"Rocket Summer." **2.** 42.
"A Scent of Sarsaparilla." **3.** 53.
"The Scythe." **1.** 25.
"The Sea Shell." **4.** 40.
"The Settlers." **2.** 43.
"The Skeleton." **1.** 25; **2.** 43.
"The Small Assassin." **2.** 43.
"The Strawberry Window." **2.** 43; **3.** 53.
"The Summer Night." **2.** 43; **3.** 53.
"There Was an Old Woman." **1.** 25.
"There Will Come Soft Rains." **2.** 43; **3.** 53.
"The Third Expedition." **2.** 43.
"To the Chicago Abyss." **3.** 53.
"Tomorrow's Child." **3.** 53.
"Uncle Einar." **1.** 25; **3.** 53.
"Usher II." **2.** 43; **3.** 53.
"The Vacation." **3.** 53.
"The Veld." **5.** 41.
"The Watchful Poker Chip of H. Matisse." **1.** 25.
"Way in the Middle of the Air." **1.** 25; **2.** 43.
"The Wilderness." **2.** 43.
"The Wind." **1.** 25; **3.** 53.
"The Women." **3.** 53.
"The Wonderful Ice Cream Suit." **1.** 25.
"Ylla." **3.** 53.
"Zero Hour." **1.** 25; **3.** 53.

MARION ZIMMER BRADLEY

"The Wind People." **3.** 53.

ERNEST BRAMAH

"The Eastern Mystery." **4.** 40.
"The Strange Case of Cyril Bycourt." **4.** 40.

FORBES BRAMBLE

"Holiday." **5.** 41.

RAUL BRANDÃO

"The Thief and His Little Daughter." **3 ed.** 71.

WILLEM BRANDT

"The Candle." **3.** 54.

H. C. BRANNER

"Aegteskab." **3 ed.** 71.
"Anxiety." **3 ed.** 71.
"De blaa Undulater." **3 ed.** 71.
"Graenselandet." **3 ed.** 71.
"En halv Alen Vand" [same as "Boheme"]. **3 ed.** 71.
"Ingeborg." **3 ed.** 71.
"Kameliadamen." **3 ed.** 71.
"The Mountain." **3 ed.** 71.
"Om lidt er vi borte." **3 ed.** 71.
"Pengemag." **3 ed.** 71.
"Röde Heste i Sneen." **3 ed.** 71.
"Shagpiben." **3 ed.** 72.
"Sidst i August." **3 ed.** 72.
"Skibet." **3 ed.** 72.
"To Minutters Stilhed." **3 ed.** 72.
"De tre Musketerer." **3 ed.** 72.

HOWARD C. BRASHERS

"Crack, Crash Orange Flame." **1.** 25.

JOHANNA and GÜNTHER BRAUN

"The Mistake Factor." **5.** 41.

RICHARD BRAUTIGAN

"The Armored Car." **3 ed.** 72.
"The Betrayed Kingdom." **3 ed.** 72.
"Corporal." **3 ed.** 72.
"Forgiven." **3 ed.** 72.
"Homage to the San Francisco YMCA." **1.** 25; **3.** 54.
"The Kool-Aid Wino." **2.** 43.
"1/3, 1/3, 1/3." **3 ed.** 72.
"The Post Offices of Eastern Oregon." **3 ed.** 72; **4.** 40.
"Revenge of the Lawn." **3 ed.** 72.
"A Short History of Oregon." **3 ed.** 72.
"1692 Cotton Mather Newsreel." **3 ed.** 72.
"The Wild Birds." **3 ed.** 72.
"Winter Rug." **4.** 40.
"The World War I Los Angeles Airplane." **3 ed.** 72; **1.** 25; **2.** 43.

BERTOLT BRECHT

"Augsburger Kreidekreis." **3 ed.** 73.
"Das Experiment." **2.** 43.
"Der Soldat von La Ciotat." **2.** 43.

CLEMENS BRENTANO

"Brave Kasperl and Beautiful Annerl" [same as "Brave Casper and Beautiful Annie"]. **3 ed.** 73; **1.** 25; **2.** 44; **3.** 54.
"The Chronicle of the Traveling Student." **2.** 44.
"Gockel, Hinkel, and Gaskeleia" [originally "Gockel and Hinkel"]. **2.** 44; **3.** 54.
"Lieblingslied der Geizigen." **3 ed.** 73.
"Die mehreren Wehlmüller." **3 ed.** 73.

BESSIE BREUER

"Home Is a Place." **3 ed.** 73.

MILES BREUER

"Paradise and Iron." **1.** 26.

GREGORIO BRILLANTES

"The Distance to Andromeda." **5.** 41.
"Faith, Love, Time and Dr. Lazaro." **5.** 41.

GEORG BRITTING

"Der Schneckenweg." **3 ed.** 73.

MAX BROD

"Tod den Toten." **3.** 54.

HAROLD BRODKEY

"Sentimental Education." **3 ed.** 73.

LOUIS BROMFIELD

"Death in Monte Carlo." **3.** 54.
"The End of the Road." **3.** 54.
"The Life of Vergie Winters." **3.** 54.
"Miss Mehaffy." **3.** 54.
"The Old House." **3.** 54.
"Up Ferguson Way." **3.** 55.

CHARLOTTE BRONTË

"The Secret." **1.** 26.

CHRISTINE BROOKE-ROSE

"Go When You See the Green Man Walking." **4.** 41.

ALICE BROWN

"At Sudleigh Fair." **3 ed.** 73; **2.** 44.
"The Book of Love." **3 ed.** 73.
"A Day Off." **3 ed.** 73.
"Dooryards." **3 ed.** 74; **5.** 42.
"The End of All Living." **3 ed.** 74.
"Farmer Eli's Vacation." **3 ed.** 74.
"The Flat Iron Lot." **5.** 42.
"A Flower in April." **3 ed.** 74.
"Gardener Jim." **3 ed.** 74.
"Honey and Myrrh." **5.** 42.
"Horn o' the Moon." **3 ed.** 74; **5.** 42.
"A Last Assembling." **3 ed.** 74; **2.** 44; **5.** 42.
"A Meeting in the Market Place." **3 ed.** 74.
"Natalie Blayne." **3 ed.** 74.
"The Other Mrs. Dill." **3 ed.** 74.
"A Righteous Bargain." **3 ed.** 74.
"Rosamund in Heaven." **3 ed.** 74.
"A Sea Change." **3 ed.** 74.
"A Second Marriage." **3 ed.** 74; **5.** 42.
"The Way of Peace." **2.** 44; **4.** 41.
"A Winter's Courting." **3 ed.** 74.

CHARLES BROCKDEN BROWN

"Death of Cicero, A Fragment." **3 ed.** 75; **3.** 55.
"Jessica." **2.** 44.
"A Lesson on Concealment." **3 ed.** 75.
"The Man at Home." **3 ed.** 75.
"Memoirs of Carwin the Biloquist." **3 ed.** 75.

FREDRIC BROWN

"Answer." **3.** 55.
"Arena." **3.** 55.

ROSELLEN BROWN

"Good Housekeeping." **4.** 41.

JOHN ROSS BROWNE

"A Dangerous Journey." **2.** 44.

MICHAEL BROWNSTEIN

"The Plot to Save the World." **3 ed.** 75.

HETHIN BRÚ

"Alone on Lítla Dímun." **3 ed.** 75.
"Emanuel." **3 ed.** 75.
"Halgir." **3 ed.** 75.
"The Hermits." **3 ed.** 75.
"The Light." **3 ed.** 75.
"Sheep Fold." **3 ed.** 75.
"A Tall Tale." **3 ed.** 75.
"The White Church." **3 ed.** 75.

MARTA BRUNET

"Aguas abajo." **5.** 42.
"Encrucijada de ausencias." **5.** 42.
"Una mañana cualquiera." **5.** 42.
"La niña que quiso ser estampa." **5.** 42.
"La otra voz." **5.** 42.
"Piedra callada." **5.** 42.
"Soledad de la sangre." **3.** 55; **5.** 42.
"Un trapo de piso." **5.** 42.

JOHN BRUNNER

"Host Age." **2.** 44.
"Judas." **3 ed.** 76.
"Nobody Axed You." **3.** 55.
"Thou Good and Faithful." **2.** 44.
"Web of Everywhere." **2.** 44.
"The Windows of Heaven." **3 ed.** 76.

KATHARINE BRUSH

"Birthday Party." **3 ed.** 76.
"Night Club." **2.** 45.

VALERY BRUSOV

"Republic of the Southern Cross." **3 ed.** 76.

EDWARD BRYANT

"2.46593." **5.** 43.

WILLIAM CULLEN BRYANT

"A Border Tradition." **3.** 55.
"The Indian Spring." **3.** 55.
"The Legend of the Devil's Pulpit." **3.** 55.
"Medfield." **3.** 55.

ALFREDO BRYCE ECHENIQUE

"El Papa Guido Sin Número." **5.** 43.
"Pepi Monkey y Ia Educatión de su hermana." **5.** 43.
"With Jimmy in Paracas." **5.** 43.

JOHN BUCHAN

"The Grave of Ashtaroth." **3.** 56.
"No-Man's Land." **3.** 46.

GEORG BÜCHNER

"Lenz." **3 ed.** 76; **1.** 26.

PEARL S. BUCK

"The Enemy." **5.** 43.
"Enough for a Lifetime." **3 ed.** 76.
"The First Wife." **3 ed.** 76.
"The Rainy Day." **3 ed.** 76.
"Repatriated." **3 ed.** 76.
"The Revolutionist." **3 ed.** 76.

ERNEST BUCKLER

"Last Delivery Before Christmas." **2.** 45.
"A Present for Miss Merriam." **2.** 45.
"The Quarrel." **2.** 45.

F. R. BUCKLEY

"Gold-Mounted Guns." **3 ed.** 77.

ALGIS BUDRYS [ALGIRDAS JONAS BUDRYS]

"All for Love." **3.** 56.
"Nobody Bothers Gus." **3 ed.** 77.

JAMES BUECHLER

"The Proud Suitor." **3 ed.** 77.

MIKHAIL BULGAKOV

"The Adventures of Chichikov." **4.** 41.
"Diaboliad." **3.** 56; **4.** 41.
"The Extraordinary Adventures of a Doctor." **4.** 41.
"Fatal Eggs." **4.** 41.
"I Killed." **4.** 41.
"Morphine." **3.** 56; **4.** 41.
"The Murderer." **5.** 43.
"Notes on the Cuff." **3.** 56.
"No. 13, The Elpit-Rabkommun Building." **3.** 56.
"The Raid." **3.** 56; **4.** 41.
"The Red Crown." **4.** 41.

SILVINA BULLRICH

"Abnegation." **3.** 56.
"The Lover." **5.** 43.

CARLOS BULOSAN

"The Americano from Luzon." **3.** 56.
"The Capitalism of My Father." **5.** 43.
"The Gift of My Father." **5.** 43.
"Homecoming." **3.** 56.
"I Would Remember." **3.** 56.
"The Laughter of My Father." **5.** 44.
"My Father Goes to Church." **5.** 44.
"My Father Goes to Court." **5.** 44.
"My Mother's Boarders." **5.** 44.
"The Politics of My Father." **5.** 44.
"Silence." **3.** 57.
"The Soldiers Came Marching." **5.** 44.
"The Tree of My Father." **5.** 44.

EDWARD GEORGE BULWER-LYTTON

"The Haunted and the Haunters; or, the House and the Brain." **3 ed.** 77; **4.** 42.

IVAN BUNIN

"Aglaya." **2.** 45.
"Aleksey Alekseevich." **2.** 45; **5.** 44.
"Antonov Apples." **2.** 45; **3.** 57.
"The Archives." **2.** 45.
"Ash Wednesday." **2.** 45.
"A Ballad." **2.** 45.
"Brethren" [originally "A Christmas Story"]. **3 ed.** 77; **2.** 45; **3.** 57.
"By the Road." **2.** 45; **3.** 57.

"Calling Cards." **3.** 57.
"Caucasus." **2.** 45.
"Celestial Bird" [originally "Poor Is the Devil"]. **2.** 46.
"The Chapel." **2.** 46.
"Cold Autumn." **2.** 46; **3.** 57.
"A Compatriot." **2.** 46.
"Comrade Dozornyj." **2.** 47.
"Conversation at Midnight." **3 ed.** 77.
"The Cricket." **2.** 46.
"The Cup of Life." **3 ed.** 77; **2.** 46; **3.** 57.
"Dark Alleys." **2.** 46.
"The Devouring Fire." **2.** 46; **5.** 44.
"The Dreams of Chang." **2.** 46; **3.** 57.
"Elijah the Prophet." **2.** 46.
"The Endless Spring" [same as "The Eternal Spring"]. **2.** 46; **3.** 57.
"An Epitaph." **3.** 57.
"Ermil" [originally "Crime"]. **2.** 46.
"The Eve." **2.** 46.
"The Father." **5.** 44.
"Fedosevna." **2.** 46.
"The Fog." **2.** 46.
"A Gay Farmhouse." **2.** 47; **3.** 57.
"Gedali." **5.** 44.
"The Gentleman from San Francisco." **3 ed.** 77; **2.** 47; **3.** 57; **4.** 42.
"The Goddess of Reason." **2.** 47.
"God's Tree" [same as "The Tree of God"]. **2.** 47, 49.
"The Gold Mine." **3.** 57.
"Gotami." **3.** 57.
"The Grammar of Love." **3 ed.** 78; **2.** 47; **3.** 57.
"Holy Mountains." **2.** 47.
"I Say Nothing." **2.** 47.
"Ida." **2.** 47; **3.** 57; **5.** 44.
"Ignat." **2.** 47.
"In an Alien Land" [same as "Away from Home"]. **2.** 47.
"In Autumn." **2.** 47; **3.** 58.
"In the Field" [originally "Lazy Bones"]. **2.** 47.
"In the Fruit Orchard." **2.** 47.
"In the Summer House" [same as "At the Dacha"]. **2.** 47.
"Ioann the Weeper." **2.** 47; **3.** 58.
"Justice in Parentheses." **5.** 44.
"Kastryuk." **2.** 47; **3.** 58.
"Kazimir Stanislavovich." **2.** 48.
"The King." **5.** 44.
"The Last Day." **3.** 58.
"The Last Rendezvous" [same as "The Last Meeting"]. **2.** 48.
"A Letter." **5.** 44.
"Light Breathing." **2.** 48; **3.** 58; **4.** 42; **5.** 45.
"Line and Color." **5.** 45.
"Looped Ears" [same as "Knotted Ears" or "Thieves' Ears"]. **2.** 48; **3.** 58.
"The Mad Artist." **5.** 45.
"Mitya's Love." **2.** 48; **3.** 58; **5.** 45.
"The Mordvinian Sarafan." **2.** 48.
"The Mowers." **3.** 58.
"Muza." **2.** 48.
"Natalie." **3.** 58.
"The New Growths." **2.** 48.
"News from Home." **2.** 48.
"Night" [originally "Cicadas"]. **2.** 48; **3.** 58.
"The Night of Denial." **2.** 48; **3.** 58.
"A Nocturnal Conversation." **2.** 48; **3.** 58.
"An Old Man" [same as "An Ancient Man"; originally "One Hundred Eight"]. **2.** 48.
"Old Shloime." **5.** 45.
"On the Field of Honor." **5.** 45.
"The Passing." **5.** 45.
"The Pines." **2.** 48; **3.** 58; **5.** 45.
"A Premature Spring." **2.** 49.
"The Prince Among Princes." **2.** 49.
"Rusya." **2.** 49.
"The Sacrifice." **2.** 49.
"Saints." **3.** 58.
"The School Master" [same as "The Teacher"]. **2.** 49.
"The Seekers." **2.** 49.
"The Son." **2.** 49; **5.** 45.
"A Spring Evening." **2.** 49; **3.** 58.
"Sunstroke." **2.** 49; **3.** 58.
"Tan'ka." **2.** 49.
"Tanya." **2.** 49. **3.** 58.
"An Unknown Friend." **5.** 45.
"Visiting Cards." **2.** 49.
"The Weed." **2.** 49.
"The Yelagin Affair" [same as "The Elagin Affair"]. **2.** 46, 50; **3.** 59; **5.** 45.
"Zakhar Vorobyov" [same as "Zaxar Vorob'ev"]. **2.** 50.

H. C. BUNNER

"The Pettibone 'Brolly." **4.** 42.

ANTHONY BURGESS

"The Muse: A Sort of SF Story." **3 ed.** 78.

THOMAS BURKE

"The Chink and the Child." **3 ed.** 78.

YEHUDA BURLA

"Luna." **3.** 59.

DAVID BURN

"The Three Sisters." **4.** 42.

EDWARD BURNE-JONES

"The Cousins." **4.** 42.
"A Story of the North." **4.** 42.

WHIT BURNETT

"Sherrel." **3 ed.** 78.

EDGAR RICE BURROUGHS

"The Mouthpiece of Zitu." **3.** 59.

WILLIAM BURROUGHS

"The Beginning Is Also the End." **1.** 26.
"23 Skidoo Eristic Elite." **3 ed.** 78.

ROBERT WILSON BURTON

"Improvisatore: The Wonderful Shower of Frogs." **4.** 42.

WILHELM BUSCH

"Edward's Dream." **5.** 45.

ELLIS PARKER BUTLER

"Pigs Is Pigs." **1.** 26.

JOHN K. BUTLER

"The Saint in Silver." **4.** 42.

OCTAVIA E. BUTLER

"Bloodchild." **4.** 43.
"Crossover." **4.** 43.
"Near of Kin." **4.** 43.

DINO BUZZATI

"A Drop." **3.** 59.
"Fear at La Scala." **5.** 45.
"The Seven-Storied Hospital." **5.** 45.

VASILY BYKOV

"His Battalion." **2.** 50.
"Obelisk." **2.** 50.
"Sotnikov." **3.** 59.

C. E. B. [unidentified]

"A Celestial Tragedy." **2.** 50.

JUAN DE LA CABADA

"El grillo crepuscular." **4.** 43.

FERNÁN CABALLERO

"The Daughter of the Sun." **1.** 26.
"The Flower of Ruins." **1.** 26.
"Silence in Life and Pardon in Death." **1.** 26.
"Time Is Longer Than Fortune." **1.** 26.
"The Two Friends." **1.** 26.

JAMES BRANCH CABELL

"The Choices." **3 ed.** 78.
"In Necessity's Mortar." **3 ed.** 78.
"In the Second April." **3 ed.** 78.
"The Rat-Trap." **3 ed.** 78.
"The Sestina." **3 ed.** 78.
"Simon's Hour." **3 ed.** 78.
"The Tenson." **3 ed.** 78.

GEORGE WASHINGTON CABLE

"Attalie." **3 ed.** 79.
"Au Large." **3 ed.** 79.
"Belles Demoiselles Plantation." **3 ed.** 79; **1.** 27; **5.** 46.
"Café des Exilés." **3 ed.** 79; **5.** 46.
"Don Joaquin." **3 ed.** 79.
"The Entomologist." **3 ed.** 79.
"The 'Haunted House' in Royal Street." **3 ed.** 79.
"Jean-ah Poquelin." **3 ed.** 79; **1.** 27; **3.** 59; **5.** 46.
"Madame Délicieuse." **3 ed.** 79; **5.** 46.
"Madame Delphine." **3 ed.** 79.
"Posson Jone'," **3 ed.** 79; **5.** 46.

"'Sieur George." **3 ed.** 79–80; **5.** 46.
"The Solitary" [originally "Gregory's Island"]. **3 ed.** 80; **1.** 27.
"The Story of Bras-Coupé." **1.** 27.
"The Taxidermist." **3 ed.** 80.
"'Tite Poulette." **3 ed.** 80; **5.** 46.

LYDIA CABRERA

"The Devil's Treasurer." **3.** 59.
"La Loma de Mambiala." **3.** 59.
"Se hace ebó." **4.** 43.
"The Sweet Potato Thief." **3.** 60.

GUILLERMO CABRERA INFANTE

"At the Great Echo." **3.** 60.
"Un rato de tenmealla." **3.** 60.
"Undertow." **5.** 46.
"Water of Memory." **5.** 46.

VÍCTOR CÁCERES LARA

"Paludismo." **5.** 46.

ABRAHAM CAHAN

"The Apostate of Chego-Chegg." **1.** 27; **3.** 60.
"Circumstances." **1.** 27; **3.** 60.
"The Daughter of Avrom Leib" [". . . Reb Avrom Leib"]. **1.** 27; **3.** 60.
"Dumitru and Sigrid." **1.** 27; **3.** 60.
"Fanny and Her Suitors" [same as "Fanny's Khasonim"]. **1.** 27.
"A Ghetto Wedding." **1.** 27; **3.** 60.
"The Imported Bridegroom." **1.** 27; **3.** 60.
"A Marriage by Proxy: A Story of the City." **1.** 27.
"A Providential Match" [same as "Mottke Arbel and His Romance"]. **1.** 27; **3.** 60.
"Rabbi Eliezer's Christmas." **1.** 28; **3.** 60.
"Rafael Naarizokh Becomes a Socialist." **1.** 28.
"A Sweatshop Romance." **1.** 28.
"Tzinchadzi of the Catskills." **1.** 28; **3.** 60.

ERSKINE CALDWELL

"August Afternoon." **3 ed.** 80; **3.** 61.
"Blue Boy." **3 ed.** 80.
"Country Full of Swedes." **3 ed.** 80.
"Daughter." **3 ed.** 80; **1.** 28.
"The Growing Season." **3 ed.** 80.
"Indian Summer." **3 ed.** 80.
"Kneel to the Rising Sun." **3 ed.** 80; **1.** 28.
"Knife to Cut the Cornbread With." **2.** 50.
"The Lonely Day." **3 ed.** 80.
"Masses of Men." **3 ed.** 80.
"My Old Man's Baling Machine." **3 ed.** 80.
"The Negro in the Well." **3 ed.** 80.
"The People vs. Abe Lathan, Colored." **3 ed.** 81.
"The Sacrilege of Alan Kent." **3 ed.** 81.
"Saturday Afternoon." **3 ed.** 81.
"Savannah River Payday." **3 ed.** 81.
"Slow Death." **1.** 28.
"The Sunfield." **3 ed.** 81.
"A Swell Looking Girl." **3 ed.** 81.
"Where the Girls Were Different." **1.** 28.
"Yellow Girl." **3 ed.** 81.

HORTENSE CALISHER

"Heartburn." **3 ed.** 81.
"If You Don't Want to Live I Can't Help You." **4.** 43.
"The Old Stock." **5.** 46.
"The Rabbi's Daughter." **4.** 43.
"The Scream on Fifty-Seventh Street." **1.** 28.
"Time, Gentlemen." **4.** 43.
"The Watchers." **4.** 43.

MORLEY CALLAGHAN

"Amuck in the Bush." **3 ed.** 81.
"Ancient Lineage." **3 ed.** 81; **5.** 47.
"An Autumn Penitent." **3 ed.** 81.
"The Blue Kimono." **3 ed.** 81.
"A Cap for Steve." **3 ed.** 81; **2.** 50.
"The Cheat's Remorse." **3 ed.** 81.
"A Cocky Young Man." **3 ed.** 82.
"A Country Passion." **3 ed.** 82.
"The Enchanted Pimp." **3.** 61.
"An Escapade." **3 ed.** 82.
"The Faithful Wife." **3 ed.** 82.
"Father and Son." **3 ed.** 82.
"Getting on in the World." **3 ed.** 82; **3.** 61.
"A Girl with Ambition." **3 ed.** 82.
"In His Own Country." **3 ed.** 82.
"It Had to Be Done." **3 ed.** 82.
"Last Spring They Came Over." **3 ed.** 82; **5.** 47.
"The Life of Sadie Hall." **3 ed.** 82.
"The Loved and the Lost." **3 ed.** 82.
"Mr. and Mrs. Fairbanks." **3 ed.** 82.

"Now That April's Here." **3 ed.** 82.
"A Predicament." **3 ed.** 82.
"A Princely Affair." **3 ed.** 83.
"The Red Hat." **3 ed.** 83.
"A Sick Call." **3 ed.** 83; **2.** 50; **5.** 47.
"Soldier Harmon." **3 ed.** 83.
"Two Fishermen." **3 ed.** 83.
"A Wedding Dress." **3 ed.** 83.
"The Young Priest." **2.** 50.

ITALO CALVINO

"The Adventure of a Motorist." **3.** 61.
"The Adventure of a Photographer." **4.** 43; **5.** 47.
"The Adventure of a Poet." **3.** 61.
"The Adventure of a Reader." **3.** 61.
"The Adventure of a Soldier." **3.** 61.
"All at One Point." **3 ed.** 83; **5.** 47.
"The Argentina Ant." **5.** 47.
"The Baron in the Trees." **4.** 43; **5.** 47.
"Big Fish, Little Fish." **3.** 61.
"Blood, Sea." **5.** 47.
"The Canary Prince." **3.** 61.
"The Cloven Viscount." **4.** 44; **5.** 47.
"The Contemplation of the Stars." **5.** 47.
"Crystals." **5.** 47.
"The Dinosaurs." **5.** 47.
"The Distance of the Moon." **3.** 61; **5.** 47.
"A Goatherd at Lunch." **3.** 61.
"The Hen of the Department." **3.** 61.
"How Much Should We Bet?" **4.** 44.
"Last Comes the Crow." **4.** 44; **5.** 47.
"My Aquatic Uncle." **5.** 48.
"The Nonexistent Knight." **4.** 44; **5.** 48.
"The Peasant." **3.** 61.
"Priscilla." **5.** 48.
"Reading a Wave." **5.** 48.
"A Sign of Space." **3.** 62; **4.** 44.
"Smog." **5.** 48.
"The Spiral." **3.** 62.
"The Watcher." **5.** 48.
"Without Colors." **5.** 48.

ANNE CAMERON

"Copper Woman." **5.** 48.
"Old Magic." **5.** 48.

JOHN W. CAMPBELL

"Atomic Power." **3.** 62.
"Forgetfulness." **3.** 62.
"The Invaders." **4.** 44.
"Islands of Space." **3.** 62.
"The Last Evolution." **2.** 50.
"The Machine." **1.** 28; **3.** 62.
"The Mightiest Machine." **3.** 62.
"Night" [originally under pseudonym Don A. Stuart]. **3.** 62.
"Rebellion." **3.** 62.
"Twilight" [originally under pseudonym Don A. Stuart]. **1.** 28; **3.** 62; **4.** 44.
"When the Atoms Failed." **5.** 48.
"Who Goes There?" [originally under pseudonym Don A. Stuart]. **3.** 62.

MEG CAMPBELL

"Just Saying You Love Me Doesn't Make It So." **2.** 50; **3.** 62.

RAMSEY CAMPBELL

"Before the Storm." **5.** 48.
"The Cellars." **5.** 48.
"The Chimney." **4.** 44.
"Down There." **4.** 44.
"The End of a Summer Day." **5.** 48.
"The Sneering." **4.** 44.
"The Trick." **4.** 44.

DAVID CAMPTON

"At the Bottom of the Garden." **5.** 48.

ALBERT CAMUS

"The Adulterous Woman." **3 ed.** 83; **2.** 51; **3.** 63; **4.** 44; **5.** 49.
"The Fall." **3 ed.** 84–86; **1.** 29; **2.** 51; **3.** 63; **4.** 45; **5.** 49.
"The Fire." **3 ed.** 86.
"The Growing Stone." **3 ed.** 87; **1.** 29; **2.** 51; **3.** 63; **4.** 45; **5.** 49.
"The Guest." **3 ed.** 87; **1.** 29; **2.** 51–52; **3.** 63; **4.** 45; **5.** 49.
"Jonas, or The Artist at Work." **3 ed.** 87–88; **1.** 29; **2.** 52; **3.** 63; **4.** 45; **5.** 49.
"The Renegade." **3 ed.** 88; **1.** 29; **2.** 52–53; **3.** 64; **4.** 45; **5.** 49.
"The Silent Men." **3 ed.** 88; **2.** 53; **3.** 64; **4.** 45; **5.** 49.
"The Stranger." **3 ed.** 88–92; **1.** 29–30; **2.** 53; **3.** 64; **4.** 45–46; **5.** 49–50.

KAREL ČAPEK

"The Death of the Baron Granada." **3.** 64.
"The Disappearance of Actor Benda." **3.** 64.
"The Farm Murder." **3.** 64.
"The Footprints." **3.** 64.
"The Fortune-Teller." **3.** 64.
"The Last Judgment." **3.** 64.
"The Post Office Crime." **3.** 64.

KAREL and JOSEF ČAPEK

"The Living Flame." **4.** 46.

TRUMAN CAPOTE

"Among the Paths of Eden." **3 ed.** 92; **2.** 54.
"Brooklyn." **2.** 54.
"Children on Their Birthdays." **3 ed.** 92; **2.** 54.
"A Christmas Memory." **3 ed.** 93; **2.** 54; **3.** 65; **5.** 50.
"La Côte Basque." **2.** 54.
"Dazzle." **2.** 54.
"A Diamond Guitar." **3 ed.** 93; **2.** 54.
"The Headless Hawk." **3 ed.** 93; **2.** 54.
"House of Flowers." **3 ed.** 93; **2.** 54.
"Jug of Silver." **3 ed.** 93; **2.** 54; **3.** 65.
"Kate McCloud." **2.** 54.
"Master Misery." **3 ed.** 93; **1.** 30; **2.** 54.
"A Mink of One's Own." **2.** 54.
"Miriam." **3 ed.** 93; **2.** 54–55; **3.** 65; **4.** 46; **5.** 50.
"Mojave." **2.** 55.
"My Side of the Matter." **2.** 55; **5.** 50.
"Preacher's Legend." **2.** 55.
"Shut a Final Door." **3 ed.** 93; **2.** 55.
"A Tree of Night." **3 ed.** 93; **1.** 30; **2.** 55.
"Unspoiled Monsters." **2.** 55.
"The Walls Are Cold." **2.** 55.

EMILIO CARBALLIDO

"La caja vacía." **2.** 55.
"El cubilete." **2.** 55.
"Danza antigua." **2.** 55.
"La desterrada." **2.** 55.
"Las flores blancas." **2.** 55.
"A Half-Dozen Sheets." **2.** 55.
"Los huéspedes." **2.** 55.
"La paz después del combate." **2.** 56.
"Los prodijios." **2.** 56.

PETER CAREY

"The Fat Man in History." **1.** 30.
"Peeling." **5.** 50.

WILLIAM CARLETON

"The Battle of the Factions." **3.** 65; **4.** 46.
"The Broken Oath." **2.** 56; **3.** 65.
"The Brothers." **2.** 56; **3.** 65.
"The Castle of Aughentain, or Legend of the Brown Goat." **4.** 46.
"Condy Cullen; or, The Excisemen Defeated." **3.** 65.
"Confessions of a Reformed Ribbonman." **3.** 65; **4.** 67.
"The Death of a Devotee." **2.** 56.
"Denis O'Shaughnessy Going to Maynooth." **2.** 56; **3.** 65; **4.** 46.
"Dinner at Helen's." **5.** 50.
"The Donagh, or the Horse Stealers." **2.** 56; **3.** 65.
"Father Butler." **2.** 56; **3.** 65; **4.** 46.
"The Funeral and the Party Fight." **3.** 65; **4.** 46.
"The Geography of an Irish Oath." **3.** 66.
"The Hedge School." **2.** 56; **3.** 66; **4.** 46; **5.** 50.
"The History of a Chimney Sweep." **2.** 56.
"The Illicit Distiller, or The Force of Conscience." **2.** 56; **3.** 66.
"An Irish Wedding." **2.** 56.
"Jane Sinclair, or the Fawn of Springvale." **4.** 46.
"Lachlin Murray and the Blessed Candle." **2.** 56.
"Larry M'Farland's Wake." **3.** 66.
"A Legend of Knockmany." **3.** 66; **4.** 46.
"The Lianhan Shee, An Irish Superstition." **2.** 56; **3.** 66; **4.** 46.
"The Lough Derg Pilgrim." **2.** 56; **3.** 66; **4.** 47.
"Mary Murray the Irish Matchmaker." **3.** 66.
"The Materialist." **2.** 56.
"The Midnight Mass." **2.** 57; **3.** 66; **4.** 47.
"Neal Malone." **3.** 66.
"Ned M'Keown." **4.** 47.
"Party Fight." **2.** 57.
"Phelim O'Toole's Courtship." **2.** 57; **3.** 66; **4.** 47.
"Phil Purcel, the Pig-Driver." **2.** 57; **3.** 66.

"A Pilgrimage to Patrick's Purgatory." **1.** 30; **3.** 66.
"The Poor Scholar." **2.** 57; **3.** 66; **4.** 47; **5.** 50.
"The Priest's Funeral." **2.** 57.
"The Rival Kempers." **4.** 47.
"Shane Fadh's Wedding." **3.** 66; **4.** 47.
"The Station." **2.** 57; **3.** 67; **4.** 47.
"The Three Tasks." **3 ed.** 94; **4.** 47.
"Tom Gressiey, the Irish Senachie." **3.** 67.
"Tubber Derg, or The Red Well" [expansion of story originally titled "The Landlord and the Tenant"]. **3.** 67.
"Wildgoose Lodge" [originally "Confessions of a Reformed Ribbonman"]. **1.** 30; **3.** 67.

EDWARD CARPENTER

"Narayan." **5.** 50.

ALEJO CARPENTIER

"El año 59." **1.** 30.
"The Chosen." **4.** 47.
"Los convidados de plata." **1.** 30.
"The Fugitives." **2.** 57; **4.** 47; **5.** 50–51.
"The High Road of St. James." **2.** 57; **3.** 67; **4.** 47; **5.** 51.
"Histoire de Lunes." **3.** 67.
"Journey to the Source" [same as "Journey to the Seed"]. **1.** 31; **2.** 57; **4.** 48; **5.** 51.
"Like the Night." **4.** 48; **5.** 51.
"Lord, Praised Be Thou." **1.** 31.
"Manhunt." **3 ed.** 94; **1.** 31; **5.** 51–52.
"Moonstruck." **4.** 48.
"Morning Service." **4.** 48; **5.** 52.

TOMÁS CARRASQUILLA

"San Antoñito." **5.** 52.

ROCH CARRIER

"The Nun Who Returned to Ireland." **4.** 48.

LEONORA CARRINGTON

"The Debutante." **5.** 52.

MIGUEL DE CARRÓN

"Astros y besos." **5.** 52.
"Un contraste." **5.** 52.
"De la guerra." **5.** 52.
"En familia." **5.** 52.
"El error." **5.** 53.
"Inocencia." **5.** 53.
"La noche virtuosa." **5.** 53.
"El rebaño." **5.** 53.
"La última voluntad." **5.** 53.
"El viudo." **5.** 53.

ANGELA CARTER

"Black Venus." **5.** 53.
"The Bloody Chamber." **4.** 48.
"The Cabinet of Edgar Allan Poe." **5.** 53.
"Our Lady of the Massacre." **5.** 53.

CLEVE CARTMILL

"Deadline." **5.** 53.

RAYMOND CARVER

"After the Denim." **5.** 53.
"Are You a Doctor?" **2.** 57; **5.** 53.
"The Bath." **4.** 48; **5.** 53.
"Bicycles, Muscles, Cigarettes." **5.** 53.
"Boxes." **5.** 54.
"The Bridle." **5.** 54.
"The Calm." **4.** 48; **5.** 54.
"Careful." **5.** 54.
"Cathedral." **4.** 48; **5.** 54.
"Chef's House." **5.** 54.
"Collectors." **2.** 57; **5.** 54.
"The Compartment." **5.** 54.
"Distance." **5.** 54.
"The Ducks." **5.** 54.
"Dummy." **5.** 54.
"Elephant." **5.** 54.
"Fat." **5.** 54.
"The Father." **2.** 57; **5.** 54.
"Feathers." **5.** 54.
"Fever." **5.** 54.
"The Fling." **5.** 55.
"Furious Seasons." **5.** 55.
"Gazebo." **5.** 55.
"Harry's Death." **5.** 55.
"How About This?" **5.** 55.
"I Could See the Smallest Things." **5.** 55.
"The Idea." **2.** 58; **5.** 55.
"Jerry and Molly and Sam." **5.** 55.
"The Lie." **5.** 55.
"Mine." **5.** 55.
"Mr. Coffee and Mr. Fixit." **5.** 55.
"Neighbors." **2.** 58; **5.** 55.

"Night School." **5.** 55.
"Nobody Said Anything." **5.** 55.
"One More Thing." **5.** 55.
"Pastoral." **5.** 55.
"Popular Mechanics." **5.** 55.
"Preservation." **5.** 56.
"Put Yourself in My Shoes." **2.** 58; **5.** 56.
"Sacks." **5.** 56.
"A Serious Talk." **5.** 56.
"Signals." **5.** 56.
"Sixty Acres." **5.** 56.
"A Small, Good Thing." **4.** 49; **5.** 56.
"So Much Water So Close to Home." **5.** 56.
"The Student's Wife." **5.** 56.
"Tell the Women We're Going." **5.** 56.
"They're Not Your Husband." **5.** 56.
"The Train." **4.** 49; **5.** 56.
"Vitamins." **5.** 56.
"What Do You Do in San Francisco?" **5.** 56.
"What Is It?" **5.** 56.
"What We Talk About When We Talk About Love." **5.** 56–57.
"What's in Alaska?" **2.** 58; **5.** 56.
"Where I'm Calling From." **5.** 57.
"Why Don't You Dance?" **5.** 57.
"Why, Honey?" **5.** 57.
"Will You Please Be Quiet, Please?" **2.** 58.

JOYCE CARY

"The Breakout." **3 ed.** 94.
"Bush River." **3 ed.** 94.

CALVERT CASEY

"En el Potosí." **1.** 31.
"In partenza." **1.** 31.
"Polacca brillante." **1.** 31.
"El regreso." **1.** 31.

R. V. CASSILL

"And in My Heart." **3 ed.** 94.
"The Biggest Band." **1.** 31.
"Fracture." **3 ed.** 94.
"Happy Marriage." **3 ed.** 94.
"Larchmont Is Not the World." **3 ed.** 95.
"This Hand, These Talons." **3 ed.** 95.

ROSARIO CASTELLANOS

"Aceite guapo." **5.** 57.
"The Caprice Waltz." **3.** 67; **5.** 57.
"Cooking Lesson." **5.** 57.
"Ephemeral Friendships." **5.** 57.
"Family Album." **5.** 57.
"Fleeting Friends." **5.** 57.
"Guests in August." **5.** 57.
"Lección de cocina."**5.** 57.
"A Man of Destiny." **5.** 58.
"La muerte del tigre." **5.** 58.
"La rueda del hambriento." **5.** 58.
"Sunday." **5.** 58.
"La tregua." **1.** 31; **5.** 58.
"The Widower Roman." **5.** 58.

WILLA CATHER

"The Affair at Grover Station." **3.** 67.
"Alexandra." **5.** 58.
"Ardessa." **3 ed.** 95; **3.** 67.
"Before Breakfast." **3 ed.** 95; **3.** 68; **4.** 49; **5.** 58.
"Behind the Singer Tower." **3 ed.** 95; **3.** 68; **5.** 58.
"The Best Years." **3 ed.** 95; **4.** 49; **5.** 58.
"The Bohemian Girl." **3 ed.** 95; **3.** 68; **4.** 49; **5.** 58.
"The Bookkeeper's Wife." **3.** 68.
"The Burglar's Christmas." **4.** 49; **5.** 58.
"The Clemency of the Court." **3 ed.** 95; **2.** 58; **3.** 68; **5.** 58.
"Coming, Aphrodite!" [originally "Coming, Eden Bower!"]. **3 ed.** 95–96; **3.** 68; **4.** 49; **5.** 58.
"Consequences." **3.** 68; **4.** 49.
"The Count of Crow's Nest." **3.** 68; **5.** 58–59.
"The Dance at Chevalier's." **3.** 68.
"A Death in the Desert." **3 ed.** 96; **3.** 68; **5.** 59.
"The Diamond Mine." **3 ed.** 96; **3.** 68.
"El Dorado: A Kansas Recessional." **3 ed.** 96; **3.** 68.
"Double Birthday." **3 ed.** 96; **3.** 68; **5.** 59.
"Eleanor's House." **3 ed.** 96; **2.** 58; **3.** 68; **5.** 59.
"The Elopement of Allen Poole." **3 ed.** 96; **3.** 68; **5.** 59.
"The Enchanted Bluff." **3 ed.** 96; **1.** 31; **3.** 68.
"Eric Hermannson's Soul." **3 ed.** 96; **3.** 68; **5.** 59.
"The Fear That Walks by Noonday." **3.** 69; **4.** 49.

"Flavia and Her Artists." **3 ed.** 96; **3.** 69; **5.** 59.
"The Garden Lodge." **3 ed.** 97; **3.** 69; **4.** 49; **5.** 59.
"A Gold Slipper." **3 ed.** 97; **3.** 69; **5.** 59.
"Her Boss." **3 ed.** 97; **3.** 69.
"Jack-a-Boy." **3.** 69; **5.** 59.
"The Joy of Nelly Deane." **3 ed.** 97; **3.** 69; **5.** 59.
"Lou, the Prophet." **3 ed.** 97; **2.** 58; **3.** 69.
"The Marriage of Phaedra." **3 ed.** 97; **3.** 69; **4.** 49; **5.** 59.
"The Namesake." **3 ed.** 97; **3.** 69; **5.** 59.
"Nanette, An Aside." **3 ed.** 97; **3.** 69.
"Neighbour Rosicky." **3 ed.** 97–98; **1.** 31; **2.** 58; **3.** 69; **4.** 49; **5.** 59.
"A Night at Greenway Court." **3.** 69.
"The Old Beauty." **3 ed.** 98; **1.** 31; **3.** 69; **4.** 49; **5.** 59.
"Old Mrs. Harris." **3 ed.** 98; **3.** 69; **5.** 60.
"On the Divide." **3 ed.** 98; **2.** 58; **3.** 69; **4.** 50.
"On the Gull's Road." **3.** 70; **5.** 60.
"Paul's Case." **3 ed.** 98; **1.** 32; **2.** 58; **3.** 70; **4.** 50; **5.** 60.
"Peter." **3 ed.** 99; **2.** 58; **3.** 70; **5.** 60.
"The Professor's Commencement." **3 ed.** 99; **3.** 70; **5.** 60.
"The Profile." **3 ed.** 99; **3.** 70; **5.** 60.
"A Resurrection." **3.** 70.
"Scandal." **3 ed.** 99; **3.** 70.
"The Sculptor's Funeral." **3 ed.** 99; **3.** 70.
"The Sentimentality of William Tavener." **3.** 70.
"A Son of the Celestial." **3 ed.** 99.
"The Song of the Lark." **3 ed.** 99.
"The Strategy of the Were-Wolf Dog." **3.** 70.
"A Tale of the White Pyramid." **5.** 60.
"Tom Outland's Story." **3 ed.** 99; **2.** 58.
"Tommy, the Unsentimental." **3 ed.** 99; **5.** 60.
"The Treasure of Far Island." **3 ed.** 99; **3.** 70; **5.** 60.
"Two Friends." **3 ed.** 99; **3.** 70; **4.** 50; **5.** 60.
"Uncle Valentine." **3 ed.** 99; **3.** 70; **5.** 60.
"A Wagner Matinée." **3 ed.** 100; **2.** 58; **3.** 70; **4.** 50; **5.** 61.
"The Way of the World." **3.** 70.
"The Willing Muse." **3 ed.** 100; **3.** 71; **5.** 61.

MARY HARTWELL CATHERWOOD

"Career of a Prairie Farmer." **4.** 50.
"The Little Renault." **4.** 50.
"The Monument to the First Mrs. Smith." **4.** 50.
"The Spirit of an Illinois Town." **4.** 50.

W. A. CAWTHORNE

"The Kangaroo Islanders." **3 ed.** 100.

CAMILO JOSÉ CELA

"Don Anselmo." **3 ed.** 100.
"La lata de galletas del Chirlerín Marcial, randa de parlos." **5.** 61.
"Marcelo Brito." **3 ed.** 100.
"The Mysterious Murder on Blanchard Street." **3 ed.** 100.

PAUL CELAN

"Dialogue in the Mountains." **3 ed.** 100.

BLAISE CENDRARS [FRÉDÉRIC SAUSER]

"Le cercle du diamant." **2.** 59.
"Morganni Nameh." **2.** 59.
"Paris, Port-de-Mer." **2.** 59.
"La Tour Eiffel sidérale." **2.** 59.

ROBERT W. CHAMBERS

"The Demoiselle d'Ys." **2.** 59; **4.** 50.
"In the Court of the Dragon." **4.** 50.
"The Key to Grief." **4.** 50.
"The Maker of Moons." **3.** 71.
"The Mask." **4.** 50.
"The Messenger." **4.** 50.
"The Repairer of Reputations." **2.** 59; **4.** 50.
"The Silent Land." **4.** 51.
"The White Shadow." **4.** 51.
"The Yellow Sign." **4.** 51.

ADELBERT VON CHAMISSO

"Peter Schlemihls Wundersame Geschichte." **3 ed.** 100; **1.** 32; **3.** 71; **5.** 61.

JEFFERY PAUL CHAN

"Auntie Tsia Lays Dying." **3.** 71.
"The Chinese in Faifa." **5.** 61.
"Jackrabbit." **3.** 71; **5.** 61.

RAYMOND CHANDLER

"Bay City Blues." **3.** 71; **4.** 51.
"Blackmailers Don't Shoot." **3.** 71; **4.** 51.
"English Summer." **4.** 51.
"Goldfish." **4.** 51.
"Guns at Cyrano's." **4.** 51.
"I'll Be Waiting." **3 ed.** 101; **2.** 59; **4.** 51.
"Killer in the Rain." **4.** 51.
"The King in Yellow." **4.** 51.
"The Lady in the Lake." **3.** 71; **4.** 51.
"Mandarin's Jade." **3.** 71; **4.** 51.
"Nevada Gas." **4.** 51.
"No Crime in the Mountains." **3.** 71; **4.** 51.
"Pearls Are a Nuisance." **3.** 71.
"Red Wind." **3.** 72; **4.** 52.
"Spanish Blood." **4.** 52.
"Try the Girl." **3.** 72; **4.** 52.

EILEEN CHANG

"Blockade." **1.** 32.
"Jasmine Tea." **1.** 32.

CHANG HSI-KUO

"The Leader." **2.** 59.
"Red Boy." **2.** 59.

CHANG T'IEN

"After Her Departure." **1.** 32.
"The Bulwark." **1.** 32.
"The Mid-Autumn Festival." **1.** 32.
"On the Journey." **1.** 32.
"Spring Breeze." **1.** 32.

CHAO LIEN [YU DAFU] (see YU DAFU)

CHAO SHU-LI

"The Marriage of Hsiao Erh-hei." **1.** 32.

SUZY McKEE CHARNAS

"Scorched Supper on New Niger." **4.** 52.

MARY ELLEN CHASE

"Marigolds." **3 ed.** 101.
"A Return to Constancy." **3 ed.** 101.
"Sure Dwelling." **3 ed.** 101.

FRANÇOIS-RENÉ DE CHATEAUBRIAND

"Abencérraje." **3 ed.** 101; **1.** 33.
"Atala." **3 ed.** 101; **1.** 33; **2.** 59; **3.** 72; **4.** 52; **5.** 61.
"René." **3 ed.** 101–02; **1.** 33; **2.** 59–60; **3.** 72; **4.** 52; **5.** 61.

PADDY CHAYEFSKY

"A Few Kind Words from Newark." **1.** 33.
"The Giant Fan." **1.** 33.

JOHN CHEEVER

"The Angel of the Bridge." **1.** 33; **2.** 60; **3.** 72.
"Artemis, the Honest Well Digger." **2.** 60; **3.** 72; **4.** 52.
"The Bella Lingua." **1.** 33; **3.** 72.
"Boy in Rome." **2.** 60; **3.** 72.
"The Brigadier and the Golf Widow." **2.** 60; **3.** 72.
"Brimmer." **2.** 60.
"The Brothers." **2.** 60; **4.** 52.
"The Bus to St. James's." **3.** 73.
"Chaste Clarissa." **4.** 52.
"Christmas Is a Sad Season for the Poor." **3.** 73.
"Clancy in the Tower of Babel." **3.** 73; **4.** 52.
"Clementina." **1.** 33; **2.** 60; **3.** 73.
"The Common Day." **1.** 33; **4.** 52.
"The Country Husband." **3 ed.** 102; **1.** 33; **2.** 60; **3.** 73; **5.** 61.
"The Cure." **2.** 60.
"The Day the Pig Fell into the Well." **3.** 73.
"The Death of Justina." **1.** 33; **2.** 60; **3.** 73; **4.** 53; **5.** 62.
"An Educated American Woman." **2.** 60.
"The Embarkment for Cythera." **3.** 73.
"The Enormous Radio." **3 ed.** 102; **1.** 34; **2.** 60; **3.** 73; **4.** 53; **5.** 62.
"Expelled." **2.** 60; **5.** 62.
"The Five-Forty-Eight." **2.** 60; **3.** 73.
"The Fourth Alarm." **1.** 34; **2.** 61; **3.** 73.
"Gee-Gee." **2.** 61.
"The Geometry of Love." **3.** 73.
"Goodbye, My Brother." **3 ed.** 102; **1.** 34; **2.** 61; **3.** 74; **4.** 53.
"The Hartleys." **2.** 61.
"The Housebreaker of Shady Hill." **1.** 34; **2.** 61; **3.** 74.

"The Jewels of the Cabots." **2.** 61; **3.** 74.
"Just Tell Me Who It Was." **2.** 61; **3.** 74.
"The Leaves, the Lion-Fish, and the Bear." **5.** 62.
"The Lowboy." **2.** 61; **3.** 74; **4.** 53.
"Marito in Citta." **3.** 74.
"Metamorphoses." **2.** 61; **3.** 74.
"Miscellany of Characters That Will Not Appear." **2.** 61.
"The Music Teacher." **1.** 34; **2.** 61.
"O City of Broken Dreams." **3.** 74.
"O Youth and Beauty!" **1.** 34; **2.** 61; **3.** 74.
"The Ocean." **3.** 74.
"Percy." **2.** 61.
"The Pot of Gold." **3.** 74.
"Publick House." **2.** 61.
"Reunion." **5.** 62.
"The Scarlet Moving Van." **1.** 34; **2.** 61; **3.** 74; **4.** 53; **5.** 62.
"The Seaside Houses." **1.** 34; **2.** 61; **3.** 75; **5.** 62.
"The Season of Divorce." **5.** 62.
"The Sorrows of Gin." **3.** 75; **5.** 62.
"The Summer Farmer." **2.** 62; **3.** 75.
"The Superintendent." **3.** 75.
"The Survivor." **2.** 62.
"The Swimmer." **3 ed.** 102; **1.** 34; **2.** 62; **3.** 75; **4.** 53; **5.** 62.
"Torch Song." **2.** 62; **4.** 53.
"The Trouble of Marcie Flint." **2.** 62; **3.** 75.
"A Vision of the World." **1.** 34; **3.** 75; **5.** 62.
"A Woman Without a Country." **2.** 62.
"The World of Apples." **1.** 34; **2.** 62; **3.** 75.
"The Worm in the Apple." **2.** 62.
"The Wrysons." **1.** 34; **2.** 62; **3.** 75.

ANTON CHEKHOV

"About Love." **3 ed.** 102; **2.** 62; **5.** 63.
"After the Theatre." **3 ed.** 102.
"Agafya." **3 ed.** 102; **1.** 34; **5.** 63.
"Anna on the Neck." **3 ed.** 102; **1.** 34; **5.** 63.
"An Anonymous Story." **3 ed.** 102; **2.** 62; **5.** 63.
"The Antagonists." **3 ed.** 103.
"Anyuta." **3 ed.** 103; **1.** 35; **5.** 63.
"Ariadna." **3 ed.** 103; **1.** 35; **2.** 62; **5.** 63.
"An Artist's Story." **3 ed.** 103.
"At a Country House." **3 ed.** 103.
"At Home" [same as "The Homecoming"]. **3 ed.** 103; **1.** 35; **2.** 62.
"At Sea—A Sailor's Story." **3.** 76.
"An Attack of Nerves." **3 ed.** 103; **1.** 35.
"Beautiful Women" [same as "The Beauties"]. **3 ed.** 103; **1.** 35.
"The Bet." **3 ed.** 103; **3.** 76.
"The Betrothed" [same as "The Bride"]. **3 ed.** 103; **2.** 62, 63; **3.** 76; **5.** 63.
"Big Volodya and Little Volodya." **1.** 35.
"The Birthday Party." **5.** 63.
"The Bishop." **3 ed.** 103–04; **1.** 35; **2.** 62; **4.** 53; **5.** 63.
"The Black Monk." **3 ed.** 104; **2.** 63; **3.** 76; **4.** 53; **5.** 63.
"The Boys." **3 ed.** 104.
"The Butterfly." **3 ed.** 104.
"A Case History." **5.** 64.
"The Chameleon." **3 ed.** 104; **2.** 63.
"Champagne." **5.** 64.
"The Chemist's Wife." **3 ed.** 104.
"The Chorus Girl." **3 ed.** 104; **5.** 64.
"The Cook's Marriage." **3 ed.** 104.
"The Crooked Mirror." **3 ed.** 104.
"The Darling." **3 ed.** 104–05; **1.** 35; **2.** 63; **4.** 53; **5.** 64.
"The Daughter of Albion." **4.** 53.
"The Death of a Civil Servant." **3 ed.** 105.
"Difficult People." **5.** 64.
"A Doctor's Visit." **3 ed.** 105; **5.** 64.
"Dreams." **3 ed.** 105; **1.** 35; **2.** 63.
"A Dreary Story" [same as "A Boring Story," "A Dull Story," or "A Tedious Story"]. **3 ed.** 105; **1.** 35; **2.** 63; **4.** 53; **5.** 64.
"The Duel." **3 ed.** 105–06; **1.** 35; **2.** 63; **4.** 54; **5.** 64.
"Easter Eve." **3 ed.** 106; **1.** 35; **4.** 54; **5.** 64.
"Enemies." **3 ed.** 106; **1.** 35.
"The Examining Magistrate." **3 ed.** 106.
"Fat and Thin." **3 ed.** 106; **2.** 63.
"The Fish." **3 ed.** 106; **5.** 64.
"A Fragment." **2.** 63.
"From the Diary of a Violent-Tempered Man." **4.** 54.
"A Gentleman Friend." **3 ed.** 106; **1.** 35; **4.** 54.
"Gooseberries." **3 ed.** 106–07; **1.** 36; **2.** 63; **4.** 54; **5.** 64.
"The Grasshopper" [same as "La Cigale," or "The Flutterer," or "A Great Man";

originally "The Philistines"]. **3 ed.** 107; **1.** 36; **2.** 63; **5.** 64.
"Grisha." **3 ed.** 107; **2.** 63.
"Gusev." **3 ed.** 107; **1.** 36; **2.** 63; **5.** 64.
"Happiness." **3 ed.** 107; **1.** 36; **5.** 65.
"The Head Gardener's Story." **3.** 76.
"Heartache." **3 ed.** 107.
"A Horse Name." **1.** 36.
"The House with the Mezzanine." **3 ed.** 107; **1.** 36; **2.** 63; **5.** 65.
"The Huntsman" [same as "The Gamekeeper"]. **3 ed.** 107; **1.** 36; **5.** 65.
"In Exile." **3 ed.** 107; **3.** 76.
"In Spring." **3 ed.** 107.
"In the Cart." **2.** 64; **5.** 65.
"In the Ravine" [same as "In the Gully"]. **3 ed.** 107–08; **1.** 36; **2.** 64; **3.** 76; **4.** 54; **5.** 65.
"Ionych." **3 ed.** 108; **1.** 36.
"Ivanov." **5.** 65.
"The Kiss." **3 ed.** 108; **1.** 36; **2.** 64; **5.** 65.
"The Lady of the Manor." **3 ed.** 108.
"The Lady with the Dog" [same as "The Lady with the Lapdog," "The Lady with the Pet Dog," or "The Lady with the Small Dog"]. **3 ed.** 108; **1.** 36; **2.** 64; **3.** 76; **4.** 54; **5.** 65.
"The Lament" [same as "Misery"]. **3 ed.** 108, 109; **1.** 37; **2.** 64; **3.** 76; **4.** 54.
"Late-Blooming Flowers." **3 ed.** 108.
"The Letter." **3 ed.** 108.
"Lights." **3 ed.** 108; **1.** 37; **2.** 64.
"Live Merchandise." **3 ed.** 109.
"The Lottery Ticket." **3 ed.** 109.
"The Man in a Case" [same as "The Man in a Shell"]. **3 ed.** 109; **2.** 64; **5.** 65.
"Melyuzga." **2.** 64.
"Mire." **2.** 64.
"A Misfortune." **3 ed.** 109; **1.** 37; **2.** 64.
"My Anniversary." **3 ed.** 109.
"My Life." **3 ed.** 109; **1.** 37; **2.** 64; **5.** 65.
"My Wife." **5.** 65.
"Name Day" [same as "Name Party"]. **3 ed.** 109; **5.** 65.
"The Native Corner." **2.** 64.
"Neighbours." **3 ed.** 109; **4.** 54.
"A Nervous Breakdown." **3 ed.** 109; **3.** 76.
"The New Villa." **3 ed.** 109; **2.** 64.
"A Nightmare." **3 ed.** 109.
"Ninochka." **3 ed.** 109.
"Old Age." **3 ed.** 109.
"On Official Business" [same as "On Official Duty"]. **3 ed.** 110; **5.** 65.
"On the Cart." **1.** 37.
"On the Road." **3 ed.** 110; **2.** 65; **5.** 65–66.
"One Man's Meat." **3 ed.** 110.
"One's Own Corner." **3 ed.** 110.
"The Order of St. Anne." **5.** 66.
"Oysters." **3 ed.** 110; **2.** 65.
"The Party." **3 ed.** 110; **1.** 37; **4.** 54.
"Peasant Wives." **3 ed.** 110.
"Peasants." **3 ed.** 110; **1.** 37; **2.** 65; **3.** 76; **4.** 54; **5.** 66.
"Polinka." **3 ed.** 110.
"The Princess." **3 ed.** 110; **5.** 66.
"Requiem." **3 ed.** 110.
"A Romance with a Double-Bass." **3 ed.** 111.
"Rothschild's Fiddle." **3 ed.** 111; **2.** 65; **4.** 55.
"The Runaway." **3 ed.** 111.
"The Russian Master." **5.** 66.
"The Schoolmistress." **3 ed.** 111.
"The Service of the Dead." **3 ed.** 111.
"The Shooting Party." **3 ed.** 111; **5.** 66.
"Sleepy." **3 ed.** 111; **2.** 65; **5.** 66.
"Small Fry." **3 ed.** 111.
"Sorrow." **3 ed.** 111; **1.** 37.
"The Steppe." **3 ed.** 111; **1.** 37; **2.** 65; **4.** 55; **5.** 66.
"The Story of an Unknown Person." **3 ed.** 111; **5.** 66.
"The Story of Miss N. N." **2.** 65.
"The Student." **3 ed.** 111–12; **1.** 37; **4.** 55; **5.** 66.
"A Tale." **2.** 65.
"The Teacher of Literature." **3 ed.** 112; **1.** 37.
"Terror." **5.** 66.
"Thieves." **3 ed.** 112; **2.** 65.
"The Three Sisters." **5.** 66.
"Three Years." **3 ed.** 112; **1.** 37; **5.** 66.
"A Trifle from Real Life" [same as "A Trifling Occurrence"]. **3 ed.** 112; **2.** 65; **3.** 76; **5.** 66.
"The Trousseau." **3 ed.** 112.
"Two in One." **3 ed.** 112.
"Typhus." **2.** 65; **5.** 67.
"Under-Officer Prishibeyev." **3 ed.** 112.
"An Unpleasantness." **3 ed.** 112.
"An Upheaval." **1.** 37.
"Vanka." **3 ed.** 112; **1.** 37; **2.** 65.
"Verochka." **3 ed.** 112–13; **2.** 65; **5.** 67.

"Vint." **3 ed.** 113.
"A Visit to Friends" [same as "A Visit to a Friend"]. **3 ed.** 113; **1.** 37.
"Volodya" [originally "His First Love"]. **3 ed.** 113; **2.** 65.
"Ward No. 6." **3 ed.** 113; **1.** 38; **2.** 66; **3.** 76; **4.** 55; **5.** 67.
"The Wife" [same as "Zena"]. **3 ed.** 113.
"The Witch." **3 ed.** 113; **2.** 66; **5.** 67.
"A Woman's Kingdom." **3 ed.** 113; **1.** 38; **5.** 67.

CHEN JO-HSI

"Big Blue Fish." **2.** 66.
"Black Cat with Gray Eyes." **2.** 66.
"Ching-ching's Birthday." **2.** 66.
"Hsin Chuang." **2.** 66.
"Keng Erh in Peking." **2.** 66.
"The Last Performance." **2.** 66.
"Pa-li's Journey." **2.** 66.
"Spring Comes Late." **2.** 66.
"Subway." **2.** 66.
"Uncle Ch'in-chih." **2.** 66.

CH'EN YING-CHEN

"A Certain Afternoon." **5.** 67.
"The Country Village Teacher." **2.** 66.
"Forever Terra." **5.** 67.
"Mountain Path." **5.** 67.
"My Younger Brother K'ang Hsiung." **2.** 67.
"Poor, Poor Dumb Mouths." **2.** 67.
"A Race of Generals." **2.** 67.

MAXINE CHERNOFF

"Don't Send Poetry, Send Money." **5.** 67.

CHARLES W. CHESNUTT

"Aunt Mimy's Son." **2.** 67.
"Baxter's Procrustes." **3 ed.** 114; **2.** 67; **4.** 55.
"The Bouquet." **3 ed.** 114; **2.** 67.
"A Busy Day in a Lawyer's Office." **3 ed.** 114.
"Cicely's Dream." **1.** 38; **2.** 67.
"The Conjurer's Revenge." **3 ed.** 114; **1.** **38;** **3.** 77; **5.** 67.
"Dave's Neckliss." **2.** 67; **4.** 55; **5.** 67.
"The Doll." **3 ed.** 114; **2.** 67.
"The Dumb Witness." **4.** 55.
"Evelyn's Husband." **2.** 67.
"The Goophered Grapevine." **3 ed.** 114; **1.** 38; **2.** 67; **3.** 77; **5.** 68.
"The Gray Wolf's Ha'nt." **3 ed.** 114; **1.** 38; **2.** 67; **3.** 77; **5.** 68.
"Her Virginia Mammy." **3 ed.** 114; **1.** 38; **2.** 67; **4.** 55.
"Hot-Foot Hannibal." **3 ed.** 114–15; **1.** 38; **3.** 77; **5.** 68.
"How Dasdy Came Through." **3 ed.** 115.
"Lonesome Ben." **4.** 55.
"Mandy Oxendine." **2.** 67.
"The March of Progress." **2.** 67.
"The Marked Tree." **4.** 55.
"Mars Jeems's Nightmare." **3 ed.** 115; **1.** 38; **2.** 68; **3.** 77; **5.** 68.
"A Matter of Principle." **3 ed.** 115; **1.** 38; **2.** 68; **3.** 77.
"Mr. Taylor's Funeral." **3 ed.** 115.
"The Orgin [sic] of the Hatchet Story." **3 ed.** 115.
"The Partners." **2.** 68.
"The Passing of Grandison." **3 ed.** 115; **1.** 38; **2.** 68.
"Paul Marchand, F.M.C." **2.** 68.
"Po' Sandy." **3 ed.** 115; **1.** 38; **2.** 68; **3.** 77; **5.** 68.
"The Prophet Peter." **3 ed.** 115.
"The Quarry." **2.** 68.
"The Rainbow Chasers." **2.** 68.
"The Sheriff's Children." **3 ed.** 115; **1.** 38; **2.** 68; **5.** 68.
"Sis' Becky's Pickaninny." **3 ed.** 115; **1.** 38; **3.** 77; **5.** 68.
"A Tight Boot." **3 ed.** 115.
"Tom's Warm Welcome." **3 ed.** 116.
"Uncle Peter's House." **3 ed.** 116.
"Uncle Wellington's Wives." **3 ed.** 116; **2.** 68.
"A Victim of Heredity." **4.** 55.
"The Web of Circumstance." **3 ed.** 116; **1.** 39; **2.** 68; **3.** 77.
"The Wife of His Youth." **3 ed.** 116; **1.** 39; **2.** 68; **3.** 77; **4.** 55.

GILBERT KEITH CHESTERTON

"The Blast of the Book." **3.** 77.
"The Blue Cross." **3 ed.** 116.
"The Chief Mourner of Marne." **4.** 56.
"The Duel of Dr. Hirsch." **3.** 77.
"The Ghost of Gideon Wise." **3.** 77.

"The Green Man." **3 ed.** 116.
"The Hammer of God." **3 ed.** 116.
"The Invisible Man." **4.** 56.
"The Miracle of Moon Crescent." **3.** 77; **4.** 56.
"The Mistake of the Machine." **3.** 78.
"The Paradise of Thieves." **3.** 78.
"The Queer Feet." **3 ed.** 116.
"The Resurrection of Father Brown." **3.** 78.
"The Scandal of Father Brown." **3.** 78.
"The Secret Garden." **3.** 78.
"The Three Tools of Death." **4.** 56.
"The Yellow Bird." **3 ed.** 116.

RONALD CHETWYND-HAYES

"The Brats." **5.** 68.
"My Mother Married a Vampire." **5.** 68.
"Why?" **5.** 68.

CHIANG HUNG-CHIAO

"The Coward." **2.** 68.

CHIANG KUEI [WANG I-CHIEN]

"Ah-yüan." **3 ed.** 116.
"The Shoe That Didn't Fit." **3 ed.** 116.

CH'IEN CHUNG-SHU

"Cat." **1.** 39; **2.** 69.
"God's Dream." **2.** 69.
"Inspiration." **1.** 39.
"Souvenir." **1.** 39; **2.** 69.

CHIKAMATSU SHŪKŌ

"A Snowy Day." **5.** 68.

LYDIA MARIA CHILD

"Chocorua's Curse." **4.** 56.
"Hilda Silfverling." **4.** 56.
"Hobomok." **4.** 56.
"A Legend of the Falls of St. Anthony." **4.** 56.
"She Waits in the Spirit Land." **4.** 56.

FRANK CHIN

"Food for All His Dead." **3.** 78; **5.** 69.
"Goong Hai Fot Choy." **3.** 78.

IGNACY CHODZKO

"The Guardian Angel." **3 ed.** 117.
"The Heir's Return." **3 ed.** 117.
"The Jubilee." **3 ed.** 117.
"The Last Court Session." **3 ed.** 117.
"My Grandfather's House." **3 ed.** 117.
"Samovar." **3 ed.** 117.

KATE CHOPIN

"Alexander's Wonderful Experience." **4.** 56.
"At Chênière Caminada." **2.** 69; **4.** 56.
"At the 'Cadian Ball." **3 ed.** 117; **4.** 56.
"Athénaïse." **3 ed.** 117; **2.** 69; **3.** 78; **4.** 56–57.
"Azélie." **2.** 69; **4.** 57.
"La Belle Zoraïde." **2.** 69; **4.** 57.
"Beyond the Bayou." **2.** 69.
"Cavanelle." **4.** 57.
"Charlie." **3 ed.** 117; **4.** 57.
"Désirée's Baby." **3 ed.** 117; **1.** 39; **2.** 69; **3.** 78; **4.** 57.
"A Dresden Lady in Dixie." **3.** 78.
"An Egyptian Cigarette." **4.** 57.
"Elizabeth Stock's One Story." **4.** 57.
"A Family Affair." **4.** 57.
"Fedora." **2.** 69; **4.** 57.
"The Gentleman from New Orleans." **4.** 57.
"A Gentleman of Bayou Teche." **4.** 57.
"The Godmother." **4.** 57.
"The Going Away of Liza." **2.** 69; **3.** 78.
"The Haunted Chamber." **4.** 57.
"Her Letters." **3.** 78; **4.** 57.
"In and Out of Old Natchitoches." **3 ed.** 117; **4.** 58.
"In Sabine." **3 ed.** 117; **3.** 78; **4.** 58.
"The Kiss." **4.** 58.
"A Lady of Bayou St. John." **3.** 78; **4.** 58.
"Lilacs." **3 ed.** 117; **2.** 69; **4.** 58.
"Loka." **2.** 69; **3.** 79; **4.** 58.
"Love on the Bon-Dieu." **2.** 70; **3.** 79; **4.** 58.
"Madame Célestin's Divorce." **4.** 58.
"Madame Martel's Christmas Eve." **4.** 58.
"Ma'ame Pélagie." **2.** 70; **4.** 58.
"The Maid of St. Phillippe." **3.** 79.
"A Matter of Prejudice." **3.** 79; **4.** 58.
"Miss McEnders." **3 ed.** 117; **4.** 58.
"Mrs. Mobry's Reason." **4.** 58.
"A Morning Walk." **3.** 79.

"Nég Créol." **4.** 58.
"The Night Came Slowly." **4.** 58.
"A Night in Acadie." **4.** 58.
"A No-Account Creole." **3 ed.** 118; **4.** 59.
"Ozème's Holiday." **3 ed.** 118; **4.** 59.
"A Pair of Silk Stockings." **4.** 59; **5.** 69.
"A Point at Issue." **3 ed.** 118; **3.** 79; **4.** 59.
"Polly." **4.** 59.
"Regret." **3 ed.** 118; **3.** 79; **4.** 59; **5.** 69.
"A Respectable Woman." **2.** 70; **3.** 79; **4.** 59.
"The Return of Alcibiade." **4.** 59.
"Ripe Figs." **3.** 79.
"A Sentimental Soul." **2.** 70; **4.** 59.
"A Shameful Affair." **3.** 79; **4.** 59.
"The Storm." **3 ed.** 118; **2.** 70; **3.** 79; **4.** 59.
"The Story of an Hour." **3 ed.** 118; **2.** 70; **3.** 79; **4.** 59.
"Suzette." **4.** 59.
"Tante Cat'rinette." **4.** 59.
"Ti Démon." **4.** 59.
"Two Portraits." **4.** 60.
"The Unexpected." **3.** 79.
"Vagabonds." **3 ed.** 118; **2.** 70; **4.** 60.
"A Visit to Avoyelles." **3.** 79; **4.** 60.
"A Vocation and a Voice." **3 ed.** 118; **2.** 70; **4.** 60.
"The White Eagle." **3.** 80; **4.** 60.
"Wiser Than a God." **3 ed.** 118; **3.** 80; **4.** 60.

MICHAL CHOROMANSKI

"The Banal Tale." **3 ed.** 118.
"The Cynical Tale." **3 ed.** 118.
"The Incredible Tale." **3 ed.** 118.
"The Insane Tale." **3 ed.** 118.

CHOU CH'ÜAN-P'ING

"His Confession." **3.** 80.

PIOTR CHOYNOWSKI

"A Deed." **3 ed.** 118.
"The Five Sulerzycki Gentlemen." **3 ed.** 118.
"The Voyevod's Christmas Eve." **3 ed.** 119.

AGATHA CHRISTIE

"The Capture of Cerberus." **2.** 70.
"Tragedy of Marsdon Manor." **4.** 60.
"The Under Dog." **2.** 70.
"Where There's a Will." **2.** 70.

CHU HSI-NING

"Molten Iron." **2.** 70.

SADEQ CHUBAK

"A Bouquet." **3.** 80.
"The Burning of Omar." **3.** 80.
"The First Day in the Grave." **3.** 80.
"Flowers of Flesh." **3.** 80; **5.** 69.
"The Glass Eye." **3.** 80; **5.** 69.
"Gravediggers." **3.** 80; **5.** 69.
"Impoliteness." **3.** 80.
"The Last Lamp." **3.** 80.
"The Maroon Dress." **3.** 80; **5.** 69.
"The Monkey Whose Master Had Died." **3.** 80; **5.** 69.
"Monsieur Ilyas." **3.** 81; **5.** 69.
"The Purple Dress." **3.** 81.
"Under the Red Light." **3.** 81; **5.** 69.

CHUNG LI-HO

"Oleander." **2.** 71.

KAY CICELLIS

"The Way to Colonus." **3 ed.** 119.

CHARLES-ALBERT CINGRIA

"Le petit labyrinthe harmonique." **2.** 71.

CLARÍN [LEOPOLDO ALAS]

"El caballero de la mesa redonda." **5.** 70.
"The Conversion of Chiripa." **3.** 4; **5.** 70.
"Cuervo." **5.** 70.
"El diablo en Semana Santa." **5.** 70.
"El doctor Pértinax." **5.** 70.
"Las dos cajas." **5.** 70.
"El dúo de la tos." **4.** 4; **5.** 70.
"The Golden Rose." **5.** 70.
"Madrid, June 1882." **3.** 4.
"Una medianía." **5.** 70.
"Mi entierro." **5.** 70.
"La mosca sabia." **5.** 70.
"Para vicios." **5.** 70.

"Pipá." **4.** 4; **5.** 70–71.
"La Reina Margarita." **5.** 71.
"Snob." **5.** 71.
"Superchería." **5.** 71.
"Zurita." **5.** 71.

WALTER VAN TILBURG CLARK

"The Anonymous." **3 ed.** 119; **1.** 39.
"The Buck in the Hills." **3 ed.** 119; **1.** 39.
"Hook." **3 ed.** 119; **1.** 39; **5.** 71.
"The Indian Well." **3 ed.** 119; **1.** 39.
"The Portable Phonograph." **3 ed.** 119; **1.** 39; **2.** 71.
"The Rapids." **3 ed.** 119; **1.** 39.
"The Watchful Gods." **3 ed.** 119–20; **1.** 40; **2.** 71.
"Why Don't You Look Where You're Going?" **3 ed.** 120.
"The Wind and the Snow of Winter." **3 ed.** 120; **1.** 40.

ARTHUR C. CLARKE

"Breaking Strain." **3.** 81.
"Critical Mass." **3.** 81.
"The Curse." **3.** 81.
"The Defenestration of Erminstrude Inch." **3.** 81.
"Encounter at Dawn." **3.** 81.
"Hide and Seek." **3.** 81.
"History Lesson." **3.** 81.
"The Lion of Comarre." **3.** 81.
"The Man Who Ploughed the Sea." **3.** 81.
"A Meeting with Medusa." **1.** 40; **3.** 81.
"Moving Spirit." **3.** 81.
"The Next Tenants." **3.** 81.
"The Nine Billion Names of God." **1.** 40; **3.** 82.
"The Pacifist." **3.** 82.
"The Parasite." **3.** 82.
"Patent Pending." **3.** 82.
"The Reluctant Orchid." **3.** 82.
"Rescue Party." **3.** 82.
"The Road to the Sea" [originally "Seeker of the Sphynx"]. **3.** 82.
"Robin Hood, F.R.S." **3.** 82.
"Saturn Rising." **3.** 82.
"The Sentinel." **3.** 82.
"Silence, Please." **3.** 82.
"The Songs of Distant Earth." **3.** 82.
"The Star." **3 ed.** 120; **1.** 40; **2.** 71; **3.** 82; **4.** 60; **5.** 71.
"Summer on Icarus." **1.** 40; **3.** 83.
"Superiority." **3.** 83.
"Time's Arrow." **3.** 83.
"Trouble with Time." **3.** 83.
"The Ultimate Melody." **3.** 83.
"What Goes Up." **3.** 83.

AUSTIN CLARKE

"Four Stations in His Circle." **3 ed.** 120.
"The Motor Car." **3 ed.** 120.
"They Heard a Ringing of Bells." **4.** 60.

MARCUS CLARKE

"La Béguine." **5.** 71.
"The Gypsies of the Sea." **5.** 71.
"Holiday Peak." **5.** 71.
"Human Repetends." **5.** 71.
"Hunted Down." **5.** 71.
"A Mining Township." **5.** 72.
"The Mystery of Major Molineux." **5.** 72.
"Pretty Dick." **2.** 71; **5.** 72.
"An Up-Country Township." **5.** 72.

HAL CLEMENT

"Fireproof." **4.** 60.
"Impediment." **3.** 83.

LUCILLE CLIFTON

"The Magic Mama." **2.** 71.

MILDRED CLINGERMAN

"The Day of the Green Velvet Cloak." **3.** 83.
"A Red Heart and Blue Roses." **5.** 72.

STANTON A. COBLENTZ

"Manna from Mars." **3.** 83.

MANUEL COFRIÑO LÓPEZ

"Dania." **5.** 72.
"Magda, el mar, el aire." **5.** 72.
"El milagro de la lluvia." **5.** 72.
"Mirna." **5.** 72.
"Para leer mañana." **5.** 72.
"Tiempo de cambio." **5.** 72.

MATT COHEN

"Columbus and the Fat Lady." **3 ed.** 120.
"The Cure." **3.** 83.
"Johnny Crackle Sings." **2.** 71; **3.** 83.
"Korsoniloff." **2.** 72; **3.** 83.
"Vogel." **2.** 72; **3.** 83.

JOHN REECE COLE

"It Was So Late." **3.** 84.
"The Sixty-Nine Club." **3.** 84.
"Up at the Mammoth." **3.** 84.

SIDONIE-GABRIELLE COLETTE

"Bella-Vista." **3.** 84.
"The Cat." **3 ed.** 120; **3.** 84; **4.** 61.
"Chance Acquaintances." **3.** 84.
"Chéri." **3 ed.** 120; **3.** 84; **4.** 61; **5.** 72.
"Duo." **3 ed.** 121; **3.** 84.
"L'Enfant malade." **3 ed.** 121.
"Gigi." **3.** 84; **4.** 61; **5.** 72.
"The Hidden Woman." **5.** 73.
"The Kepi." **3.** 84.
"The Last of Chéri." **3 ed.** 121; **3.** 84; **5.** 73.
"The Patriarch." **2.** 72.
"The Photographer's Missus." **3.** 84.
"The Rainy Moon." **3.** 84.
"The Secret Woman." **3.** 84.
"The Tender Shoot." **2.** 72; **3.** 84; **5.** 73.
"Le Toutounier." **3 ed.** 121; **3.** 85.

ALFREDO COLLADO MARTELL

"Guillo 'el Holandes.'" **5.** 73.
"The Last Adventure of Patito Feo." **5.** 73.

JOHN COLLIER

"After the Ball." **3.** 85.
"Another American Tragedy." **3.** 85.
"Back for Christmas." **3.** 85.
"Bottle Party." **2.** 72.
"The Chaser." **2.** 72; **3.** 85; **4.** 61.
"De Mortuis." **3 ed.** 121; **2.** 72; **3.** 85.
"The Devil George and Rosie." **3.** 85.
"Evening Primrose." **3.** 85.
"Fallen Star." **3.** 85.
"The Frog Prince." **3.** 85.
"Gavin O'Leary." **3.** 85.
"Green Thoughts." **2.** 72.
"The Invisible Dove of Strathpheen Island." **3.** 85.
"Mary." **3.** 85.
"A Matter of Taste." **3.** 85.
"The Right Side." **3.** 85.
"Romance Lingers, Adventure Lives." **3.** 85.
"Sleeping Beauty." **3.** 86.
"Special Delivery." **3.** 86.
"Three Bears Cottage." **4.** 61.
"Thus I Refute Beelzy." **3 ed.** 121; **4.** 61.
"Variation on a Theme." **3.** 86.
"Wet Saturday." **1.** 40; **3.** 86.
"Witch's Money." **3.** 86.
"Without Benefit of Galsworthy." **3.** 86.

[WILLIAM] WILKIE COLLINS

"Anne Rodway." **3.** 86.
"The Biter Bit." **3.** 86.
"Blow Up with the Brig!" **2.** 72.
"Brother Griffin's Story of Mad Monckton." **2.** 72; **4.** 61.
"Brother Morgan's Story of the Dead Hand." **4.** 61.
"The Double-Bedded Room." **2.** 72.
"The Dream Woman." **3.** 86.
"Miss Jéromette and the Clergyman." **4.** 61.
"Plot in Private Life." **3.** 86.
"The Spectre of Tappington." **3.** 86.
"A Terribly Strange Bed." **2.** 72; **5.** 73.
"The Yellow Mask." **4.** 61.

FRANK APPLETON COLLYMORE

"Mark Learns Another Lesson." **4.** 61.
"Shadows." **4.** 62.
"The Snag." **4.** 62.

CYRUS COLTER

"The Beach Umbrella." **3 ed.** 121.
"A Chance Meeting." **3 ed.** 121.
"A Man in the House." **3 ed.** 121.
"Moot." **3 ed.** 121.

PADRAIC COLUM

"Eilis: A Woman's Story." **3 ed.** 121.
"The Flute Player's Story." **3 ed.** 122; **4.** 62.

ALEX COMFORT

"The Martyrdom of the House." **3 ed.** 122.

SARAH COMSTOCK

"Ways That Are Dark." **2.** 72.

ENRIQUE CONGRAINS MARTÍN

"Cuatro pisos, mil esperanzas." **3 ed.** 122.
"Lima, hora cero." **3 ed.** 122.
"El niño de junto al cielo." **5.** 73.

EVAN S. CONNELL

"The Anatomy Lesson." **3 ed.** 122.
"Arcturus." **3 ed.** 122.
"The Fisherman from Chihuahua." **3 ed.** 122.
"Guatemala." **3 ed.** 122.
"St. Augustine's Pigeon." **3 ed.** 122.
"The Trellis." **3 ed.** 122.
"The Walls of Avila." **3 ed.** 122.
"The Yellow Raft." **3 ed.** 122.

RICHARD CONNELL

"The Most Dangerous Game." **3 ed.** 122; **1.** 40; **2.** 73; **4.** 62; **5.** 73.

JOSEPH CONRAD

"Amy Foster." **3 ed.** 123; **1.** 40; **2.** 73; **3.** 86; **4.** 62; **5.** 73.
"An Anarchist." **3 ed.** 123; **2.** 73; **4.** 62.
"Because of the Dollars." **3 ed.** 123; **3.** 86.
"The Black Mate." **3 ed.** 124; **3.** 86; **4.** 62; **5.** 73–74.
"The Brute." **3 ed.** 124; **3.** 86; **5.** 74.
"Il Conde." **3 ed.** 124; **2.** 73; **3.** 87.
"The Duel." **3 ed.** 124–25; **2.** 73; **4.** 62.
"The End of the Tether." **3 ed.** 125; **1.** 40; **2.** 73; **3.** 87; **4.** 62; **5.** 74.
"Falk." **3 ed.** 125–26; **1.** 41; **2.** 73; **3.** 87; **4.** 62; **5.** 74.
"Freya of the Seven Isles." **3 ed.** 126; **1.** 41; **2.** 73; **3.** 87.
"Gaspar Ruiz." **3 ed.** 126; **4.** 62.
"Heart of Darkness." **3 ed.** 126–33; **1.** 41; **2.** 73–74; **3.** 87–88; **4.** 62–64; **5.** 74–75.
"The Idiots." **3 ed.** 133–34; **2.** 74; **3.** 88; **4.** 64; **5.** 75.
"The Informer." **3 ed.** 134; **1.** 41; **2.** 74; **4.** 64.
"The Inn of the Two Witches." **3 ed.** 134; **3.** 88; **4.** 64; **5.** 75.
"Karain." **3 ed.** 134; **1.** 41–42; **2.** 74; **3.** 88; **5.** 76.
"The Lagoon." **3 ed.** 134–35; **1.** 42; **2.** 74–75; **3.** 88; **4.** 64; **5.** 76.
"An Outcast of the Islands." **2.** 75; **3.** 88.
"An Outpost of Progress." **3 ed.** 135–36; **1.** 42; **2.** 75; **3.** 89; **4.** 64; **5.** 76.
"The Partner." **3 ed.** 136; **3.** 89.
"The Planter of Malata." **3 ed.** 136; **2.** 75; **3.** 89; **4.** 64.
"Prince Roman." **3 ed.** 136; **3.** 89.
"The Rescue." **4.** 64.
"The Return." **3 ed.** 136; **1.** 42; **2.** 75; **3.** 89; **4.** 64; **5.** 76.
"The Secret Sharer." **3 ed.** 136–39; **1.** 42; **2.** 75; **3.** 89; **4.** 64–65; **5.** 76.
"The Shadow Line." **3 ed.** 139–40; **1.** 42; **2.** 75; **3.** 89; **4.** 65; **5.** 76.
"A Smile of Fortune." **3 ed.** 140; **2.** 75; **3.** 90; **4.** 65.
"The Tale." **3 ed.** 140–41; **2.** 75; **3.** 90; **5.** 76.
"Tomorrow." **3 ed.** 141; **2.** 75; **5.** 76.
"Typhoon." **3 ed.** 141–42; **1.** 42; **2.** 76; **3.** 90; **4.** 65; **5.** 76–77.
"The Warrior's Soul." **3 ed.** 142; **3.** 90.
"Youth." **3 ed.** 142–43; **1.** 43; **2.** 76; **3.** 90; **4.** 65; **5.** 77.

BENJAMIN CONSTANT

"Adolphe." **3 ed.** 143; **1.** 43; **2.** 76; **3.** 90; **5.** 77.

C. W. CONTESSA

"Meister Dietrich." **3 ed.** 144.

GONZALO CONTRERAS

"Naves quemadas." **5.** 77.

ROSE TERRY COOKE

"Alcedema Sparks; or Old and New." **3.** 90.
"Cal Culver and the Devil." **3 ed.** 144.
"Clary's Trial." **3.** 91.
"Dely's Cow." **4.** 65.
"Doom and Dan." **3.** 91; **4.** 65.
"Eben Jackson." **4.** 65.
"Freedom Wheeler's Controversy with Providence." **3 ed.** 144; **3.** 91; **4.** 65.

"How Celia Changed Her Mind." **2.** 76; **3.** 91; **4.** 66.
"Love." **3.** 91.
"Miss Beulah's Bonnet." **4.** 66.
"Miss Lucinda." **4.** 66.
"Mrs. Flint's Married Experience." **3.** 91; **4.** 66.
"The Mormon's Wife." **3.** 91.
"My Visitation." **4.** 66.
"Polly Mariner, Tailoress." **3 ed.** 144; **2.** 76; **3.** 91; **4.** 66.
"The Ring Fetter." **3.** 91; **4.** 66.
"Some Account of Thomas Tucker." **4.** 66.
"Tenty Scran." **4.** 66.
"Too Late." **3.** 91; **4.** 66.
"The Valley of Childish Things." **4.** 66.

ROBERT COOVER

"Aesop's Forest." **4.** 66.
"The Babysitter." **3 ed.** 144; **1.** 43; **2.** 76; **3.** 91; **4.** 66; **5.** 77.
"Beginnings." **2.** 76.
"A Brief Encounter." **4.** 67.
"The Brother." **3 ed.** 144; **2.** 76; **3.** 91; **4.** 67; **5.** 77.
"The Cat in the Hat for President." **2.** 77.
"The Dead Queen." **2.** 77; **4.** 67.
"The Door: A Prologue of Sorts." **3.** 91; **4.** 67.
"The Elevator." **1.** 43; **2.** 77; **3.** 91; **4.** 67; **5.** 77.
"The Gingerbread House." **2.** 77; **3.** 92; **4.** 67.
"The Hat Act." **2.** 77; **3.** 92.
"In a Train Station." **2.** 77; **3.** 92; **5.** 77.
"J's Marriage." **2.** 77; **3.** 92; **4.** 67; **5.** 78.
"The Kid." **2.** 77.
"Klee Dead." **2.** 77; **3.** 92; **5.** 78.
"The Leper's Helix." **3 ed.** 144; **2.** 77; **3.** 92; **4.** 67.
"Love Scene." **2.** 77.
"Lucky Pierre and the Music Lesson." **2.** 77.
"McDuff on the Mound." **2.** 77.
"The Magic Poker." **2.** 77; **3.** 92; **4.** 67.
"The Marker." **2.** 77; **3.** 92; **4.** 67; **5.** 78.
"The Milkmaid of Samaniago." **2.** 78; **3.** 92.
"Morris in Chains." **2.** 78; **3.** 92; **4.** 67.
"Panel Game." **2.** 78; **3.** 92; **4.** 67; **5.** 78.
"The Pedestrian Accident." **3 ed.** 144; **2.** 78; **3.** 92.
"Quenby and Ola, Swede and Carl." **2.** 78; **3.** 92; **4.** 67; **5.** 78.
"Rip Awake." **2.** 78.
"Romance of the Thin Man and the Fat Lady." **2.** 78; **3.** 92.
"Scene for Winter." **2.** 78; **3.** 92.
"The Second Son." **2.** 78.
"Spanking the Maid." **3.** 92; **4.** 67.
"A Theological Position." **2.** 78.
"The Wayfarer." **3.** 93; **5.** 78.
"Whatever Happened to Gloomy Gus of the Chicago Bears?" **2.** 78; **4.** 67.
"You Must Remember This." **4.** 68.

JACK COPE

"A Crack in the Sky." **3 ed.** 144.

A. E. COPPARD

"Adam and Eve and Pinch Me." **3 ed.** 144; **2.** 78.
"Arabesque." **3 ed.** 144.
"Emergency Exit." **3 ed.** 144.
"The Field of Mustard." **3.** 93.
"Fifty Pounds." **3 ed.** 145.
"The Higgler." **3 ed.** 145; **2.** 78; **3.** 93.
"Olive and Camilla." **3 ed.** 145.
"The Watercress Girl." **3 ed.** 145.
"A Wildgoose Chase." **3 ed.** 145.
"Willie Waugh." **3 ed.** 145.

DANIEL CORKERY

"The Awakening." **5.** 78.
"Carrig-an-Afrinn" [same as "The Mass Rock"]. **2.** 78; **4.** 68.
"The Eyes of the Dead." **3.** 93; **5.** 78.
"Joy." **4.** 68.
"A Looter of the Hills." **5.** 78.
"On the Heights." **4.** 68.
"The Ploughing of Leaca-Na-Naomh." **4.** 68.
"The Priest." **2.** 79.
"The Serenade." **5.** 78.
"Storm-Struck." **4.** 68.
"Vision." **5.** 78.
"The Wager." **4.** 68.
"The Wraith of the Kilronans." **5.** 78.

JULIO CORTÁZAR

"After Breakfast." **3 ed.** 146; **4.** 69; **5.** 78.
"Ahí pero dónde, cómo." **5.** 78.
"All Fires the Fire." **1.** 43–44; **2.** 79; **5.** 79.
"Apocalypse at Solentiname." **5.** 79.
"Around the Day in Eighty Worlds." **5.** 79.
"At Your Service." **1.** 44.
"Axolotl." **1.** 44; **2.** 79; **3.** 93; **4.** 68; **5.** 79.
"The Band." **1.** 44; **3.** 93; **5.** 79.
"Bestiary." **1.** 44; **3.** 93; **5.** 79.
"Blow-Up" [originally "Las babas del diablo"]. **3 ed.** 145; **1.** 44; **2.** 79; **3.** 93; **4.** 68–69; **5.** 79–80.
"Los buenos servicios." **3 ed.** 145; **1.** 44.
"Cambio de luces." **3.** 94; **4.** 69.
"La caricia más profunda." **3 ed.** 145; **5.** 80.
"Cefalea." **1.** 44–45; **4.** 69; **5.** 80.
"Circe." **1.** 45; **3.** 94; **4.** 69; **5.** 80.
"Clone." **3.** 94.
"The Condemned Door." **3 ed.** 145; **5.** 80.
"Continuity of Parks." **1.** 45; **2.** 79; **3.** 94; **4.** 69; **5.** 80.
"Deshoras." **5.** 80.
"Diario para un cuento." **5.** 80.
"The Distances." **3 ed.** 146; **1.** 45; **4.** 69; **5.** 80.
"End of the Game." **3 ed.** 146; **1.** 45; **2.** 79; **5.** 80.
"Estación de la mano." **5.** 81.
"The Face of the Medal." **3.** 94; **4.** 69.
"Footsteps in the Footprints." **3.** 95; **5.** 81.
"The Gates of Heaven." **3 ed.** 146; **1.** 45; **3.** 94; **4.** 69; **5.** 81.
"Graffiti." **3.** 94; **4.** 69; **5.** 81.
"The Health of the Sick Ones." **3.** 94; **5.** 81.
"Historia." **3.** 94.
"Homage to a Young Witch." **1.** 45.
"House Taken Over." **1.** 45; **2.** 79; **3.** 94; **4.** 69; **5.** 81.
"The Idol of the Cyclades." **5.** 81.
"In the Name of Bobby." **5.** 81.
"Instructions for John Howell." **3 ed.** 146; **1.** 45; **2.** 79; **4.** 70.
"The Isle at Noon." **3 ed.** 146; **1.** 45; **5.** 81.
"The Journey." **5.** 82.
"Junto al Río Cenizas de Rosa." **3.** 94.
"Letter to a Girl in Paris." **3.** 94; **4.** 70; **5.** 82.
"Letters from Mama." **3 ed.** 145; **4.** 69; **5.** 82.
"Liliana llorando." **5.** 82.
"The Maenads." **3.** 94; **4.** 70; **5.** 82.
"Manuscript Found in a Pocket." **2.** 79; **4.** 70; **5.** 82.
"Mobile." **3 ed.** 146; **5.** 82.
"Moebius Strip." **4.** 70.
"Neck of the Black Kitten." **1.** 44; **2.** 79. **4** 70; **5.** 82.
"The Night Face Up." **1.** 45; **2.** 79; **3.** 94; **5.** 82.
"No se culpe a nadie." **4.** 70; **5.** 82.
"Nurse Cora." **1.** 46; **5.** 82–83.
"Omnibus." **1.** 46; **4.** 70; **5.** 83.
"Orientation of Cats." **5.** 83.
"The Other Heaven." **3 ed.** 146; **1.** 46; **5.** 83.
"Pesadillas." **5.** 83.
"The Phases of Severo." **1.** 46.
"A Place Called Kindberg." **1.** 46; **5.** 82.
"Press Clippings." **5.** 83.
"The Pursuer." **1.** 46; **2.** 80; **3.** 95; **4.** 70; **5.** 83.
"Relato con un fondo de agua." **5.** 83.
"Reunion." **1.** 46; **3.** 95; **5.** 83.
"Reunión con un cículo rojo." **3.** 95.
"The River." **1.** 46; **5.** 83–84.
"Satarsa." **5.** 84.
"Second Time Around." **3.** 95; **5.** 84.
"Secret Weapons." **3 ed.** 145; **1.** 46; **2.** 80; **5.** 84.
"Siesta." **3 ed.** 146; **5.** 84.
"Silvia." **3 ed.** 146; **5.** 84.
"Someone Walks Around." **5.** 84.
"The Southern Throughway." **3 ed.** 145; **1.** 46; **3.** 95; **5.** 84.
"Story with Spiders." **4.** 70.
"Summer." **3.** 95.
"Torito." **1.** 46; **5.** 84.
"Trade Winds." **3.** 95; **4.** 70.
"Usted se tendió a tu lado." **3.** 95; **5.** 84.
"Los venenos." **5.** 84.
"Verano." **2.** 80; **3.** 95; **5.** 85.
"A Walk Among the Cages." **5.** 83.
"We Love Glenda So Much." **3.** 95; **4.** 70; **5.** 85.
"Witch." **5.** 85.
"With True Pride." **5.** 85.
"A Yellow Flower." **1.** 46; **5.** 85.

ODYLO COSTA FILHO

"A Faca e o Rio." **3.** 95.

MARK COSTELLO

"Murphy's Xmas." **1.** 46; **5.** 85.

JOHN COULTER

"Boy at a Prayer Meeting." **2.** 80.
"The Catholic Walk." **2.** 80.
"Dinner Hour at the Mill." **2.** 80.
"Muskoka Respite." **2.** 80.

JAMES COURAGE

"Flowers on the Table." **3.** 95.

PETER COWAN

"Drift." **3.** 96.
"The Empty Street." **3 ed.** 146.
"The Red-Backed Spider." **3.** 96.
"The Tractor." **3 ed.** 146.
"The Unploughed Land." **3.** 96.

JAMES GOULD COZZENS

"Eyes to See." **1.** 47.

HUBERT CRACKANTHORPE

"Anthony Garstin's Courtship." **1.** 47.
"Battledore and Shuttlecock." **3 ed.** 147.
"A Commonplace Chapter." **1.** 47.
"A Dead Woman." **1.** 47.
"Étienne Mattou." **1.** 47.
"A Fellside Tragedy." **3 ed.** 147.
"Gaston Lalanne's Child." **1.** 47.
"In Cumberland" [originally "Study in Sentiment"]. **1.** 47.
"Lisa-la-Folle." **1.** 47.
"Modern Melodrama." **1.** 47.
"Profiles." **1.** 47.
"Saint-Pé." **1.** 47.
"The Struggle for Life." **1.** 47.
"Trevor Perkins." **1.** 47.
"The Turn of the Wheel." **3 ed.** 147; **1.** 47.
"The White Maize." **1.** 47.
"Yew Trees and Peacocks." **1.** 48.

DINAH MULOCK CRAIK

"Parson Garland's Daughter." **3.** 96.

STEPHEN CRANE

"And If He Wills, We Must Die." **3 ed.** 147.
"The Angel Child." **3 ed.** 147.
"Billie Atkins Went to Omaha" [same as "An Excursion Ticket"]. **3 ed.** 147.
"The Blue Hotel." **3 ed.** 147–49; **1.** 48; **2.** 80; **3.** 96; **4.** 70–71; **5.** 85.
"The Bride Comes to Yellow Sky." **3 ed.** 149–50; **1.** 48; **2.** 80–81; **3.** 96; **4.** 71; **5.** 85.
"The Charge of William B. Perkins." **3 ed.** 150.
"The City Urchin and the Chaste Villagers." **3 ed.** 150.
"The Clan of No-Name." **3 ed.** 150–51; **2.** 81; **4.** 71; **5.** 85.
"The Cry of a Huckleberry Pudding." **3 ed.** 151.
"Dan Emmonds." **3 ed.** 151.
"Death and the Child." **3 ed.** 151; **2.** 81; **3.** 96; **5.** 85.
"An Episode of War." **3 ed.** 151; **2.** 81; **5.** 85.
"An Experiment in Luxury." **3 ed.** 151; **3.** 96.
"An Experiment in Misery." **3 ed.** 151–52; **1.** 48; **2.** 81; **3.** 97; **5.** 85–86.
"Five White Mice." **3 ed.** 152; **1.** 48; **2.** 81; **4.** 71; **5.** 86.
"Flanagan and His Short Filibustering Adventure." **4.** 71.
"Four Men in a Cave." **3 ed.** 152; **5.** 86.
"George's Mother." **3 ed.** 152; **2.** 81; **3.** 97; **4.** 71; **5.** 86.
"God Rest Ye, Merry Gentlemen [sic]." **3 ed.** 152.
"A Grey Sleeve." **3 ed.** 153.
"His New Mittens." **3 ed.** 153; **5.** 86.
"The Holler Tree." **3 ed.** 153.
"Horses—One Dash." **3 ed.** 153; **1.** 49; **2.** 81; **5.** 86.
"An Illusion in Red and White." **2.** 81.
"In the Tenderloin." **3 ed.** 153.
"An Indiana Campaign." **3 ed.** 153; **5.** 86.
"Just Plain Private Nolan." **3 ed.** 153.
"Killing His Bear." **3 ed.** 153; **3.** 97; **5.** 86.
"The King's Favor." **3 ed.** 153.
"A Little Pilgrim" [same as "A Little Pilgrimage"]. **3 ed.** 153; **1.** 48.
"The Little Regiment." **3 ed.** 153; **5.** 86.

"The Lover and the Telltale." **3 ed.** 153.
"Lynx-Hunting." **3 ed.** 153.
"Maggie: A Girl of the Streets." **3 ed.** 153–55; **1.** 48; **2.** 81; **3.** 97; **4.** 71; **5.** 86.
"Making an Orator." **3 ed.** 155.
"A Man and Some Others." **3 ed.** 155; **2.** 81; **5.** 86.
"Manacles." **3 ed.** 155.
"Marines Signalling under Fire at Guantanamo." **3 ed.** 155.
"The Men in the Storm." **3 ed.** 156; **3.** 97.
"The Mesmeric Mountain." **3 ed.** 156.
"The Monster." **3 ed.** 156; **1.** 48–49; **2.** 81; **3.** 97; **4.** 71; **5.** 86.
"Moonlight on the Snow." **3 ed.** 157; **1.** 49; **2.** 81; **3.** 97.
"A Mystery of Heroism." **3 ed.** 157; **5.** 86.
"The Octopus." **3.** 97.
"An Ominous Baby." **3 ed.** 157.
"The Open Boat." **3 ed.** 157–59; **1.** 49; **2.** 81–82; **3.** 97; **4.** 71; **5.** 86–87.
"The Pace of Youth." **3 ed.** 159; **5.** 87.
"The Price of the Harness." **3 ed.** 159; **2.** 82; **5.** 87.
"The Reluctant Voyagers." **3.** 98.
"A Self-Made Man." **3 ed.** 159.
"Shame." **3 ed.** 159.
"Showing Off." **3 ed.** 159.
"The Silver Pageant." **2.** 82.
"The Siren." **3 ed.** 160.
"The Squire's Madness." **3 ed.** 160.
"A Tent in Agony." **3 ed.** 160.
"The Third Violet." **3 ed.** 160; **1.** 49.
"Three Miraculous Soldiers." **3 ed.** 160; **1.** 49; **2.** 82.
"The Trial, Execution and Burial of Homer Phelps." **3 ed.** 160.
"Twelve O'Clock." **3 ed.** 160; **1.** 49.
"Uncle Jake and the Bell-Handle." **3 ed.** 160; **2.** 82; **3.** 98.
"The Upturned Face." **3 ed.** 160; **1.** 49; **2.** 82; **3.** 98; **5.** 87.
"The Veteran." **5.** 87.
"Virtue in War." **3 ed.** 160.
"War Memories." **3 ed.** 160.
"When Man Falls, a Crowd Gathers." **5.** 87.
"Why Did the Young Clerk Swear? Or, The Unsatisfactory French." **3 ed.** 160.
"The Wise Men." **5.** 87.

WILLIAM F. CRANE

"The Year 1899." **3.** 98.

FRANCIS MARION CRAWFORD

"The Dead Smile." **3 ed.** 161; **4.** 71.
"Man Overboard." **4.** 72.
"The Screaming Skull." **4.** 72.
"The Upper Berth." **4.** 72.

ROBERT CREELEY

"The Book." **3 ed.** 161; **1.** 49.
"A Death." **3 ed.** 161.
"The Dress." **3 ed.** 161.
"The Grace." **1.** 49.
"Mr. Blue." **3 ed.** 161.
"The Séance. **3 ed.** 161.
"The Unsuccessful Husband." **3 ed.** 161; **1.** 49.

ARTHUR SHEARLY CRIPPS

"Amor Filius Misericordiae." **3 ed.** 161.
"Art Thou for Us, or for Our Adversaries?" **3 ed.** 161.
"The Black-Faced Lamb." **3 ed.** 161.
"A Bowed Head." **3 ed.** 161.
"The Burnt Offering." **3 ed.** 161.
"Charnwood Forest." **3 ed.** 161.
"Crimson and Snow White." **3 ed.** 161.
"Death in April." **3 ed.** 162.
"Fern Seed." **3 ed.** 162.
"In Blue and White." **3 ed.** 162.
"The Last Fence." **3 ed.** 162.
"The Leper Windows." **3 ed.** 162.
"A Lost Saint." **3 ed.** 162.
"The Miracle of the Nativity." **3 ed.** 162.
"New Light on an Old Champion." **3 ed.** 162.
"The Old Boy." **3 ed.** 162.
"On the Night of the Nativity." **3 ed.** 162.
"The Open Way." **3 ed.** 162.
"Our Lady of the Lake." **3 ed.** 162.
"The Place of Pilgrimage." **3 ed.** 162.
"The Riding of the Red Horse." **3 ed.** 162.
"The Scales of Passion." **3 ed.** 162.
"Times Go by Turns." **3 ed.** 162.
"A Trader's Story." **3 ed.** 162.
"Veld Fires." **3 ed.** 162.

LAURENCE CRITCHELL

"Flesh and Blood." **3 ed.** 163.

GASTÃO CRULS

"Meu Sósia." **2.** 82.

CUBENA [CARLOS GUILLERMO WILSON]

"The Family." **2.** 82; **3.** 98.
"The Little African Grandmother." **2.** 82.

ELIZABETH CULLINAN

"The Voices of the Dead." **2.** 82.

RAY CUMMINGS

"The Girl in the Golden Atom." **3.** 98.
"Tama of the Light Country." **3.** 98.

ROBERT BONTINE CUNNINGHAME GRAHAM

"Animula Vagula." **3.** 98.
"Christie Christison." **3.** 98.
"The Gold Fish." **3.** 98.
"A Hegira." **2.** 82.
"Snaekoll's Saga." **3.** 98.

GEORGE CUOMO

"A Part of the Bargain." **3 ed.** 163.
"Sing, Choir of Angels." **3 ed.** 163.
"Sophisticated Lady." **3 ed.** 163.

DANIEL CURLEY

"A Story of Love, Etc." **2.** 83.
"Who, What, When, Where—Why?" **3.** 99.

MICHAL CZAJKOWSKI

"The Battle of Moloczki." **3 ed.** 163.
"The Cavalry." **3 ed.** 163.
"The Proposal of a Zaporog Cossack." **3 ed.** 163.

MARIA DABROWSKA

"A Change Came O'er the Scenes of My Dream." **3 ed.** 163.
"Consolation." **3 ed.** 163.
"Father Philip." **3 ed.** 163.
"Little John." **3 ed.** 163.
"Lucia from Pukucice." **3 ed.** 163.
"Miss Winczewska." **3 ed.** 163.
"A Piece of Glass." **3 ed.** 164.
"The Third Autumn." **3 ed.** 164.
"The Triumph of Dionysius." **3 ed.** 164.
"A Village Wedding." **3 ed.** 164.
"The Wild Plant." **3 ed.** 164.

IGNACY DABROWSKI

"Twilight." **3 ed.** 164.

CYRIL DABYDEEN

"Memphis." **4.** 72.

BERNARD DADIÉ

"The Black Loincloth." **5.** 87.
"The Confession." **3.** 99.
"The Death of Men." **3.** 99.
"The Light of the Setting Sun." **3.** 99.
"The Pitcher." **3.** 99.
"The Saltworks of the Old Woman of Amafi." **3.** 99.
"Spider and His Son." **3.** 99.
"Spider, Bad Father." **3.** 99.
"Taweloro." **3.** 99.

ULADZIMIR DADZIJONAU

"Bielaziersk Diary." **3.** 99.

STIG DAGERMAN

"The Hanging Tree." **3.** 99.
"The Man Condemned to Death." **3.** 99.
"Our Nocturnal Resort." **3.** 99.
"Where Is My Iceland Jumper?" **3.** 99.

ROALD DAHL

"An African Story." **5.** 87.
"Ah! Sweet Mystery of Life, at Last I've Found Thee." **5.** 87.
"Beware of the Dog." **5.** 87.
"Bitch." **5.** 87.
"The Bookseller." **5.** 87.
"The Boy Who Talked to Animals." **5.** 87.
"The Butler." **5.** 88.
"The Champion of the World." **5.** 88.
"Claud's Dog." **5.** 88.
"Death of an Old, Old Man." **5.** 88.
"Dip in the Pool." **5.** 88.
"Edward the Conqueror." **5.** 88.
"Galloping Foxley." **5** 88.

"Genesis and Catastrophe" [same as "A Fine Son"]. **3 ed.** 164; **5.** 88.
"Georgy Porgy." **5.** 88.
"The Great Automatic Grammatisator." **5.** 88.
"The Great Switcheroo." **5.** 88.
"The Hitchhiker." **5.** 88.
"Kalina." **5.** 88.
"Lamb to Slaughter." **4.** 72; **5.** 88.
"The Landlady." **5.** 88.
"The Last Act." **5.** 88.
"Madame Rosette." **5.** 88.
"Man from the South." **5.** 88.
"The Mildenhall Treasure." **5.** 89.
"Mr. Botibol." **5.** 89.
"Mrs. Bixby and the Colonel's Coat." **5.** 89.
"My Lady Love, My Dove." **5.** 89.
"Neck." **5.** 89.
"Nunc Dimittis" [originally "The Devious Bachelor"]. **5.** 89.
"Only This." **5.** 89.
"Parson's Pleasure." **5.** 89.
"Pig." **5.** 89.
"Poison." **5.** 89.
"Royal Jelly." **4.** 72; **5.** 89.
"The Ruins." **5.** 89.
"Shot Down in Libya" [originally "A Piece of Cake"]. **5.** 89.
"Skin." **5.** 89.
"The Soldier." **5.** 89.
"Someone Like You." **5.** 89.
"The Sound Machine." **5.** 89.
"The Swan." **5.** 90.
"Taste." **5.** 90.
"They Shall Not Grow Old." **5.** 90.
"Vengeance Is Mine, Inc." **5.** 90.
"The Visitor." **4.** 72; **5.** 90.
"The Way up to Heaven." **5.** 90.
"William and Mary." **5.** 90.
"The Wish." **5.** 90.
"The Wonderful Story of Henry Sugar" [originally "The Amazing Eyes of Kuda Bux"]. **4.** 72; **5.** 90.
"Yesterday Was Beautiful." **5.** 90.

HANS DAIBER

"It Is Written." **3.** 100.

VLADIMIR DAL [pseudonym COSSACK LUGANSKY]

"The Gypsy Girl." **3.** 100.
"Schlemiel." **3.** 100.
"Vakkh Sidorov Chaikin." **4.** 72.

SEPTIMUS DALE

"The Little Girl Eater." **5.** 90.

CARROLL JOHN DALY

"The False Burton Combs." **4.** 72.

LÉON DAMAS

"Sur un air de guitare." **3 ed.** 164.

ACHMED [AHMAT] DANGOR

"Waiting for Leila." **3.** 100; **5.** 90.

YURI DANIEL

"Hands." **3 ed.** 164.

GUSTAW DANILOWSKI

"Behind the Wall." **3 ed.** 164.

GABRIELE D'ANNUNZIO

"The Idolators." **3.** 100.

RUBÉN DARÍO

"The Blue Bird." **4.** 72.
"The Case of Señorita Amelia." **3.** 100.
"Cuento de Noche Buena." **3.** 100.
"The Death of the Empress of China." **3.** 100; **4.** 73.
"El fardo." **4.** 73.
"La pesadilla de Honorio." **3.** 100.
"The Ruby." **4.** 73; **5.** 90.
"Thanathopía." **3.** 100.
"The Three Magian Queens." **3.** 100.
"The Tree of King David." **4.** 73.
"Verónica." **3.** 101.

ELEANOR DARK

"Urgent Call." **1.** 49.
"Water in Moko Creek." **1.** 50.
"Wheels." **1.** 50.
"Wind." **1.** 50.

KAMALA DAS

"Sanatan Chaudhuri's Wife." **4.** 73.
"The Tattered Blanket." **4.** 73.

KISHOREE DAS

"Husband, the Supreme Teacher." **2.** 83.
"Manihara." **2.** 83.
"Million Birds." **2.** 83.
"Sangeeta's Father." **2.** 83.
"Wild Peacock." **2.** 83.

MANOJ DAS

"Birds in the Twilight." **3.** 101.
"The Brothers." **3.** 101.
"The Crocodile's Lady." **3 ed.** 164.
"Farewell to the Ghost." **3 ed.** 165.
"The Kite." **3.** 101.
"Lakshmi's Adventure." **3.** 101.
"The Last I Heard of Them." **3 ed.** 165.
"A Letter from the Last Spring." **3 ed.** 165.
"Mystery of the Missing Cap." **3 ed.** 165; **3.** 101.
"A Song for Sunday." **3 ed.** 165.
"The Story of Baba Chakradhari." **3 ed.** 165.
"Tragedy." **3 ed.** 165.
"A Trip into the Jungle." **3 ed.** 165.

RAI KRISHNA DAS

"Secrets of Ramani." **3.** 101.

ALPHONSE DAUDET

"La Chèvre de M. Seguin." **5.** 91.
"Father Gaucher's Elixir." **3 ed.** 165.
"The Girl in Arles." **3 ed.** 165.
"Poet Mistral." **3 ed.** 165.

MAX DAUTHENDEY

"Das Abendrot zu Seta." **3 ed.** 165.
"Auf dem Weg zu den Eulenkäfigen." **3 ed.** 165.
"Die Segelboote von Yabase im Abend heimkehren sehen." **3 ed.** 165.
"Der unbeerdigte Vater." **3 ed.** 165.
"Unter den Totentürmen." **3 ed.** 165.
"Zur Stunde der Maus." **3 ed.** 166.

GUY DAVENPORT

"Apples and Pears." **3.** 101; **5.** 91.
"The Bowmen of Shu." **3.** 101.
"The Chain." **3.** 101; **5.** 91.
"Fifty-Seven Views of Fujiyama." **3.** 101.

AVRAM DAVIDSON

"Dagon." **4.** 73.
"Sacheverell." **4.** 73.
"What Strange Stars and Skies." **4.** 73.

FRANK DALBY DAVIDSON

"Blood Will Tell." **3 ed.** 166.
"Fathers and Sons." **3 ed.** 166; **2.** 83.
"Fields of Cotton." **2.** 83.
"Further West." **2.** 83.
"The Good Herdsman." **2.** 83.
"Here Comes the Bride." **2.** 83.
"Lady with a Scar." **3 ed.** 166; **2.** 83.
"A Letter from Colleen." **3 ed.** 166; **2.** 83.
"Meet Darkie Hoskins." **2.** 83.
"The Night Watch." **2.** 84.
"Nobody's Kelpie." **3 ed.** 166; **2.** 84.
"Return of the Hunter." **3 ed.** 166; **2.** 84.
"The Road to Yesterday." **3 ed.** 166; **2.** 84.
"Sojourners." **2.** 84.
"Soldier of Fortune." **2.** 84.
"Tank-Sinkers." **3 ed.** 166; **2.** 84.
"Transition." **2.** 84.
"The Wasteland." **2.** 84.
"The Woman at the Mill." **3 ed.** 166; **2.** 84.
"The Yarns Men Tell." **3 ed.** 166; **2.** 84.

RHYS DAVIES

"Canute." **2.** 84.
"The Dilemma of Catherine Fuchsias." **2.** 84.
"I Will Keep Her Company." **4.** 73.
"Nightgown." **2.** 84.

ROBERTSON DAVIES

"Eisengrin." **5.** 91.

DAN DAVIN

"Below the Heavens." **3.** 101.
"Growing Up." **3.** 102.
"The Locksmith Laughs Last." **3.** 102.
"Mortal." **3.** 102.
"Not Substantial Things." **3.** 102.
"Psychological Warfare at Cassino." **3.** 102.
"The Quiet One." **3.** 102.
"That Golden Time." **3.** 102.
"The Wall of Doors." **3.** 102.

CHANDLER DAVIS

"To Still the Drums." **5.** 91.

H. L. DAVIS

"Extra Gang." **1.** 50.
"Homestead Orchard." **1.** 50.
"The Kettle of Fire." **1.** 50.
"Old Man Isbell's Wife." **1.** 50.
"Open Winter." **1.** 50.
"Shiloh's Waters." **1.** 50.
"World of Little Doves." **2.** 84.

REBECCA HARDING DAVIS

"John Lamar." **3.** 102.
"Life in the Iron Mills." **4.** 73.
"The Wife's Story." **4.** 73.

RICHARD HARDING DAVIS

"The Deserter." **1.** 50.
"Eleanore Cuyler." **2.** 85.
"The Exiles." **2.** 85.
"Guy Fawkes Night." **5.** 91.
"Her First Appearance." **2.** 85.
"The Men of Zanzibar." **2.** 85.
"My Buried Treasure." **2.** 85.
"The Other Woman." **2.** 85.
"Ranson's Folly." **2.** 85.
"The Reporter Who Made Himself King." **2.** 85.
"An Unfinished Story." **2.** 85.
"The Vagrant." **2.** 85.
"Van Bibber's Burglar." **2.** 85.

EMMA F. DAWSON

"The Dramatic in My Destiny." **2.** 85; **3.** 102.

JENNIFER DAWSON

"Hospital Wedding." **4.** 74.

DAZAI OSAMU

"Admonition." **3 ed.** 166.
"An Almanac of Pain." **4.** 74.
"An Appeal to the Authorities." **1.** 50.
"Bankruptcy." **3 ed.** 166.
"Bottomless Abyss." **3 ed.** 166.
"Cherries." **3 ed.** 166.
"The Crackling Mountain." **3 ed.** 166.
"Family Happiness." **3 ed.** 167.
"The Father." **3 ed.** 167.
"Female Bandits." **3 ed.** 167.
"Fifteen Years." **4.** 74.
"Forsaking the Old Woman." **3 ed.** 167.
"The Garden." **4.** 74.
"Das Gemeine." **3 ed.** 167.
"Going Home." **4.** 74.
"The Great Red Drum." **3 ed.** 167.
"Great Strength." **3 ed.** 167.
"He Is Not What He Was." **3 ed.** 167.
"Hometown." **4.** 74.
"The Indictment." **3 ed.** 167.
"Landlord for a Generation." **3 ed.** 167.
"Mermaid Sea." **3 ed.** 167.
"Metamorphosis." **3 ed.** 167; **2.** 85.
"Monkey Island." **3 ed.** 167.
"Monkey-Face Lad." **3 ed.** 167.
"The Monkey's Grave." **3 ed.** 167.
"Mount Yoshino." **3 ed.** 167.
"Obligation." **3 ed.** 167.
"One Hundred Views of Mount Fuji." **4.** 74.
"Osan." **3 ed.** 167.
"Poor Mosquito." **4.** 74.
"A Record of the Autumn Wind." **4.** 74.
"The Refined Man." **3 ed.** 168.
"River of the Naked." **3 ed.** 168.
"Romanesque." **3 ed.** 168.
"Run Melos." **3 ed.** 168.
"A Sound of Hammering." **5.** 91.
"The Split-Tongue Sparrow." **3 ed.** 168.
"Stubborn in Poverty." **3 ed.** 168.
"Thinking of Zenzo." **4.** 74.
"Those Two and Their Pathetic Mother." **3 ed.** 168.
"Villon's Wife." **3 ed.** 168; **4.** 74; **5.** 91.

L. SPRAGUE DE CAMP

"The Blue Giraffe." **3.** 102.
"The Green Magician." **3.** 102.
"Hyperpilosity." **3.** 102.
"The Wall of Serpents." **3.** 103.

L. SPRAGUE DE CAMP and ROBERT E. HOWARD

"The Road of Eagles." **3.** 103.

DESIDERIO T. DEFERIA

"Man Is Indeed a Slave." **5.** 91.

MIRIAM ALLEN DE FORD

"The Crib Circuit." **3.** 103.
"The Eel." **3.** 103.

JOHN W. DE FOREST

"The Apotheosis of Ki." **3.** 103.
"Della." **5.** 92.
"A Gentleman of the Old South." **3.** 103.
"The Lauson Tragedy." **5.** 92.

SALVADOR M. DE JESÚS

"Lágrimas de mangle." **5.** 92.
"La otra hija de Jairo." **5.** 92.

M. DELAFIELD [EDMÉE ELIZABETH MONICA DE LA PASTURE]

"Appreciation." **4.** 74.
"Not Yet." **4.** 74.
"The Spoilers." **4.** 74.

SIDONIE DE LA HOUSSAYE

"The Adventures of Françoise and Suzanne." **1.** 50.
"Alix de Morainville." **1.** 50.
"The Young Aunt with White Hair." **1.** 51.

WALTER DE LA MARE

"A. B. O." **2.** 86.
"All Hallows." **3.** 103.
"The Almond Tree." **3.** 103.
"The Creatures." **4.** 75.
"Crewe." **2.** 86.
"Crossings." **3.** 103.
"The Dancing Princess." **3.** 103.
"The Green Room." **3.** 103.
"The Guardian." **3 ed.** 168.
"An Ideal Craftsman." **3.** 103.
"In the Forest." **3 ed.** 168.
"The Looking Glass." **3 ed.** 168.
"Maria-Fly." **3 ed.** 168.
"Miss Duveen." **3.** 103.
"Miss Jemima." **3.** 104.
"Missing." **3.** 104.
"Mr. Kempe." **2.** 86.
"A Mote." **4.** 75.
"Out of the Deep" [originally "The Bell"]. **3 ed.** 168; **2.** 86; **3.** 104.
"A Recluse." **3 ed.** 168; **2.** 86; **3.** 104.
"The Riddle." **3 ed.** 168; **3.** 104; **4.** 75.
"Seaton's Aunt." **3 ed.** 168; **2.** 86; **3.** 104; **4.** 75.
"The Trumpet." **2.** 86.

MARGARET DELAND

"The Eliots' Katy." **4.** 75.
"How COULD She!" **4.** 75.
"The Waiting Hand." **4.** 75.

SAMUEL R. DELANY

"Cage of Brass." **3.** 104.
"Corona." **3.** 104.
"Dog in a Fisherman's Net." **3.** 104.
"Driftglass." **3.** 104; **5.** 92.
"High Weir." **3.** 104.
"Night and the Loves of Joe Dicostanzo." **3.** 104.
"Power of the Nail." **3.** 104.
"The Star Pit." **3.** 104.
"The Tale of Dragons and Dreamers." **4.** 75.
"The Tale of Gorgik." **4.** 75.
"The Tale of Old Venn." **4.** 75.
"The Tale of Potters and Dragons." **4.** 75.
"We in Some Strange Power's Employ, Move on a Rigorous Line" [same as "Lines of Power"]. **3.** 104.

MAZO DE LA ROCHE [MAZO ROCHE]

"A Boy in the House." **1.** 51.
"Buried Treasure." **1.** 51.
"D' Ye Ken John Peele?" **1.** 51.
"The Son of a Miser: How Noel Caron of St. Loo Proved That He Was No Pinch-Penny." **1.** 51.
"The Spirit of the Dance." **1.** 51.
"The Thief of St. Loo: An Incident in the Life of Antoine O'Neill, Honest Man." **1.** 51.

CHARLOTTE DELBO

"Spectres mes compagnons." **5.** 92.

AUGUSTO MARIO DELFINO

"The Confidant." **4.** 75.
"The Telephone." **3.** 105; **4.** 76.

ANTONIO DELGADO

"Continuous Time." **4.** 76.
"José Destino." **4.** 76.
"The Lost Space." **4.** 76.

"The Luminous Scar." **4.** 76.
"The Radiance of Fire." **4.** 76.

LESTER DEL REY

"The Day Is Done." **3.** 105.
"The Faithful." **5.** 92.
"Helen O'Loy." **3.** 105; **4.** 76.
"Instinct." **2.** 86.
"Nerves." **3.** 105.
"Though Dreamers Die." **2.** 86.

MANUEL DEL TORO

"My Father." **5.** 92.

PHILANDER DEMING

"John's Trial." **3 ed.** 169.

MARCO DENEVI

"The Butterfly." **3.** 105.

LESTER DENT

"Read 'Angelfish.'" **3.** 105.
"Sail." **3.** 105.

AUGUST DERLETH

"Alannah." **4.** 76.
"The Dark Boy." **4.** 76.
"The Extra Child." **4.** 76.

FEDERICO DE ROBERTO

"La Cocotte." **3.** 105.

ANITA DESAI

"Games at Twilight." **5.** 92.
"Sale." **5.** 93.
"Scholar and Gypsy." **5.** 93.
"Studies in the Park." **5.** 93.
"Surface Texture." **5.** 93.

SUZANNE DESCHEVAUX-DUMESNIL

"F——." **1.** 51.

KUSUMAVATI DESHPANDE

"Wet and Shiny." **3 ed.** 169.

SHASHI DESHPANDE

"The Intrusion." **4.** 76.

VLADAN DESNICA

"Florjanović." **1.** 51.
"Oko." **1.** 51.
"Summer Vacation During the Winter." **1.** 51.

A. J. DEUTSCH

"A Subway Named Moebius." **4.** 77.

CHARLES DE VET and KATHARINE MacLEAN

"Second Game." **3.** 106.

MAHASVETA DEVI

"Breast-Giver." **5.** 93.
"Draupadi." **2.** 86; **5.** 93.

AUGUSTO D'HALMAR [AUGUSTO GEOMINE THOMPSON]

"In the Province." **3.** 106; **5.** 93.

AHMADOU MAPADÉ DIAGNE

"Malic's Three Wishes." **3.** 106.

ABELARDO DÍAZ ALFARO

"Bagazo." **5.** 93.
"Los perros." **5.** 93.

JESÚS DÍAZ RODRÍGUEZ

"El cojo." **1.** 51.
"No hay Dios que resista esto." **1.** 51.
"No matarás." **1.** 52.
"El polvo a la mitad." **1.** 52.

RAMÓN DÍAZ SÁNCHEZ

"La virgen no tiene cara." **3.** 106.

EMILIO DÍAZ VALCÁRCEL

"La mente en blanco." **5.** 93.
"The Soldier Damián Sánchez." **5.** 93.
"Two Men." **5.** 93.

OLIVE DIBERT

"A Chinese Lily." **2.** 86.

PHILIP K. DICK

"A. Lincoln, Simulacra." **3.** 106.
"Adjustment Team." **5.** 94.
"Autofac." **2.** 87; **5.** 94.
"Beyond Lies the Wub." **5.** 94.
"Cantata 140." **5.** 94.
"Colony." **5.** 94.
"The Cosmic Poachers." **5.** 94.
"The Days of Perky Pat." **3.** 106.
"The Defenders." **2.** 87; **3.** 106; **4.** 77.
"The Electric Ant." **2.** 87; **3.** 106; **5.** 94.
"Exhibit Piece." **5.** 94.
"Faith of Our Fathers." **3.** 106; **4.** 77; **5.** 94.
"The Father-Thing." **3.** 107; **5.** 94.
"The Hanging Stranger." **5.** 94.
"Human Is." **5.** 94.
"If There Were No Benny Cemoli." **3.** 107.
"The Imposter." **3.** 107.
"Jon's World." **4.** 77.
"The Little Movement." **3.** 107.
"Man, Android and Machine." **3.** 107.
"Misadjustment." **5.** 94.
"The Mold of Yancy." **5.** 94.
"Nanny." **5.** 94.
"Oh To Be a Blobel." **5.** 94.
"Precious Artifact." **5.** 95.
"The Preserving Machine." **3 ed.** 169; **2.** 87.
"Rautawaara's Case." **5.** 95.
"Roog." **5.** 95.
"Second Variety." **2.** 87; **3.** 107.
"Small Town." **5.** 95.
"The Stand-By Job." **3 ed.** 169.
"Time Pawn." **5.** 95.
"To Serve the Master." **3.** 107.
"The Variable Man." **5.** 95.
"War Game." **3 ed.** 169.
"A World of Talent." **5.** 95.

CHARLES DICKENS

"The Black Veil." **3 ed.** 169; **3.** 107.
"The Boarding-House." **3.** 107.
"The Bride's Chamber." **3.** 107.
"A Confession Found in a Prison in the Time of Charles the Second." **3 ed.** 169.
"The Drunkard's Death." **3.** 107.
"George Silverman's Explanation." **3 ed.** 169; **3.** 107.
"Main Line; The Boy at Mugby." **4.** 77.
"Mrs. Lirripet's Legacy." **3.** 107.
"Mrs. Lirripet's Lodging." **3.** 107.
"No Thoroughfare." **3 ed.** 169.
"No. 1 Branch Line—The Signalman" [same as "The Signalman"]. **2.** 87; **3.** 107; **4.** 77; **5.** 95.
"The Stroller's Tale." **4.** 77.
"To Be Read at Dusk." **5.** 95.

FRANCIS J. DICKIE

"The Creed of Ah Sin." **2.** 87.

GORDON DICKSON

"Computers Don't Argue." **4.** 77.
"Jean Dupres." **5.** 95.

JOAN DIDION

"When Did Music Come This Way? Children, Dear, Was It Yesterday?" **2.** 87.

PIETRO DI DONALDO

"Christ in Concrete." **3 ed.** 169.

ELMER DIKTONIUS

"The Boy and the Halter." **4.** 77.
"Broad Back." **4.** 77.
"The Child Killed the Knife." **4.** 77.
"The Chimera" [originally "They and It"]. **4.** 78.
"The Elk Bullet." **4.** 78.
"Hang Yourself, You Damned Kid!" **4.** 78.
"Josef and Sussan." **4.** 78.
"Mama." **4.** 78.
"96%." **4.** 78.
"Veikko, Little Slaughterer's Helper." **4.** 78.

ISAK DINESEN [BARONESS KAREN BLIXEN]

"Alexander the Great." **3 ed.** 170.
"Alkmene." **3 ed.** 170; **5.** 95.
"Babette's Feast." **3 ed.** 170; **3.** 108; **5.** 95.
"The Bear and the Kiss." **5.** 95.
"The Blank Page." **3 ed.** 170; **2.** 87; **3.** 108; **4.** 78.
"The Blue Jar." **5.** 96.
"The Blue Stones." **5.** 96.

"The Cardinal's First Tale." **3 ed.** 170; **4.** 78; **5.** 96.
"The Cardinal's Third Tale." **3 ed.** 170; **1.** 52; **2.** 87; **3.** 108; **5.** 96.
"Carnival." **3.** 108; **4.** 78; **5.** 96.
"The Caryatids." **3 ed.** 170; **2.** 88; **5.** 96.
"The Cloak." **3 ed.** 170.
"A Consolatory Tale." **3 ed.** 170; **1.** 52; **2.** 88.
"Converse at Night in Copenhagen." **3 ed.** 170; **3.** 108.
"Copenhagen Season." **3 ed.** 170; **3.** 108; **5.** 96.
"A Country Tale." **3 ed.** 170.
"The Deluge at Norderney." **3 ed.** 170–71; **2.** 88; **5.** 96.
"The Diver." **3 ed.** 171; **5.** 96.
"The Dreamers." **3 ed.** 171; **5.** 96.
"The Dreaming Child." **3 ed.** 171.
"Echoes." **3 ed.** 171; **5.** 96.
"Ehrengard." **3 ed.** 171.
"Familien de Cats." **3 ed.** 171.
"The Fish." **3 ed.** 171; **5.** 96.
"Grjotgard Alvesøn and Aud." **3.** 108.
"The Hermits." **3.** 108.
"The Heroine." **3 ed.** 171; **2.** 88; **5.** 96.
"The Immortal Story." **3 ed.** 171; **5.** 96.
"The Invincible Slave Owners." **3 ed.** 171; **5.** 96.
"The Last Day." **5.** 96.
"The Monkey." **3 ed.** 171–72; **2.** 88; **3.** 108; **4.** 78.
"Of Secret Thoughts and of Heaven." **3 ed.** 172.
"The Old Chevalier." **3 ed.** 172; **3.** 108; **5.** 96.
"The Pearls." **3 ed.** 172; **2.** 88.
"Peter and Rosa." **3 ed.** 172; **2.** 88; **5.** 97.
"The Ploughman." **3.** 108.
"The Poet." **3 ed.** 172; **5.** 97.
"The Ring." **3 ed.** 172; **1.** 52; **2.** 88.
"The Roads Round Pisa." **3 ed.** 172; **2.** 88; **4.** 78; **5.** 97.
"The Sailor-Boy's Tale." **3 ed.** 172; **2.** 88; **5.** 97.
"Second Meeting." **5.** 97.
"Sorrow-Acre." **3 ed.** 172; **1.** 52; **3.** 108; **5.** 97.
"The Supper at Elsinore." **3 ed.** 172; **5.** 97.
"Tales of Two Old Gentlemen." **5.** 97.
"Tempest." **3 ed.** 172; **3.** 108.
"Uncle Seneca." **5.** 97.
"The Wine of the Tetrarch." **3 ed.** 173.
"The Young Man with the Carnation." **3 ed.** 173; **2.** 88.

DING LING

"After He Left." **3.** 109.
"A Certain Night." **1.** 52; **2.** 88; **3.** 109.
"The Day Before New Year's Day." **3.** 109.
"The Diary of Miss Sophie." **1.** 52; **3.** 109.
"Du Wanxiang." **2.** 88.
"Flight." **3.** 109.
"Flood." **3.** 109.
"From Night Till Daybreak." **3.** 109.
"In the Hospital." **4.** 78.
"Mengke." **3.** 109.
"Miss Amao." **3.** 109.
"The Net of the Law." **3.** 109.
"New Faith." **3.** 109.
"New Year's Day." **3.** 109.
"Night." **2.** 88; **3.** 109.
"On a Small Steamboat." **3.** 109.
"One Day." **3.** 109.
"The People's Artist Li Bu." **3.** 109.
"A Secret Visitor on a Moonlit Night." **3.** 109.
"A Small Room in Qingyun Lane." **3.** 110.
"A Suicide's Diary." **3.** 110.
"Tian Family Village." **3.** 110.
"We Need *Zawen*." **3.** 110.
"When I Was in Xia Village." **3.** 110.
"Yecao." **3.** 110.
"Yuan Guangfa." **3.** 110.

BIRAGO DIOP

"The Antelope and the Two Hunters." **4.** 79.
"Bad Company." **4.** 79.
"Bouki and His Egg." **3.** 110.
"Bouki, Boarder." **3.** 110.
"The Breasts." **3.** 110.
"The Bull of Bouki." **3.** 110.
"The Calabashes of Kouss." **3.** 110.
"Dof Diop." **3.** 110.
"The Folly of the Dervish." **3.** 110.
"The Hind and the Two Hunters." **3.** 110.
"Khary Gaye." **3.** 110.
"Samba of the Night." **3.** 111.
"Sarzan." **3.** 111; **4.** 79.

THOMAS DISCH

"The Asian Shore." **5.** 97.
"Planet of the Rapes." **5.** 97.

STEPHEN DIXON

"Fourteen Stories." **3.** 111.
"Goodbye to Goodbye." **3.** 111.
"Time to Go." **3.** 111.

ASSIA DJEBAR [FATIMA-ZOHRA IMALAYEN]

"Algerian Women in Their Quarters." **3.** 111.

ALFRED DÖBLIN

"Die Ermordung einer Butterblume." **3 ed.** 173.

E. L. DOCTOROW

"The Foreign Legation." **5.** 97.
"The Hunter." **5.** 97.
"The Leather Man." **5.** 97–98.
"Lives of the Poets." **5.** 98.
"Willi." **5.** 98.
"The Writer in the Family." **5.** 98.

HEIMITO VON DODERER

"Divertimento V." **2.** 89.
"Divertimento IV." **2.** 89.
"Divertimento I." **2.** 89.
"Divertimento VI." **2.** 89.
"Divertimento III." **2.** 89.
"Encounter at Dawn." **2.** 89.
"Jutta Bamberger." **2.** 89.
"A Person of Porcelain." **2.** 89.
"The Torment of the Leather Pouches." **2.** 89.
"Trethofen." **2.** 89.
"The Trumpets of Jericho." **2.** 89.
"Two Lies, or Classical Tragedy in a Village." **2.** 89.

MARY DODGE

"Our Contraband." **3.** 111.

EMMA DOLUJANOFF

"La correría del venado." **5.** 98.
"El huellero." **5.** 98.
"María Galdina." **5.** 98.
"Siéntate Teófilo." **5.** 98.

EDWARD DONAHOE

"Head by Scopas." **3 ed.** 173.

JAMES PATRICK DONLEAVY

"At Longitude and Latitude." **2.** 89; **4.** 79.
"Dear Hugo." **4.** 79.
"Dear Sylvia." **4.** 79.
"Franz F." **4.** 79.
"Gustav G." **4.** 79.
"It Was My Chimes." **4.** 79.
"The Romantic Life of Alphonse A." **2.** 90; **4.** 79.
"The Saddest Summer of Samuel S." **3 ed.** 173; **4.** 79.
"Whither Wigwams." **4.** 79.

JOSÉ DONOSO

"Ana María." **2.** 90; **5.** 98.
"Celebration on a Grand Scale." **2.** 90.
"Charleston." **2.** 90.
"China." **2.** 90.
"The Closed Door." **2.** 90.
"Gaspard de la nuit." **5.** 98.
"Green Atom Number Five." **5.** 98.
"The Güerro." **2.** 90; **3.** 111; **5.** 98.
"El hombrecito." **5.** 98.
"A Lady." **2.** 90; **3.** 111.
"Namesakes." **2.** 90.
"Paseo." **2.** 90; **3.** 111; **5.** 99.
"Pasos en la noche." **5.** 99.
"Santelices." **1.** 52; **2.** 90; **3.** 111; **5.** 99.
"Summertime" [same as "Summering"]. **1.** 52; **2.** 90.
"Two Letters." **2.** 90.
"Veraneo." **5.** 99.
"Walk." **1.** 52.

SONDRA DORMAN

"Building Block." **3.** 112.

JOHN DOS PASSOS

"Revolution." **5.** 99.
"Romantic Education." **5.** 99.

FYODOR DOSTOEVSKY

"Another Man's Wife and the Husband Under the Bed." **3 ed.** 173.
"Bobok." **1.** 52; **2.** 90.
"A Boy at Christ's Christmas Party." **2.** 91.

"A Christmas Party and a Wedding" [same as "A Christmas Tree and a Wedding"]. **3 ed.** 173; **2.** 91.
"The Citizen." **3 ed.** 173.
"The Crocodile." **3 ed.** 174; **3.** 112.
"The Double." **3 ed.** 174; **1.** 53; **2.** 91; **3.** 112; **4.** 79; **5.** 99.
"The Dream of a Ridiculous Man." **3 ed.** 174–75; **1.** 53; **2.** 91; **4.** 80.
"The Duel." **5.** 99.
"The Eternal Husband." **1.** 53; **4.** 80; **5.** 99.
"A Faint Heart" [same as "A Weak Heart"]. **3 ed.** 175; **1.** 54; **2.** 91.
"The Friend of the Family" [same as "The Village of Stepanchikov and Its Inhabitants"]. **3 ed.** 175; **1.** 54.
"The Gambler." **3 ed.** 175; **1.** 53; **3.** 112.
"A Gentle Creature" [same as "A Meek One"]. **3 ed.** 175, 177; **1.** 53; **2.** 91; **4.** 80.
"The Grand Inquisitor." **3 ed.** 175–76; **1.** 53; **2.** 91; **3.** 112; **4.** 80.
"An Honest Thief." **3 ed.** 176; **1.** 53.
"The Landlady." **3 ed.** 176–77; **1.** 53; **2.** 91.
"A Little Hero." **3 ed.** 177; **1.** 53; **2.** 91.
"Mr. Prokharchin." **3 ed.** 177; **1.** 53; **2.** 91; **3.** 112; **5.** 99.
"A Nasty Story" [same as "A Disgraceful Affair"]. **4.** 80.
"Notes from Underground." **3 ed.** 177–79; **1.** 53–54; **2.** 91–92; **3.** 112; **4.** 80; **5.** 99.
"A Novel in Nine Letters." **3 ed.** 179; **1.** 54.
"The Peasant Marey." **3 ed.** 179; **1.** 54; **2.** 92; **4.** 80; **5.** 99.
"Polzunkov." **3 ed.** 179–80; **1.** 54; **5.** 100.
"Stavrogin's Confession." **3 ed.** 180.
"Uncle's Dream." **3 ed.** 180; **1.** 54; **3.** 113.
"An Unpleasant Predicament." **3 ed.** 180.
"The Verdict." **3 ed.** 180.
"White Nights." **3 ed.** 180; **1.** 54; **2.** 92; **4.** 80.

ELLEN DOUGLAS

"Hold On." **3 ed.** 180; **3.** 113.
"The House on the Bluff." **3 ed.** 180.
"I Just Love Carrie Lee." **3.** 113.
"Jesse." **3.** 113.

FREDERICK DOUGLASS

"The Heroic Slave." **3.** 113.

COLEMAN DOWELL

"If Beggars Were Horses." **3.** 113.
"The Moon, the Owl, My Sister." **3.** 113.
"My Father Was a River." **3.** 113.

J. HYATT DOWNING

"Rewards." **3 ed.** 180.

ERNEST DOWSON

"Apple Blossom in Brittany." **3 ed.** 180.
"The Diary of a Successful Man." **3 ed.** 180.
"The Dying of Francis Donne." **3 ed.** 181.

ARTHUR CONAN DOYLE

"The Adventure of Black Peter." **4.** 81.
"The Adventure of Charles Augustus Milverton." **4.** 81.
"The Adventure of Silver Blaze." **4.** 81; **5.** 100.
"The Adventure of the Abbey Grange." **4.** 81.
"The Adventure of the Beryl Coronet." **4.** 81.
"The Adventure of the Blanched Soldier." **4.** 81; **5.** 100.
"The Adventure of the Blue Carbuncle." **4.** 81.
"The Adventure of the Brice-Partington Plan." **4.** 81.
"The Adventure of the Cardboard Box." **4.** 81.
"The Adventure of the Copper Beeches." **4.** 81.
"The Adventure of the Creeping Man." **4.** 81.
"The Adventure of the Crooked Man." **4.** 81.
"The Adventure of the Dancing Men." **4.** 81.
"The Adventure of the Devil's Foot." **4.** 81; **5.** 100.
"The Adventure of the Dying Detective." **4.** 81.
"The Adventure of the Empty House." **4.** 82; **5.** 100.

"The Adventure of the Engineer's Thumb." **4.** 82; **5.** 100.
"The Adventure of the *Gloria Scott.*"**4.** 82.
"The Adventure of the Golden Pince-Nez." **4.** 82.
"The Adventure of the Greek Interpreter." **4.** 82.
"The Adventure of the Illustrious Client." **4.** 82.
"The Adventure of the Lion's Mane." **4.** 82.
"The Adventure of the Mazarin Stone." **4.** 82.
"The Adventure of the Missing Three-Quarter." **4.** 82; **5.** 100.
"The Adventure of the Naval Treaty." **4.** 82.
"The Adventure of the Noble Bachelor." **3.** 113; **4.** 82.
"The Adventure of the Norwood Builder." **4.** 82.
"The Adventure of the Priory School." **3.** 114; **4.** 82; **5.** 100.
"The Adventure of the Red Circle." **4.** 82; **5.** 100.
"The Adventure of the Reigate Squire." **4.** 82; **5.** 101.
"The Adventure of the Resident Patient." **4.** 82; **5.** 101.
"The Adventure of the Retired Colourman." **4.** 82.
"The Adventure of the Second Stain." **4.** 83; **5.** 101.
"The Adventure of the Shoscombe Old Place." **4.** 83.
"The Adventure of the Six Napoleons." **4.** 83.
"The Adventure of the Solitary Cyclist." **4.** 83.
"The Adventure of the Speckled Band." **3 ed.** 181; **1.** 55; **2.** 92; **3.** 113; **4.** 83; **5.** 101.
"The Adventure of the Stockbroker's Clerk." **4.** 83.
"The Adventure of the Sussex Vampire." **4.** 83.
"The Adventure of the Three Gables." **4.** 83.
"The Adventure of the Three Garridebs." **4.** 83.
"The Adventure of the Three Students." **4.** 83.
"The Adventure of the Veiled Lodger." **4.** 83.
"The Adventure of the Yellow Face." **2.** 92; **4.** 83.
"The Adventure of Wisteria Lodge." **2.** 92; **4.** 83.
"The Boscombe Valley Mystery." **4.** 83.
"The Brazilian Cat." **4.** 83.
"The Captain of the Polestar." **5.** 100.
"A Case of Identity." **4.** 83.
"The Case of Lady Sannox." **2.** 92.
"Danger." **4.** 83.
"The Disappearance of Lady Frances Carfax." **1.** 54; **4.** 84.
"The Disintegration Machine." **4.** 84.
"The Final Problem." **4.** 84; **5.** 100.
"The Five Orange Pips." **2.** 92; **4.** 84; **5.** 101.
"His Last Bow." **4.** 84; **5.** 101.
"The Horror of the Heights." **4.** 84.
"The Hound of the Baskervilles." **2.** 92; **4.** 84.
"The Last Adventure of the Brigadier." **4.** 84.
"The Lost Special." **5.** 101.
"The Man with the Twisted Lip." **4.** 84.
"The Man with the Watches." **5.** 101.
"The Musgrave Ritual." **3.** 113; **4.** 84; **5.** 101.
"The New Catacomb." **2.** 92.
"The Problem at Thor Bridge." **4.** 84.
"The Red-Headed League." **4.** 84; **5.** 101.
"The Ring of Thoth." **4.** 84.
"A Scandal in Bohemia." **1.** 55; **4.** 84.
"The Sign of Four." **4.** 84.
"A Study in Scarlet." **4.** 84.
"The Terror of Blue John Gap." **4.** 85.
"When the World Screamed." **4.** 85; **5.** 101.

LYNN DOYLE [LESLIE A. MONTGOMERY]

"Sham Fight." **3 ed.** 181.

MARGARET DRABBLE

"Crossing the Alps." **3 ed.** 181; **3.** 114; **4.** 85.
"A Day in the Life of a Smiling Woman." **3.** 114; **4.** 85.
"The Gifts of War." **3.** 114; **4.** 85.
"Hassan's Tower." **3.** 114; **4.** 85.

"Homework." **4.** 85.
"A Pyrrhic Victory." **3.** 114; **4.** 85.
"The Reunion" [same as "Faithful Lovers"]. **3.** 114; **4.** 85.
"A Success Story." **3.** 114; **4.** 85.
"A Voyage to Cythera." **3 ed.** 181; **3.** 114; **4.** 85.

DAVID DRAKE

"Something Had To Be Done." **5.** 101.

THEODORE DREISER

"Butcher Rogaum's Door." **1.** 55; **2.** 92; **3.** 114.
"Chains" [originally "Love"]. **2.** 92; **3.** 115; **4.** 85.
"Convention." **4.** 85.
"The Cruise of the *Idlewild*." **3 ed.** 181; **4.** 85.
"A Doer of the Word." **3.** 115.
"Fine Furniture." **4.** 85.
"Free." **3.** 115; **4.** 86.
"Fulfilment." **2.** 93; **4.** 86.
"The Hand." **4.** 86.
"Khat." **4.** 86.
"The Lost Phoebe." **3 ed.** 181; **1.** 55; **3.** 115; **4.** 86.
"McEwen of the Shining Slave Makers" [same as "The Shining Slave Makers"]. **1.** 55; **2.** 93; **3.** 115; **4.** 86; **5.** 102.
"Marriage—For One." **3.** 115; **4.** 86.
"Married." **3.** 115; **4.** 86.
"The Mercy of God." **4.** 86.
"Nigger Jeff." **1.** 55; **2.** 93; **3.** 115; **4.** 86; **5.** 102.
"The Old Neighborhood." **4.** 86.
"Old Rogaum and His Theresa." **4.** 86.
"The Prince Who Was a Thief." **4.** 86.
"St. Columbia and the River." **4.** 86.
"Sanctuary." **4.** 86.
"The Second Choice." **3.** 115; **4.** 86.
"The Shadow" [originally "Jealousy"]. **3.** 115; **4.** 86.
"Solution." **4.** 87.
"A Start in Life." **4.** 87.
"A Story of Stories." **4.** 87; **5.** 102.
"Tabloid Tragedy." **4.** 87.
"The Tithe of the Lord." **4.** 87.
"Typhoon." **3 ed.** 181; **4.** 87.
"The Victor." **3 ed.** 181; **4.** 87.
"When the Old Century Was New." **1.** 55; **2.** 93; **4.** 87.
"Will You Walk into My Parlor?" **4.** 87.

ANNETTE VON DROSTE-HÜLSHOFF

"Bei uns zu Lande auf dem Lande." **3 ed.** 181.
"Joseph: Eine Kriminalgeschichte." **3 ed.** 182.
"Die Judenbuche." **3 ed.** 182; **1.** 55; **2.** 93; **3.** 115; **4.** 87; **5.** 102.
"Ledwina." **3 ed.** 182.

NIKOLAI DUBOV

"Escape." **3.** 115.

IHNAT DUBROUSKI

"The Komsomol Writer Solam Alejchem." **3.** 116.

ANDRE DUBUS

"Adultery." **5.** 102.
"Andromache." **5.** 102.
"Anna." **5.** 102.
"The Blackberry Patch." **5.** 102.
"Blessings." **5.** 102.
"Cadence." **5.** 102.
"Corporal of Artillery." **5.** 102.
"The Dark Men." **5.** 102.
"Deaths at Sea." **5.** 103.
"The Doctor." **3 ed.** 182; **5.** 103.
"Dressed Like Summer Leaves." **5.** 103.
"The Fat Girl." **5.** 103.
"A Father's Story." **5.** 103.
"Finding a Girl in America." **5.** 103.
"Going Under." **5.** 103.
"Graduation." **5.** 103.
"His Lover." **5.** 103.
"Killings." **5.** 103.
"Land Where My Fathers Died." **5.** 103.
"Molly." **5.** 103.
"My Life." **5.** 103.
"Rose." **5.** 103.
"Separate Flights." **5.** 103.
"The Shooting." **5.** 103.
"The Sorrowful Mysteries." **5.** 104.
"Townies." **5.** 104.
"We Don't Live Here Anymore." **5.** 104.
"The Winter Father." **5.** 104.

GUADALUPE DUEÑAS

"The Story of Mariquita." **1.** 55; **3.** 116.

MAURICE DUGGAN

"Along Rideout Road That Summer." **3 ed.** 182; **3.** 116; **4.** 87; **5.** 104.
"Blues for Miss Laverty." **3.** 116.
"The Deposition." **4.** 87.
"For the Love of Rupert." **3.** 116.
"Riley's Handbook." **4.** 87.
"Salvation Sunday." **3.** 116.
"The Wits of Willie Graves." **3.** 116.

GEORGE DUHAMEL

"Candide's Last Voyage." **3 ed.** 182.
"The Carter." **3 ed.** 182.
"Meeting Salavin Again." **3 ed.** 182.
"The Origin and Prosperity of Monkeys." **3 ed.** 182.
"The Wreck." **3 ed.** 182.

ALEXANDRE DUMAS, PÈRE

"Blanche de Beaulieu." **3 ed.** 183.
"Souvenirs d'Antony." **3 ed.** 183.

HENRY DUMAS

"Ark of Bones." **5.** 104.
"Fon." **5.** 104.
"Harlem." **5.** 104.
"Rope of Wind." **5.** 104.
"The Voice." **5.** 104.

PAUL LAURENCE DUNBAR

"At Shaft 11." **2.** 93.
"The Boy and the Bayonet." **2.** 93.
"A Council of State." **2.** 93.
"The Finding of Zach." **2.** 93.
"The Independence of Silas Bollender." **3 ed.** 183.
"The Last Fiddling of Mordaunt's Jim." **2.** 93.
"The Lynching of Jube Benson." **2.** 93.
"Mr. Cornelius Johnson, Office-Seeker." **2.** 93.
"One Man's Fortunes." **2.** 93.
"The Scapegoat." **1.** 56; **2.** 93.
"The Strength of Gideon." **2.** 94.
"Viney's Free Papers." **2.** 94.

ALICE DUNBAR-NELSON

"The Goodness of Saint Rocque." **4.** 87.
"Little Miss Sophie." **4.** 88.
"Mr. Baptiste." **4.** 88.
"M'sieu Fortier's Violin." **4.** 88.
"A Story of Vengeance." **4.** 88.
"Titee." **4.** 88.
"Tony's Wife." **4.** 88.
"Violets." **4.** 88.
"The Woman." **4.** 88.

QUINCE DUNCAN

"Ancestral Myths." **3.** 116.
"La rebelión Pocomita." **3.** 116.
"The Signalman's Light." **3.** 116.

SARA JEANNETTE DUNCAN

"The Hesitation of Miss Anderson." **3.** 117.
"An Impossible Ideal." **3.** 117.
"A Mother in India." **3.** 117.
"The Pool in the Desert." **3.** 117.

ROGER DUNKLEY

"A Problem Called Albert." **5.** 104.

ASHLEY SHEUN DUNN

"No Man's Land." **3.** 117.

LORD DUNSANY [EDWARD JOHN MORETON DRAX PLUNKETT]

"The Sword of Welleran." **5.** 105.
"Two Bottles of Relish." **3 ed.** 183; **1.** 56; **3.** 117; **4.** 88.

MARGUERITE DURAS [MARGUERITE DONADIEU]

"Le Boa." **3 ed.** 183.
"Les Chantiers." **3 ed.** 183.
"Madame Dodin." **3 ed.** 183.
"Mr. Andesman's Afternoon." **5.** 105.
"Moderato cantabile." **3 ed.** 183; **1.** 56; **2.** 94; **3.** 117; **5.** 105.

FRIEDRICH DÜRRENMATT

"Christmas." **3 ed.** 183; **1.** 56.
"The Director." **3 ed.** 183.
"The Dog." **3 ed.** 184.

"The Judge and His Executioner." **3 ed.** 184; **1.** 56.
"Once a Greek." **3 ed.** 184.
"The Picture of Sisyphus." **3 ed.** 184.
"Pilate." **3 ed.** 184.
"The Pledge." **3 ed.** 184.
"Das Sterben der Pythia." **2.** 94.
"The Suspicion." **3 ed.** 184.
"The Torturer." **3 ed.** 184; **1.** 56.
"The Town." **3 ed.** 184.
"The Trap" [originally "The Nihilist"]. **3 ed.** 184.
"The Tunnel." **3 ed.** 184; **1.** 56.

ADOLF DYGASINSKI

"A Trip with Mademoiselle Jourdan." **3 ed.** 184.

EDWARD DYSON

"A Golden Shanty." **4.** 88.

WARREN EARLE

"In Re State vs. Forbes." **3.** 117.

SARIF EASMON

"The Black Madonna." **5.** 105.
"The Feud." **5.** 105.
"For Love of Theresa." **5.** 105.
"Koya." **5.** 105.
"No. 2 to Maia's Tailor." **5.** 105.
"Under the Flamboyante Tree." **5.** 105.

EDITH EATON

"The Chinese Lily." **3.** 118.
"Her Chinese Husband." **3.** 118.
"The Inferior Woman." **3.** 118.
"Story of One White Woman Who Married a Chinese." **3.** 118.

JACOB HAR EBEN

"Boaz of Dupra." **3 ed.** 184.

MARIA VON EBNER-ESCHENBACH

"Er lasst die Hand küssen." **3 ed.** 184; **1.** 56.
"Der Erstgeborene." **3 ed.** 185.
"First Confession." **4.** 88.
"Die Freiherrn von Gemperlein." **3 ed.** 185.
"Mašlans Frau." **3 ed.** 185.
"Das Schädliche." **3 ed.** 185.

AQUILEO J. ECHEVERRÍA

"Acuarlas." **5.** 105.

ESTEBAN ECHEVERRÍA

"The Matador." **3 ed.** 185; **3.** 118; **5.** 106.

MARIA EDGEWORTH

"Angelina; ou l'Amie Inconnue." **3 ed.** 185; **2.** 94; **3.** 118.
"The Bracelets." **2.** 94.
"The Contrast." **2.** 94.
"False Key." **2.** 94.
"Forester." **2.** 94.
"The Good Aunt." **2.** 94.
"The Good French Governess." **2.** 94.
"The Grateful Negro." **2.** 94.
"Lame Jervas." **2.** 94.
"Lazy Lawrence." **2.** 95.
"The Lottery." **2.** 95.
"Madame de Fleury." **2.** 95.
"The Manufacturers." **2.** 95.
"The Modern Griselda." **2.** 95.
"Orlandino." **2.** 95.
"Tomorrow." **2.** 95.

HALIDE EDIP-ADIVAR

"Everyday Men: The Pumpkin-Seed Seller." **1.** 56.

WALTER D. EDMONDS

"The Death of Red Peril." **3 ed.** 185.

AMELIA B. EDWARDS

"The Eleventh of March." **4.** 88.
"A Night on the Border of the Black Forest." **4.** 89.
"The Phantom Coach." **4.** 89.
"The Professor's Story." **4.** 89.
"The Story of a Clock." **4.** 89.
"The Treasure Isle." **4.** 89.

CATERINA EDWARDS

"The Last Young Man." **4.** 89.

HARRY STILLWELL EDWARDS

"Elder Brown's Backslide." **3 ed.** 185.
"His Defense." **3 ed.** 185.

GEORGE EGERTON [MARY CHAVELITA BRIGHT]

"A Lost Masterpiece: A City Mood, August '93." **4.** 89.
"The Regeneration of Two." **5.** 106.
"Wedlock." **5.** 106.

GÜNTER EICH

"Züge im Nebel." **3 ed.** 185.

JOSEPH VON EICHENDORFF

"Dürande Castle." **3 ed.** 186.
"Die Entführung." **3 ed.** 186; **3.** 118.
"From the Life of a Good-for-Nothing." **3 ed.** 186; **1.** 57; **2.** 95; **3.** 118; **4.** 89.
"The Marble Statue." **3 ed.** 186; **1.** 57.
"Much Ado About Nothing." **3 ed.** 186.

CYPRIAN O. D. EKWENSI

"African Alchemist." **3.** 118.
"Death on the Bus." **3.** 118.
"Glittering City." **4.** 89.
"Lokotown" [same as "Loco Town"]. **3.** 118; **4.** 89.
"Stranger from Lagos." **4.** 89.

ASGHAR ELAHI

"The Holy Day of Ashura." **3.** 119.

M. BARNARD ELDERSHAW [MARJORIE BARNARD and FLORA ELDERSHAW]

"The Plover." **3 ed.** 187.
"Shipwreck." **3 ed.** 187.

SUZETTE HADEN ELGIN

"For the Sake of Grace." **5.** 106.

GEORGE ELIOT [MARY ANN EVANS]

"Amos Barton" [same as "The Sad Fortunes of Amos Barton"]. **3 ed.** 187; **2.** 95; **3.** 119; **4.** 90; **5.** 106.
"Brother Jacob." **3.** 119; **4.** 89–90.
"Janet's Repentance." **3 ed.** 187; **2.** 95; **3.** 119; **4.** 90; **5.** 106.
"The Lifted Veil." **3 ed.** 187; **2.** 95; **3.** 119; **4.** 90; **5.** 106.
"Mr. Gilfil's Love Story." **3 ed.** 187; **3.** 119; **4.** 90; **5.** 106.

SALVADOR ELIZONDO

"History According to Pao Cheng." **3.** 119.

SERGIO ELIZONDO

"Coyote, Tonight." **4.** 90.
"The Flowers." **4.** 90.
"I Shouldn't Have Danced That Night." **4.** 90.
"Lugar." **4.** 90.
"Quien le manda." **4.** 90.
"Rose, the Flute." **4.** 90.
"So Here I Am To Die." **4.** 90.
"Solitude with an Intruding Word." **4.** 90.
"Ur." **4.** 90.

STANLEY ELKIN

"Among the Witnesses." **4.** 91.
"The Bailbondsman." **3.** 120; **4.** 91.
"The Condominium." **4.** 91.
"The Conventional Wisdom." **3.** 120.
"Fifty Dollars." **2.** 95; **3.** 120.
"I Look Out for Ed Wolfe." **1.** 57; **2.** 96; **3.** 120.
"In the Alley." **2.** 96; **3.** 120.
"The Making of Ashenden." **4.** 91; **5.** 106.
"On a Field, Rampant." **3.** 120.
"The Party." **2.** 96; **3.** 120.
"Plot." **5.** 106.
"A Poetics for Bullies." **2.** 96; **3.** 120; **4.** 91.
"A Sound of Distant Thunder." **2.** 96; **3.** 120.

GEORGE P. ELLIOTT

"The NRACP." **1.** 57.
"Sandra." **3 ed.** 187.

SARAH BARNWELL ELLIOTT

"As a Little Child." **2.** 96.
"An Ex-Brigadier." **2.** 96.
"Fortune's Vassals." **2.** 96.

"Hands All Round." **2.** 96.
"Hybrid Roses." **2.** 96.
"An Idle Man." **2.** 96.
"An Incident." **2.** 96.
"Mrs. Gollyhaw's Candy-Stew." **2.** 96.
"Readjustments." **2.** 96.
"A Simple Heart." **2.** 96.
"Some Data." **2.** 96.
"Squire Kayley's Conclusions." **2.** 97.
"Stephen's Margaret." **2.** 97.
"*We* People." **2.** 97.
"Without the Courts." **2.** 97.

HARLAN ELLISON

"Adrift Just Off the Coast of Langerhans." **2.** 97.
"All the Sounds." **1.** 57.
"Along the Scenic Route." **1.** 57.
"Back to the Drawing Boards." **1.** 57.
"Basilisk." **1.** 57.
"Battlefield." **1.** 57.
"The Beast That Shouted Love at the Heart of the World." **1.** 57.
"A Boy and His Dog." **1.** 58; **2.** 97; **3.** 120; **4.** 91; **5.** 107.
"Catman." **1.** 58; **3.** 120.
"The Crackpots." **1.** 58.
"Croatoan." **1.** 58; **3.** 120.
"The Deathbird." **1.** 58; **2.** 97; **3.** 120; **4.** 91; **5.** 107.
"Deeper Than the Darkness." **1.** 58.
"Delusion for a Dragon Slayer." **1.** 58; **2.** 97.
"I Have No Mouth and I Must Scream." **1.** 58; **2.** 97; **3.** 120; **5.** 107.
"Knox." **1.** 58.
"Night Vigil." **1.** 58.
"One Life." **1.** 58.
"Paingod." **1.** 58.
"The Place with No Name." **1.** 58; **2.** 97; **3.** 121.
"Pretty Maggie Moneyeyes." **1.** 58.
"Punky and the Yale Men." **1.** 58.
"The Region Between." **5.** 107.
"Repent, Harlequin! Said the Ticktockman." **3 ed.** 187; **1.** 59; **3.** 121.
"The Resurgence of Miss Ankle-Strap Wedgie." **3.** 121.
"Run for the Stars." **1.** 59; **3.** 121.
"Santa Claus vs. S.P.I.D.E.R." **3.** 121.
"Silent in Gehenna." **1.** 59; **3.** 121.
"The Silver Corridor." **1.** 59.
"Status Quo at Troyden's." **1.** 59.
"Wanted in Surgery." **1.** 59.
"Worlds to Kill." **1.** 59; **3.** 121.

RALPH ELLISON

"Afternoon." **3 ed.** 187; **1.** 59; **2.** 97.
"And Hickman Arrives." **2.** 97.
"Backwacking: A Plea to the Senator." **2.** 97.
"Battle Royal." **3 ed.** 188; **1.** 59; **2.** 97–98; **3.** 121; **4.** 91; **5.** 107.
"The Birthmark." **3 ed.** 188; **1.** 59; **2.** 98.
"Cadillac Flambé." **2.** 98.
"A Coupla Scalped Indians." **1.** 59; **2.** 98.
"Did You Ever Dream Lucky?" **2.** 98.
"Flying Home." **3 ed.** 188; **1.** 59; **2.** 98; **3.** 121; **5.** 107.
"Heine's Bull." **2.** 98.
"In a Strange Country." **1.** 59.
"It Always Breaks Out." **2.** 98.
"Juneteenth." **2.** 98.
"King of the Bingo Game." **3 ed.** 188; **1.** 59–60; **2.** 98; **3.** 121; **4.** 91.
"Mister Toussan." **3 ed.** 188; **1.** 60; **2.** 98.
"Night-Talk." **2.** 98.
"Out of the Hospital and Under the Bar." **2.** 98.
"The Roof, the Steeple, and the People." **2.** 98.
"Slick Gonna Learn." **3 ed.** 188; **2.** 99.
"A Song of Innocence." **2.** 99.
"Sweet-the-Monkey." **2.** 99.
"That I Had the Wings." **3 ed.** 188; **1.** 60; **2.** 99.

MIRIAM ELSTON

"A Mess of Things." **4.** 91.

ANWAR ENAVATULLAH

"The Unravelled Knot." **3 ed.** 188.

ENCHI FUMIKO

"Boxcar of Chrysanthemums." **5.** 107.

GEORGE A. ENGLAND

"The Empire of the Air." **1.** 60.
"June 6, 2016." **1.** 60.

PER OLOV ENQUIST

"After the Classical Highpoints." **3.** 121.
"The Anxiety of the Loyal Souls." **3.** 121.
"Balance in Santa Monica." **3.** 121.
"From a Guinea Pig's Life." **3.** 122.
"The Tracks in the Sea of Tranquillity." **1.** 60; **3.** 122.

ELIZABETH ENRIGHT

"I Forgot Where I Was." **3 ed.** 188.
"The Sardillion." **3 ed.** 188.

NAZLI ERAY

"Monte Kristo." **5.** 107.

LOUISE ERDRICH

"The Red Convertible." **5.** 107.
"Saint Marie." **5.** 108.

PAUL ERNST

"The Blind Man." **3 ed.** 188.
"Das Eisenbahnwägelchen." **3 ed.** 189.
"Förster und Wilddieb." **3 ed.** 189.
"Das Opfer der Frau." **3 ed.** 189.
"Das Porzellangeschirr." **3 ed.** 189.
"Die Quittung." **3 ed.** 189.
"Second Vision." **3 ed.** 189.
"Das streitige Gut." **3 ed.** 189.
"The Wife of the Signalman." **3 ed.** 189.

CONCHA ESPINA

"The Foundling." **2.** 99.
"The Girl Who Disappeared." **2.** 99.
"The Gray File." **2.** 99.
"Love's Cure." **2.** 99.
"The Man and the Mastiff." **2.** 99.
"Marilis." **2.** 99.
"The Prince of Song." **2.** 99.
"Rural Tragedy." **2.** 99.
"Talín." **2.** 99.
"Wax Flame." **2.** 99.

AHMED ESSOP

"The Commandment." **5.** 108.
"Film." **3.** 122.
"Gerry's Brother." **3.** 122.
"The Hajji." **3.** 122.
"Mr. Moonreddy." **3.** 122.

DENNIS ETCHISON

"The Dead Line." **4.** 92.
"Deathtracks." **4.** 92.
"It Will Be Here Soon." **4.** 92.
"The Late Shift." **4.** 92.
"Sitting in the Corner, Whimpering Quietly." **4.** 92.
"Wet Season." **4.** 92.

CARADOC EVANS

"Be This Her Memorial." **4.** 92.
"The Blast of God." **3 ed.** 189.
"The Earth Gives All and Takes All." **3 ed.** 189.
"A Father in Sion." **4.** 92.
"Joseph's House." **2.** 99.
"Taffy at Home." **4.** 92.
"The Woman Who Sowed Iniquity." **4.** 92.

KLAUS EWERT EVERWYN

"Description of an Industrial Accident." **3 ed.** 189.

JOHN K. EWERS

"Carew's Place." **3.** 122.

SAIT FAIK

"Love Letter." **1.** 60.
"The Man Who Doesn't Know What a Tooth or a Toothache Is." **1.** 60.
"Sivriada Night." **1.** 60.

WILLIAM FAIN

"Harmony." **3 ed.** 189.

ZOË FAIRBANKS

"Relics." **5.** 108.

PAUL W. FAIRMAN

"Invasion from the Deep." **5.** 108.

PAUL P. FARIS

"The Cup That Told." **2.** 100.

PHILIP JOSÉ FARMER

"After King Kong Fell." **2.** 100.
"The Captain's Daughter." **2.** 100.
"Don't Wash the Carats." **3.** 122.

"Father." **3.** 122; **4.** 92.
"The God Business." **1.** 60.
"The Lovers." **3.** 122; **5.** 108.
"My Sister's Brother." **2.** 100.
"The Öogenesis of Bird City." **3.** 122.
"Prometheus." **3.** 122.
"Riders of the Purple Wage." **3.** 122.
"Sketches Among the Ruins of My Mind." **3.** 123.
"Son." **1.** 60; **3.** 123.

JAMES T. FARRELL

"The Benefits of American Life." **3 ed.** 190.
"Clyde." **3 ed.** 190.
"Helen, I Love You." **3 ed.** 190.
"Jim O'Neill." **2.** 100.
"Joe Eliot." **2.** 100.
"The Sisters." **3 ed.** 190.
"Studs." **3.** 123.
"When Boyhood Dreams Come True." **3.** 123.

HOWARD FAST

"The Day of Victory." **3 ed.** 190.

WILLIAM FAULKNER

"Ad Astra." **3 ed.** 190; **3.** 123; **4.** 92.
"Adolescence." **4.** 93.
"Afternoon of a Cow." **4.** 93.
"All the Dead Pilots." **3 ed.** 190; **3.** 123; **4.** 93.
"Artist at Home." **3 ed.** 190; **4.** 93.
"Barn Burning." **3 ed.** 190–91; **1.** 61; **2.** 100; **3.** 123; **4.** 93; **5.** 108.
"The Bear." **3 ed.** 191–96; **1.** 61; **2.** 100-01; **3.** 123–24; **4.** 93; **5.** 108.
"A Bear Hunt." **3 ed.** 196; **4.** 93.
"Beyond." **4.** 93.
"The Big Shot." **4.** 93.
"Black Music." **3 ed.** 196; **1.** 61; **3.** 124; **4.** 93.
"The Brooch." **3 ed.** 196; **4.** 93.
"By the People." **4.** 93.
"Carcassonne." **1.** 61; **2.** 101; **3.** 124; **4.** 93.
"Centaur in Brass." **3 ed.** 196; **4.** 93–94.
"A Courtship." **3 ed.** 196–97; **2.** 101; **4.** 94.
"Crevasse." **3 ed.** 197; **3.** 124.
"A Dangerous Man." **4.** 94.
"Death Drag." **3 ed.** 197; **4.** 94.
"Delta Autumn." **3 ed.** 197–98; **1.** 61; **2.** 101; **3.** 124; **4.** 94; **5.** 109.
"Dr. Martino." **3 ed.** 198; **1.** 61; **4.** 94.
"Dry September." **3 ed.** 198; **1.** 61; **2.** 101; **3.** 124; **4.** 94; **5.** 109.
"Elly." **3 ed.** 198; **4.** 94.
"An Error in Chemistry." **3 ed.** 198; **2.** 101; **3.** 124.
"Evangeline." **4.** 94.
"The Fire and the Hearth." **3 ed.** 198–99; **1.** 61; **2.** 101; **3.** 124; **4.** 94; **5.** 109.
"Fool About a Horse." **4.** 94.
"Fox Hunt." **3 ed.** 199; **4.** 94.
"Go Down, Moses." **3 ed.** 199; **1.** 61; **2.** 101; **3.** 124; **4.** 95; **5.** 109.
"Gold Is Not Always." **3 ed.** 199.
"Golden Land." **3 ed.** 199; **1.** 62; **2.** 101; **3.** 125.
"Hair." **3 ed.** 200; **4.** 95.
"Hand upon the Waters." **3 ed.** 200; **2.** 101; **3.** 125; **4.** 95.
"Honor." **3.** 125.
"The Hound." **3 ed.** 200; **4.** 95.
"Idyll in the Desert." **4.** 95.
"A Justice." **3 ed.** 200; **3.** 125; **4.** 95.
"The Kid Learns." **4.** 95.
"Knight's Gambit." **3 ed.** 200; **1.** 62; **2.** 102; **3.** 125; **4.** 95; **5.** 109.
"Landing in Luck." **4.** 95.
"The Leg." **3.** 125; **4.** 95.
"The Liar." **4.** 95.
"Lion." **3 ed.** 200.
"Lizards in Jamshyd's Courtyard." **4.** 96.
"Lo!" **3 ed.** 200; **4.** 96.
"Love." **4.** 96.
"Mirrors of Chartres Street." **4.** 96.
"Miss Zilphia Gant." **3 ed.** 200; **4.** 96; **5.** 109.
"Mr. Acarius." **3 ed.** 200; **4.** 96.
"Mistral." **3 ed.** 200; **2.** 102; **5.** 109.
"Monk." **3 ed.** 200; **2.** 102; **3.** 125; **4.** 96.
"Moonlight." **4.** 96.
"Mountain Victory." **3 ed.** 200; **3.** 125; **4.** 96; **5.** 109.
"Mule in the Yard." **3.** 125; **4.** 96; **5.** 109.
"My Grandmother Millard." **3 ed.** 201; **3.** 125; **4.** 96.
"A Name for the City." **4.** 96.
"Notes on a Horsethief." **4.** 96.
"Nympholepsy" [originally "The Hill"]. **2.** 102; **4.** 95, 96.

"An Odor of Verbena." **3 ed.** 201; **1.** 62; **2.** 102; **4.** 96.
"Old Man." **3 ed.** 201; **1.** 62; **2.** 102; **3.** 125.
"The Old People." **3 ed.** 201; **1.** 62; **2.** 102; **3.** 125–26; **4.** 97; **5.** 109.
"Once Aboard the Lugger." **1.** 62; **3.** 126.
"Out of Nazareth." **4.** 97.
"Pantaloon in Black." **3 ed.** 202; **1.** 62; **2.** 102; **3.** 126; **4.** 97; **5.** 109.
"Pennsylvania Station." **4.** 97.
"A Portrait of Elmer." **4.** 97.
"The Priest." **4.** 97.
"Race at Morning." **3 ed.** 202; **4.** 97; **5.** 110.
"Raid." **3 ed.** 202; **2.** 102; **3.** 126.
"Red Leaves." **3 ed.** 202; **1.** 62; **2.** 102; **4.** 97.
"Retreat." **3 ed.** 202; **3.** 126.
"A Return." **4.** 97.
"Riposte in Tertio." **3 ed.** 202.
"The Rosary." **2.** 102.
"A Rose for Emily." **3 ed.** 203–04; **1.** 62; **2.** 102–03; **3.** 126; **4.** 97; **5.** 110.
"Sepulture South: Gaslight." **3 ed.** 204; **4.** 96.
"Shall Not Perish." **3 ed.** 205; **3.** 126; **4.** 97.
"Shingles for the Lord." **3 ed.** 205; **3.** 126; **4.** 97.
"Skirmish at Sartoris." **3 ed.** 205; **2.** 103.
"Smoke." **3 ed.** 205; **2.** 103; **3.** 126; **4.** 97–98.
"Snow." **5.** 110.
"Spotted Horses." **3 ed.** 205; **1.** 62; **2.** 103; **3.** 127; **4.** 98; **5.** 110.
"The Tall Men." **3 ed.** 205–06; **1.** 62; **3.** 127; **4.** 98; **5.** 110.
"That Evening Sun." **3 ed.** 206–07; **1.** 62–63; **2.** 103; **3.** 127; **4.** 98; **5.** 110.
"That Will Be Fine." **4.** 98.
"There Was a Queen." **3 ed.** 207; **3.** 127; **4.** 98.
"Thrift." **2.** 103; **3.** 127; **4.** 98.
"Tomorrow." **3 ed.** 207; **2.** 103; **3.** 127; **4.** 98.
"Turnabout." **3 ed.** 207; **3.** 127; **4.** 98.
"Two Dollar Wife." **3 ed.** 207.
"Two Soldiers." **3 ed.** 207; **3.** 127; **4.** 98.
"Uncle Willy." **3 ed.** 207; **1.** 63; **2.** 103; **3.** 127; **4.** 98; **5.** 110.
"Vendee." **3 ed.** 207; **3.** 127; **5.** 110.
"Victory." **3 ed.** 208; **3.** 127; **4.** 98; **5.** 110.
"Was." **3 ed.** 208; **1.** 63; **2.** 103; **3.** 127; **4.** 98; **5.** 110.
"Wash." **3 ed.** 208; **1.** 63; **2.** 103; **4.** 98.
"The Wild Palms." **4.** 99.
"The Wishing Tree." **4.** 99.
"With Caution and Dispatch." **3.** 127.
"Yo Ho and Two Bottles of Rum." **4.** 99.

ARTHUR HUFF FAUSET

"Symphonesque." **2.** 104.

JESSIE REDMON FAUSET

"Double Trouble." **2.** 104.
"Emmy." **2.** 104.
"Mary Elizabeth." **2.** 104.
"The Sleeper Wakes." **2.** 104; **4.** 99.

IRVIN FAUST

"Jake Bluffstein and Adolf Hitler." **1.** 63.
"Roar Lion Roar." **1.** 63; **5.** 110.

BRIAN FAWCETT

"Lowers." **5.** 111.

JOHN RUSSELL FEARN

"The Brain of Light." **3.** 128.

KONSTANTIN FEDIN

"Transvaal." **3.** 128.

MORDECAI ZEV FEIERBERG

"In the Evening." **3 ed.** 208.
"The Shadows." **3 ed.** 209.
"Whither." **4.** 99.

BEPPE FENOGLIO

"The Whirlpool." **4.** 99.

CRISTINA FERNÁNDEZ CUBAS

"Los altillos de Brumal." **5.** 111.
"Lúnula and Violeta." **5.** 111.
"Mi hermana Elba." **5.** 111.
"La noche de Jezebel." **5.** 111.
"El provocador de imágenes." **5.** 111.
"El reloj de Bagdad." **5.** 111.

"The Southern Hemisphere." **5.** 111.
"La ventana del jardín." **5.** 111.

JESÚS FERNÁNDEZ SANTOS

"Although I Don't Know Your Name." **3.** 128.
"Apartment." **3.** 128.
"The Bicycle." **3.** 128.
"Climbing the Tower." **3.** 128.
"Interview." **3.** 128.
"The Long Journey of the Monstrance." **3.** 128.
"Pablo on the Threshold." **3.** 128.
"Premature Ruin." **3.** 128.
"The Shadow of the Horse." **3.** 128.
"The Snail." **3.** 128.
"Story of the Dean." **3.** 128.
"The Strike Child." **3.** 128.
"Within Sight of an Old Lady." **3.** 128.

ROSARIO FERRÉ

"In Defense of the White Bird." **3.** 129.
"Mercedes Benz 220SL." **4.** 99.
"When Women Love Men." **3.** 129; **4.** 99.
"The Youngest Doll." **3.** 129; **4.** 99.

RAMÓN FERREIRA

"Cita a las nueve." **5.** 111.

JORGE FERRETIS

"Hombres en tempestad." **5.** 112.

JACQUES FERRON

"Cadieu." **3 ed.** 209.
"Les Méchins." **2.** 104.

LESLIE FIEDLER

"The Dancing of Reb Hershl with the Withered Hand." **3 ed.** 209.
"The First Spade in the West." **3 ed.** 209; **1.** 63; **4.** 99.
"The Last Jew in America." **1.** 63; **4.** 99.
"The Last WASP in the World." **1.** 63; **4.** 100.
"Let Nothing You Dismay." **3 ed.** 209.
"Nobody Ever Dies from It." **4.** 100.
"Nude Croquet." **3 ed.** 209; **4.** 100.
"Pull Down Vanity." **3 ed.** 209; **4.** 100.

EDWIN FIGUEROA

"Lolo Manco." **5.** 112.
"Raíz amarga." **5.** 112.
"El sol de los muertos." **5.** 112.

AMANDA FINCH

"Back Trail: A Novella of Love in the South." **4.** 100.

RODERICK FINDLAY
(see RODERICK FINLAYSON)

TIMOTHY FINDLEY

"Daybreak at Pisa." **5.** 112.
"Dinner Among the Amazons." **5.** 112.
"Hello Cheeverland, Goodbye." **5.** 112.
"Lemonade." **5.** 112.
"Losers, Finders, Strangers at the Door." **5.** 112.
"Out of the Silence." **5.** 112.
"War." **5.** 112.
"What Mrs. Felton Knew." **5.** 112.

IAN HAMILTON FINLAY

"National Assistance Money." **4.** 100.

RODERICK FINLAYSON

"Jim and Miri." **1.** 63.
"A Man of Good Religion." **3 ed.** 209.

CHARLES FINNEY

"The Captivity." **4.** 100.
"The Door." **4.** 100.
"The Life and Death of a Western Gladiator." **4.** 100.
"The Magician Out of Manchuria." **4.** 100.

LESLIE FISH

"The Deadly Innocence, or 'The End of the Hurt/Comfort Syndrome.'" **5.** 112.

CLAY FISHER [HENRY W. ALLEN]

"Ghost Town." **3.** 129.
"Pretty Face." **3.** 129.

DOROTHY CANFIELD FISHER

"The Apprentice." **3 ed.** 209.
"The Bedquilt." **3 ed.** 209.
"Flint and Fire." **3 ed.** 209.
"The Knot Hole." **2.** 104.

RUDOLPH FISHER

"The City of Refuge." **3 ed.** 210; **2.** 104; **3.** 129; **5.** 113.
"Common Meter." **3 ed.** 210; **1.** 64; **2.** 104; **5.** 113.
"Dust." **2.** 104.
"Ezekiel." **2.** 104.
"Fire by Night." **2.** 105.
"Guardian of the Law." **2.** 105.
"High Yaller." **3 ed.** 210; **2.** 105; **3.** 129.
"Lindy Hop." **2.** 105.
"Miss Cynthie." **3 ed.** 210; **2.** 105; **5.** 113.
"The Promised Land." **3 ed.** 210; **2.** 105.
"Ringtail." **2.** 105; **5.** 113.
"The South Lingers On." **2.** 105.

STEVE FISHER

"Shanghai Butterfly: A Short, Short Story." **3.** 129.

F. SCOTT FITZGERALD

"Absolution." **3 ed.** 210; **1.** 64; **2.** 105; **3.** 129; **4.** 100.
"The Adjuster." **3 ed.** 210; **3.** 130.
"An Alcoholic Case." **5.** 113.
"Author's House." **3 ed.** 210.
"The Baby Party." **3 ed.** 211; **1.** 64; **2.** 105; **5.** 113.
"Babylon Revisited." **3 ed.** 210–11; **1.** 64; **2.** 105; **3.** 130; **4.** 100–01; **5.** 113.
"Basil and Cleopatra." **3 ed.** 211; **2.** 106.
"Benediction." **2.** 106.
"Bernice Bobs Her Hair." **2.** 106; **3.** 130; **4.** 101; **5.** 113.
"The Bowl." **2.** 106.
"The Bridal Party." **3 ed.** 211; **3.** 130.
"The Camel's Back." **5.** 113.
"The Captured Shadow." **3 ed.** 211.
"Crazy Sunday." **3 ed.** 211–12; **2.** 106; **3.** 130; **5.** 113.
"The Curious Case of Benjamin Button." **2.** 106.
"The Cut-Glass Bowl." **3 ed.** 212; **1.** 64.
"Design in Plaster." **3 ed.** 212.
"The Diamond as Big as the Ritz." **3 ed.** 212; **1.** 64; **2.** 106; **3.** 130.
"Dice, Brass Knuckles & Guitar." **3.** 130.
"Family in the Wind." **3 ed.** 212; **1.** 64; **3.** 130.
"Financing Finnegan." **3.** 130.
"First Blood." **3 ed.** 212.
"Forging Ahead." **3 ed.** 212.
"The Freshest Boy." **3 ed.** 212; **2.** 106; **3.** 131.
"Fun in the Artist's Studio." **3 ed.** 212.
"Gods of Darkness." **2.** 106.
"He Thinks He's Wonderful." **3 ed.** 212.
"Head and Shoulders." **5.** 113.
"Her Last Case." **5.** 113.
"The Ice Palace." **3 ed.** 212–13; **2.** 106; **3.** 131.
"In the Darkest Hour." **2.** 106.
"Jacob's Ladder." **3 ed.** 213; **3.** 131.
"The Jelly-Bean." **3 ed.** 213; **2.** 106; **3.** 131.
"The Last of the Belles." **3 ed.** 213; **2.** 106; **3.** 131.
"The Lost Decade." **3.** 131.
"Magnetism." **3.** 131.
"Majesty." **2.** 106.
"A Man in the Way." **3 ed.** 213.
"May Day." **3 ed.** 213; **1.** 64; **2.** 106; **3.** 131.
"Myra Meets His Family." **5.** 114.
"A New Leaf." **3.** 131; **5.** 114.
"A Night at the Fair." **3 ed.** 213; **2.** 107.
"No Harm Trying." **3 ed.** 213.
"O Russet Witch!" **4.** 101.
"The Offshore Pirate." **3 ed.** 213; **3.** 131.
"One Interne." **3 ed.** 213.
"One Trip Abroad." **3 ed.** 213–14; **2.** 107; **3.** 131.
"The Ordeal." **3 ed.** 214; **2.** 107.
"Our Own Movie Queen." **3.** 131.
"Outside the Cabinet-Maker's." **3 ed.** 214; **3.** 131.
"Pat Hobby's Christmas Wish." **3 ed.** 214.
"Pat Hobby's College Days." **5.** 114.
"Pat Hobby's Secret." **3 ed.** 214.
"A Patriotic Short." **3 ed.** 214.
"The Perfect Life." **3 ed.** 214; **2.** 107.
"The Pierian Springs." **3 ed.** 214.
"The Popular Girl." **3.** 131.
"Presumption." **3.** 132.
"Rags Martin-Jones and the Pr-nce of W-les." **3.** 132.

"The Rich Boy." **3 ed.** 214; **1.** 64; **2.** 107; **3.** 132; **4.** 101; **5.** 114.
"The Rough Crossing." **3 ed.** 214–15; **2.** 107.
"The Scandal Detectives." **3 ed.** 215.
"The Sensible Thing." **3 ed.** 215; **3.** 132.
"A Short Trip Home." **3 ed.** 215.
"The Sisters." **2.** 107.
"Six of One—." **3 ed.** 215.
"The Spire and the Gargoyle." **3.** 132.
"The Swimmers." **3 ed.** 215; **3.** 132.
"That Kind of Party." **3 ed.** 215; **2.** 107.
"Three Acts of Music." **3.** 132.
"Two Old-Timers." **3 ed.** 215.
"Two Wrongs." **3 ed.** 215.
"Winter Dreams." **3 ed.** 215; **1.** 64; **2.** 107; **3.** 132; **4.** 101.
"A Woman with a Past." **3 ed.** 215.

ZELDA SAYRE FITZGERALD

"A Couple of Nuts." **1.** 64.
"Miss Ella." **1.** 65.

CHARLES MACOMB FLANDRAU

"Wanderlust." **2.** 107.

GUSTAVE FLAUBERT

"Bibliomanie." **3 ed.** 216.
"Bouvard and Pécuchet." **3 ed.** 216; **1.** 65; **2.** 107–08; **3.** 132; **4.** 101; **5.** 114.
"Chevrin." **3 ed.** 216.
"Chronique Normande du dixième siècle." **3 ed.** 216.
"La dernière heure." **3 ed.** 216.
"Deux mains sur une couronne." **3 ed.** 216.
"La femme du monde." **3 ed.** 216.
"La fiancée et la tombe." **3 ed.** 216.
"La grande dame et le joueur de vielle." **3 ed.** 216.
"Hérodias." **3 ed.** 216–17; **1.** 65; **2.** 108; **3.** 132–33; **4.** 101.
"Une leçon d'histoire naturelle." **3 ed.** 217.
"Le main de fer." **3 ed.** 217.
"Matteo Falcone." **3 ed.** 217.
"Mémoires d'un fou." **3 ed.** 217.
"Le Moine des Chartreux." **3 ed.** 217.
"Le mort de Marguerite de Bourgogne." **3 ed.** 217.
"St. Julien." **3 ed.** 217–18; **1.** 65; **2.** 108; **3.** 133; **4.** 101–02; **5.** 114.
"San Pietro Ormano." **3 ed.** 218.
"Un secret de Philippe Prudent." **3 ed.** 218.
"A Simple Heart." **3 ed.** 218–19; **1.** 65; **2.** 108; **3.** 133; **4.** 102; **5.** 114.
"Smarh." **3 ed.** 219.

PAUL FLEHR [FREDERIK POHL]

"A Life and A/Half." **5.** 114.

ANTONIO FOGAZZARO

"Eden Anto." **1.** 65.
"The Fiasco of Maestro Chieco." **1.** 65.

MARTHA FOLEY

"One with Shakespeare." **3 ed.** 219.

RUBEM FONSECA

"The Exterminator." **3.** 133.
"Happy New Year." **5.** 114.
"Large Intestine." **5.** 115.

THEODOR FONTANE

"Grete Minde." **3.** 133.

MARY HALLOCK FOOTE

"A Cloud on the Mountain." **2.** 108.
"The Cup of Trembling." **3 ed.** 219; **2.** 108.
"The Fate of a Voice." **2.** 108.
"Friend Barton's 'Concern.'" **3 ed.** 219; **2.** 108.
"Gideon's Knock." **2.** 108.
"The Harshwood Bride." **3 ed.** 219.
"How the Pump Stopped at the Morning Watch." **3 ed.** 219; **2.** 108.
"In Exile." **3 ed.** 219; **2.** 108.
"The Maid's Progress." **3 ed.** 219; **2.** 108.
"Maverick." **3 ed.** 219.
"On a Side Track." **3 ed.** 219.
"The Picture in the Fire-Place Bedroom." **2.** 109.
"Pilgrims to Mecca." **3 ed.** 219; **2.** 109.
"The Rapture of Hetty." **3 ed.** 219.
"The Story of Alcázar." **3 ed.** 219; **2.** 109.
"A Story of the Dry Season." **2.** 109.
"A Touch of Sun." **3 ed.** 219; **2.** 109.
"The Trumpeter." **3 ed.** 220; **2.** 109.
"The Watchman." **3 ed.** 220; **2.** 109.

SHELBY FOOTE

"Child by Fever." **2.** 109; **3.** 133.
"The Freedom Kick." **3.** 133.
"A Marriage Portion." **3.** 133.
"Pillar of Fire." **3.** 133.
"Rain Down Home." **3.** 134.
"Ride Out." **3.** 134.
"The Sacred Mound." **3.** 134.

XAVIER FORNERET

"À neuf heures à Paris." **3 ed.** 220.
"Un Oeil entre deux yeux." **3 ed.** 220.
"Un Rêve c'est." **3 ed.** 220.

DAVID FORREST

"The Keeper of the Night." **3 ed.** 220.

E. M. FORSTER

"Albergo Empedocle." **3 ed.** 220; **1.** 65; **2.** 109; **3.** 134.
"Ansell." **1.** 65; **3.** 134; **5.** 115.
"Arthur Snatchfold." **1.** 66; **2.** 109; **3.** 134; **5.** 115.
"The Celestial Omnibus." **3 ed.** 220; **1.** 66; **2.** 109; **3.** 134; **4.** 102; **5.** 115.
"The Classical Annex." **1.** 66; **2.** 109.
"Co-ordination" [originally "Cooperation"]. **3 ed.** 221; **3.** 134.
"The Curate's Friend." **3 ed.** 221; **2.** 109; **3.** 134; **4.** 102; **5.** 115.
"Dr. Woolacott." **1.** 66; **2.** 110; **3.** 134.
"The Eternal Moment." **3 ed.** 221; **1.** 66; **2.** 110; **3.** 134; **5.** 115.
"The Life To Come." **2.** 110; **3.** 135; **5.** 115.
"Little Imber." **3.** 135.
"The Machine Stops." **3 ed.** 221; **1.** 66; **2.** 110; **3.** 135; **4.** 102; **5.** 115.
"Mr. Andrews." **3 ed.** 221–22; **3.** 135; **5.** 115.
"The Obelisk." **1.** 66; **2.** 110; **3.** 135.
"The Other Boat." **1.** 66; **2.** 110; **3.** 135; **4.** 102; **5.** 115.
"Other Kingdom." **3 ed.** 222; **2.** 110; **3.** 135; **4.** 102; **5.** 115.
"The Other Side of the Hedge." **3 ed.** 222; **1.** 66; **3.** 135.
"The Point of It." **3 ed.** 222; **1.** 66; **2.** 110; **3.** 135; **4.** 102.
"The Purple Envelope." **1.** 66; **3.** 135.
"The Purple Hat." **2.** 110.
"Ralph and Tony." **3.** 135.
"The Road from Colonus." **3 ed.** 222–23; **1.** 66; **2.** 110; **3.** 136; **4.** 102; **5.** 115.
"The Rock." **3.** 136.
"The Story of a Panic." **3 ed.** 223; **1.** 66; **2.** 110; **3.** 136; **4.** 102; **5.** 115.
"The Story of the Siren." **3 ed.** 223–24; **2.** 111; **3.** 136.
"The Tomb of Pletone." **5.** 115.
"The Torque." **1.** 66; **2.** 111; **3.** 136.
"What Does It Matter?" **1.** 66; **2.** 111; **3.** 136.

KEITH FORT

"The Coal Shoveller." **3 ed.** 224.

JOHN FOWLES

"The Cloud." **2.** 111; **3.** 136; **4.** 102; **5.** 116.
"The Ebony Tower." **2.** 111; **3.** 136; **4.** 103; **5.** 116.
"Eliduc." **3.** 136; **4.** 103.
"The Enigma." **2.** 111; **3.** 137; **5.** 116.
"Poor Koko." **2.** 111; **3.** 137; **4.** 103; **5.** 116.

JOHN FOX

"The Army of the Callahan." **3 ed.** 224.
"The Battle-Prayer of Parson Small." **3 ed.** 224.
"Christmas for Big Ames." **3 ed.** 224.
"Christmas Night with Satan." **3 ed.** 224.
"A Crisis for the Guard." **3 ed.** 224.
"A Cumberland Vendetta." **3 ed.** 224; **3.** 137.
"The Goddess of Happy Valley." **3 ed.** 224.
"Grayson's Baby." **3 ed.** 224; **3.** 137.
"The Last Stetson." **3.** 137.
"A Message of Sand." **3.** 137.
"A Mountain Europa." **3 ed.** 224; **3.** 137.
"On Hell-fer-Sartain Creek." **3 ed.** 224.
"On the Road to Hell-for-Sartain." **3 ed.** 224.
"The Pardon of Becky Day." **3 ed.** 224.
"The Pope of Big Sandy." **3 ed.** 225.
"Preaching on Kingdom Come." **3.** 137.
"A Purple Rhododendron." **3 ed.** 225; **3.** 137.
"A Trick o' Trade." **3.** 137.

GEORGES FRADIER

"Empedocles in Bogota." **3.** 137.

MEDARDO FRAILE

"El álbum." **5.** 116.
"La cabezota." **5.** 116.

JANET FRAME

"The Bedjacket." **3.** 137.
"The Birds Began to Sing." **3.** 138.
"A Boy's Will." **3 ed.** 225.
"Dossy." **3.** 138.
"Keel and Kool." **1.** 67; **2.** 111; **3.** 138.
"The Lagoon." **1.** 67; **2.** 111.
"Miss Gibson and the Lumber Room." **3 ed.** 225; **3.** 138.
"A Note on the Russian War." **3.** 138.
"The Reservoir." **1.** 67.
"Summer." **3.** 138.
"Swans." **1.** 67; **3.** 138.
"Two Sheep." **3 ed.** 225.

HANS FRANCK

"Die Südsee-Insel." **3 ed.** 225.
"Taliter?" **3 ed.** 225.

LEONHARD FRANK

"Die Kriegswitwe." **2.** 111.
"Das Liebespaar." **2.** 111.
"Der Vater." **2.** 112.

ULRICH FRANK [ULLA WOLFF]

"Simon Eichelkatz." **5.** 116.

RAYMOND FRASER

"The Actor." **5.** 116.
"Bertha and Bill." **5.** 116.
"A Cold Frosty Morning." **5.** 116.
"The Janitor's Wife." **5.** 116.
"The Newbridge Sighting." **5.** 117.
"On the Bus." **5.** 117.
"The Quebec Prison." **5.** 117.
"Spanish Jack." **5.** 117.
"They Came Here to Die." **5.** 117.

MARY E. WILKINS FREEMAN

"Amanda and Love." **1.** 67.
"The Apple Tree." **3 ed.** 225.
"Arethusa." **3 ed.** 225; **3.** 138.
"The Balking of Christopher." **3 ed.** 225.
"Christmas Jenny." **2.** 112; **3.** 138; **5.** 117.
"A Church Mouse." **3 ed.** 225; **3.** 138.
"A Conflict Ended." **3 ed.** 225; **3.** 138.
"Evelina's Garden." **3 ed.** 225; **4.** 103.
"A Gala Dress." **3 ed.** 226; **3.** 138.
"A Gatherer of Simples." **3.** 138.
"Gentian." **3 ed.** 226; **3.** 138.
"The Great Pine." **3 ed.** 226; **3.** 138.
"The Hall Bedroom." **4.** 103.
"An Honest Soul." **3 ed.** 226; **3.** 138.
"An Independent Thinker." **3 ed.** 226.
"The Little Maid." **2.** 112.
"The Long Arm." **3.** 139.
"The Lost Ghost." **4.** 103.
"The Love of Parson Lord." **3.** 139.
"Luella Miller." **4.** 103.
"A Mistaken Charity." **3.** 139.
"A New England Nun." **3 ed.** 226; **2.** 112; **3.** 139; **4.** 103.
"A New England Prophet." **3 ed.** 226.
"An Object of Love." **5.** 117.
"Old Lady Pingree." **3 ed.** 226.
"Old Woman Magoun." **3.** 139; **5.** 117.
"On the Walpole Road." **3 ed.** 226; **3.** 139.
"One Good Time." **3.** 139.
"A Patient Waiter." **3.** 139.
"A Poetess." **3.** 139.
"The Revolt of Mother." **3 ed.** 226; **2.** 112; **3.** 139; **5.** 117.
"The Selfishness of Amelia." **3.** 139.
"The Shadows on the Wall." **4.** 103.
"Sister Liddy." **3 ed.** 226; **3.** 139.
"A Solitary." **3.** 139.
"The Southwest Chamber." **4.** 103.
"A Symphony in Lavender." **3 ed.** 226; **3.** 139.
"A Taste of Honey." **3 ed.** 226.
"The Three Old Sisters and the Old Beau." **3 ed.** 226.
"Two Friends." **5.** 117.
"Two Old Lovers." **3 ed.** 226; **3.** 140.
"Up Primrose Hill." **3.** 140.
"The Vacant Lot." **4.** 103.
"A Village Lear." **3 ed.** 227; **3.** 140.
"A Village Singer." **3.** 140.
"A Wayfaring Couple." **3 ed.** 227.
"The White Birch." **3 ed.** 227.
"The Wind in the Rose Bush." **4.** 103.

CELIA FREMLIN

"Don't Be Frightened." **2.** 112.
"The Quiet Game." **5.** 117.

ALICE FRENCH

"Mrs. Finlay's Elizabethan Chair." **4.** 103.
"Tommy and Thomas." **4.** 104.
"Trusty, No. 49." **3 ed.** 227.

HERMAN JAN FRIEDERICY

"The Counselor." **3.** 140.

BRUCE JAY FRIEDMAN

"Brazzaville Teen-ager." **3 ed.** 227.
"The Canning of Mother Dean." **3 ed.** 227.
"Far from the City of Class." **3 ed.** 227.
"A Foot in the Door." **3 ed.** 227.
"The Humiliation." **3 ed.** 227.
"The Imposing Proportions of Jean Shrimpton." **3 ed.** 227.
"The Investor." **3 ed.** 227.
"The Man They Threw out of Jets." **3 ed.** 227.
"Show Biz Connections." **3 ed.** 227.
"The Subversive." **3 ed.** 227.
"When You're Excused, You're Excused." **1.** 67.
"Yes, We Have No Ritchard." **3 ed.** 228.

BRIAN FRIEL

"Among the Ruins." **1.** 67; **2.** 112.
"The Diviner." **2.** 112.
"The Flower of Kiltymore." **2.** 112.
"Foundry House." **3 ed.** 228; **1.** 67; **2.** 112.
"The Gold in the Sea." **2.** 112.
"The Highwayman and the Saint." **2.** 112.
"The Illusionists." **2.** 113.
"Johnny and Mick." **2.** 113.
"Mr. Sing My Heart's Delight." **2.** 113.
"My Father and the Sergeant." **2.** 113.
"The Potato Gatherers." **2.** 113.
"The Saucer of Larks." **2.** 113.
"The Widowhood System." **3 ed.** 228.

MAX FRISCH

"Antwort aus der Stille." **3.** 140.

BARBARA FRISCHMUTH

"Let It Be." **2.** 113; **5.** 117.
"Tree of the Forgotten Dog." **2.** 113; **5.** 118.

ROBERT FROST

"The Cockerel Buying Habit." **3 ed.** 228.
"A Just Judge." **3 ed.** 228.
"Old Welch Goes to Show." **3 ed.** 228.
"The Original and Only." **3 ed.** 228.
"The Same Thing Over and Over." **3 ed.** 228.
"Trap Nests." **3 ed.** 228.

DANIEL FUCHS

"The Amazing Mystery of Storick, Dorschi, Pflaumer, Inc." **2.** 113.
"The Apathetic Bookie Joint." **2.** 113.
"A Clean Quiet House." **2.** 113.
"Crap Game." **2.** 113.
"Ecossaise, Berceuse, Polonaise." **2.** 113.
"The First Smell of Spring, and Brooklyn." **2.** 113.
"A Girl Like Cele." **2.** 113.
"The Golden West." **2.** 114.
"Love in Brooklyn." **2.** 114.
"The Man from Mars." **2.** 114.
"Man in the Middle of the Ocean." **2.** 114.
"The Morose Policeman." **2.** 114.
"Okay, Mr. Pappendas, Okay." **2.** 114.
"People on a Planet." **2.** 114.
"There's Always Honolulu." **2.** 114.
"Twilight in Southern California." **2.** 114; **3.** 140.

CARLOS FUENTES

"All Cats Are Gray." **2.** 114.
"Aura." **2.** 114; **3.** 140.
"Chac Mool." **3 ed.** 228; **1.** 67; **3.** 140; **5.** 118.
"The Cost of Life." **3 ed.** 228; **2.** 114; **3.** 141; **5.** 118.
"The Doll Queen." **3 ed.** 228; **2.** 114; **3.** 141; **5.** 118.
"The Gods Speak" [same as "By the Mouth of the Gods"]. **3 ed.** 228–29; **1.** 67; **3.** 141.
"In a Flemish Garden" [same as "Tlactocatzine, the One from the Flemish Garden"]. **3 ed.** 229; **2.** 114; **3.** 141; **4.** 104; **5.** 118.
"In Defense of Trigolibia." **3 ed.** 229; **3.** 141.
"Litany of the Orchids." **3 ed.** 229; **3.** 141.
"The Man Who Invented Gunpowder." **3 ed.** 229; **3.** 141.

"Mother's Day." **5.** 118.
"El muñeco." **3 ed.** 229.
"The Old Morality." **3 ed.** 229; **5.** 118.
"Pantera en jazz." **3 ed.** 229.
"Pastel rancio." **3 ed.** 229.
"A Pure Soul." **3 ed.** 229; **3.** 141.
"These Were Palaces." **3.** 141; **5.** 118.
"To the Sea Serpent" [same as "To the Snake of the Sea"]. **3 ed.** 229; **5.** 118.
"Trigo errante." **3 ed.** 229.
"The Two Helens." **3 ed.** 229; **1.** 67–68; **3.** 141; **5.** 118.
"What Fortune Brought." **3 ed.** 229; **2.** 115; **3.** 141.

NORBERTO FUENTES

"Captain Descalzo." **3.** 141.

HENRY BLAKE FULLER

"Dr. Gowdy and the Squash." **3 ed.** 229–30; **3.** 141; **5.** 118.
"The Downfall of Abner Joyce." **3 ed.** 230; **3.** 142; **5.** 119.
"The Greatest of These." **3 ed.** 230.
"Little O'Grady vs. the Grindstone." **3 ed.** 230; **3.** 142.
"Pasquale's Picture." **5.** 119.
"The Pilgrim Sons." **5.** 119.
"Waldo Trench Regains His Youth." **3 ed.** 230.

FÜRUZAN [total name]

"My Cinemas." **5.** 119.

JAQUES FUTRELLE

"The Flying Eye." **1.** 68.

CARLOS GAGINI

"La bruja de Miramar." **5.** 119.

ERNEST J. GAINES

"Bloodline." **3 ed.** 230; **3.** 142; **4.** 104.
"Just Like a Tree." **3 ed.** 230; **3.** 142; **4.** 104; **5.** 119.
"A Long Day in November." **3 ed.** 230; **1.** 68; **3.** 142; **4.** 104; **5.** 119.
"The Sky Is Gray." **3 ed.** 230; **2.** 115; **3.** 142; **4.** 104.
"Three Men." **3.** 142; **4.** 104.

ZONA GALE

"Bridal Pond." **3 ed.** 230.

SERGIO GALINDO

"Cena en Dorrius." **5.** 119.
"Heaven Knows." **4.** 104.
"Querido Jim." **5.** 119.
"El tío Quintín." **5.** 119.

MAVIS GALLANT

"About Geneva." **5.** 119.
"Acceptance of Their Ways." **1.** 68; **3.** 142; **5.** 120.
"August." **5.** 120.
"An Autobiography." **5.** 120.
"An Autumn Day." **5.** 120.
"Bernadette." **3.** 142; **5.** 120.
"Bonaventure." **5.** 120.
"The Colonel's Child." **5.** 120.
"The Cost of Living." **4.** 104; **5.** 120.
"The Deceptions of Marie-Blanche." **5.** 120.
"Ernst in Civilian Clothes." **5.** 120.
"A Flying Start." **5.** 120.
"The Four Seasons." **4.** 104; **5.** 120.
"From the Fifteenth District." **3.** 142.
"The Ice Wagon Going Down the Street." **3.** 142; **5.** 120.
"In the Tunnel." **5.** 120.
"In Youth Is Pleasure." **4.** 105; **5.** 120.
"Irina." **3.** 142.
"Its Image in the Mirror." **3.** 142; **4.** 105; **5.** 121.
"The Latehomecomers." **5.** 121.
"The Legacy." **3 ed.** 230.
"Lena." **5.** 121.
"Luk and His Father." **4.** 105.
"Malcolm and Bea." **4.** 105; **5.** 121.
"The Moabitess." **3.** 143; **5.** 121.
"The Moslem Wife." **4.** 105; **5.** 121.
"My Heart Is Broken." **3.** 143; **5.** 121.
"The Old Friends." **5.** 121.
"Orphans' Progress." **3 ed.** 230; **4.** 105.
"The Other Paris." **4.** 105; **5.** 121.
"Overhead in a Balloon." **5.** 121.
"The Pegnitz Junction." **3.** 143; **4.** 105; **5.** 121.
"Potter." **5.** 121.
"The Remission." **5.** 121.
"Saturday." **5.** 121.

"Señor Pinedo." **5.** 121.
"Speck's Idea." **5.** 122.
"Sunday Afternoon." **3.** 143.
"An Unmarried Man." **3.** 143.
"Varieties of Exile." **5.** 122.
"Virus X." **5.** 122.
"Wing's Chips." **5.** 122.

RÓMULO GALLEGOS

"The Beggar's Sweetheart." **5.** 122.
"The Miracle of the Year." **5.** 122.
"The Prop." **5.** 122.

JOAQUÍN GALLEGOS LARA

"Era la mamá." **5.** 122.

PAUL GALLICO

"The Enchanted Doll." **3 ed.** 231.

RAYMOND Z. GALLUN

"Hotel Cosmos." **3.** 143.
"Old Faithful." **3.** 143.

JOHN GALSWORTHY

"The Apple Tree." **3 ed.** 231; **5.** 122.
"Danäe." **3.** 143.
"The Japanese Quince." **3 ed.** 231; **1.** 68; **2.** 115; **5.** 122.
"The Juryman." **3 ed.** 231.
"Justice." **3 ed.** 231.
"A Knight." **5.** 122.
"A Man of Devon." **5.** 122.
"Manna." **3 ed.** 231.
"Quality." **3 ed.** 231.
"Salvation of a Forsythe." **3 ed.** 231; **5.** 122.
"The Silence." **5.** 122.
"A Stoic." **5.** 123.
"Ultima Thule." **3 ed.** 231.

JOHN GALT

"A Rich Man." **5.** 123.
"The Seamstress." **4.** 105.

EULALIA GALVARRIATO

"Descanso en primavera." **5.** 123.
"La espera." **5.** 123.
"Final de jornada." **5.** 123.
"La gota de agua." **5.** 123.
"Los hijos." **5.** 123.
"Un niño sueña." **5.** 123.
"Raíces bajo el agua." **5.** 123.
"Tantos días cualquiera." **5.** 123.
"Los zapatos blancos." **5.** 123.

ELENA GAN [pseudonym ZINAIDA R-VA]

"The Ideal." **3.** 143.

SEVER GANSOVSKII

"The Day of Wrath." **3.** 143.

GAO XIAOSHENG

"Li Shunda Builds a House." **4.** 105.

EUGENE GARBER

"The Poets." **5.** 123.

YOLANDA A. GARCÍA

"Ellipses." **4.** 105.

VENTURA GARCÍA CALDERÓN

"Juventud." **3 ed.** 231.

GABRIEL GARCÍA MÁRQUEZ

"Artificial Roses." **1.** 68; **5.** 123–24.
"Baltazar's Wonderful Afternoon." **1.** 68; **2.** 115; **3.** 143; **5.** 124.
"Big Mama's Funeral." **3 ed.** 515; **1.** 68; **2.** 115; **3.** 144; **4.** 105; **5.** 124.
"Bitterness for Three Sleepwalkers." **1.** 68; **3.** 144.
"Blacamán the Good, Vendor of Miracles." **1.** 69; **2.** 115; **3.** 144; **4.** 106; **5.** 124.
"Chronicle of a Decade Foretold." **5.** 124.
"The Day After Saturday." **3 ed.** 231; **1.** 69; **3.** 144; **5.** 124, 126.
"Death Constant Beyond Love." **1.** 69; **2.** 115; **3.** 144; **5.** 124.
"Eva Is Inside Her Cat." **1.** 69; **5.** 124.
"Eyes of a Blue Dog." **1.** 69; **3.** 144.
"The Handsomest Drowned Man in the World." **1.** 69; **2.** 115; **3.** 144; **4.** 106; **5.** 125.
"The Incredible and Sad Tale of Innocent Eréndira and Her Heartless Grand-

mother." **1.** 69; **2.** 115–16; **3.** 144; **4.** 106; **5.** 125.
"The Last Voyage of the Ghost Ship." **1.** 69; **2.** 116; **3.** 144; **5.** 125.
"Leaf Storm." **5.** 125–26.
"Monologue of Isabel Watching It Rain in Macondo." **3.** 144; **5.** 126.
"Montiel's Widow." **1.** 69; **4.** 106; **5.** 126.
"Nabo, the Black Who Made the Angels Wait." **1.** 69; **2.** 116; **3.** 144; **5.** 126.
"The Night of the Curlews." **1.** 69; **5.** 126.
"One Day After Saturday." **1.** 69; **5.** 126.
"One of These Days." **1.** 69; **3.** 144; **4.** 106; **5.** 126.
"The Other Rib of Death." **1.** 69.
"The Sea of Lost Time." **1.** 69; **2.** 116; **3.** 145; **5.** 126.
"Someone Has Disturbed the Roses" [same as "Someone Has Been Disarranging These Roses"]. **1.** 69; **3.** 145.
"Tale of a Castaway." **3.** 145; **5.** 126.
"There Are No Thieves in This Town." **1.** 70; **3.** 145.
"The Third Resignation." **1.** 70; **2.** 116; **3.** 145.
"Tubal-Cain Forges a Star." **1.** 70.
"Tuesday Siesta" [same as "Tuesday Nap"]. **3 ed.** 232; **1.** 70; **3.** 145; **4.** 106; **5.** 126–27.
"A Very Old Man with Enormous Wings." **1.** 70; **2.** 116; **3.** 145; **4.** 106; **5.** 127.

JOAQUÍN GARCÍA MONGE

"Tres viejos." **5.** 127.

FRANCISCO GARCÍA PAVÓN

"La novena." **5.** 127.

JESÚS GARDEA

"The Sun You Are Watching." **4.** 106.

ERLE STANLEY GARDNER

"In Round Figures." **3.** 144.

JOHN GARDNER

"The Art of Living." **3.** 145.
"Come on Back." **3.** 145.
"Dragon, Dragon." **3.** 145.
"The Griffin and the Wise Old Philosopher." **3.** 145.
"Gudgekin the Thistle Girl." **3.** 146.
"John Napper Sailing Through the Universe." **3.** 146.
"The Joy of the Just." **3.** 146.
"King Gregor and the Fool." **3.** 146.
"The King's Indian." **3.** 146.
"The Library Horror." **3.** 146.
"Muriel." **3.** 146.
"The Music Lover." **3.** 146.
"Nimram." **3.** 146.
"Pastoral Care." **3.** 146.
"The Pear Tree." **3.** 146.
"Queen Louisa." **3.** 146.
"The Ravages of Spring." **3.** 146.
"Redemption." **3.** 147; **4.** 106.
"Stillness." **3.** 147.
"The Tailor and the Giant." **3.** 147.
"The Temptation of St. Ivo." **3.** 147.
"Trumpeter." **3.** 147.
"Vlemk the Box-Painter." **3.** 147.
"The Warden." **3.** 147.

HAMLIN GARLAND

"Among the Corn Rows." **3 ed.** 232; **2.** 116.
"A Branch Road." **3 ed.** 232; **2.** 116.
"A Common Case." **3 ed.** 232.
"The Creamery Man." **3 ed.** 232.
"Daddy Deering." **3 ed.** 232.
"A Day's Pleasure." **3 ed.** 232.
"Drifting Crane." **4.** 107.
"Hippy the Dare-Devil" [originally "Story of Hippy"]. **2.** 116.
"The Iron Khiva." **2.** 116.
"John Boyle's Conclusion." **3 ed.** 232.
"The Land of the Straddle-Bug." **3 ed.** 232.
"A Meeting in the Foothills" [originally "A Girl from Washington"]. **3 ed.** 232.
"Mrs. Ripley's Trip." **3 ed.** 232; **2.** 116.
"The New Medicine House." **4.** 107.
"Ol' Pap's Flaxen" [expanded to become *A Little Norsk*]. **3 ed.** 232.
"The Return of a Private." **3 ed.** 232; **2.** 116.
"Rising Wolf—Ghost Dancer." **3 ed.** 232.
"The Silent Eaters." **3 ed.** 233; **1.** 70; **2.** 117; **4.** 107.
"The Sitting Bull's Visit." **2.** 117.

"The Spartan Mother." **2.** 117.
"The Story of Howling Wolf." **3 ed.** 233.
"Ten Years Dead." **3 ed.** 232.
"Under the Lion's Paw." **3 ed.** 233; **2.** 117; **3.** 147; **5.** 127.
"Up the Coulé." **3 ed.** 233; **2.** 117; **3.** 147.

ISABEL GARMA

"Consagración y secuestro." **5.** 127.
"El hombre que pintaba la verdad." **5.** 127.
"El pueblo de los seres taciturnos." **5.** 127.
"Y cuando las pascuas fueron de sangre." **5.** 128.

RICHARD GARNETT

"The Demon Pope." **4.** 107.
"The Dumb Oracle." **4.** 107.

GEORGE GARRETT

"An Evening Performance." **5.** 128.

ELENA GARRO

"La culpa es de los tlaxcaltecas." **4.** 107; **5.** 128.
"El día que fuimos perros." **5.** 128.

VSEVOLOD GARSHIN

"The Action at Ayaslar." **2.** 117.
"The Bears." **2.** 117.
"The Coward." **2.** 117.
"Four Days." **3 ed.** 233.
"From the Reminiscences of Private Ivanov." **3 ed.** 233.
"The Incident." **3 ed.** 233.
"The Meeting." **3 ed.** 233; **2.** 117.
"Nadezhda Nikolaevna." **3 ed.** 233.
"Night." **3 ed.** 233; **2.** 117.
"The Red Flower." **3 ed.** 233.

DANIEL GARZA

"Everybody Knows Tobie." **2.** 117.

PIERRE GASCAR

"The Animals." **3 ed.** 234.
"The Dogs." **3 ed.** 234.
"The Horses." **3 ed.** 234.
"The House of Blood." **3 ed.** 234.
"The Season of the Dead." **3 ed.** 234.

A. B. GASKELL

"Holiday." **3.** 147.
"Tell Me the Old Old Story." **3.** 147.
"Who Steals My Purse." **3.** 147.

ELIZABETH CLEGHORN GASKELL

"Christmas Storms and Sunshine." **2.** 117.
"Cousin Phillis." **2.** 117; **4.** 107.
"The Crooked Branch" [originally "The Ghost in the Garden"]. **2.** 118; **3.** 148.
"Crowley Castle." **3.** 148.
"Curious If True." **2.** 118.
"A Dark Night's Work." **2.** 118; **3.** 148.
"The Doom of the Griffiths." **2.** 118.
"French Life." **4.** 107.
"The Grey Woman." **2.** 118; **3.** 148; **4.** 107.
"Half a Life-Time Ago." **2.** 118; **3.** 148; **4.** 107.
"The Heart of John Middleton." **1.** 70; **3.** 148.
"Libbie Marsh's Three Eras." **2.** 118; **3.** 148; **4.** 107.
"Lizzie Leigh." **3.** 148; **4.** 108.
"Lois the Witch." **2.** 118; **3.** 148; **4.** 108.
"The Manchester Marriage." **3.** 148; **4.** 108.
"Mr. Harrison's Confession." **2.** 118; **3.** 148; **4.** 108.
"The Moorland Cottage." **2.** 118; **3.** 148.
"Morton Hall." **2.** 118; **3.** 148.
"My French Master." **2.** 118.
"My Lady Ludlow." **2.** 118; **3.** 148; **4.** 108.
"The Old Nurse's Story." **2.** 119; **3.** 148.
"The Poor Clare." **2.** 119; **3.** 149; **4.** 108.
"Right at Last" [originally "The Sin of a Father"]. **2.** 119.
"The Sexton's Hero." **1.** 70; **2.** 119.
"Six Weeks at Heppenheim." **3.** 149.
"The Squire's Story." **2.** 119.
"The Well of Pen-Morfa." **3.** 149.

WILLIAM GASS

"Icicles." **3 ed.** 234; **1.** 70; **3.** 149; **4.** 108.
"In the Heart of the Heart of the Country." **3 ed.** 234; **1.** 70; **3.** 149; **4.** 108; **5.** 128.
"Mrs. Mean." **3.** 149; **4.** 108.
"Order of Insects." **1.** 70; **2.** 119; **3.** 149; **4.** 108; **5.** 128.

"The Pedersen Kid." **3 ed.** 234; **1.** 70; **3.** 149; **4.** 108.
"William Master's Lonesome Wife." **3.** 149.

THÉOPHILE GAUTIER

"L'Âme de la maison ou la Vie et la Mort d'un Grillon." **3 ed.** 234.
"Arria Marcella, souvenir de Pompeii." **3 ed.** 234; **1.** 71.
"Avatar." **1.** 71.
"The Coffeepot." **3 ed.** 234; **4.** 108.
"The Dead Leman" [same as "The Beautiful Vampire," "Clarimonde," or "The Dead Lover"]. **3 ed.** 234–35; **1.** 71; **5.** 128.
"Elias Wildmanstadius." **3 ed.** 235.
"Fortunio." **3 ed.** 235; **1.** 71.
"Jettatura." **3 ed.** 235.
"King Candaule." **3 ed.** 235; **1.** 71.
"The Mummy's Foot." **1.** 71; **3.** 149.
"The Mummy's Tale." **1.** 71.
"Omphale." **3 ed.** 235; **1.** 71.
"One of Cleopatra's Nights." **3 ed.** 235; **1.** 71.
"Onuphrius." **3 ed.** 235.
"Spirite." **1.** 71.
"La Toison d'or." **3 ed.** 235.
"The Twin Knight." **1.** 71; **5.** 128.

SALLY GEARHART

"Krueva and the Pony." **4.** 109.

MAURICE GEE

"A Glorious Morning, Comrade." **3.** 149.
"The Losers." **3.** 149.
"Right Hand Man." **3.** 150.
"A Sleeping Face." **3.** 150.

IOSIF GERASIMOV

"The Nightingales." **3.** 150.

KATHARINE F. GEROULD

"The Great Tradition." **3 ed.** 235.
"Wesendonck." **3 ed.** 235.

WIRT GERRARE

"The Girl from Iloilo: A Picturesque Story of the Orient." **2.** 119.

BILL GERRY

"Understand What I Mean?" **3 ed.** 235.

LEWIS GRASSIC GIBBON [JAMES LESLIE MITCHELL]

"Cartaphilus." **4.** 109.
"Clay." **4.** 109.
"Dawn in Alarlu." **4.** 109.
"Daybreak." **4.** 109.
"Dieneke's Dream" [originally "Thermopylae"]. **4.** 109.
"The Floods of Spring." **4.** 109.
"Forsaken." **4.** 109.
"Gift of the River." **4.** 109.
"Greenden." **4.** 109.
"If You Sleep in the Moonlight." **4.** 109.
"It Is Written." **4.** 109.
"The Lost Constituent." **4.** 109.
"The Passage of the Dawn." **4.** 109.
"Revolt" [originally "One Man with a Dream"]. **4.** 109.
"Road to Freedom." **4.** 110.
"Smeddum." **4.** 110.

ANDRÉ GIDE

"Geneviève." **3 ed.** 235.
"El Hadj." **3 ed.** 236; **2.** 119; **5.** 129.
"The Immoralist." **3 ed.** 236–37; **1.** 71–72; **2.** 119; **3.** 150; **4.** 110; **5.** 129.
"Isabelle." **3 ed.** 237; **3.** 150; **4.** 110; **5.** 129.
"The Pastoral Symphony." **3 ed.** 237–38; **1.** 72; **2.** 119–20; **3.** 150; **4.** 110; **5.** 129.
"The Return of the Prodigal Son." **3 ed.** 238; **1.** 72.
"Robert." **3 ed.** 239.
"Theseus." **3 ed.** 240.

ENRIQUE GIL GILBERT

"El malo." **5.** 129.

MARGARET GIBSON GILBOORD

"Considering Her Condition." **4.** 110.
"Making It." **4.** 110.

ELLEN GILCHRIST

"Revenge." **3.** 150; **4.** 110.
"There's a Garden of Eden." **3.** 150; **4.** 110.

"Travelers." **3.** 150; **4.** 110.
"Victory Over Japan." **5.** 129.

ALFRED GILLESPIE

"The Evil Eye." **5.** 130.

PENELOPE GILLIATT

"Nobody's Business." **4.** 110.

CHARLOTTE PERKINS GILMAN

"The Giant Wistaria." **3.** 150; **5.** 130.
"The Rocking Chair." **3.** 151.
"When I Was a Witch." **5.** 130.
"The Yellow Wallpaper." **2.** 120; **3.** 151; **4.** 111; **5.** 130.

JEAN GIONO

"The Corn Dies." **3 ed.** 240.
"Solitude de la pitié." **3 ed.** 240.

JEAN GIRAUDOUX

"Don Manuel the Lazy." **3.** 151.
"Ice Palace." **3.** 151.
"The Last Dream of Edmond About." **3.** 151.
"The Mirage Bessines." **3.** 151.
"The Sign." **3.** 151.

JOSÉ MARÍA GIRONELLA

"Death of the Sea." **3 ed.** 241.
"Goya and the Mountain." **3 ed.** 241.
"Miracle in the Town." **3 ed.** 241.
"The Red Egg." **3 ed.** 241.
"Ryki, Bird-King." **3 ed.** 241.
"The Suicidal Twin and His Brother." **3 ed.** 241.
"Three Plates on the Table" [same as "Wishing Becomes Reality"]. **3 ed.** 241.

GEORGE GISSING

"Comrades in Arms." **3.** 151.
"Fleet-Footed Hester." **2.** 120.
"House of Cobwebs." **3 ed.** 241; **3.** 151.
"Humplebee." **3 ed.** 241.
"The Invincible Curate." **5.** 130.
"Joseph." **5.** 130.
"A Poor Gentleman." **3 ed.** 241.
"The Schoolmaster's Vision." **3.** 151.
"A Victim of Circumstances." **3.** 152.

ELLEN GLASGOW

"The Artless Age." **3 ed.** 241; **1.** 72; **2.** 120.
"Between Two Shores." **3 ed.** 241; **3.** 152.
"Dare's Gift." **3 ed.** 242; **1.** 72; **2.** 120; **3.** 152.
"The Difference." **1.** 72; **2.** 120; **3.** 152.
"The Greatest Good." **5.** 130.
"Jordan's End." **3 ed.** 242; **1.** 72; **2.** 120; **3.** 152.
"The Past." **1.** 72; **2.** 120; **3.** 152.
"A Point in Morals." **3 ed.** 242; **3.** 152.
"The Professional Instinct." **3 ed.** 242; **1.** 72; **2.** 120; **3.** 152.
"Romance and Sally Byrd." **1.** 72; **2.** 121; **3.** 152.
"The Shadowy Third." **1.** 72; **2.** 121; **3.** 152.
"Thinking Makes It So." **1.** 72; **2.** 121; **3.** 152.
"Whispering Leaves." **3 ed.** 242; **1.** 72; **2.** 121; **3.** 152.
"A Woman of Tomorrow." **3.** 152.

GERALD M. GLASKIN

"The Return." **5.** 130.

SUSAN GLASPELL

"The Busy Duck." **3 ed.** 242.
"The Escape." **3 ed.** 242.
"The Hearing Ear." **3 ed.** 242.
"A Jury of Her Peers." **3 ed.** 242; **1.** 73; **3.** 153; **4.** 111; **5.** 131.
"Pollen." **4.** 111.
"The Preposterous Motive." **3 ed.** 242.

JOHN GLASSCO

"The Black Helmet." **3.** 153.
"The Fulfilled Destiny of Electra." **3.** 153.

JACOB GLATSTEIN

"Abishag." **3.** 153.
"Citizen God." **3 ed.** 242.

BRUNO GLUCHOWSKI

"The Water Cannon." **3 ed.** 242.

PATRICIA GLYNN

"Bo and Be." **4.** 111.

URI NISSAN GNESSIN

"Genia." **4.** 111.
"In the Garden." **4.** 111.

ARTHUR DE GOBINEAU

"Adélaïde." **5.** 131.
"Akrivie Phrangopoulo." **5.** 131.
"Mademoiselle Irnois." **5.** 131.
"A Traveling Life." **5.** 131.
"The War with the Turcomans." **5.** 131.

RUMER GODDEN

"Down Under the Thames." **3 ed.** 243.
"The Little Black Ram." **3 ed.** 243.
"The Oyster." **3 ed.** 243.
"The Red Doe." **3 ed.** 243.
"Time Is a Stream." **3 ed.** 243.
"Why Not Live Sweetly." **3 ed.** 243.

DAVID GODFREY

"The Hard-Headed Collector." **3 ed.** 243.
"River Two Blind Jacks." **4.** 111.

GAIL GODWIN

"Dream Children." **5.** 131.
"Layover." **2.** 121.
"Some Side Effects of Time Travel." **2.** 121.
"A Sorrowful Woman." **3 ed.** 243.

TOM GODWIN

"The Cold Equation." **3.** 153; **4.** 111.

WILLIAM GODWIN, JR. [pseudonym SYPHAX]

"The Executioner." **3 ed.** 243.

ALBRECHT GOES

"Unruhige Nacht." **3 ed.** 243.

FERDYNAND GOETEL

"The Child Who Was Murdered." **3 ed.** 244.
"My Husband Is Dying." **3 ed.** 244.
"The Pilgrim of Karapet." **3 ed.** 244.

JOHANN WOLFGANG VON GOETHE

"Fairy Tale." **3 ed.** 244; **1.** 73; **2.** 121; **5.** 131.

NIKOLAI GOGOL

"The Carriage." **3 ed.** 244; **1.** 73; **2.** 121; **4.** 112.
"Christmas Eve." **3 ed.** 244; **1.** 73.
"The Diary of a Madman." **3 ed.** 244; **1.** 73; **2.** 121; **3.** 153; **5.** 131.
"A Dread Wild Boar." **3 ed.** 244.
"The Enchanted Spot" [same as "The Enchanted Place"]. **3 ed.** 245; **1.** 73.
"Ivan Fyodorovich Shponka and His Aunt." **3 ed.** 245; **1.** 73; **2.** 121; **3.** 153; **5.** 131.
"Kolyaska." **3 ed.** 245; **2.** 121.
"Leaving the Theater." **3 ed.** 245.
"The Lost Letter." **3 ed.** 245; **1.** 73; **3.** 153.
"The May Night, or The Drowned Woman." **3 ed.** 245; **1.** 73; **3.** 153.
"The Nevsky Prospect." **3 ed.** 245; **1.** 73; **2.** 122; **3.** 154; **4.** 112; **5.** 131.
"The Nose." **3 ed.** 245–46; **1.** 73; **2.** 122; **3.** 154; **5.** 132.
"Old World Landowners." **3 ed.** 246; **1.** 74; **2.** 122; **5.** 132.
"The Overcoat." **3 ed.** 246–47; **1.** 74; **2.** 122; **3.** 154; **4.** 112; **5.** 132.
"The Portrait." **3 ed.** 247; **1.** 74; **2.** 122; **3.** 154.
"The Quarrel Between Ivan Ivanovich and Ivan Nikoforovich." **3 ed.** 247; **1.** 74; **2.** 122; **3.** 154; **5.** 132.
"Rome." **3 ed.** 247–48; **1.** 74.
"St. John's Eve." **3 ed.** 248; **1.** 74; **2.** 122; **3.** 154.
"The Sorochinsty Fair." **3 ed.** 248; **1.** 74; **2.** 122; **3.** 154.
"Taras Bulba." **3 ed.** 248; **1.** 74; **2.** 123; **3.** 154; **5.** 132.
"The Teacher." **3 ed.** 248.
"A Terrible Vengeance." **3 ed.** 248; **1.** 74; **2.** 123; **3.** 154.
"The Two Ivans." **3 ed.** 248.
"Viy." **3 ed.** 248; **1.** 74; **2.** 123; **3.** 155; **5.** 132.

HERBERT GOLD

"The Heart of the Artichoke." **3 ed.** 249.
"A Selfish Story." **3.** 155.
"Susanna at the Beach." **3 ed.** 249.

"Where a Man Dwells." **3 ed.** 249.
"The Witch." **3 ed.** 249.

WILLIAM GOLDING

"Clonk Clonk." **4.** 112; **5.** 132.
"Envoy Extraordinary." **3 ed.** 249; **4.** 112; **5.** 132.
"The Inheritors." **4.** 112.
"The Scorpion God." **4.** 112; **5.** 132.

MEÏR GOLDSCHMIDT

"Aron and Esther." **1.** 74.
"Avrohmehe Nattergal." **1.** 75.
"The Battle of Marengo." **1.** 75.
"Bewitched, No. 1." **1.** 75.
"A Christmas in the Country." **1.** 75.
"The Fickle Girl on Graahede." **1.** 75.
"God's Angel from Rørvig." **1.** 75.
"The Last Lucifer Match." **1.** 75.
"Maser." **1.** 75.
"Paolo and Giovanna." **1.** 75.
"The Photographs and Mephistopheles." **1.** 75.
"Poison." **1.** 75.

WITOLD GOMBROWICZ

"Adventures on the Banbury." **3 ed.** 249.
"Five Minutes Before Sleep." **3 ed.** 249.
"A Supper at the Countess Kotlubaj's." **3 ed.** 249.

GERTRUDIS GÓMEZ DE AVELLANEDA

"The Baroness of Joux." **2.** 123.
"The Beautiful Toda and the Twelve Wild Boars." **2.** 123.
"The Cacique of Tumerqué." **2.** 123.
"The Lady of Amboto." **2.** 123.
"The Water Nymph of the Blue Lake." **2.** 123.
"The White Vulture." **2.** 123.

RAMÓN GÓMEZ DE LA SERNA

"The After-Dinner Guest." **3 ed.** 249.
"Aunt Martha." **3 ed.** 249.
"Beltran's Daughter." **3 ed.** 249.
"The Blind Man and the Courtesan." **3 ed.** 249.
"Blue Cholera." **3 ed.** 249.
"The Bottle and the Candlestick." **3 ed.** 250.
"The Cheerful Barbershop." **3 ed.** 250.
"The Christmas Crib-Maker." **3 ed.** 250.
"Christmas Eve, 2500 A.D." **3 ed.** 250.
"A Christmas Story About a Stained Glass Window." **3 ed.** 250.
"The Defender of the Cemetery." **3 ed.** 250.
"The Diseased One." **3 ed.** 250.
"Doña Juana the Mad." **3 ed.** 250.
"Doña Urraca of Castile." **3 ed.** 250.
"The Explorers." **3 ed.** 250.
"The Fatal Lady." **3 ed.** 250.
"Fear of the Sea." **3 ed.** 250.
"The Fragrance of the Mimosas." **3 ed.** 250.
"The Gentleman from Olmedo." **3 ed.** 250.
"A Gift for the Doctor." **3 ed.** 250.
"The Great Grippe Victim." **3 ed.** 250.
"The Greenhouse." **3 ed.** 250.
"His Liver Presented Itself." **3 ed.** 250.
"The Hypersensitive Woman." **3 ed.** 251.
"Ildefonso Cuadrado." **3 ed.** 251.
"Leopold and Teresa." **3 ed.** 251.
"The Malice of the Acacia Flowers." **3 ed.** 251.
"The Man in the Gallery." **3 ed.** 251.
"The Man with Big Feet." **3 ed.** 251.
"María Yarsilovna." **3 ed.** 251.
"The Master of the Atom." **3 ed.** 251.
"The Millionaire's Son." **3 ed.** 251.
"Of Another Race." **3 ed.** 251.
"Olvido." **3 ed.** 251.
"One Cup Short." **3 ed.** 251.
"The Opera Glasses and the Glove." **3 ed.** 251.
"Pandora's Box." **3 ed.** 251.
"Postponement of Destiny." **3 ed.** 251.
"The Recluse of Burgos." **3 ed.** 251.
"The Red-Head." **3 ed.** 251.
"The Roughnecks." **3 ed.** 251.
"The Russian." **3 ed.** 252.
"The Sated One." **3 ed.** 252.
"The Seven Princes of Lara." **3 ed.** 252.
"She + She − He + He." **3 ed.** 252.
"The Snow Coat." **3 ed.** 252.
"The Storm." **3 ed.** 252.
"The Surrealist Son." **3 ed.** 252.
"That Novel." **3 ed.** 252.
"Tonight in Russia." **3 ed.** 252.
"The Town of the Brunette." **3 ed.** 252.

"The Trials and Adventures of a Non-Hatter." **3 ed.** 252.
"The Triangular House." **3 ed.** 252.
"The Turk with the Spikenard." **3 ed.** 252.
"The Turkey Hen." **3 ed.** 252.
"The Two Sailors." **3 ed.** 252.
"The Vegetarian." **3 ed.** 252.
"The Virgin Painted Red." **3 ed.** 252.
"The White-Bearded Old Man." **3 ed.** 252.
"The Widow and the Widower's Toast." **3 ed.** 253.
"The Woman Abandoned in the Flea Market." **3 ed.** 253.
"The Woman Who Dressed Like a Man." **3 ed.** 253.
"The Woman with the Twangy Voice." **3 ed.** 253.
"Women of Assignation." **3 ed.** 253.
"The Young Alcira." **3 ed.** 253.

PEDRO A. GÓMEZ VALDERRAMA

"La aventura de la nieve." **5.** 132.

WIKTOR GOMULICKI

"A Quintet." **3 ed.** 253.
"Under the Umbrella." **3 ed.** 253.

IVAN GONCHAROV

"A Cruel Illness." **3 ed.** 253.
"A Happy Error." **3 ed.** 253.

DAVID J. GONZÁLEZ

"The Proletarian." **4.** 112.

JOSÉ LUIS GONZÁLEZ

"Una cajo de plumo que no se podía abrir." **5.** 132.
"La carta." **5.** 133.
"En el fondo del caño hay un negrito." **5.** 133.
"La noche que volvimos a ser gente." **2.** 123; **4.** 113.

N. V. M. GONZALEZ

"Where's My Baby Now?" **3 ed.** 253.

MANUEL GONZÁLEZ ZELLEDÓN

"El clis de sol." **5.** 133.

PAUL GOODMAN

"The Architect from New York." **3 ed.** 253.
"A Prayer for Dew." **3 ed.** 254.

NADINE GORDIMER

"Ah, Woe Is Me." **3 ed.** 255; **5.** 133.
"The Amateur." **3 ed.** 254.
"Another Part of the Sky." **3 ed.** 254.
"A Bit of Young Life." **3 ed.** 254.
"The Catch." **3 ed.** 254.
"Charmed Lives." **3 ed.** 254.
"Check Yes or No." **3 ed.** 254.
"A Chip of Glass Ruby." **3.** 155; **4.** 113.
"The Defeated." **3 ed.** 254.
"Enemies." **3 ed.** 254.
"Face from Atlantis." **3 ed.** 254.
"Friday's Footprint." **3 ed.** 254.
"The Gentle Art." **3 ed.** 254.
"Happy Event." **3 ed.** 254.
"Horn of Plenty." **3 ed.** 254.
"The Hour and the Years." **3 ed.** 254.
"An Image of Success." **3 ed.** 255.
"Is There Nowhere Else Where We Can Meet?" **3 ed.** 255; **3.** 155; **4.** 113; **5.** 133.
"The Kindest Thing to Do." **3 ed.** 255.
"Little Willie." **4.** 113.
"Livingstone's Companions." **3 ed.** 255; **1.** 75; **2.** 123.
"Message in a Bottle." **3 ed.** 255.
"Monday Is Better Than Sunday." **3 ed.** 255.
"No Place Like—." **3 ed.** 255.
"Our Bovary." **3 ed.** 255.
"Out of Season." **3 ed.** 255.
"The Prisoner." **3 ed.** 255.
"A Satisfactory Settlement." **3 ed.** 255.
"Six Feet of the Country." **3 ed.** 255; **5.** 133.
"The Smell of Death and Flowers." **2.** 124; **4.** 113.
"The Soft Voice of the Serpent." **3 ed.** 255.
"Something Out There." **4.** 113; **5.** 133.
"A Style of Her Own." **3 ed.** 255.
"Tenants of the Last Tree House." **3 ed.** 255.
"The Termitary." **3.** 155.
"Town and Country Lovers." **5.** 133.
"The Train from Rhodesia." **3 ed.** 255; **1.** 75; **4.** 113.
"The Umbilical Cord." **3 ed.** 256.

"La Vie Boheme." **3 ed.** 256.
"A Watcher of the Dead." **3 ed.** 256.
"Which New Era Would That Be?" **3 ed.** 256.
"The White Goddess and the Mealie Question." **3 ed.** 256.
"Why Haven't You Written?" **3 ed.** 256.

CAROLINE GORDON

"All Lovers Love the Spring." **3 ed.** 256.
"The Brilliant Leaves." **3 ed.** 256.
"The Burning Eyes." **3 ed.** 256.
"The Captive." **3 ed.** 256–57.
"Emmanuele! Emmanuele!" **3 ed.** 257.
"The Enemies." **3 ed.** 257.
"The Forest of the South." **3 ed.** 257.
"Hear the Nightingale Sing." **3 ed.** 257.
"Her Quaint Honor." **3 ed.** 257.
"The Ice House." **3 ed.** 257.
"The Last Day in the Field." **3 ed.** 257; **2.** 124; **3.** 155; **4.** 113.
"The Long Day." **3 ed.** 257.
"Mr. Powers." **3 ed.** 257.
"A Narrow Heart: The Portrait of a Woman." **3 ed.** 258.
"Old Red." **3 ed.** 258.
"The Olive Garden." **3 ed.** 258; **4.** 113.
"One Against Thebes" [complete reworking of "Summer Dust"]. **3 ed.** 258; **4.** 113.
"One More Time." **3 ed.** 258; **4.** 113.
"The Petrified Woman." **3 ed.** 258.
"The Presence." **3 ed.** 258; **4.** 113.
"Strange Children." **3 ed.** 258.
"Summer Dust." **3 ed.** 258–59.
"To Thy Chamber Window, Sweet." **3 ed.** 259.
"Tom Rivers." **3 ed.** 259.

MAXIM GORKY

"At the Salt Marsh." **3 ed.** 259.
"Boles." **3 ed.** 259.
"Chelkash." **3 ed.** 259; **3.** 155; **4.** 114; **5.** 133.
"The Coachman." **3 ed.** 259.
"Creatures That Once Were Men." **3 ed.** 259.
"He Ran Off." **3 ed.** 259.
"The Hermit." **1.** 75.
"Kain and Artem" [same as "Kain and Artyom"]. **3 ed.** 259; **5.** 133.
"Karamora." **3 ed.** 259.
"Konovalov." **3 ed.** 259.
"Makar Chudra." **3 ed.** 259; **3.** 155.
"Man." **5.** 133.
"The Mistake." **3 ed.** 259; **5.** 133.
"My Fellow Traveller." **3 ed.** 259.
"Nilushka." **3.** 155.
"Old Izergil." **3 ed.** 260.
"On the Rafts." **3 ed.** 260; **3.** 155.
"One Autumn Evening." **3 ed.** 260.
"The Orlovs." **3 ed.** 260.
"Out of Boredom." **3 ed.** 260.
"A Rolling Stone." **3 ed.** 260.
"Song of the Falcon." **5.** 133.
"The Story of a Hero." **3 ed.** 260.
"A Tale of Unrequited Love." **3 ed.** 260.
"Twenty-Six Men and a Girl." **3 ed.** 260; **3.** 155; **4.** 114.
"Vanka Mazin." **3 ed.** 260.

ANGÉLICA GORODISCHER

"And the Vacant Street." **5.** 134.
"The End of a Dynasty or The Natural History of Ferrets." **5.** 134.
"Portrait of the Empress." **5.** 134.
"El señor Caos." **5.** 134.
"Sensatez de circulo." **5.** 134.
"That's How the South Is." **5.** 134.

JOHN GOSS

"Bird Song." **3 ed.** 260.

JEREMIAS GOTTHELF [ALBERT BITZIUS]

"The Black Spider." **3 ed.** 260; **1.** 75; **5.** 134.

WILLIAM GOYEN

"The Armadillo Basket." **2.** 124.
"Bridge of Music, River of Sand." **2.** 124.
"Children of Old Somebody." **1.** 76; **2.** 124.
"The Enchanted Nurse." **1.** 76.
"Ghost and Flesh, Water and Dirt." **3 ed.** 260; **2.** 124.
"The Grasshopper's Burden." **3 ed.** 260; **1.** 76.
"The Letter in the Cedarchest." **3 ed.** 261; **2.** 124.
"The Moss Rose." **1.** 76.
"Nests in a Stone Image." **1.** 76.

"Old Wildwood." **1.** 76; **2.** 124.
"Pore Perrie." **1.** 76; **2.** 124; **3.** 156.
"The Rescue." **1.** 76.
"A Shape of Light." **2.** 124.
"The Thief Coyote." **2.** 124.
"The White Rooster." **3 ed.** 261; **2.** 124.
"Zamour" [originally "A Tale of Inheritance"]. **2.** 124.

JUAN GOYTISOLO

"Autumn in the Port When It Drizzles." **3 ed.** 261.
"Face and Cross." **3 ed.** 261.
"The Friends." **3 ed.** 261.
"The Guard." **3 ed.** 261.
"Here Below." **3 ed.** 261.
"The Night Patrol." **3 ed.** 261.
"Suburbs." **3 ed.** 261.
"The Voyage." **3 ed.** 261.

PATRICIA GRACE

"Letters from Whetu." **3.** 156.
"Parade." **3.** 156.
"Valley." **3.** 156.
"A Way of Talking." **5.** 134.

LAURENCE GRAFFTEY-SMITH

"The Locket." **5.** 134.

KENNETH GRAHAME

"The Secret Drawer." **3 ed.** 261.

EDWIN GRANBERRY

"A Trip to Czardis." **3 ed.** 261–62.

DANIIL A. GRANIN

"A Personal Opinion." **5.** 134.
"Return Ticket." **3.** 156.

DAVID GRANT

"The Bats." **5.** 134.

GORDON GRANT

"The Provocation of Ah Sing." **2.** 124; **3.** 156.

GÜNTER GRASS

"The Advantages of Wind Hens." **3 ed.** 262.
"Five Birds." **3 ed.** 262.
"The Left-Handers." **3 ed.** 262.

THOMAS COLLEY GRATTAN

"The Priest and the Garde-du-Corps." **5.** 135.

SHIRLEY ANN GRAU

"The Beach Party." **3 ed.** 262; **2.** 125; **3.** 156.
"The Bright Day." **2.** 125; **3.** 156.
"Eight O'Clock One Morning." **2.** 125.
"Fever Flower." **2.** 125; **3.** 156; **4.** 114.
"For a Place in the Sun." **3.** 156.
"The Fragile Age." **3.** 156.
"The Girl with the Flaxen Hair." **2.** 125; **3.** 157.
"The Homecoming." **2.** 125.
"Joshua." **2.** 125; **4.** 114.
"The Land and the Water." **3 ed.** 262; **2.** 125.
"The Last Gas Station." **2.** 125.
"Letting Go." **3.** 157.
"The Lonely April." **2.** 125.
"The Lonely One." **3.** 157.
"The Longest Day." **3 ed.** 262.
"The Man Outside." **2.** 125.
"Miss Yellow Eyes." **2.** 125; **3.** 157; **4.** 114.
"One Summer." **2.** 125; **3.** 157.
"The Other Way." **2.** 125.
"The Patriarch." **2.** 125; **3.** 157.
"Sea Change." **3 ed.** 262; **2.** 125.
"The Shadow Land." **3.** 157.
"So Many Worlds." **3.** 157.
"Stanley." **3 ed.** 262; **3.** 157.
"Summer Shore." **3.** 157.
"The Thieves" [originally "The Man Below"]. **2.** 125.
"The Things You Keep." **3.** 157.
"Three." **2.** 126.
"The Way Back." **3 ed.** 262; **2.** 126.
"The Way of a Man." **2.** 126.
"White Girl, Fine Girl." **2.** 126; **3.** 157; **4.** 114.
"The Wind Shifting West." **2.** 126; **3.** 157.

JOHN GRAY

"The Great Worm." **3.** 157.
"The Person in Question." **3.** 157.

JULIAN GREEN

"The Apprentice Psychiatrist." **3 ed.** 262.
"Christine." **3 ed.** 262.
"The Keys of Death." **3 ed.** 262.
"Léviathan." **3 ed.** 263.
"Pilgrim on the Earth." **3 ed.** 263; **3.** 158.

MORAG GREEN

"Under the Flagstone." **5.** 135.

A. GREENBERG

"Don Nahum." **3 ed.** 263.

ALVIN GREENBERG

"Delta q." **4.** 114.
"Disorder and Belated Sorrow: A Shadow Play." **4.** 114.

GRAHAM GREENE

"Across the Bridge." **3 ed.** 263; **4.** 114.
"The Basement Room." **3 ed.** 263; **1.** 76; **2.** 126; **3.** 158; **4.** 114; **5.** 135.
"The Blue Film." **1.** 76.
"Brother." **3 ed.** 263; **2.** 126.
"A Chance for Mr. Lever." **3.** 158; **4.** 114.
"Cheap in August." **3.** 158; **4.** 114.
"The Destructors." **3 ed.** 263; **1.** 76; **3.** 158; **4.** 114–15; **5.** 135.
"Dream of a Strange Land." **3.** 158; **4.** 115.
"A Drive in the Country." **3.** 158; **4.** 115.
"The End of the Party." **3 ed.** 264; **3.** 158; **4.** 115.
"The Hint of an Explanation." **3 ed.** 264; **3.** 158; **4.** 115; **5.** 135.
"I Spy." **3.** 158; **4.** 115.
"The Innocent." **3 ed.** 264; **2.** 126; **5.** 135.
"A Little Place Off the Edgeware Road." **3.** 158.
"The Lottery Ticket." **3.** 158.
"The Second Death." **3 ed.** 264; **4.** 115.
"Under the Garden." **3 ed.** 264; **3.** 158; **4.** 115; **5.** 135.
"A Visit to Morin." **3 ed.** 264; **3.** 158; **4.** 115; **5.** 135.

JOSEPH GREENE

"Encounter with a Carnivore." **5.** 135.

LEE GREGOR

"Heavy Planet." **3.** 159.

IRINA GREKOVA [ELENA SERGEEVNA VENCEL]

"Beyond the Entryway." **2.** 126.
"Ladies' Hairdresser." **2.** 126; **3.** 398.
"On Trial." **3.** 159.

ZANE GREY

"Avalanche." **3 ed.** 264.
"Canyon Walls." **3 ed.** 264.
"Monty Price's Nightingale." **3 ed.** 264.
"The Secret of Quaking Asp Cabin." **3 ed.** 264.

GERALD GRIFFIN

"The Aylmers of Bally-Aylmer." **5.** 135.
"The Barber of Bantry." **1.** 76; **5.** 135.
"The Black Birds and the Yellow Hammers." **1.** 76.
"Card Drawing." **1.** 76; **4.** 115; **5.** 135.
"The Great House." **1.** 77.
"The Half-Sir." **1.** 77; **3.** 159; **4.** 115; **5.** 136.
"The Hand and the Word." **5.** 136.
"A Night at Sea." **1.** 77.
"Sir Dowling O'Hartigan." **1.** 77.
"Suil Dhuv, or The Coiner." **5.** 136.
"Touch My Honour, Touch My Life." **1.** 77.
"The Village Ruin." **1.** 77.

GEORGE GRIFFITH

"The Lord of Labour." **1.** 77.

DMITRI GRIGOROVICH

"Karelin's Dream." **3 ed.** 265.
"The Village." **3 ed.** 265.

FRANZ GRILLPARZER

"The Poor Player." **3 ed.** 265–66; **1.** 77; **2.** 126–27; **3.** 159; **5.** 136.

HANS GRIMM

"Dina." **3 ed.** 266.
"The Life of Johnny Neukwa." **3.** 159.

ALEXANDR GRIN [ALEXANDER STEPANOVICH GRINEVSKY]

"The Lanfier Colony." **2.** 127.
"Oranges." **2.** 127.
"Reno Island." **2.** 127.
"Scarlet Sails." **1.** 77.

FREDERICK PHILIP GROVE [FELIX PAUL GREVE]

"The Boat." **3 ed.** 266.
"The Desert." **3 ed.** 266.
"Snow." **3 ed.** 266; **5.** 136.

BEATRIZ GUIDO

"Diez vueltas a la manzana." **3.** 159.
"Takeover." **5.** 136.

WYMAN GUIN

"Beyond Bedlam." **3 ed.** 266.

NEIL M. GUNN

"Blaeberrie." **3 ed.** 266.
"Dance of the Stones." **3 ed.** 266.
"Down to the Sea." **3 ed.** 266.
"Henry Drake Goes Home." **3 ed.** 266.
"Love's Dialectic." **3 ed.** 266.
"The Moor." **3 ed.** 266.
"Paper Boats." **3 ed.** 266.
"Such Stuff as Dreams." **3 ed.** 267.
"Symbolical." **3 ed.** 267.
"The Tax Gatherer." **4.** 115.
"Whistle for Bridge." **3 ed.** 267.

GURAZADA APPARAO

"Kanyaka." **1.** 77.
"Reform." **1.** 78.

ELENA GURO

"So Life Goes." **4.** 115.

RALPH GUSTAFSON

"The Human Fly." **2.** 127.
"The Paper-Spike." **2.** 127.
"The Pigeon." **2.** 127; **5.** 136.
"Shower of Gold." **2.** 127.
"Snow." **2.** 127.
"Summer Storm." **2.** 127.
"Surrey Harvest." **2.** 127.
"The Tangles of Neaera's Hair." **2.** 127.
"The Vivid Air." **2.** 127.

A[LFRED] B[ERTRAM] GUTHRIE

"The Image." **3.** 159.
"Loco." **3.** 160.

MANUEL GUTÍERREZ NÁJERA

"After the Races." **3.** 160; **5.** 136–37.
"At the Hippodrome." **3.** 160.

HUMBERTO GUZMÁN

"Ariel" [originally "Bad Dreams"]. **4.** 116.
"The Clock." **4.** 116.

MARTÍN LUIS GUZMÁN

"La fiesta de las balas." **5.** 137.

NICOMEDES GUZMÁN

"A Coin in the River." **1.** 78.

ROWLEY HABIB

"The Visitors." **3 ed.** 267.

J. B. HALDANE

"The Last Judgment." **2.** 127.

JOE HALDEMAN

"A Mind of His Own." **3.** 160.
"Summer Lease." **3.** 160.
"Tricentennial." **3.** 160.

NANCY HALE

"Rich People." **3 ed.** 267.

THOMAS CHANDLER HALIBURTON

"The Witch of Inky Dell." **4.** 116.

J. PARSONS HALL

"All Her Own Fault." **3 ed.** 267.
"Poor Mary Ann." **3 ed.** 267.
"The Reserved Husband." **3 ed.** 267.
"The Slave of the Needle." **3 ed.** 267.

JAMES HALL

"The Backwoodsman." **3 ed.** 267.
"The Dark Maid of Illinois." **3.** 160.
"The War Belt." **1.** 78.

OAKLEY HALL

"Horseman." **5.** 137.

S. C. HALL

"Kelly the Piper." **4.** 116.

TAK HALLUS

"The Linguist." **3.** 160.

FRIEDRICH HALM

"Die Freundinnen." **3 ed.** 267.
"Das Haus an der Veronabrücke." **3 ed.** 268.
"Die Marzipan-Lise." **3 ed.** 268.

ALBERT HALPER

"A Farewell to the Rising Sun." **2.** 128.
"On the Shore." **2.** 128.
"Prelude." **2.** 128.

LESLIE HALVARD

"Arch Anderson." **2.** 128.
"Belcher's Hod." **2.** 128.
"No Use Blaming Him." **2.** 128.

EDMOND HAMILTON

"The Comet Doom." **5.** 137.
"Devolution." **3.** 160.
"The Island of Unreason." **3.** 160.
"The Man Who Evolved." **1.** 78.

MARION E. HAMILTON

"Wong." **2.** 128.

DASHIELL HAMMETT

"The Big Knock-Over." **3.** 161; **4.** 116.
"Corkscrew." **3.** 161; **4.** 116.
"Dead Yellow Women." **3.** 161; **4.** 116.
"The Farewell Murder." **4.** 116.
"Fly Paper." **3.** 161; **4.** 116.
"The Gatewood Caper." **4.** 116.
"The Girl with the Silver Eyes." **3.** 161; **5.** 137.
"The Golden Horseshoe." **3.** 161; **4.** 116.
"The Gutting of Couffignal." **4.** 116.
"The House in Turk Street." **3.** 161; **4.** 117.
"The Main Death." **4.** 117.
"The Man Who Killed Dan Odams." **4.** 117.
"One Hour." **3.** 161.
"$106,000 Blood Money." **4.** 117.
"The Scorched Face." **4.** 117.
"The Tenth Clew." **4.** 117.
"This King Business." **3.** 161; **4.** 117.
"Tom, Dick, or Harry." **3.** 161.
"The Whosis Kid." **4.** 117; **5.** 137.

KNUT HAMSUN [KNUT PEDERSEN]

"Secret Suffering." **3.** 161.
"Under the Autumn Star." **3 ed.** 268; **1.** 78.

PETER HANDKE

"Der Chinese des Schmerzes." **3.** 161.
"Greeting the Board of Directors." **3.** 161.
"Kindergeschichte." **2.** 128.
"Der kurze Brief zum langen Abschied." **3.** 162.
"Die linkshändige Frau." **2.** 128.
"Martial Law." **3.** 162.
"The Peddler." **3.** 162.
"Wunschlose Unglück." **2.** 128; **3.** 162.

BARRY HANNAH

"Love Too Long." **3.** 162.
"Testimony of Pilot." **3.** 162.
"Water Liars." **3.** 162.

CARL HANSEN

"Prosperity." **3.** 162.

MARTIN A. HANSEN

"The Birds." **1.** 78.
"The Bridegroom's Oak." **1.** 78.
"Early Morning." **1.** 78.
"The Easter Bell." **1.** 78.
"The Gardener, the Beast, and the Child." **1.** 78.

"Haavn." **1.** 78.
"The Homecoming." **1.** 78.
"The Man from the Earth." **1.** 79.
"The Messenger." **1.** 79.
"The Midsummer Festival." **1.** 79.
"Night in March." **1.** 79.
"The Owl." **1.** 79.
"The Righteous One." **1.** 79.
"Sacrifice." **1.** 79.
"September Fog." **1.** 79.
"The Soldier and the Girl." **1.** 79.
"The Thornbush." **1.** 79.
"Tirad." **1.** 79.
"The Waiting Room." **1.** 79.

JAMES HANSON

"Behind the Devil Screen." **2.** 128; **3.** 162.
"The Divorce of Ah Lum." **2.** 129.
"The Princess and the Pauper." **2.** 129.
"The Winning of Josephine Chang." **2.** 129.

YAHYA HAQQI

"Abu Fuda." **3.** 162.
"As Though." **3.** 162.
"Filla, Mishmish, Lulu." **3.** 162.
"The First Lesson." **3.** 163.
"A Glass House." **3.** 163.
"The Holy Man Is Not Confused." **3.** 163.
"Irony, or The Man with the Black Face." **3.** 163.
"The Mosque Mat." **3.** 163.
"People and People." **3.** 163.
"The Perfume Bottle." **3.** 163.
"A Photograph." **3.** 163.
"The Protest." **3.** 163.
"The Saint's Lamp" [same as "The Lamp of Umm Hashim"]. **3.** 163; **5.** 137.
"Sale!!!" **3.** 163.
"The Spiral Staircase." **3.** 163.
"A Story from Prison." **3.** 163.
"The Ten Commandments for the Vegetable Market." **3.** 163.
"The Turkey." **3.** 163.
"The Vacant Bed." **3.** 163.

WILL[IAM] N[ATHANIEL] HARBEN

"Abrum, Ca'line and Asphalt" [originally "The Matrimonial Troubles of Abraham and Caroline"]. **2.** 129.
"The Heresy of Abner Calihan." **3 ed.** 268; **2.** 129.
"A Humble Abolitionist." **2.** 129.
"Jim Trundle's Crisis." **3 ed.** 268; **2.** 129.
"A Prophet Without Honor." **2.** 129.
"A Rural Visitor." **2.** 129.
"The Sale of Uncle Rastus." **2.** 129.
"The Tender Link." **2.** 129.
"The Tragic Story of Sunset Rock, Tennessee." **2.** 129.
"The Whipping of Uncle Henry." **3 ed.** 268; **2.** 129.

THOMAS HARDY

"Absent-Mindedness in a Parish Choir." **3 ed.** 268.
"Alicia's Diary." **3.** 164.
"Andrew Satchel and the Parson and Clerk." **3.** 164.
"Anna, Lady Baxby." **3.** 164.
"Barbara of the House of Grebe." **3 ed.** 268; **2.** 129; **3.** 164.
"A Changed Man." **3.** 164.
"The Committeeman of 'The Terror.'" **3 ed.** 268; **2.** 130.
"The Distracted Preacher." **3 ed.** 268; **3.** 164; **4.** 117.
"The Doctor's Legend." **3 ed.** 268; **2.** 130.
"The Duchess of Hamptonshire." **2.** 130; **3.** 164.
"The Duke's Reappearance." **3.** 164.
"Enter a Dragoon." **3.** 164.
"Fellow-Townsmen." **3.** 164.
"A Few Crusted Characters." **3 ed.** 268.
"The Fiddler of the Reels." **3 ed.** 268–69; **2.** 130; **3.** 164; **5.** 137.
"The First Countess of Wessex." **3.** 164.
"For Conscience's Sake." **3.** 164.
"The Grave by the Handpost." **2.** 130.
"The History of the Hardcomes." **3.** 164.
"The Honourable Laura." **3.** 164.
"How I Built Myself a House." **5.** 137.
"An Imaginative Woman." **3 ed.** 269; **3.** 164; **4.** 117; **5.** 137.
"Interlopers at the Knap." **3.** 165; **5.** 138.
"The Lady Icenway." **3.** 165.
"Lady Mottisfont." **3.** 165.
"The Lady Penelope." **3.** 165.
"The Marchioness of Stonehenge." **3 ed.** 269; **3.** 165.

"The Melancholy Hussar of the German Legion." **3.** 165.
"A Mere Interlude." **1.** 79; **2.** 130; **3.** 165.
"Netty Sargent's Copyhold." **3.** 165.
"Old Mrs. Chundle." **1.** 79.
"On the Western Circuit." **3 ed.** 269; **1.** 79; **3.** 165; **5.** 138.
"Our Exploits at West Poley." **3.** 165; **4.** 117.
"The Romantic Adventures of a Milkmaid." **3 ed.** 269; **1.** 80; **2.** 130; **3.** 165.
"The Son's Veto." **4.** 117; **5.** 138.
"Squire Petrick's Lady." **3 ed.** 269; **3.** 165.
"The Superstitious Man's Story." **3.** 165.
"The Three Strangers." **3 ed.** 269; **2.** 130; **3.** 165; **5.** 138.
"To Please His Wife." **3 ed.** 269; **3.** 165.
"Tony Kytes, the Arch-Deceiver." **2.** 130; **3.** 165.
"A Tradition of the Year Eighteen Hundred and Four." **3 ed.** 269; **3.** 165; **4.** 117.
"A Tragedy of Two Ambitions." **3 ed.** 269–70; **2.** 130; **3.** 166; **4.** 117.
"A Tryst at an Ancient Earthwork." **3.** 166.
"The Waiting Supper." **3 ed.** 270; **3.** 166.
"What the Shepherd Saw." **2.** 130; **3.** 166.
"The Winters and the Palmleys." **3.** 166.
"The Withered Arm." **3 ed.** 270; **2.** 130; **3.** 166; **4.** 117; **5.** 138.

CHARLES R. HARKER

"The Revenge of a Heathen." **2.** 130; **3.** 166.

CHARLES L. HARNESS

"The New Reality." **3.** 166.

FRANK HARRIS

"The Best Man in Garotte." **3 ed.** 270.
"Elder Conklin." **3 ed.** 270.
"First Love." **3 ed.** 270.
"A Fool's Paradise." **3 ed.** 270.
"A French Artist." **3 ed.** 270.
"Gulmore the Boss." **3 ed.** 270.
"In the Vale of Tears." **3 ed.** 270.
"The Interpreter." **3 ed.** 270.
"The Irony of Chance." **3 ed.** 270.
"Love Is My Sin." **3 ed.** 270.
"A Modern Idyll." **3 ed.** 270.
"Profit and Loss." **3 ed.** 270.
"The Sheriff and His Partner." **3 ed.** 271.
"The Yellow Ticket." **3 ed.** 271.

GEORGE WASHINGTON HARRIS

"Contempt of Court—Almost." **3.** 166.
"Dad's Dog School." **3.** 166.
"Eaves-Dropping a Lodge of Free-Masons." **5.** 138.
"Frustrating a Funeral." **1.** 80; **5.** 138.
"Old Skissim's Middle Boy." **1.** 80.
"Sut at a Negro Night Meeting." **5.** 138.
"Sut Lovingood's Daddy, Acting Horse." **3.** 166; **5.** 138.
"Taurus in Lynchburg Market." **3.** 166.

JOEL CHANDLER HARRIS

"Ananias." **3 ed.** 271.
"Aunt Fountain's Prisoner." **3.** 166.
"Blue Dave." **3.** 167.
"The Cause of the Difficulty." **3 ed.** 271; **3.** 167.
"A Conscript's Christmas." **3.** 167.
"Daddy Jake, the Runaway." **3.** 167.
"Flingin' Jim and His Fool-Killer." **3.** 167.
"Free Joe and the Rest of the World." **3 ed.** 271; **3.** 167.
"Little Compton." **3 ed.** 271.
"The Making of a Statesman." **3.** 167.
"Mingo." **3 ed.** 271; **3.** 167.
"Mom Bi: Her Friends and Her Enemies." **3 ed.** 271.
"The Reason Why." **3.** 167.
"Rosalie." **3.** 167.
"Trouble on Lost Mountain." **3.** 167.
"Where's Duncan?" **3 ed.** 271; **3.** 167.

WILSON HARRIS

"Couvade." **3 ed.** 271.
"Fences upon the Earth." **3.** 167.
"Kanaima." **3 ed.** 271.
"Tomorrow." **3.** 167.
"Yurokon." **3.** 167.

HARRY HARRISON

"The Streets of Ashkelon." **3.** 168.

WILLIAM HARRISON

"Roller Ball Murder." **3.** 168.

BRET HARTE

"The Ancestors of Peter Atherly." **2.** 131.
"Convert of the Mission." **2.** 131.
"The Devotion of Enríquez." **2.** 131.
"An Episode of Fiddletown." **3.** 168.
"The Idyl of Red Gulch." **3 ed.** 271.
"The Legend of Monte del Diablo." **2.** 131.
"The Luck of Roaring Camp." **3 ed.** 271–72; **5.** 138.
"M'liss." **5.** 138.
"The Outcasts of Poker Flat." **3 ed.** 272.
"The Passing of Enríquez." **3 ed.** 272; **2.** 131.
"A Pupil of Chestnut Ridge." **2.** 131.
"The Queen of Pirate Isle." **3.** 168.
"See Yup." **3.** 168.
"Tennessee's Partner." **3 ed.** 272; **1.** 80; **2.** 131; **3.** 168.
"Three Vagabonds of Trinidad." **3.** 168.
"Wan Lee, the Pagan." **3.** 168.

L[ESLIE] P[OLES] HARTLEY

"A Beautiful Character." **3.** 168.
"Conrad and the Dragon." **1.** 80; **3.** 168.
"The Crossways." **1.** 80; **3.** 168.
"Fall in at the Double." **1.** 80.
"Friends of the Bridegroom." **3.** 168.
"The Ghost Writer." **4.** 118.
"The Island." **3.** 168.
"The Killing Bottles." **1.** 80.
"Mr. Blandfoot's Picture." **3.** 169.
"Night Fears." **3.** 169.
"Pains and Pleasures." **1.** 80.
"*Per Far l'Amore.*" **3.** 169.
"Please Do Not Touch." **1.** 80.
"Podolo." **3.** 169.
"A Portrait." **3.** 169.
"The Prayer." **1.** 80.
"The Price of the Absolute." **3.** 169.
"The Pylon." **1.** 80.
"A Sentimental Journey." **3.** 169.
"The Shadow on the Wall." **4.** 118.
"Someone in the Lift." **1.** 80.
"A Summons." **1.** 80.
"The Telephone Call." **3.** 169.
"Travelling Grave." **3 ed.** 272.
"Up the Garden Path." **3.** 169.
"A Very Present Help." **3.** 169.
"The Visitor from Down Under." **4.** 118.
"W.S." **3.** 169; **4.** 118.
"The White Wand." **3.** 169.

WILLIAM FRYER HARVEY

"The Arms of Mrs. Egan." **4.** 118.
"August Heat." **4.** 118.
"The Beast with Five Fingers." **4.** 118.
"The Clock." **4.** 118.
"The Follower." **4.** 118.
"Sambo." **4.** 118.

JAROSLAV HAŠEK

"The Cynological Institute." **3.** 169.
"An Honest Finder." **3.** 169.
"The School for the State Police." **3.** 169.
"The Story of a Good Swedish Soldier." **3.** 169.
"The Struggle for the Soul." **3.** 169.

GERALD HASLAM

"Ace Low." **5.** 138.
"Before Dishonor." **5.** 138.
"California Christmas." **5.** 139.
"Companeros." **5.** 139.
"Cowboys." **5.** 139.
"Crossing the Valley." **5.** 139.
"The Doll." **5.** 139.
"Dust." **5.** 139.
"Earthquake Summer." **5.** 139.
"The Great Kern County Gator Hunt." **5.** 139.
"Growing Up at Babe's." **5.** 139.
"Happily Ever After." **5.** 139.
"Hawk Flights: An American Fable." **5.** 139.
"Heat." **5.** 139.
"Hey, Okie!" **5.** 139.
"Home to America." **5.** 139.
"The Horned Toad." **5.** 139.
"Jimmie Eight." **5.** 139.
"Joaquin." **5.** 139.
"The Killing Pen." **5.** 140.
"The King of Skateland." **5.** 140.
"The Last Roundup." **5.** 140.
"Mad Stone." **5.** 140.
"Man of the Year." **5.** 140.
"Matinee." **5.** 140.
"Medicine." **5.** 140.
"Oil Town Rumble: The Young Men of Taft." **5.** 140.
"A Prison of Words." **5.** 140.
"Return, Prodigal." **5.** 140.
"Rider." **5.** 140.

"Sally Let Her Bangs Hang Down." **5.** 140.
"She's My Rock." **5.** 140.
"Smile." **5.** 140.
"So Slender a Splint of Song." **5.** 140.
"Sojourner." **5.** 140.
"Someone Else's Life." **5.** 140.
"The Souvenir." **5.** 141.
"Sweet Reason." **5.** 141.
"Trophies." **5.** 141.
"Vengeance." **5.** 141.
"Voice of a Place: The Great Central Valley." **5.** 141.
"The Wages of Sin." **5.** 141.
"Walls." **5.** 141.
"Who Can Write What." **5.** 141.
"Widder Maker." **5.** 141.
"Wild Goose: Memories of a Valley Summer." **5.** 141.

WILHELM HAUFF

"Die Betterin vom Pont des Arts." **3 ed.** 272.
"Othello." **3 ed.** 272.
"The Picture of the Kaiser." **3 ed.** 272.

MILDRED HAUN

"Barshia's Horse He Made, It Flew." **3 ed.** 272.

GERHART HAUPTMANN

"The Bassgeige." **5.** 141.
"Carnival." **3 ed.** 272; **1.** 81; **2.** 131; **3.** 170.
"Galahad." **5.** 141.
"Der Ketzer von Soana." **3 ed.** 273; **3.** 170; **5.** 141.
"The Miracle of the Sea." **3 ed.** 273; **3.** 170.
"Phantom." **3 ed.** 273.
"Der Schuss im Park." **3 ed.** 273.
"Signalman Thiel." **3 ed.** 273; **1.** 81; **2.** 131; **3.** 170; **5.** 141.

HAZEL H. HAVERMALE

"The Canton Shawl." **2.** 131; **3.** 170.

JOHN HAWKES

"Charivari." **3 ed.** 273; **2.** 131; **3.** 170.
"The Goose on the Grave." **3 ed.** 273; **3.** 170.
"The Grandmother." **3 ed.** 273; **3.** 170.
"The Nearest Cemetery." **3 ed.** 273; **3.** 170.
"The Owl." **3 ed.** 273; **2.** 132; **3.** 170; **4.** 118.
"A Song Outside." **3.** 171.
"The Traveler." **3.** 171.

NATHANIEL HAWTHORNE

"Alice Doane's Appeal." **3 ed.** 274; **1.** 81; **2.** 132; **3.** 171; **4.** 118–19; **5.** 142.
"The Ambitious Guest." **3 ed.** 274; **1.** 81; **2.** 132; **3.** 171; **4.** 119.
"The Ancestral Footstep." **2.** 132; **5.** 142.
"The Antique Ring." **3 ed.** 275.
"The Artist of the Beautiful." **3 ed.** 275–76; **1.** 81; **3.** 171; **4.** 119; **5.** 142.
"The Birthmark." **3 ed.** 276–77; **1.** 81; **2.** 132; **3.** 171; **4.** 119; **5.** 142.
"The Canterbury Pilgrims." **3 ed.** 277; **2.** 132.
"The Celestial Railroad." **3 ed.** 278; **4.** 119.
"Chipping with a Chisel." **3 ed.** 278.
"The Christmas Banquet." **3 ed.** 278; **5.** 142.
"David Swann: A Fantasy." **3 ed.** 278.
"The Devil in Manuscript." **3 ed.** 278; **1.** 81; **2.** 132; **3.** 171; **4.** 119.
"Dr. Heidegger's Experiment." **3 ed.** 278–79.
"Drowne's Wooden Image." **3 ed.** 279; **1.** 81–82; **5.** 142.
"Earth's Holocaust." **3 ed.** 279; **1.** 82; **2.** 132; **4.** 119.
"Edward Randolph's Portrait." **3 ed.** 279; **1.** 82; **3.** 171; **4.** 119; **5.** 142.
"Egotism; or, The Bosom Serpent." **3 ed.** 279; **4.** 119–20.
"Endicott and the Red Cross." **3 ed.** 279–80; **1.** 82; **3.** 172; **4.** 120; **5.** 142.
"Ethan Brand." **3 ed.** 280–82; **1.** 82; **2.** 133; **3.** 172; **4.** 120; **5.** 142.
"Fancy's Show Box." **3 ed.** 282; **1.** 82; **5.** 142.
"Feathertop." **3 ed.** 282; **1.** 82; **2.** 133; **5.** 143.
"Fire Worship." **3 ed.** 282–83.
"Footprints on the Seashore." **5.** 143.
"The Gentle Boy." **3 ed.** 283; **3.** 172; **4.** 120; **5.** 143.

"The Gray Champion." **3 ed.** 283–84; **1.** 82; **2.** 133; **3.** 172; **5.** 143.
"The Great Carbuncle." **3 ed.** 284.
"The Great Stone Face." **3 ed.** 284.
"The Hall of Fantasy." **3 ed.** 284; **2.** 133; **3.** 172.
"The Haunted Mind." **3 ed.** 284–85; **1.** 82; **2.** 133; **3.** 172.
"The Hollow of the Three Hills." **3 ed.** 285; **1.** 82; **2.** 133; **3.** 172.
"Howe's Masquerade." **3 ed.** 285; **1.** 82; **3.** 172; **4.** 120.
"The Intelligence Office." **3 ed.** 285.
"Lady Eleanore's Mantle." **3 ed.** 285; **1.** 82–83; **3.** 173; **4.** 120; **5.** 143.
"The Lily's Quest." **3 ed.** 285; **3.** 173.
"Little Annie's Ramble." **4.** 120; **5.** 143.
"The Man of Adamant." **3 ed.** 286; **3.** 173; **5.** 143.
"The Maypole of Merry Mount." **3 ed.** 286–87; **1.** 83; **2.** 133; **3.** 173; **4.** 120; **5.** 143.
"The Minister's Black Veil." **3 ed.** 287–88; **1.** 83; **2.** 133; **3.** 173; **4.** 120; **5.** 143.
"Mr. Higginbotham's Catastrophe." **3 ed.** 288; **1.** 83; **3.** 173; **4.** 120.
"Mrs. Bullfrog." **3 ed.** 288; **4.** 120; **5.** 143.
"Monsieur du Miroir." **3 ed.** 288–89; **2.** 133.
"My Kinsman, Major Molineux." **3 ed.** 289–91; **1.** 83; **2.** 133–34; **3.** 173; **4.** 120–21; **5.** 143–44.
"The New Adam and Eve." **3 ed.** 291; **2.** 134; **4.** 121; **5.** 144.
"The Old Apple Dealer." **3 ed.** 291.
"Old Esther Dudley." **3 ed.** 291–92; **1.** 83; **3.** 174; **4.** 121; **5.** 144.
"Old Ticonderoga." **5.** 144.
"An Old Woman's Tale." **3 ed.** 292; **2.** 134; **3.** 174.
"The Paradise of Children." **4.** 121.
"Peter Goldthwaite's Treasure." **3 ed.** 292; **1.** 83; **2.** 134.
"The Procession of Life." **3 ed.** 292; **5.** 144.
"The Prophetic Pictures." **3 ed.** 292; **1.** 84; **2.** 134; **3.** 174; **4.** 121; **5.** 144.
"Rappaccini's Daughter." **3 ed.** 292–94; **1.** 84; **2.** 134; **3.** 174; **4.** 121; **5.** 144.
"Roger Malvin's Burial." **3 ed.** 294–95; **1.** 84; **2.** 134; **3.** 174; **4.** 121; **5.** 144.
"A Select Party." **3 ed.** 295; **3.** 174.
"The Seven Vagabonds." **3 ed.** 295; **3.** 174.
"The Shaker Bridal." **3 ed.** 295–96; **3.** 174; **5.** 145.
"The Snow Image." **3 ed.** 296; **3.** 174; **4.** 121.
"Sunday at Home." **3 ed.** 296.
"Sylph Etherege." **3 ed.** 296; **2.** 134.
"The Threefold Destiny." **3 ed.** 296; **4.** 121; **5.** 145.
"The Village Uncle." **3 ed.** 296; **2.** 134.
"A Virtuoso's Collection." **3 ed.** 296.
"Wakefield." **3 ed.** 296–97; **1.** 84; **2.** 134; **3.** 175; **4.** 122; **5.** 145.
"The Wedding Knell." **3 ed.** 297; **1.** 84; **5.** 145.
"The White Old Maid." **3 ed.** 297.
"The Wives of the Dead" [same as "The Two Widows"]. **3 ed.** 297; **2.** 134; **3.** 175.
"Young Goodman Brown." **3 ed.** 297–301; **1.** 85; **2.** 134–35; **3.** 175; **4.** 122; **5.** 145.

JOHN HAY

"The Blood Seedling." **3 ed.** 301; **1.** 85.
"The Foster-Brother." **3 ed.** 301; **1.** 85.
"Kane and Abel." **3 ed.** 301; **1.** 85.
"Shelby Cabell." **3 ed.** 301; **1.** 85.

HAYASHI FUMIKO

"Late Chrysanthemums." **3.** 175; **5.** 145.

ERNEST HAYCOCK

"On Bakeoven Grade." **5.** 145.
"Stage to Lordsburg." **5.** 145.

KATE SIMPSON HAYES

"Aweena." **4.** 122.
"An Episode at Clarke's Crossing." **3.** 176.
"The La-de-dah from London." **4.** 122.

MUHAMMAD HUSAYN HAYKAL

"The Atonement for the Sin of True Love." **2.** 135.
"Love Is Blind." **2.** 135.
"The Power of Passionate Love." **2.** 135.

HAIM [HAYIM] HAZAZ

"Aristotle." **4.** 122.
"A Flowing River." **3 ed.** 301.
"Harat Olam." **3.** 176.

"Rahamim the Porter." **5.** 146.
"The Sermon." **3 ed.** 301; **2.** 135; **3.** 176; **5.** 146.

BESSIE HEAD

"The Collector of Treasures." **4.** 122.
"The Deep River: A Story of Ancient Tribal Migration." **4.** 122; **5.** 146.
"Heaven Is Not Closed." **3.** 176; **5.** 146.
"Jacob." **4.** 122.
"Life." **5.** 146.
"Snapshots of a Wedding." **4.** 122.
"The Special One." **4.** 123.
"The Wind and a Boy." **4.** 123.

FRIEDRICH HEBBEL

"Anna." **3 ed.** 301.
"Barbier Zitterlein." **3 ed.** 301.
"The Cow." **3 ed.** 302; **1.** 85.
"Der Rubin." **3 ed.** 302.
"Schnock." **3 ed.** 302.

ANNE HÉBERT

"The Coral Dress." **3.** 176; **5.** 146.
"The Death of Stella." **3 ed.** 302; **2.** 135; **3.** 176; **5.** 146.
"Dominique's Angel." **3.** 176.
"A Grand Marriage." **3 ed.** 302; **3.** 176; **4.** 123.
"The House on the Esplanade." **3.** 176; **5.** 146.
"The Spring Time of Catherine." **3 ed.** 302; **3.** 176.
"The Torrent." **3 ed.** 302; **2.** 135; **3.** 176.
"The Wooden House." **3 ed.** 302.

EDITH HECHT

"His First Client." **2.** 135.

SADEQ HEDAYAT

"The Abyss." **3.** 177.
"The Antichrist's Donkey." **3.** 177.
"Buried Alive." **2.** 136.
"Dash Akul." **3.** 177.
"David the Hunchback." **3.** 177.
"Dead End." **3.** 177.
"The Elder Sister." **3.** 177.
"The Fire Worshipper." **3.** 177.
"The Ghouls" [same as "Eaters of the Dead"]. **3.** 177.
"The Legalizer." **3.** 177.
"The Man Who Killed His Passions." **2.** 136; **3.** 177.
"The Patriot." **3.** 177.
"The Stray Dog." **3.** 177.
"Three Drops of Blood." **2.** 136.
"Tulip." **3.** 177.
"The Woman Who Lost Her Man." **3.** 177.

THOMAS HEGGEN

"Night Watch." **3 ed.** 302.

HEINRICH HEINE

"The Baths of Lucca." **1.** 85.
"Florentine Night." **1.** 85; **2.** 136.
"From the Memoirs of Herr Schnabelewopski." **1.** 85.
"Die Harzreise." **1.** 85.
"The Journey from Munich to Genoa." **1.** 86.
"The Rabbi of Bacherach." **1.** 86.

WILLIAM HEINESEN

"Arcadian Afternoon." **3 ed.** 302.
"Ascension." **3 ed.** 302.
"Atalanta." **3 ed.** 302.
"The Ballad of Double-Simon and Kildse-Kalsa." **3 ed.** 303.
"Doda." **3 ed.** 303.
"Don Juan of the Blubber Works." **3 ed.** 303.
"Gamaliel's Bewitchment." **3 ed.** 303.
"The Gryla." **3 ed.** 303.
"The Heavens Smile." **3 ed.** 303.
"The Hour of the Wolf." **3 ed.** 303.
"Knives." **3 ed.** 303.
"Leonard and Lenora." **3 ed.** 303.
"The Madman's Garden." **3 ed.** 303.
"The Modern Age." **3 ed.** 303.
"The Moon over Mount Horeb." **3 ed.** 303.
"The Night of the Storm." **3 ed.** 303.
"The Rush of the River." **3 ed.** 303.
"Smoking Mirror." **3 ed.** 303.
"The Soul." **3 ed.** 303.
"The Story of the Poet Lin Pe and His Tame Crane." **3 ed.** 303.
"Tartaros." **3 ed.** 304.
"The Virgin Birth." **3 ed.** 304.
"The Winged Darkness." **3 ed.** 304; **1.** 86.

ROBERT A. HEINLEIN

"All You Zombies." **3 ed.** 304; **2.** 136; **3.** 178; **5.** 146.
"And He Built a Crooked House." **1.** 86.
"Blowups Happen." **3 ed.** 304; **2.** 136; **5.** 146.
"By His Bootstraps." **3 ed.** 304; **1.** 86; **2.** 136; **5.** 146.
"Common Sense." **3 ed.** 304.
"Coventry." **3 ed.** 304; **1.** 86; **2.** 136.
"Destination Moon." **3 ed.** 304.
"The Elephant Circuit." **2.** 136.
"The Future Revisited." **3 ed.** 304.
"Gentlemen, Be Seated." **1.** 86.
"The Green Hills of Earth." **1.** 86.
"Gulf." **3 ed.** 304; **2.** 136; **3.** 178.
"If This Goes On." **3 ed.** 304; **1.** 86; **5.** 146.
"Jerry Is a Man." **3 ed.** 304; **2.** 136.
"Let There Be Light." **3 ed.** 304; **2.** 136.
"Life-Line." **3 ed.** 304; **1.** 86; **2.** 136.
"Logic of Empire." **2.** 137.
"Lost Legion." **2.** 137.
"Magic, Inc." [originally "The Devil Makes the Law"]. **1.** 86; **2.** 136.
"The Man Who Sold the Moon." **3 ed.** 304; **2.** 137.
"The Man Who Travelled in Elephants." **1.** 86.
"The Menace from Earth." **3 ed.** 305; **2.** 137.
"Misfit." **3 ed.** 305; **1.** 86; **2.** 137.
"My Object All Sublime." **3 ed.** 305.
"Project Nightmare." **2.** 137; **5.** 147.
"Requiem." **1.** 86; **2.** 137; **5.** 147.
"The Roads Must Roll." **5.** 147.
"Searchlight." **1.** 87.
"Sky Lift." **1.** 87; **2.** 137.
"Solution Unsatisfactory." **3 ed.** 305; **2.** 137; **5.** 147.
"Space Jockey." **1.** 87.
"They." **3 ed.** 305; **1.** 87; **2.** 137; **3.** 178; **4.** 123.
"Universe." **3 ed.** 305; **1.** 87; **2.** 137.
"The Unpleasant Profession of Jonathan Hoag." **3 ed.** 305; **2.** 137.
"Waldo." **3 ed.** 305; **1.** 87; **2.** 137; **3.** 178.
"We Also Walk Dogs." **1.** 87.
"The Year of the Jackpot." **1.** 87; **2.** 137.

LILLIAN HELLMAN

"Julia." **2.** 137.

MARK HELPRIN

"A Dove of the East." **5.** 147.
"Ellis Island." **5.** 147.
"A Jew of Persia." **5.** 147.
"North Light." **5.** 147.
"The Schreuderspitze." **5.** 147.

ERNEST HEMINGWAY

"After the Storm." **3 ed.** 305; **1.** 87; **2.** 138.
"An Alpine Idyll." **3 ed.** 305–06; **1.** 87; **2.** 138; **3.** 178; **5.** 147.
"The Ash-Heels Tendon." **4.** 123.
"Banal Story." **3 ed.** 306; **2.** 138.
"The Battler." **3 ed.** 306; **1.** 87; **2.** 138; **3.** 178; **4.** 123; **5.** 147.
"Big Two-Hearted River." **3 ed.** 306–07; **1.** 87; **2.** 138; **3.** 178; **4.** 123; **5.** 147.
"The Butterfly and the Tank." **3 ed.** 307.
"A Canary for One." **3 ed.** 307–08; **2.** 138; **4.** 123.
"The Capital of the World." **3 ed.** 308; **1.** 87; **2.** 138; **4.** 123.
"Cat in the Rain." **3 ed.** 308; **1.** 87; **2.** 138; **3.** 178; **4.** 124; **5.** 147–48.
"Che Ti Dice La Patria?" **3 ed.** 308; **4.** 124.
"A Clean, Well-Lighted Place." **3 ed.** 308–10; **1.** 88; **2.** 138–39; **3.** 179; **4.** 124; **5.** 148.
"Cross-Country Snow." **3 ed.** 310; **2.** 139; **3.** 179; **5.** 148.
"Crossing the Mississippi." **2.** 139.
"The Current." **4.** 124.
"The Dangerous Summer." **3 ed.** 310.
"A Day's Wait." **3 ed.** 310–11; **2.** 139; **3.** 179.
"The Denunciation." **3 ed.** 311; **2.** 139; **5.** 148.
"The Doctor and the Doctor's Wife." **3 ed.** 311; **1.** 88; **2.** 139; **3.** 179; **4.** 124; **5.** 148.
"The End of Something." **3 ed.** 311–12; **2.** 139; **3.** 179.
"The Faithful Bull." **1.** 88; **2.** 139; **5.** 148.
"Fathers and Sons." **3 ed.** 312; **1.** 88; **2.** 139; **3.** 179; **4.** 124; **5.** 148.

"Fifty Grand." **3 ed.** 312; **2.** 139; **3.** 179; **4.** 124; **5.** 148.
"The Gambler, the Nun, and the Radio." **3 ed.** 312–13; **1.** 88; **2.** 139; **3.** 179; **4.** 124.
"Get a Seeing-Eye Dog." **3 ed.** 313; **4.** 124; **5.** 148.
"God Rest You Merry, Gentlemen." **3 ed.** 313; **1.** 88; **5.** 148.
"The Good Lion." **1.** 88; **2.** 139; **5.** 148.
"Hills Like White Elephants." **3 ed.** 313; **1.** 88; **2.** 140; **3.** 179–80; **4.** 124; **5.** 148.
"Homage to Switzerland." **3 ed.** 313; **2.** 140.
"In Another Country." **3 ed.** 314; **2.** 140; **3.** 180; **4.** 124; **5.** 149.
"Indian Camp." **3 ed.** 314–15; **1.** 88; **2.** 140; **3.** 180; **4.** 124–25; **5.** 149.
"The Indians Move Away." **2.** 140.
"The Killers." **3 ed.** 315–16; **1.** 88–89; **2.** 140; **3.** 180; **4.** 125; **5.** 149.
"The Last Good Country." **2.** 140; **3.** 180; **5.** 149.
"The Light of the World." **3 ed.** 316; **1.** 89; **2.** 140; **4.** 125.
"A Man of the World." **3 ed.** 317; **2.** 141.
"The Mercenaries." **4.** 125.
"Mr. and Mrs. Elliot." **3 ed.** 317; **4.** 125.
"The Mother of a Queen." **3 ed.** 317; **3.** 180.
"My Old Man." **3 ed.** 317; **2.** 141; **3.** 180; **4.** 125.
"A Natural History of the Dead." **3 ed.** 317; **2.** 141; **3.** 180; **4.** 125.
"Night Before Battle." **3 ed.** 317.
"Night Before Landing." **2.** 141; **3.** 180.
"Nobody Ever Dies." **3 ed.** 317; **1.** 89; **5.** 149.
"Now I Lay Me." **3 ed.** 317–18; **2.** 141; **3.** 180; **4.** 125; **5.** 149.
"The Old Man and the Sea." **3 ed.** 318–21; **1.** 89; **2.** 141; **3.** 180; **4.** 125; **5.** 149.
"Old Man at the Bridge." **3 ed.** 321–22; **4.** 125.
"On the Quai at Smyrna." **3 ed.** 322; **1.** 89; **2.** 141; **3.** 181; **4.** 125; **5.** 149.
"One Reader Writes." **3 ed.** 322.
"Out of Season." **3 ed.** 322; **4.** 126; **5.** 149.
"A Pursuit Race." **3 ed.** 322; **3.** 181; **4.** 126.
"The Revolutionist." **3 ed.** 322; **1.** 89; **5.** 149.
"The Sea Change." **3 ed.** 322; **2.** 141; **4.** 126.
"The Short Happy Life of Francis Macomber." **3 ed.** 322–25; **1.** 89–90; **2.** 141–42; **3.** 181; **4.** 126; **5.** 150.
"A Simple Enquiry." **3 ed.** 325.
"The Snows of Kilimanjaro." **3 ed.** 325–27; **1.** 90; **2.** 142; **3.** 181; **4.** 126; **5.** 150.
"Soldier's Home." **3 ed.** 327; **1.** 90; **2.** 142; **3.** 181; **4.** 126; **5.** 150.
"The Strange Country." **5.** 150.
"The Summer People." **4.** 126.
"Ten Indians." **3 ed.** 327; **2.** 142; **3.** 181; **5.** 150.
"Three Shots." **1.** 90; **2.** 142; **4.** 126.
"The Three-Day Blow." **3 ed.** 327; **1.** 90; **2.** 142; **3.** 181; **5.** 150.
"Today Is Friday." **3 ed.** 328; **4.** 126.
"The Undefeated." **3 ed.** 328; **2.** 142; **4.** 126; **5.** 150.
"Under the Ridge." **3 ed.** 328; **1.** 90.
"Up in Michigan." **3 ed.** 328; **3.** 181; **4.** 127.
"A Very Short Story." **3 ed.** 328; **4.** 127.
"The Visiting Team." **4.** 127.
"A Way You'll Never Be." **3 ed.** 328–29; **2.** 142; **3.** 181; **4.** 127; **5.** 150.
"Wine of Wyoming." **3 ed.** 329; **2.** 142; **3.** 181; **5.** 150.

AMY HEMPEL

"In the Cemetery Where Al Jolson Is Buried." **5.** 150.

ZENNA HENDERSON

"J-Line to Nowhere." **3.** 181.
"Things." **5.** 150.

PEDRO HENRÍQUEZ UREÑA

"El peso falso." **4.** 127.
"La sombra." **4.** 127.

WILL HENRY [HENRY W. ALLEN]

"A Bullet for Billy the Kid." **3.** 182.
"The Friendship of Red Fox." **3.** 182.
"The Ghost Wolf of Thunder Mountain." **3.** 182.
"The Pale Eyes." **3.** 182.
"Peace of the Pony Soldiers." **3.** 182.
"River of Decision." **3.** 182.
"The Tallest Indian in Toltepec." **3.** 182.

FRANK HERBERT

"Cease Fire." **3.** 182.
"Operation Syndrome." **3.** 182.
"The Priests of Psi." **3.** 182.
"Seed Stock." **3.** 182.
"Skylark." **3.** 182.
"The Tactful Saboteur." **3.** 182.

JOSEPHINE HERBST

"As a Fair Young Girl." **4.** 127.
"Dry Sunday in Connecticut." **4.** 127.
"The Elegant M. Gason." **4.** 127.
"The Golden Egg." **4.** 127.
"Hunter of Doves." **4.** 127.
"The Last Word." **4.** 127.
"The Man of Steel." **4.** 127.

JOSEPH HERGESHEIMER

"Asphodel." **3 ed.** 329.
"Bread." **3 ed.** 329.
"The Crystal Chandelier." **3 ed.** 329.
"The Great Wall." **3 ed.** 329.
"Juju." **3 ed.** 329.
"A Little Number in Piqué." **3 ed.** 329.
"Oak." **3 ed.** 329.
"Rosemary Roselle." **3 ed.** 329.

STEPHAN HERMLIN

"The Commandant." **1.** 90.
"Journey of a Painter in Paris." **1.** 90.
"The Way of the Bolsheviks." **1.** 90.

GYULA HERNÁDI

"Deszkakolostor." **4.** 128.

EFRÉM HERNÁNDEZ

"Crossouts." **3.** 182.
"Nicomaco Closed In." **3.** 183.

FELISBERTO HERNÁNDEZ

"El acomodador." **5.** 151.
"El balcón." **5.** 151.
"La casa inundador." **5.** 151.
"El cocodrilo." **5.** 151.
"Las dos historias." **5.** 151.
"La envenedada." **5.** 151.
"Historia de un cigarillo." **5.** 151.
"Las hortensias." **5.** 151.
"Menos Julia." **5.** 151.
"Muebles el canario." **5.** 151.
"Nadie encendía las lámparas." **5.** 151.
"Tal vez un movimiento." **5.** 151.
"Úrsula." **5.** 151.
"El vestido blanco." **5.** 152.

LUIS HERNÁNDEZ AQUINO

"Aire de guazábara." **5.** 152.
"Un enigma y una clave." **5.** 152.

ALFONSO HERNÁNDEZ CATÁ

"Ninety Days." **3.** 183.

JUAN LUIS HERRERO

"Isla de Pinos." **1.** 90.

JOHN HERSEY

"The Death of Buchan Walsh." **3.** 183.
"A Fable South of Cancer." **3.** 183.
"The Pen." **3.** 183.
"A Short Wait." **3.** 183.
"Why Were You Sent Out Here?" **3.** 183.

ALEXANDER HERZEN

"Dr. Krupov." **3.** 183.
"Elena." **3.** 183.
"The Legend." **3.** 183.
"Notes of a Certain Young Man." **3.** 183.
"The Thieving Magpie." **3 ed.** 329; **3.** 183.

HERMANN HESSE

"Bird." **3.** 183.
"A Child's Soul." **3 ed.** 329–30; **1.** 90.
"Diary from a Health Resort" [same as "Guest at a Spa" or "Kurgast"]. **3 ed.** 330.
"Heumond." **3 ed.** 330.
"Iris." **3 ed.** 330.
"Journey to the East." **3 ed.** 330; **1.** 91; **2.** 143.
"King Yu." **3 ed.** 330.
"Klein and Wagner." **3 ed.** 330.
"Klingsor's Last Summer." **3 ed.** 330–31; **1.** 91; **2.** 143.
"Kurgast" [same as "Diary from a Health Resort" or "Guest at a Spa"]. **3 ed.** 331.
"Pictor's Metamorphoses." **3.** 184.
"The Poet." **3 ed.** 331; **4.** 128.

"Report from Normalia." **3.** 184.
"Siddhartha." **3 ed.** 331; **1.** 91; **2.** 143; **3.** 184; **4.** 128; **5.** 152.
"The Steep Road." **3 ed.** 331.
"The Trip to Nuremberg." **3 ed.** 331.
"Youth, Beautiful Youth." **3 ed.** 331–32.

GEORG HEYM

"An Afternoon." **3.** 184.
"The Fifth of October." **3.** 184.
"Jonathan." **3 ed.** 332.
"The Lunatic Asylum." **1.** 91; **3.** 184.
"Shakleton's Diary." **3.** 184.
"The Thief." **3.** 184.

PAUL HEYSE

"L'Arrabiata." **3 ed.** 332.
"David and Jonathan." **3 ed.** 332.
"Furia." **3 ed.** 332.
"Geteiltes Herz." **3 ed.** 332.
"Grenzen der Menschheit." **3 ed.** 332.
"Die Hexe vom Korso." **3 ed.** 332.
"Himmlische und irdische Liebe." **3 ed.** 332.
"The Last Centaur." **3 ed.** 332.
"Mädchen von Treffi." **3 ed.** 332.
"Nino and Maso." **3 ed.** 332.
"Die Stickerin von Treviso." **3 ed.** 332.
"Unvergessbare Worte." **3 ed.** 332.
"Der verlorene Sohn." **3 ed.** 332.
"Der Weihnachtsfund." **3 ed.** 332.

DU BOSE HEYWARD

"The Brute." **3 ed.** 333.
"Dorothy Grumpet, Graduate Lady." **3 ed.** 333.
"The Half Pint Flask." **2.** 143.
"The Winning Loser." **3 ed.** 333.

ROBERT [SMYTHE] HICHENS

"How Love Came to Professor Guildea." **4.** 128.
"The Lost Faith." **4.** 128.
"The Sin of Envy." **4.** 128.

THOMAS WENTWORTH HIGGINSON

"The Monarch of Dreams." **3 ed.** 333.

PATRICIA HIGHSMITH

"Hamsters vs. Websters." **5.** 152.
"Harry: A Ferret." **5.** 152.

HIGUCHI ICHIYŌ

"A Buried Life." **3.** 184.
"Child's Play." **2.** 143.
"Clouds in Springtime." **2.** 143.
"Comparing Heights." **5.** 152.
"Encounters on a Dark Night." **2.** 143.
"Growing Up." **3.** 184; **5.** 152.
"In Obscurity." **2.** 143.
"Nightingale in the Grove." **3.** 184.
"Old-Fashioned Credit Accounts, Modern Cash on the Line." **2.** 143.
"On the Last Day of the Year." **2.** 143; **3.** 184.
"Separate Ways." **2.** 143; **4.** 128.
"The Sound of the Koto." **2.** 143.
"The Thirteenth Night." **2.** 144.
"Troubled Waters." **2.** 144.

WOLFGANG HILDESHEIMER

"A World Ends." **3 ed.** 333.

SUSAN HILL

"The Albatross." **3.** 185.
"The Custodian." **3.** 185; **4.** 128.
"The Peacock." **3.** 185.
"Somerville." **3.** 185.

CHESTER HIMES

"Crazy in the Stir." **1.** 91.
"Da—Da—Dee." **1.** 91.
"He Knew." **1.** 91.
"Headwaiter." **1.** 91.
"Heaven Has Changed." **1.** 91.
"His Last Day." **1.** 91.
"Lunching at the Ritzmore." **1.** 91.
"Mama's Missionary Money." **1.** 91.
"A Nigger." **1.** 92.
"Pork Chop Paradise." **1.** 92.
"Prediction." **1.** 92; **4.** 128.
"Prison Mass." **1.** 92.
"So Softly Smiling." **1.** 92.
"Tang." **1.** 92.
"To What Red Hell?" **1.** 92.
"Two Soldiers." **1.** 92.

JAMES HINTON

"Mediators to the Goatherd." **3 ed.** 333.

ZINAIDA HIPPIUS

"All Is for the Worse." **3.** 185.
"Born Too Early." **3.** 185.
"He Is White." **3.** 185.

HIRADE SHŪ

"The Plan." **3.** 185.
"The Rebels." **3.** 185.
"The Way of the Brutes." **3.** 185.

HIROTSU RYŪRŌ

"The Love Suicide at Imado." **3.** 185.

HO TAO-SHENG

"The Apprentice." **3.** 185.

JACK HODGINS

"Ladies and Gentlemen, The Fabulous Barclay Sisters." **4.** 129.
"Separation." **4.** 129.
"Spit Delaney's Island." **4.** 129.

WILLIAM HOPE HODGSON

"The Baumoff Explosion" [originally "Eloi, Eloi, Lama Sabachthani"]. **4.** 129.
"The Gateway of the Monster." **3.** 186.
"The Hog." **3.** 186; **4.** 129.
"The Whistling Room." **3.** 186.

SIGURD HOEL

"The Dream." **3.** 186.
"The Idiot." **3.** 186.
"Love One Another." **3.** 186.
"The Murderer." **3.** 186.
"Nothing." **3.** 186.
"The Old Ones on the Hill." **3.** 186.
"Spleen." **3.** 186.
"The Star." **3.** 186.

CHARLES FENNO HOFFMAN

"Queen Meg." **1.** 92.

E[RNST] T[HEODOR] A[MADEUS] HOFFMANN

"Account of the Life of a Noted Man." **3 ed.** 333.
"The Adventure of New Year's Night" [same as "New Year's Eve Adventure"]. **3 ed.** 333, 336; **1.** 92; **2.** 144; **3.** 186; **4.** 130.
"Der Artushof." **3 ed.** 333.
"Automata." **3 ed.** 333; **1.** 92.
"The Baron of B." **1.** 92.
"The Choice of a Bride." **3 ed.** 333.
"The Contest of the Minstrels." **3 ed.** 333–34.
"Counselor Krespel" [same as "The Story of Krespel"]. **3 ed.** 334; **1.** 92–93; **2.** 144; **4.** 129.
"The Cousin's Corner Window." **3 ed.** 334; **4.** 129.
"The Cremona Violin." **3.** 186.
"Datura Fastuosa." **3.** 186.
"The Deserted House." **3 ed.** 334; **1.** 93; **3.** 187.
"Doge and Dogaressa." **3.** 187.
"Don Juan." **2.** 144.
"The Doubles." **2.** 144.
"The Enemy." **3 ed.** 334; **4.** 129.
"The Entail." **3 ed.** 334; **4.** 129; **5.** 152.
"A Fragment from the Life of Three Friends." **4.** 129.
"Gambler's Luck." **3 ed.** 334.
"The Golden Pot." **3 ed.** 334; **1.** 93; **3.** 187; **4.** 129; **5.** 152–53.
"Die Haimatochare." **3 ed.** 334.
"The Hold." **3 ed.** 334.
"Ignaz Denner." **3 ed.** 335; **3.** 187; **5.** 153.
"The Jesuit Church in G." **3 ed.** 335.
"The King's Bride." **3 ed.** 335; **3.** 187; **4.** 130.
"Knight Gluck." **3 ed.** 335; **2.** 144; **3.** 187.
"Little Zaches Called Cinnabar." **3 ed.** 335; **2.** 144.
"The Lost Reflection." **3 ed.** 335; **2.** 144.
"The Loved One." **3 ed.** 335.
"Luck." **3 ed.** 335.
"Mademoiselle de Scudery." **3 ed.** 335; **1.** 93; **2.** 144–45; **3.** 187; **5.** 153.
"The Magnetizer." **3 ed.** 335; **2.** 145.
"Die Marquise de la Privadière." **3 ed.** 335.
"Master Floh." **3 ed.** 335–36; **2.** 145; **3.** 187.

"Master Johannes Wacht." **3 ed.** 336.
"Master Martin the Cooper and His Assistants." **3 ed.** 336.
"The Mines of Falun." **3 ed.** 336; **2.** 145; **4.** 130; **5.** 153.
"The Mysterious Child." **3 ed.** 336.
"Nutcracker and Mouse King." **3 ed.** 336; **2.** 145.
"The Pause." **1.** 93.
"The Poet and the Composer." **3 ed.** 336.
"The Primogeniture." **3 ed.** 336.
"Princess Brambilla." **3 ed.** 336; **1.** 93; **2.** 145; **3.** 187.
"The Recovery." **3 ed.** 336.
"The Sandman." **3 ed.** 336–37; **1.** 93; **2.** 145; **3.** 187; **4.** 130; **5.** 153.
"Serapion." **3 ed.** 337; **4.** 130.
"Signor Formica." **3 ed.** 337.
"The Sinister Guest" [same as "The Uncanny Guest"]. **3 ed.** 337; **2.** 145.
"The Strange Sufferings of a Theatre Director." **3 ed.** 337.
"The Uncanny Guest" [same as "The Sinister Guest"]. **2.** 145.
"The Vow." **3 ed.** 337.
"Der Zusammenhang der Dinge." **5.** 153.

HUGO VON HOFMANNSTHAL

"Horseman's Story." **3 ed.** 337; **1.** 93–94; **2.** 145.
"Summer Time." **2.** 145.
"Tale of the Merchant' s Son and His Servant." **1.** 94.
"The Tale of the 672nd Night." **2.** 145; **3.** 188.
"Under the Copper-Beech Tree." **1.** 94.
"Die Wege und die Begegnungen." **1.** 94.

DAVID HOGAN [FRANK GALLAGHER]

"The Leaping Trout." **3 ed.** 337.

DESMOND HOGAN

"A Poet and an Englishman." **3.** 188.

ROBERT J. HOGAN

"The Case of the Six Coffins." **3.** 188.

JAMES HOGG

"The Adventures of Basil Lee." **3.** 188.
"The Adventures of Captain John Lochy." **3.** 188.
"The Barber of Duncow." **1.** 94; **3.** 188.
"The Brownie of the Black Haggs." **3.** 188.
"The Cameronian Preacher's Tale." **1.** 94; **3.** 188.
"Cousin Mattie." **3.** 188.
"George Dobson's Expedition to Hell." **3.** 188.
"Mary Burnet." **1.** 94.
"Mr. Adamson of Laverhope." **1.** 94.
"The Mysterious Bride." **3.** 188.
"Strange Letter of a Lunatic." **3.** 189.
"The Surpassing Adventures of Allan Gordon." **3.** 189.
"Tibby Hyslop's Dream." **1.** 94.
"Tibby Johnston's Wraith." **3.** 189.

GRO HOLM

"Life on the Løstøl Farm." **3.** 189.

EDUARDO LADISLAO HOLMBERG

"El ruiseñor y el artista." **2.** 146.

HUGH HOOD

"An Allegory of Man's Fate." **3.** 189.
"Around Theatres." **4.** 130.
"Bicultural Angela." **4.** 130.
"Breaking Off." **3.** 189.
"Flying a Red Kite." **3.** 189.
"Going Out as a Ghost." **3.** 189.
"The Good Listeners." **3.** 189.
"The Hole." **3.** 189.
"Light Shining Out of Darkness." **4.** 130.
"Looking Down from Above." **3.** 189; **4.** 130.
"None Genuine Without This Signature." **3.** 189.
"One Way North and South." **4.** 130.
"Predictions of Ice." **4.** 130.
"The River Behind Things." **4.** 130.
"The Sportive Centre of Saint Vincent de Paul." **4.** 131.
"Starting Again on Sherbrooke Street." **4.** 131.
"Thanksgiving: Between Junetown and Caintown." **3.** 189.
"Three Halves of a House." **3.** 189.

"The Village Inside." **4.** 131.
"The Woodcutter's Third Son." **3.** 189.

MARY HOOD

"Finding the Chain." **5.** 153.

JOHNSON JONES HOOPER

"The 'Tallapoonsy Vollantares' Meet the Enemy." **1.** 94.

PAUL HORGAN

"The Candy Colonel." **3.** 190.
"The Captain's Watch." **3.** 190.
"National Honeymoon." **3.** 190.
"The Peach Stone." **3.** 190.
"The Surgeon and the Nun." **3.** 190.

HORI TATSUO

"The Beautiful Village." **3.** 190.
"The Fake Rubens." **3.** 190.
"The Holy Family." **3.** 190.

CLYDE HOSEIN

"I'm a Presbyterian, Mr. Kramer." **4.** 131.

LUCILA HOSILLOS

"Baptism-Escape." **5.** 153.

BRANT HOUSE

"Curse of the Mandarin's Fan." **3.** 190.

JAMES HOWARD

"The Director." **3.** 190.

ROBERT ERVIN HOWARD

"Beyond the Black River." **3.** 190; **5.** 153.
"Black Canaan." **3.** 190; **5.** 154.
"The Black Stone." **3.** 191.
"The Blonde Goddess of Bal Sagoth." **3.** 191.
"By This Axe I Rule." **5.** 154.
"The Dark Man." **5.** 154.
"The Devil in Iron." **3.** 191.
"The Footfall Within." **5.** 154.
"For the Love of Barbara Allen." **5.** 154.
"The Frost Giant's Daughter" [originally "Gods of the North"]. **3.** 191.
"The God in the Bowl." **3.** 191.
"The Grey God Passes." **5.** 154.
"The Hour of the Dragon." **4.** 131.
"Jewels of Gwahlur." **3.** 191.
"Kings of the Night." **3.** 191.
"The Mansion of Unholy Magic." **3.** 191.
"Men of the Shadows." **5.** 154.
"The Mirrors of Tuzun Thune." **5.** 154.
"The Moon of Skulls." **5.** 154.
"Nekht Semerkeht." **5.** 154.
"The People of the Black Circle." **3.** 191.
"The Phoenix on the Sword" [revision of "By This Axe I Rule"]. **3.** 191; **4.** 131.
"Pigeons from Hell." **3.** 191; **5.** 154.
"The Pool of the Black One." **3.** 191.
"Queen of the Black Coast." **3.** 191; **5.** 154.
"Red Nails." **3.** 191; **5.** 154.
"Red Shadows." **3.** 191; **5.** 154.
"Rogues in the House." **3.** 191; **5.** 154.
"The Scarlet Ruse." **3.** 192.
"The Shadow Kingdom." **3.** 192; **5.** 154.
"The Shadow of the Vulture." **5.** 155.
"Shadows in the Moonlight." **3.** 192.
"Shadows in Zamboula." **3.** 192.
"The Skull of Silence." **5.** 155.
"The Slithering Shadow." **3.** 192.
"The Thunder-Rider." **3.** 192; **5.** 155.
"The Tower of the Elephant." **3.** 192.
"The Treasure of Tranicos." **3.** 192.
"The Vale of Lost Women." **3.** 192; **5.** 155.
"The Valley of the Lost." **5.** 155.
"The Valley of the Worm." **4.** 131; **5.** 155.
"Wings in the Night." **3.** 192; **5.** 155.
"A Witch Shall Be Born." **3.** 192; **5.** 155.
"Worms of the Earth." **3.** 192; **5.** 155.

ROBERT ERVIN HOWARD and L. SPRAGUE DE CAMP

"The Road of Eagles." **3.** 192.

SIDNEY HOWARD

"The God They Left Behind Them." **2.** 146.
"The Homesick Lady." **2.** 146.
"A Likeness of Elizabeth." **2.** 146.
"Mrs. Vietch: A Segment of Biography." **2.** 146.
"The Stars in Their Courses." **2.** 146.
"Such Women as Ellen Steele." **2.** 146.
"Transatlantic." **2.** 146.

E. W. HOWE

"Doctor Gilkerson." **3 ed.** 337.

WILLIAM DEAN HOWELLS

"A Circle in the Water." **3.** 193.
"A Difficult Case." **1.** 94.
"Editha." **3 ed.** 338; **2.** 146; **5.** 155.
"His Apparition." **2.** 146.
"How I Lost a Wife." **4.** 131.
"Niagara Revisited." **4.** 131.
"The Pearl." **3.** 193.
"A Romance of Real Life." **3 ed.** 338.
"A Sleep and a Forgetting." **1.** 94; **3.** 193.

MARY HOWITT

"The Lost White Woman." **4.** 131.

BOHUMIL HRABAL

"Palaverers." **2.** 146.

HSIAO HUNG [same as XIAO HONG or ZHANG NAIYING]

"At the Foot of the Mountain." **1.** 95.
"The Bridge." **1.** 95.
"A Cry in the Wilderness." **1.** 95.
"Flight from Danger." **1.** 95.
"Hands." **1.** 95.
"On the Oxcart." **1.** 95.
"Vague Expectations." **1.** 95.

HSÜ SHIH-HENG

"Punishment." **3.** 193.

RICARDA HUCH

"Der letzte Sommer." **3 ed.** 338.

W[ILLIAM] H[ENRY] HUDSON

"Dead Man's Plack." **3.** 193.
"Marta Riquelme." **3.** 193; **4.** 131.
"Niño Diablo." **3.** 193.
"An Old Thorn." **3.** 193.
"El Ombú." **3.** 193; **4.** 131.
"Pelino Viera's Confession." **3.** 193.
"Story of a Piebald Horse." **3.** 193.

LANGSTON HUGHES

"Berry." **3 ed.** 338.
"Big Meeting." **3 ed.** 338.
"Blessed Assurance" [originally "Du, Meine Zuversicht"]. **3 ed.** 338.
"The Blues I'm Playing." **3 ed.** 338; **1.** 95; **3.** 194.
"Christmas Song." **3 ed.** 338.
"Conversation on the Corner." **3.** 194.
"Cora Unashamed." **3 ed.** 338; **3.** 194.
"Father and Son." **3 ed.** 338; **1.** 95; **3.** 194.
"Feet Live Their Own Life." **5.** 155.
"A Good Job Gone." **3 ed.** 338.
"Home" [originally "The Folks at Home"]. **3 ed.** 338.
"Jazz, Jive and Jam." **3.** 194.
"Little Dog." **3 ed.** 339; **3.** 194.
"Luani of the Jungles." **3.** 194.
"Mary Winowsky." **3 ed.** 339.
"Mother and Child." **3 ed.** 339.
"On the Road." **3 ed.** 339.
"On the Way Home." **3 ed.** 339.
"One Christmas Eve." **3 ed.** 339.
"Passing." **3 ed.** 339.
"Poor Little Black Fellow." **3 ed.** 339.
"Powder-White Face." **3 ed.** 339.
"Professor." **3 ed.** 339.
"Red-Headed Baby." **3 ed.** 339.
"Rejuvenation Through Joy." **3 ed.** 339.
"Sailor Ashore." **3 ed.** 339.
"Slave on the Block." **3 ed.** 339; **5.** 155.
"Slice Him Down." **3 ed.** 340.
"Something in Common." **3 ed.** 340.
"'Tain't So." **3 ed.** 340.
"Ways and Means." **3 ed.** 340.
"Who's Passing for Who?" **3 ed.** 340.

RICHARD HUGHES

"The Cart." **3 ed.** 340; **4.** 132.
"Jungle." **4.** 132.
"Llwyd." **3 ed.** 340; **4.** 132.
"Lochinvárovič." **4.** 132.
"Monoculism: A Fable." **4.** 132.
"Poor Man's Inn." **3 ed.** 340.

TED HUGHES

"The Rain Horse." **3.** 194.
"The Thought Fox." **5.** 155.

JESSLYN H. HULL

"A Yellow Angel." **2.** 147.

WILLIAM HUMPHREY

"A Job of the Plains." **3.** 194; **4.** 132.

JAMES GIBBONS HUNEKER

"Pan." **3 ed.** 340.

T. A. G. HUNGERFORD

"Green Grow the Rushes." **4.** 132.
"Wong Chu and the Queen's Letterbox." **4.** 132.

HAMLEN HUNT

"Tonight We Eat Leaning." **3 ed.** 340.

ZORA NEALE HURSTON

"Behold de Rib." **4.** 132.
"Black Death." **1.** 95.
"Drenched in Light." **3 ed.** 341; **2.** 147; **5.** 156.
"The Gilded Six-Bits." **3 ed.** 341; **2.** 147; **5.** 156.
"John Redding Goes to Sea." **3 ed.** 341; **2.** 147; **3.** 194.
"Muttsy." **2.** 147; **5.** 156.
"Spunk." **3 ed.** 341; **2.** 147; **3.** 194; **5.** 156.
"Sweat." **3 ed.** 341; **1.** 95; **5.** 156.

INTIZĀR HUSAIN

"The Dolorous City." **2.** 147.
"The Lost Ones." **2.** 147.
"The Stairway." **2.** 147.
"The Yellow Cur." **2.** 147.

ALDOUS HUXLEY

"After the Fireworks." **3 ed.** 341.
"Chawdron." **3 ed.** 341.
"The Claxtons." **3 ed.** 341.
"A Country Walk." **3 ed.** 341.
"Cynthia." **3 ed.** 341.
"The Death of Lully." **3 ed.** 341.
"Eupompus Gave Splendour to Art by Numbers." **3 ed.** 341.
"The Farcical History of Richard Greenow." **3 ed.** 341.
"Frad." **3 ed.** 341.
"The Gioconda Smile." **3 ed.** 341–42.
"Green Tunnels." **3 ed.** 342.
"Happily Ever After." **3 ed.** 342; **1.** 95.
"Happy Families." **3 ed.** 342.
"Little Mexican." **3 ed.** 342.
"Nuns at Luncheon." **3 ed.** 342.
"The Rest Cure." **3 ed.** 342.
"Sir Hercules." **3 ed.** 342.
"The Tillotson Banquet." **3 ed.** 342.
"Two or Three Graces." **3 ed.** 342; **3.** 194.
"Uncle Spencer." **3 ed.** 342.
"Young Archimedes." **3 ed.** 342; **3.** 195.

HWANG CHUN-MING

"Days of Looking at the Sea." **2.** 147.
"The Drowning of an Old Cat." **2.** 148.
"The Fish." **2.** 148.
"The Gong." **2.** 148.
"His Son's Big Doll." **2.** 148.
"Ringworms." **2.** 148.
"The Story of Ch'ing-fan Kung." **2.** 148.

IBUSE MASUJI

"The Carp." **5.** 156.
"The Charcoal Bus." **3.** 195.
"Chōhei on an Uninhabited Island." **5.** 156.
"Chōhei's Grave." **5.** 156.
"Confinement." **5.** 156.
"The Day of a Memorial Service for a Bell." **5.** 156.
"The Far-Worshiping Commander." **3.** 195.
"The Fire God." **5.** 156.
"A General Account of Aogashima." **5.** 156.
"A Guide to the Ravine." **5.** 156.
"Kuchisuke's Valley." **5.** 156.
"Lieutenant Lookeast." **5.** 157.
"Morikichi from Beppu Village on Oki Island." **5.** 157.
"Papaya." **5.** 157.
"Pilgrim's Inn." **5.** 157.
"Plum Blossom by Night." **5.** 157.
"The River." **5.** 157.
"Sawan on the Roof." **5.** 157.
"The Sutra Case." **5.** 157.
"A Talk with Abu Bakr." **5.** 157.
"Wabisuke." **5.** 157.
"A Young Girl's Wartime Diary." **5.** 157.

JORGE ICAZA

"Disorientation." **5.** 157.
"Interpretation." **5.** 157.
"Thirst." **5.** 157.
"Whelps." **5.** 157.

YUSUF [YOUSSEF] IDRIS

"Addiction." **3.** 195.
"An Affair of Honour." **3.** 195.
"Ahmad of the Local Council." **3.** 195.
"The Aorta." **3.** 195.
"The Bottom of the City." **2.** 149.
"Bus Stop." **3.** 195.
"Caught Red-Handed." **3.** 195.
"The Chair Bearer." **3.** 195.
"The Cheapest of Nights." **3.** 195.
"City Dregs." **5.** 158.
"The Concave Mattress." **3.** 195.
"The Curtain." **3.** 195.
"The Deception." **3.** 195.
"A Dining Table." **3.** 195.
"The Dromedary Riders." **3.** 195.
"The End of the World." **3.** 196.
"Farahat's Republic." **2.** 148; **3.** 196; **5.** 158.
"Five Hours." **3.** 196.
"The Fourth Case." **2.** 148.
"The Game." **3.** 196.
"The Glance." **3.** 196.
"The Greatest Sin." **3.** 196.
"A Ground Whisper." **3.** 196.
"The Hermaphrodite." **3.** 196.
"House of Flesh." **5.** 158.
"Impossible." **3.** 196.
"The Incident." **3.** 196.
"A Job." **3.** 196.
"The Journey." **3.** 196; **4.** 132.
"The Machine." **3.** 196.
"The Major Operation." **3.** 196.
"The Master of Egypt." **3.** 196.
"The Miracle." **3.** 196.
"Mother of the World." **3.** 196.
"Old Age Without Madness." **3.** 197.
"The Omitted Letter." **4.** 132; **5.** 158.
"On Cellophane Paper." **3.** 197.
"The Ow Ow Language." **3.** 197.
"The People." **3.** 197.
"The Point." **3.** 197.
"Sayyed's Father." **2.** 148.
"She." **3.** 197.
"The Sin." **3.** 197.
"The Sphinx." **3.** 197.
"A Story with a Thin Voice." **3.** 197.
"A Summer Night." **3.** 197.
"Sunset March." **3.** 197.
"The Sweetness of the Soul." **3.** 197.
"The Swing." **3.** 197.
"The Syren." **3.** 197.
"To Asyut." **3.** 197.
"Upon My Word of Honour and My Honesty." **3.** 197.
"Was It Really Necessary to Turn on the Light, Lili?" **3.** 197.
"The Wish." **3.** 198.

WITI IHIMAERA

"Catching-Up." **4.** 133.
"Fire on Greenstone." **4.** 133.
"The Greenstone Patu." **3.** 198.
"Halcyon." **3.** 198.
"The House with Sugarbag Windows." **4.** 133.
"I, Ozymandias." **4.** 133.
"The Truth of the Matter." **3.** 198; **4.** 133.
"The Whale." **3.** 198; **4.** 133.

IKEDA MASUO

"To the Aegean Sea." **5.** 158.

IKUTA KIZAN

"The City." **3.** 198.

NATALIYA ILYINA

"The Return." **3.** 198.

EUGÈNE IONESCO

"The Colonel's Photograph." **4.** 133.
"Oriflamme." **3.** 198.
"Rhinoceros." **1.** 95–96; **2.** 148.

JOHN IRVING

"Lost in New York." **4.** 133.
"The Pension Grillparzer." **4.** 133.
"Vigilance." **4.** 133.

WASHINGTON IRVING

"The Adalantado of the Seven Cities." **2.** 148.
"The Adventure of My Aunt." **3 ed.** 343; **2.** 148; **3.** 198; **5.** 158.
"The Adventure of My Uncle." **3 ed.** 343; **2.** 149; **3.** 198; **5.** 158.
"The Adventure of the German Student." **3 ed.** 343; **1.** 96; **2.** 149; **3.** 198; **4.** 133; **5.** 158.

"The Adventure of the Mason." **2.** 149.
"The Adventure of the Mysterious Picture." **3 ed.** 343; **2.** 149; **3.** 199; **5.** 158.
"The Adventure of the Mysterious Stranger." **3 ed.** 343.
"The Angler." **3 ed.** 343.
"Annette Delarbre." **3 ed.** 343; **4.** 133.
"The Bold Dragoon." **3 ed.** 343; **3.** 199.
"Buckthorne and His Friends." **4.** 134.
"Buckthorne, or The Young Man of Great Expectations." **3 ed.** 343.
"The Devil and Tom Walker." **3 ed.** 343; **2.** 149; **4.** 134; **5.** 158.
"Dolph Heyliger." **3 ed.** 343; **2.** 149; **3.** 199; **4.** 134; **5.** 158.
"The Italian Banditti." **4.** 134.
"The Legend of Prince Ahmed al Kamel." **3 ed.** 343; **2.** 149.
"The Legend of Sleepy Hollow." **3 ed.** 344; **1.** 96; **2.** 149; **3.** 199; **4.** 134; **5.** 158.
"The Legend of the Rose of the Alhambra." **3 ed.** 344.
"The Legend of the Three Beautiful Princesses." **2.** 149.
"The Legend of the Two Discreet Statues." **2.** 149.
"The Little Man in Black." **4.** 134.
"The Pride of the Village." **3 ed.** 344.
"Rip Van Winkle." **3 ed.** 344–45; **1.** 96; **2.** 149; **3.** 199; **4.** 134; **5.** 159.
"The Spectre Bridegroom." **3 ed.** 345; **1.** 96; **2.** 149; **3.** 199; **4.** 134.
"The Storm Ship." **2.** 150; **5.** 159.
"The Story of the Young Italian." **3 ed.** 345; **2.** 150; **4.** 134; **5.** 159.
"The Story of the Young Robber." **3 ed.** 345; **1.** 96; **5.** 159.
"The Stout Gentleman." **2.** 150.
"The Student of Salamanca." **3 ed.** 345; **2.** 150.
"The Wife." **3 ed.** 345–46.
"Wolfert Webber." **3 ed.** 346; **2.** 150; **3.** 199; **5.** 159.

CHRISTOPHER ISHERWOOD

"Ambrose." **1.** 96.
"The Hero." **1.** 96.
"On Ruegen Island." **1.** 96.
"Prater Violet." **3 ed.** 346.

ISHIKAWA JUN

"The Beautiful Woman." **3.** 199.
"Fugen." **3.** 199.
"The Golden Legend." **3.** 199.
"The Jesus of the Burned-Out Site." **3.** 199.
"The Song of Mars." **3.** 199.

FAZIL ABDULOVICH ISKANDER

"Constellation of the Goat-Buffalo." **3.** 200.
"My Uncle Had the Highest Principles." **3.** 200.
"On a Summer Day." **2.** 150.
"The Story of Old Xabug's Mule." **5.** 159.

MANJERI S. ISVARAN

"At His Nativity." **1.** 97.
"Consummation." **1.** 97.
"Immersion." **5.** 159.
"Sivaratri." **1.** 97.

VSEVOLOD IVANOV

"The Kid." **3 ed.** 346.
"Runaway Island." **3 ed.** 346.

IZUMI KYŌKA

"Night Patrolman." **3.** 200.
"Noble Blood, Heroic Blood." **3.** 200.
"The Operating Room." **3.** 200.
"A Song Under Lanterns." **3.** 200.

CHARLES JACKSON

"The Boy Who Ran Away." **3 ed.** 346.

SHIRLEY JACKSON

"After You, My Dear Alphonse." **3 ed.** 346; **1.** 97.
"The Beautiful Stranger." **1.** 97.
"The Bus." **1.** 97.
"Charles." **1.** 97.
"The Daemon Lover" [originally "The Phantom Lover"]. **1.** 97; **2.** 150; **4.** 134.
"Flower Garden." **1.** 97; **2.** 150.
"The Island." **1.** 97.
"The Little House." **1.** 97.
"The Lottery." **3 ed.** 346; **1.** 97; **2.** 150; **3.** 200; **4.** 134–35; **5.** 159.
"On the House." **1.** 97.

"The Possibility of Evil." **1.** 98.
"The Rock." **1.** 98.
"Seven Types of Ambiguity." **2.** 150.
"The Summer People." **3 ed.** 347; **1.** 98.
"The Tooth." **3.** 200.
"The Villager." **1.** 98.
"The Visit." **1.** 98; **4.** 135.
"The Witch." **3 ed.** 347.

W[ILLIAM] W[YMARK] JACOBS

"The Monkey's Paw." **2.** 150; **4.** 135.
"The Three Sisters." **4.** 135.

JENS PETER JACOBSEN

"Doctor Faust." **2.** 151.
"Mrs. Fönss." **2.** 151.
"Mogens." **2.** 151.
"The Plague in Bergamo." **2.** 151.
"A Shot in the Fog." **2.** 151.
"Strangers." **2.** 151.
"There Should Have Been Roses" [same as "From the Sketchbook"]. **2.** 151.
"Two Worlds." **2.** 151.

DAN JACOBSON

"Beggar My Neighbour." **3 ed.** 347; **2.** 151.
"The Zulu and the Zeide." **3 ed.** 347; **2.** 151.

RICARDO JAIMES FREYRE

"Justicia india." **5.** 159.

SVAVA JAKOBSDÓTTIR

"Accident." **1.** 98.

SAYYID MUHAMMAD ALI JAMAL-ZADEH

"The Bear Hug." **4.** 135.
"Every Man to His Deserts." **4.** 135.
"Mulla Qurban-Ali's Confession." **4.** 135.
"Persian Is Sugar." **4.** 135.
"The Politician." **4.** 135.
"Veylan Al-Dawleh." **4.** 135.

BRIAN JAMES

"Bungally." **3 ed.** 347.
"Coming Down from Tip-Top." **3 ed.** 347.
"Dolf." **3 ed.** 347.
"Jacob's Escape." **3 ed.** 347.
"Joe Waite's Lantern." **3 ed.** 347.
"Prayers for Rain." **3 ed.** 347.
"The Reign of Eugene Ham." **3 ed.** 347.
"Untimely Aid." **3 ed.** 347.

C[YRIL] L[IONEL] R[OBERT] JAMES

"La Divina Pastora." **4.** 135.
"Triumph." **4.** 136; **5.** 160.

HENRY JAMES

"The Abasement of the Northmores." **3 ed.** 347–48; **4.** 136; **5.** 160.
"Adina." **3 ed.** 348; **1.** 98.
"The Altar of the Dead." **3 ed.** 348; **1.** 98; **4.** 136; **5.** 160.
"The Aspern Papers." **3 ed.** 348–49; **1.** 98; **2.** 151; **3.** 200; **4.** 136; **5.** 160.
"At Isella." **3 ed.** 349; **4.** 136.
"The Author of 'Beltraffio.'" **3 ed.** 349–50; **3.** 200; **4.** 136; **5.** 160.
"The Beast in the Jungle." **3 ed.** 350–52; **1.** 98–99; **2.** 151–52; **3.** 201; **4.** 136; **5.** 160.
"The Beldonald Holbein." **3 ed.** 352; **1.** 99; **2.** 152; **4.** 137; **5.** 160.
"The Bench of Desolation." **3 ed.** 352–53; **1.** 99; **2.** 152; **3.** 201; **4.** 137; **5.** 160.
"Benvolio." **3 ed.** 353; **1.** 99; **2.** 152.
"The Birthplace." **3 ed.** 353; **1.** 99; **3.** 201; **4.** 137; **5.** 160.
"Broken Wings." **3 ed.** 353; **1.** 99; **4.** 137; **5.** 161.
"Brooksmith." **3 ed.** 353–54; **1.** 99; **4.** 137; **5.** 161.
"A Bundle of Letters." **3 ed.** 354; **1.** 99; **3.** 201; **4.** 137; **5.** 161.
"The Chaperon." **3 ed.** 354; **1.** 99; **4.** 137.
"Collaboration." **3 ed.** 354; **1.** 100; **5.** 161.
"Covering End." **3 ed.** 354; **1.** 100; **3.** 201; **4.** 137; **5.** 161.
"The Coxon Fund." **3 ed.** 354; **1.** 100; **4.** 137; **5.** 161.
"Crapy Cornelia." **3 ed.** 354; **1.** 100; **4.** 137; **5.** 161.
"Crawford's Consistency." **3 ed.** 354–55; **3.** 201; **4.** 137.
"Daisy Miller." **3 ed.** 355–56; **1.** 100; **2.** 152; **3.** 201; **4.** 137–38; **5.** 161.
"A Day of Days." **3 ed.** 356–57; **1.** 100; **2.** 152.

"The Death of the Lion." **3 ed.** 357; **1.** 100; **2.** 152; **4.** 138; **5.** 161.
"De Grey." **3 ed.** 357; **2.** 152; **4.** 138.
"The Diary of a Man of Fifty." **3 ed.** 357; **1.** 100; **2.** 152.
"The Escape." **3 ed.** 357.
"Eugene Pickering." **3 ed.** 357–58; **1.** 100; **2.** 152; **4.** 138.
"Europe." **3 ed.** 358; **4.** 138.
"The Figure in the Carpet." **3 ed.** 358–59; **1.** 100; **2.** 153; **3.** 202; **4.** 138; **5.** 161.
"Flickerbridge." **3 ed.** 359; **1.** 100; **2.** 153; **4.** 138.
"Fordham Castle." **3 ed.** 359; **1.** 100; **2.** 153; **4.** 138.
"Four Meetings." **3 ed.** 359–60; **1.** 100; **2.** 153; **4.** 138; **5.** 161.
"The Friends of the Friends" [originally "The Way It Came"]. **3 ed.** 360; **1.** 101; **3.** 202; **4.** 138; **5.** 162.
"Gabrielle de Bergerac." **3 ed.** 360; **4.** 138.
"Georgina's Reasons." **3 ed.** 360; **1.** 101.
"The Ghostly Rental." **3 ed.** 360–61; **3.** 202; **4.** 138; **5.** 162.
"The Given Case." **3 ed.** 361; **5.** 162.
"Glasses." **3 ed.** 361; **1.** 101; **4.** 139; **5.** 162.
"The Great Condition." **3 ed.** 361; **3.** 202; **4.** 139; **5.** 162.
"The Great Good Place." **3 ed.** 361; **1.** 101; **2.** 153; **3.** 202; **4.** 139; **5.** 162.
"Greville Fane." **3 ed.** 361–62; **1.** 101; **4.** 139; **5.** 162.
"Guest's Confession." **3 ed.** 362; **1.** 101; **4.** 139.
"Hugh Merrow." **5.** 162.
"The Impressions of a Cousin." **3 ed.** 362; **1.** 101.
"In the Cage." **3 ed.** 362; **1.** 101; **2.** 153; **3.** 202; **4.** 139; **5.** 162.
"An International Episode." **3 ed.** 362–63; **1.** 101; **3.** 202; **4.** 139.
"John Delavoy." **3 ed.** 363; **1.** 101; **2.** 153; **3.** 202; **4.** 139; **5.** 162.
"The Jolly Corner." **3 ed.** 363–64; **1.** 101; **2.** 153; **3.** 202–03; **4.** 139; **5.** 162.
"Julia Bride." **3 ed.** 364; **1.** 102; **4.** 139.
"Lady Barberina." **3 ed.** 364–65; **3.** 203; **4.** 139.
"A Landscape Painter." **3 ed.** 365; **2.** 154; **4.** 140; **5.** 162.
"The Last of the Valerii." **3 ed.** 365; **1.** 102; **2.** 154; **3.** 203; **4.** 140.
"The Lesson of the Master." **3 ed.** 365–66; **1.** 102; **2.** 154; **3.** 203; **4.** 140; **5.** 162.
"The Liar." **3 ed.** 366; **1.** 102; **2.** 154; **3.** 203; **4.** 140; **5.** 162.
"A Light Man." **3 ed.** 366; **2.** 154; **4.** 140.
"A London Life." **3 ed.** 366; **4.** 140.
"Longstaff's Marriage." **3 ed.** 366; **2.** 154.
"Lord Beaupré." **3 ed.** 367; **4.** 140.
"Louisa Pallant." **3 ed.** 367; **1.** 102; **3.** 203; **4.** 140; **5.** 163.
"Madame de Mauves." **3 ed.** 367–68; **1.** 102; **2.** 154; **3.** 203; **4.** 140; **5.** 163.
"The Madonna of the Future." **3 ed.** 368; **1.** 102; **2.** 154; **4.** 140.
"The Marriages." **3 ed.** 368; **1.** 102; **3.** 203; **4.** 140; **5.** 163.
"Master Eustace." **3 ed.** 368; **1.** 102; **3.** 203.
"Maud-Evelyn." **3 ed.** 368–69; **1.** 102; **2.** 154; **4.** 140; **5.** 163.
"The Middle Years." **3 ed.** 369; **1.** 102; **3.** 203; **4.** 140; **5.** 163.
"Miss Gunton of Poughkeepsie." **3 ed.** 369; **2.** 154; **4.** 140; **5.** 163.
"Mrs. Medwin." **3 ed.** 369; **1.** 102; **4.** 141; **5.** 163.
"Mrs. Temperly." **1.** 102.
"The Modern Warning" [originally "The Two Countries"]. **3 ed.** 369; **1.** 103; **3.** 203.
"Mora Montravers." **3 ed.** 369; **1.** 103; **3.** 203; **4.** 141.
"A Most Extraordinary Case." **3 ed.** 369–70; **2.** 154; **4.** 141; **5.** 163.
"My Friend Bingham." **3 ed.** 370; **2.** 155; **3.** 204; **4.** 141.
"A New England Winter." **3 ed.** 370; **1.** 103.
"The Next Time." **3 ed.** 370; **2.** 155; **3.** 204; **4.** 141; **5.** 163.
"Nona Vincent." **3 ed.** 370; **2.** 155; **4.** 141.
"Osborne's Revenge." **3 ed.** 370; **2.** 155.
"Owen Wingrave." **3 ed.** 370–71; **1.** 103; **3.** 204; **4.** 141.
"Pandora." **3 ed.** 371; **1.** 103; **4.** 141; **5.** 163.
"The Papers." **3 ed.** 371; **1.** 103; **2.** 155; **3.** 204; **5.** 163.
"A Passionate Pilgrim." **3 ed.** 371; **1.** 103; **2.** 155; **5.** 163.

"Paste." **3 ed.** 371–72; **1.** 103; **2.** 155; **3.** 204; **4.** 141; **5.** 163.
"The Patagonia." **3 ed.** 372; **1.** 103; **4.** 141; **5.** 163.
"The Path of Duty." **3 ed.** 372; **1.** 103; **3.** 204.
"The Pension Beaurepas." **3 ed.** 372; **1.** 103; **4.** 141; **5.** 164.
"The Point of View." **3 ed.** 372; **1.** 103.
"Poor Richard." **3 ed.** 372; **1.** 103; **2.** 155; **5.** 164.
"The Private Life." **3 ed.** 372–73; **4.** 141.
"A Problem." **3 ed.** 373.
"Professor Fargo." **3 ed.** 373; **1.** 103; **2.** 155; **3.** 204; **4.** 141.
"The Pupil." **3 ed.** 373–74; **1.** 103–04; **2.** 155; **3.** 204; **4.** 141; **5.** 164.
"Pyramus and Thisbe." **3 ed.** 374.
"The Real Right Thing." **2.** 155; **4.** 141; **5.** 164.
"The Real Thing." **3 ed.** 374–75; **1.** 104; **2.** 155; **3.** 204; **4.** 141–42; **5.** 164.
"The Romance of Certain Old Clothes." **3 ed.** 375; **1.** 104; **3.** 205; **4.** 142.
"Rose-Agathe." **1.** 104.
"A Round of Visits." **3 ed.** 375–76; **2.** 155; **4.** 142; **5.** 164.
"The Siege of London." **3 ed.** 376; **3.** 205; **4.** 142.
"Sir Dominick Ferrand." **3 ed.** 376.
"Sir Edmund Orme." **3 ed.** 376; **1.** 104; **3.** 205; **4.** 142.
"The Solution." **3 ed.** 376; **1.** 104.
"The Special Type." **3 ed.** 376; **5.** 164.
"Still Waters." **3 ed.** 376.
"The Story in It." **3 ed.** 376; **1.** 104; **2.** 155; **3.** 205; **4.** 142; **5.** 164.
"The Story of a Masterpiece." **3 ed.** 376–77; **2.** 156; **3.** 205; **4.** 142; **5.** 164.
"The Story of a Year." **3 ed.** 377; **1.** 104; **2.** 156; **5.** 164.
"The Sweetheart of M. Briseux." **3 ed.** 377; **2.** 156.
"The Third Person." **3 ed.** 377; **4.** 142; **5.** 164.
"The Tone of Time." **3 ed.** 377; **1.** 104; **2.** 156; **5.** 164.
"A Tragedy of Error." **3 ed.** 377; **2.** 156; **3.** 205; **5.** 164.
"Travelling Companions." **3 ed.** 377–78; **1.** 104; **3.** 205.
"The Tree of Knowledge." **3 ed.** 378; **1.** 104; **2.** 156; **4.** 142; **5.** 164.
"The Turn of the Screw." **3 ed.** 378–83; **1.** 104–05; **2.** 156–57; **3.** 205; **4.** 142–43; **5.** 164–65.
"The Two Faces." **3 ed.** 383; **1.** 105; **4.** 143; **5.** 165.
"The Velvet Glove." **3 ed.** 383; **1.** 105; **2.** 157; **3.** 205; **4.** 143; **5.** 165.
"Washington Square." **3 ed.** 383–84; **1.** 105; **2.** 157; **3.** 206; **4.** 143; **5.** 165.
"The Wheel of Time." **3 ed.** 384; **4.** 143.

M[ONTAGUE] R[HODES] JAMES

"After the Dark in the Playing Field." **3.** 206.
"The Ash-Tree." **3 ed.** 384; **2.** 157.
"Casting the Runes." **3.** 206.
"Count Magnus." **2.** 157.
"The Diary of Mr. Poynter." **3 ed.** 384; **3.** 206.
"An Episode of Cathedral History." **3.** 206.
"The Mezzotint." **2.** 157; **3.** 206; **5.** 165.
"Number 13." **3.** 206.
"Oh, Whistle and I'll Come to You, My Lad." **5.** 165.
"The Rose Garden." **3.** 206.
"The Uncommon Prayer Book." **3.** 206.

P. D. JAMES

"The Girl Who Loved Graveyards." **4.** 143.
"Great-Aunt Allie's Flypapers." **4.** 143.
"Moment of Power." **4.** 143.
"Murder, 1986." **4.** 143.
"The Murder of Santa Claus." **4.** 144.
"A Very Desirable Residence." **4.** 144.
"The Victim." **4.** 144.

AMALIA JAMILIS

"Night Work." **3.** 206.
"Los trabajos nocturnos." **3.** 206.

KRISTOFER JANSON

"Wives, Submit Yourselves Unto Your Husbands." **3.** 207.

TOVE JANSSON

"Cedric." **3.** 207.
"The Doll's House." **3.** 207.
"The Fir Tree." **3.** 207.

"The Invisible Child." **3.** 207.
"The Listener." **3.** 207.
"Locomotive." **3.** 207.
"Wolves." **3.** 207.

JOHN E. JENKINS

"Ginx's Baby." **1.** 105.

JOHANNES V. JENSEN

"Dolores." **3.** 207.
"Louison." **3.** 207.
"Vanished Forests." **3.** 207.
"Wombwell." **3.** 207.

JEROME K. JEROME

"Blasé Billy." **3 ed.** 384.
"The Choice of Cyril Harjohn." **3 ed.** 384.
"In Remembrance of John Ingerfield, and of Anne, His Wife." **3 ed.** 385.
"Johnson and Emily, or the Faithful Ghost." **3 ed.** 385.
"Malvina Brittany." **3 ed.** 385.
"The Man Who Went Wrong." **3 ed.** 385.
"The Materialization of Charles Mivanway." **3 ed.** 385.
"The Passing of the Third Floor Back." **3 ed.** 385.
"The Philosopher's Joke." **3 ed.** 385.
"The Soul of Nicholas Snyders." **3 ed.** 385.
"The Woman of the Saeter." **3 ed.** 385.

DOUGLAS JERROLD

"Ephraim Rue: The Victim of Society." **3 ed.** 385.
"A Lay of St. Gengulphus." **3 ed.** 385.
"The Lesson of Life." **3 ed.** 385.
"The Mayor of Hole-Cum-Corner." **3 ed.** 385.
"Mr. Peppercorn at Home." **3 ed.** 385.
"The Papers of a Gentleman-at-Arms." **3 ed.** 385.
"The Preacher Parrot." **3 ed.** 385.
"The Sick Giant and the Doctor Dwarf." **3 ed.** 386.
"A Wine Cellar." **3 ed.** 386.

SARAH ORNE JEWETT

"Andrew's Fortune." **3 ed.** 386; **2.** 157.
"Aunt Cynthy Dallett." **3 ed.** 386.
"An Autumn Holiday." **3 ed.** 386; **2.** 157.
"The Best China Saucer." **2.** 157.
"Beyond the Toll-Gate." **2.** 157.
"A Bit of Shore Life." **3 ed.** 386; **2.** 157.
"A Born Farmer." **3 ed.** 386; **4.** 144.
"The Captains." **2.** 157.
"The Circus at Denby." **2.** 157.
"The Confession of a House-Breaker." **3 ed.** 386; **3.** 207.
"The Courting of Sister Wisby." **3 ed.** 386; **2.** 158; **3.** 207; **4.** 144.
"Cunner-Fishing." **2.** 158; **3.** 208.
"A Dark Night." **3 ed.** 386.
"The Dulham Ladies." **3 ed.** 386; **2.** 158.
"A Dunnet Shepherdess." **3 ed.** 386; **2.** 158.
"An Every-Day Girl." **3 ed.** 387; **4.** 144.
"The Failure of David Berry." **2.** 158.
"Fame's Little Day." **3 ed.** 387.
"Farmer Finch." **3 ed.** 387; **4.** 144.
"The First Sunday in June." **3 ed.** 387.
"The Flight of Betsey Lane." **3 ed.** 387; **2.** 158; **4.** 144.
"The Foreigner." **3 ed.** 387; **2.** 158; **3.** 208; **4.** 144.
"From a Mournful Village." **3.** 208.
"A Garden Story." **3 ed.** 387; **4.** 144.
"The Girl with the Cannon Dresses." **3 ed.** 387; **2.** 158.
"The Gray Man." **3 ed.** 387.
"The Gray Mills of Farley." **3 ed.** 387.
"The Green Bowl." **3 ed.** 387; **4.** 144.
"The Growtown 'Bugle.'" **3 ed.** 387.
"A Guest at Home." **3 ed.** 387; **2.** 158; **4.** 144.
"The Guests of Mrs. Timms." **3 ed.** 388; **2.** 158.
"The Hiltons' Holiday." **3 ed.** 388.
"The Honey Tree." **3 ed.** 388.
"In a Country Practice." **3 ed.** 388.
"In Dark New England Days." **2.** 158; **3.** 208.
"In Shadow." **2.** 158.
"Jenny Garrow's Lovers." **3 ed.** 388; **2.** 158.
"The King of Folly Island." **3 ed.** 388; **2.** 158.
"Lady Ferry." **3 ed.** 388; **4.** 144.
"A Landlocked Sailor." **3 ed.** 388.
"The Landscape Chamber." **3 ed.** 388; **2.** 158.
"A Late Supper." **2.** 158.
"Law Lane." **3 ed.** 388; **2.** 159.

"A Lost Lover." **3 ed.** 388; **2.** 159.
"Luck of the Bogans." **4.** 144.
"Marsh Rosemary." **3 ed.** 388.
"Martha's Lady." **3 ed.** 388; **2.** 159; **4.** 145.
"Miss Chauncey." **2.** 159.
"Miss Manning's Minister." **3 ed.** 388.
"Miss Peck's Promotion." **3 ed.** 388; **2.** 159; **4.** 145.
"Miss Sydney's Flowers." **2.** 159; **4.** 145.
"Miss Tempy's Watchers." **3 ed.** 389; **2.** 159; **4.** 145.
"Mr. Bruce." **2.** 159.
"The Mistress of Sydenham Plantation." **3 ed.** 389; **2.** 159.
"My Lady Brandon and the Widow Jim." **2.** 159.
"Nancy's Doll." **2.** 159.
"A Native of Winby." **3 ed.** 389.
"A Neighbor's Landmark." **3 ed.** 389.
"The New Methuselah." **3 ed.** 389.
"A New Parishioner." **3 ed.** 389.
"An October Ride." **3.** 208.
"The Only Rose." **3 ed.** 389; **2.** 159; **3.** 208.
"Paper Roses." **3 ed.** 389.
"The Parshley Celebration." **3 ed.** 389.
"The Passing of Sister Barsett." **3 ed.** 389.
"Peach-Tree Joe." **3 ed.** 389.
"Peg's Little Child." **3 ed.** 389.
"A Pinch of Salt." **3 ed.** 389.
"A Player Queen." **4.** 145.
"The Queen's Twin." **3 ed.** 389; **4.** 145.
"The Shipwrecked Buttons." **2.** 159.
"The Shore House." **2.** 159.
"Sister Peacham's Turn." **3 ed.** 389.
"A Sorrowful Guest." **3 ed.** 390.
"A Spring Sunday." **3 ed.** 390.
"The Spur of the Moment." **3 ed.** 390.
"A Stage Tavern." **3 ed.** 390.
"Stolen Pleasures." **3 ed.** 390.
"Three Friends." **4.** 145.
"Tom's Husband." **3 ed.** 390; **2.** 159.
"A Village Shop." **2.** 159; **4.** 145.
"The Waiting Place." **2.** 160.
"A White Heron." **3 ed.** 390; **1.** 105–06; **2.** 160; **3.** 208; **4.** 145; **5.** 165.
"William's Wedding." **3 ed.** 390; **4.** 145.

RUTH PRAWER JHABVALA

"A Bad Woman." **5.** 166.
"A Course of English Studies." **5.** 166.
"An Experience of India." **5.** 166.
"The Housewife." **5.** 166.
"How I Became a Holy Mother." **4.** 145.
"Rose Petal." **5.** 166.

JIANG ZILONG

"A Factory Secretary's Diary." **4.** 146.
"Manager Qiao Assumes Office." **4.** 146.
"More About Manager Qiao." **4.** 146.

JIBRAN KHALIL JIBRAN

"Martha of the Village of Ban." **4.** 146.
"The Shout of Graves." **4.** 146.

JIN HE

"Re-encounter." **4.** 146.

NICK JOAQUÍN

"Guardia de Honor." **4.** 146.

B. S. JOHNSON

"A Few Selected Sentences." **3.** 208.

COLIN JOHNSON

"A Missionary Would I Have Been." **4.** 146; **5.** 166.

DOROTHY JOHNSON

"The Hanging Tree." **3.** 208; **5.** 166.
"Laugh in the Face of Danger." **3.** 208.
"Lost Sister." **3.** 208.
"A Man Called Horse." **3.** 208; **5.** 166.
"Prairie Kid." **3.** 209.
"Scars of Honor." **3.** 209.
"A Time of Greatness." **3.** 209.
"The Unbeliever." **3.** 209.
"War Shirt." **3.** 209.

JOSEPHINE JOHNSON

"John, Chapter VI." **3 ed.** 390.
"Safe." **3 ed.** 390.

LESLIE T. JOHNSON

"Seeker of To-Morrow." **3.** 209.

UWE JOHNSON

"An Absence" [originally "Eine Reise wegwohin, 1960"]. **3 ed.** 390.
"Osterwasser." **3.** 209.
"A Tavern Vanishes." **3 ed.** 390.

RICHARD MALCOLM JOHNSTON

"An Adventure of Mr. Joel Boozle." **2.** 160.
"The Combustion of Jim Rakestraw." **2.** 160.
"The Early Majority of Mr. Thomas Watts." **2.** 160.
"The Expensive Treat of Colonel Moses Grice." **1.** 106; **2.** 160.
"The Goosepond School." **1.** 106; **2.** 160.
"How Mr. Bill Williams Took the Responsibility." **1.** 106; **2.** 160.
"Investigations Concerning Mr. Jonas Lively." **2.** 160.
"Mr. Fortner's Marital Claims." **3 ed.** 391; **1.** 106; **2.** 160.
"Mr. Neelus Peeler's Conditions." **1.** 106; **2.** 160.
"Mr. Williamson Slippey and His Salt." **1.** 106.
"Old Friends and New Friends." **3 ed.** 391; **2.** 160.
"The Pursuit of Mr. Adiel Slack." **2.** 160.
"The Various Languages of Billy Moon." **2.** 160.

C. I. JOHNSTONE

"Mrs. Mark Luke; or, West Country Exclusive." **5.** 166.

ELIZABETH JOLLEY

"Grasshopper." **4.** 146.
"Hilda's Wedding." **4.** 146.
"Liberation." **4.** 146.
"Paper Children." **4.** 147.
"Two Men Running." **4.** 147.

GAYL JONES

"Asylum." **4.** 147.
"Return: A Fantasy." **3.** 209.
"White Rat." **1.** 106; **4.** 147.
"The Women." **4.** 147.

GWYN JONES

"Bad Blood." **4.** 147.
"The Brute Creation." **4.** 147.
"The Green Island." **4.** 147.
"Where My Dark Lover Lies." **4.** 147.
"A White Birthday." **4.** 147.

H. R. JONES

"Suicide Durkee's Last Ride." **5.** 166.

JAMES JONES

"A Bottle of Cream." **2.** 160.
"Greater Love." **2.** 161.
"The Ice-Cream Headache." **2.** 161.
"Just Like the Girl." **2.** 161.
"The Pistol." **2.** 161.
"The Temper of Steel." **2.** 161.
"The Tennis Game." **2.** 161.
"Two Legs for the Two of Us." **2.** 161.
"The Valentine." **2.** 161.
"The Way It Is." **2.** 161.

NEIL JONES

"The Jameson Satellite." **3.** 209.

RAYMOND F. JONES

"Noise Level." **2.** 161.

WILLIAM JONES

"Anaska Mimiwina." **3.** 209.
"Lydie." **3.** 209.

NEIL JORDAN

"A Love." **2.** 161.

GABRIEL JOSIPOVICI

"Contiguities." **4.** 147.
"Little Words." **4.** 147.
"Second Person Looking Out." **4.** 147.

JAMES JOYCE

"After the Race." **3 ed.** 391; **1.** 106; **2.** 161; **3.** 210; **4.** 148; **5.** 167.
"Araby." **3 ed.** 391–93; **1.** 106–07; **2.** 162; **3.** 210; **4.** 148; **5.** 167.
"The Boarding House." **3 ed.** 393; **1.** 107; **2.** 162; **3.** 210; **4.** 148; **5.** 167.
"Clay." **3 ed.** 393–95; **1.** 107; **2.** 162; **3.** 210; **4.** 148; **5.** 167.
"Counterparts." **3 ed.** 395; **1.** 107; **2.** 162; **3.** 210–11; **4.** 148.
"The Dead." **3 ed.** 395–98; **1.** 107; **2.** 162; **3.** 211; **4.** 148; **5.** 167.
"An Encounter." **3 ed.** 398–99; **1.** 107; **2.** 162; **3.** 211; **4.** 149; **5.** 168.

"Eveline." **3 ed.** 399–400; **1.** 107; **2.** 163; **3.** 211–12; **4.** 149; **5.** 168.
"Grace." **3 ed.** 400–01; **1.** 107; **2.** 163; **3.** 212; **4.** 149; **5.** 168.
"Ivy Day in the Committee Room." **3 ed.** 401–02; **1.** 107; **2.** 163; **3.** 212; **4.** 149; **5.** 168.
"A Little Cloud." **3 ed.** 402; **1.** 107; **2.** 163; **3.** 212; **4.** 149; **5.** 168.
"A Mother." **3 ed.** 402–03; **1.** 108; **2.** 163; **3.** 212; **4.** 149; **5.** 168.
"A Painful Case." **3 ed.** 403–04; **1.** 108; **2.** 163; **3.** 212–13; **4.** 149; **5.** 168.
"The Sisters." **3 ed.** 404–05; **1.** 108; **2.** 163; **3.** 213; **4.** 149; **5.** 168–69.
"Two Gallants." **3 ed.** 405–06; **1.** 108; **2.** 163; **3.** 213; **4.** 149.

FRANZ KAFKA

"Before the Law." **3 ed.** 406; **2.** 163; **3.** 213; **4.** 149; **5.** 169.
"Ein Besuch im Bergwerk." **3 ed.** 406; **5.** 169.
"Blumfeld, an Elderly Bachelor." **3 ed.** 406; **1.** 108; **3.** 213; **4.** 150; **5.** 169.
"The Bridge." **3.** 213; **5.** 169.
"The Bucket Rider." **3 ed.** 406.
"The Burrow." **3 ed.** 407; **1.** 108; **2.** 164; **3.** 213–14; **4.** 150; **5.** 169.
"The Cares of a Family Man." **3 ed.** 407–08; **1.** 108; **2.** 164; **3.** 214; **4.** 150; **5.** 169.
"Children on a Country Road." **3 ed.** 408; **2.** 164.
"A Common Confusion." **3 ed.** 408.
"The Conscription of Troops" [same as "The Levy of Troops"]. **3 ed.** 408, 416.
"Conversation with a Praying Man" [same as "Conversation with a Supplicant"]. **3 ed.** 408; **3.** 214.
"A Country Doctor." **3 ed.** 408–09; **1.** 108; **2.** 164; **3.** 214; **4.** 150; **5.** 169.
"Description of a Struggle." **3 ed.** 409; **2.** 164; **3.** 214; **4.** 150; **5.** 169.
"A Dream." **3 ed.** 410; **3.** 214.
"Eleven Sons." **3 ed.** 410; **2.** 164; **5.** 170.
"First Sorrow." **3 ed.** 410; **3.** 214; **5.** 170.
"A Fratricide." **3 ed.** 410; **1.** 108; **2.** 164; **4.** 150.
"The Giant Mole" [originally "The Village School Teacher"]. **3 ed.** 410; **1.** 111; **2.** 164; **3.** 214.
"Give It Up!" **3 ed.** 410; **3.** 214; **5.** 170.
"The Great Wall of China." **3 ed.** 410–11; **1.** 108–09; **2.** 164; **3.** 215; **4.** 150; **5.** 170.
"Homecoming." **3.** 215.
"A Hunger Artist." **3 ed.** 411–12; **1.** 109; **2.** 164–65; **3.** 215; **4.** 150; **5.** 170.
"The Hunter Gracchus." **3 ed.** 412; **1.** 109; **2.** 165; **3.** 215; **4.** 151; **5.** 170.
"A Hybrid" [same as "A Crossbreed"]. **3 ed.** 412; **4.** 151; **5.** 170.
"An Imperial Message." **3 ed.** 412; **3.** 215; **5.** 170.
"In Our Synagogue." **3 ed.** 412.
"In the Gallery." **3 ed.** 412–13; **1.** 109; **2.** 165; **3.** 215; **4.** 151; **5.** 170.
"In the Penal Colony." **3 ed.** 413–14; **1.** 109; **2.** 165; **3.** 215; **4.** 151; **5.** 170.
"Investigations of a Dog." **3 ed.** 414; **1.** 109; **2.** 165; **3.** 215; **4.** 151; **5.** 170.
"Jackals and Arabs." **3 ed.** 414; **2.** 165; **5.** 170.
"Josephine the Singer." **3 ed.** 414–15; **1.** 109; **2.** 165; **3.** 216; **4.** 151; **5.** 171.
"The Judgment." **3 ed.** 415–16; **1.** 109–10; **2.** 165; **3.** 216; **4.** 151; **5.** 171.
"The Knock on the Manor Gate." **3 ed.** 416; **2.** 166.
"A Little Fable." **3.** 216; **5.** 171.
"A Little Woman." **3 ed.** 416; **3.** 216; **5.** 171.
"The Married Couple." **3 ed.** 416.
"Memoirs of the Kalda Railroad." **3 ed.** 416.
"The Merchant Messner." **3 ed.** 417.
"Metamorphosis." **3 ed.** 417–19; **1.** 110; **2.** 166; **3.** 216–17; **4.** 151–52; **5.** 171.
"My Neighbor." **3 ed.** 419; **3.** 217; **5.** 171.
"The New Advocate." **3 ed.** 419; **1.** 110; **5.** 171.
"The Next Village." **3 ed.** 419; **5.** 171.
"An Old Page" [same as "An Old Manuscript"]. **3 ed.** 419; **2.** 166; **5.** 171–72.
"On a Little Railway in Russia." **3 ed.** 419.
"On the Tram." **3 ed.** 420; **5.** 172.
"Poseidon." **4.** 152.
"Prometheus." **3 ed.** 420; **4.** 152; **5.** 172.
"A Report to an Academy." **3 ed.** 420; **1.** 110; **2.** 166; **3.** 217; **4.** 152; **5.** 172.

"The Silence of the Sirens." **3 ed.** 420; **1.** 111; **2.** 166; **4.** 152; **5.** 172.
"The Spinning Top." **3 ed.** 416; **3.** 217; **5.** 172.
"Das Stadtwappen." **3 ed.** 420.
"The Stoker." **3 ed.** 420–21; **1.** 111; **5.** 172.
"Testimonials" [same as "Guarantors"]. **3.** 217.
"Unhappiness." **4.** 152; **5.** 172.
"Wedding Preparations in the Country." **3 ed.** 421; **3.** 217; **5.** 172.
"The White Horse." **3 ed.** 421.

NORMAN KAGAN

"The Mathenauts." **4.** 152.

AMALIA KAHANA-CARMON

"The Bright Light." **5.** 172.
"If I Found Favor in Your Eyes." **5.** 172.
"Neima Sasson Writes Poems." **5.** 172.
"To Build Herself a Home in the Land of Shinar." **5.** 172.

KAJII MOTOJIRO

"The Ascension of K." **2.** 166.
"The Lemon." **2.** 166; **3.** 217.
"The Scroll of Darkness." **2.** 166.
"Under the Cherry Tree." **2.** 166.

KAMBAYASHI AKATSUKI

"At St. John's Hospital." **3.** 217.
"The Fields." **3.** 217.

KAMELESHWAR [entire name]

"King Nirbansta." **3.** 217.

KAMURA ISOTA

"The Night of July 22nd." **3.** 218.
"The Torments of Karma." **3.** 218.

KANAI MIEKO

"Platonic Love." **5.** 173.

NIKOLAY KARAMZIN

"Anecdote." **3 ed.** 421.
"The Island of Bornholm." **3.** 218.
"A Knight of Our Time." **3 ed.** 421.
"Martha the Mayoress" [same as "Marfa . . ."]. **3 ed.** 421.
"My Confession." **3 ed.** 421.
"Poor Liza." **5.** 173.
"The Sensitive and the Cold." **3 ed.** 421.

MUSTAI KARIM

"A Long, Long Childhood." **3.** 218.

HERMANN KASACK

"The Dream of Death." **3 ed.** 421.
"Fälschungen." **3 ed.** 421.

KASAI ZENZŌ

"In the Same Boat." **5.** 173.
"A Mad Drunk's Monologue." **5.** 173.
"Morning Pilgrimage." **5.** 173.
"The Oppressed One." **5.** 173.
"A Stillbirth." **5.** 173.
"An Unhappy Father." **5.** 173.
"With the Children on My Hands" [same as "With the Children in Tow"]. **3.** 218; **5.** 173.
"Wriggling Creatures." **5.** 173.
"Young Oak Leaves" [same as "Young Pasania Leaves"]. **3.** 218; **5.** 173.

IVAN KATAEV [KATAYEV]

"Milk." **3.** 219.
"Under Clear Skies." **4.** 153.

VALENTIN KATAEV [KATAYEV]

"At Night." **3.** 218.
"The Child." **3.** 218.
"The Drum." **3.** 218.
"The Father." **3.** 218.
"Fire." **3.** 218.
"The Flag." **3.** 218.
"The Gold Nib." **3.** 218.
"In Winter." **3.** 219.
"The Iron Ring." **3.** 219.
"Kranz's Experiment." **3.** 219; **4.** 153.
"Our Father Who Art in Heaven." **3 ed.** 421.
"Rodion Zhukov." **3.** 219.
"Sir Henry and the Devil." **3.** 219.
"Things." **3.** 219.
"Violet." **3.** 219.

NAIM KATTAN

"Les Bagages." **3.** 219.
"L'Étude." **3.** 219.
"La Fin du voyage." **3.** 219.
"L'Hôtel." **3.** 219.
"Rue Abou Nouas." **3.** 219.
"Le Substitut." **3.** 219.
"Sur le Balcon." **3.** 219.
"Les Yeux fermés." **3.** 220.

STEVE KATZ

"43." **3.** 220.
"Trip." **3.** 220.

PATRICK KAVANAGH

"The Lay of the Crooked Knight." **2.** 166.

VENIAMIN KAVERIN

"Engineer Shvarts." **3.** 220.

KAWABATA YASUNORI

"Crystal Fantasies." **3.** 220.
"The House of the Sleeping Beauties." **5.** 173.
"The Izu Dancer." **3 ed.** 422; **3.** 220; **5.** 173.
"Lyric Poem." **3.** 220.
"A Man Who Does Not Smile." **1.** 111.
"The Moon in the Water." **2.** 167; **3.** 220; **4.** 153.
"Of Birds and Beasts." **2.** 167; **3.** 220.
"One Arm." **2.** 167; **5.** 174.
"Reencounter." **2.** 167.

EMMANUIL KAZAKEVICH

"The Blue Notebook." **3.** 220.
"Enemies." **3.** 220.

YURI KAZAKOV

"Adam and Eve." **3 ed.** 422; **2.** 167.
"Antlers." **3 ed.** 422.
"Autumn in the Woods." **3 ed.** 422.
"Here Comes a Dog." **3 ed.** 422.
"Morning Calm." **3 ed.** 422.
"The Outsider." **3 ed.** 422.
"The Smell of Bread." **3.** 220.

WELDON KEES

"Applause." **4.** 153.
"The Ceremony." **4.** 153.
"Downward and Away." **4.** 153.
"Escape in Autumn." **4.** 153.
"The Evening of the Fourth of July." **4.** 153.
"Gents 50¢; Ladies 25¢." **4.** 153.
"I Should Worry." **4.** 153.
"The Life of the Mind." **4.** 153.
"A Man to Help." **4.** 153.
"Mrs. Lutz." **4.** 153.
"The Sign Painters." **4.** 154.
"So Cold Outside." **4.** 154.
"This Is Home." **4.** 154.
"Three Pretty Nifty Green Suits." **4.** 154.
"A Walk Home." **4.** 154.

DAVID H. KELLER

"The Feminine Metamorphosis." **3.** 221.
"The God Wheel." **3.** 221.
"The Menace." **1.** 111.
"The Revolt of the Pedestrians." **1.** 111; **3.** 221.
"Tree of Evil." **3.** 221.
"The Yeast Men." **3.** 221.

GOTTFRIED KELLER

"Die Berlocken." **3 ed.** 422.
"Clothes Make the Man." **3 ed.** 422; **1.** 111; **5.** 174.
"The Dance Legend." **3 ed.** 422.
"Dietegen." **3 ed.** 423; **4.** 154.
"Don Correa." **3 ed.** 423.
"Dorothea's Flower-Basket." **3 ed.** 423.
"Eugenia." **3 ed.** 423.
"Das Fähnlein der sieben Aufrechten." **3 ed.** 423.
"Der Geistersehen." **3 ed.** 423.
"Der Landvogt von Greifensee." **3 ed.** 423; **2.** 167.
"The Misused Love Letter." **3 ed.** 423; **5.** 174.
"Der Narr auf Manegg." **3 ed.** 423.
"Pankraz der Schmoller." **3 ed.** 423.
"The Poor Baroness." **3 ed.** 423.
"Regine." **3 ed.** 423.
"Regula Amrain and Her Youngest Son." **3 ed.** 423.
"Der Schlimm-heilige." **3 ed.** 423.

"Der Schmied seines Glückes." **3 ed.** 423.
"The Three Righteous Comb-Makers." **3 ed.** 424; **1.** 111; **3.** 221; **4.** 154.
"Ursula." **3 ed.** 424.
"Das Verloren Lachen." **3 ed.** 424; **2.** 167.
"A Village Romeo and Juliet." **3 ed.** 424; **1.** 111; **2.** 167; **4.** 154.
"The Virgin and the Devil." **3 ed.** 424.
"The Virgin and the Nun." **3 ed.** 425.
"The Virgin as Knight." **3 ed.** 425.

WILLIAM MELVIN KELLEY

"Cry for Me." **3.** 221.
"The Poker Party." **1.** 111.

E. LINCOLN KELLOGG

"A Partly Celestial Tale." **2.** 167; **3.** 221.

MAEVE KELLY

"The Last Campaign." **2.** 167.

MICHAEL KERNAN

"The Doll Named Silvio." **5.** 174.

KEN ELTON KESEY

"Abdul and Ebenezer." **3.** 221.
"The Day After Superman Died." **3.** 221.
"Search for the Secret Pyramid." **3.** 221.
"Thrice-Thrown Tranny-Man or Ogre at Palo Alto High School." **3.** 222.
"Tools from My Chest." **3.** 222.

DANIEL KEYES

"Flowers for Algernon." **1.** 111; **2.** 168.

EDUARD VON KEYSERLING

"Der Beruf." **3 ed.** 425.

DANIIL KHARMS [DANIIL IVANOVICH YUVACHEV]

"The Cashier." **3.** 222.
"Elizabeth Bam." **5.** 174.
"The Old Woman." **3.** 222; **5.** 174.
"Vindication." **5.** 174.

LEONARD KIBERA

"It's a Dog's Share in Our Kinshasa." **1.** 112.
"Silent Song." **1.** 112.
"The Stranger." **1.** 112.
"The Tailor." **1.** 112.

VIRGINIA KIDD and JAMES BLISH

"On the Wall of the Lodge." **3.** 222.

BENEDICT KIELY

"A Ball of Malt and Madame Butterfly." **3 ed.** 425; **5.** 174.
"Blackbird in a Bramble Bough." **2.** 168; **3.** 222.
"A Bottle of Brown Sherry." **3 ed.** 425.
"A Cow in the House." **3 ed.** 425.
"Down Then by Derry." **2.** 168.
"God's Own People." **5.** 174.
"A Great God's Angel Standing." **3 ed.** 425; **3.** 222.
"Heroes in the Dark House." **3 ed.** 425.
"Homes on the Mountain." **3 ed.** 425.
"The House in Jail Square." **3 ed.** 425.
"A Journey to the Seven Streams." **3 ed.** 425.
"The Little Bishop." **3 ed.** 425.
"The Little Wrens and Robins." **3 ed.** 425.
"Maiden's Leap." **5.** 174.
"The Pilgrims." **3 ed.** 426.
"A Room in Linden." **2.** 168; **5.** 174.
"The Shortest Way Home." **3 ed.** 426.
"Soldier, Red Soldier." **3 ed.** 426.
"Ten Pretty Girls." **3 ed.** 426.
"A View from the Treetop." **3 ed.** 426.
"The White Wild Bronco." **3 ed.** 426; **2.** 168.

KIKUO ITAYA

"The Pilgrimage of the Curse." **3.** 222.
"The Robber and the Flute." **3.** 222.

SIEW YUE KILLINGLEY

"Everything's Arranged." **4.** 154.
"A Question of Dowry." **4.** 154.

LEE KILLOUGH

"The Existential Man." **3.** 222.
"The Lying Ear." **3.** 222.

KICHUNG KIM

"A Homecoming." **3.** 223.

JAMAICA KINCAID

"At the Bottom of the River." **4.** 154.
"Girl." **5.** 175.
"In the Night." **4.** 155.
"A Walk to the Jetty." **4.** 155.
"What Have I Been Doing Lately?" **4.** 155.
"Windless." **5.** 175.

GRACE KING

"The Balcony." **2.** 168.
"Bayou L'Ombre." **3.** 223.
"Bonne Maman." **2.** 168.
"The Chevalier Alain de Triton." **3.** 223.
"A Crippled Hope." **3 ed.** 426; **2.** 168; **3.** 223.
"Destiny." **2.** 168.
"A Domestic Interior." **3.** 223.
"A Drama of Three." **3.** 223.
"Earthlings." **3.** 223.
"La Grande Demoiselle." **2.** 168; **3.** 223.
"Grandmother's Grandmother." **3.** 223.
"Joe." **3.** 223; **4.** 155.
"The Little Convent Girl." **2.** 168.
"Making Progress." **2.** 168.
"Mardriléne; or, The Festival of the Dead." **5.** 175.
"Monsieur Motte." **5.** 175.
"A Quarrel with God." **2.** 168.
"The Story of a Day." **2.** 168; **3.** 223.

STEPHEN KING

"Apt Pupil." **5.** 175.
"Body." **5.** 175.
"Breathing Method." **5.** 175.
"Children of the Corn." **3.** 223; **5.** 175.
"I Am the Doorway." **5.** 175.
"Jerusalem's Lot." **5.** 175.
"Last Rung on the Ladder." **5.** 175.
"The Mangler." **5.** 175.
"Night Surf." **5.** 175.
"Rita Hayworth and Shawshank Redemption." **5.** 176.

SUSAN PETIGRU KING

"The Best of Friends." **3.** 223.
"A Male Flirt." **3.** 224.
"A Man of Honor." **3.** 224.
"Old Maidism vs. Marriage." **3.** 224.
"Sylvia's World." **3.** 224.

MAXINE HONG KINGSTON

"The Ghost-Mate." **5.** 176.
"On Mortality." **3.** 224.

W[ILLIAM] P[ATRICK] KINSELLA

"The Ballad of the Public Trustee." **5.** 176.
"Barefoot and Pregnant in Des Moines." **5.** 176.
"Baseball Spurs." **5.** 176.
"The Battery." **5.** 176.
"The Bear Went Over the Mountain." **5.** 176.
"Black Wampum." **5.** 176.
"Caraway." **5.** 176.
"Dr. Don." **5.** 176.
"Fiona the First." **5.** 176.
"First Names and Empty Pockets." **5.** 176.
"The Four-Sky-Thunder Bundle." **5.** 176.
"Fugitives." **5.** 176.
"Horse Collars." **5.** 176.
"Indian Joe." **5.** 177.
"Jokemaker." **5.** 177.
"Lark Song." **5.** 177.
"The Last Pennant Before Armageddon." **5.** 177.
"The Managers." **5.** 177.
"The Mother's Dance." **5.** 177.
"The Night Mammy Mota Tied the Record." **5.** 177.
"Panache." **5.** 177.
"Parts of the Eagle." **5.** 177.
"Pretend Dinners." **5.** 177.
"The Rattlesnake Express." **5.** 177.
"Scars." **5.** 177.
"Shoeless Joe Jackson Comes to Iowa." **5.** 177.
"Sister Ann of the Cornfields." **5.** 177.
"The Thrill of the Grass." **5.** 177.
"Weasels and Ermines." **5.** 177.
"Yellow Scarf." **5.** 177.

RUDYARD KIPLING

"The Arrest of Lieutenant Golightly." **3 ed.** 426.
"As Easy as A. B. C." **3 ed.** 426; **3.** 224; **5.** 178.
"At the End of the Passage." **3 ed.** 426; **2.** 169; **3.** 224; **4.** 155; **5.** 178.
"At the Pit's Mouth." **3 ed.** 426.
"Aunt Ellen." **3 ed.** 426.

"Baa, Baa, Black Sheep." **3 ed.** 426; **2.** 169; **5.** 178.
"Beauty Spots." **3 ed.** 427; **3.** 224.
"Below the Mill Dam." **1.** 112; **5.** 178.
"Bertram and Bimi." **5.** 178.
"Beyond the Pale." **3 ed.** 427; **2.** 169; **3.** 224; **4.** 155; **5.** 178.
"Black Jack." **3 ed.** 427; **3.** 224.
"Bread Upon the Waters." **3 ed.** 427.
"The Bridge-Builders." **3 ed.** 427; **3.** 224; **4.** 155; **5.** 178.
"The Bronckhorst Divorce Case." **3 ed.** 427.
"Brother Square-Toes." **3 ed.** 427.
"Brugglesmith." **3 ed.** 427.
"The Brushwood Boy." **3 ed.** 427; **3.** 224; **4.** 155; **5.** 178.
"The Bull That Thought." **3 ed.** 427–28; **3.** 224; **4.** 155; **5.** 178.
"By Word of Mouth." **4.** 155.
"The Captive." **4.** 155.
"The Children of the Zodiac." **3 ed.** 428; **3.** 224; **5.** 178.
"The Church That Was at Antioch." **3 ed.** 428; **1.** 112; **3.** 224; **5.** 178.
"Cold Iron." **3 ed.** 428.
"The Comprehension of Private Copper." **3 ed.** 428; **1.** 112.
"A Conference of the Powers." **3 ed.** 428.
"The Conversion of Aurelian McGoggin." **3 ed.** 428.
"The Conversion of St. Wilfred." **5.** 178–79.
"The Courting of Dinah Shadd." **3 ed.** 428; **3.** 225.
"Dayspring Mishandled." **3 ed.** 428; **1.** 112; **3.** 225; **4.** 155; **5.** 179.
"Debits and Credits." **4.** 155.
"The Devil and the Deep Sea." **3 ed.** 429; **5.** 179.
"The Disturber of Traffic." **3 ed.** 429.
"The Dog Hervey." **3 ed.** 429; **1.** 112; **5.** 179.
"The Dream of Duncan Parrenness." **2.** 169; **5.** 179.
"The Drums of the Fore and Aft." **3 ed.** 429.
"Dymchurch." **5.** 179.
"East and West." **3 ed.** 429.
"The Edge of the Evening." **3 ed.** 429; **2.** 169.
"The Enemies to Each Other." **3 ed.** 429; **3.** 225.
"The Enlightenments of Pagett, M.P." **3 ed.** 429; **4.** 156.
"An Error in the Fourth Dimension." **3 ed.** 429.
"The Eye of Allah." **3 ed.** 429; **3.** 225; **5.** 179.
"Fairy-Kist." **3 ed.** 429; **5.** 179.
"False Dawn." **3 ed.** 429.
"The Finest Story in the World." **3 ed.** 430; **5.** 179.
"A Friend of the Family." **3 ed.** 430.
"Friendly Brook." **3 ed.** 430; **1.** 112; **2.** 169.
"A Friend's Friend." **3 ed.** 430.
"The Galley-Slave." **2.** 169.
"The Gardener." **3 ed.** 430; **1.** 112; **2.** 169; **3.** 225; **5.** 179.
"The Gate of the Hundred Sorrows." **5.** 179.
"Georgie Porgie." **3.** 225.
"An Habitation Enforced." **3 ed.** 430; **1.** 112; **5.** 179.
"Haunted Subalterns." **4.** 156.
"The Head of the District." **3 ed.** 430; **2.** 169; **4.** 156.
"His Chance in Life." **2.** 169; **4.** 156; **5.** 179.
"His Private Honour." **3 ed.** 430; **3.** 225.
"The Horse-Marines." **3.** 225.
"The House Surgeon." **3 ed.** 430; **1.** 112; **5.** 179.
"How Fear Came." **3 ed.** 430.
"In the House of Suddhoo." **3 ed.** 430–31.
"In the Interests of the Brethren." **3 ed.** 431; **5.** 179.
"In the Presence." **3 ed.** 431.
"In the Rukh." **3 ed.** 431.
"In the Same Boat." **3 ed.** 431; **1.** 112; **5.** 180.
"The Janeites." **3 ed.** 431.
"The Judgment of Dungara." **2.** 169; **5.** 180.
"Kaa's Hunting." **3 ed.** 431.
"The Killing of Hatim Tai." **4.** 156.
"The King's Ankus." **3 ed.** 431.
"The Knife and the Naked Chalk." **3 ed.** 431; **5.** 180.
"The Legs of Sister Ursula." **3 ed.** 431.
"The Limitations of Pambe Serang." **5.** 180.

"Lispeth." **2.** 169; **5.** 180.
"Little Foxes." **3 ed.** 431; **4.** 156.
"Love-o'-Women." **3 ed.** 431; **5.** 180.
"The Madness of Private Ortheris." **3 ed.** 431; **2.** 169; **3.** 225.
"A Madonna of the Trenches." **3 ed.** 431; **1.** 112; **3.** 225; **5.** 180.
"The Maltese Cat." **3 ed.** 431; **5.** 180.
"The Man Who Was." **3 ed.** 432.
"The Man Who Would Be King." **3 ed.** 432; **1.** 113; **2.** 169; **3.** 225; **4.** 156; **5.** 180.
"The Manner of Men." **3.** 225; **5.** 180.
"The Mark of the Beast." **3 ed.** 432; **4.** 156; **5.** 180.
"Marklake Witches." **3.** 225.
"Mary Postgate." **3 ed.** 432; **1.** 113; **3.** 225; **4.** 156; **5.** 180.
"A Matter of Fact." **5.** 180.
"The Miracle of Purun Shagat." **3 ed.** 432; **5.** 181.
"The Miracle of St. Jubanus." **3.** 225; **5.** 181.
"Miss Youghal's Sais." **5.** 181.
"Mrs. Bathurst." **3 ed.** 432–33; **1.** 113; **2.** 170; **3.** 226; **5.** 181.
"The Moral Reformers." **3 ed.** 433.
"My Son's Wife." **3 ed.** 433; **1.** 113; **3.** 226; **4.** 156.
"My Sunday at Home." **3 ed.** 433.
"Naboth." **3 ed.** 433.
"Namgay Doola." **3 ed.** 433.
"On Greenhow Hill." **3 ed.** 433; **2.** 170; **3.** 226; **5.** 181.
"On the City Wall." **3 ed.** 433; **3.** 226; **5.** 181.
"On the Gate." **3 ed.** 433; **5.** 181.
".007." **3 ed.** 433.
"The Other Man." **3 ed.** 433.
"The Phantom Rickshaw." **3 ed.** 433; **2.** 170; **4.** 156; **5.** 181.
"Pig." **3 ed.** 433–34.
"A Priest in Spite of Himself." **3 ed.** 434.
"The Prophet and the Country." **3 ed.** 434; **2.** 170.
"The Puzzler." **1.** 113.
"The Record of Badalia Herodsfoot." **3 ed.** 434.
"Red Dog." **3 ed.** 434.
"The Rescue of Pluffles." **3 ed.** 434.
"The Return of Imray" [same as "The Recrudescence of Imray"]. **3 ed.** 434; **2.** 170; **4.** 156; **5.** 181.
"A Sahibs' War." **3 ed.** 434.
"The Satisfaction of a Gentleman." **3 ed.** 434.
"Sea Constables: A Tale of '15." **3 ed.** 434; **1.** 113; **3.** 226.
"The Ship That Found Herself." **3 ed.** 434; **5.** 181.
"Simple Simon." **5.** 181.
"The Son of His Father." **2.** 170.
"The Story of Muhammad Din." **3 ed.** 434; **5.** 181.
"The Strange Ride of Morrowbie Jukes." **3 ed.** 434; **1.** 113; **2.** 170; **4.** 156; **5.** 181.
"Swept and Garnished." **3 ed.** 434; **1.** 113; **2.** 170; **5.** 182.
"Teem." **3 ed.** 434.
"The Tender Achilles." **3 ed.** 435; **5.** 182.
"They." **3 ed.** 435; **1.** 113; **3.** 226; **4.** 156; **5.** 182.
"Three and—an Extra." **5.** 182.
"The Threshold." **5.** 182.
"Thrown Away." **5.** 182.
"The Tie." **3 ed.** 435.
"To Be Filed for Reference." **3 ed.** 435; **2.** 170.
"Tods' Amendment." **3 ed.** 435.
"The Tomb of His Ancestors." **3 ed.** 435; **3.** 226; **5.** 182.
"The Tree of Justice." **3 ed.** 435; **3.** 226.
"Uncovenanted Mercies." **3 ed.** 435; **3.** 226; **5.** 182.
"Unprofessional." **3 ed.** 435; **1.** 113; **3.** 226.
"The Village That Voted the Earth Was Flat." **3 ed.** 435; **5.** 182.
"The Vortex." **1.** 113.
"A Wayside Comedy." **3 ed.** 435; **1.** 113; **5.** 182.
"The White Seal." **3 ed.** 436.
"William the Conqueror." **3 ed.** 436; **5.** 182.
"Wireless." **3 ed.** 436; **2.** 170; **5.** 182.
"The Wish House." **3 ed.** 436; **1.** 113; **2.** 170; **3.** 226; **4.** 157; **5.** 182.
"With the Night Mail." **3 ed.** 436.
"Without Benefit of Clergy." **3 ed.** 436; **3.** 226; **4.** 157; **5.** 182.
"The Woman in His Life." **1.** 113; **5.** 182.
"Wressley of the Foreign Office." **3 ed.** 436.

RUSSELL KIRK

"Ex Tenebris." **4.** 157.
"Lost Lake." **4.** 157.
"The Princess of All Lands." **4.** 157.
"The Reflex-Man of Whinnymuir Close." **4.** 157.
"Saviorgate." **4.** 157.
"Skyberia." **4.** 157.

SARAH KIRSCH

"Merkwürdiges Beispiel weiblicher Entschlossheit." **3.** 226.

PERRI KLASS

"Not a Good Girl." **4.** 157.

A. M. KLEIN

"The Bells of Sobor Spasitula." **5.** 183.

T. E. D. KLEIN

"Black Man with a Horn." **4.** 157.
"Children of the Kingdom." **4.** 157.
"Events at Poroth Farm." **4.** 157.
"Petey." **4.** 157.

HEINRICH VON KLEIST

"The Beggar Woman of Locarno." **3 ed.** 436; **1.** 113–14; **3.** 227.
"The Duel." **3 ed.** 437; **1.** 114; **2.** 170; **3.** 227; **4.** 158; **5.** 183.
"The Earthquake in Chile." **3 ed.** 437; **1.** 114; **2.** 170; **3.** 227; **4.** 158; **5.** 183.
"The Engagement in Santo Domingo." **3 ed.** 437; **1.** 114; **3.** 227; **4.** 158; **5.** 183.
"The Foundling." **3 ed.** 437–38; **1.** 114–15; **2.** 170–71; **3.** 227; **4.** 158; **5.** 183.
"The Marquise of O—." **3 ed.** 438; **1.** 115; **3.** 227; **4.** 159; **5.** 183.
"Michael Kohlhaas." **3 ed.** 438–39; **1.** 115; **2.** 171; **3.** 227; **4.** 159; **5.** 183.
"St. Cecilia or the Power of Music." **3 ed.** 439; **1.** 115; **2.** 171; **3.** 227; **4.** 159.
"Über das Marionettentheater." **5.** 183.

ALEXANDER KLUGE

"Eingemachte Elefantenwünsche." **5.** 183.
"Lernprozessen mit tödlichem Ausgang." **3.** 227–28.
"Ein Liebesversuch." **5.** 184.

EDWARD KNATCHBULL-HUGESSON

"The Pig-Faced Queen." **5.** 184.

NIGEL KNEALE

"Oh, Mirror, Mirror." **5.** 184.

DAMON FRANCIS KNIGHT

"The Country of the Kind." **5.** 184.
"The Earth Quarter." **3.** 228.
"Masks." **3.** 228.
"Not with a Bang." **3.** 228.
"Stranger Station." **3.** 228; **5.** 184.
"To Serve Man." **3.** 228.

ERIC KNIGHT

"Flurry at the Sheep Dog Trial." **3 ed.** 439.

RAYMOND KNISTER

"The Dance at Corncob Corners." **5.** 184.
"The First Day of Spring." **5.** 184.
"Grapes." **5.** 184.
"Hackman's Night." **5.** 184.
"Indian Summer." **5.** 184.
"Innocent Man." **5.** 184.
"The Strawstack." **5.** 184.

KOBAYASHI TAKIJI

"The Factory Ship." **5.** 185.

KŌDA ROHAN

"The Bearded Samurai" [same as "The Bearded Man"]. **1.** 115; **5.** 185.
"Destiny." **1.** 116.
"Encounter with a Skull." **1.** 116; **5.** 185.
"The Five-Storied Pagoda." **5.** 185.
"Love Bodhisattva." **1.** 116.
"Snowflakes Dancing." **1.** 116.
"A Sword." **1.** 116.
"Tarōbō." **3.** 228.
"Viewing of a Painting." **1.** 116.

L. A. KOELEWIJN [NIC BEETS]

"Best Forgotten." **3.** 228.

A. KOLLONTAY

"The Love of Three Generations." **3 ed.** 439.

MANUEL KOMROFF

"Hamlet's Dagger." **3 ed.** 439.

VIKTOR KONETSKY

"A Tale About Radio Operator Kamushkin." **2.** 171.

KŌNO TAEKO

"The Last Time." **5.** 185.

MARIA KONOPNICKA

"My Children's Dolls." **3 ed.** 439.
"Smoke." **3 ed.** 439.
"The Wine Fortress." **3 ed.** 439.
"Wojciech Zapala." **3 ed.** 440.

KONSTANTIN KONSTANTINOV

"Day by Day." **3 ed.** 440.

AUGUST KOPISCH

"Ein Carnevalsfest." **3 ed.** 440.

CYRIL M. KORNBLUTH

"The Little Black Bag." **3.** 228.
"The Marching Morons." **3.** 228.
"The Mindworm." **3.** 228.

JINCY KORNHAUSER

"Melinda Falling." **5.** 185.

VLADIMIR KOROLENKO

"Makar's Dream." **3 ed.** 440.

JOSEF KORZENIOWSKI

"After Thirty Years." **3 ed.** 440.
"It's Good to Know Even This in These Hard Times." **3 ed.** 440.
"The Second Wife." **3 ed.** 440.

WILLIAM KOTZWINKLE

"Follow the Eagle." **1.** 116; **5.** 185.

MIKHAIL KOZAKOV

"The Man Who Kissed the Ground." **3 ed.** 440.

VADIM KOZHEV

"Shield and Sword." **3.** 229.

JOSEF IGNACY KRASZEWSKI

"Abracadabra." **3 ed.** 440.
"Adam." **3 ed.** 440.
"The Biography of an Organist of Sokal." **3 ed.** 440.
"The Butterfly." **3 ed.** 440.
"A Cemetery Story." **3 ed.** 441.
"A Concert in Krynica." **3 ed.** 441.
"A Country Fair in Yanovka." **3 ed.** 441.
"Old-Fashioned Letter Writing." **3 ed.** 441.
"Psiarek." **3 ed.** 441.
"The Treasure." **3 ed.** 441.
"The Woman at the Church Door." **3 ed.** 441.

HENRY KREISEL

"The Almost Meeting." **5.** 185.
"The Broken Globe." **5.** 185.

V. KRESTOVSKY [NADEZHDA KHVOSCHIUSKAYA]

"Behind the Wall." **4.** 159.
"The Teacher." **4.** 159.

ERNST KREUDER

"Phantom der Angst." **3 ed.** 441.

UYS KRIGE

"The Charcoal Burners." **3 ed.** 441.
"The Coffin." **3 ed.** 441.
"Death of a Zulu." **3 ed.** 441.
"The Dream." **3 ed.** 441.

TOM KRISTENSEN

"The Disaster." **3.** 229.
"What Is Death?" **3.** 229.

ANATOLII KRITONOSOV

"Burn, Burn Brightly." **2.** 171.

JAMES F. KRONENBERG

"The Avenging Joss." **2.** 171.

WILHELM KUCCHELBECKER

"Ado." **3.** 229.
"The Land of the Headless." **3.** 229.

MILAN KUNDERA

"The Hitchhiking Game." **3.** 229; **4.** 159; **5.** 185.
"Lost Letters." **3.** 229.

KUNIKIDA DOPPO

"Beef and Potatoes" [same as "Meat and Potatoes"]. **3.** 229; **5.** 186.
"Old Gen." **3.** 229; **4.** 159; **5.** 186.
"Spring Birds." **4.** 159.
"Unforgettable People." **3.** 229.

ALEXANDER KUPRIN

"At the Circus." **1.** 116.
"The Bracelet of Garnets" [same as "The Garnet Bracelet"]. **3 ed.** 441; **1.** 116.
"Delirium." **1.** 116.
"Emerald." **1.** 116.
"The Enquiry." **1.** 116.
"In the Dark." **1.** 116.
"The Jewess." **1.** 116.
"The Last Debut." **1.** 116.
"Off the Street." **1.** 116.
"A Quiet Life." **1.** 117.
"The River of Life." **3 ed.** 441; **1.** 117.
"Staff-Captain Rybnikow." **1.** 117.
"The Swamp." **1.** 117.

KURAHASHI YUKIMO

"Partei." **5.** 186.

KUROSHINA DENJI

"A Flock of Circling Crows." **3.** 229.
"Siberia in the Snow." **3.** 230.
"The Sleigh." **3.** 230.

HERMANN KURZ

"Die blasse Apollonia." **3 ed.** 442.
"Horoscope." **3 ed.** 442.

ISOLDE KURZ

"Anno Pestis." **3 ed.** 442.
"Die Dame von Forli." **3 ed.** 442.
"Der heilige Sebastian." **3 ed.** 442.
"Die Humanisten." **3 ed.** 442.
"Die Mär von der schönen Galiana." **3 ed.** 442.
"Schuster und Schneider." **3 ed.** 442.
"Unsere Carlotta." **3 ed.** 442.
"Die Verdammten." **3 ed.** 442.

HENRY KUTTNER

"Mimsy Were the Borogoves." **3.** 230.

HENRY KUTTNER and C[ATHERINE] L. MOORE

"Vintage Season." **2.** 171.

HAROLD SONNY LADOO

"The Quiet Peasant." **4.** 160.

OLIVER LA FARGE

"Captain Tom and Mother Carey's Chickens." **3 ed.** 442.
"Haunted Ground." **3 ed.** 442.
"North Is Black." **3 ed.** 442.
"Old Century River." **3 ed.** 442.
"La Spécialté de M. Duclos." **3 ed.** 442.

R[APHAEL] A[LOYSIUS] LAFFERTY

"All But the Words." **5.** 186.
"Among the Hairy Earthmen." **4.** 160.
"Bubbles When They Burst." **5.** 186.
"The Cliff Climbers." **5.** 186.
"Configuration of the North Shore." **5.** 186.
"Continued on the Next Rock." **5.** 186.
"Days of Grass, Days of Straw." **5.** 186.
"Hog-Belly Honey." **5.** 186.
"Interurban Queen." **5.** 186.
"Rivers of Damascus." **5.** 186.
"The Six Fingers of Time." **4.** 160.
"Slow Tuesday Night." **4.** 160.
"Thus We Frustrate Charlemagne." **5.** 186.
"The Weird World." **5.** 186.

CARMEN LAFORET

"The Cat's Secret." **2.** 171.
"The Christmas Gift." **2.** 171.
"The Condemned." **2.** 171.
"The Dead Woman." **2.** 171.
"An Engagement." **2.** 171.
"The Inferno." **2.** 172.

"The Last Night." **2.** 172.
"The Last Summer." **2.** 172.
"The Little Girl." **2.** 172.
"The Newlyweds." **2.** 172.
"Off to School." **2.** 172.
"The Photograph." **2.** 172.
"The Piano." **2.** 172.
"The Pleasure Trip." **2.** 172.
"The Return." **2.** 172.
"Rosamunda." **2.** 172.
"The Unburdening." **2.** 172.

PÄR LAGERKVIST

"The Children's Campaign." **3 ed.** 443.
"Father and I." **3 ed.** 443; **1.** 117.
"The Fragment." **3 ed.** 443.
"The Hangman." **1.** 117.
"The Lift That Went Down into Hell." **3 ed.** 443.
"Maurice Fleury." **3 ed.** 443.
"The Strange Country." **3 ed.** 443.

SELMA LAGERLÖF

"The Changeling." **3.** 230.
"Herr Arnes penningar." **3.** 230.
"The Outcast." **3.** 230.
"The Son of Ingemar." **3.** 230.
"The Story of a Country House" [same as "From a Swedish Country House"]. **3.** 230.

ENRIQUE A. LAGUERRE

"The Enemy." **3.** 230; **5.** 187.
"Pacholí." **3.** 230.
"Roots." **3.** 230.
"Shipwreck." **3.** 230; **5.** 187.

ALEX LA GUMA

"At the Portagee's." **4.** 160.
"Blankets." **2.** 172.
"Coffee for the Road." **1.** 117; **4.** 160.
"The Gladiators." **1.** 117; **2.** 172; **4.** 160.
"A Glass of Wine." **4.** 160.
"Late Edition." **4.** 160.
"The Lemon Orchard." **2.** 172; **3.** 230; **4.** 160.
"A Matter of Taste." **1.** 117; **2.** 172.
"Nocturne" [originally "Étude"]. **2.** 173; **4.** 160.
"Out of Darkness." **2.** 173; **4.** 160.
"Slipper Satin." **2.** 173; **4.** 160.
"Tattoo Marks and Nails." **3.** 231; **4.** 160.
"Thang's Bicycle." **4.** 161.
"A Walk in the Night." **2.** 173.

GEORGE LAMMING

"A Wedding in Spring." **3 ed.** 443.

TOMMASO LANDOLFI

"Gogol's Wife." **2.** 173; **3.** 231.
"Hands." **2.** 173.
"Wedding Night." **3 ed.** 443.

SPENCER LANE

"The Origin of Thought." **3.** 231.

ELISABETH LANGGÄSSER

"Beginning of the Season." **3 ed.** 443.

ROMUALDAS LANKAUSKAS

"One More Day." **3 ed.** 443.
"So Short Is the Month of August." **3 ed.** 444.
"Sprites Live in the Woods." **3 ed.** 444.
"Wandering Sand." **3 ed.** 444.

VALERY LARBAUD

"Amants, heureux amants . . . ." **2.** 173.
"Beauté, mon beau souci." **2.** 173.
"Devoirs de vacances." **2.** 173.
"Mon plus secret conseil." **2.** 173.
"La Paix et le salut." **2.** 173.

RING LARDNER

"Alibi Ike." **3 ed.** 444; **1.** 117.
"Anniversary." **3 ed.** 444; **2.** 173.
"The Battle of the Century." **3 ed.** 444.
"A Busher's Letters Home." **3 ed.** 444.
"A Caddy's Diary." **3 ed.** 444; **1.** 117.
"Champion." **3 ed.** 444; **1.** 117; **2.** 173.
"A Chip of the Old Block." **3 ed.** 444.
"Contract." **3 ed.** 444; **2.** 173.
"A Day with Conrad Green." **3 ed.** 444; **2.** 174.
"Dinner." **3 ed.** 445.
"Ex Parte." **3 ed.** 445.
"The Golden Honeymoon." **3 ed.** 445; **1.** 117; **2.** 174; **4.** 161.

"Gullible's Travels." **2.** 174.
"Haircut." **3 ed.** 445; **1.** 117; **2.** 174; **4.** 161; **5.** 187.
"Harmony." **3 ed.** 445.
"Horseshoes." **3 ed.** 445.
"Hurry Kane." **3 ed.** 446.
"I Can't Breathe." **3 ed.** 446; **1.** 118.
"Insomnia." **3 ed.** 446; **1.** 118.
"Liberty Hall." **2.** 174.
"The Love Nest." **3 ed.** 446; **2.** 174.
"The Maysville Minstrel." **3 ed.** 446; **4.** 161.
"Mr. and Mrs. Fix-It." **2.** 174.
"My Roomy." **3 ed.** 446; **1.** 118; **2.** 174.
"Nora." **3 ed.** 446.
"Now and Then." **3 ed.** 446.
"Old Folks' Christmas." **2.** 174.
"Poodle." **2.** 174.
"Reunion." **2.** 174.
"Rhythm." **3 ed.** 446; **2.** 174.
"Some Like Them Cold." **3 ed.** 446; **1.** 118; **2.** 174; **3.** 231.
"Sun Cure." **3 ed.** 446; **4.** 161.
"There Are Smiles." **3 ed.** 446.
"Three Without Doubled." **2.** 174.
"A Visit to the Garrison." **3 ed.** 447.
"Who Dealt?" **3 ed.** 447; **2.** 174.
"Zone of Quiet." **3 ed.** 447; **2.** 174; **4.** 161.

NELLA LARSEN

"Passing." **4.** 161.
"Quicksand." **4.** 161.

MAHMUT TAHIR LASHIN

"The Talk of the Village." **3.** 231.

KURD LASSWITZ

"Against the Law of the World: A Tale from the Year 3877." **3.** 231.
"Aladdin's Magic Lamp." **3.** 231.
"From the Diary of an Ant." **3.** 231.
"How the Devil Fetched the Professor." **3.** 231.
"On the Soap-Bubble." **3.** 231.
"To the Zero-Point of Existence: A Tale from the Year 2371." **3.** 232.
"The University Library." **3.** 232.

JOSÉ VICTORINO LASTARRÍA

"Rosa." **5.** 187.

IRVING LATTON

"Vacation in La Voiselle." **5.** 187.

KEITH LAUMER

"The War Against the Yukks." **5.** 187.

MARGARET LAURENCE

"A Bird in the House." **5.** 187.
"The Drummer of All the World." **3 ed.** 447; **2.** 175; **3.** 232; **4.** 161.
"A Fetish for Love." **4.** 161.
"Godman's Master." **3 ed.** 447; **2.** 175; **3.** 232; **4.** 161.
"A Gourdful of Glory." **2.** 175.
"The Half-Husky." **2.** 175.
"Horses of the Night." **4.** 162; **5.** 187.
"The Loons." **2.** 175; **5.** 187.
"Mask of the Bear." **4.** 162.
"The Merchant of Heaven." **3 ed.** 447; **2.** 175.
"Nanuk." **3 ed.** 447.
"The Perfume Sea." **3 ed.** 447; **2.** 175; **3.** 232; **4.** 162.
"The Rain Child." **2.** 175.
"The Sound of Singing." **2.** 175.
"To Set Our House in Order." **3 ed.** 447; **2.** 175; **3.** 232; **4.** 162.
"The Tomorrow-Tamer." **3 ed.** 447; **2.** 175; **3.** 232; **4.** 162.
"Uncertain Flowering." **5.** 187.
"The Voice of Adamo." **3 ed.** 447; **2.** 175; **3.** 232.

MARY LAVIN

"An Akoulina of the Irish Midlands." **1.** 118; **2.** 176; **3.** 232.
"Assigh." **3.** 232.
"At Sallygap." **3 ed.** 448; **1.** 118; **2.** 176; **3.** 232.
"The Becker Wives." **3 ed.** 448; **1.** 118; **2.** 176; **3.** 232; **5.** 188.
"Bridal Sheets." **1.** 118; **2.** 176.
"Brigid." **3.** 233.
"Brother Boniface." **3 ed.** 448.
"The Bunch of Grapes." **3 ed.** 448.

"The Cemetery." **3 ed.** 448.
"The Convert." **2.** 176; **3.** 233.
"The Cuckoo-Spit." **3 ed.** 448; **1.** 118; **2.** 176; **3.** 233.
"A Cup of Tea." **3 ed.** 448; **1.** 118.
"Eterna." **2.** 176; **3.** 233.
"A Fable." **3 ed.** 448; **3.** 233.
"The Face of Hate." **3.** 233.
"Frail Vessel." **3 ed.** 448.
"A Gentle Soul." **1.** 118; **2.** 176.
"The Great Wave." **3 ed.** 448; **1.** 118; **2.** 176; **3.** 233.
"The Green Grave and the Black Grave." **3 ed.** 448; **1.** 118; **2.** 176.
"Grief." **3 ed.** 448.
"Happiness." **3 ed.** 448; **1.** 118; **2.** 176.
"A Happy Death." **3 ed.** 448; **1.** 118; **2.** 176.
"The Haymaking." **3 ed.** 449; **2.** 176.
"Heart of Gold." **1.** 119; **2.** 176.
"In a Café." **1.** 119; **2.** 176; **3.** 233.
"In the Middle of the Fields." **3 ed.** 449; **1.** 119; **2.** 176; **3.** 233.
"The Inspector's Wife." **2.** 176.
"The Joy Ride." **3 ed.** 449.
"A Likely Story." **2.** 177.
"Lilacs." **3 ed.** 449; **2.** 177.
"Limbo." **2.** 177.
"The Little Prince." **3 ed.** 449; **1.** 119; **2.** 177.
"The Long Ago." **3 ed.** 449; **2.** 177.
"The Long Holidays." **2.** 177.
"The Lost Child." **1.** 119; **2.** 177; **3.** 233.
"Love Is for Lovers." **1.** 119; **2.** 177.
"Loving Memory." **3 ed.** 449; **1.** 119; **2.** 177.
"The Lucky Pair." **3.** 233.
"A Memory." **1.** 119; **2.** 177; **3.** 233.
"Miss Holland." **1.** 119; **2.** 177; **3.** 233.
"A Mock Auction." **1.** 119.
"A Mug of Water." **3.** 233.
"My Molly." **2.** 177.
"My Vocation." **1.** 119.
"The New Gardener." **1.** 119.
"The Nun's Mother." **2.** 177.
"An Old Boot." **1.** 119.
"One Evening." **1.** 119; **2.** 177.
"One Summer." **3 ed.** 449; **1.** 119.
"The Pastor of Six Mile Bush." **1.** 119; **2.** 177; **3.** 233.
"The Patriot Son." **3 ed.** 449; **1.** 119; **3.** 234.
"Posy." **3 ed.** 449; **2.** 177; **3.** 234.
"A Pure Accident." **1.** 120; **2.** 177.
"The Sand Castle." **3 ed.** 449; **1.** 120.
"Sarah." **3 ed.** 449; **1.** 120; **2.** 177.
"Say Could That Lady Be I?" **3 ed.** 449; **2.** 178; **3.** 234.
"Scylla and Charybdis." **3 ed.** 449.
"The Shrine." **2.** 178; **3.** 234; **5.** 188.
"A Single Lady." **3 ed.** 449; **2.** 178.
"The Small Bequest." **1.** 120; **2.** 178; **3.** 234.
"A Story with a Pattern." **3 ed.** 449; **1.** 120; **2.** 178.
"Sunday Brings Sunday." **3 ed.** 449; **1.** 120; **2.** 178.
"Tom." **1.** 120.
"Tomb of an Ancestor." **1.** 120.
"A Tragedy." **3 ed.** 450; **1.** 120.
"Trastevere." **1.** 120.
"Villa Violetta." **3.** 234.
"A Visit to the Cemetery." **3 ed.** 450.
"A Wet Day." **3.** 234.
"What's Wrong with Aubretia?" **1.** 120.
"The Widow's Son." **3 ed.** 450; **1.** 120; **2.** 178.
"The Will." **3 ed.** 450; **1.** 120; **2.** 178.
"A Woman Friend." **1.** 120; **2.** 178.
"The Yellow Beret." **1.** 120.
"The Young Girls." **2.** 178.

WARNER LAW

"The Harry Hastings Method." **2.** 178; **3.** 234.

D. H. LAWRENCE

"Adolf." **2.** 178.
"The Blind Man." **3 ed.** 450; **1.** 120; **2.** 178; **3.** 234; **4.** 162; **5.** 188.
"The Blue Moccasins." **3 ed.** 450; **3.** 234.
"The Border Line." **3 ed.** 451; **1.** 121; **2.** 178; **3.** 234; **5.** 188.
"The Captain's Doll." **3 ed.** 451; **1.** 121; **3.** 234; **4.** 162; **5.** 188.
"The Christening." **3 ed.** 451; **1.** 121; **2.** 178; **3.** 235; **5.** 188.
"Daughters of the Vicar" [originally "Two Marriages"]. **3 ed.** 451, 463; **1.** 121; **2.** 179; **3.** 235; **5.** 188.
"Delilah and Mr. Bircumshaw." **3.** 235; **5.** 188.
"A Dream of Life." **4.** 162.

"England, My England." **3 ed.** 452; **2.** 179; **3.** 235.
"Fanny and Annie." **3 ed.** 452; **2.** 179; **3.** 235.
"The Fly in the Ointment." **3 ed.** 452; **4.** 162; **5.** 188.
"The Flying Fish." **3 ed.** 452.
"The Fox." **3 ed.** 452–53; **1.** 121; **2.** 179; **3.** 235; **4.** 162; **5.** 188.
"A Fragment of Stained Glass." **3 ed.** 453; **3.** 235.
"Glad Ghosts." **3 ed.** 453.
"Goose Fair." **3 ed.** 453; **5.** 188.
"Her Turn." **3 ed.** 453; **3.** 235; **5.** 189.
"The Horse Dealer's Daughter" [originally "The Miracle"]. **3 ed.** 453; **1.** 121; **3.** 235; **4.** 162.
"In Love." **3 ed.** 454; **3.** 235.
"Jimmy and the Desperate Woman." **3 ed.** 454; **1.** 121; **2.** 179; **3.** 236.
"The Ladybird" [originally "The Thimble"]. **3 ed.** 454, 462; **1.** 121, 123; **2.** 179; **3.** 236; **4.** 162–63; **5.** 189, 190.
"The Last Laugh." **3 ed.** 454; **1.** 121; **3.** 236.
"A Lesson on a Tortoise." **4.** 163.
"Love Among the Haystacks." **3 ed.** 454; **1.** 121; **3.** 236; **4.** 163.
"The Lovely Lady." **3 ed.** 454–55; **1.** 121; **3.** 236; **5.** 189.
"The Man Who Died" [originally "The Escaped Cock"]. **3 ed.** 455–56; **1.** 121; **2.** 179; **3.** 236; **4.** 163; **5.** 189.
"The Man Who Loved Islands." **3 ed.** 456; **1.** 122; **2.** 179; **3.** 236; **4.** 163; **5.** 189.
"The Man Who Was Through with the World." **3 ed.** 456; **2.** 179.
"The Miner at Home." **2.** 179; **3.** 236; **5.** 189.
"A Modern Lover." **3 ed.** 456; **3.** 236; **4.** 163.
"Monkey Nuts." **3 ed.** 456; **3.** 236; **4.** 163.
"Mother and Daughter." **3 ed.** 456; **3.** 236.
"New Eve and Old Adam." **3 ed.** 457; **1.** 122; **3.** 236; **4.** 163.
"None of That." **3 ed.** 457; **2.** 179; **3.** 236; **5.** 189.
"Odour of Chrysanthemums." **3 ed.** 457; **1.** 122; **2.** 179–80; **3.** 237; **4.** 163; **5.** 189.
"The Old Adam." **3 ed.** 457.
"Once." **3 ed.** 457; **3.** 237.
"The Overtone." **3 ed.** 457–58; **1.** 122.
"A Prelude" [same as "A Prelude to a Happy Christmas"]. **3 ed.** 458; **3.** 237; **4.** 163; **5.** 189.
"The Primrose Path." **3 ed.** 458; **3.** 237.
"The Princess." **3 ed.** 458; **1.** 122; **2.** 180; **4.** 163.
"The Prussian Officer" [originally "Honour and Arms"]. **3 ed.** 458–59; **1.** 122; **2.** 180; **3.** 237; **4.** 163–64.
"The Rocking-Horse Winner." **3 ed.** 459–60; **1.** 122; **3.** 237; **4.** 164; **5.** 189.
"St. Mawr." **3 ed.** 460–61; **1.** 122; **2.** 180; **3.** 237; **4.** 164; **5.** 190.
"Samson and Delilah." **3 ed.** 461.
"Second Best." **3 ed.** 461; **1.** 122.
"The Shades of Spring" [originally "The Soiled Rose"]. **3 ed.** 461; **1.** 122; **2.** 180; **4.** 164.
"The Shadow in the Rose Garden." **3 ed.** 461–62; **1.** 123; **2.** 180; **4.** 164.
"A Sick Collier." **3 ed.** 462; **2.** 180; **5.** 190.
"Smile." **3 ed.** 462; **5.** 190.
"Strike Pay." **3 ed.** 462; **2.** 180; **5.** 190.
"Sun." **3 ed.** 462; **1.** 123; **2.** 180; **3.** 237.
"Things." **3 ed.** 462; **1.** 123; **2.** 180.
"The Thorn in the Flesh" [same as "Vin Ordinaire"]. **3 ed.** 462; **1.** 237; **4.** 164; **5.** 190.
"Tickets, Please" [originally "The Eleventh Commandment"]. **3 ed.** 482–83; **1.** 123; **2.** 180–81; **3.** 237; **4.** 164.
"Two Blue Birds." **3 ed.** 463; **3.** 237.
"The Undying Man." **3 ed.** 463.
"The Virgin and the Gipsy." **3 ed.** 463; **1.** 123; **2.** 181; **3.** 238.
"The White Stocking." **3 ed.** 463; **2.** 181; **3.** 238; **4.** 164; **5.** 190.
"The Wilful Woman." **5.** 190.
"Wintry Peacock." **3 ed.** 463; **1.** 123; **2.** 181.
"The Witch a la Mode." **3 ed.** 463; **1.** 123; **3.** 238; **4.** 164.
"The Woman Who Rode Away." **3 ed.** 463–64; **1.** 123; **2.** 181; **3.** 238; **4.** 164; **5.** 190.
"You Touched Me." **3 ed.** 464; **2.** 181; **3.** 238.

HENRY LAWSON

"Ah Soon." **4.** 164.
"The Babies in the Bush." **3 ed.** 464.
"Brighten's Sister-in-law." **3 ed.** 464.

"The Bush Undertaker." **3 ed.** 464; **1.** 123; **4.** 165.
"A Child in the Dark" [same as "A Child in the Dark, and a Foreign Father"]. **2.** 181; **3.** 238.
"A Double-Buggy at Lahey's Creek." **3 ed.** 464.
"The Drover's Wife." **3 ed.** 464; **1.** 123; **2.** 181; **4.** 165; **5.** 190.
"Going Blind." **2.** 181; **3.** 238.
"The Green Lady." **1.** 123.
"A Hero in Dingo Scrubs." **3 ed.** 465.
"Joe Wilson's Courtship." **3 ed.** 465.
"The Loaded Dog." **3.** 238; **4.** 165; **5.** 191.
"No Place for a Woman." **3 ed.** 465.
"Rats." **4.** 165.
"A Sketch of Mateship." **3 ed.** 465.
"Telling Mrs. Baker." **3 ed.** 465.
"The Union Buries Its Dead." **3 ed.** 465; **2.** 181; **5.** 191.
"Water Them Geraniums." **3 ed.** 465.

CAMARA LAYE

"Groit's Tale." **3.** 238.
"Les Yeux de la Statue." **1.** 123.

STEPHEN LEACOCK

"The Arrested Philanthropy of Mr. Tomlinson." **5.** 191.
"The Beacon on the Hill." **5.** 191.
"The Candidacy of Mr. Smith." **5.** 191.
"The Conjurer's Revenge." **4.** 165.
"L'Envoi: The Train to Mariposa." **4.** 165; **5.** 191.
"The Extraordinary Entanglement of Mr. Pupkin." **5.** 191.
"The Great Election in Missinaba County." **5.** 191.
"The Hostelry of Mr. Smith." **5.** 191.
"A Little Dinner with Mr. Lucullus Fyshe." **5.** 191.
"The Love Story of Mr. Peter Spillikins." **5.** 191.
"The Marine Excursion of the Knights of Pythias." **5.** 191.
"The Mariposa Bank Mystery." **5.** 191.
"The Ministrations of the Rev. Mr. Drone." **5.** 191.
"The Ministrations of the Reverend Uttermust Dumfarthing." **5.** 191.
"The Rival Churches of St. Asaph and St. Osoph." **5.** 191–92.
"The Speculations of Jefferson Thorpe." **5.** 192.
"The Whirlwind Campaign in Mariposa." **5.** 192.
"The Wizard of Finance." **5.** 192.
"The Yahi-Bahi Oriental Society of Mrs. Rasselyer-Brown." **5.** 192.

DAVID LEAVITT

"Family Dancing." **5.** 192.
"Territory." **5.** 192.

JOHN LE CARRÉ [DAVID JOHN MOORE CORNWELL]

"Dare I Weep, Dare I Mourn?" **4.** 165.
"What Ritual Is Being Observed Tonight?" **4.** 165.

JEAN-MARIE GUSTAVE LE CLÉZIO

"The Day Beaumont Became Acquainted with His Pain." **2.** 181.
"A Day in Old Age." **1.** 124; **2.** 182.
"Fever." **1.** 124; **2.** 182.
"Martin." **1.** 124; **2.** 182.

ALWYN LEE

"Something for Bradshaw's Tombstone." **2.** 182.

C. Y. LEE

"The Casanova of Kearny Street." **3 ed.** 466.

LEE KOK LIANG

"Return to Malaya." **4.** 172.
"When the Saints Go Marching." **3 ed.** 472.

VERNON LEE [VIOLET PAGET]

"Amour Dure." **2.** 182; **4.** 165.
"Dionea." **4.** 165.
"Oke of Okehurst." **2.** 182; **4.** 165.
"Prince Alberic and the Snake Lady." **4.** 165; **5.** 192.
"A Wicked Voice." **4.** 166.

JOSEPH SHERIDAN LE FANU

"An Account of Some Strange Disturbances in Aungier Street." **4.** 166.
"An Authentic Narrative of the Ghost of a Hand." **2.** 182.
"Carmilla." **3 ed.** 466; **2.** 182; **4.** 166; **5.** 192.
"A Chapter in the History of the Tyrone Family." **4.** 166.
"The Dead Sexton." **4.** 166.
"The Drunkard's Dream." **3 ed.** 466; **4.** 166.
"The Evil Guest." **3 ed.** 466; **3.** 238.
"The Familiar." **5.** 192.
"The Fortunes of Sir Robert Ardagh." **2.** 182; **4.** 166; **5.** 192.
"Green Tea." **3 ed.** 466; **2.** 182; **3.** 239; **4.** 166; **5.** 192.
"The Haunted Baronet." **2.** 182; **4.** 166.
"The Last Heir of Castle Connor." **2.** 182.
"Madame Crowl's Ghost." **4.** 166.
"Mr. Justice Harbottle." **3 ed.** 466; **2.** 183; **3.** 239; **4.** 166.
"The Murdered Cousin." **3.** 239.
"The Mysterious Lodger." **2.** 183; **4.** 166.
"The Room in the Dragon Volant." **3 ed.** 467; **3.** 239; **4.** 166.
"Sir Dominick's Bargain." **4.** 167.
"Squire Toby's Will." **4.** 167.
"A Strange Adventure in the Life of Miss Laura Mildmay." **3 ed.** 467.
"A Strange Event in the Life of Schalken the Painter." **3 ed.** 467; **4.** 167.
"The Watcher." **4.** 167; **5.** 193.
"The White Cat of Drumgunniol." **4.** 167.

URSULA K. LE GUIN

"An die Musik." **4.** 167.
"April in Paris." **4.** 167.
"The Author of the Acacia Seeds and Other Extracts from the *Journal of the Association of Therolinguistics.*" **3.** 239; **4.** 167.
"The Barrow." **4.** 167.
"The Child and the Shadow." **4.** 167.
"The Darkness Box." **4.** 167.
"The Day Before the Revolution." **2.** 183; **4.** 167.
"The Diary of the Rose." **4.** 167.
"The Dowry of Angyar." **4.** 167.
"The Eye Altering." **4.** 167.
"Field of Vision." **4.** 168.
"The Good Trip." **4.** 168.
"The House." **4.** 168.
"Imaginary Countries." **4.** 168.
"The Lady of Moge." **4.** 168.
"The Masters." **2.** 183; **5.** 193.
"Mazes." **2.** 183; **5.** 193.
"The New Atlantis." **1.** 124; **2.** 183; **3.** 239; **4.** 168; **5.** 193.
"Nine Lives." **1.** 124; **3.** 239; **4.** 168.
"The Ones Who Walk Away from Omelas." **2.** 183; **4.** 168; **5.** 193.
"The Road East." **4.** 168.
"The Rule of Names." **4.** 168.
"Selection." **4.** 168.
"Semley's Necklace." **4.** 168.
"The Stars Beyond." **4.** 168.
"A Trip to the Head." **3.** 239.
"Vaster Than Empires and More Slow." **1.** 124; **2.** 183; **3.** 239; **4.** 168.
"Winter's King." **4.** 168.
"The Word for World Is *Forest.*" **1.** 124; **4.** 169; **5.** 193.
"The Word of Unbinding." **4.** 169.

MARCUS LEHMANN

"Der Fürst von Coucy." **5.** 193.

ROSAMOND LEHMANN

"A Dream of Winter." **3.** 239.
"The Gipsy's Baby." **3.** 239.
"The Red-Haired Miss Daintreys." **3.** 239.
"When the Waters Came." **3.** 239.
"Wonderful Holiday." **3.** 240.

FRITZ LEIBER

"Adept's Gambit." **3.** 240; **4.** 169.
"Belsen Express." **3.** 240.
"Black Glass." **3.** 240.
"The Button Moulder." **3.** 240.
"Catch That Zeppelin." **3.** 240.
"Crazy Wolf." **3.** 240.
"The Girl with the Hungry Eyes." **3.** 240; **5.** 193.
"The Haunted Future." **3.** 240.
"Ill Met in Lankhmar." **3.** 240.
"Lean Times in Lankhmar." **4.** 169.
"The Lords of Quarmall." **4.** 169.
"The Man Who Made Friends with Electricity." **1.** 124.

"The Man Who Never Grew Young." **4.** 169.
"No Great Magic." **3.** 240.
"The Oldest Soldier." **3.** 240.
"Scylla's Daughter." **4.** 169.
"The Ship Sails at Midnight." **5.** 193.
"Smoke Ghost." **3.** 240.
"The Snow Women." **4.** 169.
"You're All Alone." **4.** 169.

JOHN LEIMERT

"John Thomas's Cube." **3 ed.** 467.
"The Swiss Watch." **3 ed.** 467.

MURRAY LEINSTER

"Exploration Team." **5.** 193.
"First Contact." **3.** 240.
"The Power Planet." **5.** 193.
"The Runaway Skyscraper." **3.** 240.
"Sidewise in Time." **3.** 240.

STANISLAW LEM

"The Computer That Fought a Dragon." **2.** 183.
"Do You Exist, Mr. Johns?" [same as "Are You There, Mr. Johns?"]. **3.** 241.
"The Hammer." **3.** 241.
"The Hunt." **2.** 183.
"In Hot Pursuit." **1.** 124.
"The Mask." **2.** 183; **3.** 241; **4.** 169.
"Professor A. Donda." **4.** 169.
"Professor Corcoran." **4.** 169.
"Rien du tout, ou la consequence." **4.** 169.
"The Sanatorium of Dr. Vliperdius." **2.** 183.
"The Sixth Sally." **2.** 183.
"The Washing Machine Tragedy." **4.** 169.

HENRY-RENÉ LENORMAND

"The Denizens of the Elite Bar." **3.** 241.

SIEGFRIED LENZ

"The Amusement Doctor." **2.** 184.
"Favorite Food for Hyenas." **2.** 184.
"Die Festung." **3 ed.** 467.
"Ein Haus aus lauter Liebe." **3 ed.** 467.
"Der langere Arm." **3 ed.** 467.
"The Lightship." **2.** 184.
"Mein verdrossenes Gesicht." **2.** 184.
"Opportunity for Renunciation." **2.** 184.
"Der sechste Geburtstag." **3 ed.** 467.
"Der seelische Ratgeber." **3 ed.** 467.

JOSÉ ANTONIO LÉON REY

"La casita del Alto." **5.** 194.

LEONID LEONOV

"The End of a Petty Man." **3 ed.** 467.

CONSTANTINE LEONTIEV

"A Husband's Confession." **3.** 241.
"A Summer in the Village." **3.** 241.

MIKHAIL LERMONTOV

"Shtoss" [same as "Fragment of a Story Once Begun"]. **3 ed.** 467.
"Taman." **1.** 125.

ALEXANDER LERNET-HOLENIA

"Baron Bagge." **5.** 194.
"Der Herr von Paris." **5.** 194.

NIKOLAI LESKOV

"Administrative Grace." **1.** 125; **2.** 184.
"The Alexandrite." **3 ed.** 468; **1.** 125.
"The Amazon." **1.** 125; **2.** 184.
"Ancient Psychopaths." **1.** 125.
"Antukà." **1.** 125.
"An Apparition in the Engineers' Castle." **1.** 125; **2.** 184.
"At the Edge of the World." **2.** 184.
"The Battle-Axe." **1.** 125; **4.** 170.
"The Beast." **2.** 184.
"The Beast Pen." **2.** 184.
"The Beauteous Aza." **1.** 125; **5.** 194.
"The Best Implorer of God." **2.** 184.
"The Bishop's Judgement" [same as "Episcopal Justice"]. **1.** 126; **2.** 184, 185; **5.** 194.
"Boyarin Nikita Yurievich." **1.** 125.
"Boyarinya Marfa Andreyevna." **1.** 125.
"Brahmadatta and Radovan." **1.** 125.
"The Brigand of Askelon" [same as "The Felon of Askelon"]. **1.** 126; **2.** 184; **5.** 194.
"The Bugbear." **1.** 125.
"A Cancelled Affair." **2.** 185.
"A Case That Was Dropped." **1.** 125.

"The Cattle-Pen." **1.** 125.
"Cheramour." **2.** 185.
"Christ Visits a Peasant" [same as "Christ Visits a *Muzhik*"]. **1.** 126; **2.** 185.
"The Co-Functionaries: A Bucolic Tale on a Historical Canvas." **1.** 126.
"Conscience-Stricken Danila" [same as "The Legend of Conscience-Stricken Daniil"]. **2.** 185; **5.** 194.
"The Darner" [originally "The Moscow Ace"]. **1.** 126.
"The Dead Estate." **1.** 126.
"Deathless Golovan." **2.** 185; **5.** 194.
"Deception" [originally "The Featherbrains"]. **1.** 126; **2.** 185.
"The Devil Chase" [same as "Exorcising the Devil"]. **2.** 185.
"The Enchanted Pilgrim" [same as "The Enchanted Wanderer"]. **3 ed.** 468; **1.** 126; **2.** 185; **5.** 194.
"An Enigmatic Incident in an Insane Asylum." **1.** 126.
"Figura." **1.** 126.
"Fish Soup Without Fish." **1.** 126; **2.** 185.
"The Hour of God's Will." **1.** 126; **2.** 185.
"The Improvisers." **1.** 126.
"In a Coach." **1.** 126.
"Innocent Prudentsy." **2.** 185.
"Interesting Men." **1.** 126.
"Iron Will" [same as "A Will of Iron"]. **1.** 126; **2.** 186; **4.** 170.
"A Journey with a Nihilist" [originally "Christmas Night in a Railway Carriage"]. **1.** 127.
"A Kolyvan Husband." **1.** 127; **2.** 185.
"Kotin the Provider and Platonida." **2.** 185.
"The Kreutzer Sonata." **2.** 185.
"The Lady and the Wench." **1.** 127.
"Lady Macbeth of the Mtsensk District." **3 ed.** 468; **1.** 127; **2.** 185.
"The Left-Handed Craftsman" [same as "The Lefthander" or "Lefty" but originally "The Tale of the Crosseyed Lefthander from Tula and the Steel Flea"]. **1.** 127; **2.** 186.
"Leon the Butler's Son." **1.** 127.
"The Life of a Peasant Martyress" [same as "The Life of a Peasant Woman" but originally "The Mind Takes Its Own and the Devil His Own"]. **1.** 127; **2.** 186.
"The Little Fool." **1.** 127.
"A Little Mistake." **1.** 127.
"The Little Things in a Bishop's Life." **5.** 194.
"Man of Darkness." **1.** 127.
"The Man on Watch." **3 ed.** 468.
"A Man Without Shame." **2.** 186.
"The March Hare." **2.** 186.
"The Melamed of Österreich." **1.** 127.
"The Mocker." **1.** 127.
"The Monognome." **5.** 194.
"The Mountain." **1.** 127; **2.** 186; **5.** 194.
"The Musk-Ox." **1.** 127; **2.** 186.
"Mysterious Omens." **1.** 128.
"Nightowls." **1.** 128; **2.** 186.
"Offended Before Christmas." **1.** 128.
"Pamphalon the Mountebank." **1.** 128; **5.** 194.
"Pavlin." **1.** 128.
"Pearl Necklace." **1.** 128.
"The Prince's Slanders." **2.** 186.
"A Product of Nature." **2.** 186.
"The Pustoplyasians" [same as "Idle Dancers"]. **1.** 128.
"The Pygmy" [originally "Three Good Deeds"]. **1.** 128.
"Rabbit Warren" [originally "An Invasion of Barbarians"]. **1.** 128.
"The Robber." **1.** 128.
"A Robbery." **1.** 128.
"Russian Cryptomatrimony." **1.** 128.
"The Sealed Angel." **1.** 128; **2.** 186; **4.** 170; **5.** 195.
"The Sentry." **1.** 128; **2.** 186.
"Sheramur" [originally "Children of Cain"]. **1.** 128.
"A Short History of a Case of Private Derangement." **1.** 128.
"The Spirit of Mme. de Genlis." **1.** 128.
"Spiritual Torment." **2.** 186.
"The Tale of Fedor [Theodore] the Christian and His Friend Abraham the Jew." **1.** 129; **5.** 195.
"The Tale of the God-Pleasing Woodcutter." **5.** 195.
"The Toupee Artist." **1.** 129; **2.** 186.
"The Unbaptized Priest." **1.** 129.
"The Unmercenary Engineers." **1.** 129; **2.** 186.
"Vexation of Spirit." **1.** 129.
"The Voice of Nature." **3 ed.** 468.
"The White Eagle." **1.** 129; **2.** 186; **5.** 195.
"The Wild Beast." **1.** 129.

"A Winter's Day." **1.** 129; **2.** 187.
"Yid Somersault." **1.** 129.

JEAN-TALON LESPERANCE

"Rosalba; or, Faithful to Two Lovers." **3 ed.** 468.

BRUNO LESSING [RUDOLPH BLOCK]

"The End of Our Task." **3 ed.** 468.
"The Unconverted." **3 ed.** 468.
"Urim and Turim." **3 ed.** 468.

DORIS LESSING

"The Ant Heap." **1.** 129; **4.** 170.
"Between Men." **2.** 187.
"The Black Madonna." **1.** 129; **3.** 241.
"The Day Stalin Died." **3 ed.** 468; **2.** 187.
"The De Wets Come to Kloof Grange." **3 ed.** 468; **2.** 187; **5.** 195.
"Dialogue." **3 ed.** 468; **1.** 129; **2.** 187.
"Each Other." **4.** 170; **5.** 195.
"Eldorado." **3.** 241.
"England versus England." **3 ed.** 469; **2.** 187.
"The Eye of God in Paradise." **3 ed.** 469; **4.** 170.
"Flavors of Exile." **3 ed.** 469; **4.** 170.
"Flight." **2.** 187.
"Getting Off the Altitude." **3 ed.** 469; **4.** 170.
"The Habit of Loving." **3 ed.** 469; **2.** 187.
"He." **2.** 187.
"Homage to Isaac Babel." **2.** 187; **3.** 241.
"'Leopard' George." **3 ed.** 469; **1.** 129.
"A Letter from Home." **3 ed.** 469.
"Little Tembi." **3.** 241.
"Lucy Grange." **2.** 187.
"A Man and Two Women." **3 ed.** 469; **3.** 241.
"My Father." **3.** 241.
"No Witchcraft for Sale." **3 ed.** 469.
"Not a Very Nice Story." **2.** 187; **5.** 195.
"Notes for a Case History." **3 ed.** 469; **2.** 187.
"The Nuisance." **3 ed.** 469; **2.** 187.
"The Old Chief Mshlanga." **3 ed.** 469; **1.** 129; **2.** 187; **3.** 242; **4.** 170; **5.** 195.
"Old John's Place." **3 ed.** 469; **5.** 195.
"An Old Woman and Her Cat." **4.** 170.
"One Off the Short List." **2.** 188; **3.** 242; **4.** 170; **5.** 195.
"The Other Woman." **5.** 195.
"Our Friend Judith." **2.** 188; **5.** 195.
"Out of the Fountain." **2.** 188.
"Outside the Ministry." **3 ed.** 469.
"The Pig." **2.** 188; **3.** 242; **4.** 170.
"Plants and Girls." **3 ed.** 469.
"Report on a Threatened City." **5.** 195.
"A Room." **3 ed.** 469.
"The Second Hut." **3 ed.** 469; **1.** 129; **2.** 188; **4.** 171.
"The Story of a Non-Marrying Man." **2.** 188; **4.** 171.
"Story of Two Dogs." **3 ed.** 470.
"The Sun Between Their Feet." **2.** 188.
"A Sunrise on the Veld." **3 ed.** 470; **1.** 129; **3.** 242; **4.** 171.
"The Temptation of Jack Orkney." **1.** 130; **3.** 242; **4.** 171.
"To Room Nineteen." **3 ed.** 470; **1.** 130; **2.** 188; **3.** 242; **4.** 171; **5.** 196.
"The Trinket Box." **2.** 188; **4.** 171.
"Two Potters." **3 ed.** 470; **1.** 130.
"An Unposted Love Letter." **2.** 188; **3.** 242; **5.** 196.
"Winter in July." **3 ed.** 470; **5.** 196.
"The Witness." **2.** 188.
"The Woman." **2.** 188.
"A Woman on a Roof." **3 ed.** 470; **2.** 188; **3.** 242.

MERIDEL LE SUEUR

"Annunciation." **3 ed.** 466.
"Breathe Upon These Slain." **3 ed.** 466.
"Corn Village." **4.** 171.
"Salute to Spring." **4.** 171.

ADA LEVERSON

"The Blow." **3 ed.** 470.
"Claude's Aunt." **3 ed.** 470.
"In the Change of Years." **3 ed.** 470.
"Mimosa." **3 ed.** 470.
"The Quest of Sorrow." **3 ed.** 470.
"Suggestion." **3 ed.** 470.

DENISE LEVERTOV

"Say the Word." **3 ed.** 470.

MEYER LEVIN

"Cheuing Gohm." **3.** 242.
"Molasses Tide." **3.** 242.
"A Seder." **3.** 242.

NORMAN LEVINE

"A Canadian Upbringing." **4.** 171; **5.** 196.
"Class of 1949." **5.** 196.
"The Dilettante." **5.** 196.
"The Playground." **5.** 196.
"Ringa Ringa Rosie." **5.** 196.

LUISA LEVINSON

"The Clearing." **5.** 196.

ALFRED HENRY LEWIS

"The Mills of Savage Gods." **3 ed.** 471.

ALUN LEWIS

"Acting Captain." **3.** 242.
"Almost a Gentleman." **2.** 189.
"The Children." **3.** 242.
"Cold Spell." **2.** 189; **3.** 243.
"The Death of Monga." **3.** 243.
"The Earth Is a Syllable." **3.** 243.
"The Housekeeper." **3.** 243.
"It's a Long Way to Go." **3.** 243.
"The Last Inspection." **3.** 243.
"The Orange Grove." **3 ed.** 471; **3.** 243.
"Private Jones." **3.** 243.
"The Raid." **3 ed.** 471; **3.** 243.
"The Return of Dick Turpin." **3.** 243.
"The Reunion." **3 ed.** 471.
"They Came." **3.** 243.
"They Say There's a Boat on the River." **3.** 243.
"Tudor Witch." **3 ed.** 471.
"The Wanderers." **3 ed.** 471; **2.** 189; **3.** 243.
"Ward O.3b." **3 ed.** 471; **3.** 243.

HENRY CLAY LEWIS

"The Curious Widow." **1.** 130.
"Stealing a Baby." **1.** 130.
"A Struggle for Life." **1.** 130.

JANET LEWIS

"Proserpina." **3.** 243.

O. F. LEWIS

"Alma Mater." **1.** 130.

RICHARD O. LEWIS

"The Fate Changer." **1.** 130.

SINCLAIR LEWIS

"The Hidden People." **1.** 130.
"Let's Play King." **3.** 244.
"Moths in the Arc Light." **3.** 244.
"Virga Vay and Allan Cedar." **3.** 244.
"Young Man Axelbrod." **1.** 130.

WYNDHAM LEWIS

"Beau Séjour." **3 ed.** 471; **1.** 130.
"Bestre." **1.** 131.
"Brotcotnaz." **3 ed.** 471; **1.** 131.
"Cantleman's Spring Mate." **3 ed.** 471; **1.** 131; **2.** 189; **4.** 171.
"The Cornac and His Wife." **3 ed.** 471.
"Creativity." **4.** 171.
"The Death of the Ankou." **3 ed.** 471; **1.** 131.
"Doppelgänger." **3 ed.** 472.
"The French Poodle." **1.** 131.
"My Disciple." **3 ed.** 472.
"The Rot." **3 ed.** 472.
"Sigismund." **3 ed.** 472.
"Time the Tiger." **3 ed.** 472.
"Unlucky for Pringle." **3 ed.** 472.
"The War Baby." **3 ed.** 472.

LUDWIG LEWISOHN

"The Bolshevik." **3 ed.** 472; **3.** 244.
"The Saint." **3 ed.** 472; **3.** 244.
"Writ of Divorcement." **3 ed.** 472; **3.** 244.

MEYER LIBEN

"Justice Hunger." **3 ed.** 472.

JONAS LIE

"The Nordfjord Horse." **1.** 131.
"The Søndmøre Boat" [same as "The Eight-Oared Boat"]. **1.** 131.

ENRIQUE LIHN

"Huancho y Pochocha." **4.** 172.

BALDOMERO LILLO

"Gate Number 12." **3.** 244; **5.** 196.
"The Well." **3.** 244.

LIN HWAI MIN

"Homecoming." **3.** 244.

VICTORIA LINCOLN

"Down in the Reeds by the River." **3 ed.** 472.

JAKOV LIND

"Hurrah for Freedom." **3 ed.** 473.
"Journey Through the Night." **3 ed.** 473.
"Resurrection." **3 ed.** 473.
"Soul of Wood." **3 ed.** 473; **4.** 172.

ROBERT LINDNER

"The Jet-Propelled Couch." **1.** 131.

LUCY F. LINDSAY

"Sang." **2.** 189.

LING SHU-HUA

"Embroidered Pillows." **1.** 131.
"The Eve of the Mid-Autumn Festival." **1.** 131.
"Little Liu." **1.** 131.

ERIC LINKLATER

"The Abominable Imprecation of Shepherd Alken." **4.** 172.
"Country-Born." **4.** 172.
"The Crusader's Key." **4.** 172.
"The Dancers." **4.** 172.
"The Duke." **4.** 172.
"Escape Forever." **4.** 172.
"God Likes Them Plain." **4.** 172.
"The Goose Girl." **4.** 173.
"His Majesty the Dentist." **4.** 173.
"Kind Kitty." **4.** 173.
"The Masks of Purpose." **4.** 173.
"The Redundant Miracle." **4.** 173.
"A Sociable Plover." **4.** 173.

OSMAN LINS

"The Betrothal." **3 ed.** 473.
"A Dot in the Circle." **3 ed.** 473.

CLARICE LISPECTOR

"The Body." **5.** 196.
"The Buffalo." **4.** 173; **5.** 197.
"The Chicken." **5.** 197.
"The Crime of the Mathematics Professor." **3.** 244; **4.** 173; **5.** 197.
"Daydream of a Drunken Housewife" [same as "Daydream of a Drunken Woman"]. **2.** 189; **3.** 244–45.
"Family Ties." **4.** 173.
"The Fifth Story." **4.** 173.
"Happy Anniversary." **3.** 245.
"The Imitation of a Rose." **3.** 245; **5.** 197.
"Love." **3.** 245; **4.** 173.
"The Man Who Appeared." **5.** 197.
"Miss Ruth Algrave." **4.** 173; **5.** 197.
"Por Enquanto." **5.** 197.
"Praça Mauá." **5.** 197.
"Preciousness." **3.** 245.
"A Quest for Dignity." **5.** 197.
"The Smallest Woman in the World." **3.** 245; **5.** 197.

LIU BINYAN

"At the Building Site of the Bridge." **5.** 197.

LIU XINWU

"Black Wall." **4.** 173.
"The Class Teacher" [same as "Class Counsellor"]. **4.** 173; **5.** 197.

DOROTHY LIVESAY

"The Glass House." **3 ed.** 473.

SYLVIA LIZÁRRAGO

"El Don." **4.** 174.
"Quinceañera." **4.** 174.

CHARLES LLOYD

"Special Diet." **5.** 198.

LO HUA-SHENG [HSÜ TI-SHAN]

"The Vain Labors of a Spider." **1.** 131.
"Yü-kuan." **1.** 131.

TABAN LO LIYONG

"The Uniform Man." **4.** 174.

JOSÉ BENTO MONTEIRO LOBATO

"Bracket Fungus." **3.** 245.

MARÍA LOMBARDO DE CASO

"La culebra tapó el rio." **5.** 198.

JACK LONDON

"All Gold Canyon." **1.** 132.
"And 'Frisco Kid Came Back." **3.** 245.
"The Apostate." **3 ed.** 473; **3.** 245.
"Bâtard" [originally "Diable—A Dog"]. **3 ed.** 473; **3.** 245; **4.** 174; **5.** 198.
"The Bones of Kahelili." **3 ed.** 473; **2.** 189.
"The Call of the Wild." **3 ed.** 474; **1.** 132; **2.** 189; **3.** 245; **4.** 174; **5.** 198.
"The Chinago." **3 ed.** 474; **2.** 189.
"Chris Farrington, Able Seaman." **4.** 174.
"Chun Ah Chun." **3.** 245.
"A Curious Fragment." **3 ed.** 474; **3.** 245.
"The Death of Ligoun." **3 ed.** 474.
"The Dream of Debs." **3 ed.** 474; **3.** 246.
"The Enemy of All the World." **3 ed.** 474; **3.** 246.
"The Eternity of Forms." **3.** 246.
"The God of His Fathers." **3 ed.** 474.
"Goliah." **3.** 246.
"The Great Interrogation." **3 ed.** 474; **2.** 189.
"The Grit of Woman." **3 ed.** 474.
"In a Far Country." **3 ed.** 474; **3.** 246.
"The Inevitable White Man." **3 ed.** 474.
"The Kanaka Surf." **3 ed.** 474–75; **4.** 174.
"Keesh, the Son of Keesh." **3 ed.** 475.
"Koolau the Leper." **3 ed.** 475; **5.** 198.
"The Law of Life." **3 ed.** 475; **2.** 190; **3.** 246.
"Law-Giving." **2.** 190.
"The League of Old Men." **3 ed.** 475; **5.** 198.
"Like Argus of the Ancient Times." **3 ed.** 475.
"Local Color." **3 ed.** 475.
"Love of Life." **3 ed.** 475; **2.** 190.
"The Madness of John Harned." **3.** 246.
"The Mahatma's Little Joke." **3.** 246.
"Mauki." **3 ed.** 475; **5.** 198.
"The Men of Forty-Mile." **3 ed.** 475; **2.** 190.
"The Mexican." **3 ed.** 475; **2.** 190; **3.** 246.
"The Minions of Midas." **3 ed.** 475; **3.** 246.
"An Odyssey of the North." **3 ed.** 475.
"On the Makaloa Mat." **3 ed.** 475; **5.** 198.
"A Piece of Steak." **3 ed.** 475; **1.** 132; **3.** 246.
"Planchette." **3 ed.** 476; **3.** 246.
"The Priestly Prerogative." **3 ed.** 476; **2.** 190.
"The Red One." **1.** 132; **2.** 190; **3.** 246; **4.** 174; **5.** 198.
"The Rejuvenation of Major Rathbone." **3.** 246.
"The Seed of McCoy." **3 ed.** 476.
"The Shadow and the Flash." **3 ed.** 476; **3.** 247.
"Shin Bones." **3 ed.** 476; **2.** 190.
"The Sickness of Lone Chief." **3 ed.** 476.
"The Son of the Wolf." **3 ed.** 476; **2.** 190.
"South of the Slot." **3.** 247.
"The Story of Jees Uck." **3 ed.** 476.
"The Strength of the Strong." **3 ed.** 476; **3.** 247.
"The Sun-Dog Trail." **3 ed.** 476.
"The Tears of Ah Kim." **3 ed.** 476; **2.** 190; **3.** 247.
"A Thousand Deaths." **3.** 247.
"To Build a Fire." **3 ed.** 476–77; **1.** 132; **2.** 190; **3.** 247; **4.** 174; **5.** 198.
"To the Man on Trail." **3 ed.** 477.
"Told in the Drooling Ward." **1.** 132.
"The Unexpected." **3 ed.** 477.
"The Unparalleled Invasion." **3.** 247; **5.** 198.
"The Water Baby." **3 ed.** 477; **2.** 190; **5.** 198.
"The Whale Tooth." **3 ed.** 477.
"When Alice Told Her Soul." **3 ed.** 477; **2.** 190.
"When God Laughs." **3 ed.** 477.
"When the World Was Young." **3.** 247.
"Which Make Men Remember." **3 ed.** 477; **2.** 190.
"The White Silence." **3 ed.** 477; **2.** 191; **3.** 247; **5.** 198.
"The Wife of a King." **3 ed.** 477; **1.** 132.
"The Wisdom of the Trail." **3 ed.** 477.
"The Wit of Porportuk." **3 ed.** 477; **5.** 199.
"Yah! Yah! Yah!" **3 ed.** 478.

FRANK BELKNAP LONG

"The Black Druid." **4.** 174.
"Dark Vision." **4.** 175.
"Second Night Out" [originally "The Black Dead Thing"]. **4.** 175.

AUGUSTUS BALDWIN LONGSTREET

"The Chase." **5.** 199.
"The Dance." **5.** 199.
"The Debating Society." **3.** 247.
"The Fight." **3.** 247; **5.** 199.
"The Fox Hunt." **5.** 199.
"The Gander Pulling." **5.** 199.
"Georgia Theatrics." **5.** 199.
"The Gnatville Gem." **3.** 247.
"The Horse-Swap." **3 ed.** 478; **3.** 247.
"The Mother and Her Child." **1.** 132.
"The Shooting Match." **5.** 199.
"The Song." **5.** 199.
"The Turf." **5.** 199.

BARRY LONGYEAR

"Enemy Mine." **5.** 199.

EDWARD LOOMIS

"Wounds." **3 ed.** 478.

ENRIQUE LÓPEZ ALBÚJAR

"El campeon de la muerte." **3 ed.** 478.
"El licenciado Aponte." **3 ed.** 478.

JESÚS LÓPEZ PACHECO

"Lucha contra el murciélago." **4.** 175.
"Lucha por la respiración." **4.** 175.

JOSÉ LÓPEZ PORTILLO Y ROJAS

"Reloj sin dueño." **5.** 199.

JOSÉ LÓPEZ RUBIO

"Aunt Germana." **2.** 191.

LORELLE [unidentified]

"The Battle of the Wabash." **2.** 191; **3.** 248.

H[OWARD] P. LOVECRAFT

"Arthur Jermyn" [same as "The White Ape" but originally "Facts Concerning Arthur Jermyn & His Family"]. **3.** 248.
"At the Mountains of Madness." **1.** 132; **3.** 248.
"Beyond the Wall of Sleep." **3.** 248.
"The Call of Cthulhu." **3 ed.** 478; **1.** 132; **2.** 191; **3.** 248; **4.** 175; **5.** 200.
"The Cats of Ulthar." **3.** 248.
"Celephaïs." **3.** 248.
"The Colour Out of Space." **1.** 133; **3.** 248.
"The Curse of Yig." **3.** 248.
"Dagon." **1.** 133; **3.** 248.
"The Doom That Came to Sarnath." **3.** 248.
"The Dream-Quest of Unknown Kadath." **3.** 248.
"Dreams in the Witch House." **1.** 133; **3.** 248.
"The Dunwich Horror." **1.** 133; **3.** 249; **4.** 175; **5.** 200.
"Ex Oblivione." **3.** 249.
"The Festival." **3.** 249; **5.** 200.
"From Beyond." **3.** 249.
"The Haunter of the Dark." **1.** 133; **3.** 249.
"He." **1.** 133; **3.** 249.
"Herbert West—Reanimator." **3.** 249.
"The Horror at Red Hook." **1.** 133; **3.** 249; **5.** 200.
"The Hound." **3.** 249.
"Hypnos." **3.** 249.
"Imprisoned with the Pharaohs" [originally "Under the Pyramids"]. **3.** 249.
"In the Vault." **3.** 249.
"In the Walls of Eryx." **3.** 249.
"The Lurking Fear." **3.** 249.
"Memory." **3.** 249.
"The Moon-Bog." **3.** 249.
"The Mound." **3.** 250.
"The Music of Erich Zann." **3 ed.** 478; **3.** 250; **5.** 200.
"The Nameless City." **1.** 133; **3.** 250.
"The Night Ocean." **3.** 250.
"Nyarlathotep." **3.** 250.
"The Other Gods." **1.** 133; **3.** 250.
"The Outsider." **1.** 133; **2.** 191; **3.** 250; **5.** 200.
"Pickman's Model." **1.** 133; **3.** 250.
"The Picture in the House." **1.** 133; **3.** 250.
"Polaris." **1.** 133; **3.** 250.
"The Quest of Iranon." **3.** 250.
"The Rats in the Walls." **1.** 133; **3.** 250; **5.** 200.
"The Shadow out of Time." **1.** 133; **3.** 250.
"The Shadow over Innsmouth." **1.** 133; **3.** 250; **5.** 200.
"The Shunned House." **1.** 133; **3.** 250.

"The Silver Key." **3.** 251; **5.** 200.
"The Statement of Randolph Carter." **3.** 251.
"The Strange High House in the Mist." **3.** 251.
"The Temple." **1.** 134; **3.** 251.
"The Terrible Old Man." **3.** 251; **5.** 200.
"The Thing on the Doorstep." **1.** 134; **3.** 251.
"Through the Gates of the Silver Key." **1.** 134; **3.** 251; **5.** 200.
"The Tomb." **1.** 134; **3.** 251.
"The Transition of Juan Romero." **3.** 251.
"The Tree." **3.** 251.
"The Unnamable." **3.** 251.
"What the Moon Brings." **3.** 251.
"The Whisperer in Darkness." **1.** 134; **2.** 191; **3.** 251.
"The White Ship." **2.** 191; **3.** 251; **5.** 200.

SAMUEL LOVER

"Barney O'Reirdon." **4.** 175.
"The Burial of the Tithe." **4.** 175.

MALCOLM LOWRY

"The Bravest Boat." **3 ed.** 478; **1.** 134; **2.** 191; **3.** 252; **5.** 200.
"Bulls of the Resurrection." **3 ed.** 478; **3.** 252.
"China." **3.** 252.
"Economic Conference, 1934." **3 ed.** 478.
"Elephant and Colosseum." **3 ed.** 478–79; **1.** 134; **2.** 191; **3.** 252; **5.** 200.
"Enter One in Sumptuous Armor." **3 ed.** 479.
"The Forest Path to the Spring." **3 ed.** 479; **1.** 134; **2.** 192; **3.** 252; **5.** 201.
"Ghostkeeper." **3 ed.** 479; **2.** 192; **3.** 252.
"Gin and Goldenrod." **3 ed.** 479; **1.** 134; **2.** 192; **3.** 252.
"Hotel Room in Chartres." **3 ed.** 479; **2.** 192.
"In Le Havre." **3 ed.** 479; **2.** 192.
"In the Black Hills." **2.** 192.
"June the 30th, 1934." **3.** 252.
"The Last Address." **3 ed.** 479.
"Lunar Caustic." **3 ed.** 479.
"On Board the West Hardaway." **3 ed.** 479.
"Present Estate of Pompeii." **3 ed.** 479–80; **1.** 134; **2.** 192; **3.** 252; **5.** 201.
"Strange Comfort Afforded by the Profession." **3 ed.** 480; **1.** 134; **2.** 192.
"Through the Panama." **3 ed.** 480; **1.** 134; **2.** 192; **3.** 252; **5.** 201.
"The Voyage That Never Ends." **3.** 252.

LU XINHUA

"The Wound." **4.** 175.

LU XÜN [LU HSÜN or CHOU SHU-JEN]

"Benediction." **1.** 134.
"Brothers." **1.** 134.
"Diary of a Madman." **1.** 134–35; **2.** 192; **5.** 201.
"Divorce." **1.** 135; **3.** 252.
"Dragon Boat Festival." **1.** 135.
"A Happy Family." **1.** 135.
"In a Restaurant." **1.** 135.
"In the Tavern" [same as "In the Wineshop" or "Upstairs in the Wineshop"]. **1.** 135; **4.** 175; **5.** 201.
"Kong Yiji" [same as "K'ung I-chi"]. **1.** 135; **5.** 201.
"Looking Backward to the Past." **3.** 252.
"Medicine." **1.** 135; **3.** 252; **5.** 201.
"The Misanthrope." **5.** 201.
"My Old Home." **5.** 201.
"The New Year's Sacrifice." **1.** 135; **4.** 176; **5.** 201.
"Peking Street Scene." **3.** 252.
"Remorse." **1.** 135.
"Soap." **1.** 135.
"Storm in a Teacup." **3 ed.** 480; **1.** 135.
"The Story of Hair." **5.** 201.
"Tomorrow." **5.** 201.
"The True Story of Ah Q." **1.** 135; **2.** 192; **3.** 253; **4.** 176; **5.** 201.
"A Warning to the People." **1.** 135.
"The White Light." **3 ed.** 480; **1.** 135.

OTTO LUDWIG

"Between Heaven and Earth." **3 ed.** 480.
"Erbförster." **3 ed.** 480.

LEOPOLDO LUGONES

"La lluvia de fuego." **4.** 176.
"The Pillar of Salt." **3.** 253; **4.** 176.
"Yzur." **4.** 176.

BRIAN LUMLEY

"David's Worm." **5.** 201.

GRACE LUMPKIN

"White Man." **3 ed.** 480.

PETER LUS

"My Heart Is as Black as the Soil of This Country." **3 ed.** 480.

N. LYASHKO

"The Rainbow." **3 ed.** 481.
"The Song of the Chains." **3 ed.** 481.

MARTA LYNCH

"Campo de batalla." **3.** 253.
"Entierro de carnaval." **2.** 192.
"Historía con gato." **2.** 193.
"Latin Lover." **5.** 202.
"Triptico." **2.** 193.

MIKHAS' T. LYNKOŬ

"Giovanni." **3.** 253.

HARRIS MERTON LYON

"In the Black-and-Tan." **3 ed.** 481.
"The Man with the Broken Fingers." **3 ed.** 481.
"The Riding Beggar." **3 ed.** 481.
"The 2000th Christmas." **1.** 136.
"The Weaver Who Clad the Summer." **3 ed.** 481.

ANDREW LYTLE

"Alchemy." **3 ed.** 481; **3.** 253.
"Jerico, Jerico, Jerico." **3 ed.** 481; **3.** 253.
"The Mahogany Frame." **3 ed.** 481.
"Mister McGregor." **3 ed.** 481; **2.** 193.

ROSE MACAULAY

"The Mind Is Its Own Place." **3 ed.** 482.

ROBIE MACAULEY

"The Invaders." **3 ed.** 482.

CHARLES W. McCABLE

"Only a Squaw Man—Kind Feelings Lodge in Many Unlikely Places." **2.** 193.

ANNE McCAFFREY

"Lady in the Tower." **3.** 253.

MARY McCARTHY

"Artists in Uniform." **3 ed.** 482; **2.** 193.
"The Cicerone." **3 ed.** 482.
"The Company Is Not Responsible." **3 ed.** 482.
"Cruel and Barbarous Treatment." **3 ed.** 482; **2.** 193; **3.** 253.
"The Friend of the Family." **3 ed.** 482.
"The Genial Host." **3 ed.** 482; **2.** 193.
"Ghostly Father, I Confess." **3 ed.** 482; **2.** 193.
"The Hounds of Summer." **3 ed.** 482.
"The Man in the Brooks Brothers Shirt." **3 ed.** 483; **2.** 193; **4.** 176.
"The Old Men." **3 ed.** 483.
"Portrait of the Intellectual as a Yale Man." **3 ed.** 483; **2.** 193.
"Rogue's Gallery." **3 ed.** 483; **2.** 193.
"The Unspoiled Reaction." **3 ed.** 483.
"The Weeds." **3 ed.** 483.

DOROTHY McCLEARY

"Something Jolly." **3 ed.** 483.

NELLIE McCLUNG

"The Way of the West." **4.** 176.

JOHN McCLUSKY

"Chicago Jubilee Rag." **5.** 202.

JOHN LUDLUM McCONNEL

"The Ranger's Chase." **2.** 193.

CARSON McCULLERS

"Art and Mr. Mahoney." **2.** 194.
"The Ballad of the Sad Café." **3 ed.** 483–84; **1.** 136; **2.** 194; **3.** 254; **4.** 176; **5.** 202.
"Breath from the Sky." **2.** 194.
"Correspondence." **3 ed.** 484; **2.** 194.
"A Domestic Dilemma." **3 ed.** 484; **2.** 194; **5.** 202.
"The Haunted Boy." **2.** 194.
"The Instant of the Hour After." **2.** 194.
"The Jockey." **3 ed.** 484; **1.** 136; **2.** 194.

"Like That." **2.** 194; **4.** 176.
"Madame Zilensky and the King of Finland." **2.** 194.
"The Sojourner." **3 ed.** 484–85; **1.** 136; **2.** 194.
"Sucker." **3 ed.** 485; **2.** 194.
"A Tree, A Rock, A Cloud." **3 ed.** 485; **1.** 136; **2.** 195; **3.** 254; **4.** 176.
"Who Has Seen the Wind?" **2.** 195.
"Wunderkind." **2.** 195; **5.** 202.

HUGH MacDIARMID [CHRISTOPHER MURRAY GRIEVE]

"Cerebral." **5.** 202.

ANSON MacDONALD [ROBERT HEINLEIN]

"Solution Unsatisfactory." **4.** 177; **5.** 202.

GEORGE MacDONALD

"The Broken Swords." **3 ed.** 485.
"The Castle." **3 ed.** 485.
"Cross Purposes." **3 ed.** 485.
"The Cruel Painting." **3 ed.** 485.
"The Day Boy and the Night Girl." **5.** 202.
"The Fairy Fleet" [originally "The Carasoyn"]. **3 ed.** 485.
"The Giant's Heart." **3 ed.** 485.
"The Golden Key." **3 ed.** 485; **3.** 254; **4.** 177.
"A Hidden Life." **3 ed.** 485.
"The Light Princess." **3 ed.** 485; **5.** 203.
"The Shadows." **3 ed.** 485.

JOHN D. MacDONALD

"Interlude in India." **4.** 177.
"Spectator Sport." **4.** 177.

URSULA MacDOUGALL

"Titty's Dead and Tatty Weeps." **3 ed.** 486.

IAN McEWAN

"Dead As They Come." **4.** 177.
"Disguise." **4.** 177.
"Homemade." **4.** 177.
"Reflections of a Kept Ape." **4.** 177.
"Solid Geometry." **4.** 177.

GWENDOLYN MacEWEN

"The House of the Whale." **4.** 177.
"Kingsmere." **5.** 203.
"Noman." **5.** 203.
"The Second Coming of Julian the Magician." **5.** 203.

JOHN McGAHERN

"Peaches." **2.** 195.

R. J. McGREGOR

"The Perfect Gentleman." **5.** 203.

K. H. MÁCHA

"The Evening at Bezděz." **3 ed.** 486.
"The Krkonoshe Pilgrimage." **3 ed.** 486.
"Marinka." **3 ed.** 486.

JOAQUIM MARÍA MACHADO DE ASSIS

"Adam and Eve." **3.** 254.
"Admiral's Night." **3 ed.** 486.
"Um Almôço." **3 ed.** 486.
"The Animal Game." **3 ed.** 486.
"A Captain of Volunteers." **3.** 254.
"O Caso de Vara." **3.** 254.
"The Church of the Devil." **3.** 254.
"Education of a Stuffed Shirt." **3 ed.** 486.
"Ernesto de Tal." **3 ed.** 486.
"Un Esqueleto." **3 ed.** 486.
"Father versus Mother." **3 ed.** 486.
"Final Request." **3 ed.** 486.
"Um Homem Superior." **3 ed.** 486.
"The Looking Glass." **3 ed.** 486.
"Midnight Mass." **3 ed.** 487; **3.** 254.
"The Mockery of Dates." **3.** 254.
"El Mulher Prêto." **3 ed.** 487.
"One Night." **3.** 254.
"Onze Anos Depuis." **3 ed.** 487.
"The Opera." **3.** 254.
"Pai Contra Mae." **3.** 255.
"A Parasita Azul." **3.** 255.
"Pílades e Orestes." **3 ed.** 487.
"The Psychiatrist." **3 ed.** 487.
"The Rod of Justice." **3 ed.** 487.
"The Secret Heart." **3 ed.** 487.
"Sem Olhos." **3 ed.** 487.
"Singular Occurrence." **3.** 255.
"Valério." **3 ed.** 487.
"A Woman's Arms." **3 ed.** 487.

ARTHUR MACHEN

"The Angels of Mons" [originally "The Bowmen"]. **3 ed.** 487.
"The Bright Boy." **5.** 203.
"A Fragment of Life." **4.** 178.
"The Great God Pan." **3.** 255; **4.** 178.
"The Happy Children." **5.** 203.
"The Novel of the Black Seal." **2.** 195; **4.** 178.
"The Novel of the White Powder." **3 ed.** 487; **2.** 195; **4.** 178; **5.** 203.
"Out of the Earth." **5.** 203.
"The Shining Pyramid." **3 ed.** 487; **5.** 203.
"The White People." **3 ed.** 487; **5.** 203.

VONDA N. McINTYRE

"Aztecs." **3.** 255.
"The Genius Freaks." **3.** 255.
"The Mountains of Sunset, the Mountains of Dawn." **3.** 255.
"Only at Night." **3.** 255.
"Screwtop." **3.** 255.
"Spectra." **3.** 255.
"Wings." **3.** 255.

LORENZ MACK

"A Ferryman Died." **3 ed.** 488.

CLAUDE McKAY

"The Agricultural Show." **3 ed.** 488; **5.** 203.
"Brownskin Blues." **3 ed.** 488; **1.** 136.
"Color Scheme." **5.** 204.
"Highball." **1.** 136.
"The Little Sheik." **1.** 136.
"Mattie and Her Sweetman." **1.** 136.
"Near-White." **3 ed.** 488; **1.** 136.
"The Prince of Porto Rico." **1.** 136.
"The Strange Burial of Sue." **3 ed.** 488; **1.** 136.
"Truant." **3 ed.** 488.
"When I Pounded the Pavement." **1.** 136.

RICHARD McKENNA

"Hunter, Come Home." **5.** 204.
"The Secret Place." **3.** 255.

BERNARD MacLAVERTY

"Between Two Shores." **5.** 204.
"My Dear Palestrina." **5.** 204.
"Phonefun Limited." **5.** 204.
"St. Paul Could Hit the Nail on the Head." **2.** 195; **5.** 204.
"Secrets." **2.** 195; **5.** 204.
"Umberto Verdi, Chimney-Sweep." **5.** 204.

MICHAEL McLAVERTY

"The Game Cock." **3 ed.** 488.
"Pigeons." **3 ed.** 488.
"A Schoolmaster." **3.** 256; **5.** 204.
"Stone." **3.** 256; **5.** 204.

KATHERINE McLEAN

"And Be Merry." **3.** 256.
"Contagion." **3.** 256.
"The Other." **5.** 204.

NORMAN MACLEAN

"A River Runs Through It." **2.** 195; **3.** 256.

HUGH MacLENNAN

"So All Their Praises." **4.** 178.

ALISTAIR MacLEOD

"As Birds Bring Forth the Sun." **5.** 204–05.
"The Boat." **5.** 205.
"The Closing Down of Summer." **5.** 205.
"In the Fall." **5.** 205.
"Island." **5.** 205.
"The Last Salt Gift." **5.** 205.
"The Return." **5.** 205.
"The Road to Rankin's Point." **5.** 205.
"Second Spring." **5.** 205.
"To Every Thing There Is a Season." **5.** 205.
"The Vastness of the Dark." **5.** 205.
"Vision." **5.** 205.
"Winter Dog." **5.** 205.

FIONA MACLEOD [WILLIAM SHARP]

"The Harping of Cravetheen." **4.** 178.
"Honey of the Wild Bee." **4.** 178.

SEAN MacMATHUNA

"A Straight Run down to Kilcash." **2.** 196.

JAMES ALAN McPHERSON

"Elbow Room." **4.** 178; **5.** 205.
"The Faithful." **4.** 178.
"Gold Coast." **3 ed.** 488; **1.** 136; **2.** 196; **4.** 178; **5.** 206.
"Hue and Cry." **3 ed.** 488; **5.** 206.
"Just Enough for the City." **5.** 206.
"A Loaf of Bread." **4.** 178.
"A Matter of Vocabulary." **4.** 178.
"Of Cabbages and Kings." **4.** 179.
"On Trains." **4.** 179.
"Problems of Art." **3.** 256.
"A Sense of Story." **4.** 179.
"The Silver Bullet." **4.** 179.
"A Solo Song: For Doc." **1.** 137; **4.** 179.
"The Story of a Dead Man." **4.** 179; **5.** 206.
"The Story of a Scar." **4.** 179; **5.** 206.
"Why I Like Country Music." **4.** 179.

DAVID MADDEN

"No Trace." **5.** 206.

SVEND AGE MADSEN

"Here." **1.** 137.

WILLIAM MAGINN

"The Man in the Bell." **5.** 206.

NAJIB MAHFUZ

"Al-Karnak." **5.** 206.
"The Mosque in the Alley." **5.** 206.
"Story with No Beginning and No End." **5.** 206.

MAMADALI MAHMUDOV

"The Immortal Cliffs." **5.** 206.

NORMAN MAILER

"A Calculus at Heaven." **1.** 137; **2.** 196; **5.** 207.
"The Last Night." **4.** 179.
"The Man Who Studied Yoga." **3 ed.** 488; **1.** 137; **2.** 196.
"Maybe Next Year." **2.** 196.
"The Time of Her Time." **1.** 137; **2.** 196.

XAVIER DE MAISTRE

"La Jeune Sibérienne." **3 ed.** 489.

CLARENCE MAJOR

"Art." **2.** 196.
"Dear Freud." **2.** 196.
"Escape the Close Circle." **2.** 196.
"Fish, Tomatoes, Mama & Book." **2.** 196.
"Newhouse." **2.** 196.
"Number Four." **2.** 197.
"The Pecan Pie." **2.** 197.
"The Vase and the Rose." **2.** 197.

VLADIMIR MAKANIN

"Where the Sky Met the Hills." **5.** 207.

BERNARD MALAMUD

"Angel Levine." **3 ed.** 489; **1.** 137; **2.** 197; **3.** 256; **5.** 207.
"Behold the Key." **3 ed.** 489; **1.** 137.
"Benefit Performance." **3 ed.** 489.
"The Bill." **3 ed.** 489; **4.** 179; **5.** 207.
"Black Is My Favorite Color." **3 ed.** 489; **1.** 137; **2.** 197; **3.** 256; **5.** 207.
"A Choice of Profession." **3 ed.** 489–90; **1.** 137.
"The Cost of Living." **2.** 197; **4.** 179.
"The Death of Me." **4.** 179.
"The First Seven Years." **3 ed.** 490; **1.** 137; **5.** 207.
"The German Refugee." **3 ed.** 490; **2.** 197; **3.** 256; **4.** 179.
"The Girl of My Dreams." **3 ed.** 490; **1.** 137; **3.** 257.
"Glass Blower of Venice." **3 ed.** 490; **1.** 137; **2.** 197; **4.** 179.
"Idiots First." **3 ed.** 490; **1.** 138; **2.** 197; **3.** 257; **4.** 180; **5.** 207.
"The Jewbird." **3 ed.** 490; **1.** 138; **2.** 197; **3.** 257; **4.** 180; **5.** 207.
"The Lady of the Lake." **3 ed.** 490; **1.** 138; **2.** 197; **3.** 257; **4.** 180; **5.** 207.
"The Last Mohican." **3 ed.** 490–91; **1.** 138; **2.** 198; **3.** 257; **4.** 180; **5.** 207.
"Life Is Better Than Death." **3 ed.** 491; **1.** 138.
"The Loan." **3 ed.** 491; **1.** 138; **2.** 198; **3.** 257; **5.** 207.
"The Magic Barrel." **3 ed.** 491–92; **1.** 138; **2.** 198; **3.** 257; **4.** 180; **5.** 207–08.
"The Maid's Shoes." **3 ed.** 492; **1.** 138.
"Man in the Drawer." **3.** 257; **5.** 208.
"The Mourners." **3 ed.** 492; **2.** 198; **5.** 208.

"Naked Nude." **3 ed.** 492; **1.** 138; **2.** 198; **4.** 180.
"Pictures of an Artist." **1.** 138; **2.** 198; **5.** 208.
"A Pimp's Revenge." **3 ed.** 492; **1.** 138; **2.** 198; **4.** 180; **5.** 208.
"The Place Is Different Now." **3 ed.** 492.
"The Prison." **3 ed.** 492.
"The Silver Crown." **3 ed.** 492; **1.** 138; **2.** 198; **4.** 180; **5.** 208.
"Still Life." **3 ed.** 492; **1.** 138; **2.** 198; **4.** 180; **5.** 208.
"A Summer's Reading." **3 ed.** 492.
"Take Pity." **3 ed.** 492–93; **1.** 139; **2.** 198; **4.** 180; **5.** 208.
"The Talking Horse." **2.** 198; **5.** 208.

HERBERT MALECHA

"The Trial." **3 ed.** 493.

MANOHAR MALGONKAR

"Bachcha Lieutenant." **3 ed.** 493.
"Hush." **3 ed.** 493.
"A Little Sugar—A Little Tea." **3 ed.** 493.
"Maggie." **3 ed.** 493.
"A Pinch of Snuff." **3 ed.** 493.
"A Question of Tactics." **3 ed.** 493.
"The Rise of Kistu." **3 ed.** 493.
"Suleman's Courier." **3 ed.** 493.
"This Is to Recommend." **3 ed.** 493.
"Top Cat." **3 ed.** 493.
"Two Red Roosters." **3 ed.** 493.

EDUARDO MALLEA

"La causa de Jacobo Uber, perdida." **3.** 257.
"Conversation." **3.** 257; **5.** 208.
"Human Reason." **2.** 199; **3.** 257.

McKNIGHT MALMAR

"The Storm." **3.** 257.

DAVID MALOUF

"Eustace." **3.** 258.
"The Prowler." **3.** 258.

ALBERT MALTZ

"Good-by." **1.** 139.
"The Happiest Man on Earth." **1.** 139.
"Incident on a Street Corner." **1.** 139.
"Man on a Road." **3 ed.** 493; **1.** 139.
"Season of Celebration." **1.** 139.
"The Way Things Are." **1.** 139.

BARRY MALZBERG

"The Twentieth-Century Murder Case." **3.** 258.

NADEZHDA MANDELSTAM

"The Egyptian Stamp." **3.** 258.
"The Noise of Time." **3.** 258.

ANDRÉ PIEYRE DE MANDIARGUES

"The Archaeologist." **3.** 258.
"The Capital Vision." **3.** 258; **5.** 208.
"The Diamond." **2.** 199; **3.** 258.
"The Little Stone Women." **5.** 208.
"Le Marronnier." **3.** 258.
"Le Sang de l'agneau." **3.** 258.
"La Spirale." **2.** 199.
"The Tide." **1.** 139.
"Le Tombeau d'Aubrey Beardsley." **3.** 258.

FREDERICK MANFRED

"Arrow of Love." **2.** 199.
"Country Love." **2.** 199.
"Footsteps in the Alfalfa." **2.** 199.
"Lew and Luanne." **2.** 199.
"The Mink Coat." **2.** 199.

JAMES CLARENCE MANGAN

"The Man in the Cloak." **3 ed.** 494.
"The Thirty Flasks." **3 ed.** 494.
"The Three Rings." **3 ed.** 494.

YANNIS MANGLIS

"Benghazi." **3 ed.** 494.
"The Boy with the Red Rose." **3 ed.** 494.
"Coffin." **3 ed.** 494.
"The Diving Suit." **3 ed.** 494.
"The Feast of St. Paraskevi." **3 ed.** 494.
"The Fellow Travelers." **3 ed.** 494.
"The Forest." **3 ed.** 494.
"The Gambler." **3 ed.** 494.
"Ghosts." **3 ed.** 494.
"Gypsy Wedding." **3 ed.** 494.
"Half Moon." **3 ed.** 494.
"Maaleche." **3 ed.** 494.
"Madalena." **3 ed.** 494.

"The Miracle." **3 ed.** 495.
"My Friend from Munich." **3 ed.** 495.
"The Old Man." **3 ed.** 495.
"The Partners." **3 ed.** 495.
"The Photographs." **3 ed.** 495.
"Revenge." **3 ed.** 495.
"The Secret of Captain Antonis the Bear." **3 ed.** 495.
"The Sluggard." **3 ed.** 495.
"A Strange Fellow." **3 ed.** 495.
"The Twins." **3 ed.** 495.
"The Wanderer." **3 ed.** 495.
"The Wedding." **3 ed.** 495.
"When You Fight for Freedom." **3 ed.** 495.

RALPH MANHEIM

"The Girl Who Loved Seders." **3 ed.** 495.

JOHN STREETER MANIFOLD

"Smoko with the Balkans." **1.** 139.

HEINRICH MANN

"Auferstehung." **3 ed.** 496.
"Die Branzilla." **3 ed.** 496.
"Contessina." **3.** 259.
"Kobes." **3 ed.** 496.
"The Marvelous." **2.** 199.
"Pippo Spano." **3 ed.** 496; **2.** 199; **5.** 208–09.
"Resignation." **3 ed.** 495; **2.** 199.
"The Tyrant." **3 ed.** 496.

KLAUS MANN

"Le Dernier Cri." **1.** 139.
"The Monk." **1.** 139.
"Three Star Hennessy." **1.** 139.

THOMAS MANN

"At the Prophet's." **3 ed.** 496; **4.** 180.
"The Bajazzo." **2.** 200.
"The Black Swan." **3 ed.** 496; **4.** 180.
"Blood of the Walsungs." **3 ed.** 497; **1.** 140; **2.** 200; **4.** 181.
"Death." **3 ed.** 497; **4.** 181.
"Death in Venice." **3 ed.** 497–500; **1.** 140; **2.** 200; **3.** 259; **4.** 181; **5.** 209.
"The Dilettante" [same as "The Clown"]. **3 ed.** 500; **4.** 181.
"Disillusionment." **3 ed.** 500; **2.** 200; **4.** 181.
"Disorder and Early Sorrow." **3 ed.** 500–01; **1.** 140; **2.** 200; **3.** 259; **4.** 181.
"Fallen." **3 ed.** 501; **1.** 140; **2.** 200; **4.** 181.
"The Fight Between Jappe and Do Escobar." **3 ed.** 501; **4.** 181.
"Gladius Dei." **3 ed.** 501; **1.** 140; **3.** 259; **4.** 181.
"A Gleam." **3 ed.** 501; **4.** 181.
"The Hungry." **2.** 200; **4.** 181.
"The Infant Prodigy." **3 ed.** 501–02; **1.** 140; **2.** 200; **4.** 181.
"Little Herr Friedemann." **3 ed.** 502; **2.** 200; **4.** 181.
"Little Lizzy." **3 ed.** 502; **4.** 182.
"Luischen." **2.** 200.
"A Man and His Dog." **3 ed.** 502–03; **4.** 182.
"Mario and the Magician." **3 ed.** 503–04; **1.** 140–41; **2.** 201; **3.** 259; **4.** 182; **5.** 209.
"Railway Accident." **3 ed.** 504; **2.** 201; **3.** 259; **4.** 182.
"Revenge." **2.** 200; **4.** 182.
"Royal Highness." **2.** 201.
"The Tables of the Law." **3 ed.** 504; **4.** 182.
"Tobias Mindernickel." **3 ed.** 504; **2.** 201; **4.** 182.
"Tonio Kröger." **3 ed.** 504–05; **1.** 141; **2.** 201; **3.** 259; **4.** 182; **5.** 209.
"The Transposed Heads." **3 ed.** 505–06; **2.** 201; **3.** 260; **4.** 182; **5.** 209.
"Tristan." **3 ed.** 506; **2.** 201; **3.** 260; **4.** 182.
"The Wardrobe." **3 ed.** 506; **2.** 201; **3.** 260; **4.** 182.
"The Way to the Churchyard" [same as "The Way to the Cemetery"]. **3 ed.** 506; **4.** 182.
"A Weary Hour." **3 ed.** 506–07; **4.** 182.
"The Will to Happiness." **3 ed.** 507; **1.** 141; **2.** 201; **3.** 260; **4.** 183.

BALRAJ MANRA

"The Box of Matches." **2.** 201.

CAPTAIN MANSFIELD [given name unknown]

"A Deal in Dope." **2.** 201.

KATHERINE MANSFIELD [KATHERINE BEAUCHAMP]

"An Advanced Lady." **4.** 183; **5.** 209.
"All Serene." **3 ed.** 507.
"The Aloe" [retitled "Prelude"]. **5.** 209.
"The Apple Tree." **3 ed.** 507.
"At Lehmann's." **3 ed.** 507; **1.** 141; **3.** 260; **4.** 183; **5.** 209.
"At the Bay." **3 ed.** 507; **1.** 141; **2.** 202; **3.** 260; **4.** 183; **5.** 210.
"Bains Turcs." **3 ed.** 507; **1.** 141; **3.** 260.
"Bank Holiday." **1.** 141.
"The Baron." **3 ed.** 507; **1.** 141.
"A Birthday." **3 ed.** 507; **1.** 141; **3.** 260; **4.** 183; **5.** 210.
"A Blaze." **5.** 210.
"Bliss." **3 ed.** 508; **2.** 202; **3.** 260; **4.** 183; **5.** 210.
"Brave Love." **3.** 260.
"The Canary." **3 ed.** 508.
"Carnation." **1.** 141.
"The Child-Who-Was-Tired." **3 ed.** 508; **4.** 183; **5.** 210.
"A Cup of Tea." **3 ed.** 508; **5.** 210.
"The Daughters of the Late Colonel." **3 ed.** 508–09; **1.** 142; **2.** 202; **3.** 260; **4.** 183; **5.** 210.
"A Dill Pickle." **3 ed.** 509; **3.** 260; **4.** 183; **5.** 210.
"The Doll's House." **3 ed.** 509; **1.** 142; **3.** 260; **4.** 183; **5.** 210.
"The Education of Audrey." **1.** 142.
"Die Einsame." **1.** 142; **3.** 260.
"The Escape." **3 ed.** 509; **1.** 142; **4.** 183; **5.** 210.
"A Fairy Story." **3.** 261.
"Feuille d'Album." **3 ed.** 509.
"The Flower." **3.** 261.
"The Fly." **3 ed.** 509–10; **1.** 142; **3.** 261; **5.** 210.
"Frau Brechenmacher Attends a Wedding." **3 ed.** 510; **1.** 142; **3.** 261; **4.** 183; **5.** 210.
"The Garden Party." **3 ed.** 510–11; **1.** 142; **3.** 261; **4.** 183; **5.** 210–11.
"Germans at Meat." **3 ed.** 511; **1.** 142; **3.** 261; **5.** 211.
"Her First Ball." **3 ed.** 511; **2.** 202; **3.** 261; **4.** 184; **5.** 211.
"Honeymoon." **3 ed.** 511.
"How Pearl Buttons Was Kidnapped." **3 ed.** 511; **1.** 142; **4.** 184; **5.** 211.
"An Ideal Family." **3 ed.** 511; **5.** 211.
"An Indiscreet Journey." **3 ed.** 511; **1.** 142.
"Je ne Parle Pas Français." **3 ed.** 512; **1.** 142; **2.** 202; **4.** 261; **5.** 211.
"A Journey to Bruges." **3 ed.** 512.
"The Lady's Maid." **3 ed.** 512; **2.** 202; **3.** 261.
"The Life of Ma Parker." **3 ed.** 512; **2.** 202; **3.** 261; **4.** 184; **5.** 211.
"The Little Girl." **3.** 261; **4.** 184; **5.** 211.
"The Little Governess." **3 ed.** 512; **3.** 261; **5.** 211.
"The Man Without a Temperament." **3 ed.** 512; **2.** 202; **3.** 261; **5.** 211.
"Marriage à la Mode." **3 ed.** 512; **1.** 142; **5.** 211.
"A Married Man's Story." **2.** 202; **3.** 261; **4.** 184; **5.** 211.
"Millie" [expanded to become "The Woman at the Store"]. **3 ed.** 512; **3.** 262; **5.** 211.
"Miss Brill." **3 ed.** 512–13; **1.** 142–43; **2.** 202; **3.** 262; **4.** 184; **5.** 211.
"Mr. and Mrs. Dove." **3 ed.** 513.
"Mr. Reginald Peacock's Day." **3 ed.** 513.
"The Modern Soul." **1.** 143; **3.** 262; **5.** 211.
"My Potplants." **3.** 262.
"New Dresses." **3 ed.** 513; **1.** 143; **3.** 262; **4.** 184; **5.** 211.
"Ole Underwood." **3 ed.** 513; **3.** 262.
"Pension Séguin." **3 ed.** 513; **1.** 143.
"Pictures" [originally "The Common Round"]. **3 ed.** 508, 513; **1.** 143; **3.** 262; **5.** 212.
"Poison." **3 ed.** 513; **5.** 212.
"Prelude" [originally "The Aloe"]. **3 ed.** 513; **1.** 143; **2.** 202; **3.** 262; **4.** 184; **5.** 209, 212.
"Psychology." **3 ed.** 513.
"Revelations." **3 ed.** 514; **5.** 212.
"The Singing Lesson." **3 ed.** 514; **1.** 143.
"The Sister of the Baroness." **1.** 143; **5.** 212.
"Six Years After." **1.** 143.
"Sixpence." **5.** 212.
"Something Childish but Very Natural." **3 ed.** 514; **2.** 202.
"Spring Picture." **1.** 143.
"The Stranger." **3 ed.** 514; **1.** 143; **3.** 262; **5.** 212.
"A Suburban Fairy Tale." **1.** 143.
"Sun and Moon." **3 ed.** 514; **1.** 143.

"The Swing of the Pendulum." **3 ed.** 514; **1.** 143.
"Taking the Veil." **1.** 143.
"This Flower." **1.** 143.
"The Tiredness of Rosabel." **3 ed.** 514; **1.** 144; **2.** 202; **4.** 184.
"A Truthful Adventure." **1.** 144.
"Violet." **1.** 144.
"The Voyage." **3 ed.** 514; **2.** 203; **3.** 262.
"A Wedding." **3 ed.** 514.
"What You Please." **3.** 262.
"The Wind Blows." **3 ed.** 514; **1.** 144; **2.** 203.
"The Woman at the Store" [originally, in shorter form, "Millie"]. **3 ed.** 514; **1.** 144; **2.** 203; **3.** 262; **5.** 212.
"The Young Girl." **1.** 144; **2.** 203.
"Youth." **5.** 212.

SAADAT HASAN MANTO

"By God." **3.** 263.
"Cold Meat." **3.** 263.
"Last Salute." **3.** 263.
"Mozel." **3.** 263.
"Open Up." **3.** 263.
"A Tetwal Dog." **3.** 263.
"Toba Tek Singh." **3.** 263.

DON JUAN MANUEL

"La mujer brava." **3 ed.** 515.

MAO DUN [same as MAO TUN or MAO TUNG; also SHEN YEN-PING]

"Autumn Harvest." **1.** 144.
"Autumn in Kuling." **1.** 144; **4.** 184.
"Creation." **1.** 144.
"Haze." **4.** 184.
"Lin Ch'ung the Leopard Head." **4.** 184.
"Spring Silkworms." **1.** 144.
"Stone Tablet." **4.** 184.
"Suicide." **1.** 144; **4.** 184.
"A Woman." **4.** 184.

RENÉ MARAN

"Deux Amis." **4.** 185.
"L'Homme qui attend." **4.** 185.
"Peines de Coeur." **4.** 185.

JUANITO MARCELLA

"The Cry of One Pierced by a Lance." **5.** 212.

WILLIAM MARCH

"Aesop's Last Fable." **1.** 144.
"The Arrogant Shoat." **4.** 185.
"Bill's Eyes." **4.** 185.
"The Borax Bottle." **4.** 185.
"Dirty Emma." **4.** 185.
"The Female of the Fruit Fly." **4.** 185.
"George and Charlie." **4.** 185.
"A Great Town for Characters." **4.** 185.
"A Haircut in Toulouse." **3 ed.** 515; **4.** 185.
"Happy Jack." **4.** 185.
"He Sits There All Day Long." **4.** 185.
"The Holly Wreath." **4.** 185.
"I'm Crying with Relief." **4.** 185.
"The Last Meeting." **4.** 185.
"The Little Wife." **3 ed.** 515; **4.** 186.
"A Memorial to the Slain." **4.** 186.
"Miss Daisy." **4.** 186.
"Not Very—Subtle." **4.** 186.
"October Island." **4.** 186.
"One Way Ticket." **4.** 186.
"The Patterns That Gulls Weave." **4.** 186.
"Personal Letter." **3 ed.** 515; **4.** 186.
"Runagate Niggers." **4.** 186.
"She Talks Good Now." **4.** 186.
"The Shoe Drummer." **4.** 186.
"A Shop in St. Louis, Missouri." **4.** 186.
"A Short History of England." **4.** 186.
"The Slate." **4.** 186.
"Snowstorm in the Alps." **4.** 186.
"The Static Sisters." **4.** 186.
"A Sum in Addition." **3 ed.** 515.
"This Heavy Load." **4.** 186.
"Time and Leigh Brothers." **4.** 187.
"To the Rear." **4.** 187.
"The Toy Bank." **4.** 187.
"Transcribed Album of Familiar Music." **4.** 187.
"The Tune the Old Cow Died To." **4.** 187.
"The Unploughed Patch." **4.** 187.
"Upon the Dull Earth Dwelling." **4.** 187.
"Whistles." **4.** 187.
"The Wood Nymph." **4.** 187.
"Woolen Drawers" [same as "Woolen Underwear" or "Mrs. Joe Cotton"]. **4.** 187.
"You and Your Sister." **4.** 187.

PESACH MARCUS

"Higher and Higher." **1.** 144.

ROBERTO MARIANI

"Rillo." **4.** 187.
"Riverita." **4.** 187.
"Toulet." **4.** 187.
"Uno." **4.** 187.

JUAN MARIN

"Black Port." **1.** 145.
"A Flight into Mystery." **1.** 145.
"Julian Aranda's Death." **1.** 145.
"Lazarus." **1.** 145.
"The Man at the Funeral." **1.** 145.
"The Man Hunt." **1.** 145.
"Nuptial." **1.** 145.
"Percival Lawrence's Crime." **1.** 145.

JOSÉ MARÍN CAÑAS

"Coto." **4.** 187.
"Rota la ternura." **5.** 212.

HUMBERTO MARIOTTI

"Into the Deep, Into the Deep." **3.** 263.

MARKANDEYA [full name]

"The Loss of Karmnasha." **3.** 263.

WALLACE MARKFIELD

"The Country of the Crazy Horse." **2.** 203.

VLADIMIR MARMARZIN

"Pushpull." **3.** 263.

JOHN P. MARQUAND

"Deep Water." **3 ed.** 515.
"The End Game." **3 ed.** 515.
"Good Morning, Major." **3 ed.** 515.

RENÉ MARQUÉS

"The Blue Kite." **2.** 203.
"The Child in the Tree." **2.** 203.
"The Crucifixion of Miss Bunning." **2.** 203.
"Death." **2.** 203; **4.** 188; **5.** 212.
"The Dragon's Hour." **2.** 203.
"Fear." **2.** 203.
"In a City Called San Juan." **2.** 203.
"In the Stern There Lies a Body." **2.** 203; **4.** 188.
"The Informer." **2.** 203.
"Island in Manhattan." **2.** 203.
"The Knife and the Stone." **2.** 204.
"The Little Miracle of Saint Anthony." **2.** 204.
"The Oath." **2.** 204.
"Purification on Christ Street." **2.** 204.
"La sala." **5.** 212.
"Three Men Near the River." **2.** 204; **5.** 213.
"Two Turns of the Key and a Guardian Angel" [same as ". . . Archangel"]. **2.** 204; **4.** 188.

DON MARQUIS

"The Ancient Mariner." **2.** 204.
"The Glass Eater's Story." **2.** 204.
"The Magic Melody." **2.** 204.
"Miss Higginbotham Declines." **2.** 204.
"The Report of a Trial Which Was Not Printed." **2.** 204.
"The Saddest Man." **2.** 204.
"Satan Goes to Church." **2.** 204.
"Twiller Van Durden's Miracle." **2.** 204.

JULIO MARRERO NUÑEZ

"Requiem for a Soldier of the King of Spain." **5.** 213.

JOYCE MARSHALL

"The Old Woman." **3 ed.** 515.

PAULE MARSHALL

"Barbados." **1.** 145; **3.** 264.
"Brazil." **3.** 264.
"British Guiana." **3.** 264.
"Brooklyn." **1.** 145; **3.** 264.
"Reena." **3 ed.** 516; **2.** 204; **3.** 264; **4.** 188.
"Some Get Wasted." **4.** 188.
"To Da-duh in Memoriam." **1.** 145; **3.** 264; **4.** 188.
"The Valley Between." **3.** 264.

ADAM MARS-JONES

"Bathpool Park." **4.** 188.
"Hooshi-mi." **4.** 188.
"Lantern Lecture." **4.** 188.

CLAIRE MARTIN

"C'est raté." **3.** 264.
"Femmes." **3.** 264.

GEORGE R. R. MARTIN

"A Song for Lya." **5.** 213.

FRANCISCO MARTÍNEZ

"A Story." **4.** 188.

GREGORIO MARTÍNEZ

"The Cross of Bolivar." **5.** 213.

EZEQUIEL MARTINEZ ESTRADA

"Examen sin conciencia." **2.** 205.

MASAMUNE HAKUCHŌ

"Autumn of This Year." **2.** 205.
"By the Inlet." **2.** 205.
"Clay Doll." **2.** 205.
"A Dangerous Character." **3.** 264.
"The Dead and the Living." **2.** 205.
"Discord and Harmony." **2.** 205.
"Dust." **2.** 205.
"Early Summer This Year." **2.** 205.
"Elder Brother Rii." **2.** 205.
"Ghost Picture." **2.** 205.
"Hell." **2.** 205.
"I Killed a Man, and Yet." **2.** 205.
"Illusion." **2.** 205.
"Nightmare." **2.** 205.
"Old Friend." **2.** 205.
"Peace of Mind." **2.** 206.
"The Smell of the Cowshed." **2.** 206.
"Solitude." **2.** 206.
"Spring This Year." **2.** 206.
"Suffocation." **2.** 206.
"Various People." **2.** 206.
"Wasted Effort." **2.** 206.
"Whither?" **2.** 206.

BOBBIE ANN MASON

"The Climber." **5.** 213.
"Detroit Skyline, 1949." **5.** 213.
"Drawing Names." **5.** 213.
"Gooseberry Winter." **3.** 265.
"Graveyard Day." **3.** 265; **5.** 213.
"A New-Wave Format." **3.** 265.
"The Ocean." **5.** 213.
"Offerings." **3.** 265.
"Old Things." **3.** 265; **5.** 213.
"Private Lies." **3.** 265.
"Residents and Transients." **3.** 265; **5.** 213.
"The Retreat." **3.** 265; **5.** 213.
"The Rookers." **3.** 265.
"Shiloh." **3.** 265; **5.** 214.
"Still Life with Watermelon." **3.** 265.

RICHARD MATHESON

"Drink My Blood." **5.** 214.
"Pattern for Survival." **5.** 214.
"Return." **3 ed.** 516.
"Trespass" [originally "Mother by Protest"]. **3.** 265.

JOHN MATHEUS

"Anthropoi." **2.** 206.
"Fog." **2.** 206.

SHAILESH MATIYANI

"Married Women." **3.** 265.

ANTUN GUSTAV MATOŠ

"The Balcony." **2.** 206.

MTUTUZELI MATSHOBA

"A Pilgrimage to the Isle of Makana." **3.** 266.
"Three Days in the Land of a Dying Illusion." **5.** 214.

BRANDER MATTHEWS

"An Interview with Miss Marlenspuyk." **5.** 214.

JAMES MATTHEWS

"A Case of Guilt." **5.** 214.
"The Park." **3.** 266.

ANA MARÍA MATUTE

"The Apprentice." **3 ed.** 516.
"The Beautiful Dawn." **3 ed.** 516.
"Bernardino." **3 ed.** 516.
"The Birds." **3 ed.** 516.

"The Black Sheep." **3 ed.** 516.
"The Boy Next Door." **3 ed.** 516.
"The Boy Who Found a Violin in the Granary." **3 ed.** 516.
"The Boy Who Was the Devil's Friend." **3 ed.** 516.
"The Boy Whose Friend Died." **3 ed.** 516.
"The Boys." **3 ed.** 516.
"The Celebration." **3 ed.** 516.
"Christmas for Carnavalito." **3 ed.** 516.
"Coal Dust." **3 ed.** 516.
"Conscience." **3 ed.** 517.
"The Cotton Field." **3 ed.** 517.
"The Dead Boys." **4.** 188.
"Doing Nothing." **3 ed.** 517.
"The Dry Branch." **3 ed.** 517.
"Fausto." **3 ed.** 517.
"A Few Kids." **3 ed.** 517; **4.** 189.
"The Fire." **3 ed.** 517; **5.** 214.
"The Friend." **3 ed.** 517.
"The Good Children." **3 ed.** 517.
"The Island." **3 ed.** 517.
"King of the Zennos." **3 ed.** 517.
"The Laundress' Son." **3 ed.** 517.
"The Little Blue-Eyed Negro." **3 ed.** 517.
"The Lost Dog." **3 ed.** 517.
"The Merry-Go-Round." **3 ed.** 517.
"The Metalworker." **3 ed.** 517.
"Miss Vivian." **3 ed.** 517.
"Mr. Clown." **3 ed.** 518.
"The Moon." **3 ed.** 518.
"News of Young K." **3 ed.** 518.
"No tocar." **3 ed.** 518.
"The Ones from the Store." **3 ed.** 518.
"The Pastry Shop Window." **3 ed.** 518.
"The Rabble." **3 ed.** 518.
"Rather a Sword." **3 ed.** 518.
"Reason." **3 ed.** 518.
"The Repentant One." **3 ed.** 518.
"The Rescue." **3 ed.** 518.
"Roads." **3 ed.** 518.
"The Round." **3 ed.** 518.
"The Schoolmaster." **3 ed.** 518.
"Shadows." **3 ed.** 518.
"Sin of Omission." **3 ed.** 518; **5.** 214.
"The Son." **3 ed.** 518.
"A Star on Her Skin." **3 ed.** 519.
"Thirst and the Child." **3 ed.** 519.
"The Treasure." **3 ed.** 519.
"The Trees." **3 ed.** 519.
"The Ugly Girl." **3 ed.** 519.

W. SOMERSET MAUGHAM

"The Artistic Temperament of Stephen Carey." **3 ed.** 519.
"The Back of Beyond." **3 ed.** 519.
"A Bad Example." **3 ed.** 519.
"Before the Party." **3 ed.** 519.
"The Colonel's Lady." **3 ed.** 519; **2.** 206; **4.** 189.
"The Creative Impulse." **3 ed.** 519.
"Daisy." **3 ed.** 519.
"A Domiciliary Visit." **4.** 189.
"The Door of Opportunity." **3 ed.** 519.
"The Facts of Life." **3 ed.** 519; **3.** 266.
"The Fall of Edward Barnard." **3 ed.** 519–20; **5.** 214.
"Fear." **3 ed.** 520.
"The Force of Circumstance." **3 ed.** 520.
"The Human Element." **3 ed.** 520.
"Jane." **3 ed.** 520.
"The Kite." **4.** 189.
"The Letter." **2.** 206.
"The Lion's Skin." **3 ed.** 520.
"Mackintosh." **3 ed.** 520; **2.** 206; **4.** 189.
"Miss King." **4.** 189.
"Mr. Know-All." **3 ed.** 520; **5.** 215.
"The Outstation." **3 ed.** 520; **1.** 145; **2.** 207; **4.** 189.
"P & O." **2.** 207.
"The Pool." **3 ed.** 520.
"Princess September and the Nightingale." **3 ed.** 520.
"Rain" [same as "Sadie Thompson"]. **3 ed.** 520–21; **2.** 207; **3.** 266; **4.** 189; **5.** 215.
"Red." **3 ed.** 521.
"Sanatorium." **3 ed.** 521; **1.** 145; **2.** 207.
"The Taipan." **5.** 215.
"The Traitor." **3 ed.** 521.
"The Treasure." **3 ed.** 521.
"The Unconquered." **3 ed.** 521; **4.** 189.
"The Vessel of Wrath." **3 ed.** 521.
"Virtue." **3 ed.** 521.
"Winter Cruise." **4.** 189.
"The Yellow Streak." **3 ed.** 521; **2.** 207.

MARIE K. MAULE

"A Week with a New Woman." **3.** 266.

GUY DE MAUPASSANT

"All Over." **3 ed.** 521.
"Allouma." **5.** 215.
"Amour." **3 ed.** 521.

"The Apparition." **3 ed.** 521.
"At Sea." **3 ed.** 522.
"The Avenger." **3 ed.** 522.
"Le Baptême." **3.** 266.
"Bed No. 29." **3 ed.** 522.
"Berthe." **5.** 215.
"The Bringer of Sleep." **3 ed.** 522.
"By Horseback." **3 ed.** 522.
"The Chair Mender." **4.** 189.
"Christmas Night." **2.** 207.
"A Corsican Bandit." **3 ed.** 522.
"Un Coup d'état." **5.** 215.
"A Coward." **3 ed.** 522.
"The Cripple." **3 ed.** 522.
"Darkness." **3 ed.** 522; **2.** 207.
"Decorated." **3 ed.** 522.
"The Devil." **3 ed.** 522.
"A Divorce Case." **3 ed.** 522.
"Don Juan." **2.** 207.
"Le Donneur d'eau bénite." **5.** 215.
"Dreams." **3 ed.** 522.
"The Drowned Man" [same as "Lost at Sea"]. **3 ed.** 522.
"Duchoux." **3 ed.** 522.
"A Duel." **3 ed.** 522.
"Epiphany." **3.** 266.
"A Family Affair." **3 ed.** 523.
"Fear." **3 ed.** 523.
"Fly: Recollections of a Boatman." **3 ed.** 523.
"The Hand." **5.** 215.
"Happiness." **3 ed.** 523.
"The Hautots, Father and Son." **3 ed.** 523.
"He?" **3 ed.** 523; **2.** 207.
"The Horla." **3 ed.** 523; **2.** 207; **3.** 266; **5.** 215.
"In the Wood." **3 ed.** 523.
"The Inheritance." **3 ed.** 523.
"The Inn." **3 ed.** 523.
"The Jewels." **3 ed.** 523; **2.** 207.
"Little Roque" [same as "Little Louise Roque"]. **3 ed.** 523.
"The Lock of Hair." **3 ed.** 524; **2.** 208.
"A Mad Man." **3 ed.** 524.
"The Mad Woman." **3 ed.** 524.
"Madame Hermet." **5.** 215.
"Madame Tellier's House." **3 ed.** 524; **3.** 266.
"Mademoiselle Cocotte." **3 ed.** 524.
"Mademoiselle Fifi." **3 ed.** 524; **5.** 215.
"Mademoiselle Perle." **3 ed.** 524.
"The Mask." **3 ed.** 524.
"Miss Harriet." **3.** 266; **4.** 189; **5.** 215.
"Monsieur Parent." **3 ed.** 524.
"Moonlight." **3 ed.** 524.
"Mount of Olives." **3 ed.** 524.
"My Uncle Jules." **3 ed.** 524.
"The Necklace." **3 ed.** 524–25; **1.** 145; **2.** 208; **3.** 267; **4.** 189.
"A Night's Entertainment." **3 ed.** 525.
"Old Amiable." **3 ed.** 525.
"The Olive Orchard." **3.** 267.
"On the Journey." **3 ed.** 525; **4.** 190.
"The Orphan." **5.** 216.
"Une Partie de campagne." **2.** 208.
"Paul's Woman." **3 ed.** 525; **2.** 208.
"A Piece of String." **3 ed.** 525; **3.** 267; **5.** 216.
"The Protector." **3 ed.** 525.
"Queen Hortense." **3 ed.** 525; **5.** 216.
"The Rondoli Sisters." **3 ed.** 525.
"The Rosebush of Madame Husson." **4.** 190.
"The Savage Mother." **3 ed.** 525; **2.** 208.
"Simon's Papa." **3 ed.** 526.
"The Skinned Hand." **3 ed.** 526; **5.** 216.
"The Spasm." **3 ed.** 526.
"Story of a Farm Girl." **3 ed.** 526.
"Story of Christmas." **2.** 208.
"Suicides." **3 ed.** 526.
"Tallow Ball." **3 ed.** 526; **2.** 208; **3.** 266.
"The Test." **3 ed.** 526.
"A Trick." **3.** 267.
"Two Friends" [same as "A Fishing Excursion"]. **3 ed.** 526.
"Two Little Soldiers." **3 ed.** 526.
"Useless Beauty." **3 ed.** 526.
"The Victim." **3 ed.** 526.
"Waiter, A Bock." **3 ed.** 526.
"Who Knows?" **3 ed.** 527; **4.** 190.
"A Widow." **5.** 216.
"The Will." **3 ed.** 527.
"Yvette." **3 ed.** 527; **3.** 267.

FRANÇOIS MAURIAC

"Conte de Noël." **3 ed.** 527.
"Coups de Couteau." **3 ed.** 527.
"Le Démon de la connaissance." **3 ed.** 527.
"Insomnia." **3 ed.** 527; **3.** 267.
"Rank." **3 ed.** 527.
"Thérèse à l'hôtel." **3 ed.** 527.
"Thérèse chez le docteur." **3 ed.** 527.

"Thérèse Desqueyroux." **3 ed.** 527; **1.** 146; **2.** 208; **4.** 190.
"Young Man in Chains." **3 ed.** 528.

ANDRÉ MAUROIS

"Le Départ." **3 ed.** 528.

WILLIAM MAXWELL

"The Absent-Minded Heart." **3 ed.** 528.

KARL MAY

"Abdahn Effendi." **3.** 267.
"Schamah." **3.** 267.

WILLIAM STARBUCK MAYO

"The Astonishing Adventure of James Botello." **2.** 208.
"The Captain's Story." **2.** 208.
"Don Sebastian: A Tale from the Chronicles of Portugal." **2.** 208.
"A Legend of the Cape de Verdes." **2.** 208.
"The Pious Constancy of Inez de Mencia Mont-Roy." **2.** 209.
"A Real Pirate." **2.** 209.

E. K. MEANS

"The Late Figger Bush." **3 ed.** 528.

CHRISTOPHER MECKEL

"Drusch, the Happy Magician." **3.** 267.
"A Man Came to Me." **3.** 267.
"Mr. Ucht." **3.** 267.
"The Shadow." **3.** 268.

DOLORES MEDIO

"Andrés." **3 ed.** 528.
"The Bellboy." **3 ed.** 528.
"A Cape for Braulio." **3 ed.** 528.
"The Courtyard." **3 ed.** 528.
"Five Letters from Germany." **3 ed.** 528.
"Giddy-up, Nicolas." **3 ed.** 528.
"The Hand Organ." **3 ed.** 528.
"The Handful of Dry Grass." **3 ed.** 528.
"Hi, Boss!" **3 ed.** 528.
"Injustice." **3 ed.** 529.
"The Last Toy Drum." **3 ed.** 529.
"Little Miguel's Baby Carriage." **3 ed.** 529.
"The Marten." **3 ed.** 529.
"Miracle in Santaolaya." **3 ed.** 529.
"Mr. Garcia." **3 ed.** 529.
"Nina." **3 ed.** 529.
"Pause." **3 ed.** 529.
"The Picture." **3 ed.** 529.
"The Second Time." **3 ed.** 529.
"Shall We Go, Timotheo?" **3 ed.** 529.
"The Strongest One." **3 ed.** 529.
"Teresa, A Solo Composed of Memories for a Man." **3 ed.** 529.
"Tomorrow." **3 ed.** 529.
"Unpunished Crime." **3 ed.** 529.
"Uphill." **3 ed.** 529.

S. P. MEEK

"The Red Peril." **5.** 216.

AHARON MEGGED

"The Name." **3.** 268.

HERMAN MELVILLE

"The Apple-Tree Table." **3 ed.** 529–30; **1.** 146; **2.** 209; **3.** 268; **5.** 216.
"Bartleby the Scrivener." **3 ed.** 530–33; **1.** 146–47; **2.** 209; **3.** 268; **4.** 190; **5.** 216–17.
"The Bell-Tower." **3 ed.** 533–34; **1.** 147; **2.** 210; **4.** 190–91.
"Benito Cereno." **3 ed.** 534–38; **1.** 147–48; **2.** 210; **3.** 268–69; **4.** 191; **5.** 217.
"Billy Budd." **3 ed.** 538–44; **1.** 148; **2.** 210–11; **3.** 269; **4.** 191; **5.** 217.
"Cock-A-Doodle-Doo!" **3 ed.** 544–45; **1.** 148–49; **2.** 211; **3.** 270; **4.** 191; **5.** 217–18.
"Daniel Orme." **3 ed.** 545; **5.** 218.
"The Encantadas." **3 ed.** 545–46; **1.** 149; **2.** 211; **3.** 270; **4.** 191; **5.** 218.
"The Fiddler." **3 ed.** 546; **1.** 149; **2.** 211.
"The Happy Failure." **3 ed.** 546; **1.** 149.
"I and My Chimney." **3 ed.** 546–47; **1.** 149; **2.** 211; **3.** 270; **5.** 218.
"Jimmy Rose." **3 ed.** 547; **1.** 149; **5.** 218.
"The Lightning-Rod Man." **3 ed.** 547–48; **1.** 149; **2.** 211; **4.** 191; **5.** 218.
"The Paradise of Bachelors and the Tartarus of Maids." **3 ed.** 548; **1.** 149; **2.** 211; **3.** 270; **4.** 192; **5.** 218.
"The Piazza." **3 ed.** 548–49; **1.** 149–50; **2.** 211; **4.** 192; **5.** 218.

"Poor Man's Pudding and Rich Man's Crumbs." **3 ed.** 549; **1.** 150.
"The Two Temples." **3 ed.** 549; **1.** 150; **3.** 270; **5.** 219.

ALFRED MENDES

"Boodhoo." **5.** 219.

MIGUEL MÉNDEZ [same as C. MIGUEL MÉNDEZ or M. MIGUEL MÉNDEZ]

"Estillo." **4.** 192.
"Tata Casehua." **4.** 192; **5.** 219.

ALVARO MENÉNDEZ LEAL [same as ALVARO MENÉN DESLEAL]

"Fire and Ice." **5.** 219.
"A Rope of Nylon and Gold." **3.** 270.

PORFIRIO MENESES

"Contrabando." **3 ed.** 549.

GEORGE MEREDITH

"The Case of General Opler and Lady Camper." **3 ed.** 550.
"The House on the Beach." **3 ed.** 550.
"The Tale of Chloe." **3 ed.** 550.

PROSPER MÉRIMÉE

"The Blue Room." **3 ed.** 550; **1.** 150.
"The Capture of the Redoubt." **3 ed.** 550; **1.** 150; **4.** 192.
"Carmen." **3 ed.** 550; **1.** 150.
"Colomba." **3 ed.** 550; **1.** 150; **4.** 192.
"La Double Méprise. **3 ed.** 550; **1.** 150.
"The Etruscan Vase." **3 ed.** 550; **1.** 150; **3.** 270.
"Federigo." **1.** 150.
"The Game of Backgammon." **3 ed.** 550; **1.** 150.
"Lokis." **1.** 150.
"Mateo Falcone." **3 ed.** 550; **1.** 150.
"Venus of Ille." **3 ed.** 550; **1.** 150–51; **4.** 192.
"La Vision de Charles XI." **3 ed.** 551; **1.** 150.

JUDITH MERRIL

"Daughters of Earth." **3.** 270; **5.** 219.
"Peeping Tom." **3.** 270.
"Stormy Weather." **3.** 270.
"That Only a Mother." **3.** 271; **5.** 219.

JAMES MERRILL

"Driver." **3.** 271.
"Peru: The Landscape Game." **3.** 271.

ABRAHAM MERRITT

"Burn, Witch, Burn!" **4.** 192.
"The Conquest of the Moon Pool." **3.** 271; **4.** 193.
"The Face in the Abyss." **4.** 193.
"The Metal Monster." **4.** 193.
"The Moon People." **3.** 271.
"The Moon Pool." **4.** 193.
"The People of the Pit." **3.** 271; **4.** 193.
"The Ship of Ishtar." **4.** 193.
"Three Lines of Old French." **3.** 271; **4.** 193.
"Through the Dragon Glass." **3.** 271.
"The Woman of the Wood." **3.** 271; **4.** 193.

W. S. MERWIN

"The Locker Room." **3 ed.** 551.

JOHN METCALF

"A Bag of Cherries." **4.** 193.
"The Beef Curry." **4.** 193.
"Beryl." **3.** 271; **4.** 193.
"Biscuits." **4.** 193.
"The Children Green and Golden." **4.** 193.
"Dandelions." **4.** 193.
"Early Morning Rabbits." **3.** 271.
"The Eastmill Reception Centre." **4.** 193; **5.** 219.
"The Estuary." **4.** 193; **5.** 219.
"Gentle as Flowers Make the Stones." **3.** 271; **4.** 194; **5.** 219.
"Geography of the House." **4.** 194.
"The Girl in Gingham." **3.** 271.
"The Happiest Days." **4.** 194.
"I've Got It Made." **4.** 194.
"Keys and Watercress." **3.** 272; **4.** 194.
"The Lady Who Sold Furniture." **3.** 272; **4.** 194; **5.** 220.

"Our Mr. Benson." **4.** 194.
"Playground." **4.** 194.
"Polly Ongle." **4.** 194; **5.** 220.
"The Practice of the Craft." **4.** 194.
"Pretty Bay." **4.** 194.
"Private Parts." **3.** 272.
"A Process of Time." **4.** 194.
"Single Gents Only." **4.** 194; **5.** 220.
"The Strange Aberration of Mr. Ken Smythe." **4.** 194.
"The Teeth of My Father." **3.** 272; **4.** 194; **5.** 220.
"A Thing They Wear." **4.** 194.
"The Tide Line." **3.** 272; **4.** 195.
"A Toy Called Peter Dog." **4.** 195.
"Travelling Northward." **5.** 220.
"Walking Around the City." **4.** 195.
"The Years in Exile." **3.** 272; **4.** 195; **5.** 220.

JOHN METCALFE [WILLIAM JOHN METCALFE]

"The Feasting Dead." **4.** 195.
"The Firing-Chamber." **4.** 195.
"Funeral March of a Marionette." **5.** 220.

ELIZA METEYARD

"Lucy Dean, the Noble Needlewoman." **3.** 272.

CHARLOTTE MEWS

"A White Night." **5.** 220.

CONRAD FERDINAND MEYER

"The Amulet." **3 ed.** 551; **1.** 151; **4.** 195; **5.** 220.
"Angela Borgia." **3 ed.** 551; **1.** 151.
"Gustav Adolf's Page." **3 ed.** 551; **1.** 151; **5.** 220.
"Der Heilige." **3 ed.** 551; **1.** 151.
"The Monk's Wedding." **3 ed.** 551–52; **1.** 151; **2.** 211.
"Plautus in the Convent." **3 ed.** 552; **4.** 195.
"Die Richterin." **3 ed.** 552; **1.** 151; **2.** 212.
"Der Schuss von der Kanzel." **3 ed.** 552; **1.** 151.
"The Sufferings of a Boy." **3 ed.** 551; **1.** 151; **2.** 212; **5.** 220.
"Die Versuchung des Pescara." **3 ed.** 552; **1.** 151.

CORD MEYER

"Waves of Darkness." **3 ed.** 552.

VICTOR MEYER-ECKHARDT

"Die Gemme." **3 ed.** 552.

GUSTAV MEYRINK

"The Urn of St. Gingolph." **5.** 220.

LEONARD MICHAELS

"City Boy." **3.** 272.

O. E. MIDDLETON

"The Crows." **3.** 272.
"The Loners." **3.** 272.
"A Married Man." **3.** 272.
"A Means of Soaring." **3.** 272.
"Not for a Seagull." **3 ed.** 552.
"The Will to Win." **3.** 272.

RICHARD MIDDLETON

"The Bird in the Garden." **3 ed.** 552.
"Fate and the Artist." **3 ed.** 552.
"The Ghost Ship." **3 ed.** 552.
"A Tragedy in Little." **3 ed.** 553.

JOSÉ RODRIGUES MIGUÉIS

"The Accident." **3.** 273.
"Beleza Orgulhosa." **3.** 273.
"Perdão, Frau Schwartz!" **3.** 273.

MIKHAIL MIKHAĬLOVICH ROSHCHIN

"Reminiscence." **3.** 273.

KÁLMÁN MIKSZÁTH

"The Big Spender." **1.** 151.
"The First Narrative." **1.** 151.
"The Golden Maid." **1.** 152.
"Lapaj, the Famous Bagpiper." **1.** 152.
"The Late Lamb." **1.** 152.
"The Lottery." **1.** 152.
"The Novel of Two Manors." **1.** 152.
"Pali Szűcs's Luck." **1.** 152.

"Poor János Gelyi's Horses." **1.** 152.
"The Queen's Skirt." **1.** 152.
"The Second Narrative." **1.** 152.
"That Black Stain." **1.** 152.
"That Which Poisons the Soul." **1.** 152.
"The Virgin Mary of Gozon." **1.** 152.
"Where Has Magda Gal Gone?" **1.** 152.

GEORGE MILBURN

"The Apostate." **3 ed.** 553.
"A Pretty Cute Little Stunt." **3 ed.** 553.
"The Wish Book." **3 ed.** 553.

PIERRE MILLE

"Barnavaux, général." **2.** 212.
"Barnavaux, homme d'état." **2.** 212.
"Les Chinois." **2.** 212.
"Le Dieu." **2.** 212.
"L'Evadé." **2.** 212.
"The Hare." **3.** 273.
"La Précaution inutile." **2.** 212.
"Un Prêtre qui pécha." **2.** 212.
"Ramary and Kétaka." **3.** 273.
"Le Romancero." **2.** 212.
"The Victory." **3.** 273.

ARTHUR MILLER

"Fame." **3 ed.** 553.
"Fitter's Night." **3 ed.** 553.
"I Don't Need You Any More." **3 ed.** 553.
"Monte Sant' Angelo." **3 ed.** 553; **1.** 152.
"Please Don't Kill Anything." **3 ed.** 553.
"The Prophecy." **3 ed.** 553.
"A Search for a Future." **3 ed.** 553.

HENRY MILLER

"Circe." **2.** 212.
"Dawn Travellers." **2.** 212.
"A Devil in Paradise." **4.** 195.
"Jabberwhorl Cronstadt." **4.** 195.

P. SCHUYLER MILLER

"The Cave." **1.** 152; **5.** 221.

SUE MILLER

"Tyler and Brina." **5.** 221.

WALTER M. MILLER

"Anybody Else Like Me?" **3 ed.** 553; **3.** 273.
"The Big Hunger." **1.** 153; **2.** 212.
"Big Joe and the Nth Generation" [same as "It Takes a Thief"]. **2.** 213; **3.** 273.
"Blood Bank." **1.** 153; **2.** 213; **3.** 273; **4.** 195.
"Check and Checkmate." **1.** 153; **2.** 213.
"Cold Awakening." **1.** 153; **2.** 213.
"Command Performance." **1.** 153; **2.** 213.
"Conditionally Human." **1.** 153; **2.** 213; **3.** 273.
"Crucifixus Etiam." **1.** 153; **2.** 213; **3.** 273.
"The Darfsteller." **2.** 213; **3.** 274.
"Dark Benediction." **1.** 153; **2.** 213; **3.** 274; **4.** 196.
"Death of a Spaceman" [same as "Memento Homo"]. **1.** 153; **2.** 213.
"Dumb Waiter." **2.** 213; **3.** 274; **4.** 196.
"The Hoofer." **1.** 153; **2.** 213.
"I Made You." **1.** 153; **2.** 213.
"No Moon for Me." **1.** 153; **2.** 214.
"Please Me Plus Three." **1.** 153; **2.** 214.
"Secret of the Death Dome." **2.** 214.
"Six and Ten Are Johnny." **1.** 153; **2.** 214.
"The Soul-Empty Ones." **1.** 153; **2.** 214.
"The Ties That Bind." **1.** 153; **2.** 214.
"The Yokel." **1.** 153; **2.** 214.
"You Triflin' Skunk." **4.** 196.

STEPHEN MINOT

"Journey to Ocean Grove." **3 ed.** 554.

SUSAN MINOT

"Lust." **5.** 221.

MISHIMA YUKIO

"The Boy Who Wrote Poetry." **3.** 274.
"The Cigarette." **3.** 274.
"Death in Midsummer." **5.** 221.
"Love in the Morning." **2.** 214.
"Onnagata." **5.** 221.
"Patriotism." **3 ed.** 554; **1.** 154; **2.** 214; **3.** 274; **4.** 196; **5.** 221.
"The Priest and His Love." **2.** 214.
"The Sea and the Sunset." **2.** 214.
"Seven Bridges." **2.** 214.
"Three Million Yen." **5.** 221.

DONALD G. MITCHELL

"Boldo's Story." **4.** 196.
"The Bride of the Ice-King." **4.** 196.
"The Petit Soulier." **4.** 196.
"Wet Day at an Irish Inn." **4.** 196.

IRENE MUSILLO MITCHELL

"Scenes from the Thistledown Theatre." **1.** 154.

JULIAN MITCHELL

"Can I Go Now?" **4.** 196.

S. WEIR MITCHELL

"The Autobiography of a Quack." **3 ed.** 554.
"The Case of George Dedlow." **3 ed.** 554.
"The Fourteenth Guest." **3 ed.** 554.
"Hephzibah Guinness." **3 ed.** 554.
"A Madeira Party." **3 ed.** 554.
"A Man and a Woman." **3 ed.** 554.
"Miss Helen." **3 ed.** 554.
"The Sins of the Fathers." **3 ed.** 554.
"Thee and You." **3 ed.** 554.
"Was He Dead?" **3 ed.** 554.

W. O. MITCHELL

"The Liar Hunter." **4.** 196.

NAOMI MITCHISON

"Round with the Boats." **4.** 196.

PREMENDRA MITRA

"The Great Big City." **3 ed.** 555.

WILLIAM ("BLOKE") MODISANE

"The Situation." **3.** 274.

NICHOLASA MOHR

"Herman and Alice." **5.** 221.
"Love with Aleluya." **5.** 221.
"Mr. Mendelsohn." **5.** 221.
"The Perfect Little Flower Girl." **5.** 221.
"Uncle Claudio." **5.** 221.
"A Very Special Pet." **5.** 222.

FERENC MOLNÁR

"The Coal Pilferers." **2.** 214.
"The Gnome and the Princess." **2.** 215.
"Music." **2.** 215.
"Princess Olga at the Funeral." **2.** 215.
"The Secret of the Aruwima Forest." **2.** 215.

N[AVARRO] SCOTT MOMADAY

"The Well." **4.** 197.

NICHOLAS MONSARRAT

"Heavy Rescue." **4.** 196.

C. E. MONTAGUE

"Action." **3 ed.** 555.

JOHN MONTAGUE

"A Ball of Fire." **3.** 274.
"A Change of Management." **2.** 214; **3.** 274.
"The Cry." **3 ed.** 555; **3.** 274.
"Death of a Chieftain." **3 ed.** 555; **3.** 274.
"The New Enamel Bucket." **3.** 274.
"An Occasion of Sin." **3.** 274.
"The Oklahoma Kid." **3.** 274.
"The Road Ahead." **3.** 275.
"That Dark Accomplice." **3.** 275.

EUGENE MONTALE

"Butterfly of Dinard." **2.** 215.
"English Gentleman." **2.** 215.

CARLOS MONTEMAYOR

"Nora." **4.** 197.
"Old Story." **4.** 197.

AUGUSTO MONTERROSO

"Mr. Taylor." **3.** 275.

BRIAN MOORE

"Catholics." **3.** 275.
"Grieve for the Dear Departed." **2.** 215; **5.** 222.
"Lion of the Afternoon." **2.** 215.
"Next Thing Was Kansas." **2.** 215.
"Off the Track." **2.** 215.

"Sassenach." **2.** 215.
"The Sight." **2.** 215.
"Uncle T." **3 ed.** 555; **2.** 215; **3.** 275; **5.** 222.

C[ATHERINE] L[UCILLE] MOORE

"Black God's Kiss." **3.** 275; **4.** 197.
"Black God's Shadow." **3.** 275; **4.** 197.
"The Bright Illusion." **1.** 154; **4.** 197.
"Daemon." **4.** 197.
"Fruit of Knowledge." **4.** 197.
"Greater Glories." **4.** 197.
"Greater Than Gods." **3.** 275.
"Judgment Night." **3.** 275.
"No Woman Born." **1.** 154; **3.** 275.
"Shambleau." **2.** 216; **3.** 275; **5.** 222.

GEORGE MOORE

"Agnes Lahens." **3 ed.** 555.
"Albert Nobbs." **3 ed.** 555; **1.** 154.
"Alms-Giving." **3 ed.** 555; **3.** 276.
"The Clerk's Quest." **3 ed.** 555; **3.** 276.
"The Curse of Julia Cahill" [same as "Julia Cahill's Curse"]. **3 ed.** 556; **1.** 154; **3.** 276; **5.** 222.
"The Exile." **3 ed.** 556; **1.** 154; **3.** 276.
"Fugitives" [late coalescence of "In the Clay" and "The Way Back," below]. **3 ed.** 556.
"Henrietta Marr" [an expansion of "Mildred Lawson"]. **3 ed.** 556; **1.** 154.
"Home Sickness." **3 ed.** 556; **3.** 276; **4.** 197.
"In the Clay" [later part of "Fugitives," above]. **3 ed.** 556; **1.** 154; **3.** 276.
"A Letter to Rome." **1.** 154; **3.** 276.
"Liadin and Curithir." **1.** 154.
"Mildred Lawson" [originally "An Art Student"; later expanded to become "Henrietta Marr," above]. **3 ed.** 556; **1.** 154.
"Peronnik the Fool." **1.** 155.
"A Play-House in the Waste." **3 ed.** 556; **3.** 276.
"Priscilla and Emily Lofft." **3 ed.** 556; **1.** 155.
"Sarah Gwynn." **3 ed.** 556; **1.** 155.
"So on He Fares." **3 ed.** 556; **1.** 155; **3.** 276.
"Some Parishioners." **3 ed.** 556; **1.** 155; **3.** 276.
"The Way Back" [later part of "Fugitives," above]. **3 ed.** 556; **1.** 155; **3.** 276.
"The Wedding Gown." **3 ed.** 556; **1.** 155; **3.** 276.
"The Wild Goose." **3 ed.** 556; **1.** 155; **5.** 222.
"Wilfred Holmes." **3 ed.** 557; **1.** 155.
"The Window." **1.** 155; **3.** 276; **4.** 197.

WARD MOORE

"Flying Dutchman." **5.** 222.
"Lot." **5.** 222.
"Lot's Daughter." **5.** 222.

FRANK MOORHOUSE

"The American, Paul Jonson." **1.** 155.
"Dell Goes into Politics." **2.** 216.
"The Dutch Letter." **2.** 216.
"The Everlasting Secret Family." **2.** 216.
"The Girl from the Family of Man." **4.** 198.
"Imogene Continued." **2.** 216.
"The Machine Gun." **1.** 155.
"The Town Philosophers' Banquet." **2.** 216.

ALBERTO MORAVIA

"Agostino." **3 ed.** 557.
"The Automaton." **3 ed.** 557.
"The Chase." **3.** 276.
"The Chimpanzee." **3 ed.** 557.
"The Chinese Vase." **3 ed.** 557.
"The Comics." **3 ed.** 557.
"Crime at the Tennis Club." **3 ed.** 557.
"Disobedience" [same as "Luca"]. **3 ed.** 557.
"Going to the People." **3 ed.** 557.
"In a Strange Land." **3 ed.** 557.
"Measurements." **3 ed.** 557.
"Mother's Boy." **3 ed.** 557.
"The Negro and the Old Man with the Bill-Hook." **3 ed.** 557.
"Rain in May." **3 ed.** 557.
"Scatter-Brains." **3 ed.** 557.
"A Sick Boy's Winter." **3 ed.** 558.
"Tired Courtesan." **3 ed.** 558.

HANNAH MORE

"The History of Diligent Dick." **4.** 198.
"The Lancashire Collier-Girl." **4.** 198.

LOUIS MOREAU

"The Face." **3 ed.** 558.

CARLOS MARTÍNEZ MORENO

"Biography." **3.** 277.

MARVEL MORENO

"Algo tan feo en la vida de una señora bien." **5.** 222.
"La noche feliz de Madame Yvonne." **5.** 222.

MORI ŌGAI

"The Abe Family" [same as "The Abe Clan"]. **3 ed.** 558; **2.** 216; **3.** 277.
"As If." **3 ed.** 558.
"The Boat on the River Takase." **3 ed.** 558.
"The Courier." **3 ed.** 558.
"The Dancing Girl." **3 ed.** 558; **3.** 277; **5.** 223.
"Delusions." **3.** 277; **5.** 223.
"Exorcising Demons." **3 ed.** 558.
"Fumizukai." **2.** 216.
"Half a Day." **3 ed.** 558; **3.** 277.
"Hanako." **3 ed.** 558; **3.** 277.
"The Japanese Neptune." **5.** 223.
"Kuriyama Daizan." **3 ed.** 558.
"The Last Phrase." **3 ed.** 558.
"The Last Testament of Okitsu Yagoemon" [same as "The Last Will and Testament . . ."]. **3 ed.** 558; **2.** 216; **3.** 277.
"Living Alone." **3 ed.** 558.
"Ōshio Heihachirō." **2.** 216.
"Play." **3 ed.** 559.
"A Record of Froth on the Water." **3 ed.** 559.
"The Revenge of Gojiingahara." **2.** 216.
"Sahashi Jingorō." **3 ed.** 559; **2.** 216.
"Sakai jiken." **2.** 216.
"Sanshō the Bailiff" [same as "Sanshō the Steward"]. **3 ed.** 559; **1.** 155.
"Sleeping Late." **3 ed.** 559.
"The Snake." **3 ed.** 559.
"Tower of Silence." **3.** 277.
"Tsuge Shirōzaemon." **3 ed.** 559; **2.** 216.
"Under Reconstruction." **3 ed.** 559; **3.** 277; **5.** 223.
"Yasui's Wife." **3 ed.** 559.

EDUARD MÖRIKE

"The Farmer and His Son." **3 ed.** 559.
"The Hand of Jezerte." **3 ed.** 559.
"Lucie Gelmeroth." **3 ed.** 559.
"Mozart on the Way to Prague." **3 ed.** 559; **1.** 155; **2.** 217; **4.** 198.
"The Stuttgart Hutzelmännlein." **3 ed.** 560.
"The Treasure." **3 ed.** 560.

A. G. MORRIS

"Panahard and Mr. Snaith." **3 ed.** 560.

WILLIAM MORRIS

"A Dream." **1.** 156; **5.** 223.
"Frank's Sealed Letter." **2.** 217; **4.** 198; **5.** 223.
"Gertha's Lovers." **1.** 156; **3.** 277; **4.** 198; **5.** 223.
"Golden Wings." **1.** 156.
"The Hill of Venus." **5.** 223.
"The Hollow Land." **1.** 156; **3.** 277; **4.** 198; **5.** 223.
"Lindenborg Pool." **1.** 156; **3.** 277.
"The Ring Given to Venus." **2.** 217.
"The Story of the Glittering Plain." **1.** 156; **2.** 217.
"The Story of the Unknown Church." **1.** 156; **2.** 217; **4.** 198; **5.** 223.
"Svend and His Brethren." **1.** 156; **4.** 198; **5.** 223.
"The Water of the Wondrous Isles." **2.** 217.
"The Well at the World's End." **2.** 217.
"The Wood Beyond the World." **2.** 217.

WRIGHT MORRIS

"Love Among the Cannibals." **3 ed.** 560.
"The Ram in the Thicket." **2.** 217; **3.** 278.
"Real Losses, Imaginary Gains." **3.** 278.

JOHN MORRISON

"The Battle of Flowers." **3 ed.** 560.
"The Lonely One." **3 ed.** 560.
"The Sleeping Doll." **3 ed.** 560.
"To Margaret." **3 ed.** 560.

TONI MORRISON

"1919." **2.** 217; **3.** 278.
"SEEMOTHERMOTHERISVERYNICE." **2.** 217.
"Sula." **3.** 278.

YIGAL MOSENSOHN

"Corporal Sonnenberg." **3 ed.** 560.
"Sergeant Green." **3 ed.** 560.
"Sheep." **3 ed.** 560.

MOTI NANDY

"Coming to the Town." **2.** 217.
"The United Front." **2.** 218.

WILLARD MOTLEY

"The Almost White Boy." **1.** 156.
"The Beautiful Boy." **3 ed.** 560.
"Bedroom Scene." **3 ed.** 561.
"The Beer Drinkers." **3 ed.** 561.
"The Boy." **1.** 156.
"The Boy Grows Up." **3 ed.** 561; **1.** 156.
"Boy Meets Boy." **3 ed.** 561.
"The Concert." **3 ed.** 561.
"Father Burnett's Vestry." **3 ed.** 561.
"How the Road Was Built" [revised to be Chap. VI of *Knock on Any Door*]. **3 ed.** 561.
"Needles." **3 ed.** 561.
"Niño de Noche." **3 ed.** 561.
"Street Walker." **3 ed.** 561.
"V-Female." **3 ed.** 561.
"Weasel Takes a Woman." **3 ed.** 561.

MARY T. MOTT

"Poor Ah Toy." **2.** 218; **3.** 278.

FRIEDRICH HEINRICH KARL DE LA MOTTE FOUQUÉ

"Undine." **3.** 278.

LAZLO MOUSSONG

"Orugananda." **5.** 223.

EZEKIEL MPHAHLELE

"Across Down Stream." **1.** 156.
"A Ballad of Oyo." **1.** 156.
"The Barber of Bariga." **1.** 156.
"Down the Quiet Street." **1.** 156.
"Grieg on a Stolen Piano." **1.** 157; **2.** 218.
"He and the Cat." **1.** 157; **2.** 218.
"In Corner B." **1.** 157.
"The Leaves Were Falling." **1.** 157.
"The Living and Dead." **3 ed.** 561; **1.** 157; **2.** 218.
"Man Must Live." **2.** 218.
"The Master of Doornvlei." **1.** 157; **3.** 278.
"Mrs. Plum." **1.** 157; **3.** 278; **4.** 198.
"Out Brief Candle." **1.** 157.
"A Point of Identity." **1.** 157.
"Reef Train." **1.** 157.
"The Suitcase." **1.** 157.
"Tomorrow You Shall Reap." **1.** 157.
"We'll Have Dinner at Eight." **1.** 157; **3.** 278.
"The Woman." **1.** 157.
"The Woman Walks Out." **1.** 157.

SLAWOMER MROZEK

"Art." **3 ed.** 561.

WILLIAM MUDFORD

"The Iron Shroud." **5.** 223.

MANUEL MÚJICA LÁINEZ

"La galera." **5.** 224.
"La gran favorita." **5.** 224.
"La hechizada." **5.** 224.
"El hombrecito del azulejo." **5.** 224.
"El ilustre amor." **3.** 278.
"La navegantes." **5.** 224.
"La princesa de los camafeos." **5.** 224.
"El rey artificial." **5.** 224.
"El rey picapedrero." **5.** 224.

ROSA MULHOLLAND

"The Hungry Death." **3.** 279.

CHARLES MUNGOSHI

"The Coming of the Dry Season." **3.** 279.

ALICE MUNRO

"Accident." **5.** 224.
"Age of Faith." **5.** 224.
"At the Other Place." **3.** 279; **5.** 224.
"Baptizing." **5.** 224.
"Bardon Bus." **4.** 198; **5.** 224.

"A Basket of Strawberries." **5.** 224.
"The Beggar Maid." **3.** 279; **5.** 225.
"Boys and Girls." **3 ed.** 562; **2.** 218; **4.** 199; **5.** 225.
"Chaddeleys and Flemings." **5.** 225.
"Circle of Prayer." **5.** 225.
"Connection." **4.** 199; **5.** 225.
"Dance of the Happy Shades." **1.** 157; **3.** 279; **5.** 225.
"The Dangerous One." **5.** 225.
"Day of the Butterfly" [originally "Good-bye, Myra"]. **1.** 158; **3.** 279; **5.** 225.
"The Dimensions of a Shadow." **5.** 225.
"Dulse." **4.** 199; **5.** 225.
"The Edge of Town." **3.** 279; **5.** 225.
"Eskimo." **5.** 225.
"Executioners." **5.** 225.
"The Ferguson Girls Must Never Marry." **5.** 225.
"Fits." **5.** 226.
"Forgiveness in Families." **3.** 279; **5.** 226.
"The Found Boat." **5.** 226.
"Hard-Luck Stories." **4.** 198; **5.** 226.
"Heirs of the Living Body." **5.** 226.
"Home." **3.** 279; **5.** 226.
"How Could I Do That?" **5.** 226.
"How I Met My Husband." **3.** 279; **5.** 226.
"The Idyllic Summer." **5.** 226.
"Images." **3.** 279; **5.** 226.
"Jesse and Meribeth." **5.** 226.
"Labour Day Dinner." **4.** 199; **5.** 226.
"Marrakesh." **3.** 279; **4.** 199; **5.** 226.
"Material." **2.** 218; **3.** 280; **4.** 199; **5.** 226–27.
"Memorial." **3.** 280; **5.** 227.
"Miles City, Montana." **5.** 227.
"Mischief." **5.** 227.
"Mrs. Cross and Mrs. Kidd." **5.** 227.
"Monsieur les Deux Chapeaux." **5.** 227.
"The Moon in the Orange Street Skating Rink." **5.** 227.
"The Moons of Jupiter." **4.** 199; **5.** 227.
"The Office." **3 ed.** 562; **3.** 280; **5.** 227.
"The Ottawa Valley." **2.** 218; **3.** 280; **4.** 199; **5.** 227.
"An Ounce of Cure." **3.** 280; **5.** 227.
"The Peace of Utrecht." **3.** 280; **5.** 227.
"Postcard." **5.** 227.
"Privilege." **3.** 280.
"The Progress of Love." **5.** 228.
"Providence." **5.** 228.
"Prue." **5.** 228.
"A Queer Streak." **5.** 228.
"Red Dress—1946." **5.** 228.
"The Shining House." **3 ed.** 562; **5.** 228.
"Simon's Luck." **5.** 228.
"Something I've Been Meaning to Tell You." **3.** 280; **4.** 199; **5.** 228.
"The Spanish Lady." **3.** 280; **4.** 199; **5.** 228.
"Spelling." **4.** 199; **5.** 228.
"The Stone in the Field." **3.** 280; **4.** 199; **5.** 228.
"Story for Sunday." **3.** 280; **5.** 228.
"Sunday Afternoon." **5.** 228.
"Tell Me Yes or No." **2.** 218; **3.** 280; **5.** 228.
"Thanks for the Ride." **3.** 280; **5.** 228–29.
"The Time of Death." **1.** 158; **5.** 229.
"A Trip to the Coast." **5.** 229.
"The Turkey Season." **5.** 229.
"Visitors." **5.** 229.
"Walker Brothers Cowboys." **3 ed.** 562; **5.** 229.
"Walking on Water." **3.** 280; **4.** 199; **5.** 229.
"White Dump." **5.** 229.
"Who Do You Think You Are?" **3.** 281; **5.** 229.
"The Widower." **5.** 229.
"Winter Wind." **1.** 158; **4.** 199; **5.** 229.
"Wood." **5.** 229.

IRIS MURDOCH

"Venus, Cupid, Folly, and Time." **3.** 281.

MARY NOAILLES MURFREE [pseudonym CHARLES EGBERT CRADDOCK]

"A-Playin' of Old Sledge at the Settlemint [sic]." **3 ed.** 562.
"Bushwhackers." **3 ed.** 562.
"The Casting Vote." **3 ed.** 562.
"The Dancin' Party at Harrison's Cove." **3 ed.** 562.
"Drifting Down Lost Creek." **3 ed.** 562.
"The 'Harnt' That Walks Chilhowee." **3 ed.** 562.
"The Mystery of Witch-Face Mountain." **3 ed.** 562.
"The Panther of Jolton's Ridge." **3 ed.** 562.
"The Phantom of Bogue Holauba." **3 ed.** 562.

"The Phantoms of the Foot-Bridge." **3 ed.** 563.
"The Raid of the Guerilla." **3 ed.** 563.
"The Riddle of the Rocks." **3 ed.** 563.
"The Romance of Sunrise Rock." **3 ed.** 563.
"Star in the Valley." **3 ed.** 563.
"Taking the Blue Ribbon at the County Fair." **3 ed.** 563.
"The Visitants from Yesterday." **3.** 281.

AMADO JESÚS MURO [CHESTER E. SELZER]

"Ay, Chihuahua." **4.** 200.
"Cecilia Rosas." **4.** 200.
"María Tepache." **4.** 200.
"My Aunt Dominga." **4.** 200.
"My Grandfather's Brave Songs." **4.** 200.
"Street of the Crazy Women." **4.** 200.
"Sunday in Little Chihuahua." **4.** 200.

ROBERT MUSIL

"The Blackbird." **1.** 158; **2.** 218; **4.** 200.
"The Enchanted House." **2.** 218.
"Das Fliegenpapier." **2.** 219.
"Grigia." **3 ed.** 563; **1.** 158; **3.** 281; **4.** 200; **5.** 229.
"The Perfection of Love" [same as "The Completion of Love"]. **3 ed.** 563; **1.** 158; **2.** 219; **3.** 281; **4.** 200; **5.** 230.
"The Portuguese Lady." **3 ed.** 563; **1.** 158; **2.** 219; **3.** 281; **4.** 200; **5.** 230.
"The Temptation of Silent Veronica." **3 ed.** 564; **1.** 158; **2.** 218; **4.** 200; **5.** 230.
"Tonka." **3 ed.** 564; **1.** 158; **2.** 219; **4.** 201; **5.** 230.

ALFRED DE MUSSET

"Les Deux Maîtresses." **3 ed.** 564; **2.** 219.
"Emmeline." **3 ed.** 564.
"Mimi Pinson." **3 ed.** 564.
"Le Secret de Javotte." **3 ed.** 564.

MBULELO VIZIKHUNGO MZAMANE

"My Cousin and His Pick-up." **5.** 230.
"The Soweto Bride." **3.** 281.

FRANZ NABL

"The Find." **2.** 219.

VLADIMIR NABOKOV

"The Admiralty Needle." **3 ed.** 564.
"An Affair of Honor" [originally "The Scoundrel"]. **3 ed.** 564; **1.** 158; **3.** 282.
"The Assistant Producer." **3 ed.** 565.
"The Aurelian." **3 ed.** 565.
"Bachmann." **3 ed.** 565; **1.** 158.
"Christmas." **1.** 159; **3.** 282.
"A Christmas Story." **3 ed.** 565; **1.** 159.
"The Circle." **3 ed.** 565.
"Cloud, Castle, Lake" [originally "Cloud, Lake, Tower"]. **3 ed.** 565; **5.** 230.
"Conversation Piece" [same as "Double Talk, 1945"]. **3 ed.** 565; **1.** 159.
"A Dashing Fellow." **3 ed.** 565; **1.** 159.
"The Defense" [originally "The Luzhin Defense"]. **3 ed.** 565.
"Details of Sunset." **1.** 159.
"The Doorbell." **3 ed.** 565; **1.** 159.
"The Eye." **3 ed.** 565.
"The Fight." **3 ed.** 565; **1.** 159.
"First Love." **3 ed.** 565; **3.** 282.
"A Forgotten Poet." **3 ed.** 565.
"A Guide to Berlin" [same as "A Guidebook . . ."]. **3 ed.** 565; **1.** 159; **2.** 219.
"Krug." **3.** 282.
"Lance." **5.** 230.
"The Leonardo." **2.** 219; **4.** 201.
"A Letter That Never Reached Russia." **1.** 159.
"Letter to Russia." **3 ed.** 566.
"Lik." **3.** 282; **5.** 230.
"Lips to Lips." **3 ed.** 566; **5.** 230.
"Mademoiselle O." **3.** 282.
"The Magician." **3 ed.** 566.
"A Matter of Chance." **1.** 159.
"Music." **3 ed.** 566.
"Notification." **3 ed.** 566.
"A Nursery Tale." **1.** 159.
"The Offense." **3 ed.** 566.
"The Passenger." **1.** 159.
"Perfection." **3 ed.** 566.
"Pnin." **2.** 219.
"Port." **3 ed.** 566; **1.** 159.
"The Potato Elf." **3 ed.** 566; **1.** 159; **3.** 282.
"The Razor." **3 ed.** 566; **1.** 159.
"Recruitment." **3 ed.** 566.
"The Return of Chorb." **3 ed.** 566; **1.** 159; **5.** 231.

"Scenes from the Life of a Double Monster." **3 ed.** 566; **2.** 220.
"Signs and Symbols." **3 ed.** 566; **1.** 159; **2.** 220; **3.** 282; **4.** 201; **5.** 231.
"Spring in Fialta." **3 ed.** 566; **1.** 160; **3.** 282; **4.** 201; **5.** 231.
"The Storm." **1.** 160.
"Terra Incognita." **3.** 282.
"Terror." **3 ed.** 567; **1.** 160; **3.** 282; **4.** 201.
"That in Aleppo Once . . . ." **3 ed.** 567; **2.** 220; **3.** 282; **5.** 231.
"Time and Ebb." **3 ed.** 567.
"Torpid Smoke." **3.** 282; **5.** 231.
"Triangle in a Circle." **3 ed.** 567.
"Tyrants Destroyed." **2.** 220; **3.** 282.
"Ultima Thule." **3.** 283.
"The Vane Sisters." **3 ed.** 567; **1.** 160; **2.** 220; **3.** 283; **5.** 231.
"A Visit to the Museum." **3 ed.** 567; **3.** 283.
"The Windows of the Mint." **3.** 283.

NAGAI KAFŪ

"Behind the Prison." **3.** 283.
"The Bill Collector." **3.** 283.
"Clouds" [originally "Dissipation"]. **3.** 283.
"The Decoration." **3.** 283.
"Diary of One Who Returned to Japan." **3.** 283.
"Flower Basket." **3.** 283.
"Flower Vase." **3.** 283.
"Hydrangea." **3.** 283.
"Journey Alone." **3.** 283.
"Night Plovers." **3.** 283.
"The Peony Garden." **3.** 284.
"Pleasure." **3.** 284.
"The River Sumida." **1.** 160; **5.** 231.
"A Strange Tale from East of the River." **5.** 231.
"Summer Dress." **3.** 284.
"A Swirl of Pine Needles." **3.** 284.
"A Tale of a Nettle Tree." **3.** 284.
"A Toast." **3.** 284.

AMRIT LAL NAGAR

"Problems of Truthfulness." **3.** 284.

YURI NAGIBIN

"The Chase." **2.** 220.
"Chetunov, Son of Chetunov." **2.** 220.
"Echoes." **3.** 284.
"The Fiery Archpriest." **5.** 231.
"A Man and a Road." **2.** 220.

RABBI BRATYLAV NAHAM

"A Story About a Clever Man and a Simple Man." **3 ed.** 567.

MIKHAIL NAIMY [same as MIKHAIL NUAYMA]

"Her New Year." **4.** 201; **5.** 231.

V[IDIADHAR] S[URAJPRASAD] NAIPAUL

"A Christmas Story." **1.** 160; **3.** 284; **5.** 232.
"Circus at Luxor." **5.** 232.
"The Enemy." **1.** 160.
"A Family Reunion." **5.** 232.
"A Flag on the Island." **3 ed.** 567; **5.** 232.
"Gopi." **1.** 160.
"Greenie and Yellow." **3 ed.** 567; **5.** 232.
"Gurudeva." **1.** 160.
"Hat." **5.** 232.
"Heart." **3 ed.** 567.
"In a Free State." **3 ed.** 567; **5.** 232.
"Love, Love, Love Alone." **5.** 232.
"Man-man." **3 ed.** 567.
"The Mourners." **1.** 160; **5.** 232.
"My Aunt Gold Teeth." **1.** 160; **5.** 232.
"The Night Watchman's Occurrence Book." **3.** 284.
"The Old Man." **5.** 232.
"One out of Many." **3 ed.** 567; **1.** 160; **5.** 232.
"Potatoes." **5.** 232.
"A Second Visit." **5.** 232.
"Tell Me Who to Kill." **3 ed.** 568; **1.** 160; **5.** 232–33.
"The Tramp at Piraeus." **5.** 233.
"Until the Soldiers Came." **5.** 233.

NAKAGAMI KENJI

"The Promontory." **5.** 233.
"The Sea of Kareki." **5.** 233.

NAKAJIMA ATSUSHI

"The Disciple." **3.** 284.

NAKAYAMA GISHŪ

"The Last Days of Tinian." **3.** 285.

LILIKA NAKOS

"And the Child Lied." **3.** 285.
"The Cat." **3.** 285.
"Elenitsa." **3.** 285.
"God's Garden." **3.** 285.
"The Little Servant." **3.** 285.
"Love." **3.** 285.
"Maternity." **3.** 285.
"The Story of the Virginity of Miss Tade." **3.** 285.

ZOFIA NALKOWSKA

"Happiness." **3 ed.** 568.

R. K. NARAYAN

"Annamalai." **3.** 285.
"Another Community." **3.** 285.
"An Astrologer's Day." **5.** 233.
"A Breach of Promise." **3 ed.** 568; **5.** 233.
"A Breath of Lucifer." **3.** 285.
"Dodu." **4.** 201.
"Gateman's Gift." **3.** 285.
"Half-a-Rupee Worth." **3.** 285.
"A Horse and Two Goats." **3 ed.** 568; **2.** 220; **3.** 286; **4.** 201.
"The Martyr's Corner." **3.** 286.
"Ranga." **4.** 201.
"The Roman Image." **5.** 233.
"The Seventh House." **3.** 286.
"Trail of the Green Blazer." **3.** 286.
"Uncle." **3.** 286; **4.** 201.
"Under the Banyan Tree." **5.** 233.
"Wife's Holiday." **3.** 286.

ISAAC R. NATHANSON

"The World Aflame." **5.** 233.

NATSUME SŌSEKI

"Botchan." **5.** 233.
"The Grass Pillow." **5.** 233.
"Hearing Things." **5.** 234.
"The 'Storm Day.'" **5.** 234.
"Ten Nights of Dreams." **5.** 234.
"The Wintry Blast." **5.** 234.

J. L. NAVARRO

"Blue Day on Main Street." **4.** 201.
"Cutting Mirrors." **4.** 202.
"Frankie's Last Wish." **4.** 202.
"Weekend." **4.** 202.

NJABULO NDEBELE

"The Music of the Violin." **3.** 286.
"Uncle." **5.** 234.

JOHN NEAL

"Courtship." **1.** 161.
"David Whicher." **1.** 161.
"The Haunted Man." **1.** 161.
"The Ins and Outs." **1.** 161.
"Otter-Bag, the Oneida Chief." **1.** 161; **4.** 202.
"Robert Steele." **1.** 161.
"The Utilitarian." **1.** 161.
"The Young Phrenologist." **1.** 161.

JOHN G. NEIHARDT

"The Alien." **3.** 286.
"Beyond the Spectrum." **3.** 286.
"The End of a Dream." **3.** 286.
"The Fading of a Shadow Flower." **3.** 286; **5.** 234.
"The Heart of a Woman." **3.** 286.
"The Look in the Face." **3.** 286; **5.** 234.
"Mignon." **3.** 286.
"A Prairie Borgia." **3.** 286.
"The Red Roan Mare." **3.** 287.
"The Scars." **3.** 287.
"The Singer of the Ache." **3.** 287.
"Vylin." **3.** 287.
"The White Wakunda." **3.** 287.

BOZHENA NĚMCOVÁ

"Babs." **3 ed.** 568.
"The Castle and the Village." **3 ed.** 568.
"Karla." **3 ed.** 568.
"Poor People." **3 ed.** 568.
"Wild Bára." **3 ed.** 568.

GÉRARD DE NERVAL [GÉRARD LABRUNIE]

"The Bewitched Hand." **5.** 234.
"The Golden Ass." **2.** 220.
"L'Histoire de la reine du matin et de Soli-

man, prince des Génies." **3 ed.** 568; **2.** 220.
"L'Histoire du Calife Hakem." **2.** 220.
"The Illuminists." **2.** 221.
"Jemmy." **3 ed.** 568.
"The Marquis de Fayolle." **3 ed.** 568; **2.** 221.
"Le Roi de Bicêtre." **2.** 221.
"The Singular Biography of Raoul Spifame." **2.** 221.
"Sylvie." **1.** 161; **2.** 221; **3.** 287; **4.** 202.

AMADO NERVO

"Las Casas." **5.** 234.
"Diálogos pitagóricos: La proxima encarnación." **5.** 234.

EDITH NESBIT

"The Bristol Bowl." **5.** 234.
"The Cockatoucan." **3.** 287.
"Melisande." **3.** 287.
"Whereyouwantogoto." **3.** 287.

JAY NEUGEBOREN

"Something Is Rotten in the Borough of Brooklyn." **3.** 287.

F. TERRY NEWMAN

"Marius the Doll." **5.** 235.

FRANCES NEWMAN

"Rachel and Her Children." **2.** 221.

MARTIN ANDERSEN NEXØ

"An' Mari's Journey." **4.** 202.
"Awash." **4.** 202.
"Fate." **4.** 202.
"Fraenke." **4.** 202.
"Good Fortune." **4.** 202.
"Gossamer." **4.** 202.
"The Idiot." **4.** 202.
"The Lottery-Swede." **4.** 202.
"The Musical Pig." **4.** 203.
"The Old Bachelor's Story." **4.** 203.
"Paradise." **4.** 203.
"Payday." **4.** 203.
"The Smith from Dyndeby." **4.** 203.
"The Walls." **4.** 203.

JAMES NGUGI

"A Meeting in the Dark." **3 ed.** 569.

NGUGI WA THIONG'O

"And the Rain Came Down." **2.** 221.
"Minutes of Glory." **2.** 221.
"The Mubenzi Tribesman." **2.** 221.

NI I-TE

"On the Bank of the River." **3.** 287.
"A Poor Scholar." **3.** 287.

DJIBRIL TAMSIR NIANE

"Kakandé." **3.** 288.

ZYGMUNT NIEDZWIECKI

"The Eyes." **3 ed.** 569.
"A Fable." **3 ed.** 569.
"Marinated Fish." **3 ed.** 569.
"The Quarrelsome Woman." **3 ed.** 569.
"The Winning Number." **3 ed.** 569.

ANDRZEJ NIEMOJEWSKI

"Ptak." **3 ed.** 569.

ANAÏS NIN

"The All-Seeing." **3 ed.** 569; **2.** 221.
"Birth." **1.** 161; **2.** 221; **3.** 288.
"Bread and Wafer." **2.** 221.
"The Café." **2.** 222.
"The Child Born out of the Fog." **2.** 222.
"Hejda." **1.** 161; **2.** 222; **3.** 288; **5.** 235.
"Houseboat." **2.** 222; **3.** 288.
"Je Suis le Plus Malade des Surrealistes." **2.** 222.
"The Labyrinth." **2.** 222; **3.** 288.
"Lilith." **3.** 288.
"The Maya." **3.** 288.
"The Mohican." **2.** 222.
"The Mouse." **1.** 161; **2.** 222.
"Ragtime." **1.** 161; **2.** 222; **3.** 288.
"Sabina." **2.** 222.
"The Sealed Room." **2.** 222.
"Stella." **1.** 162; **2.** 222; **3.** 288.
"This Hunger." **2.** 222.
"Under a Glass Bell." **3 ed.** 569; **2.** 222; **3.** 288.
"The Voice." **1.** 162; **2.** 222; **3.** 288.

"Waste of Timelessness." **3.** 288.
"Winter of Artifice" [originally "Lilith"]. **1.** 162; **2.** 223; **3.** 288.

HUGH NISSENSON

"The Blessing." **4.** 203.
"The Crazy Old Man." **4.** 203.
"The Law." **4.** 203.
"The Prisoner." **4.** 203.

DER NISTER [PINKHES KAHANOVITSH]

"Under the Fence." **4.** 203.

LARRY NIVEN

"Neutron Star." **2.** 223.
"Rammer." **3.** 288.
"The Soft Weapon." **5.** 235.
"Three Vignettes: Grammar Lesson." **3.** 289.

LARRY NIXON

"Inconstant Moon." **3.** 289.

LEWIS NKOSI

"The Prisoner." **3.** 289.

CHARLES NODIER

"La Fée aux miettes." **3 ed.** 569.
"The Four Talismans." **3 ed.** 569.
"Franciscus Columna." **3 ed.** 569.
"Une Heure ou la vision." **3 ed.** 570.
"L'Histoire d'Hélène Gillet." **3 ed.** 570.
"L'Histoire du Calife Hakem." **3 ed.** 570.
"L'Homme et la fourmi." **3 ed.** 570.
"Ines de Las Sierras." **3.** 289.
"Jean Sbogar." **3 ed.** 570.
"Jean-François Les Bau-Bleus." **3 ed.** 570.
"Légende de Soeur Béatrix." **3 ed.** 570.
"Lydie or the Resurrection." **3 ed.** 570.
"Mademoiselle de Marsas." **3 ed.** 570.
"Paul or the Resemblance." **3 ed.** 570.
"Le Peintre de Saltzbourg." **3 ed.** 570.
"La plus petite des pantouffles." **3 ed.** 570.
"Le Songe d'or." **3 ed.** 570.
"Trilby." **3 ed.** 570.

FRANK NORRIS

"After Strange Gods." **2.** 223; **3.** 289.
"'As Long As Ye Both Shall Live.'" **3.** 289.
"A Case for Lombroso." **3 ed.** 570; **4.** 203.
"A Deal in Wheat." **3 ed.** 570–71.
"Dying Fires." **3 ed.** 571; **3.** 289.
"Grettir at Drangey." **3 ed.** 571.
"Grettir at Thorhall-stead." **3 ed.** 571.
"His Single Blessedness." **3 ed.** 571.
"Lauth." **3 ed.** 571.
"A Reversion to Type." **4.** 203.
"The Salvation Boom in Matabeleland." **3 ed.** 571.
"This Animal of Buldy Jones." **2.** 223.
"Thoroughbred." **2.** 223.
"Toppan" [originally "Unequally Yoked"]. **3 ed.** 571.
"Travis Hallett's Halfback." **2.** 223.

CYPRIAN NORWID

"Ad leones." **3 ed.** 571.
"The Bracelet." **3 ed.** 571.
"Civilization." **3 ed.** 571.
"Dominic." **3 ed.** 571.
"The Kind Guardian, or Bartlomiej Becomes Alphonse." **3 ed.** 571.
"Lord Singleworth's Secret." **3 ed.** 571.
"Menego." **3 ed.** 571.
"Stigma." **3 ed.** 571.

LINO NOVÁS CALVO

"'Allies' and 'Germans.'" **2.** 223; **3.** 289; **4.** 204.
"Angusola and the Knives." **2.** 223.
"A Bad Man." **2.** 223; **4.** 204.
"Between Neighbors." **2.** 223.
"A Bum." **2.** 223; **4.** 204.
"Can't Really Say." **4.** 204.
"The Cow on the Rooftop." **1.** 162; **2.** 223.
"The Dark Night of Ramón Yendía." **1.** 162; **2.** 223; **4.** 204; **5.** 235.
"Down in Copey." **2.** 224.
"The Execution of Fernández." **2.** 224; **4.** 204.
"A Finger on Him" [same as "Don't Lay a Finger on Him"]. **1.** 162; **2.** 224; **4.** 204.
"The First Lesson." **2.** 224; **4.** 204.
"The Flutist." **4.** 204.
"The Grandmother Queen and Her Nephew Delfín." **1.** 162; **2.** 224; **4.** 204.

"Hold That Man Down!" [same as "Tie That Man Down!"]. **2.** 225; **4.** 204.
"I Don't Know What to Say." **3.** 289.
"In the Key" [same as "On the Key" or "On the Island"]. **2.** 224; **4.** 205.
"The Invisible Husband." **2.** 224; **4.** 204.
"Long Island." **2.** 224; **4.** 204.
"The Moon Ceremony." **4.** 204.
"My Uncle Antón Luna." **2.** 224; **4.** 204.
"The Night the Dead Came out to Haunt Us" [same as "The Night the Dead Came Forth"]. **2.** 224; **4.** 205.
"The Ninth Moon." **2.** 224.
"No le sé desil." **5.** 235.
"No One to Kill." **1.** 162; **2.** 224.
"The Oquendo Family." **2.** 224.
"The Other Key." **1.** 162; **2.** 224.
"Palm Key." **1.** 162; **2.** 224; **4.** 204.
"The Place That's Calling Me." **2.** 224; **4.** 205.
"The Reed: A Cuban Story." **4.** 205.
"The Room for Dying." **2.** 224; **4.** 205.
"A Ruined Man." **2.** 225.
"The Secret of Narciso Campana." **2.** 225; **4.** 205.
"A Singular Encounter." **2.** 225; **4.** 205.
"A Sip of Coffee." **4.** 205.
"The Spider Man." **2.** 225; **4.** 205.
"A Thinking Man" [same as "The Thinking Head"]. **2.** 225; **4.** 205.
"The Vine." **2.** 225.
"The Vision of Tamaría." **2.** 225; **4.** 205.
"Worse Than a Hell." **2.** 225; **4.** 205.

PHILLIP FRANCIS NOWLAN

"The Air Lords of Han." **3.** 289.

BETH NUGENT

"City of Boys." **5.** 235.

FLORA NWAPA

"The Chief's Daughter." **4.** 205.
"The Child Thief." **2.** 225.
"Daddy, Don't Strike the Match." **4.** 205.
"The Delinquent Adults." **2.** 225; **4.** 205.
"Jide's Story." **2.** 225.
"The Loss of Eze." **2.** 225; **4.** 205.
"My Soldier Brother." **2.** 225.
"The Road to Benin." **2.** 225; **4.** 206.
"This Is Lagos." **2.** 225; **4.** 206.
"The Traveller." **2.** 225; **4.** 206.
"A Wife's Dilemma." **4.** 206.
"Wives at War." **4.** 206.

JOYCE CAROL OATES

"Accomplished Desires." **2.** 226; **4.** 206.
"All the Good People I've Left Behind." **4.** 206.
"An American Adventure." **4.** 206.
"An American Dream." **4.** 206.
". . . & Answers." **2.** 226; **4.** 206.
"Archways." **2.** 226; **4.** 206.
"The Assailant." **4.** 206.
"Assault." **2.** 226; **4.** 206.
"At the Seminary." **1.** 162; **3.** 290; **4.** 206; **5.** 235.
"The Blessing." **4.** 206.
"Blindfold." **2.** 226.
"Bloodstains." **4.** 206.
"Blood-Swollen Landscape." **4.** 207.
"Bodies." **3 ed.** 572; **2.** 226; **4.** 207; **5.** 235.
"Boy and Girl." **4.** 207.
"Boys at a Picnic." **4.** 207.
"By the North Gate." **2.** 226.
"The Census Taker." **2.** 226; **4.** 206.
"Ceremonies." **4.** 207.
"The Children." **1.** 162; **4.** 207; **5.** 235.
"Convalescing." **4.** 207.
"Crossing the Border." **4.** 207.
"Customs." **4.** 207.
"The Daughter." **4.** 207.
"The Dead." **3 ed.** 572; **1.** 162; **4.** 207; **5.** 236.
"A Descriptive Catalogue." **2.** 226.
"Détente." **5.** 236.
"Did You Ever Slip on Red Blood?" **1.** 162; **2.** 226.
"DOUBLE TRAGEDY STRIKES TENNESSEE HILL FAMILY." **4.** 207.
"The Dreaming Woman." **4.** 207.
"The Dungeon." **4.** 207.
"Dying." **4.** 207.
"The Dying Child." **4.** 207.
"Edge of the World." **4.** 207.
"Exile." **4.** 208.
"Extraordinary Popular Delusions." **4.** 208.
"Eye-Witness." **4.** 208.
"Famine Country." **4.** 208.
"The Fine White Mist of Winter." **4.** 208.
"First Views of the Enemy." **2.** 226; **4.** 208.
"Four Summers." **2.** 226; **4.** 208.

"Free." **2.** 226.
"Getting and Spending." **4.** 208.
"Gifts." **4.** 208.
"The Girl." **1.** 163.
"The Girl at the Edge of the Ocean." **4.** 208.
"The Going-Away Party." **4.** 208.
"The Golden Madonna." **4.** 208.
"The Hallucination." **4.** 208.
"The Heavy Sorrow of the Body." **4.** 208.
"Hello Fine Day Isn't It." **4.** 208.
"How I Contemplated the World from the Detroit House of Correction and Began My Life Over Again." **1.** 163; **2.** 227; **3.** 290; **4.** 208; **5.** 236.
"I Must Have You." **4.** 208.
"Images." **4.** 209.
"In the Old World." **2.** 227; **4.** 209.
"In the Region of Ice." **2.** 227; **3.** 290; **4.** 209; **5.** 236.
"In the Warehouse." **2.** 227.
"An Incident in the Park." **4.** 209.
"The Lady with the Pet Dog." **2.** 227; **3.** 290; **4.** 209; **5.** 236.
"Landscape of Neutral Colors." **4.** 209.
"Last Days." **5.** 236.
"The Leap." **4.** 209.
"The Loves of Franklin Ambrose." **3 ed.** 572.
"Loving/Losing/Loving a Man." **2.** 227; **4.** 209.
"The Madwoman." **4.** 209.
"Magna Mater." **2.** 227; **4.** 209.
"The Man That Turned into a Statue." **4.** 209.
"The Man Whom Women Adored." **5.** 236.
"The Maniac." **2.** 227; **4.** 209.
"Matter and Energy." **4.** 209.
"The Metamorphosis" [originally "Others' Dreams"]. **1.** 163; **2.** 227; **4.** 209.
"My Warszawa: 1980." **5.** 236.
"Narcotic." **1.** 163.
"Normal Love." **1.** 163; **2.** 227; **4.** 210; **5.** 236.
"Norman and the Killer." **2.** 227; **4.** 210.
"Old Budapest." **5.** 236.
"Our Wall." **5.** 236.
"Out of Place." **2.** 227.
"Pastoral Blood." **1.** 163; **2.** 227; **3.** 290; **4.** 210; **5.** 236.
"Plagiarized Material." **2.** 227.
"Plot." **3 ed.** 572; **4.** 210.
"The Precipice." **4.** 210.
"A Premature Autobiography." **4.** 210.
"Problems of Adjustment in Survival of Natural/Unnatural Diseases." **4.** 210.
"Psychiatric Services." **4.** 210.
"Puzzle." **1.** 163; **4.** 210; **5.** 236.
"Queen of Night." **4.** 210.
"Rewards of Fame." **2.** 227.
"River Rising." **4.** 210.
"Ruth." **4.** 210.
"The Sacred Marriage." **4.** 210; **5.** 237.
"The Sacrifice." **4.** 210.
"The Scream." **4.** 210.
"Sentimental Journey." **4.** 210.
"Shame." **4.** 211.
"Small Avalanche." **2.** 228.
"The Snowstorm." **4.** 211.
"The Son of God and His Sorrow." **2.** 228.
"Stalking." **4.** 211.
"Stigmata." **2.** 228; **4.** 211.
"The Survival of Childhood." **2.** 228; **4.** 211.
"Swamps." **2.** 228.
"Sweet Love Remembered." **2.** 228; **4.** 211.
"Through the Looking Glass." **4.** 211.
"The Tryst." **4.** 211.
"The Turn of the Screw." **4.** 211; **5.** 237.
"29 Inventions." **4.** 211.
"Unmailed, Unwritten Letters." **2.** 228; **4.** 211.
"Unpublished Fragments." **4.** 211.
"Upon the Sweeping Flood." **2.** 228.
"Voyage to Rosewood." **4.** 211.
"Waiting." **1.** 163; **2.** 228; **4.** 211.
"Walden." **4.** 211.
"Walled City." **4.** 211.
"Wednesday's Child." **4.** 212.
"What Death with Love Should Have to Do." **4.** 212.
"What Is the Connection Between Men and Women?" **2.** 228; **4.** 212.
"The Wheel of Love." **5.** 237.
"Where Are You Going, Where Have You Been?" **3 ed.** 572; **1.** 163; **2.** 228; **3.** 290; **4.** 212; **5.** 237.
"Where I Live and What I Live For." **2.** 228.
"Wild Saturday." **3 ed.** 572; **2.** 229; **4.** 212; **5.** 237.
"Year of Wonders." **4.** 212.
"You." **3 ed.** 572; **2.** 229; **4.** 212; **5.** 237.

ŌBA MINAKO

"The Three Crabs." **5.** 237.

EDNA O'BRIEN

"Irish Revel." **3 ed.** 572.
"An Outing." **3 ed.** 572.
"The Rug." **3 ed.** 572.

FITZ-JAMES O'BRIEN

"The Diamond Lens." **3 ed.** 572; **4.** 212; **5.** 237.
"From Hand to Mouth." **4.** 212.
"A Legend of Barlagh Cave." **5.** 237.
"The Lost Room." **5.** 238.
"The Pot of Tulips." **3 ed.** 572.
"Seeing the World." **5.** 238.
"A Terrible Night." **4.** 212.
"What Was It?—A Mystery." **3 ed.** 572; **4.** 212.
"The Wondersmith." **3 ed.** 572; **4.** 212.

FLANN O'BRIEN

"Donagate." **3 ed.** 573.
"John Duffy's Brother." **3 ed.** 573; **3.** 290.
"The Marble Crown." **3 ed.** 573.
"Two in One." **3 ed.** 573.

TIM O'BRIEN

"Going after Cacciato." **5.** 238.

SIGBJØRN OBSTFELDER

"Autumn." **3.** 290.
"Liv." **3.** 290.
"The Plain." **3.** 290.
"The Unknown One." **3.** 291.

SILVINA OCAMPO

"Autobiography of Irene." **5.** 238.
"La casa de azúcar." **5.** 238.
"Esparanza en Flores." **5.** 238.
"Keif." **5.** 238.
"La liebre dorada." **5.** 238.
"Malva." **5.** 238.
"Mimoso." **5.** 238.
"Nueve Perros." **5.** 238.
"La paciente y el médico." **4.** 213.
"The Photographs." **4.** 212.
"El vestido de terciopelo." **5.** 238.
"El vestido verde aceituna." **5.** 238.
"Las vestiduras pelgrosas." **5.** 238.

PADRAIC O'CONAIRE

"Paidin Mhaire." **2.** 229.
"The Woman on Whom God Put His Hand." **2.** 229.
"The Woman Who Was Made to Suffer." **2.** 229.

EDWIN O'CONNOR

"Parish Reunion." **3 ed.** 573.

FLANNERY O'CONNOR

"The Artificial Nigger." **3 ed.** 573–74; **1.** 163; **2.** 229; **3.** 291; **4.** 213; **5.** 239.
"The Barber." **3 ed.** 574; **1.** 164; **4.** 213.
"The Capture" [originally "The Turkey"]. **3 ed.** 574; **1.** 166; **3.** 293; **5.** 239, 242.
"A Circle in the Fire." **3 ed.** 574; **1.** 164; **2.** 229; **4.** 213; **5.** 239.
"The Comforts of Home." **3 ed.** 574–75; **1.** 164; **3.** 291; **4.** 213; **5.** 239.
"The Crop." **3 ed.** 575; **1.** 164; **5.** 239.
"The Cross." **3.** 291.
"The Displaced Person." **3 ed.** 575–76; **1.** 164; **2.** 229; **3.** 291; **4.** 213–14; **5.** 239.
"The Enduring Chill." **3 ed.** 576; **1.** 164; **2.** 229; **4.** 214; **5.** 239.
"Enoch and the Gorilla." **1.** 164.
"Everything That Rises Must Converge." **3 ed.** 576–77; **1.** 164; **2.** 229; **3.** 291; **4.** 214; **5.** 239.
"The Geranium." **1.** 164; **2.** 230; **3.** 291; **4.** 214; **5.** 240.
"Good Country People." **3 ed.** 577; **1.** 164; **2.** 230; **3.** 292; **4.** 214; **5.** 240.
"A Good Man Is Hard to Find." **3 ed.** 577–79; **1.** 165; **2.** 230; **3.** 292; **4.** 214–15; **5.** 240.
"Greenleaf." **3 ed.** 579; **1.** 165; **2.** 230; **3.** 292; **4.** 215; **5.** 240.
"The Heart of the Park." **1.** 165.
"Judgement Day." **3 ed.** 579; **1.** 165; **2.** 230; **3.** 292; **4.** 215; **5.** 240.
"The Lame Shall Enter First." **3 ed.** 579–80; **1.** 165; **3.** 292; **4.** 215; **5.** 241.
"A Late Encounter with the Enemy." **3 ed.** 580; **4.** 215; **5.** 241.
"The Life You Save May Be Your Own." **3**

ed. 580–81; **1.** 165; **2.** 230; **4.** 215; **5.** 241.
"The Misfit." **5.** 241.
"Parker's Back." **3 ed.** 581; **1.** 165; **2.** 231; **3.** 292–93; **4.** 215; **5.** 241.
"The Partridge Festival." **3 ed.** 581; **4.** 215; **5.** 241.
"The Peeler." **1.** 165.
"Revelation." **3 ed.** 581–82; **1.** 165; **2.** 231; **3.** 293; **4.** 215–16; **5.** 241.
"The River." **3 ed.** 582; **1.** 165; **2.** 231; **3.** 293; **4.** 216; **5.** 241.
"A Stroke of Good Fortune" [originally "Woman on the Straits"]. **3 ed.** 582; **1.** 165; **2.** 231; **4.** 216; **5.** 242.
"A Temple of the Holy Ghost." **3 ed.** 582–83; **1.** 166; **2.** 231; **3.** 293; **4.** 216; **5.** 242.
"The Train" [revised to become a chapter of *Wise Blood*]. **3 ed.** 583; **1.** 166; **3.** 293; **4.** 216; **5.** 242.
"A View of the Woods." **3 ed.** 583; **1.** 166; **2.** 231; **3.** 293; **4.** 216; **5.** 242.
"Why Do the Heathen Rage?" **1.** 166.
"The Wildcat." **1.** 166; **4.** 216; **5.** 242.
"You Can't Be Any Poorer Than Dead" [expanded to become first chapter of *The Violent Bear It Away*]. **1.** 166.

FRANK O'CONNOR [MICHAEL FRANCIS O'DONOVAN]

"Achilles Heel." **1.** 166.
"An Act of Charity." **1.** 166.
"After Fourteen Years." **1.** 166; **3.** 293; **4.** 216.
"The American Wife." **3 ed.** 583.
"The Babes in the Wood." **4.** 216.
"Bones of Contention." **1.** 166.
"The Bridal Night." **1.** 166; **2.** 231.
"The Cheapjack." **3 ed.** 583.
"The Cheat." **1.** 166; **3.** 293.
"The Conversion." **3.** 293.
"The Corkerys." **1.** 166.
"Counsel of Oedipus." **1.** 166.
"The Custom of the Country." **3.** 293; **4.** 216–17.
"Daydreams." **1.** 167.
"Don Juan (Retired)." **1.** 167.
"Don Juan's Temptation." **3.** 294.
"The Drunkard." **3 ed.** 583; **1.** 167; **2.** 231; **3.** 294; **5.** 242.
"The Duke's Children." **3.** 294.
"The Eternal Triangle." **1.** 167.
"Expectation of Life." **1.** 167; **3.** 294.
"Father and Son." **1.** 167.
"First Confession." **3 ed.** 583; **1.** 167; **2.** 232; **3.** 294.
"The Frying Pan." **3.** 294; **4.** 217.
"The Genius." **1.** 167.
"The Grand Vizier's Daughter." **1.** 167.
"Guests of the Nation." **3 ed.** 584; **1.** 167; **3.** 294; **4.** 217; **5.** 242.
"The Holy Door." **1.** 167; **2.** 232; **3.** 294; **4.** 217.
"The House That Johnny Built." **1.** 167; **4.** 217.
"The Idealist." **3.** 294; **4.** 217.
"The Impossible Marriage." **1.** 167.
"In the Train." **3 ed.** 584; **1.** 167; **2.** 232; **3.** 294; **4.** 217.
"Jerome." **3.** 294; **4.** 217.
"Jo." **3.** 294.
"Judas." **3 ed.** 584; **1.** 167; **2.** 232.
"Jumbo's Wife." **3.** 294.
"A Life of Your Own." **1.** 168.
"The Little Mother." **4.** 217.
'The Long Road to Ummera." **1.** 168; **2.** 232.
"Lost Fatherland." **4.** 217.
"The Luceys." **1.** 168; **3.** 295; **4.** 217.
"Mac's Masterpiece." **3 ed.** 584; **3.** 295.
"The Mad Lomasneys." **3 ed.** 584; **1.** 168; **2.** 232; **3.** 295.
"The Majesty of the Law." **3 ed.** 584; **1.** 168; **2.** 232; **3.** 295; **4.** 217.
"The Man of the House." **3 ed.** 584.
"The Man of the World." **1.** 168; **3.** 295; **4.** 217.
"The Masculine Principle." **3.** 295.
"Masculine Protest." **3.** 295.
"The Mass Island." **1.** 168; **3.** 295; **5.** 242.
"Michael's Wife." **1.** 168; **2.** 232.
"A Minority." **3.** 295.
"The Miser." **2.** 232.
"A Mother's Warning." **2.** 232.
"Music When Soft Voices Die." **1.** 168.
"My Da." **4.** 217.
"My First Protestant." **3.** 295; **4.** 218.
"My Oedipus Complex." **3 ed.** 584; **1.** 168; **2.** 232; **3.** 295; **4.** 218.
"The New Teacher." **2.** 232.
"News for the Church." **2.** 232; **3.** 295.
"Nightpiece with Figures." **3.** 295; **4.** 218.

"The Old Faith." **3.** 295; **4.** 218.
"Out-and-Out Free Gift." **1.** 168.
"The Paragon." **1.** 168.
"The Party." **1.** 168.
"The Patriarch." **3 ed.** 584; **2.** 232.
"Peasants." **1.** 168; **2.** 232; **4.** 218.
"The Pretender." **3 ed.** 585; **1.** 168.
"Requiem." **1.** 169.
"A Romantic" [in collection *Bones of Contention*]. **2.** 233.
"A Romantic" [different story in collection *More Stories*]. **2.** 233.
"The School for Wives." **1.** 169.
"The Sentry." **1.** 169.
"September Dawn." **1.** 169; **2.** 233; **3.** 295; **4.** 218.
"A Set of Variations." **1.** 169; **4.** 218.
"Song Without Words." **1.** 169; **4.** 218.
"The Star That Bids the Shepherd Fold." **1.** 169; **2.** 233; **3.** 295; **4.** 218.
"The Stepmother." **1.** 169.
"The Study of History." **3 ed.** 585.
"The Teacher's Mass." **1.** 169; **2.** 233.
"The Thief." **1.** 169; **3.** 296.
"A Torrent Damned." **3.** 296; **4.** 218.
"The Ugly Duckling." **4.** 218.
"Unapproved Route." **1.** 169; **5.** 242.
"Uprooted." **3 ed.** 585; **1.** 169; **2.** 233; **3.** 296; **4.** 218.
"Vanity." **1.** 169.

JOSEPH OCRUTNI

"Rumkowsky." **3 ed.** 585.

ODA SAKUNOSUKE

"The State of the Times." **3.** 296.

EUNICE ODIO

"Once There Was a Man." **5.** 243.

VLADIMIR FËDROVICH ODOEVSKY

"Beethoven's Last Quartet." **3 ed.** 585.
"A City Without Name." **3 ed.** 585.
"The Dead Body That Belonged to No One Knew Whom." **3 ed.** 585.
"Elsa." **3 ed.** 585.
"How Collegiate Councillor Ivan Bogdanovich Otnoshenie Was Unable to Offer Holiday Greetings to His Superior on Easter Sunday." **3 ed.** 585.
"How Dangerous It Is for Girls to Walk in Groups on the Nevskij Prospekt." **3 ed.** 585.
"The Improvisor." **3 ed.** 585.
"Kosmorama." **3 ed.** 585.
"Opere del Cavaliere Giambatista Piranesi." **3 ed.** 586.
"Princess Mimi." **3.** 296.
"The Salamander." **3 ed.** 586.
"Sebastian Bach." **3 ed.** 586; **3.** 296.
"The Sylph." **3 ed.** 586; **3.** 296.

LAWRENCE O'DONNELL [CATHERINE L. MOORE]

"The Children's Hour." **1.** 169.
"Vintage Season." **1.** 169.

ŌE KENZABURŌ

"Aghwee the Sky Monster." **5.** 243.
"The Catch." **1.** 170.
"Cheers." **5.** 243.
"A Dark River, Heavy Oars." **5.** 243.
"The Day He Himself Shall Wipe My Tears Away." **5.** 243.
"Father, Where Are You Going?" **5.** 243.
"Lavish Are the Dead." **5.** 243.
"Leap Before You Look." **5.** 243.
"A Political Boy Is Now Dead." **5.** 243.
"Prize Stock." **5.** 243.
"Sheep." **3 ed.** 586; **5.** 243.
"A Strange Job." **5.** 243.
"Teach Us to Outgrow Our Madness." **5.** 243–44.

JULIA O'FAOLAIN

"Daughters of Passion." **4.** 218.
"Melancholy Baby." **4.** 218.
"We Might See Sights." **4.** 218.

SEAN O'FAOLAIN

"Admiring the Scenery." **3 ed.** 586; **1.** 170.
"Angels and Ministers of Grace." **4.** 219.
"The Bombshop." **3 ed.** 586; **5.** 244.
"A Born Genius." **3 ed.** 586; **4.** 219.
"The Bosom of the Country." **3.** 296.
"A Broken World." **3 ed.** 586; **1.** 170; **3.** 296; **4.** 219; **5.** 244.
"Childybawn." **3 ed.** 586.
"Discord." **3 ed.** 586.
"The End of the Record." **5.** 244.

"Falling Rocks, Narrowing Road, Cul-de-sac, Stop." **5.** 244.
"Feed My Lambs." **4.** 219.
"Fugue." **3 ed.** 586; **3.** 296; **4.** 219; **5.** 244.
"The Fur Coat." **3 ed.** 586.
"The Heat of the Sun." **3.** 296.
"How to Write a Short Story." **3.** 296.
"The Human Thing." **4.** 219.
"Hymeneal." **5.** 244.
"I Remember! I Remember!" **3 ed.** 586; **3.** 296; **4.** 219.
"In the Bosom of the Country." **4.** 219; **5.** 244.
"An Inside-Outside Complex." **3.** 297; **4.** 219.
"The Kitchen." **2.** 233; **4.** 219.
"Lady Lucifer." **3 ed.** 587; **3.** 297.
"A Letter." **5.** 244.
"Lilliput." **3 ed.** 587.
"Lord and Master." **5.** 244.
"Lovers of the Lake." **3 ed.** 587; **1.** 170; **2.** 233; **3.** 297; **4.** 219; **5.** 244.
"The Man Who Invented Sin." **3 ed.** 587; **2.** 233; **3.** 297; **4.** 219; **5.** 244.
"Midsummer Night Madness." **3 ed.** 587; **1.** 170; **3.** 297; **4.** 219.
"Murder at Cobbler's Hulk." **2.** 233; **5.** 244.
"No Country for Old Men." **3 ed.** 587; **4.** 219.
"The Old Master." **3 ed.** 587; **5.** 244.
"One Man, One Boat, One Girl." **5.** 244.
"One Night in Turin." **3.** 297; **4.** 219.
"One True Friend." **3 ed.** 587.
"Our Fearful Innocence." **3.** 297; **4.** 219.
"The Patriot." **3 ed.** 587; **3.** 297; **4.** 220.
"A Shadow, Silent as a Cloud." **3 ed.** 587.
"The Silence of the Valley." **3 ed.** 587; **1.** 170; **3.** 297; **4.** 220; **5.** 245.
"Sinners." **3 ed.** 587.
"The Small Lady." **3 ed.** 587; **1.** 170.
"The Sugawn Chair." **3 ed.** 588.
"Teresa." **3 ed.** 588; **5.** 245.
"The Time of Their Lives." **3.** 297.
"A Touch of Autumn in the Air." **3 ed.** 588; **3.** 297; **5.** 245.
"The Trout." **5.** 245.
"Two of a Kind." **4.** 220.
"Unholy Living and Half Dying." **3 ed.** 588.
"Up the Bare Stairs." **3 ed.** 588; **2.** 233; **4.** 220; **5.** 245.
"The Younger Generation." **4.** 220.

LIAM O'FLAHERTY

"The Bath." **1.** 170.
"The Black Rabbit." **3 ed.** 588.
"The Blackbird's Mate." **1.** 170.
"Blood Lust." **3.** 297.
"The Blow." **3.** 297.
"The Caress." **3 ed.** 588; **1.** 170; **4.** 220.
"The Child of God." **4.** 220.
"The Conger Eel." **3 ed.** 588.
"The Cow's Death." **3 ed.** 588.
"The Ditch." **1.** 170.
"The Fairy Goose." **3 ed.** 588; **1.** 170; **4.** 220.
"The Fall of Joseph Timmins." **5.** 245.
"Galway Bay." **3 ed.** 588; **1.** 170; **3.** 297; **4.** 220.
"Going into Exile." **1.** 171; **2.** 233; **3.** 298; **4.** 220.
"The Hawk." **3 ed.** 588; **1.** 171.
"His First Flight." **3 ed.** 588.
"The Inquisition." **1.** 171.
"The Landing." **4.** 220.
"The Letter." **1.** 171.
"Mackerel for Sale." **5.** 245.
"Milking Time." **1.** 171.
"The Mirror." **3 ed.** 588; **1.** 171.
"The Mountain Tavern." **1.** 171; **3.** 298.
"The Oar." **4.** 220.
"The Outcast." **1.** 171; **3.** 298.
"The Parting." **1.** 171.
"The Pedlar's Revenge." **1.** 171.
"The Post Office." **3 ed.** 589; **1.** 171.
"Proclamation." **1.** 171.
"The Reaping Race." **3 ed.** 589.
"Red Barbara." **3 ed.** 589; **1.** 171.
"The Rockfish." **3 ed.** 589; **1.** 171.
"The Salted Goat." **5.** 245.
"Sport: The Kill." **1.** 171.
"Spring Sowing." **3 ed.** 589; **1.** 171.
"A Strange Disease." **1.** 171.
"The Stream." **3 ed.** 589.
"The Tent." **1.** 172; **3.** 298.
"The Terrorist." **1.** 172.
"Three Lambs." **3 ed.** 589.
"The Tramp." **1.** 172; **5.** 245.
"Trapped." **3 ed.** 589; **4.** 220.

"Two Lovely Beasts." **3 ed.** 589; **3.** 298; **4.** 220.
"The Tyrant." **1.** 172.
"Unclean." **1.** 172.
"The Wave." **3 ed.** 589.
"The Wedding." **3 ed.** 589.
"The Wild Goat's Kid." **4.** 220.
"The Wounded Cormorant." **3 ed.** 589; **1.** 172.

GRACE OGOT

"Elizabeth." **2.** 233.
"The Family Doctor." **4.** 220.
"Fishing Village." **4.** 221.
"The Honourable Minister." **2.** 234; **4.** 221.
"The Island of Tears." **4.** 221.
"Karatina." **4.** 221.
"Land Without Thunder." **4.** 221.
"The Middle Door." **4.** 221.
"The Old White Witch." **2.** 234; **4.** 221.
"The Other Woman." **2.** 234; **4.** 221.
"The Rain Came." **4.** 221.
"Tekayo." **4.** 221.
"The Wayward Father." **4.** 221.
"The White Veil." **2.** 234; **4.** 221.

OGURI FŪYŌ

"Big Sister's Little Sister." **3.** 298.
"Cold and Flaming." **3.** 298.
"Lazy Woman." **3.** 298.
"Making Up for Bed." **3.** 298.

JOHN O'HARA

"Agatha." **3.** 298.
"All the Girls He Wanted." **3 ed.** 589.
"Alone." **3.** 298.
"Andreas." **2.** 234.
"Appearances." **3.** 298.
"Are We Leaving Tomorrow?" **3 ed.** 589.
"Assistant." **3.** 298.
"The Bucket of Blood." **3.** 298.
"A Case History." **2.** 234.
"The Chink in the Armor." **3 ed.** 589.
"The Clear Track." **3.** 299.
"Conversation in the Atomic Age." **3 ed.** 590.
"Days." **3.** 299.
"Decision." **3 ed.** 590.
"Do You Like It Here?" **3 ed.** 590; **4.** 221.
"The Doctor's Son." **3 ed.** 590; **2.** 234; **3.** 299.
"Ella and the Chinee." **3.** 299.
"The Engineer." **2.** 234.
"Family Evening." **3.** 299.
"A Family Party." **5.** 245.
"The Father." **3.** 299.
"A Few Trips and Some Poetry." **3 ed.** 590; **2.** 234; **3.** 299.
"The Gangster." **3 ed.** 590.
"The General." **3.** 299.
"The Girl on the Baggage Truck." **3 ed.** 590; **2.** 234.
"The Gunboat and Madge." **3.** 299.
"Horizon." **3 ed.** 590.
"How Can I Tell You?" **3.** 299.
"Imagine Kissing Peter." **3 ed.** 590; **2.** 234.
"James Francis and the Star." **2.** 234; **3.** 299.
"The Lesson." **3.** 299.
"The Madeline Wherry Case." **3.** 299.
"Miss W." **3 ed.** 590.
"Most Gorgeous Thing." **3.** 299.
"Natica Jackson." **3.** 299.
"Nineteen Minutes Away." **2.** 234.
"Nothing Missing." **3.** 299.
"Over the River and Through the Woods." **3 ed.** 590; **3.** 299.
"Pat Collins." **2.** 234.
"The Pig." **3.** 300.
"The Pioneer Hep-Cat." **3.** 300.
"Price's Always Open." **3 ed.** 590.
"Radio." **3 ed.** 590.
"Saturday Lunch." **3.** 300.
"The Sharks." **3.** 300.
"The Skeleton." **2.** 234.
"Someone to Trust." **3 ed.** 590.
"Sterling Silver." **3.** 300.
"Summer's Day." **3 ed.** 590.
"Sunday Morning." **3.** 300.
"The Time Element." **3.** 300.
"Transaction." **3 ed.** 590.
"The Twinkle in His Eye." **3.** 300.
"We're Friends Again." **3 ed.** 590; **2.** 235.
"Yostie." **3.** 300.

O. HENRY [WILLIAM SYDNEY PORTER]

"According to Their Lights." **3 ed.** 591; **5.** 245.
"The Atavism of John Tom Little Bear." **3 ed.** 591.

"Blind Man's Holiday." **3 ed.** 591.
"Brickdust Row." **5.** 245.
"The Caballero's Way." **3 ed.** 591.
"The Call of the Tame." **3 ed.** 591.
"The Chair of Philanthromathematics." **3 ed.** 591.
"A Chaparral Christmas Gift." **3 ed.** 591.
"The Complete Life of John Hopkins." **3 ed.** 591; **5.** 245.
"The Cop and the Anthem." **4.** 221; **5.** 245.
"The Duel." **3 ed.** 591.
"The Duplicity of Hargraves." **3 ed.** 591.
"The Enchanted Profile." **3.** 300.
"The Ferry of Unfulfillment." **5.** 246.
"The Fool-Killer." **3 ed.** 591.
"The Furnished Room." **3 ed.** 591; **2.** 235.
"The Gift of the Magi." **3 ed.** 591; **3.** 300.
"The Green Door." **3 ed.** 591; **5.** 246.
"The Guilty Party." **5.** 246.
"The Handbook of Hymen." **3 ed.** 591.
"The Hiding of Black Bill." **3 ed.** 592.
"The Last Leaf." **3 ed.** 592.
"Let Me Feel Your Pulse." **3 ed.** 592.
"A Lickpenny Lover." **5.** 246.
"The Lonesome Road." **3 ed.** 592.
"Lost on Dress Parade." **3 ed.** 592.
"A Madison Square Arabian Night." **5.** 246.
"Mammon and the Archer." **5.** 246.
"Man About Town." **5.** 246.
"The Memento." **3 ed.** 592.
"The Miracle of Lava Canyon" [same as "An Afternoon Miracle"]. **3 ed.** 592.
"A Municipal Report." **3 ed.** 592; **1.** 172; **5.** 246.
"The Passing of Black Eagle." **3 ed.** 592.
"Past One at Rooney's." **5.** 246.
"The Pendulum." **3 ed.** 592; **5.** 246.
"The Poet and the Peasant." **3 ed.** 592.
"The Proof of the Pudding." **3 ed.** 592; **5.** 246.
"The Ransom of Mack." **3 ed.** 592.
"The Roads We Take." **3 ed.** 592.
"Romance of a Busy Broker." **5.** 246.
"The Rose of Dixie." **3 ed.** 592.
"Roses, Ruses and Romance." **5.** 246.
"The Shamrock and the Palm." **2.** 235.
"The Skylight Room." **5.** 246.
"The Snow Man." **3 ed.** 593.
"The Social Triangle." **5.** 246.
"Thimble, Thimble." **3 ed.** 593.
"The Third Ingredient." **5.** 246.
"Tobin's Palm." **5.** 246.
"The Venturers." **3 ed.** 593.
"Vereton Villa." **3 ed.** 593.
"The Voice of the City." **5.** 247.
"While the Auto Waits." **3 ed.** 593; **2.** 235; **5.** 247.
"The Whirligig of Life." **3 ed.** 593.
"The Yellow Day." **5.** 247.

OKAMOTO KANOKO

"Mother and Son, a Lyric." **3.** 300.

SEUMAS O'KELLY

"At the Burning of the Sod." **3 ed.** 593.
"Both Sides of the Pond." **3 ed.** 593; **4.** 221.
"The Building." **3 ed.** 593.
"The Gray Lake." **3 ed.** 593.
"Nan Hogan's House." **4.** 222.
"The Prodigal Daughter." **3 ed.** 593; **4.** 222.
"The Rector." **4.** 222.
"The Story of a Spell." **4.** 222.
"The Weaver's Grave." **3 ed.** 593; **2.** 235; **3.** 300; **4.** 222; **5.** 247.
"The White Goat." **3 ed.** 593.

PETER OLDALE

"The Problem Child." **5.** 247.

IURIĬ [JURY] KARLOVICH OLESHA

"The Chain." **3 ed.** 593.
"The Cherry Pit" [same as "The Cherry Stone"]. **3.** 301; **4.** 222.
"Envy." **3 ed.** 594.
"In Summer." **3 ed.** 594.
"Liompa." **3.** 301.
"Love." **3 ed.** 594.

MARGARET OLIPHANT

"A Christmas Tale." **4.** 222.
"Earthbound." **3.** 301.
"The Land of Darkness." **4.** 222.
"The Land of Suspense." **4.** 222.
"The Library Window." **3.** 301; **4.** 222; **5.** 247.
"Old Lady Mary." **3.** 301.

"The Open Door." **3.** 301.
"Queen Eleanor and Fair Rosamond." **3.** 301.

CHAD OLIVER

"Rite of Passage." **3.** 301.

DIANE OLIVER

"Neighbors." **3 ed.** 594; **2.** 235.

ANTONIO OLIVER FRAU

"Chemán el Correcostas." **5.** 247.
"Juan Perdío." **5.** 247.

BOB OLSEN

"The Space Marines and the Slaves." **5.** 247.

TILLIE OLSEN

"Hey Sailor, What Ship?" **3 ed.** 594; **4.** 222; **5.** 247.
"I Stand Here Ironing." **3 ed.** 594; **2.** 235; **3.** 301; **4.** 222; **5.** 247–48.
"O Yes." **3 ed.** 594; **2.** 235; **4.** 223; **5.** 248.
"Requa." **3.** 301; **5.** 248.
"Tell Me a Riddle." **3 ed.** 594; **1.** 172; **2.** 235; **3.** 301; **4.** 223; **5.** 248.

JUAN CARLOS ONETTI

"The Album." **3.** 302.
"As Sad as She." **3.** 302.
"Avenida de mayo—Diagonal—Avenida de Mayo." **1.** 172; **2.** 236.
"Dreaded Hell." **3 ed.** 594; **5.** 248.
"A Dream Come True." **3 ed.** 594; **3.** 302; **4.** 223; **5.** 248.
"Esbjerg, on the Coast." **3 ed.** 594; **3.** 302.
"The Face of Misfortune." **3 ed.** 594; **1.** 172.
"The House in the Sand." **3 ed.** 594.
"El infierno tan temido." **3.** 302.
"Jacob and the Other." **2.** 236; **5.** 248.
"The Knight of the Rose." **3.** 302.
"Masquerade." **3 ed.** 595.
"The Nameless Tomb." **3 ed.** 595.
"El posible Baldi." **1.** 172; **2.** 236.
"Welcome, Bob." **3 ed.** 595; **5.** 248.

OLIVER ONIONS

"The Beckoning Fair One." **3 ed.** 595; **2.** 236; **4.** 223; **5.** 248.
"The Honey in the Wall." **4.** 223.
"The Master of the House." **4.** 223.
"The Rosewood Door." **4.** 223.
"The Woman in the Way." **4.** 223.

JAMES OPPENHEIM

"Slag." **1.** 172.

YOLANDA OREAMUNO

"High Valley." **5.** 248.
"The Tide Returns at Night." **5.** 248.

VLADIMIR ORLOVSKY

"The Revolt of the Atoms." **5.** 249.

GEORGE ORWELL [ERIC BLAIR]

"Animal Farm." **3 ed.** 595–96; **1.** 173; **3.** 302; **4.** 223; **5.** 249.

ELIZA ORZESZKOWA

"The Chain Links." **3 ed.** 596.
"The Generous Lady." **3 ed.** 596.
"On a Winter Evening." **3 ed.** 596.
"The Strong Samson." **3 ed.** 596.
"Whose Fault Is It?" **3 ed.** 596.

CAROLYN OSBORN

"A Horse of Another Color." **4.** 224.
"Reversals." **4.** 224.

JOHN A. OSKINSON

"Only the Master Shall Praise." **3.** 302.

SEMBÉNE OUSMANE

"Le Mandat." **5.** 249.
"Ses Trois Jours." **3 ed.** 596.
"Vehi-Ciosane." **3 ed.** 596.

V. OVECHKIN

"One of the Many." **3 ed.** 596.
"Praskovya Maksimovna." **3 ed.** 596.

WAYNE D. OVERHOLSER

"Book L'arnin' and the Equalizer." **3.** 302.
"The Steadfast." **3.** 302.

MICHELE OWENS

"We Find Harris Again." **5.** 249.

AMOS OZ

"Crusade." **3.** 303.
"Lands of the Jackal." **2.** 236.
"Late Love." **2.** 236.
"Longing." **4.** 224.
"My Michael." **2.** 236.
"The Nomads and the Viper." **3 ed.** 596; **2.** 236; **5.** 249.
"Repair of the World." **2.** 236.
"Strange Fire." **5.** 249.
"The Trappist Monastery." **5.** 249.
"Upon This Evil Earth." **5.** 249.
"The Way of the Wind." **5.** 249.

OZAKI KAZUO

"Various Kinds of Bugs." **3.** 303.

OZAKI KŌYŌ

"The Erotic Confessions of Two Nuns." **3.** 303.

CYNTHIA OZICK

"At Fumicaro." **5.** 249.
"Bloodshed." **3.** 303; **4.** 224; **5.** 250.
"The Doctor's Wife." **5.** 250.
"Dreams of Jewish Magic/The Magic of Jewish Dreams." **5.** 250.
"An Education." **5.** 250.
"Envy; or, Yiddish in America." **1.** 173; **3.** 303; **4.** 224; **5.** 250.
"Levitation." **4.** 224; **5.** 250.
"A Mercenary." **4.** 224; **5.** 250.
"The Pagan Rabbi." **5.** 250–51.
"Puttermesser and Xanthippe." **3.** 303; **5.** 251.
"Puttermesser: Her Work History, Her Ancestry, Her Afterlife." **5.** 251.
"Rosa." **4.** 224; **5.** 251.
"The Sewing Harem." **5.** 251.
"The Shawl." **4.** 224; **5.** 251.
"Shots." **5.** 251.
"The Suitcase." **2.** 236; **4.** 224.
"Usurpation (Other People's Stories)." **1.** 173; **3.** 303; **4.** 224; **5.** 251.
"Virility." **1.** 173; **4.** 224; **5.** 251.

PA CHIN [BA JIN or LI FEI-KAN]

"The Cross of Love." **3.** 303.
"The Days When the Snow Melts." **3.** 303.
"Dog." **3.** 303.
"Father and Son." **3.** 303.
"First Love." **3.** 304.
"The General." **3.** 304.
"A Girl and Her Cat." **3.** 304.
"A Good Man." **3.** 304.
"Man." **3.** 304.
"Mrs. Landlady." **3.** 304.
"Mona Lisa." **3.** 304.
"Monsieur Robert." **3.** 304.
"Piglet and Chickens." **3.** 304.
"Revenge." **3.** 304.
"Sinking Down." **3.** 304.
"Star." **3.** 304.
"A Woman." **3.** 304.
"Yuliana." **3.** 304.

CRISTINA PACHECO

"La dicha conyugal." **5.** 251.
"La esclavitud." **5.** 252.
"Esposa y mártir." **5.** 252.
"Los trabajos perdidos." **5.** 252.

JOSÉ EMILIO PACHECO

"August Afternoon." **4.** 224; **5.** 252.
"The Bullfight." **4.** 225.
"El castillo en la aguja." **2.** 236; **5.** 252.
"La cautiva." **5.** 252.
"Civilization and Barbarism." **3.** 304; **5.** 252.
"Cuando sali de La Habana, válgame Dios." **4.** 225; **5.** 252.
"The Fierce Sport of Bullfighting." **3.** 305; **4.** 225; **5.** 252.
"Jericó." **5.** 252.
"Langenhaus." **5.** 252.
"La luna decapitada." **5.** 252.
"The Night of the Immortal." **3.** 305.
"Parque de diversiones." **4.** 225; **5.** 252.
"El principio del placer." **5.** 253.
"Tenga para que se entretenda." **5.** 253.
"El viento distante." **5.** 253.

NANCY HUDDLESTON PACKER

"Early Morning, Lonely Ride." **5.** 253.

LEWIS PADGETT [CATHERINE L. MOORE and HENRY KUTTNER]

"Minsy [sic] Were the Borogroves [sic]." **4.** 225.
"Piggy Bank." **1.** 173.
"The Proud Robot." **3.** 305.
"The Twonky." **1.** 173.
"When the Bough Breaks." **1.** 173; **3.** 305.

JO PAGANO

"The Disinherited." **3 ed.** 597.

P. K. PAGE

"The Green Bird." **5.** 253.

THOMAS NELSON PAGE

"Marse Chan." **3 ed.** 597; **1.** 173; **2.** 237; **4.** 225.
"Meh Lady." **3 ed.** 597; **1.** 173.
"No Haid Pawn." **3 ed.** 597; **1.** 173.
"Ole 'Stracted." **3 ed.** 597; **1.** 173.
"Unc' Edinburg's Drowndin'." **3 ed.** 597.

PAI HSIEN-YUNG

"Lament for Bygone Days." **2.** 237.

BARRY PAIN [BARRY ERIC ODELL PAIN]

"The Diary of a God." **4.** 225.
"The Glass of Supreme Moments." **4.** 225.
"The Moon-Slave." **4.** 225.
"The Tree of Death." **4.** 225.

ALBERT B. PAINE

"The Black Hands." **1.** 173.

RALPH PAINE

"The Freshman Fullback." **4.** 225.

GRACE PALEY

"A Conversation with My Father." **2.** 237; **3.** 305; **4.** 226; **5.** 253.
"Distance." **2.** 237; **3.** 305.
"Enormous Changes at the Last Minute." **2.** 237.
"Faith in a Tree." **3.** 305.
"Faith in the Afternoon." **2.** 237.
"Friends." **3.** 305.
"Goodbye and Good Luck." **3 ed.** 597; **5.** 253.
"The Immigrant Story." **2.** 237.
"In Time Which Made Monkeys of Us All." **3.** 305.
"An Interest in Life." **4.** 226.
"An Irrevocable Diameter." **4.** 226.
"The Long-Distance Runner." **2.** 237; **3.** 305.
"The Loudest Voice." **2.** 237; **5.** 253.
"Love." **5.** 253.
"The Pale Pink Roast." **4.** 226.
"Ruth and Edie." **5.** 253.
"Somewhere Else." **5.** 254.
"A Subject of Childhood." **3.** 305.
"The Used-Boy Raisers." **1.** 174; **3.** 305.
"Wants." **2.** 237.

CLEMENTE PALMA

"Anacreon Intoxicated." **5.** 254.
"Aventura del hombre que no nació." **5.** 254.
"The Butterflies." **5.** 254.
"Los canastos." **3 ed.** 597; **5.** 254.
"The Carnival of Flowers." **5.** 254.
"The Child Prodigy." **5.** 254.
"The Creed of a Drunk." **5.** 254.
"Cuento de marionetes." **5.** 254.
"En el carretón." **5.** 254.
"Female Vampires." **5.** 254.
"The Fifth Gospel." **5.** 254.
"Una historia vulgar." **3 ed.** 597; **5.** 254.
"El hombre del cigarillo." **3 ed.** 597; **5.** 254.
"Idealismos." **5.** 254.
"The Last Faun." **5.** 254.
"Leyendas de haschisch." **3 ed.** 597; **5.** 254.
"Lina's Eyes." **3.** 306; **5.** 254.
"Love Note." **5.** 255.
"Mythological Fantasies." **5.** 255.
"The Necromancer." **5.** 255.
"Parábola." **5.** 255.
"Un paseo extraño." **3 ed.** 597; **5.** 255.
"Prince Alacrán." **5.** 255.
"Las queridas de humo." **5.** 255.
"Tengo una gata blanca." **5.** 255.
"The Tragic Day." **5.** 255.
"La ultima rubia." **5.** 255.

"Walpurgis." **5.** 255.
"The White Farm." **3.** 306; **5.** 255.

RICARDO PALMA

"Broadside and Counter-Broadside." **3.** 306.

CHARLES H. PALMER

"Citizen 505." **3.** 306.

VANCE PALMER

"The Catch." **5.** 255.
"Father and Son." **5.** 255.
"The Foal." **3 ed.** 598; **5.** 255.
"Josie." **5.** 255.
"Mathieson's Wife." **5.** 255.
"The Rainbow Bird." **3 ed.** 598.
"The Red Truck." **5.** 256.

W. H. PALMER

"A Woman." **3.** 306.

IVAN I. PANAEV

"Actaeon." **4.** 226.
"The Boudoir of a Fashionable Lady." **3.** 306.
"She Will Be Happy." **3.** 306.

BREECE D'J PANCAKE

"Hollow." **4.** 226.
"The Honored Dead." **4.** 226.
"The Scrapper." **4.** 226.
"Trilobites." **4.** 226.

ALEXANDROS PAPADIAMANDIS

"Christos Milionis." **5.** 256.

JAN PARANDOWSKI

"Aegean Civilization." **3 ed.** 598.
"Cherry." **3 ed.** 598.
"A Conversation with a Shadow." **3 ed.** 598.
"Encyclopedists." **3 ed.** 598.
"Lascaux." **3 ed.** 598.
"Max von Trott." **3 ed.** 598.
"The Mediterranean Hour." **3 ed.** 598.
"Miedzy lampa a switem." **3 ed.** 598.
"The Milestone." **3 ed.** 598.
"The Olympic Wreath." **3 ed.** 598.
"The Phonograph." **3 ed.** 598.
"Poczajow." **3 ed.** 598.
"The Prayer of Aristides." **3 ed.** 598.
"Rodecki." **3 ed.** 598.
"Roscher." **3 ed.** 599.
"Tableau." **3 ed.** 599.
"The Telescope of Galileo." **3 ed.** 599.

EMILIA PARDO BAZÁN

"Accidente." **1.** 14.
"La dama joven." **2.** 237.
"The Drop of Blood." **5.** 256.
"Jesusa." **1.** 14.
"Náufragas." **2.** 237.
"La niña mártir." **1.** 14; **2.** 237.

DOROTHY PARKER

"The Banquet of Crow." **1.** 174.
"Big Blonde." **3 ed.** 599; **1.** 174; **3.** 306; **4.** 226.
"But the One on the Right." **2.** 238.
"Clothe the Naked." **1.** 174.
"Iseult of Brittany." **4.** 226.
"Mr. Durant." **3 ed.** 599; **3.** 306.
"The Sexes." **3 ed.** 599.
"Soldier of the Republic." **1.** 174.
"Standard of Living." **3 ed.** 599.
"Such a Pretty Little Picture." **1.** 174.
"A Telephone Call." **3 ed.** 599.
"Too Bad." **1.** 174; **3.** 306.
"The Waltz." **5.** 256.
"Wonderful Old Gentleman." **3.** 307.
"You Were Perfectly Fine." **3 ed.** 599.

ELIZABETH PARSONS

"The Nightingales Sing." **1.** 174.

MARIANO PASCUAL

"The Major's Story." **4.** 227.

JOAQUÍN PASOS

"The Poor Angel." **2.** 238.

BORIS PASTERNAK

"Aerial Ways." **3 ed.** 599.
"The Cave." **3 ed.** 599.
"The Childhood of Luvers." **3 ed.** 599–600; **3.** 307; **5.** 256.

"The History of a Contraoctave." **3 ed.** 600.
"The Last Summer." **3 ed.** 600.
"Letters from Tula." **3 ed.** 600.
"The Narrative." **3 ed.** 600.
"The Sign of Apelles." **3 ed.** 600.
"Tale." **1.** 174.

KENNETH PATCHEN

"Bury Them in God." **1.** 174.

WALTER PATER

"Apollo in Picardy." **3 ed.** 600; **5.** 256.
"The Child in the House." **3 ed.** 600; **4.** 227; **5.** 256.
"Denys L'Auxerrois." **3 ed.** 600; **5.** 256.
"Duke Carl of Rosenmold." **3 ed.** 600; **5.** 256.
"Emerald Uthwart." **3 ed.** 601; **5.** 256.
"An English Poet." **3 ed.** 601.
"Gaudioso, the Second." **3 ed.** 601.
"Sebastian Van Storck." **3 ed.** 601; **1.** 174; **5.** 256.

ALAN PATON

"Death of a Tsotsi." **3 ed.** 601.
"Debbie Go Home." **3 ed.** 601.
"A Drink in the Passage." **3 ed.** 601.
"Ha'penny." **3 ed.** 601.
"Life for a Life." **3 ed.** 601.
"Sponono." **3 ed.** 601.
"The Waste Land." **3 ed.** 601.

FRANCES GRAY PATTON

"A Piece of Bread." **3 ed.** 601.

GEORGE PATTULO

"The More Abundant Life." **3 ed.** 602.

JAMES KIRKE PAULDING

"Cobus Yerks." **3.** 307.
"The Dumb Girl." **3 ed.** 602; **3.** 307.
"The Little Dutch Sentinel of the Manhadoes." **3.** 307.

GUDRUN PAUSEWANG

"Der Weg nach Tongay." **3 ed.** 602.

NIKOLAI PAVLOV

"The Demon." **3.** 307.
"The Name Day Party." **3.** 307; **4.** 227.
"Yataghan." **3.** 307.

MANUEL PAYNO

"Amor secreto." **5.** 256.

ROBERTO J. PAYRÓ

"The Devil in Pago Chico." **3.** 307.

THOMAS LOVE PEACOCK

"Headlong Hall." **5.** 257.

R. J. PEARSALL

"The Revelation." **2.** 238; **3.** 307.

PATRICK H. PEARSE

"Barbara." **3 ed.** 602.
"The Dearg-Daol." **3 ed.** 602.
"Eoineen of the Birds." **3 ed.** 602.
"Iosagan." **3 ed.** 602.
"The Keening Woman" [originally "Brigid of the Wind"]. **3 ed.** 602.
"The Mother." **3 ed.** 602.
"The Priest." **3 ed.** 602.
"The Singer." **3 ed.** 602.
"The Thief." **3 ed.** 602.
"The Wood." **3 ed.** 602.

MARTIN PEARSON [DONALD A. WOLLHEIM]

"Private World." **4.** 227.

JONATHAN PENNER

"Emotion Recollected in Tranquillity." **5.** 257.

JOSÉ MARÍA DE PEREDA

"Coats of Arms and Bags of Money." **3 ed.** 603.
"The End of a Race." **3 ed.** 603.
"The Levy." **3 ed.** 603.
"Un sabio." **5.** 257.

S. J. PERELMAN

"Call Me Monty and Grovel Freely." **1.** 175.
"Dial 'H' for Heartburn." **1.** 175.
"The Idol Eye." **5.** 257.

IZHAK [ITZHAK] LEIB PERETZ

"The Adventures of a Melody." **3 ed.** 603.
"The Apron." **2.** 238.
"Between Two Mountains." **3.** 308.
"Bontsha the Silent." **3 ed.** 603.
"Bontsie Shvayg." **3.** 308.
"The Defense of the Accused." **2.** 238.
"Devotion Without End." **1.** 175.
"Hear, O Israel." **3 ed.** 603.
"If Not Higher." **3 ed.** 603.
"An Informer." **2.** 238.
"The Kabbalists." **3 ed.** 603.
"The Love Affair." **2.** 238.
"The Magician." **3.** 308.
"The Mental Ward." **2.** 238.
"The Messenger." **2.** 238.
"The Mute." **2.** 238.
"A Night of Terror." **2.** 238.
"No Luck." **2.** 238.
"The Pious Cat." **5.** 257.
"A Question." **2.** 238.
"The Reader." **2.** 238.
"Seven Years of Plenty" [same as "The Trust"]. **2.** 239; **3.** 308.
"The Shtaymil." **2.** 239.
"The Sick Boy." **2.** 239.
"A Strange Being." **2.** 239.
"The Woman Mrs. Hannah." **2.** 239.
"A Woman's Wrath." **2.** 239.

RAMÓN PÉREZ DE AYALA

"Miguelín y Margarita." **5.** 257.

BENITO PÉREZ GALDÓS

"El pórtico de la gloria." **1.** 175.
"The Streetcar Novel." **3.** 308.

CRISTINA PERI ROSSI

"El museo de los esfuerzos inútiles." **5.** 257.
"Unidentified Flying Objects." **5.** 257.

ISAAC PERLOW

"In Thy Blood Live." **3 ed.** 603.

ALEKSEY ALEKSEENVICH PEROVSKY [pseudonym ANTHONY POGORELSKY] [See ANTHONY POGORELSKY]

S. PERSOV

"The Outcome." **3 ed.** 603.

WLODZIMIERZ PERZYNSKI

"The Laundry of Conscience." **3 ed.** 603.
"The Perishing World." **3 ed.** 603.

JULIA PETERKIN

"Ashes." **3 ed.** 604; **1.** 175; **3.** 308.
"Finding Peace." **3.** 308.
"Green Thursday." **1.** 175; **3.** 308.
"Meeting." **1.** 175.
"Missie." **3.** 308.
"The Red Rooster." **1.** 175.
"Son." **3.** 309.
"A Sunday." **1.** 175; **3.** 309.

LEVI S. PETERSON

"Road to Damascus." **5.** 258.

HARRY MARK PETRAKIS

"The Wooing of Ariadne." **2.** 239.

ANN LANE PETRY

"Has Anybody Here Seen Miss Dora Dean?" **5.** 258.
"In Darkness and Confusion." **3 ed.** 604; **5.** 258.
"Miss Muriel." **3 ed.** 604; **5.** 258.
"Mother Africa." **5.** 258.
"The New Mirror." **5.** 258.
"The Witness." **1.** 175; **2.** 239.

ANTHONY PHELPS

"Hier, hier encore . . .." **3.** 309.

ELIZABETH STUART PHELPS

"An Angel over the Right Shoulder." **2.** 239; **5.** 258.
"At Bay." **3.** 309.
"A Brave Girl." **3.** 309.
"Comrades." **3.** 309.
"The Girl Who Could Not Write a Composition." **3.** 309.
"Hannah Colby's Chance." **3.** 309.
"His Soul to Keep." **3.** 309.
"Margaret Bronson." **3.** 309.
"No News." **3.** 309.
"The Sacred Fire." **3.** 309.
"Sweet Home Road." **3.** 309.
"The True Woman." **3.** 309.
"Twenty-Four: Four." **3.** 309.
"What Was the Matter?" [originally "What Did She See With?"]. **3.** 310.
"A Woman's Pulpit." **3.** 310.

LUDWIG PHILIPPSON

"Die Marannen." **5.** 258.

JAYNE ANNE PHILLIPS

"Cheers." **5.** 258.
"Counting." **5.** 258.
"Souvenir." **5.** 258.

LOIS PHILLIPS

"The Loop of Time." **5.** 258.

PETER PHILLIPS

"Lost Memory." **3.** 310.

THOMAS HAL PHILLIPS

"The Shadow of an Arm." **3 ed.** 604.

PI I-HUNG

"Children after Divorce." **2.** 239.

WILLIAM PICKENS

"The Vengeance of the Gods." **1.** 175.

HELEN W. PIERSON

"Chips." **3.** 310.
"In Bonds." **3.** 310.
"My Heart." **3.** 310.
"Queen's Good Work." **3.** 310.

ALBERT PIKE

"A Mexican Tale." **2.** 239.

RAYMOND PILLAI

"Muni Deo's Devil." **4.** 227.
"To Market, To Market." **4.** 227.

THAKAZHI SIVASANKARA PILLAI

"The Flood." **3 ed.** 604.

BORIS PIL'NYAK

"The Bridegroom Cometh." **3.** 310.
"Krasnoye derevo." **2.** 240.
"A Story of the Unextinguished Moon." **3.** 310.
"The Third Capital." **3.** 310.
"A Whole Lifetime." **3.** 310.
"A Year in Their Life." **3.** 310.

VIRGILIO PIÑERA

"The Album." **5.** 259.
"Allegations Against the Uninstalled Bathtub." **4.** 227.
"The Great Baro." **3.** 310.
"The Puppet." **3.** 311.

PING HSIN [HSIEH WAN-YING]

"Since Her Departure." **1.** 176.
"The West Wind." **1.** 176.

NÉLIDA PIÑON

"Trophy Room." **3.** 311.

DAVID PINSKI

"Beruria." **3 ed.** 604.
"The Wall." **3 ed.** 604.
"Zerubabel." **3 ed.** 604.

HAROLD PINTER

"Tea Party." **3 ed.** 604.

H. BEAM PIPER

"Omnilingual." **4.** 227.

LUIGI PIRANDELLO

"An Annuity for Life." **1.** 176.
"A Breath." **1.** 176.
"By Himself." **1.** 176.
"Candelora." **1.** 176.
"The Captive" [same as "Captivity"]. **1.** 176; **3.** 311.
"The Choice." **1.** 176.
"Ciaula scopre la Luna." **1.** 176.
"A Day." **1.** 176.
"The Destruction of Man." **1.** 176.
"The Difficulty of Living Like This." **5.** 259.
"The Doctor's Duty." **2.** 240.
"Double Tombs for Two." **1.** 176.
"The Epistle Singer." **2.** 240; **5.** 259.
"The First Night." **5.** 259.
"Flight." **1.** 176.
"The Fly." **1.** 176.
"The Gentle Touch of Death." **1.** 176.
"Happiness." **1.** 176.
"The Haunted House" [same as "Granella's House"]. **3 ed.** 605.
"Horse in the Moon." **2.** 240.
"The Husband's Revenge." **3.** 311.
"I Have So Much to Tell You." **2.** 240.
"If . . . ." **2.** 240.
"The Illustrious Corpse." **1.** 177.
"In Silence." **1.** 177.
"It's Nothing Serious." **3.** 311.
"The Jar." **3 ed.** 605; **3.** 311.
"The Journey" [same as "The Trip"]. **1.** 177; **2.** 240.
"Juggler's Balls." **1.** 177.
"Let's Burn the Hay." **2.** 240.
"Let's Not Think About It Any More." **2.** 240.
"The Light of the Other House." **3 ed.** 605; **2.** 240.
"The Little Fan." **3 ed.** 605; **1.** 177.
"The Little Garden." **1.** 177.
"A Little Wine." **5.** 259.
"The Long Dress." **1.** 177.
"A Mere Formality." **1.** 177.
"Mortal Remains." **1.** 177.
"Near Death." **2.** 240.
"Nothing." **1.** 177.
"Old Music." **1.** 177.
"Prima Notte." **3 ed.** 605.
"Puberty." **5.** 259.
"The Readied Room." **5.** 604; **2.** 240.
"Remedy: Geography." **1.** 177.
"The Rose." **1.** 177.
"Schoolmistress Boccarmè." **1.** 177.
"Scialle Nero." **1.** 177.
"The Shrine." **1.** 177.
"Sicilian Honor." **3.** 311.
"Stefano Giogli, uno e due." **1.** 177.
"The Straw Bird" [same as "The Stuffed Bird"]. **1.** 177; **2.** 240.
"Sunlight and Shadow." **5.** 259.
"There's Someone Who Is Laughing." **1.** 178.
"The Tragedy of a Character." **1.** 178.
"The Train Has Whistled." **2.** 240.
"The Trap." **1.** 178.
"The Truth." **2.** 240.
"The Umbrella." **1.** 178.
"Visit." **1.** 178.
"Visiting the Sick." **1.** 178; **5.** 259.
"A Voice." **5.** 259.
"War." **3 ed.** 605; **2.** 241; **4.** 228.
"The Wave." **1.** 178.
"The Wet Nurse." **1.** 178.
"The Wheelbarrow." **1.** 178; **2.** 241; **4.** 228.
"When I Was Mad." **1.** 178.
"World News." **1.** 178.
"The Wreath." **1.** 178.

PUDUMAI PITHAN

"Redemption." **3 ed.** 605.

SYLVIA PLATH

"The Brink." **4.** 228.
"The Daughters of Blossom Street." **3 ed.** 605.
"The Fifteen-Dollar Eagle." **3 ed.** 605.
"The Fifty-Ninth Bear." **3 ed.** 605.
"In the Mountains." **4.** 228.
"Johnny Panic and the Bible of Dreams." **3 ed.** 605; **4.** 228.
"Stone Boy with Dolphin." **4.** 228.
"Sunday at the Mintons'." **4.** 228.
"Sweetie-Pie and the Gutter Men." **4.** 228.
"Tongues of Stone." **4.** 228.
"The Wishing Box." **3 ed.** 605; **4.** 228.

ANDREI PLATONOV

"The Epifan Locks." **3.** 311.
"Makar the Doubtful." **4.** 228.

WILLIAM PLOMER

"Bed Number Seventeen." **3 ed.** 605.
"Black Peril." **3 ed.** 606.
"A Brutal Sentimentalist." **3 ed.** 606.
"The Child of Queen Victoria." **3 ed.** 606.
"Down on the Farm." **3 ed.** 606.
"Ever Such a Nice Boy." **3 ed.** 606.
"Folk Tale." **3 ed.** 606.
"The Island." **3 ed.** 606.
"Local Colour." **3 ed.** 606.
"Mother Kamchatka: or Mr. Mainchance in Search of the Truth." **3 ed.** 606.
"A Museum Piece." **3 ed.** 606.
"Nakamura." **3 ed.** 606.
"Nausicaa." **3 ed.** 606.
"The Night Before the War." **3 ed.** 606.
"No Ghost." **3 ed.** 606.
"The Owl and the Pussy Cat." **3 ed.** 606.
"A Piece of Good Luck." **3 ed.** 606.
"The Portrait of an Emperor." **3 ed.** 606.
"Portraits in the Nude." **3 ed.** 606.
"The Sleeping Husband." **3 ed.** 607.
"Stephen Jordan's Wife." **3 ed.** 607.
"Thy Neighbor's Creed." **3 ed.** 607.
"Ula Masonda." **3 ed.** 607; **2.** 241.
"A Wedding Guest." **3 ed.** 607.
"When the Sardines Came." **3 ed.** 607; **2.** 241.

JAMES PLUNKETT

"A Walk Through the Summer." **3.** 311.

ERNEST M. POATE

"Phantom Footsteps." **3.** 311.

EDGAR ALLAN POE

"The Angel of the Odd." **3 ed.** 607; **1.** 178; **3.** 312.
"The Assignation." **3 ed.** 607; **2.** 241; **3.** 312; **4.** 228–29; **5.** 259.
"The Balloon Hoax." **3 ed.** 607.
"Berenice." **3 ed.** 608; **1.** 178; **2.** 241; **3.** 312; **4.** 229; **5.** 259.
"The Black Cat." **3 ed.** 608; **1.** 178–79; **2.** 241; **3.** 312; **4.** 229; **5.** 260.
"Bon-Bon." **3 ed.** 608; **3.** 312; **5.** 260.
"The Business Man." **3.** 312.
"The Cask of Amontillado." **3 ed.** 609–10; **1.** 179; **2.** 241; **3.** 312; **4.** 229; **5.** 260.
"The Colloquy of Monos and Una." **3 ed.** 610; **1.** 179; **3.** 312; **4.** 229; **5.** 260.
"The Conversation of Eiros and Charmion." **3 ed.** 610; **3.** 313; **4.** 229; **5.** 260.
"A Descent into the Maelström." **3 ed.** 610–11; **1.** 179; **2.** 241; **3.** 313; **4.** 229; **5.** 260.
"The Devil in the Belfry." **3 ed.** 611; **1.** 179; **3.** 313.
"Diddling Considered as One of the Exact Sciences." **3 ed.** 611.
"The Domain of Arnheim." **3 ed.** 611; **1.** 179; **2.** 242; **3.** 313; **4.** 229; **5.** 260.
"A Dream." **5.** 260.
"The Duc de l'Omelette." **3 ed.** 611; **1.** 179; **4.** 229.
"Eleonora." **3 ed.** 611–12; **1.** 179; **3.** 313; **4.** 229.
"The Facts in the Case of M. Valdemar." **3 ed.** 612; **3.** 313; **4.** 229; **5.** 260–61.
"The Fall of the House of Usher." **3 ed.** 612–15; **1.** 179–80; **2.** 242; **3.** 313; **4.** 230; **5.** 261.
"Four Beasts in One." **3 ed.** 615; **1.** 180.
"The Gold Bug." **3 ed.** 615–16; **1.** 180; **2.** 242; **3.** 314; **4.** 230; **5.** 261.
"Hop-Frog." **3 ed.** 616; **1.** 180; **2.** 242; **3.** 314; **5.** 261.
"How to Write a Blackwood Article." **3 ed.** 616; **3.** 314.
"The Imp of the Perverse." **3 ed.** 616; **1.** 180; **2.** 242; **3.** 314; **4.** 230; **5.** 261.
"The Island of the Fay." **3 ed.** 616; **1.** 180; **3.** 314; **4.** 230.
"King Pest." **3 ed.** 616; **3.** 314; **5.** 261.
"Landor's Cottage." **3 ed.** 616; **3.** 314; **4.** 230; **5.** 261.
"The Landscape Garden." **3.** 314.
"Ligeia." **3 ed.** 616–18; **1.** 180; **2.** 242–43; **3.** 314–15; **4.** 230–31; **5.** 262.
"The Lighthouse." **3 ed.** 618.
"Lionizing." **3 ed.** 618.
"The Literary Life of Thingum Bob, Esq." **3 ed.** 618.
"Loss of Breath." **3 ed.** 618; **1.** 180; **2.** 243; **4.** 231; **5.** 262.
"The Man of the Crowd." **3 ed.** 619; **2.** 243; **3.** 315; **4.** 231; **5.** 262.

"The Man That Was Used Up." **3 ed.** 619; **1.** 180; **2.** 243; **4.** 231; **5.** 262.
"MS. Found in a Bottle." **3 ed.** 619; **1.** 180; **3.** 315; **4.** 231; **5.** 262.
"The Masque of the Red Death." **3 ed.** 619–20; **1.** 180; **2.** 243; **3.** 315; **4.** 231; **5.** 262.
"Mellonta Tauta." **3 ed.** 620; **3.** 315; **5.** 262.
"Mesmeric Revelation." **3 ed.** 620; **3.** 315; **4.** 231.
"Metzengerstein." **3 ed.** 620–21; **3.** 315; **4.** 231; **5.** 262.
"Morella." **3 ed.** 621; **1.** 180; **2.** 243; **3.** 315; **5.** 262–63.
"The Murders in the Rue Morgue." **3 ed.** 621; **1.** 181; **2.** 243; **3.** 315; **4.** 231; **5.** 263.
"The Mystery of Marie Roget." **3 ed.** 621–22; **2.** 243; **3.** 315; **5.** 263.
"The Narrative of Arthur Gordon Pym." **3 ed.** 622–23; **1.** 181; **2.** 243–44; **3.** 316; **4.** 232; **5.** 263.
"Never Bet the Devil Your Head." **3 ed.** 623; **5.** 263.
"The Oblong Box." **3 ed.** 623; **4.** 232.
"The Oval Portrait." **3 ed.** 624; **1.** 181; **2.** 244; **4.** 232; **5.** 263–64.
"The Pit and the Pendulum." **3 ed.** 624; **1.** 181; **2.** 244; **3.** 316; **4.** 232; **5.** 264.
"The Power of Words." **3 ed.** 624; **4.** 232; **5.** 264.
"A Predicament." **3 ed.** 624; **1.** 181; **2.** 244; **3.** 316; **5.** 264.
"The Premature Burial." **3 ed.** 624; **3.** 316; **4.** 232; **5.** 264.
"The Purloined Letter." **3 ed.** 625; **1.** 182; **2.** 244; **3.** 316; **4.** 232; **5.** 264.
"The Scythe of Time." **3 ed.** 625.
"Shadow—A Parable." **3 ed.** 625; **3.** 316; **5.** 264.
"Silence—A Fable." **3 ed.** 625; **1.** 182.
"Some Words with a Mummy." **3 ed.** 625; **5.** 265.
"The Spectacles." **3 ed.** 625; **1.** 182; **4.** 232; **5.** 265.
"The Sphinx." **3 ed.** 625; **1.** 182; **2.** 244; **4.** 232.
"The System of Doctor Tarr and Professor Fether." **3 ed.** 625–26; **1.** 182; **2.** 244; **3.** 316; **4.** 232.
"A Tale of Jerusalem." **3 ed.** 626.
"A Tale of the Ragged Mountains." **3 ed.** 626; **2.** 244; **3.** 316.
"The Tell-Tale Heart." **3 ed.** 626–27; **1.** 182; **2.** 244; **3.** 317; **4.** 232; **5.** 265.
"Thou Art the Man." **3 ed.** 627; **4.** 233; **5.** 265.
"The Thousand-and-Second Tale of Scheherazade." **3 ed.** 627.
"Three Sundays in a Week." **3 ed.** 627; **4.** 233.
"The Unparalleled Adventures of One Hans Pfaall." **3 ed.** 627; **2.** 244; **3.** 317; **4.** 233; **5.** 265.
"Von Kempelen and His Discovery." **3 ed.** 627; **3.** 317; **4.** 233.
"William Wilson." **3 ed.** 627–28; **1.** 182; **2.** 244–45; **3.** 317; **4.** 233; **5.** 265.

MIKHAIL POGODIN

"The Deacon-Wizard." **3.** 317.
"Happiness in Misfortune." **3.** 317.
"Sokolnitsky Park." **3.** 317.

ANTHONY POGORELSKY [ALEKSEY ALEKSEENVICH PEROVSKY]

"The Baleful Consequences of an Unbridled Imagination" [same as "The Pernicious Consequences of an Uncontrolled Imagination"]. **3 ed.** 628; **3.** 308.
"The Black Chicken, or The Subterranean Dwellers." **3 ed.** 628.
"The Fifth Evening." **3 ed.** 628.
"The First Evening." **3 ed.** 628.
"The Fourth Evening." **3 ed.** 628.
"The Hypnotist." **3 ed.** 629.
"Isadore and Anyuta." **3 ed.** 629; **3.** 308.
"A Journey by Stagecoach" [same as ". . . Diligence"]. **3 ed.** 629; **3.** 308.
"The Lafertov District Poppyseed-Cake Vendor" [same as "The Poppy-Seed-Cake Woman of the Lafërtov"]. **3 ed.** 629; **3.** 308.

FREDERIK POHL

"The Abominable Earthman." **5.** 265.
"The Candle Lighter." **5.** 265.
"The Census-Taker." **5.** 265.
"The Children of the Night." **5.** 265.
"Day Million." **2.** 245.

"The Day of the Boomer Dukes." **5.** 265.
"The Day the Icicle Works Closed." **5.** 265.
"The Deadly Mission of Phineas Snodgrass." **5.** 265.
"Earth, Farewell!" **5.** 266.
"Father of the Stars." **5.** 266.
"Fermi and Frost." **5.** 266.
"The Five Hells of Orion." **5.** 266.
"The Gold at the Starbow's End." **3.** 317; **5.** 266.
"Gravy Planet." **3.** 317.
"Happy Birthday, Dear Jesus." **5.** 266.
"I Plingot, Who You?" **5.** 266.
"In the Problem Pit." **2.** 245.
"Let the Ants Try." **4.** 233; **5.** 266.
"The Man Who Ate the World." **5.** 266.
"The Mapmakers." **3.** 317; **5.** 266.
"The Merchant of Venus." **2.** 245.
"The Midas Plague." **3.** 317; **5.** 266.
"The Middle of Nowhere." **5.** 266.
"My Lady Greensleeves." **5.** 266.
"Pythians." **4.** 233.
"Rafferty's Reasons." **4.** 233; **5.** 266.
"The Richest Man in Levittown" [originally "The Bitterest Pill"]. **5.** 266.
"The Schematic Man." **5.** 266.
"Shaffery Among the Immortals." **5.** 266.
"The Snowmen." **5.** 267.
"Some Joys under the Star." **5.** 267.
"To See Another Mountain." **5.** 267.
"The Tunnel Under the World." **2.** 245; **4.** 233; **5.** 267.
"Under Two Moons." **5.** 267.
"The Waging of the Peace." **5.** 267.
"Way Up Yonder." **5.** 267.
"We Purchased People." **2.** 245.
"What to Do Till the Analyst Comes." **4.** 233.
"The Wizards of Pung's Corners." **4.** 233; **5.** 267.

FREDERIK POHL and CYRIL KORNBLUTH

"Best Friend." **5.** 267.
"The Engineer." **5.** 267.

BORIS POLEVOY

"Doctor Vera." **3.** 318.

NIKOLAY FËDROVICH POLEVOY

"The Artist." **3.** 318.
"The Felicity of Madness." **3 ed.** 629.
"The Painter." **3 ed.** 629.

JOHN POLIDORI

"The Vampyre." **3 ed.** 629; **2.** 245; **5.** 267.

WILLIAM T. POLK

"Golden Eagle Ordinary." **3.** 318.

FRANK LILLIE POLLACK

"Finis." **3.** 318.

KERIMA POLOTAN

"Cost Price." **3 ed.** 629.
"The Virgin." **3 ed.** 629.

MARIO POMILIO

"Cimitero cinesi." **5.** 267.

ELENA PONIATOWSKA

"The House in Sololoi." **3.** 318.
"Limbo." **3.** 318.
"Place Yourself, My Lovely, Between the Tie and the Whistle." **3.** 318.

JOSEF PONTEN

"Die Bockreiter." **3 ed.** 629.
"Die Uhr von Gold." **3 ed.** 629.

HENRIK PONTOPPIDAN

"Charity." **2.** 245.
"A Deathblow." **2.** 245.
"The End of a Life." **2.** 245.
"The Votive Ship" [same as "The Ship Model"]. **2.** 245.

RENÉ POPPE

"Una mita más mi General." **4.** 233.

HAL PORTER

"A Double Because It's Snowing." **4.** 233.
"Francis Silver." **3 ed.** 629.
"The Housegirl." **4.** 234.
"Otto Ruff." **3 ed.** 630.

"Say to Me Ronald." **3 ed.** 630; **4.** 234.
"They're Funny People." **4.** 234.

KATHERINE ANNE PORTER

"The Circus." **3 ed.** 630; **1.** 182; **2.** 245; **3.** 318; **4.** 234; **5.** 267.
"The Cracked Looking-Glass." **3 ed.** 630; **2.** 246; **3.** 318; **4.** 234; **5.** 268.
"A Day's Work." **3 ed.** 630; **2.** 246; **5.** 268.
"The Days Before." **3 ed.** 630.
"The Downward Path to Wisdom." **3 ed.** 631; **4.** 234; **5.** 268.
"The Fig Tree." **3 ed.** 631; **1.** 182; **2.** 246; **3.** 318; **4.** 234; **5.** 268.
"Flowering Judas." **3 ed.** 631–32; **1.** 183; **2.** 246; **3.** 319; **4.** 234; **5.** 268.
"The Grave." **3 ed.** 632–33; **1.** 183; **2.** 246; **3.** 319; **4.** 234; **5.** 268.
"Hacienda." **3 ed.** 633; **1.** 183; **3.** 319; **4.** 235; **5.** 268.
"He." **3 ed.** 633; **1.** 183; **3.** 319; **4.** 235; **5.** 268.
"Holiday." **3 ed.** 633–34; **1.** 183; **2.** 246; **3.** 319; **4.** 235; **5.** 268.
"The Jilting of Granny Weatherall." **3 ed.** 634; **1.** 183; **2.** 246; **3.** 319; **4.** 235; **5.** 268.
"The Journey." **1.** 183; **5.** 269.
"The Last Leaf." **3 ed.** 634; **2.** 246; **3.** 319.
"The Leaning Tower." **3 ed.** 634–35; **2.** 246; **4.** 235; **5.** 269.
"Magic." **3 ed.** 635; **1.** 183; **4.** 235; **5.** 269.
"María Concepción." **3 ed.** 635; **2.** 246; **3.** 319; **4.** 235; **5.** 269.
"The Martyr." **3 ed.** 635; **3.** 319; **4.** 235; **5.** 269.
"Noon Wine." **3 ed.** 635–36; **1.** 183; **2.** 246–47; **3.** 320; **4.** 235; **5.** 269.
"Old Mortality." **3 ed.** 636–37; **1.** 183; **2.** 247; **3.** 320; **4.** 235; **5.** 269.
"The Old Order." **3 ed.** 637; **1.** 183; **2.** 247; **3.** 320; **4.** 235; **5.** 269.
"Pale Horse, Pale Rider." **3 ed.** 637–38; **1.** 184; **2.** 247; **3.** 320; **4.** 236; **5.** 269.
"Rope." **3 ed.** 638; **1.** 184; **3.** 320; **5.** 269.
"The Source." **3 ed.** 638; **1.** 184; **2.** 247; **3.** 320; **5.** 269.
"That Tree." **3 ed.** 638; **2.** 247; **3.** 320; **4.** 236; **5.** 269.
"Theft." **3 ed.** 638; **1.** 184; **3.** 320; **4.** 236; **5.** 269.
"Virgin Violeta." **3 ed.** 638; **3.** 320; **4.** 236; **5.** 270.
"The Witness." **3 ed.** 639; **2.** 247; **3.** 320; **4.** 236; **5.** 270.

ESTELA PORTILLO TRAMBLEY

"The Burning." **2.** 279; **4.** 236.
"Duende." **5.** 270.
"If It Weren't for the Honeysuckle." **2.** 279; **4.** 236.
"The Paris Gown." **2.** 279; **4.** 236; **5.** 270.
"Pay the Crier." **4.** 236.
"Rain of Scorpions." **1.** 208; **4.** 236.
"Recast." **4.** 236.
"The Secret Room." **2.** 279; **4.** 237.
"The Trees." **2.** 279; **4.** 237.

ALEXANDER A. POSEY

"Jes 'Bout a Mid'lin', Sah." **3.** 320.
"Moses and Richard." **3.** 320.

RICHARD POSNER

"Vacation." **5.** 270.

MELVILLE DAVISSON POST

"An Act of God." **3 ed.** 639.
"The Adopted Daughter." **3 ed.** 639.
"The Age of Miracles." **3 ed.** 639.
"The Angel of the Lord" [originally "The Broken Stirrup"]. **3 ed.** 639.
"The Bradmoor Murder." **3 ed.** 639.
"The Corpus Delicti." **3 ed.** 639.
"The Edge of the Shadow." **3 ed.** 639.
"The Riddle." **3 ed.** 639.
"The Spread Rails." **3 ed.** 639.

JAN POTOCKI

"Princess Brambilla." **3 ed.** 639.

J. F. POWERS

"The Blessing." **3 ed.** 639.
"Blue Island." **3 ed.** 639.
"A Couple of Nights Before Christmas." **3 ed.** 640.
"Dawn." **3 ed.** 640.
"Death of a Favorite." **3 ed.** 640.
"Defection of a Favorite." **3 ed.** 640.
"The Devil Was the Joker." **3 ed.** 640.
"The Forks." **3 ed.** 640; **2.** 247.

"God Writes a Bad Hand." **3 ed.** 640.
"He Don't Plant Cotton." **3 ed.** 640–41.
"Interlude in a Bookshop." **3 ed.** 641.
"Jamesie." **3 ed.** 641.
"The Keystone." **3 ed.** 641.
"Lions, Harts, and Leaping Does." **3 ed.** 641.
"Look How the Fish Live." **3 ed.** 641.
"The Lord's Day." **3 ed.** 641; **5.** 270.
"A Losing Game." **3 ed.** 641; **2.** 247.
"The Old Bird, A Love Story." **3 ed.** 641.
"The Poor Thing." **3 ed.** 641.
"Presence of Grace." **3 ed.** 641.
"Priestly Fellowship." **3 ed.** 642.
"Prince of Darkness." **3 ed.** 642; **1.** 184.
"Renner." **3 ed.** 642.
"The Trouble." **3 ed.** 642.
"The Valiant Woman." **3 ed.** 642; **1.** 184; **3.** 320; **4.** 237; **5.** 270.
"Zeal." **3 ed.** 642.

JOHN C. POWYS

"The Mountains of the Moon." **3.** 321.
"Up and Out." **3.** 321.

T[HEODORE] F[RANCIS] POWYS

"Abraham Men." **3.** 321.
"The Baked Mole." **3.** 321.
"The Barometer." **3.** 321.
"The Blind Hen and the Earthworm." **3.** 321.
"Bottle's Path." **3 ed.** 642.
"The Bucket and the Rope." **3.** 321; **4.** 237.
"The Corpse and the Flea." **3.** 321.
"Darkness and Nathaniel." **4.** 237.
"Hester Dominy." **3.** 321.
"Jane Moller's Box." **3.** 321.
"John Pardy and the Waves." **3.** 321.
"The Left Leg." **3.** 321.
"Mr. Pim and the Holy Crumb." **3.** 321.
"The Only Penitent." **3.** 321; **4.** 237.
"The Spittoon and the Slate." **3.** 321.
"The Stone and Mr. Thomas." **3.** 321; **4.** 237.

PEDRO PRADO

"The Laugh in the Desert." **1.** 184.
"Moonlight." **1.** 184.
"Summer Picture: The Cripple." **1.** 184.
"When You Are Poor." **1.** 184.
"The Wise Woman." **1.** 184.

PRAMOEDYA ANANTA TOER

"Things Vanished." **1.** 184.

JAISHANKAR PRASAD

"Ashoka." **3.** 322.
"The Beggar Woman." **3.** 322.
"A Broken Vow." **3.** 322.
"The Chariot of the Gods." **3.** 322.
"Doubt." **3.** 322.
"Echo." **3.** 322.
"Gangster." **3.** 322.
"Jahanara." **3.** 322.
"The Liberation of Chittor." **3.** 322.
"The Lighthouse." **3.** 322.
"Madhua." **3.** 322.
"Mamata." **3.** 322.
"The Moon." **3.** 322.
"The Recluse." **3.** 322.
"Tansen." **3.** 322.

FLETCHER PRATT and LAURENCE MANNING

"City of the Living Dead." **1.** 185.

MUNSHI PREM CHAND [MUNSHI DHANPAT RAI SHRIVASTAV]

"The Bad Omen." **2.** 247.
"Battle Journey." **3.** 322.
"Brahman Sham." **3.** 323.
"The Chess Player." **1.** 185.
"The Coward." **3.** 323.
"The Co-Wives." **2.** 247.
"The Cry of the Poor." **3.** 323.
"Deliverance." **3.** 323.
"Despair." **2.** 247; **3.** 323.
"Durga Temple." **3.** 323.
"Exile." **3.** 323.
"False Courage." **3.** 323.
"A False Flame." **3.** 323.
"Fatherless Girl." **3.** 323.
"The Fine." **3.** 323.
"From Beast to Man." **3.** 323.
"The God in the Panchayat." **3.** 323.
"A Good Place in the Hereafter." **3.** 323.
"Hostility." **3.** 323.
"Kafan." **4.** 237.
"Kusum." **3.** 323.

"Madness." **3.** 323.
"Man's Highest Duty." **3.** 324.
"Miss Padma." **3.** 324.
"A Mother's Heart." **3.** 324.
"The New Marriage." **3.** 324.
"The Old Aunt." **1.** 185.
"The Plaything of Pride." **3.** 324.
"The Price of Milk." **3.** 324.
"Rani Sarandha." **3.** 324.
"Reconciliation." **3.** 324.
"Sacrifice." **3.** 324.
"The Shroud." **3.** 324.
"Temple and Mosque." **3.** 324.
"The Thakur's Well." **3.** 324.
"This Is My Country." **3.** 324.
"A Winter Night." **3.** 324.

HARRIET E. PRESCOTT

"Down the River." **3.** 324.

DONALD PRICE

"Character of a Broad." **3 ed.** 642.

REYNOLDS PRICE

"The Anniversary." **3.** 325.
"A Chain of Love." **3.** 325; **5.** 270.
"A Dog's Death." **3.** 325.
"Elegies." **3.** 325.
"Good and Bad Dreams." **3.** 325.
"The Happiness of Others." **3.** 325.
"Michael Egerton." **3.** 325.
"The Names and Faces of Heroes." **3 ed.** 643; **3.** 325.
"Scars." **3.** 325.
"A Sight of Blood." **3 ed.** 643.
"Troubled Sleep." **3.** 325.
"Truth and Lies." **3.** 325.
"Uncle Grant." **3 ed.** 643; **3.** 325.
"Waiting at Dachau." **3.** 325.
"Walking Lessons." **3 ed.** 643; **3.** 325.
"The Warrior Princess Ozimba." **3 ed.** 643; **3.** 325.

J. B. PRIESTLEY

"The Pavilion of Masks." **2.** 248; **3.** 325.

MARIYA PRILEZHAEVA

"The Pushkin Waltz." **3.** 326.

V[ICTOR] S[AWDON] PRITCHETT

"The Ape." **3 ed.** 643.
"Blind Love." **4.** 237; **5.** 270.
"The Camberwell Beauty." **2.** 248; **4.** 237; **5.** 270.
"The Corsican Inn." **4.** 237.
"The Cuckoo Clock." **5.** 271.
"The Diver." **5.** 271.
"A Family Man." **5.** 271.
"The Fly in the Ointment." **5.** 271.
"Greek Theatre Tragedy." **5.** 271.
"Handsome Is as Handsome Does." **4.** 237; **5.** 271.
"It May Never Happen." **2.** 248.
"The Liars." **5.** 271.
"Many Are Disappointed." **5.** 271.
"The Marvellous Gift." **5.** 271.
"The Night Worker." **5.** 271.
"Noise in the Doghouse." **5.** 271.
"On the Edge of the Cliff." **5.** 271.
"Page and Monarch." **5.** 271.
"Pocock Passes." **5.** 271.
"The Sailor." **3 ed.** 643; **4.** 238; **5.** 271.
"The Saint." **2.** 248; **4.** 238; **5.** 272.
"The Scapegoat." **3 ed.** 643; **5.** 272.
"The Skeleton." **5.** 272.
"The Spanish Virgin." **5.** 272.
"The Speech." **4.** 238; **5.** 272.
"The Two Brothers." **5.** 272.
"The Voice." **5.** 272.
"The Wheelbarrow." **5.** 272.
"The White Rabbit." **5.** 272.
"You Make Your Own Life." **5.** 272.

MARCEL PROUST

"Mélancolique villégiature de Mme de Breyves." **5.** 272.
"La Morte de Baldassare Silvande." **5.** 272.
"Le Petit Pan de mur jaune." **5.** 272.
"A Young Girl's Confession." **5.** 272.

AGNES L. PROVOST

"Heathen." **2.** 248.

BOLESLAW PRUS

"Antek." **3 ed.** 643.
"The Barrel-Organ." **3 ed.** 643.
"The Converted One." **3 ed.** 643.
"Graveyard Stories." **3 ed.** 643.
"The Harvest Contest." **3 ed.** 643.

"A Legend of Ancient Egypt." **3 ed.** 644.
"Mr. Wesolowski and His Walking Stick." **3 ed.** 644.
"The Saxonian Garden." **3 ed.** 644.
"Under the Fence." **3 ed.** 644.

MARÍA LUISA PUGA

"Secret, Immobile Sun." **3.** 326.

JAMES PURDY

"About Jessie Mae." **3 ed.** 644.
"Color of Darkness." **3 ed.** 644; **1.** 185; **4.** 238; **5.** 273.
"Cutting Edge." **3 ed.** 644; **1.** 185; **4.** 238.
"Daddy Wolf." **3 ed.** 644; **1.** 185.
"Don't Call Me by My Right Name." **3 ed.** 644; **1.** 185; **2.** 248; **4.** 238; **5.** 273.
"Encore." **3 ed.** 644; **5.** 273.
"Eventide." **3 ed.** 644; **1.** 185; **5.** 273.
"Everything Under the Sun." **3 ed.** 645.
"A Good Woman." **3 ed.** 645.
"Goodnight, Sweetheart." **3 ed.** 645.
"Home by Dark." **3 ed.** 645; **1.** 185.
"The Lesson." **3 ed.** 645.
"Man and Wife." **3 ed.** 645; **4.** 238; **5.** 273.
"Mr. Evening." **3 ed.** 645.
"Mrs. Benson." **3 ed.** 645.
"Night and Day." **3 ed.** 645; **5.** 273.
"Plan Now to Attend." **3 ed.** 645; **5.** 273.
"Sermon." **3 ed.** 645.
"63: Dream Palace." **3 ed.** 645; **1.** 185; **3.** 326.
"Sound of Talking." **3 ed.** 645.
"Why Can't They Tell You Why?" **3 ed.** 646; **1.** 185; **4.** 238; **5.** 273.
"You May Safely Gaze." **3 ed.** 646.
"You Reach for Your Hat." **3 ed.** 646; **4.** 238.

ALEXANDER PUSHKIN

"The Blizzard." **3.** 326; **4.** 238.
"The Captain's Daughter." **3 ed.** 646; **2.** 248.
"The Coffinmaker" [same as "The Undertaker"]. **3 ed.** 647; **2.** 248; **3.** 326, 327.
"Egyptian Nights." **3 ed.** 646; **3.** 326; **4.** 238.
"The Golden Cockerel." **2.** 248.
"The Guests Were Arriving at the Dacha." **3.** 326.
"History of the Village Goryukhino." **3 ed.** 646.
"Kirdzhali." **3.** 326.
"The Lady Peasant" [same as "The Peasant Miss"]. **3 ed.** 646; **2.** 248.
"The Lonely Cottage on Vasilevskij Island." **3 ed.** 646.
"Mistress into Maid." **2.** 248; **3.** 326.
"The Queen of Spades." **3 ed.** 646; **1.** 185–86; **2.** 249; **3.** 326–27; **4.** 238; **5.** 273.
"The Shot" [same as "The Pistol Shot"]. **3 ed.** 647; **2.** 249; **3.** 327; **4.** 239.
"The Snowstorm." **3 ed.** 647; **3.** 327.
"The Squire's Daughter." **3.** 327.
"The Stationmaster" [same as "The Post-Stage Master"]. **3 ed.** 647; **1.** 186; **2.** 249; **3.** 327; **5.** 273.
"The Tale of Tsar Saltan." **2.** 249.
"The Undertaker" [same as "The Coffinmaker"]. **3 ed.** 647; **2.** 248; **3.** 326, 327.

BARBARA PYM

"Across the Crowded Room." **4.** 239; **5.** 273.
"The Day the Music Came." **4.** 239.
"English Ladies." **4.** 239.
"Goodbye, Balkan Capital!" **4.** 239.
"So Some Tempestuous Morn . . . ." **4.** 239.
"The White Elephant." **4.** 239.

THOMAS PYNCHON

"Entropy." **3 ed.** 647; **1.** 186; **2.** 249; **3.** 327; **4.** 239; **5.** 273.
"A Journey into the Mind of Watts." **1.** 186.
"Low-Lands." **1.** 186; **2.** 249; **3.** 327; **4.** 239; **5.** 274.
"Mortality and Mercy in Vienna." **1.** 186; **2.** 249; **3.** 327; **4.** 239; **5.** 274.
"The Secret Integration." **1.** 186; **2.** 249; **3.** 327; **4.** 239; **5.** 274.
"The Small Rain." **3.** 327; **4.** 239.
"Under the Rose." **3.** 327; **4.** 239; **5.** 274.

ABD AL-HAKIM QASIM

"The Journey." **5.** 274.

QIAN ZHONGSHU

"The Cat." **3.** 328.
"God's Dream." **3.** 328.
"Inspiration." **3.** 328.
"Satan Pays an Evening Visit to Mr. Qian Zhongshu." **3.** 328.
"Souvenir." **3.** 328.

QIAO SHI

"Providing a Meal." **4.** 240.

RAYMOND QUENEAU

"A la limite de la forêt." **4.** 240.

LUIS QUERO CHIESA

"Detrás de aquella lucesita." **5.** 274.
"La protesta." **5.** 274.

ARTHUR QUILLER-COUCH

"The Mystery of Joseph Laquedem." **4.** 240.
"The Room of Mirrors." **4.** 240.

SEABURY GRANDIN QUINN

"The Jest of Warburg Tantaval." **3.** 328.

HORACIO QUIROGA

"A la deriva." **1.** 186; **3.** 328; **4.** 240.
"Anaconda." **5.** 274.
"El crimen del otro." **4.** 240.
"The Dead Man." **1.** 186; **3.** 328; **4.** 240; **5.** 274.
"The Decapitated Chicken." **3.** 328; **4.** 240.
"En la noche." **3 ed.** 647.
"The Flies." **1.** 186; **4.** 240.
"Gloria tropical." **3 ed.** 647.
"Hired Hands." **5.** 274.
"La insolación." **4.** 240.
"Juan Darién." **3.** 328; **4.** 241; **5.** 274.
"Los pescadores de vigas." **3 ed.** 647.
"Las rayas." **5.** 274.
"The Spectre." **4.** 241.
"La voluntad." **3 ed.** 647.

ESTHER RAAB

"The Days of *Hedim.*" **4.** 241.

WILHELM RAABE

"The Black Galley." **3 ed.** 647.
"Else von der Tanne." **3 ed.** 647; **2.** 249.
"Die Gänse von Bützow." **3 ed.** 647; **2.** 249.
"Gedelöcke." **3 ed.** 648; **2.** 249.
"Die Hämelschen." **3 ed.** 648; **2.** 250.
"Holunderblüte." **3 ed.** 648; **2.** 250.
"Höxter und Corvey." **3 ed.** 648; **2.** 250.
"Die Innerste." **3 ed.** 648.
"Das letzte Recht." **3 ed.** 648.
"Der Marsch nach Hause." **3 ed.** 648; **2.** 250.
"Pfister's Mill." **3.** 329.
"Der Reiches Krone." **3 ed.** 648.
"Die schwartze Galeere." **2.** 250.
"The Student from Wittenberg." **3 ed.** 648; **2.** 250.
"Zum wilden Mann." **3 ed.** 648; **1.** 187; **2.** 250.

THOMAS H. RADDALL

"Resurrection." **3.** 329.
"Triangle in Steel." **3.** 329.

MOHAN RAKESH

"Another Life." **2.** 250.
"Ek Aur Zindagi." **2.** 250.
"Miss Pall." **2.** 250.
"Savorless Sin." **1.** 187.
"The Strangers." **2.** 250.
"Suhagine." **2.** 250.
"The Wound." **2.** 250.

JUAN ANTONIO RAMOS

"Elpidia Figueroa." **5.** 275.
"Había una vez y dos son tres." **5.** 275.

FLORENCE ENGLE RANDALL

"The Watchers." **2.** 250.

RAJA RAO

"Akkaya." **5.** 275.
"Companions." **3 ed.** 648.
"The Cow of the Barricades." **3 ed.** 648; **1.** 187; **2.** 251; **4.** 241; **5.** 275.
"In Khandesh." **3 ed.** 648; **1.** 187.
"Javni." **4.** 241; **5.** 275.
"Narsiga." **3 ed.** 648; **1.** 187; **2.** 251.

"The Policeman and the Rose." **5.** 275.
"The True Story of Kanakapala, Protector of God." **3 ed.** 648.

VALENTIN GRIGOREVICH RASPUTIN

"Borrowed Time." **5.** 275.
"The Final Term." **2.** 251.
"Live and Love." **5.** 275.
"Live and Remember." **2.** 251.
"Money for Maria." **2.** 251; **5.** 275.
"The Old Woman." **5.** 275.
"Parting with Matera." **2.** 251; **3.** 329; **4.** 241; **5.** 275.
"Vasily and Vasilisa." **4.** 241.

MARJORIE KINNAN RAWLINGS

"Black Secret." **3 ed.** 648.
"Cocks Must Crow." **3 ed.** 649.
"A Crop of Beans." **3 ed.** 649.
"The Enemy." **3 ed.** 649.
"Gal Young Un." **3 ed.** 649.
"Jacob's Ladder." **3 ed.** 649.
"A Mother in Manville." **3 ed.** 649.

CHARLES READE

"Art: A Dramatic Tale." **1.** 187.
"Clouds and Sunshine." **1.** 187.

TOM REAMY

"The Detweiler Boy." **3.** 329.

PETER REDGROVE

"Mr. Waterman." **1.** 187.

ISHMAEL REED

"Cab Calloway Stands in for the Moon." **4.** 241; **5.** 275.

JOHN REED

"Endymion." **2.** 251.

KIT REED

"Winter." **5.** 276.

F. ANTON REEDS

"Forever Is Not So Long." **1.** 187.

ALEKSIEI REMIZOV

"Sisters in the Cross." **3 ed.** 649.

JOSÉ REVUELTAS

"The Abyss." **3.** 329.
"Dream Matter." **3.** 329.
"The Escape Plan." **3.** 329.
"Ezekiel, or The Massacre of the Innocents." **3.** 329.
"The Fall." **3.** 329.
"La frontera increíble." **1.** 187.
"God on This Earth." **3.** 329; **5.** 276.
"The Green Heart." **3.** 330.
"Green Is the Color of Hope." **3.** 330.
"Hegel and I." **3.** 330.
"The Hostile Sister." **3.** 330.
"How Great Is That Darkness?" **3.** 330.
"The Idiot." **3.** 330.
"The Language of the Dispossessed." **3.** 330.
"The Living God." **3.** 330.
"The Men in the Swamp." **1.** 188; **3.** 330.
"Night of Epiphany." **3.** 330.
"Pastoral Symphony." **3.** 330.
"Preferences." **3.** 330.
"Lo que solo uno escucha." **1.** 188.
"Resurrection Without Life." **3.** 330.
"The Sacred Word." **3.** 330.
"Self-Spying." **3.** 330.
"The Surrender." **3.** 330.
"To Sleep on Earth." **3.** 330.
"A Woman on Earth." **3.** 331.

ALFONSO REYES

"La cena." **2.** 251.

WLADYSLAW REYMONT

"At Dusk." **3 ed.** 649.
"The Confession." **3 ed.** 649.
"Death." **3 ed.** 649.
"The Dreamer." **3 ed.** 649.
"Franek." **3 ed.** 649.
"The Graveyard." **3 ed.** 649.
"I Have Killed." **3 ed.** 649.
"Lili" [originally "A Sacrifice"]. **3 ed.** 649.
"On a Certain Day." **3 ed.** 650.
"On the Edge." **3 ed.** 650.
"Pages of a Diary." **3 ed.** 650.
"The Pilgrimage to Jasna Gora." **3 ed.** 650.
"The Princess." **3 ed.** 650.

"The Return." **3 ed.** 650.
"Righteously." **3 ed.** 650.
"The Riot." **3 ed.** 650.
"The Shadow." **3 ed.** 650.
"Tomek Baran." **3 ed.** 650.
"Work!" **3 ed.** 650.

MACK REYNOLDS

"Pacifist." **2.** 251.
"Revolution." **2.** 251.

EUGENE MANLOVE RHODES

"Beyond the Desert." **3 ed.** 650.

JEAN RHYS [ELLA GWENDOLEN REES WILLIAMS]

"The Bishop's Feast." **5.** 276.
"Fishy Waters." **4.** 241.
"From a French Prison." **2.** 252; **5.** 276.
"Goodbye Marcus, Goodbye Rose." **2.** 252; **4.** 241.
"La Grosse Fifi." **2.** 252; **4.** 241.
"Hunger." **2.** 252.
"I Spy a Stranger." **2.** 252; **4.** 242.
"I Used to Live Here Once." **3.** 331.
"Illusion." **2.** 252; **4.** 242.
"In a Café." **2.** 252.
"Let Them Call It Jazz." **4.** 242; **5.** 276.
"The Lotus." **4.** 242.
"Mannequin." **2.** 252.
"On Not Shooting Sitting Birds." **3.** 331.
"Outside the Machine." **4.** 242.
"Rapunzel, Rapunzel." **2.** 252; **5.** 276.
"Sleep It Off, Lady." **2.** 252; **4.** 242.
"A Solid House." **4.** 242.
"The Sound of the River." **5.** 276.
"Tea with an Artist." **4.** 242.
"Tigers Are Better Looking." **2.** 252; **4.** 242; **5.** 276.
"Till September Petronella." **2.** 252; **5.** 276.
"Vienna." **2.** 252; **4.** 242.

JULIO RAMÓN RIBEYRO

"Una aventura nocturna." **3 ed.** 650.
"De color modesto." **3 ed.** 650.
"The Featherless Buzzards." **3 ed.** 650; **2.** 252; **3.** 331.
"Interior L." **2.** 252.
"La piel de un indio no cuesta cara." **3 ed.** 650.
"Silvio en el rosedal." **2.** 253.

DOROTHY RICHARDSON

"Excursion." **1.** 188.
"Nook on Parnassus." **1.** 188.
"Ordeal." **1.** 188.
"Tryst." **1.** 188.
"Visit." **1.** 188.
"Visitor." **1.** 188.

HENRY HANDEL RICHARDSON [ETHEL FLORENCE LINDESAY RICHARDSON]

"And Women Must Weep." **3.** 331.
"The Bath." **3 ed.** 651.
"The Coat." **3 ed.** 651; **3.** 331.
"The End of a Childhood." **3 ed.** 651.
"The Life and Death of Peterle Lüthy." **3 ed.** 651; **3.** 331.
"Mary Christina" [originally "Death"]. **3 ed.** 651; **3.** 331.
"The Professor's Experiment." **3 ed.** 651; **3.** 331.
"Sister Ann." **3 ed.** 651.
"Succedaneum." **3 ed.** 651; **1.** 188; **3.** 331.
"Two Hanged Women." **3.** 331.
"The Wrong Turning." **3.** 331.

JACK RICHARDSON

"In the Final Year of Grace." **5.** 276.

MORDECAI RICHLER

"The Summer My Grandmother Was Supposed to Die." **3 ed.** 651.

CONRAD RICHTER

"Brothers of No Kin." **3 ed.** 651.
"The Laughter of Leen." **3 ed.** 651.

J. H. RIDDELL

"Forewarned, Forearmed." **4.** 242.
"Hertford O'Donnell's Warning." **4.** 242.
"Nut Bush Farm." **4.** 242.
"The Old House in Vauxhall Walk." **4.** 242.
"Old Mrs. Jones." **4.** 242.
"The Open Door." **4.** 242.

"Sandy the Tinker." **4.** 243.
"A Strange Christmas Game." **4.** 243.
"Walnut-Tree House." **4.** 243.

WILHELM HEINRICH RIEHL

"Der Stadtpfeifer." **3 ed.** 651.
"Der stumme Ratsherr." **3 ed.** 651.

CARMA RIERA

"Te deix, amor, la mar com a penyora." **5.** 277.

RAINER MARIA RILKE

"The Beggar and the Proud Maiden." **3 ed.** 652.
"Die Turnstunde." **1.** 188.

MARY ROBERTS RINEHART

"The Better Man." **2.** 253.
"His Father's Son." **2.** 253.
"Lightning Never Strikes Twice." **2.** 253.
"The Second Marriage." **2.** 253.
"Seven Days." **2.** 253.
"The Tall Tree." **2.** 253.
"The Temporary Death of Mrs. Ayres." **2.** 253.
"Three Pirates of Penzance." **2.** 253.

TADEUSZ RITTNER

"The Clock." **3 ed.** 652.
"Gold." **3 ed.** 652.

RICHARD RIVE

"Advance, Retreat" [originally "Black Macbeth"]. **5.** 277.
"A Man from the Board." **5.** 277.
"Rain." **3.** 332.

TOMÁS RIVERA

" . . . And the Earth Did Not Part." **3.** 332; **4.** 243; **5.** 277.
"The Children Were Victims." **4.** 243.
"Christmas Eve." **3.** 332; **4.** 243.
"First Holy Communion." **4.** 243; **5.** 277.
"His Hands in His Pockets." **4.** 243.
"It Is Painful." **3.** 332; **4.** 243; **5.** 277.
"It Was a Silvery Night." **3.** 332; **4.** 243; **5.** 277.
"Little Children Burned." **4.** 243.
"The Lost Year." **3.** 332; **4.** 243; **5.** 277.
"The Night of the Blackout." **4.** 243; **5.** 277.
"On the Way to Texas." **4.** 243.
"The Portrait." **3.** 332.
"A Prayer." **3.** 332; **4.** 243.
"The Salamanders." **4.** 244.
"Under the House." **3.** 332; **4.** 244.
"When We Arrive." **3.** 332; **4.** 244.

AMÉLIE RIVES [PRINCESS TROUBETZKOY]

"A Brother to Dragons." **3 ed.** 652.
"Virginia of Virginia." **3 ed.** 652.

AUGUSTO ROA BASTOS

"Ajuste de cuentas." **5.** 277.
"Borrador de un informe." **3 ed.** 40; **5.** 277–78.
"Brothers." **4.** 244.
"The Carpincho Hunters." **1.** 188.
"Cigarillos Mauser." **5.** 278.
"Encounter with the Traitor." **3.** 332.
"The Excavation." **1.** 188; **3.** 333; **4.** 244.
"Kurupí.'" **5.** 278.
"Lucha hasta el alba." **3.** 333.
"Lying in State." **1.** 188.
"Niño-azuté." **5.** 278.
"Nocturnal Games." **1.** 189.
"El pájaro mosca." **2.** 253; **5.** 278.
"The Prisoner." **4.** 244; **5.** 278.
"Private Audience." **1.** 189.
"Slaughter." **1.** 189.
"To Tell a Story." **1.** 189; **3.** 333; **5.** 278.

ALAIN ROBBE-GRILLET

"Behind the Automatic Door." **3 ed.** 652; **1.** 189.
"A Corridor." **3 ed.** 652; **1.** 189.
"The Dressmaker's Dummy." **3 ed.** 652; **1.** 189.
"The Escalator." **3 ed.** 652; **1.** 189.
"The Replacement." **3 ed.** 652; **1.** 189.
"Scene." **3 ed.** 652; **1.** 189.
"The Secret Room." **3 ed.** 652–53; **1.** 189; **2.** 253; **3.** 333; **5.** 278.
"The Shore." **3 ed.** 653; **1.** 189.
"The Way Back." **3 ed.** 653; **1.** 189.
"The Wrong Direction." **3 ed.** 653; **1.** 189.

TOM ROBBINS

"The Chink and the Clock People." **5.** 278.

CHARLES G. D. ROBERTS

"The Last Barrier." **3 ed.** 653.
"The Moonlight Trail." **3 ed.** 653.
"Strayed." **5.** 278.
"When Twilight Falls on the Stump Lots." **1.** 189.

ELIZABETH MADOX ROBERTS

"The Betrothed." **3 ed.** 653.
"Death at Bearwallow." **3 ed.** 653.
"The Haunted Palace." **3 ed.** 653.
"On the Mountainside." **3 ed.** 653.

KEITH ROBERTS

"The Beautiful One." **5.** 278.
"Brother John." **5.** 279.
"The Death of Libby Maynard." **5.** 279.
"The Everything Man." **5.** 279.
"Fragments." **5.** 279.
"The God House." **5.** 279.
"The Grain Kings." **5.** 279.
"The Inner Wheel." **5.** 279.
"The Lady Margaret." **5.** 279.
"Lords and Ladies." **5.** 279.
"The Ministry of Children." **5.** 279.
"Monkey and Pru and Sal." **5.** 279.
"Rand." **5.** 279.
"The Signaller." **5.** 279.
"The Sun over a Low Hill." **5.** 279.
"Usk and Jokeman." **5.** 279.
"Weihnachtabend." **5.** 279.

FRANK M. ROBINSON

"The Fire and the Sword." **5.** 279.
"The Wreck of the Ship *John B.*" **1.** 190.

MARY ROBINSON

"Coach." **5.** 280.

RAMÓN ROCHA MONROY

"Hora cero." **4.** 244.

MERCÈ RODOREDA

"Una carta." **5.** 280.

JOSÉ RODRIGUES MIGUÉIS

"Léah." **5.** 280.

EDWARD PAYSON ROE

"Gentle Woman Roused." **4.** 244.

MANUEL ROJAS

"The Glass of Milk." **3.** 333; **5.** 280.

OCTAVIO ROMANO

"One More Rosary for Doña Marina." **4.** 244.

EMILIO ROMERO

"Balseros del Titicaca." **3 ed.** 653.

FERNANDO ROMERO

"De regreso." **3 ed.** 653.
"El nido extraño." **3 ed.** 654.
"Santos Tarqui." **3 ed.** 654.

LUIS ROMERO

"At the Edge of Time." **2.** 253.
"The Beach." **2.** 254.
"The Boat." **2.** 254.
"Elena's Birthday." **2.** 254.
"Foot Soldier's Soliloquy." **2.** 254.
"Mister Plural Anyone." **2.** 254.
"Repatriates' Soliloquy." **2.** 254.
"Sentinel's Soliloquy." **2.** 254.
"A Shadow Passed By." **2.** 254.
"They Call This Judgment . . .." **2.** 254.

LEON ROOKE

"The End of the Revolution." **4.** 244.
"Mama Tuddi Done Over." **3.** 333.

FRANK ROONEY

"Cyclists' Raid." **2.** 254.

JOÃO GUIMARÃES ROSA

"The Aldacious [sic] Navigator." **3.** 333.
"Altar Piece of St. Never." **3.** 333.
"The Appearance of the Shiny Stones." **3.** 333.
"Augusto Matraga's Hour and Turn" [same as "The Time and Turn of Au-

gusto Matraga"]. **3 ed.** 654; **3.** 334; **4.** 245.
"Buriti." **3 ed.** 654.
"Conversation Among Oxen." **3.** 334.
"The Dagobé Brothers." **3.** 334.
"Duel." **3.** 334.
"Evil Beast." **3.** 334.
"Field of the High Plain." **5.** 280.
"The Little Dust-Brown Donkey." **3.** 334.
"A Love Story." **3 ed.** 654.
"The Man with the Snake." **3.** 334.
"Message from the Mountain." **3 ed.** 654.
"The Mirror." **3.** 334.
"Much Ado." **3.** 334.
"My Friend the Fatalist." **3.** 334.
"My People" [same as "Mine Own People"]. **3 ed.** 654; **3.** 334.
"My Uncle the Jaguar." **3.** 334.
"No Man, No Woman." **3.** 334.
"Nothingness and the Human Condition." **3.** 334.
"Notorious." **3.** 334.
"Páramo." **3.** 334.
"The Return of the Prodigal Husband." **3 ed.** 654; **3.** 334.
"The Simple and Exact Story of the Captain's Donkey." **3.** 335.
"The Straw Spinners." **3.** 335.
"Tantarum, My Boss." **3.** 335.
"The Thin Edge of Happiness." **3.** 335.
"The Third Bank of the River." **3 ed.** 654; **3.** 335; **5.** 280.
"The Transient Hats." **3.** 335.
"Treetops." **3.** 335.
"With Cowboy Mariano." **3.** 335.
"Woodland Witchery." **3.** 335.
"A Young Man, Gleaming, White." **3.** 335.

ROLANDO P. ROSELL

"Reflection of the Times." **5.** 280.

ISAAC ROSENFELD

"Bazaar of the Senses." **3 ed.** 654.
"The Brigadier." **3 ed.** 654.
"The Hand That Fed Me." **3 ed.** 654; **3.** 335; **5.** 280.
"Joe the Janitor." **3.** 335.
"King Solomon." **3 ed.** 654; **3.** 335; **5.** 281.
"My Landlady." **3.** 335.

MIKHAIL MIKHAĬLOVICH ROSHCHIN

"Vospominanie." **2.** 254.

J. H. ROSNY [pseudonym JOSEPH HENRI BOEX]

"Another World." **5.** 281.
"The Shapes." **5.** 281.
"The Xipéhuz." **5.** 281.

SINCLAIR ROSS

"Circus in Town." **3 ed.** 654; **2.** 254.
"Cornet at Night." **3 ed.** 655; **2.** 254; **3.** 335.
"A Day with Pegasus." **2.** 254; **3.** 336.
"The Flowers That Killed Him." **3.** 336.
"The Lamp at Noon." **3 ed.** 655; **2.** 255; **4.** 245.
"Nell." **3.** 336.
"No Other Way." **2.** 255; **3.** 336.
"Not by Rain Alone." **3 ed.** 655.
"One's a Heifer." **2.** 255; **3.** 336.
"The Outlaw." **2.** 255.
"The Painted Door." **3 ed.** 655; **2.** 255.
"The Race." **3.** 336.

DANTE GABRIEL ROSSETTI

"Hand and Soul." **3.** 336.
"St. Agnes of Intercession." **2.** 255.

EVDOKIA ROSTOPCHINA [pseudonym CLAIRVOYANT]

"The Duel." **3.** 336.
"Rank and Money." **3.** 336.

HENRY ROTH

"At Times in Flight." **3 ed.** 655.
"Broker." **3 ed.** 655.
"The Dun Dakotas." **3 ed.** 655.

JOSEPH ROTH

"Die Legende vom heiligen Trinker." **2.** 255.

PHILIP ROTH

"The Conversion of the Jews." **3 ed.** 655; **1.** 190; **2.** 255; **3.** 336; **4.** 245; **5.** 281.
"Courting Disaster, or Serious in the Fifties." **1.** 190; **2.** 255; **3.** 336.

"Defender of the Faith." **3 ed.** 655–56; **1.** 190; **2.** 255; **3.** 337; **5.** 281.
"Eli the Fanatic." **3 ed.** 656; **1.** 190; **2.** 256; **3.** 337; **4.** 245; **5.** 281.
"Epstein." **3 ed.** 656; **1.** 190; **2.** 256; **3.** 337; **4.** 245.
"Ferdinand." **2.** 256; **3.** 337.
"Goodbye, Columbus." **3 ed.** 656; **1.** 190; **2.** 256; **3.** 337; **5.** 281.
"I Always Wanted You to Admire My Fasting; or Looking at Kafka." **1.** 190; **3.** 337.
"In Trouble." **1.** 190.
"It Was." **2.** 256; **3.** 337.
"Letting Go." **3.** 337.
"Marriage à la Mode." **3.** 337.
"My True Story." **2.** 256.
"Novotny's Pain." **3.** 337.
"On the Air." **2.** 256; **3.** 338; **4.** 245.
"The Prague Orgy." **5.** 282.
"Salad Days." **1.** 190; **2.** 256.
"Whacking Off." **3 ed.** 656.
"You Can't Tell a Man by the Song He Sings." **2.** 256.

FREDERICK ROTHERMEL

"Foo Soon, the Heathen." **2.** 256.

CONSTANCE ROURKE

"The Porch." **2.** 256.
"Portrait of a Young Woman." **2.** 257.

GABRIELLE ROY

"L'alouette." **5.** 282.
"De la truite dans l'eau glacée." **5.** 282.
"Demetrioff." **5.** 282.
"A Garden at the End of the World." **2.** 257; **3.** 338.
"The Garden in the Wind." **4.** 245.
"Hoodoo Valley." **3.** 338; **4.** 245.
"Ma grandmère tout-puissante." **3.** 338.
"La maison gardée." **5.** 282.
"La Route d'Altamont." **3.** 338.
"Le Vieillard et l'enfant." **3.** 338.
"Vincento." **5.** 282.
"Wilhelm." **3 ed.** 656.

RU ZHIJUAN

"A Mis-edited Story." **4.** 245.

MURILO RUBIÃO

"The Ex-Magician from the Minhota Tavern." **5.** 282.
"Zacarias the Pyrotechnist." **5.** 282.

HUGHES RUDD

"Miss Euayla Is the Sweetest *Thang*!" **3.** 338.

STEELE RUDD

"Starting the Selection." **3 ed.** 656.

HENRY RUFFNER

"Arnheim." **4.** 245.
"Judith Bensaddi." **4.** 246.
"Seclusaval." **4.** 246.

JUAN RULFO

"Anacleto Morones." **2.** 257; **3.** 338.
"At Daybreak." **3.** 338.
"The Burning Plain." **1.** 191; **2.** 257; **3.** 338; **4.** 246; **5.** 282.
"The Day of the Landslide." **3.** 338.
"En la madrugada." **5.** 282.
"The Heritage of Matilde Archangel." **3.** 339; **4.** 246; **5.** 282.
"The Hill of the *Comadres.*" **1.** 190; **3.** 339; **4.** 246; **5.** 282.
"Life Is Not Very Serious About Things." **3.** 339.
"Luvina." **3 ed.** 657; **1.** 191; **2.** 257; **3.** 339; **4.** 246; **5.** 283.
"Macario." **2.** 257; **3.** 339; **5.** 283.
"The Man." **1.** 191; **3.** 339; **4.** 246.
"The Night They Left Him Alone." **3.** 339; **5.** 283.
"A Night's Fragment." **3.** 339.
"No Dogs Bark." **3 ed.** 657; **1.** 191; **3.** 339; **5.** 283.
"Paso del Norte." **3.** 339.
"Remember." **3.** 339.
"Talpa." **1.** 191; **3.** 339.
"Tell Them Not to Kill Me." **3.** 339; **4.** 246; **5.** 283.
"They Gave Us the Land." **2.** 257; **3.** 339; **5.** 283.
"We Are Very Poor." **2.** 257; **3.** 338, 340; **4.** 246; **5.** 283.

PHILIPP RUNGE

"Von dem Fischer un syner Fru." **3.** 340.

DAMON RUNYON

"Baseball Hattie." **2.** 257.
"Bred for Battle." **2.** 257.

RURICOLLA [unidentified]

"The Captain's Wife." **4.** 246.

JOANNA RUSS

"Daddy's Girl." **2.** 257.
"Sword Blades and Poppy Seed." **5.** 283.
"When It Changed." **3.** 340; **5.** 283.

BERTRAND RUSSELL

"The Corsican Ordeal of Miss X." **3.** 340.
"The Infra-redioscope." **3.** 340.
"Satan in the Suburbs or Horrors Manufactured Here." **3.** 340.

ERIC FRANK RUSSELL

" . . . And Then There Were None." **3.** 340.
"Design for Great-Day." **3.** 340.
"Fast Falls the Eventide." **3.** 340.
"Metamorphosis." **3.** 340.
"Sole Solution." **3.** 341.

JOHN RUSSELL

"The Price of the Head." **3 ed.** 657.

MARK RUTHERFORD [WILLIAM HALE WHITE]

"Confessions of a Self-Tormentor." **5.** 283.
"A Dream of Two Dimensions." **5.** 283.
"The Love of Woman." **3 ed.** 657.
"Michael Trevanion." **3 ed.** 657.
"Miriam's Schooling." **3 ed.** 657.
"Mr. Whitaker's Retirement." **3 ed.** 657.
"A Mysterious Portrait." **3 ed.** 657.

HENRYK RZEWUSKI

"Prince Karol Radziwill." **3 ed.** 657.
"A Sermon at the Bar Confederacy." **3 ed.** 657.
"Tadeusz Reyten." **3 ed.** 657.
"The Zaporog Sich." **3 ed.** 657.

FERDINAND VON SAAR

"Marianne." **3 ed.** 658.
"Schloss Kostenitz." **2.** 258.
"Die Troglodytin." **3 ed.** 658.

RAMAN SABALENKA

"Always on the Road." **3.** 341.

FRED SABERHAGEN

"The Face of the Deep." **3.** 341.
"Goodlife." **1.** 191; **3.** 341.
"In the Temple of Mars." **1.** 191; **3.** 341.
"Patron of the Arts." **1.** 191; **3.** 341.
"The Peacemaker." **1.** 191; **3.** 341.
"Starsong." **3.** 341.

GHOLAMHOSAYN SA'EDI

"The Mourners of Bayal." **3.** 341.

BHISHAM SAHNI

"Chief ki Davat." **3.** 341.

JUNUS SAID

"Fidgety." **3 ed.** 658.

GEORGE SAIKO

"The Bathtub." **5.** 284.

GARTH ST. OMER

"Another Place, Another Time." **4.** 247.
"Light on the Hill." **4.** 247.

SAKARUCHI ANGO

"Under the Forest of Cherry Trees in Full Bloom." **3.** 342.

SAKI [HECTOR HUGH MUNRO]

"The Achievement of the Cat." **3 ed.** 658.
"Esmé." **3 ed.** 658; **4.** 247.
"Filboid Studge." **3 ed.** 658; **2.** 258.
"The Forbidden Buzzards." **3 ed.** 658.
"Gabriel-Ernest." **2.** 258.
"The Hounds of Fate." **3 ed.** 658.
"The Interlopers." **2.** 258.
"The Lumber Room." **3 ed.** 658; **5.** 284.
"The Mappined Life." **3 ed.** 658; **2.** 258.
"Mrs. Packletide's Tiger." **2.** 258.

"The Music on the Hill." **3 ed.** 658; **4.** 247.
"The Occasional Garden." **3 ed.** 658.
"The Open Window." **2.** 258; **4.** 247.
"The Penance." **5.** 284.
"Reginald on House Parties." **4.** 247.
"The Reticence of Lady Anne." **3 ed.** 658.
"The Scharz-Metterklume Method." **4.** 247.
"The Sheep." **3 ed.** 659.
"The She-Wolf." **3 ed.** 659; **4.** 247.
"The Soul of Laploshka." **3 ed.** 659.
"Sredni Vashtar." **3 ed.** 659; **2.** 258; **4.** 247; **5.** 284.
"The Stampeding of Lady Bastable." **3 ed.** 659.
"The Story of St. Vespaluus." **3 ed.** 659.
"The Story-Teller." **4.** 247.
"Tea." **3 ed.** 659.
"Tobermory." **3 ed.** 659; **2.** 258; **4.** 247.
"The Treasure Ship." **3 ed.** 659.

SALVADOR SALAZAR ARRUÉ [same as SALVADOR SALARRUÉ]

"La botija." **5.** 284.
"Buried Treasure." **3.** 342.

SEBASTIAN SALAZAR BONDY

"Volver al pasado." **3 ed.** 659.

CARLOS SALAZAR HERRERA

"La saca." **5.** 284.

PEDRO SALINAS

"The Breakfast." **3 ed.** 659.
"Cita de los tres." **5.** 284.
"Mundo cerrado." **5.** 284.
"The Neophyte Author." **3 ed.** 659.

J. D. SALINGER

"Blue Melody." **3 ed.** 659; **5.** 284.
"Both Parties Concerned." **3 ed.** 660.
"A Boy in France." **3 ed.** 660.
"De Daumier-Smith's Blue Period." **3 ed.** 660; **1.** 191; **2.** 258; **3.** 342; **4.** 247; **5.** 284–85.
"Down at the Dinghy." **3 ed.** 660; **1.** 191; **2.** 258; **5.** 285.
"Elaine." **3 ed.** 660; **5.** 285.
"The Fire Sermon." **2.** 259.
"For Esmé—With Love and Squalor." **3 ed.** 660–61; **1.** 192; **2.** 259; **3.** 342; **4.** 247; **5.** 285.
"Franny." **3 ed.** 661–63; **1.** 192; **2.** 259; **3.** 342; **4.** 248; **5.** 285.
"A Girl I Knew." **3 ed.** 663; **5.** 285.
"Go See Eddie." **3 ed.** 663.
"The Hang of It." **3 ed.** 663.
"Hapworth 16, 1924." **3 ed.** 663; **2.** 259; **4.** 248; **5.** 285.
"The Heart of a Broken Story." **3 ed.** 663.
"I'm Crazy." **3 ed.** 663.
"The Inverted Forest." **3 ed.** 663; **2.** 259; **5.** 285.
"Just Before the War with the Eskimos." **3 ed.** 663; **1.** 192; **2.** 259; **5.** 285.
"The Last Day of the Last Furlough." **3 ed.** 663; **2.** 259.
"The Laughing Man." **3 ed.** 663–64; **1.** 192; **2.** 259; **4.** 248; **5.** 285–86.
"The Long Debut of Lois Taggett." **3 ed.** 664; **5.** 286.
"Once a Week Won't Kill You." **3 ed.** 664; **5.** 286.
"A Perfect Day for Bananafish." **3 ed.** 664–65; **1.** 192; **2.** 259; **4.** 248; **5.** 286.
"Personal Notes of an Infantryman." **3 ed.** 665.
"Pretty Mouth and Green My Eyes." **3 ed.** 665; **1.** 192; **5.** 286.
"Raise High the Roofbeam, Carpenters." **3 ed.** 665; **2.** 259; **3.** 342; **4.** 248; **5.** 286.
"Seymour: An Introduction." **3 ed.** 665–66; **2.** 259; **3.** 342; **4.** 248; **5.** 286.
"Slight Rebellion Off Madison." **3 ed.** 666; **5.** 286.
"The Stranger." **3 ed.** 666.
"Teddy." **3 ed.** 666; **1.** 192; **2.** 259; **3.** 342; **4.** 248; **5.** 286.
"This Sandwich Has No Mayonnaise." **3 ed.** 666.
"Uncle Wiggily in Connecticut." **3 ed.** 666–67; **1.** 192; **2.** 259; **5.** 287.
"The Varioni Brothers." **3 ed.** 667; **5.** 287.
"The Young Folks." **3 ed.** 667; **5.** 287.
"A Young Girl in 1941 with No Waist at All." **3 ed.** 667; **5.** 287.
"Zooey." **3 ed.** 667–68; **1.** 192; **2.** 260; **3.** 342; **4.** 248; **5.** 287.

ANDREW SALKEY

"Anancy." **3 ed.** 668.
"How Anancy Became a Spider Individual Person." **4.** 248.

MIKHAIL EVGRAFOVICH SALTYKOV

"Glava." **3.** 342.

IVAN SAMIAKIN

"The Bridge." **3.** 343.
"The Market Woman and the Poet." **3.** 343.

LUIS RAFAEL SÁNCHEZ

"Que sabe a paraíso." **2.** 260.

ROSAURA SÁNCHEZ

"Crónica del barrio." **5.** 287.
"Una noche . . .." **5.** 287.
"Se Arremango Las Mangas." **5.** 287.

GEORGE SAND [ARMANDINE AURORE LUCILE DUPIN]

"Coax." **5.** 287.
"Le Gnome des huîtres." **5.** 287.
"Mattea." **3 ed.** 668.
"Melchior." **3 ed.** 668.
"Métella." **3 ed.** 668.
"L'Orgue." **5.** 287.
"Pictordu." **5.** 287.
"Rêveur." **5.** 288.

SCOTT SANDERS

"Touch the Earth." **3.** 343.

MARI SANDOZ

"Peachstone Basket." **3.** 343.
"The Smart Man." **2.** 260.

MANUEL SAN MARTÍN

"Salut y otros misterios." **5.** 288.

WILLIAM SANSOM

"Among the Dahlias." **3 ed.** 668; **2.** 260.
"The Biter Bit." **2.** 260.
"The Bonfire." **2.** 260.
"Building Alive." **3 ed.** 668.
"Caffs, Pools, and Bikes." **3 ed.** 669.
"A Change of Office." **3 ed.** 669.
"The Cliff." **3 ed.** 669.
"A Contest of Ladies." **2.** 260; **5.** 288.
"A Country Walk." **3 ed.** 669; **4.** 248.
"The Dangerous Age." **2.** 260.
"The Day the Life . . .." **2.** 260.
"Difficulty with a Bouquet." **3 ed.** 669.
"Episode at Gastein." **3 ed.** 669.
"Fireman Flower." **3 ed.** 669; **4.** 248; **5.** 288.
"The Forbidden Lighthouse." **3 ed.** 669.
"Friends." **3 ed.** 669.
"From the Water Junction." **3 ed.** 669.
"The Girl on the Bus." **3 ed.** 669.
"Gliding Gulls and Going People." **4.** 249.
"Hot and Cold." **3 ed.** 669.
"How Claeys Died." **3 ed.** 669; **2.** 260.
"Journey into Smoke." **3 ed.** 669.
"The Last Ride." **2.** 260.
"A Last Word." **3 ed.** 669; **2.** 260.
"Life, Death." **3 ed.** 669; **4.** 249.
"The Long Sheet." **3 ed.** 669.
"Love at First Sight." **2.** 260.
"Mama Mia." **2.** 261.
"The Man with the Moon in Him." **2.** 261.
"The Marmalade Bird." **2.** 261.
"A Mixed Bag." **3 ed.** 669.
"Murder." **3 ed.** 670.
"No Smoking in the Apron." **2.** 261.
"Old Man Alone." **3 ed.** 670; **2.** 261.
"On Stony Ground." **3 ed.** 670.
"Outburst." **3 ed.** 670.
"The Peach-House Potting-Shed." **3 ed.** 670.
"A Smell of Fear." **3 ed.** 670.
"Something Terrible, Something Lovely." **3 ed.** 670.
"Three Dogs in Sienna." **3 ed.** 670.
"Through the Quinquina Glass." **5.** 288.
"Time and Place." **3 ed.** 670.
"Time Gents, Please." **3 ed.** 670.
"To the Rescue." **2.** 261.
"Tutti Frutti." **3 ed.** 670.
"Various Temptations." **3 ed.** 670; **2.** 261.
"The Vertical Ladder." **3 ed.** 670.
"A Visit to the Dentist." **3 ed.** 670; **2.** 261.
"The Wall." **3 ed.** 670; **4.** 249; **5.** 288.
"A Waning Moon." **2.** 261; **4.** 249.
"The Witnesses." **3 ed.** 670.
"A Woman Seldom Found." **3 ed.** 670.
"The World of Glass." **3 ed.** 670.

BIENVENIDO N. SANTOS

"Be American." **3.** 343.
"The Day the Dancers Came." **3.** 343.
"Scent of Apples." **3.** 343.

SAPPER [HERMAN CYRIL MNEILE]

"The Land of Topsy-Turvy." **5.** 288.

SARBAN [JOHN W. WALL]

"Capra." **4.** 249.
"The Doll Maker." **4.** 249.
"A House of Call." **4.** 249.
"The Khan." **4.** 249.
"Ringstone." **4.** 249.
"The Trespassers." **4.** 249.

ELLEN SARGENT

"Wee Wi Ping." **2.** 261.

PAMELA SARGENT

"IMT." **3.** 343.

FRANK SARGESON

"An Attempt at an Explanation." **3.** 343.
"Beau." **5.** 288.
"City and Suburban." **4.** 249.
"The Colonel's Daughter." **3.** 343.
"Conversation with My Uncle." **5.** 288.
"A Great Day." **3.** 344.
"The Hole That Jack Dug." **3.** 344; **4.** 249; **5.** 288.
"In the Department." **3 ed.** 671.
"I've Lost My Pal." **3.** 344; **5.** 289.
"Just Trespassing, Thanks." **3.** 344; **5.** 289.
"A Man and His Wife." **3 ed.** 671.
"A Man of Good Will." **2.** 261; **5.** 289.
"Old Man's Story." **2.** 261; **3.** 344; **5.** 289.
"A Pair of Socks." **3.** 344.
"A Piece of Yellow Soap." **5.** 289.
"Sale Day." **5.** 289.
"That Summer." **5.** 289.
"Three Men." **5.** 289.
"Tod." **5.** 289.
"The Undertaker's Story." **5.** 289.
"White Man's Burden." **5.** 289.

WILLIAM SAROYAN

"Antranik of Armenia." **3 ed.** 671.
"The Ants." **3 ed.** 671.
"Aspirin Is a Member of the N. R. A." **3 ed.** 671.
"At Sundown." **3 ed.** 671.
"Baby." **3.** 344.
"The Circus." **5.** 289.
"Citizens of the Third Grade." **3 ed.** 671; **3.** 344.
"Corduroy Pants." **3 ed.** 671.
"Countryman, How Do You Like America?" **3.** 344.
"The Crusader." **3 ed.** 671.
"The Daring Young Man on the Flying Trapeze." **3.** 344.
"The Fifty-Yard Dash." **3 ed.** 671.
"The Journey and the Dream." **3.** 344.
"The Journey to Hanford." **3 ed.** 671; **5.** 289.
"Laughing Sam." **3 ed.** 671.
"Laughter." **4.** 249.
"The Living and the Dead." **3 ed.** 671.
"Love, Here Is My Hat." **1.** 192.
"The Man with the Heart in the Highlands." **3.** 344.
"My Cousin Dikran, the Orator." **3 ed.** 672.
"A Nice Old-Fashioned Romance with Love Lyrics and Everything." **5.** 289.
"O.K., Baby, This Is the World." **3 ed.** 672.
"Old Country Advice to the American Traveler." **5.** 289.
"1, 2, 3, 4, 5, 6, 7, 8." **3 ed.** 672.
"The Pomegranate Trees." **5.** 289.
"Seventy Thousand Assyrians." **3 ed.** 672.
"Some Day I'll Be a Millionaire Myself." **3 ed.** 672.
"The Summer of the Beautiful White Horse." **3 ed.** 672; **5.** 289.
"The Three Swimmers and the Grocer from Yale." **3 ed.** 672.
"The Trains." **3.** 344.
"Two Days Wasted in Kansas City." **3 ed.** 672.

JEAN-PAUL SARTRE

"L'Ange du morbide." **3.** 344.
"The Childhood of a Leader" [same as "The Making . . ."]. **3 ed.** 672; **3.** 345; **4.** 250.
"Dépaysement." **5.** 290.
"Erostratus." **3 ed.** 672; **3.** 345; **4.** 250.
"Intimacy." **3 ed.** 672; **3.** 345; **4.** 250; **5.** 290.
"The Room." **3 ed.** 672–73; **2.** 261; **3.** 345; **5.** 290.
"Strange Friendship." **3.** 345.

"The Wall." **3 ed.** 673; **3.** 345; **4.** 250; **5.** 290.

SRIPANDA SUBRAHMANYA SASTRI

"Attar of Roses." **3 ed.** 673.

WILLIAM SATCHELL

"After His Kind." **3 ed.** 673.
"The Babes in the Bush." **3 ed.** 673.
"The Black Mirror." **3 ed.** 673.
"The Divided Note." **3 ed.** 673.
"From a Northern Gumfield." **3 ed.** 673.
"The Great Unemployed Scheme." **3 ed.** 674.
"The Man Who Went North." **3 ed.** 674.
"A Martyr of Circumstantial Evidence." **3 ed.** 674.
"The Stiff 'Un." **3 ed.** 674.
"The White Girl." **3 ed.** 674.
"The Yellow Dwarf: A Tale of a Mine." **3 ed.** 674.

SATOMI TON

"Early Summer in a Certain Year." **3.** 345.

CHARLES SATTERWHITE [FREDERIK POHL]

"With Redfern on Capella XII." **5.** 290.

JOSEPHINE SAXTON

"Elouise and the Doctors of Planet Pergamon." **3.** 345.

DOROTHY L. SAYERS

"The Abominable History of the Man with Copper Fingers." **3.** 345.
"The Adventurous Exploit of the Cave of Ali Baba." **3.** 345.
"An Arrow O'er the House." **3.** 345.
"Bitter Almonds." **3.** 345.
"Blood-Sacrifice." **3.** 345.
"The Fascinating Problem of Uncle Meleager's Will." **3.** 346.
"The Incredible Elopement of Lord Peter Wimsey." **3.** 346.
"The Learned Adventure of the Dragon's Head." **3.** 346.
"The Leopard Lady." **3.** 346.
"Maher-Shalal-Hashbaz." **3.** 346.
"The Man Who Knew How." **3.** 346; **4.** 250.
"Murder at Pentecost." **3.** 346.
"The Piscatorial Farce of the Stolen Stomach." **3.** 346.
"The Poisoned Dow '08." **3.** 346.
"The Queen's Square." **3.** 346; **4.** 250.
"The Undignified Melodrama of the Bone of Contention." **3.** 346.

JOHN SAYLES

"I-80 Nebraska, M. 490—M. 205." **4.** 250.

NAT SCHACHNER

"The 100th Generation." **3.** 346.

WILHELM SCHÄFER

"Anckemann Tristan." **3 ed.** 674.
"An der Passhöhe." **3 ed.** 674.
"Die Bearnaise." **3 ed.** 674.
"Der Brief des Dichters und das Rezept des Landammanns." **3 ed.** 674.
"Das fremde Fräulein." **3 ed.** 674.
"Im letzte D-Zug-Wagen." **3 ed.** 674.
"Die Missgeschickten." **3 ed.** 674.
"Der Pflegling." **3 ed.** 674.
"The Shepherd Boy." **3 ed.** 674.
"Tabu." **3 ed.** 674.

MARY M. SCHIDELER

"Mother and the Flying Saucer." **5.** 290.

RUNAR SCHILDT

"Aapo." **1.** 192.

BERN SCHIRMER

"Sindbad's Cap." **4.** 250.

ARNO SCHMIDT

"Alexander oder was ist Wahrheit." **5.** 290.
"Caliban upon Setebos." **3.** 346; **5.** 290.
"Great Cain." **5.** 290.
"Leviathan oder die Beste der Welten." **3.** 347.
"Seascape with Pocahontas." **3.** 347.
"Die Umsiedler." **3.** 347.

JAMES K. SCHMITZ

"Grandpa." **5.** 290.
"The Witches of Karres." **3.** 347.

REINHOLD SCHNEIDER

"Las Casas vor Karl V." **3 ed.** 675.

A. J. SCHNEIDERS

"The Cannons." **3.** 347.

ZALMAN SCHNEOUR

"The Girl." **1.** 192.

ARTHUR SCHNITZLER

"An Author's Last Letter." **3.** 347.
"The Bachelor's Death." **3.** 347.
"Blumen." **1.** 193.
"Casanova's Homecoming." **3 ed.** 675.
"The Diary of Redegonda." **4.** 250.
"Doktor Gräsler, Badearzt." **3 ed.** 675.
"Flight into Darkness." **3 ed.** 675.
"Frau Beate." **3 ed.** 675.
"Frau Berta Garlan." **3 ed.** 675.
"Fräulein Else." 3 ed. 675; **1.** 193.
"Die Fremde." **3 ed.** 675.
"The Last Letters of a Litterateur." **1.** 193.
"Lieutenant Gustl." **3 ed.** 675–76; **2.** 262; **4.** 250–51.
"The Prophecy." **4.** 251.
"Rhapsody." **3 ed.** 676; **2.** 262; **4.** 251.
"Die Toten Schweigen." **3 ed.** 676.
"Die Weissagung." **3 ed.** 676.

WOLFDIETRICH SCHNURRE

"Eine Rechnung die nicht Aufgeht." **3 ed.** 676.
"Ein Versäumnis." **3 ed.** 676.

WILHELM VON SCHOLZ

"Der Kopf im Fenster." **3 ed.** 676.

MARK SCHORER

"Boy in the Summer Sun." **3 ed.** 676.
"The Face Within the Face." **3 ed.** 677; **5.** 291.
"What We Don't Know Hurts Us." **3 ed.** 677.

OLIVE SCHREINER

"The Buddhist Priest's Wife." **3 ed.** 677.
"The Dream of the Wild Bees." **3 ed.** 677.
"The Sunlight Lay Across My Bed." **3.** 347.
"Three Dreams in a Desert." **3.** 347.

FRANZ SCHUBERT

"My Dream." **2.** 262.

BRUNO SCHULZ

"August." **4.** 251.

GEORGE S. SCHUYLER

"Seldom Seen." **3.** 348.

DELMORE SCHWARTZ

"America! America!" **3 ed.** 677.
"A Bitter Farce." **3 ed.** 677.
"The Child Is the Meaning of This Life." **3 ed.** 677.
"In Dreams Begin Responsibilities." **3 ed.** 677.
"New Year's Eve." **3 ed.** 677.
"Successful Love." **3 ed.** 677.
"The World Is a Wedding." **3 ed.** 677; **1.** 193.

KURT SCHWITTERS

"Die Zwiebel." **3 ed.** 678.

MARCEL SCHWOB

"La Croisade des enfants." **5.** 291.

LEONARDO SCIASCIA

"The American Aunt." **3.** 348.
"The Death of Stalin." **3.** 348.

MOACYR SCLIAR

"A Balada do Falso Massias." **3.** 348.
"Os Profetas de Benjamin Bok." **3.** 348.

CHARLES SCOFIELD

"Fan Show's Thanksgiving." **2.** 262.

DUNCAN CAMPBELL SCOTT

"The Bobolink." **5.** 291.
"Charcoal." **2.** 262.
"The Desjardins." **2.** 262.
"Paul Farlette." **5.** 291.

EVELYN SCOTT

"Turnstile." **3 ed.** 678.

ROBIN S. SCOTT

"Who Needs Insurance?" **3.** 348.

WALTER SCOTT

"The Highland Widow." **3 ed.** 678; **4.** 251.
"My Aunt Margaret's Mirror." **2.** 262; **4.** 251.
"The Tapestried Chamber" [originally "Story of an Apparition"]. **2.** 262; **4.** 251.
"The Two Drovers." **1.** 193; **2.** 262; **3.** 348; **4.** 251.
"Wandering Willie's Tale." **2.** 262; **4.** 251; **5.** 291.

WILLIAM CHARLES SCULLY

"Afar in the Desert." **1.** 193.
"The Battle of Ezinyoseni." **1.** 193.
"By the Waters of Marah." **1.** 193.
"Chicken Wings." **1.** 193.
"Ghamba." **1.** 193.
"The Gratitude of a Savage." **1.** 193.
"The Imishologu." **1.** 193.
"Noquala's Cattle." **1.** 194.
"On Picket, An Episode of the South African War." **1.** 194.
"The Quest of the Copper." **1.** 194.
"Rainmaking." **1.** 194.
"Ukushwama." **1.** 194.
"The Vengeance of Dogolwana." **1.** 194.
"The White Hecatomb." **1.** 194.
"The Wisdom of the Serpent." **1.** 194.
"The Writing on the Rock." **1.** 194.

ALLAN SEAGER

"The Conqueror." **3 ed.** 678.
"The Old Man of the Mountain." **3 ed.** 678.
"The Street." **3.** 348.
"This Town and Salamanca." **3 ed.** 678; **3.** 348.
"The Unicorn." **3.** 348.

C. EMMERSON SEARS

"Baxter's Beat." **3.** 348.

MENDELE MOCHER SEFORIM [SHALOM YA'AKOV ABRAMOVITSH]

"In the Days of Tumult." **1.** 194.
"In the Heavenly and Earthly Assemblies." **1.** 194.
"The Old Story" [same as "There Is No God in Jacob"]. **1.** 194.

ANNA SEGHERS

"Auf dem Wege zur amerikanischen Botschaft." **3 ed.** 678.
"Aufstand der Fischer von St. Barbara." **3 ed.** 678.
"The End." **1.** 194.
"The Light on the Gallows." **4.** 251.
"The Wedding in Haiti." **4.** 251.

SANT SINGH SEKHON

"The Whirlwind." **3 ed.** 678.

HUBERT SELBY

"And Baby Makes Three." **3 ed.** 679.
"Double Feature." **4.** 251.

ESTHER SELIGSON

"Distinto mundo habitual." **4.** 252.
"Por el monte hacia le mar." **4.** 252.
"Un viento de hojas secas." **4.** 252.

RICHARD SELZER

"An Act of Faith." **3.** 349.
"The Harbinger." **3.** 349.
"Korea." **3.** 349.

OUSMANE SEMBÈNE

"Le Noire de . . .." **3.** 349.

SEGUNDO SERRANO PONCELA

"El faro." **5.** 291.
"La raya oscura." **5.** 291.

ERNEST THOMPSON SETON

"Lobo, the King of the Currumpaw." **1.** 194.

SETOUCHI HARUMI

"Lingering Affection." **5.** 291.

EFRAIM SEVELA

"The Sabbath Candleholders." **5.** 291.

MAURICE SHADBOLT

"After the Depression." **3.** 349.
"Homecoming." **3 ed.** 679.
"Knock on Yesterday's Door." **3.** 349.
"Love Story." **3.** 349.
"Maria." **3.** 349.
"The Paua Gatherers." **3.** 349.

KHOSROW SHAHANI

"The Hurricane." **3.** 349.
"Plastic Surgery." **3.** 349.

DAVID SHAHAR

"First Lesson." **5.** 292.

SHAHNON AHMAD

"Jungle Boar." **5.** 292.

ITZHAK SHAMI

"The Vengeance of the Fathers." **2.** 262.

LAMED SHAPIRO

"The Cross." **3.** 350.
"The Dead Town." **3.** 350.
"The Jewish State." **3.** 350.
"White Chalah." **3.** 350.

GEORGE BERNARD SHAW

"The Black Girl in Her Search for God." **3 ed.** 679.

IRWIN SHAW

"An Act of Faith." **3 ed.** 679; **3.** 350.
"Circle of Light." **3.** 350.
"The City Was in Total Darkness." **3.** 350.
"The Climate of Insomnia." **3.** 350.
"Dinner in a Good Restaurant." **3.** 350.
"The Dry Rock." **3 ed.** 679; **2.** 263.
"The Eighty-Yard Run." **3 ed.** 679; **2.** 263; **3.** 350.
"Faith at Sea." **3.** 350.
"Free Conscience, Void of Offense." **3.** 350.
"Full Many a Flower." **3.** 350.
"The Girls in Their Summer Dresses." **3 ed.** 679; **1.** 195; **3.** 350; **4.** 252.
"God Was Here, But He Left Early." **3.** 350.
"Goldilocks at Graveside." **3.** 351.
"The Green Nude." **3.** 351.
"The Indian in Depth of Night." **3.** 351.
"The Inhabitants of Venus." **3.** 351.
"The Kiss at Croton Falls." **3.** 351.
"The Lament of Madame Rechevsky." **3.** 351.
"Love on a Dark Street." **3.** 351.
"Main Currents in American Thought." **3 ed.** 679; **3.** 351.
"The Man Who Married a French Wife." **3.** 351.
"Medal from Jerusalem." **3.** 351.
"Mixed Doubles." **3 ed.** 680; **3.** 351.
"The Monument." **3.** 351.
"Night, Birth, and Opinion." **3.** 351.
"Part in a Play." **3.** 351.
"The Passion of Lance Corporal Hawkins." **3 ed.** 680.
"The Priest." **3.** 351.
"Residents of Other Cities." **3 ed.** 680; **3.** 351.
"Sailor off the *Bremen*." **3 ed.** 680; **3.** 351.
"Second Mortgage." **3.** 352.
"The Sunny Banks of the River Lethe." **3.** 352.
"Then We Were Three." **3.** 352.
"Tip on a Dead Jockey." **3.** 352.
"Walking Wounded." **3.** 352.
"Weep in Years to Come." **3.** 352.
"Welcome to the City." **3.** 352.
"Where All Things Wise and Fair Descend." **3.** 352.
"Whispers in Bedlam." **3.** 352.
"A Year to Learn the Language." **3.** 352.

JANET BEELER SHAW

"No Place To Be on Christmas." **5.** 292.

ROBERT SHAW

"Appointment on Prila." **3.** 352.
"Light on Other Days." **5.** 292.

ROBERT SHECKLEY

"Can You Feel Anything When I Do This?" **3.** 352.
"The Cruel Equations." **3 ed.** 680; **3.** 352.
"Hands Off!" **3.** 352.
"Love, Incorporated." **5.** 292.
"A Thief in Time." **3.** 352.
"A Ticket to Tranai." **3 ed.** 680; **5.** 292.
"Watchbird." **3.** 353.

CHARLES SHEFFIELD

"Transition Team." **3.** 353.

RACCOONA SHELDON [ALICE HASTINGS SHELDON]

"The Screwfly Solution" [also sometimes listed under JAMES TIPTREE, JR., another of SHELDON's pseudonyms]. **2.** 277; **4.** 252; **5.** 320.
"Your Faces, O My Sisters! Your Faces Filled of Light." **4.** 252.

MARY WOLLSTONECRAFT SHELLEY

"The Mortal Immortal." **4.** 252.
"The Parvenue." **3 ed.** 680.

SHEN CONGWEN [same as SHEN TS'UNG-WEN]

"Aboard and on Shore." **5.** 292.
"After Rain." **5.** 292.
"Cotton Shoes." **5.** 292.
"The Day Before He Deserted." **5.** 292.
"Dr. Ruomo." **5.** 293.
"Fishing." **5.** 293.
"Gazing at a Rainbow." **5.** 293.
"Holiday Fruit Congee." **5.** 293.
"Hsiao-hsiao." **1.** 195.
"Housewife." **5.** 293.
"Hui Ming." **1.** 195.
"In a Private School." **5.** 293.
"Living." **1.** 195.
"Long Zhu." **5.** 293.
"The Lovers." **5.** 293.
"Meijin, Baozi, and the White Kid." **5.** 293.
"Mountain Spirit." **5.** 293.
"My Primary School Education." **5.** 293.
"The New and the Old." **5.** 293.
"No. 4." **5.** 293.
"Ox." **5.** 293.
"Portrait of Eight Steeds." **5.** 293.
"Quiet." **1.** 195.
"Sansan." **5.** 293.
"Snow." **5.** 293.
"Spring." **5.** 293.
"Three Women." **5.** 294.
"Under Moonlight." **5.** 294.
"Water and Clouds." **5.** 294.

SHENG CH'I-TENG

"I Love the Black Eyes." **2.** 263.
"Impressions: Return to the Country Home." **2.** 263.
"Reflections in the Water." **2.** 263.
"Walking to the Black Bridge." **2.** 263.

PAVEL SHESTAKOV

"Fear of Heights." **5.** 294.
"Three Days in Dagerstan." **5.** 294.

LEV SHEYNIN

"The Semenchuk Affair." **3.** 353.

SHI MO [ZHAO ZHENKAI]

"On the Ruins." **4.** 252.

SHI TIESHENG

"Blacky." **4.** 252.

BORIS SHIBAEV

"Can This Be?" **3.** 353.

M. P. SHIEL [MATTHEW PHIPPS SHIELL]

"The Bride." **4.** 252.
"Xélucha." **4.** 253.

SHIGA NAOYA

"All the Way to Abashiri." **3.** 353.
"The Apprentice's God." **3 ed.** 680.
"At Kinosaki." **3 ed.** 680; **5.** 294.
"Blind Passion." **3 ed.** 680.
"The Bonfire." **5.** 294.

"A Certain Man and the Death of His Sister." **3 ed.** 680.
"Claudius's Journal" [same as "The Diary of Claudius"]. **3 ed.** 680; **1.** 195.
"Confused Head." **3 ed.** 680.
"For Grandmother." **3 ed.** 680.
"The Good-Natured Couple." **3 ed.** 681.
"Han's Crime." **3 ed.** 681.
"An Incident." **3 ed.** 681.
"The Just Ones." **3 ed.** 681.
"The Kidnapping." **3 ed.** 681.
"Kuniko." **3 ed.** 681.
"Late Autumn." **5.** 294.
"Memories of Yamashina." **5.** 294.
"Nayao's Younger Sister." **5.** 294.
"The Old Man." **3 ed.** 681; **5.** 294.
"One Morning." **3 ed.** 681.
"Otus Junkichi." **3 ed.** 681.
"The Razor." **3 ed.** 681.
"Seibei's Gourds." **3 ed.** 681; **2.** 263.
"The Shop Boy's Patron Saint." **5.** 294.
"Tree Frogs." **3 ed.** 681.

BENJAMIN PENHALLOW SHILLABER

"Christmas Hearths and Hearts." **2.** 263.
"A Life's Fortune." **2.** 263.
"Missing." **2.** 263.
"A New Year's Revery." **2.** 263.

SHIMA RINZŌ

"In the Heavy Flow." **3.** 353.
"Midnight Feast." **3.** 353.

SHIMAZAKI TŌSON

"From Shinkatamachi." **5.** 294.
"The Water-Color Painter." **5.** 294.

ISAAC SHINHAR [originally ISAAC SHOENBERG]

"The Soul of Esther Maadani." **3 ed.** 681.

SHIRSENDU MUKHOPADHYA

"Abelai." **2.** 263.

ABRAHAM SHOAR

"Benjamin Pinckas." **3 ed.** 681.
"The Wine of Elijah." **3 ed.** 681.

GERSHON SHOFFMAN

"The Barrier." **3 ed.** 682.
"No." **3 ed.** 682.
"The Ticket." **3 ed.** 682.

MIKHAIL SHOLOKHOV

"Alien Blood." **3 ed.** 682.
"The Birthmark." **3 ed.** 682.
"The Fate of a Man" [same as "A Man's Fate"]. **3 ed.** 682; **5.** 295.
"The Insult." **3 ed.** 682.
"The Science of Hatred." **3.** 353.
"The Wind." **3.** 354.

J[OSEPH] H[ENRY] SHORTHOUSE

"An Apologue." **3.** 354.
"The Baroness Helena von Saarfeld." **3.** 354.
"Ellie: The Story of a Boy and Girl." **3.** 354.
"The Marquis Jeanne Hyacinthe de St. Palaye." **3.** 354.
"A Teacher of the Violin." **3.** 354.

NAOMI SHUMWAY

"Ike and Us Moons." **3 ed.** 682.

SHYAMAL GANGOPADHYAYA

"The Fairy." **2.** 264.

HENRYK SIENKIEWICZ

"After Bread." **3 ed.** 682.
"The Angel." **3 ed.** 682.
"Bartek the Conqueror." **3 ed.** 682.
"The Charcoal Sketches." **3 ed.** 682.
"A Comedy of Errors." **1.** 195.
"From the Memoirs of a Poznan Tutor." **3 ed.** 682.
"In the Mist." **3 ed.** 683.
"Jamiol." **3 ed.** 683.
"Latarnik" [same as "The Lighthouse-Keeper"]. **3 ed.** 683.
"Lux in Tenebris Lucet." **3 ed.** 683.
"Orso" [same as "A Circus Hercules"]. **3 ed.** 683.
"Sachem." **3 ed.** 683.
"The Third One." **3 ed.** 683.
"Yanko the Musician." **3 ed.** 683.

WACLAW SIEROSZEWSKI

"The Stolen Lady." **3 ed.** 683.
"To Be or Not to Be." **3 ed.** 683.
"The Wanderers." **3 ed.** 683.

LYDIA HUNTLEY SIGOURNEY

"The Father." **3 ed.** 683; **1.** 195.
"The Patriarch." **1.** 195.

WILLIAM WIRT SIKES

"Absalom Mather." **3.** 354.

LESLIE MARMON SILKO

"Coyote and the Stro'ro'ka Dancers." **5.** 295.
"A Geronimo Story." **5.** 295.
"Lullaby." **5.** 295.
"The Man to Send Rainclouds." **5.** 295.
"Storyteller." **5.** 295.
"Tony's Story." **5.** 295.
"Yellow Woman." **2.** 264; **3.** 354; **5.** 295.

ALAN SILLITOE

"The Bike." **3 ed.** 683.
"Canals." **3 ed.** 684.
"The Decline and Fall of Frankie Buller." **3 ed.** 684; **2.** 264.
"The Disgrace of Jim Scarfdale." **3 ed.** 684.
"The Firebug." **3 ed.** 684.
"The Fishing-boat Picture." **3 ed.** 684.
"The Good Woman." **3 ed.** 684.
"Guzman, Go Home." **3 ed.** 684.
"The Loneliness of the Long-Distance Runner." **3 ed.** 684; **1.** 195; **2.** 264; **4.** 253; **5.** 295.
"The Match." **3 ed.** 684.
"Noah's Ark." **3 ed.** 684.
"On Saturday Afternoon." **3 ed.** 684.
"The Other John Peel." **3 ed.** 684.
"The Ragman's Daughter." **3 ed.** 684.
"The Revenge." **3 ed.** 685.
"To Be Collected." **3 ed.** 685.

IGNAZIO SILONE

"The Fox and the Camellias." **1.** 196.

JOSÉ ASUNCIÓN SILVA

"Pataguya." **1.** 196.

ROBERT SILVERBERG

"After the Myths Went Home." **1.** 196; **3.** 354.
"Breckenridge and the Continuum." **3.** 354.
"Caliban." **3.** 354.
"A Happy Day in 2381." **3.** 354.
"In Entropy's Jaws." **3.** 354.
"In the Group." **5.** 295.
"Mind for Business." **3.** 355.
"New Men for Mars." **3.** 355.
"Nightwings." **3.** 355.
"The Pain Peddler." **2.** 264.
"Passengers." **3.** 355; **4.** 253.
"Road to Nightfall." **3.** 355.
"Sundance." **3.** 355.
"To the Dark Star." **2.** 264.
"Translation Error." **3.** 355.
"Warm Man." **3.** 355.
"Woman's World." **1.** 196.

CLIFFORD D. SIMAK

"The Big Front Yard." **1.** 196; **3.** 355.
"City." **3.** 355.
"A Death in the House." **3.** 355.
"Desertion." **3.** 355.
"Huddling Place." **3.** 355.
"Hunger Death." **1.** 196.
"Shotgun Cure." **1.** 196.

CLIFFORD D. SIMAK and CARL JACOBI

"The Street That Wasn't There." **1.** 196.

WILLIAM GILMORE SIMMS

"Bald-Headed Bill Baulby." **4.** 253; **5.** 296.
"Caloya." **2.** 264.
"Grayling." **3.** 356.
"How Sharp Snaffles Got His Capital and Wife." **4.** 253.
"Major Rocket." **2.** 264.
"Oakatibbe." **2.** 264; **4.** 253.
"The Plank." **2.** 265.
"Ponce de Leon." **2.** 265.
"Spirit Bridegroom." **2.** 265.
"Sweet William." **2.** 265.
"The Two Camps." **1.** 196.

ROGELIO SINÁN

"La boina roja." **5.** 296.

CLIVE SINCLAIR

"Genesis." **4.** 253.
"A Moment of Happiness." **4.** 253.

MAY SINCLAIR

"Between the Lines." **1.** 196.
"The Fault." **3 ed.** 685.
"The Finding of the Absolute." **1.** 197; **4.** 253.
"The Flaw in the Crystal." **3.** 356; **4.** 253.
"The Gift." **3 ed.** 685; **1.** 197.
"A Hero of Fiction." **3 ed.** 685.
"The Intercessor." **1.** 197; **4.** 254.
"The Mahatma's Story." **4.** 254.
"The Nature of the Evidence." **4.** 254.
"The Return." **3 ed.** 685.
"The Return of the Prodigal." **3 ed.** 685.
"The Villa Desirée." **4.** 254.
"When Their Fire Is Not Quenched." **4.** 254.

I. J. SINGER

"Sand." **1.** 197.

ISAAC BASHEVIS SINGER

"The Admirer." **3.** 356.
"Alone." **3 ed.** 685; **2.** 265; **5.** 296.
"Aunt Yentl." **4.** 254.
"The Ball." **4.** 254.
"The Black Wedding." **3 ed.** 685; **1.** 197; **5.** 296.
"Blood." **3 ed.** 685; **3.** 356; **4.** 254.
"The Briefcase." **2.** 265.
"The Bus." **2.** 265.
"The Cabalist of East Broadway." **3 ed.** 685.
"The Cafeteria." **2.** 265.
"The Captive." **1.** 197.
"Caricature." **3 ed.** 685.
"Cockadoodledoo." **3 ed.** 685.
"The Colony." **2.** 265.
"A Crown of Feathers." **3.** 356; **4.** 254; **5.** 296.
"A Day in Coney Island." **2.** 265; **4.** 254.
"The Dead Fiddler." **3 ed.** 686.
"The Destruction of Kreshev." **3 ed.** 686; **2.** 265; **4.** 254; **5.** 296.
"Dreamers." **2.** 265.
"Esther Kreindel the Second." **2.** 265.
"The Fast." **3 ed.** 686.
"The Fire." **4.** 254.
"The Gentleman from Cracow." **3 ed.** 686; **3.** 356; **4.** 254; **5.** 296.
"Getzel the Monkey." **3 ed.** 686.
"Gimpel the Fool." **3 ed.** 686; **1.** 197; **2.** 265; **3.** 356; **4.** 254; **5.** 296.
"Grandfather and Grandson." **3.** 356.
"Guests on a Winter Night." **5.** 296.
"Hanka." **4.** 254.
"A Hannukah Eve in Warsaw." **2.** 265.
"Her Son." **2.** 265.
"Jachid and Jechidah." **4.** 255; **5.** 296.
"Joy." **3 ed.** 686; **5.** 296.
"The Key." **5.** 297.
"The Lantuck." **4.** 255.
"The Last Demon." **3 ed.** 686; **2.** 266; **3.** 356; **4.** 255; **5.** 297.
"The Lecture." **2.** 266; **4.** 255.
"The Letter Writer." **2.** 266; **5.** 297.
"The Little Shoemakers." **3 ed.** 686; **1.** 197; **3.** 356; **5.** 297.
"Lost." **5.** 297.
"The Man Who Came Back" [same as "The Man Who Was Called Back"]. **3 ed.** 686; **4.** 255.
"The Mirror." **3 ed.** 686–87.
"The Needle." **4.** 255.
"Old Love." **4.** 255; **5.** 297.
"An Old Man: A Chronicle" [same as "The Old Man"]. **4.** 255; **5.** 297.
"On a Wagon." **5.** 297.
"On the Sidewalk." **4.** 255.
"One Night in Brazil." **2.** 266.
"A Piece of Advice." **2.** 266.
"Power of Darkness." **2.** 266.
"Powers." **1.** 197.
"The Psychic Journey." **2.** 266.
"Sabbath in Portugal." **2.** 266.
"Sale." **4.** 255.
"Schloimele." **2.** 266.
"The Séance." **3 ed.** 687.
"The Shadow of a Crib." **3 ed.** 687; **5.** 297.
"Shiddah and Kuziba." **3 ed.** 687; **4.** 255; **5.** 297.
"Short Friday." **3 ed.** 687; **3.** 356; **4.** 255; **5.** 297.
"The Slaughterer." **3 ed.** 687.
"Something Is There." **4.** 255; **5.** 297.
"The Son from America." **5.** 297.
"The Spinoza of Market Street." **3 ed.** 687; **1.** 197; **3.** 356; **4.** 255; **5.** 297.
"Stories from Behind the Stove." **5.** 297.

"Taibele and Her Demon." **3 ed.** 687; **5.** 297.
"The Third One." **3 ed.** 687; **3.** 357.
"Two Corpses Go Dancing." **3 ed.** 687.
"Two Weddings and One Divorce." **2.** 266.
"The Unseen." **3 ed.** 687.
"The Warehouse." **5.** 298.
"A Wedding in Brownsville." **5.** 298.
"The Wife Killer: An Old Wives' Tale." **4.** 255.
"Woman Trusts Editor with Important Secret." **4.** 255.
"Yentl the Yeshiva Boy." **3 ed.** 687; **2.** 266; **4.** 256; **5.** 298.
"Zeidlus the First." **5.** 298.
"Zeitl and Rickel." **3 ed.** 687.
"Zlateh the Goat." **3.** 357; **4.** 256.

IQBAL SINGH

"When One Is in It." **3.** 357.

KHUSHWANT SINGH

"Abroad and Not-So-Innocent." **3 ed.** 688.
"A Bride for the Sahib." **3 ed.** 688.
"The Butterfly." **3 ed.** 688.
"The Constipated Frenchman." **3 ed.** 688.
"Death Comes to Daulat Ram." **3 ed.** 688.
"The Fawn." **3 ed.** 688.
"The Great Difference." **3 ed.** 688.
"India Is a Strange Country." **3 ed.** 688.
"The Insurance Agent." **3 ed.** 688.
"Karma." **3 ed.** 688; **5.** 298.
"Kusum." **3 ed.** 688.
"Little Man, You've Had a Busy Day" [same as "Man, How the Government of India Run"]. **3 ed.** 688.
"A Love Affair in London." **3 ed.** 688.
"Maiden Voyage of the *Jal Hindia.*" **3 ed.** 688.
"The Man with a Clear Conscience." **3 ed.** 688.
"The Mark of Vishnu." **3 ed.** 688.
"The Memsahib of Mandla." **3 ed.** 688.
"Mr. Kanjoos and the Great Miracle." **3 ed.** 689.
"Mr. Singh and the Color Bar." **3 ed.** 689.
"The Morning After the Night Before." **3 ed.** 689.
"My Own, My Native Land." **3 ed.** 689.
"The Portrait of a Lady." **3 ed.** 689.
"Posthumous." **3 ed.** 689.
"A Punjab Pastoral." **3 ed.** 689.
"The Rape." **3 ed.** 689.
"Rats and Cats in the House of Culture." **3 ed.** 689.
"The Red Tie." **3 ed.** 689.
"The Riot." **3 ed.** 689.
"A Town Called Alice." **3 ed.** 689.
"The Voice of God." **3 ed.** 689.
"When Sikh Meets Sikh." **3 ed.** 689.

ANDREY SINYAVSKY [ABRAM TERTZ]

"At the Circus." **3.** 357.
"Graphomaniacs." **3 ed.** 725; **3.** 357.
"The Icicle." **3.** 357.
"Pxenc." **3.** 357.
"Tenants." **3.** 357.
"Tiny Tsores." **3.** 357.
"You and I." **3.** 357.

OSBERT SITWELL

"Alive—Alive, Oh!" **3 ed.** 689.

PEDER SJÖGREN

"Tears in Your Sleep." **3 ed.** 689.

ANTONIO SKARMETA

"First Grade." **3.** 357.
"The Phone Call." **3.** 358.

IOAN SLAVICI

"Zina Zorilor." **3.** 358.

HENRY SLESAR

"After." **3.** 358.

TESS SLESINGER

"A Life in the Day of a Writer." **1.** 197.

MIKHAIL SLONIMSKY

"The Emery Machine." **4.** 256.

ANNIE TRUMBULL SLOSSON

"Anna Malann." **5.** 298.

AGNES SMEDLEY

"Cell Mates." **5.** 298.

CLARK ASHTON SMITH

"The City of the Singing Flame." **3.** 358.
"The Empire of the Necromancers." **4.** 256.
"The Master of the Asteroid." **4.** 256.

CORDWAINER SMITH [PAUL MYRON ANTHONY LINEBARGER]

"The Game of Rat and Dragon." **1.** 197; **2.** 266; **3.** 358.
"Scanners Live in Vain." **1.** 197; **3.** 358.

CORDWAINER SMITH [PAUL MYRON ANTHONY LINEBARGER] and GENEVIEVE LINEBARGER

"The Lady Who Sailed *The Soul*." **3.** 358; **4.** 172; **5.** 298.

E[DWARD] E[LMER] "DOC" SMITH

"Imperial Stars." **4.** 256.

LEE SMITH

"All the Days of Our Lives." **3.** 358; **4.** 256.
"Artists." **3.** 358; **4.** 256.
"Between the Lines." **3.** 359; **4.** 256.
"Cakewalk." **3.** 359; **4.** 256.
"Mrs. Darcy Meets the Blue-Eyed Stranger at the Beach." **3.** 359; **4.** 256.
"Saint Paul." **3.** 359; **4.** 257.

PAULINE SMITH

"Anna's Marriage." **3 ed.** 690.
"The Cart." **3 ed.** 690.
"Desolation." **3 ed.** 690.
"The Father." **3 ed.** 690; **2.** 266.
"Ludovitje." **3 ed.** 690; **2.** 266.
"The Miller." **3 ed.** 690.
"The Pain." **3 ed.** 690.
"The Pastor's Daughter." **3 ed.** 690.
"The Schoolmaster." **3 ed.** 690.
"The Sinner." **3 ed.** 690.
"The Sisters." **3 ed.** 690.

RAY SMITH

"Break-up: From the Journals of Ti-Paulo." **5.** 298.
"Cape Breton Is the Thought-Control Centre of Canada." **3 ed.** 690; **5.** 298–99.
"Colours." **5.** 299.
"A Cynical Tale." **5.** 299.
"The Dwarf in His Valley Ate Codfish." **5.** 299.
"Family Lives." **5.** 299.
"The Galoshes." **5.** 299.
"Nora Noon." **5.** 299.
"Passion." **5.** 299.
"Peril." **5.** 299.
"Raphael Anachronic." **5.** 299.
"Sarah's Summer Holiday." **5.** 299.
"Smoke." **5.** 299.
"Symbols in Agony." **5.** 299.
"Two Loves." **5.** 299.
"Were There Flowers in the Hair of the Girls Who Danced on His Grave in the Morning?" **5.** 299.

WILLIAM JOSEPH SNELLING

"The Bois Brulé." **3 ed.** 690; **1.** 198; **2.** 266–67.

ISABELO SOBREVEGA

"Pinkaw." **5.** 300.

MARIO SOLDATI

"The Window." **3 ed.** 690.

VLADIMIR ALEXANDROVICH SOLLOGUB

"A History of Two Galoshes." **3 ed.** 691.
"The Snowstorm." **4.** 257.

FËDOR SOLOGUB [FËDOR KUZ'MICH TETERNIKOV]

"Dream on the Rocks." **3.** 359.
"In Bondage." **3.** 359.
"Turandina." **3.** 359.

VLADIMIR SOLOUKHIN

"Pasha." **4.** 257.

ALEXANDER SOLZHENITSYN

"The Easter Procession." **3 ed.** 691; **1.** 198.
"For the Good of the Cause." **3 ed.** 691; **1.** 198.

"An Incident at Krechetovka Station." **3 ed.** 691; **1.** 198; **2.** 267.
"Matryona's House." **3 ed.** 691; **1.** 198; **2.** 267; **4.** 257; **5.** 300.
"The Right Hand" [later incorporated into *Cancer Ward*]. **3 ed.** 691; **1.** 198; **3.** 359; **5.** 300.
"Zakhar Kalita the Pouch." **3 ed.** 691; **1.** 198; **2.** 267; **3.** 359.

ARMONÍA SOMERS

"The Cave-In." **4.** 257.

EDITH SOMERVILLE and MARTIN ROSS [VIOLET MARTIN]

"The Finger of Mrs. Knox." **2.** 267; **3.** 359.
"Great Uncle McCarthy." **2.** 267.
"The House of Fahy." **2.** 267.
"The Last Day of Shraft." **3.** 359.
"Lisheen." **5.** 300.
"Lisheen Races, Second-Hand." **2.** 267.
"Poisson D'Avril." **2.** 267.
"The Pug-Nosed Fox." **2.** 267.
"Sharper Than a Ferret's Tooth." **2.** 267.
"Trinket's Colt." **2.** 267.
"The Waters of Strife." **2.** 267.

OREST MIKHAILOVICH SOMOV

"The Bandit." **5.** 300.
"A Command from the Other World." **3.** 359.
"An Epigraph in Place of a Title." **3.** 360.
"The Fearful Guest." **3.** 360.
"The Holy Fool." **5.** 300.
"Kikimora—The Story of a Russian Peasant on the Highroad." **3.** 360.
"Matchmaking." **3.** 360; **5.** 300.
"Mommy and Sonny." **3.** 360; **4.** 257.
"Monster." **5.** 300.
"The Suicide." **3.** 360.

SON CH'ANG-SŎP

"The Rainy Season." **5.** 300.
"The Surplus Human Being." **5.** 300.
"The Victim." **5.** 301.
"Walking in the Snow." **5.** 301.
"A Washed-Out Dream." **5.** 301.
"Writing in Blood." **5.** 301.

CASTRO SOROMENHO

"Calenga." **2.** 268.

FERNANDO SORRENTINO

"The Fetid Tale of Antulin." **2.** 268; **3.** 360.

GILBERT SORRENTINO

"The Moon in Its Flight." **3 ed.** 691; **2.** 268.

PEDRO JUAN SOTO

"Campeones." **5.** 301.
"Garabatos." **2.** 268; **5.** 301.
"Los inocentes." **5.** 301.
"Scribbles." **3.** 360.

A. E. H. SOUTHON

"The Leopard Men." **3 ed.** 691.

WOLE SOYINKA

"Egbe's Sworn Enemy." **3.** 360.
"A Tale of Two Cities" [in *Gryphon*]. **3.** 360.
"A Tale of Two Cities" [different story, same title, in *New Nigeria Forum*]. **3.** 360.

MURIEL SPARK

"Bang, Bang—You're Dead." **3 ed.** 691; **3.** 360.
"Black Madonna." **3.** 361; **4.** 257.
"Come Along, Marjorie." **3 ed.** 691.
"The Go-Away Bird." **3 ed.** 692; **1.** 198; **3.** 361.
"A Member of the Family." **3.** 361.
"Memento Mori." **1.** 198.
"The Ormolu Clock." **3.** 361.
"The Pawnbroker's Wife." **3 ed.** 692.
"The Portobello Road." **3 ed.** 692; **4.** 257.
"The Seraph and the Zambesi." **3 ed.** 692; **4.** 257.
"The Twins." **3 ed.** 692.
"You Should Have Seen the Mess." **3.** 361.

ELIZABETH SPENCER

"The Day Before." **4.** 257.
"The Eclipse." **4.** 258.
"The Finder." **4.** 258.
"The Girl Who Loved Horses." **4.** 258.

"I, Maureen." **4.** 258.
"Indian Summer." **4.** 258.
"Instrument of Destruction." **4.** 258.
"Judith Kane." **4.** 258.
"A Kiss at the Door." **4.** 258.
"Knights and Dragons." **4.** 258.
"The Light in the Piazza." **4.** 258.
"The Little Brown Girl." **4.** 258.
"Mr. McMillan." **4.** 258.
"On the Gulf." **4.** 258.
"Sharon." **4.** 258.
"Ship Island: The Story of a Mermaid." **3.** 361; **4.** 258.
"The Visit." **4.** 259.

ADRIAN SPIES

"Miri." **5.** 301.

MICKEY SPILLANE

"The Affair with the Dragon Lady." **4.** 259.
"The Bastard Bannerman." **3.** 361; **4.** 259.
"The Big Bang" [originally "Return of the Hood"]. **4.** 259.
"Everybody's Watching Me." **4.** 256.
"The Flier" [originally "Hot Cat"]. **3.** 361; **4.** 259.
"The Girl Behind the Hedge." **4.** 259.
"The Gold Fever Tapes." **4.** 259.
"I'll Die Tomorrow." **4.** 259.
"Kick It or Kill!" **3.** 361; **4.** 259.
"Killer Mine." **3.** 361; **4.** 259.
"Me, Hood!" **4.** 259.
"The Seven-Year Kill." **3.** 361; **4.** 259.
"Stand Up and Die." **4.** 259.
"Tomorrow I Die." **4.** 259.
"The Veiled Woman." **4.** 259.

NORMAN SPINRAD

"The Big Flash." **5.** 301.

HARRIET PRESCOTT SPOFFORD

"The Amber Gods." **3.** 361.
"Circumstance." **4.** 260.

CARL SPOHR

"The Final War." **5.** 301.

MARGUERITE STABLER

"The Sale of Sooy Yet." **2.** 268; **3.** 362.

JEAN STAFFORD

"And Lots of Solid Color." **4.** 260; **5.** 301.
"Bad Characters." **2.** 268; **4.** 260; **5.** 301.
"Beatrice Trueblood's Story." **4.** 260; **5.** 302.
"The Bleeding Heart." **4.** 260.
"The Captain's Gift." **4.** 260; **5.** 302.
"The Cavalier." **4.** 260.
"Caveat Emptor." **4.** 260.
"Children Are Bored on Sunday." **3 ed.** 692; **4.** 260; **5.** 302.
"The Children's Game." **4.** 260; **5.** 302.
"The Connoisseurs." **4.** 260; **5.** 302.
"Cops and Robbers." **4.** 260; **5.** 302.
"A Country Love Story." **3 ed.** 692; **4.** 260; **5.** 302.
"The Darkening Moon." **3.** 362; **4.** 260; **5.** 302.
"The Echo and the Nemesis." **4.** 261; **5.** 302.
"The End of a Career." **4.** 261; **5.** 302.
"The Healthiest Girl in Town." **4.** 261.
"The Home Front." **4.** 261.
"The Hope Chest." **4.** 261; **5.** 302.
"I Love Someone." **4.** 261; **5.** 302.
"In the Zoo." **1.** 198; **4.** 261; **5.** 302.
"An Influx of Poets." **4.** 261; **5.** 302.
"The Interior Castle." **3 ed.** 692; **3.** 362; **4.** 261; **5.** 302.
"The Liberation." **4.** 261; **5.** 302.
"Life Is No Abyss." **4.** 261; **5.** 303.
"The Lippia Lawn." **4.** 261; **5.** 303.
"Maggie Meriwether's Rich Experience." **4.** 261; **5.** 303.
"A Modest Proposal." **4.** 261; **5.** 303.
"The Mountain Day." **3.** 362; **4.** 261; **5.** 303.
"Mountain Jim." **4.** 261.
"My Blithe, Sad Bird." **4.** 261.
"Old Flaming Youth." **4.** 262.
"The Ordeal of Conrad Pardee." **4.** 262.
"The Philosophy Lesson." **4.** 262; **5.** 303.
"Polite Conversation." **4.** 262.
"A Reading Problem." **4.** 262; **5.** 303.
"A Reasonable Facsimile." **4.** 262.
"A Reunion." **3 ed.** 692; **4.** 262.
"The Scarlet Letter." **5.** 303.
"A Slight Maneuver." **4.** 262; **5.** 303.
"A Summer Day." **3 ed.** 692; **3.** 362; **4.** 262.

"The Tea Time of Stouthearted Ladies." **4.** 262.
"The Violet Rock." **4.** 262.
"The Warlock." **4.** 262; **5.** 303.
"A Winter's Tale." **4.** 262; **5.** 303.
"Woden's Day." **4.** 262; **5.** 303.

LAURENCE STALLINGS

"The Big Parade." **2.** 268.
"Gentleman in Blue." **2.** 268.
"Return to the Woods." **2.** 269.
"Turn out the Guard." **2.** 269.
"Vale of Tears." **2.** 269.

OLAF STAPLEDON

"Arms Out of Hand." **3.** 362; **4.** 262.
"The Man Who Became a Tree." **3.** 362.
"A Modern Magician." **4.** 262.

CHRISTINA STEAD

"Day of Wrath." **5.** 303.
"The Dianas." **5.** 303.
"A Household." **5.** 303.
"In Doulcemer." **5.** 303.
"The Prodigy." **5.** 304.
"The Puzzleheaded Girl." **5.** 304.
"The Rightangled Creek." **5.** 304.
"The Sensitive Goldfish." **5.** 304.
"Speculation in Lost Causes." **5.** 304.
"The Triskelion." **5.** 304.
"U. N. O. 1945." **5.** 304.

JAMES W. STEELE

"The Scout's Mistake." **2.** 269.

WILBUR DANIEL STEELE

"Always Summer." **3 ed.** 692.
"An American Comedy." **3 ed.** 692.
"The Anglo-Saxon." **3 ed.** 692.
"Arab Stuff." **3 ed.** 693.
"At Two-in-the-Bush." **3 ed.** 693.
"Autumn Bloom." **3 ed.** 693.
"A Bath in the Sea." **3 ed.** 693.
"The Black Road." **3 ed.** 693.
"Blue Murder." **3 ed.** 693.
"The Body of the Crime." **3 ed.** 693.
"Both Judge and Jury." **3 ed.** 693.
"Brother's Keeper." **3 ed.** 693.
"Bubbles." **3 ed.** 693.
"By Appointment." **3 ed.** 693.
"Can't Cross Jordan by Myself." **3 ed.** 693.
"Ching, Ching, Chinaman." **3 ed.** 693.
"Conjuh." **3 ed.** 693.
"Crocuses." **3 ed.** 693.
"The Dark Hour." **3 ed.** 693.
"A Devil of a Fellow." **3 ed.** 693.
"Down on Their Knees." **3 ed.** 693.
"A Drink of Water." **3 ed.** 694.
"Due North." **3 ed.** 694.
"Fe-Fi-Fo-Fum." **3 ed.** 694.
"Footfalls." **3 ed.** 694.
"For They Know Not What They Do." **3 ed.** 694.
"For Where Is Your Fortune Now?" **3 ed.** 694.
"From the Other Side of the South." **3 ed.** 694.
"The Gray Goose." **3 ed.** 694.
"La Guiabless." **3 ed.** 694.
"He That Hideth His Secret." **3 ed.** 694.
"How Beautiful with Shoes." **3 ed.** 694; **1.** 199.
"In the Shade of the Tree." **3 ed.** 694.
"Isles of Spice and Lilies." **3 ed.** 694.
"Ked's Hand." **3 ed.** 694.
"The Killer's Son." **3 ed.** 695.
"Land's End." **3 ed.** 695.
"A Life." **3 ed.** 695.
"Lost at Sea." **3 ed.** 695.
"Luck." **3 ed.** 695.
"The Mad." **3 ed.** 695.
"Man and Boy" [originally "Man Without a God"]. **3 ed.** 695.
"The Man Who Sat." **3 ed.** 695.
"The Man Who Saw Through Heaven." **3 ed.** 695.
"A Man's a Fool." **3 ed.** 695.
"The Marriage Kairwan." **3 ed.** 695.
"Mary Drake and Will Todd." **3 ed.** 695.
"Never Anything That Fades . . .." **3 ed.** 695; **2.** 269.
"Out of Exile." **3 ed.** 695.
"Out of the Wind." **3 ed.** 695.
"Renegade." **3 ed.** 695.
"'Romance.'" **3 ed.** 695.
"Sailor! Sailor!" **3 ed.** 695.
"The Shame Dance." **3 ed.** 696.
"Six Dollars." **3 ed.** 696.
"Sooth." **3 ed.** 696.
"Survivor." **3 ed.** 696.
"The Thinker." **3 ed.** 696.

"Tower of Sand." **3 ed.** 696.
"Two Seconds." **3 ed.** 696.
"The Wages of Sin." **3 ed.** 696.
"A Way with Women." **3 ed.** 696.
"What Do You Mean—American?" **3 ed.** 696.
"When Hell Froze." **3 ed.** 696.
"White Hands." **3 ed.** 696.
"White Horse Winter." **3 ed.** 696.
"The White Man." **3 ed.** 696.
"The Woman at Seven Brothers." **3 ed.** 696.
"The Yellow Cat." **3 ed.** 696.

WALLACE STEGNER

"Beyond the Glass Mountain." **3 ed.** 697.
"The Blue-Winged Teal." **3 ed.** 697; **1.** 199; **3.** 362.
"Carrion Spring." **1.** 199; **2.** 269.
"The Chink." **1.** 199.
"Chip Off the Old Block." **3 ed.** 697.
"The City of the Living." **3 ed.** 697; **3.** 362.
"The Double Corner." **3 ed.** 697; **3.** 362.
"Field Guide to the Western Birds." **3 ed.** 697; **1.** 199.
"Genesis." **5.** 304.
"Goin' to Town." **1.** 199.
"Maid in a Tower." **2.** 269.
"Remembering Laughter." **3 ed.** 697.
"Saw Gang." **1.** 199.
"The Traveler." **1.** 199.
"Two Rivers." **3 ed.** 697; **3.** 362.
"The View from the Balcony." **3 ed.** 697; **3.** 362.
"The Women on the Wall." **3 ed.** 697; **1.** 199; **3.** 363.

GERTRUDE STEIN

"As a Wife Has a Cow." **3.** 363.
"The Gentle Lena." **3 ed.** 697; **1.** 199; **3.** 363.
"The Good Anna." **3 ed.** 698; **1.** 199; **3.** 363.
"Melanctha." **3 ed.** 698; **1.** 199; **3.** 363; **4.** 263; **5.** 304.
"Miss Furr and Miss Skeene." **3 ed.** 698; **3.** 363.
"Nadelman." **3.** 363.
"*Q. E. D.*" **3.** 363.
"Things As They Are." **3 ed.** 698.
"A Water-fall and a Piano." **3.** 363.

JOHN STEINBECK

"Adventures in Arcademy." **5.** 304.
"The Affair at 7, Rue de M—-." **4.** 263; **5.** 304.
"Breakfast." **3 ed.** 698; **5.** 304.
"Case History." **5.** 304.
"The Case of the Hotel Ghost . . ." [same as "A Reunion at the Quiet Hotel"]. **4.** 263; **5.** 305.
"The Chrysanthemums." **3 ed.** 698–99; **1.** 200; **2.** 269; **3.** 363; **4.** 263; **5.** 305.
"The Cottage That Wasn't There." **5.** 305.
"The Days of Long Marsh." **5.** 305.
"East Third Street." **5.** 305.
"The Elf of Algiers" [originally "The Story of an Elf"]. **5.** 305.
"Fingers of Clouds." **5.** 305.
"Flight." **3 ed.** 699; **2.** 269–70; **3.** 363; **4.** 263; **5.** 305.
"The Gift" [same as "The Red Pony"]. **3 ed.** 700, 701; **1.** 200; **2.** 270; **4.** 263; **5.** 305.
"The Gifts of Iban." **5.** 305.
"The Great Mountains." **3 ed.** 700; **1.** 200; **4.** 263; **5.** 305.
"The Great Roque War." **5.** 305.
"The Harness." **3 ed.** 700; **4.** 263; **5.** 305.
"Helen Van Deventer." **4.** 263; **5.** 305.
"His Father." **4.** 263; **5.** 305.
"How Edith McGillcuddy Met R. L. Stevenson." **4.** 264; **5.** 306.
"How Mr. Hogan Robbed a Bank." **3 ed.** 700; **4.** 264; **5.** 306.
"Johnny Bear." **3 ed.** 700; **1.** 200; **4.** 264; **5.** 306.
"Junius Maltby." **5.** 306.
"The Leader of the People." **3 ed.** 700–01; **1.** 200; **2.** 270; **3.** 363; **5.** 306.
"The Lopez Sisters." **4.** 264; **5.** 306.
"The Miracle of Tepayac." **4.** 264; **5.** 306.
"Molly Morgan." **5.** 306.
"The Murder." **3 ed.** 701; **1.** 200; **3.** 364; **4.** 264; **5.** 306.
"The Nail." **5.** 306.
"The Nymph and Isobel." **5.** 306.
"The Pacific Grove Butterfly Festival." **5.** 306.
"Pat Humbert." **5.** 306.

"The Promise." **3 ed.** 701; **1.** 200; **4.** 264; **5.** 306.
"The Raid." **3 ed.** 701; **2.** 270; **4.** 264; **5.** 306.
"Raymond Banks." **5.** 306.
"St. Katy the Virgin." **3 ed.** 701–02; **1.** 200; **5.** 307.
"The Short-Short Story of Mankind" [same as "We're Holding Our Own"]. **4.** 264; **5.** 307.
"The Snake." **3 ed.** 702; **1.** 200; **2.** 270; **3.** 364; **4.** 264; **5.** 307.
"The Summer Before." **4.** 264; **5.** 307.
"The Time the Wolves Ate the Vice-Principal." **4.** 264; **5.** 307.
"Tularecito." **4.** 264; **5.** 307.
"The Vigilante." **3 ed.** 702; **4.** 264; **5.** 307.
"The White Quail." **3 ed.** 702; **1.** 200; **2.** 270; **3.** 364; **4.** 264; **5.** 307.
"The White Sisters of Fourteenth Street." **5.** 307.
"The Whiteside Family" [same as "The Whitesides"]. **4.** 264; **5.** 307.
"The Wicks Family" [same as "Shark Wicks"]. **4.** 264; **5.** 307.

JACOB STEINBERG

"Among the Silver Poplars." **2.** 270.
"The Blind Woman." **2.** 270.
"In a Nobleman's Courtyard." **2.** 270.
"The Man of Wealth." **2.** 270.
"Melon Fields." **2.** 270.
"On the Ukraine Border." **2.** 270.
"The Rabbi's Daughter." **2.** 270.

STENDHAL [MARIE HENRI BEYLE]

"The Abbess of Castro." **3 ed.** 702.
"Les Cenci." **3 ed.** 702.
"Le Coffre et le Revenant." **3 ed.** 702.
"The Duchess of Palliano." **3 ed.** 702.
"Ernestine." **3 ed.** 702.
"Le Philtre." **3 ed.** 702.
"Souvenirs d'un gentilhomme italien." **3 ed.** 702.
"Vanina Vanini." **3 ed.** 702.

JAMES STEPHENS

"Desire." **3 ed.** 703; **1.** 201.
"Etched in Moonlight." **3 ed.** 703; **1.** 201; **4.** 265.
"Hunger." **1.** 201.
"Mongan's Frenzy." **1.** 201.
"The Threepenny Piece." **4.** 265.

JAMES STERN

"The Broken Leg." **2.** 270.

CARL STERNHEIM

"Busekow." **3.** 364; **4.** 265.
"Heidenstam." **2.** 271; **3.** 364; **4.** 265.
"Die Laus." **4.** 265.
"Meta." **2.** 271; **3.** 364; **4.** 265.
"Napoleon." **4.** 265.
"Posinsky." **2.** 271; **4.** 265.
"Schuhlin." **3.** 364; **4.** 265.
"Die Schwestern Stork." **4.** 265.
"Ulrike." **2.** 271; **4.** 265.
"Vanderbilt." **3.** 364.

ROBERT LOUIS STEVENSON

"The Beach of Falesá." **3 ed.** 703; **2.** 271; **3.** 364; **4.** 265.
"The Body Snatchers." **3 ed.** 703; **4.** 265.
"The Bottle Imp." **3 ed.** 703; **4.** 265.
"Edifying Letters of the Rutherford Family." **3.** 364.
"The Force." **2.** 271.
"The House of Eld." **3 ed.** 703; **3.** 364.
"A Lodging for the Night." **3 ed.** 703; **2.** 271; **3.** 364.
"The Man Who Was Loved." **2.** 271.
"Markheim." **3 ed.** 703–04; **2.** 271; **3.** 364.
"The Merry Men." **3 ed.** 704; **3.** 364; **4.** 266; **5.** 307.
"The Misadventures of John Nicholson." **3 ed.** 704.
"Olalla." **3 ed.** 704; **1.** 201; **2.** 271; **3.** 365.
"An Old Song." **3.** 365.
"Providence and the Guitar." **3 ed.** 704.
"The Sinking Ship." **4.** 266.
"The Sire de Maletroit's Door." **3 ed.** 704; **4.** 266.
"The Strange Case of Dr. Jekyll and Mr. Hyde." **3 ed.** 704–05; **1.** 201; **2.** 271; **3.** 365; **4.** 266; **5.** 307–08.
"The Suicide Club." **4.** 266.
"Thrawn Janet." **3 ed.** 705; **2.** 271; **4.** 266.
"The Treasure of Franchard." **3 ed.** 705.
"The Waif Woman." **3 ed.** 705.
"Weir of Hermiston." **5.** 308.
"Will o' the Mill." **3 ed.** 705; **4.** 266.

ROBERT LOUIS STEVENSON and FANNY STEVENSON

"The Squire of Dames." **4.** 266.
"The Superfluous Mansion." **4.** 266.
"Zero's Tale of the Explosive Bomb." **4.** 266.

THE STEVENSONS [no further identification]

"Chinatown: My Land of Dreams." **2.** 271; **3.** 365.

DOUGLAS STEWART

"Carnival." **3 ed.** 705.
"A Girl with Red Hair." **3 ed.** 705.
"Give Us This Day." **3 ed.** 705.
"The Three Jolly Foxes." **3 ed.** 705.
"The Whare." **3 ed.** 705.

RAMONA STEWART

"The Promise." **3 ed.** 705.

ADALBERT STIFTER

"Abdias." **3 ed.** 706; **1.** 201; **3.** 365.
"Aragonite." **3 ed.** 706; **4.** 267.
"Brigitta." **3 ed.** 706; **1.** 201; **3.** 365.
"Chips off the Old Block." **3 ed.** 706; **1.** 201.
"The *Condor.*" **3 ed.** 706; **1.** 201.
"Confidence." **3.** 365.
"The Elderly Bachelor." **3 ed.** 706; **1.** 201; **3.** 365; **4.** 267.
"Fools' Castle." **3 ed.** 707; **3.** 366.
"The Forest Path." **3 ed.** 707.
"The Fountain in the Woods." **3 ed.** 707; **1.** 201; **4.** 267.
"Der fromme Spruch." **3 ed.** 707; **3.** 366.
"Granite." **3 ed.** 707; **1.** 202; **3.** 366; **4.** 267.
"The Inscribed Fir Tree." **3 ed.** 707.
"The Kiss of Sentze." **3 ed.** 707; **3.** 366.
"Limestone." **3 ed.** 707–08; **1.** 202; **3.** 366; **4.** 267.
"Mica." **3 ed.** 708; **3.** 366; **4.** 267; **5.** 308.
"The Old Seal." **3 ed.** 708; **2.** 272; **3.** 366.
"The Pitch-Burner." **3 ed.** 708; **4.** 267.
"The Primeval Forest." **3 ed.** 708; **3.** 366; **4.** 267.
"Prokopus." **3 ed.** 708; **3.** 366.
"Rock Crystal." **3 ed.** 708; **3.** 366; **4.** 267.
"The Second-Hand Market." **2.** 272.
"The Sisters" [same as "Two Sisters"]. **3 ed.** 708.
"Turmaline." **3 ed.** 708; **1.** 202; **3.** 366; **4.** 267.
"Two Widows." **3 ed.** 708.
"The Village on the Heath." **3 ed.** 709.
"The Wanderer in the Forest." **3 ed.** 709; **1.** 202; **3.** 366.
"Wild Flowers." **3 ed.** 709.

FREDERIC J. STIMSON

"Dr. Materialismus." **3 ed.** 709.

GRANT STOCKBRIDGE [NORVELL W. PAGE?]

"Dragon Lord of the Underworld." **3.** 366.

FRANK R. STOCKTON

"Amos Kilbright: His Adscititious Experiences." **4.** 267.
"The Bee-Man of Orn." **2.** 272.
"The Buller-Podington Compact." **3 ed.** 709.
"The Christmas Shadrach." **2.** 272.
"Derelict, A Tale of the Wayward Sea." **2.** 272.
"The Governor-General." **3 ed.** 709.
"The Great Staircase at Landover Hall." **3 ed.** 709.
"The Griffin and the Minor Canon." **3 ed.** 709; **2.** 272; **4.** 268.
"The Knife That Killed Po' Hancy." **2.** 272; **4.** 268.
"The Lady, or the Tiger?" **3 ed.** 709; **2.** 272.
"My Translataphone." **2.** 272.
"Old Pipes and the Dryad." **3 ed.** 709.
"The Reformed Pirate." **3 ed.** 709.
"The Slight Mistake." **3 ed.** 710.
"A Story of Champaigne." **3 ed.** 710.
"A Tale of Negative Gravity." **4.** 268.
"The Transferred Ghost." **3 ed.** 710.
"The Water-Devil." **2.** 272.

BRAM STOKER [ABRAHAM STOKER]

"Dracula's Guest." **5.** 308.
"The Judge's House." **4.** 268.
"The Secret of the Growing Gold." **4.** 268.

ELIZABETH WHEELER STONE

"The Widow's Son." **4.** 268.

LESLIE F. STONE

"The Conquest of Gola." **3.** 367.

WILLIAM LEETE STONE

"The Grave of the Indian King." **5.** 308.
"Mercy Disborough: A Tale of the Witches." **5.** 308.
"The Skeleton Hand." **5.** 308.
"The Spectre Fire-Ship." **5.** 308.

TOM STOPPARD [TOMAS STRAUSSLER]

"Life, Times: Fragments." **4.** 268; **5.** 308.
"Reunion." **4.** 268; **5.** 309.
"The Story." **4.** 268; **5.** 309.

THEODOR STORM

"Abseits." **3 ed.** 710.
"Am Kamin." **3 ed.** 710.
"Der Amtschirurgus-Heimkehr." **3 ed.** 710.
"Aquis Submersus." **3 ed.** 710; **1.** 202; **4.** 268.
"Auf dem Staatshof." **3 ed.** 710; **2.** 272; **4.** 268.
"Auf der Universität." **3 ed.** 710.
"Beim Vetter Christian." **3 ed.** 711.
"Ein Bekenntnis." **3 ed.** 711; **3.** 367.
"Bötjer Basch." **3 ed.** 711.
"Carsten Curator." **3 ed.** 711.
"A Chapter in the History of Grieshuus." **3 ed.** 711.
"A Doppelgänger." **3 ed.** 711; **5.** 309.
"Draussen im Heidedorf." **3 ed.** 711.
"Drüben am Markt." **3 ed.** 711.
"Eekenhof." **3 ed.** 711.
"A Festival at Haderslevhuus" [same as "Another Lembeck"]. **3 ed.** 711.
"Ein grünes Blatt." **3 ed.** 711.
"Eine Halligfahrt." **3 ed.** 712.
"Hans und Heinz Kirch." **3 ed.** 712; **5.** 309.
"Der Herr Etatsrad." **3 ed.** 712.
"Hinzelmeier." **3 ed.** 712.
"Im Brauerhause." **3 ed.** 712.
"Im Nachbarhaus links." **3 ed.** 712.
"Im Schloss." **3 ed.** 712.
"Im Sonnenschein." **3 ed.** 712.
"Immensee." **3 ed.** 712; **4.** 269.
"In St. Jürgen." **3 ed.** 712.
"John Riew." **3 ed.** 712.
"Eine Malerarbeit." **3 ed.** 712.
"Marthe and Her Clock." **3 ed.** 712; **3.** 367.
"Pole Poppenspäler." **3 ed.** 712; **1.** 202.
"Posthuma." **3 ed.** 713.
"Psyche." **3 ed.** 713.
"Die Regentrude." **3 ed.** 713; **4.** 269.
"Renate." **3 ed.** 713.
"The Rider of the White Horse." **3 ed.** 713; **1.** 202; **4.** 269; **5.** 309.
"Schweigen." **3 ed.** 713.
"Die Söhne des Senators." **3 ed.** 713.
"Späte Rosen." **3 ed.** 713.
"Veronika." **3 ed.** 714.
"Viola tricolor." **3 ed.** 714.
"Von jenseit des Meeres." **3 ed.** 714.
"Waldwinkel." **3 ed.** 714.
"Zum Wald- und Wasserfreude." **3 ed.** 714.

ALFONSINA STORNI

"Catalina." **2.** 272.
"A Crisis." **2.** 273.
"Cuca in Six Episodes." **2.** 273.
"An Elegant Soul." **2.** 273.
"A Letter." **2.** 273.
"Letter from a Bride-To-Be." **2.** 273.
"Letter to a Young Friend." **2.** 273.
"My School." **2.** 273.
"Refined Cruelty." **2.** 273.
"A Swallow." **2.** 273.
"Two Cents' Worth of Psychology." **2.** 273.

RANDOLPH STOW

"The Arrival at the Homestead: A Mind-Film." **4.** 269.
"Dokónikan." **3.** 367; **4.** 269.
"Magic." **3 ed.** 714; **3.** 367; **4.** 269.

HARRIET BEECHER STOWE

"The Deacon's Dilemma; or The Use of the Beautiful." **3.** 367.
"The Minister's Housekeeping." **3 ed.** 714.
"The Yankee Girl." **3.** 367.

EMIL STRAUSS

"Frau Kampe." **3 ed.** 714.
"Der Laufen." **3 ed.** 714.
"Der Schleier." **3 ed.** 714.
"Der Skorpion." **3 ed.** 714.
"Unterwegs." **3 ed.** 714.

T. S. STRIBLING

"Passage to Benares." **3.** 367.

AUGUST STRINDBERG

"Above the Clouds." **4.** 269.
"Bad Luck." **3.** 367.
"Battle of the Brains." **3.** 367.
"The Boarders." **1.** 202.
"The Breadwinner." **3.** 367.
"The Conquering Hero and the Fool." **4.** 269.
"A Criminal." **4.** 269.
"The Criminal Disposition." **4.** 269.
"The Customs Agent." **3.** 368; **4.** 269.
"A Doll's House." **4.** 269.
"A Funeral." **4.** 270.
"The Golden Helmet in the Alleberg." **4.** 270.
"Half a Sheet of Paper." **4.** 270.
"Higher Alms." **4.** 270.
"In Midsummer Days." **4.** 270.
"Is It Not Enough?" **4.** 270.
"The Isle of Bliss." **3.** 368.
"The Mysteries of Tobacco." **4.** 270.
"A Nursery Tale." **3.** 368.
"The Old and the New." **3.** 368.
"The Pastor's Moose." **4.** 270.
"Paul and Peter." **4.** 270.
"The Pilot's Trouble." **4.** 270.
"The Price of Grain." **3.** 368.
"The Quarantine Master's Second Story." **3.** 368.
"Remorse." **3.** 368.
"The Reward of Virtue." **3.** 368.
"The Romantic Organist of Ran Island." **3.** 368; **4.** 270.
"The Seagull." **4.** 270.
"The Silver Marsh." **3.** 368; **4.** 270.
"The Story of Jubal Who Had No 'I.'" **4.** 270.
"The Tailor Had to Give a Dance." **4.** 270.
"Tschandala." **3.** 368.
"Unwelcome." **4.** 270.
"The Victim." **3.** 368.
"A Witch." **3.** 368.

DAVID STRINGER

"High Eight." **1.** 202.

ANDRZEJ STRUG

"From a Friend." **3 ed.** 715.
"An Idyll." **3 ed.** 715.
"Nightmare." **3 ed.** 715.
"Prologue." **3 ed.** 715.
"The Soldier from St. Beat." **3 ed.** 715.

ARKADY STRUGATSKY and BORIS STRUGATSKY

"Almost the Same." **3.** 369.
"The Conspirators." **3.** 369.
"Far Rainbow." **5.** 309.
"The Fellow from Hell." **3.** 369.
"The Kid." **3.** 369; **4.** 270.

DON A. STUART [JOHN W. CAMPBELL]

"The Machine." **5.** 309.
"Night." **3.** 369; **5.** 309.
"Twilight." **3.** 369; **5.** 309.
"Who Goes There?" **3.** 369.

JESSE STUART

"Angel in the Pasture." **3 ed.** 715.
"Another April." **3 ed.** 715; **1.** 203; **5.** 309.
"Another Hanging." **3 ed.** 715; **1.** 203; **3.** 369.
"As Ye Sow, So Shall Ye Reap." **5.** 309.
"Battle Keaton Dies." **3 ed.** 715.
"The Bellin' of the Bride." **3 ed.** 715.
"Betwixt Life and Death" [also "Between . . ."]. **3 ed.** 715; **1.** 203.
"The Blue Tick Pig." **3 ed.** 715.
"Clearing in the Sky." **3 ed.** 715; **1.** 203.
"Corbie." **3 ed.** 715.
"Dark Winter." **3 ed.** 715.
"Frog Trouncin' Contest." **3 ed.** 716; **1.** 203; **3.** 369.
"Hair." **3 ed.** 716.
"Hot-Collared Mule." **5.** 310.
"Huey, the Engineer." **3 ed.** 716.
"Men of the Mountains." **3 ed.** 716.
"My Father Is an Educated Man." **3.** 369.

"Nest Egg." **3 ed.** 716.
"One of God's Oddlings." **3 ed.** 716.
"Rain on Tanyard Hollow." **1.** 203; **2.** 273; **5.** 310.
"The Slipover Sweater." **3 ed.** 716.
"A Stall for Uncle Jeff." **1.** 203.
"The Storm." **3 ed.** 716; **2.** 273.
"Sylvania Is Dead." **3 ed.** 716; **1.** 203.
"Testimony of Trees." **1.** 203.
"This Farm for Sale." **1.** 203; **5.** 310.
"Tim." **3 ed.** 716.
"Uncle Jeff." **3 ed.** 716.
"Walk in the Moon Shadows." **5.** 310.
"Word and Flesh." **1.** 203.
"Zeke Hammertight." **3 ed.** 716.

RUTH McENERY STUART

"Uncle Mingo's 'Speculations.'" **3 ed.** 716.

THEODORE STURGEON

"Affair with a Great Monkey." **3.** 369.
"Baby Is Three." **4.** 271.
"Bianca's Hands." **4.** 271.
"Bright Segment." **3.** 369.
"Brownshoes" [originally "The Man Who Learned Loving"]. **3.** 369.
"Bulkhead." **1.** 203.
"Dazed." **3.** 370.
"The Education of Drusilla Strange." **3.** 370.
"Extrapolation." **1.** 203; **3.** 370.
"Fear Is a Business." **3.** 370.
"Grammy Won't Knit." **5.** 310.
"The Hurkle Is a Happy Beast." **3.** 370.
"Hurricane Trio." **3.** 370.
"It." **3.** 370.
"Killdozer." **5.** 310.
"Make Room for Me." **3.** 370.
"Maturity." **3.** 370.
"Memorial." **3.** 370; **5.** 310.
"Microcosmic God." **3.** 370; **5.** 310.
"Mr. Costello, Hero." **3.** 370.
"Morality." **3.** 370.
"Need." **4.** 271.
"Never Underestimate." **3.** 370; **5.** 310.
"The Other Celia." **3.** 370.
"The Other Man." **3.** 371.
"Poker Face." **3.** 371.
"Rule of Three." **1.** 204; **3.** 371.
"The Sex Opposite." **3.** 371.
"The Silken-Swift." **3.** 371.
"The Skills of Xanadu." **3.** 371; **5.** 310.
"Slow Sculpture." **3.** 371.
"Stars Are the Styx." **3.** 371.
"Thunder and Roses." **3 ed.** 716; **3.** 371; **5.** 310.
"Tiny and the Monster." **3.** 371.
"To Here and the Easel." **3.** 371.
"A Touch of Strange." **3.** 371.
"The Touch of Your Hand." **1.** 204; **3.** 371.
"Twink." **1.** 204; **3.** 371.
"The Wages of Synergy." **5.** 310.
"A Way Home." **3.** 371.
"What Dead Men Tell." **3.** 371.
"When You Care, When You Love." **3.** 372.
"The World Well Lost." **3.** 372.

WILLIAM STYRON

"The Enormous Window" [originally "Autumn"]. **3 ed.** 717.
"The Long March." **3 ed.** 717; **2.** 273; **3.** 372; **5.** 310.
"Marriott the Marine." **3.** 372.
"This Is My Daughter." **2.** 273.

SU MANSHU [PEV MANDJU or SU JIAN]

"Tale of Crimson Silk." **3 ed.** 717.

AUSTOLIO SUAREZ

"Intimations of Redemption." **5.** 311.

JORGE SUÁREZ

"El llanto del impuesto." **4.** 271.

SUBRAMANI [entire name]

"Marigolds." **4.** 271.
"Tell Me Where the Train Goes." **4.** 271.

RUTH SUCKOW

"Auntie Bissel." **3 ed.** 718.
"The Best of the Lot." **4.** 271.
"The Daughter." **3 ed.** 718.
"Eltha." **3 ed.** 718; **3.** 372; **5.** 311.
"Eminence." **3 ed.** 718.
"Four Generations." **3 ed.** 718; **3.** 372.
"Golden Wedding." **3 ed.** 718.
"Good Pals." **3 ed.** 718.

"A Homecoming." **3 ed.** 718.
"A Little Girl's World." **3 ed.** 718.
"Mame." **3 ed.** 718.
"The Man of the Family." **3 ed.** 718.
"Memorial Eve." **5.** 311.
"Merrittville." **5.** 311.
"Midwestern Primitive." **3 ed.** 718.
"Mrs. Kemper." **3 ed.** 718.
"Mrs. Vogel and Ollie." **3 ed.** 718; **3.** 372; **5.** 311.
"One of Three Others." **5.** 311.
"A Pilgrim and a Stranger." **3 ed.** 719.
"Renters." **3 ed.** 719.
"Retired." **3.** 372.
"A Rural Community." **3 ed.** 719; **3.** 372.
"A Start in Life." **3 ed.** 719; **2.** 274.
"Uprooted." **3 ed.** 719; **3.** 372.
"The Valentine Box." **3 ed.** 719.
"What Have I." **3 ed.** 719.

HERMANN SUDERMANN

"Die Reise nach Tilsit." **3 ed.** 719; **2.** 274.

RUBÉN SUELDO GUEVARA

"El fugitivo." **3 ed.** 719.

SUI SIN FAR [EDITH EATON]

"A Chinese Ishmael." **2.** 274; **3.** 372.

RONALD SUKENICK

"The Birds." **1.** 204; **2.** 274; **4.** 271.
"The Death of the Novel." **3 ed.** 719; **4.** 271.
"Momentum." **3 ed.** 719; **3.** 372; **4.** 271.
"One Every Minute." **3 ed.** 719.
"The Permanent Crisis." **3 ed.** 720; **4.** 271.
"Roast Beef—A Slice of Life." **3 ed.** 720.
"The Sleeping Gypsy." **3 ed.** 720; **4.** 272.
"What's Your Story?" **3 ed.** 720; **4.** 272.

PYOTR SUMAROKOV

"Coquetry and Love." **3.** 373.

PER OLOF SUNDMAN

"The Controller." **3.** 373.
"The Drummer." **3.** 373.
"The Hunters II." **3.** 373.
"Ivory." **3.** 373.
"Negotiation." **3.** 373.
"The Observer." **3.** 373.
"The Rooster." **3.** 373.
"The Seekers." **3.** 373.
"Seeking a Road." **3.** 373.
"The Skier." **3.** 373.
"The Sports Fisherman." **3.** 373.
"The Strangers." **3.** 373.
"The Stylite." **3.** 373.
"Summer Night." **3.** 373.

SUNG-YEH

"The Hound Yung-nu." **3.** 374.

SUNIL GANGOPADHYAY

"Drought." **2.** 274.
"The Man Who Wanted to Be Free." **2.** 274.
"One Side of Revenge." **2.** 274.

CÈLIA SUNYOL

"L'Homme de les fires." **5.** 311.

JULES SUPERVIELLE

"The Adolescent." **3 ed.** 720; **2.** 274.
"Antoine-du-Desert." **3 ed.** 720.
"Les Bonshommes du Cire." **2.** 274.
"A Child." **2.** 274.
"L'Enfant de la haute mer." **1.** 204.
"L'Enlèvement d'Europe." **2.** 274.
"La Femme Retrouvée." **3 ed.** 720.
"Le Heron Garde-Boeuf." **3 ed.** 720.
"L'Inconnue de Seine." **3 ed.** 720.
"Der Kuhreiher." **2.** 275.
"The Minotaur." **2.** 275; **4.** 272.
"Le Modèle des Epoux." **2.** 275.
"Noah's Ark." **2.** 275.
"Orpheus." **2.** 275.
"The Ox and the Ass of the Crèche." **3 ed.** 720; **2.** 275.
"Vacances." **3 ed.** 720.

ABRAHAM SUTZKEVER

"Green Aquarium." **3.** 374.

ITALO SVEVO [ETTORE SCHMITZ]

"Argo and His Master." **3 ed.** 720.
"Generous Wine." **1.** 204.
"The Hoax." **3 ed.** 720; **1.** 204; **2.** 275.
"The Mother." **3 ed.** 721; **1.** 204.

"The Murder on the Via Belpoggio." **2.** 275.
"Short Sentimental Journey." **1.** 204.
"The Story of the Nice Old Man and the Pretty Girl." **3 ed.** 721; **1.** 204; **2.** 275.
"This Indolence of Mine." **3 ed.** 721.

HARVEY SWADOS

"Just One of the Boys." **3 ed.** 721.

GLADYS SWAN

"Black Hole." **5.** 311.
"Getting an Education." **5.** 311.

GRAHAM SWIFT

"Learning to Swim." **5.** 311.

ARTHUR SYMONS

"The Life and Adventures of Lucy Newcome." **4.** 272.

RABINDRANATH TAGORE

"The Atonement." **1.** 204.
"Cloud and Sun." **1.** 204.
"The Devotee." **1.** 204.
"The Editor." **1.** 205.
"The Girl Between." **1.** 205.
"A Lapse of Judgment." **3 ed.** 721.
"One Night." **1.** 205.
"The Postmaster." **1.** 205.
"Punishment." **3 ed.** 721.
"Rashmoni's Son." **1.** 205.
"The Return of Khokababu." **1.** 205.
"The Troublemaker." **1.** 205.
"We Crown Thee King." **1.** 205.
"A Wife's Letter." **1.** 205.

JOHN TAINE [ERIC TEMPLE BELL]

"Black Goldfish." **4.** 272.
"The Ultimate Catalyst." **3.** 374.

TAKAHASHI MICHITSUNA

"Killing Time." **5.** 312.
"The Sky of September." **5.** 312.

TAKAHASHI TAKAKO

"Doll Love." **5.** 312.

TAKEDA RINTARŌ

"The Tune of Treason." **3.** 374.
"Violence." **3.** 374.

ZAKARIYA TAMIR

"The Face of the Moon." **5.** 312.

BENJAMIN TAMMUZ

"A Roll of Canvas." **3 ed.** 721.

TANIZAKI JUN'ICHIRŌ

"Account of Spring Breeze and Autumn Rain." **3.** 374.
"Aguri." **2.** 275.
"The Bridge of Dreams." **2.** 275; **3.** 374; **5.** 312.
"The Kylin." **3.** 374.
"A Matter of Taste." **4.** 272.
"Secrets of Lord Bushu." **2.** 275.
"Sorrow of a Heretic." **3.** 374.
"The Story of Tomoda and Matsunaga." **3.** 374.
"The Tale of Shunkin." **5.** 312.
"Tattoo." **1.** 205; **2.** 275; **4.** 272; **5.** 312.

AHMET HAMDI TANPINAR

"The Dream of Abdullah Efendi." **4.** 272.
"Master of the House." **4.** 272.
"Old-Fashioned Clothes." **4.** 272.
"A Road." **4.** 272.
"Tahsin of Erzurum." **4.** 273.

BOOTH TARKINGTON

"The Veiled Feminists of Atlantis." **5.** 312.

VALERY TARSIS

"Ward No. 7." **4.** 273.

ALLEN TATE

"The Immortal Woman." **3 ed.** 721.
"The Migration." **3 ed.** 721.

TAYAMA KATAI

"One Cold Morning." **2.** 275.
"Perpetual Calendar." **3.** 374.

ELIZABETH TAYLOR

"The Blush." **4.** 273.
"A Dedicated Man." **4.** 273.
"Girl Reading." **4.** 273.
"Hester Lilly." **4.** 273.
"The Letter Writers." **4.** 273.
"Swan Moving." **4.** 273.

PETER TAYLOR

"Allegiance." **3 ed.** 722.
"At the Drugstore." **3 ed.** 722; **2.** 276.
"Bad Dreams." **3 ed.** 722; **5.** 312.
"The Captain's Son." **2.** 276; **5.** 313.
"A Cheerful Disposition." **3 ed.** 722.
"Cookie." **3 ed.** 722; **5.** 313.
"Daphne's Lover." **2.** 276; **5.** 313.
"The Dark Walk." **3 ed.** 722.
"Dean of Men." **1.** 205; **5.** 313.
"The End of the Play." **3 ed.** 722.
"The Fancy Woman." **3 ed.** 722; **5.** 313.
"First Heat." **5.** 313.
"Friend and Protector." **3 ed.** 722; **5.** 313.
"The Gift of the Prodigal." **5.** 313.
"Guests." **3 ed.** 722; **5.** 313.
"The Hand of Emmagene." **2.** 276; **5.** 313.
"Heads of Houses." **3 ed.** 722.
"Her Need." **5.** 313.
"In the Miro District." **2.** 276; **5.** 313.
"The Instruction of a Mistress." **5.** 313.
"Je Suis Perdu." **3 ed.** 722; **5.** 314.
"The Lady Is Civilized." **3 ed.** 722.
"The Little Cousin." **3 ed.** 723.
"A Long Fourth." **3 ed.** 723; **2.** 276; **5.** 314.
"Miss Lenora When Last Seen." **3 ed.** 723; **2.** 276; **5.** 314.
"Mrs. Billingsby's Wine." **3 ed.** 723.
"Nerves." **3 ed.** 723.
"1939." **3 ed.** 723; **5.** 314.
"The Old Forest." **5.** 314.
"The Other Times." **3 ed.** 723; **5.** 314.
"An Overwhelming Question." **3 ed.** 723.
"The Party." **3 ed.** 723.
"Porte-Cochere." **3 ed.** 723.
"Rain in the Heart." **3 ed.** 723.
"Reservations." **3 ed.** 723; **5.** 314.
"The School Girl." **3 ed.** 723.
"The Scoutmaster." **3 ed.** 723; **5.** 314.
"Sky Line." **3 ed.** 724; **5.** 314.
"A Spinster's Tale." **3 ed.** 724; **5.** 314.
"A Strange Story." **3 ed.** 724.
"Their Losses." **3 ed.** 724; **3.** 375.
"There." **3 ed.** 724.
"Three Heroines." **5.** 314.
"The Throughway." **3 ed.** 724; **5.** 314.
"Two Ladies in Retirement." **3 ed.** 724; **5.** 314.
"Two Pilgrims." **3 ed.** 724; **5.** 314.
"Uncles." **3 ed.** 724.
"Venus, Cupid, Folly and Time." **3 ed.** 724; **3.** 375; **5.** 315.
"A Walled Garden." **3 ed.** 724.
"What You Hear from 'Em?" **3 ed.** 724; **2.** 276; **5.** 315.
"A Wife of Nashville." **3 ed.** 724; **1.** 205.

HERNANDO TÉLLEZ

"Just Lather, That's All." **3.** 375.

JODOCUS D. T. TEMME

"The Hallbauer Woman." **5.** 315.
"Who Was the Murderer?" **5.** 315.

VLADIMIR FËDOROVICH TENDRIAKOV

"An Exceptional Event." **4.** 273.
"The Night after Graduation." **2.** 276.
"Potholes." **2.** 276.
"Three, Seven, Ace." **3.** 375.
"The Trial." **3.** 375; **4.** 273.
"Twenty Years Late." **2.** 276.
"The Windfall." **2.** 276.

WILLIAM TENN

"Betelgeuse Bridge." **3.** 375.
"The Discovery of Morniel Mathaway." **3.** 375.
"Down Among the Dead Men." **3.** 375.
"It Ends with a Flicker." **3.** 375.
"The Liberation of Earth." **3 ed.** 725; **3.** 375.
"The Masculinist Revolt." **5.** 315.
"Medusa Was a Lady." **3.** 375.
"Null-P." **3 ed.** 725; **3.** 375.
"Venus and the Seven Sexes." **3.** 376.
"Winthrop Was Stubborn" [originally "Time Waits for Winthrop"]. **3.** 376.

ABRAM TERTZ [pseudonym ANDREY SINYAVSKY] [See ANDREY SINYAVSKY]

KAZIMIERZ TETMAJER

"To Heaven." **3 ed.** 725.

WILLIAM MAKEPEACE THACKERAY

"Dennis Haggarty's Wife." **3 ed.** 725.
"Frank Berry's Wife." **5.** 315.
"The Ravenswing." **5.** 315.

OCTAVE THANET

"The Bishop's Vagabond." **3 ed.** 725.

DOUGLAS THAYER

"Opening Day." **5.** 315.
"Under the Cottonwoods." **5.** 315.

JIM THEIS

"The Eye of Argon." **5.** 315.

CAN THEMBA

"The Suit." **3.** 376.

GEORGE THEOTOKAS

"The Daemon." **3 ed.** 725.
"Euripides Pendozalis." **3 ed.** 725.
"Everything's in Order." **3 ed.** 726.
"Leonis." **3 ed.** 726.

YVES THÉRIAULT

"La fleur qui faisait un son." **1.** 205.

AUDREY THOMAS

"Aquarius." **5.** 316.
"Aunt Hettie James and the Gates of the New Jerusalem." **5.** 316.
"Dead Man's Body." **5.** 316.
"Déjeuner sur l'Herbe." **4.** 273.
"Green Stakes for the Garden." **5.** 316.
"If One Green Bottle." **5.** 316.
"Kill Day on the Government Wharf." **5.** 316.
"A Monday Dream." **5.** 316.
"Munchmeyer." **5.** 316.
"One Is One and All Alone." **5.** 316.
"Out in the Midday." **4.** 273.
"Rapunzel." **5.** 316.
"Salon des Refusés." **5.** 316.
"Two in the Bush." **4.** 273.
"A Winter's Tale." **4.** 274; **5.** 316.
"Xanadu." **5.** 316.

DYLAN THOMAS

"An Adventure from a Work in Progress." **3 ed.** 726.
"Adventures in the Skin Trade." **3 ed.** 726.
"After the Fair." **3 ed.** 726.
"Anagram" [originally "Mr. Tritas on the Rocks"]. **3 ed.** 726.
"Ballad of the Long-Legged Bait." **3 ed.** 726.
"The Burning Baby." **3 ed.** 726.
"A Child's Christmas in Wales." **3 ed.** 726.
"The Dress." **3 ed.** 726.
"The Enemies." **3 ed.** 726.
"The Fight." **2.** 276.
"The Followers." **3 ed.** 726–27.
"Gaspar, Melchior, Balthasar." **3 ed.** 727.
"The Holy Six." **3 ed.** 727.
"The Horse's Ha." **3 ed.** 727.
"How to Be a Poet." **3 ed.** 727.
"In the Direction of the Beginning." **3 ed.** 727.
"Just Like Little Dogs." **3 ed.** 727.
"The Lemon." **3 ed.** 727.
"The Map of Love." **3 ed.** 727; **3.** 376.
"The Mouse and the Woman." **3 ed.** 727.
"One Warm Saturday." **3 ed.** 727.
"The Orchards." **3 ed.** 727.
"Patricia, Edith, and Arnold." **3 ed.** 727–28.
"The Peaches." **3 ed.** 728; **1.** 206; **5.** 316.
"Prologue to an Adventure." **3 ed.** 728.
"A Prospect of the Sea." **3 ed.** 728.
"The School for Witches." **3 ed.** 728.
"A Story." **3 ed.** 728; **1.** 206.
"The Tree." **3 ed.** 728.
"The True Story." **3 ed.** 728.
"The Vest." **3 ed.** 728.
"A Visit to Grandpa." **3 ed.** 728; **3.** 376.
"The Visitor." **3 ed.** 728.

THOMAS THOMPSON

"A Shore for the Sinking." **3 ed.** 729.

HENRY DAVID THOREAU

"Baker Farm." **3 ed.** 729.

THOMAS BANGS THORPE

"The Big Bear of Arkansas." **3 ed.** 729; **5.** 316–17.
"The Devil's Summer Retreat in Arkansaw." **5.** 317.

JAMES THURBER

"Am Not I Your Rosalind?" **3 ed.** 729; **5.** 317.
"Back to the Grades." **3 ed.** 729.
"The Beast in the Dingle." **3 ed.** 729; **3.** 376.
"The Black Magic of Barney Haller." **3.** 376; **5.** 317.
"A Box to Hide In." **3 ed.** 729; **5.** 317.
"The Breaking Up of the Winships." **3 ed.** 730; **3.** 376; **5.** 317.
"A Call on Mrs. Forrester." **3.** 376.
"The Cane in the Corridor." **3 ed.** 730.
"The Car We Had to Push." **3 ed.** 730; **3.** 376.
"The Case for the Daydreamer." **3 ed.** 730.
"The Case of Dimity Ann." **5.** 317.
"The Cases of Blue Ploermell." **3 ed.** 730.
"The Catbird Seat." **3 ed.** 730; **1.** 206; **2.** 277; **3.** 376; **4.** 274; **5.** 317.
"A Couple of Hamburgers." **3 ed.** 730; **2.** 277; **3.** 376; **5.** 317.
"The Curb in the Sky." **5.** 317.
"The Departure of Emma Inch." **5.** 317.
"Doc Marlowe." **3 ed.** 730.
"Draft Board Nights." **3 ed.** 730.
"The Evening's at Seven." **5.** 317.
"Everything Is Wild." **3 ed.** 730.
"The Fairly Intelligent Fly." **3.** 376.
"The Figgerin' of Aunt Wilma." **5.** 317.
"File and Forget." **3 ed.** 731.
"A Final Note on Chanda Bell." **3 ed.** 731; **5.** 317.
"A Friend of the Earth." **3 ed.** 731.
"A Friend to Alexander." **3 ed.** 731; **3.** 377; **5.** 317.
"The Greatest Man in the World." **3 ed.** 731; **1.** 206; **2.** 277; **3.** 377; **5.** 318.
"Here Come the Tigers." **3 ed.** 731.
"The Imperturbable Spirit." **5.** 318.
"The Indian Sign." **5.** 318.
"The Interview." **3 ed.** 731; **5.** 318.
"Josephine Has Her Day." **3 ed.** 731.
"The Lady on 142." **5.** 318.
"The Last Clock." **3 ed.** 731; **3.** 377.
"The Little Girl and the Wolf." **3 ed.** 731.
"The Luck of Jad Peters." **3 ed.** 731; **5.** 318.
"The Macbeth Murder Mystery." **3 ed.** 731; **3.** 377.
"The Man Who Hated Moonbaum." **5.** 318.
"Menace in May." **3 ed.** 731; **5.** 318.
"Mr. Preble Gets Rid of His Wife." **3 ed.** 731; **5.** 318.
"More Alarms at Night." **3 ed.** 732.
"The Moth and the Star." **3.** 377.
"The Mouse Who Went to the Country." **3.** 377.
"The Night the Bed Fell." **3 ed.** 732; **3.** 377.
"The Night the Ghost Got In." **3 ed.** 732.
"One Is a Wanderer." **3 ed.** 732; **5.** 318.
"The Ordeal of Mr. Matthews." **3 ed.** 732.
"The Other Room." **3 ed.** 732; **5.** 318.
"A Portrait of Aunt Ida." **3 ed.** 732.
"The Private Life of Mr. Bidwell." **3 ed.** 732; **5.** 318.
"The Remarkable Case of Mr. Bruhl." **3 ed.** 732.
"The Secret Life of Walter Mitty." **3 ed.** 732–33; **2.** 277; **3.** 377; **4.** 274; **5.** 318.
"The Sheep in Wolf's Clothing." **3.** 377.
"The Shrike and the Chipmunk." **3.** 377.
"Smashup." **3 ed.** 733; **5.** 318.
"Something to Say." **3 ed.** 733; **5.** 318.
"Tea at Mrs. Armsby's." **5.** 318.
"Teacher's Pet." **3 ed.** 733; **5.** 318.
"The Tiger Who Understood People." **3.** 377.
"The Two Turkeys." **3.** 377.
"The Unicorn in the Garden." **3 ed.** 733; **3.** 377; **5.** 319.
"The Very Proper Gander." **3.** 377.
"The Whip-Poor-Will." **3 ed.** 733; **5.** 319.
"The Wood Duck." **3 ed.** 733.
"You Could Look It Up." **3 ed.** 733; **1.** 206; **5.** 319.

JOHANN LUDWIG TIECK

"Die Ahnenprobe." **3 ed.** 733.
"Death of the Poet." **3 ed.** 733.
"The Elves." **3 ed.** 733; **2.** 277.
"The Enchanted Castle." **3 ed.** 734.
"Der fünfzehnte November." **3 ed.** 734.
"Die Gemälde." **3 ed.** 734.
"Die Gesellschaft auf dem Lande." **3 ed.** 734.
"Die Klausenburg." **3 ed.** 734.
"Des Lebens Überfluss." **3 ed.** 734.
"Love Magic." **3 ed.** 734; **5.** 319.
"The Moon-Possessed." **3 ed.** 734.
"Die Reisenden." **3 ed.** 734.
"Der Runenberg." **3 ed.** 734; **3.** 378; **5.** 319.
"Die Verlobung." **3 ed.** 734.
"The Witches' Sabbath." **3 ed.** 734.

TILUMANYA [entire name]

"Rice from the Beards." **3.** 378.

ROSEMARY TIMPERLEY

"Street of the Blind Donkey." **5.** 319.

JAMES TIPTREE, JR. [ALICE HASTINGS SHELDON]

"Afternoon." **3.** 378.
"All the Kinds of Yes." **4.** 274; **5.** 319.
"Amberjack." **4.** 274.
"And I Awoke and Found Me Here on the Cold Hill's Side." **3.** 378; **4.** 274; **5.** 319.
"And I Have Come upon This Place by Lost Ways." **4.** 274.
"And So On, And So On." **4.** 274.
"Beam Us Home." **3.** 378; **4.** 274.
"Beyond the Dead Reef." **4.** 274.
"Birth of a Salesman." **3.** 378.
"The Boy Who Waterskied to Forever." **4.** 274.
"Excursion Fare." **4.** 274.
"Faith." **3.** 378.
"Faithful to Thee, Terra, in Our Fashion." **4.** 275.
"Forever to a Hudson's Bay Blanket." **3.** 378; **4.** 275.
"The Girl Who Was Plugged In." **4.** 275.
"Help" [originally "Pupa Knows Best"]. **3.** 378.
"Her Smoke Rose Up Forever." **4.** 275.
"Houston, Houston, Do You Read?" **2.** 277; **3.** 378; **4.** 275; **5.** 319.
"I'll Be Waiting for You When the Swimming Pool Is Empty." **3.** 379; **4.** 275.
"I'm Too Big, But I Love to Play." **3.** 379; **4.** 275.
"The Last Flight of Dr. Ain." **3.** 379; **4.** 275.
"Lirios: A Tale of the Quintana Roo." **3.** 379; **4.** 275.
"Love Is the Plan, the Plan Is Death." **2.** 277; **4.** 275; **5.** 319.
"Mama Comes Home" [originally "The Mother Ship"]. **2.** 277; **3.** 379; **4.** 275.
"The Milk of Paradise." **4.** 275.
"A Momentary Taste of Being." **3.** 379; **4.** 275.
"Mother in the Sky with Diamonds." **3.** 379; **4.** 275.
"On the Last Afternoon." **4.** 276; **5.** 319.
"Out of the Everywhere." **4.** 276.
"Painwise." **5.** 320.
"The Peacefulness of Vivyan." **3.** 379; **4.** 276.
"The Psychologist Who Wouldn't Do Awful Things to Rats." **3.** 379; **5.** 320.
"The Screwfly Solution" [also sometimes listed under RACCOONA SHELDON, another of SHELDON's pseudonyms]. **2.** 277; **4.** 252; **5.** 320.
"She Waits for All Men Born." **3.** 379; **4.** 276.
"Slow Music." **4.** 276; **5.** 320.
"The Snows Are Melting, the Snows Are Gone." **3.** 379; **4.** 276.
"A Source of Innocent Merriment." **4.** 276.
"Time Sharing Angel." **5.** 320.
"We Who Stole the Dream." **4.** 276; **5.** 320.
"With Delicate Mad Hands." **3.** 379; **4.** 276; **5.** 320.
"The Women Men Don't See." **3.** 379; **4.** 276; **5.** 320.
"Your Haploid Heart." **3.** 379; **4.** 276; **5.** 320.

VLADIMIR TITOV [pseudonym TIT KOSMOKRATOV]

"The Isolated Little House of Vasilievsky Island." **3.** 379.

J[OHN] R[ONALD] R[EUEL] TOLKIEN

"Farmer Giles of Ham." **3.** 380.
"Leaf by Niggle." **2.** 277; **3.** 380.
"Of Beren and Lúthien." **3.** 380.
"Quenta Silmarillion." **3.** 380.

ALEKSEY KONSTANTINOVICH TOLSTOY

"Amena." **3 ed.** 735.
"Artemy Semyonovich Bervenkovsky." **3 ed.** 735.
"La Famille du Vourdalak." **3 ed.** 735.
"Le Rendezvous dans trois cents ans." **3 ed.** 735.
"The Russian Character." **4.** 276.
"The Vampire." **3 ed.** 735.

LEO TOLSTOY

"After the Ball." **3.** 380.
"Albert." **3 ed.** 735; **4.** 276.
"The Candle." **3 ed.** 735.
"A Captive in the Caucasus." **3 ed.** 735.
"The Cossacks." **5.** 320.
"The Death of Ivan Ilych." **3 ed.** 735–36; **1.** 206; **2.** 277–78; **3.** 380; **4.** 276–77; **5.** 320–21.
"The Devil." **3 ed.** 736; **4.** 277.
"Family Happiness." **3 ed.** 736; **1.** 206; **2.** 278; **4.** 277; **5.** 321.
"Father Sergii." **3.** 381; **5.** 321.
"God Sees the Truth but Waits." **3 ed.** 736; **1.** 206; **5.** 321.
"Hadji Murat." **3 ed.** 736; **1.** 206–07; **2.** 278; **4.** 277; **5.** 321.
"How Much Land Does a Man Need?" **1.** 207.
"The Kreutzer Sonata." **3 ed.** 737; **1.** 207; **4.** 277; **5.** 321.
"A Landowner's Morning." **1.** 207; **5.** 321.
"Lucerne." **3 ed.** 737; **4.** 277.
"Master and Man." **5.** 321.
"Polikushka." **1.** 207; **2.** 278; **3.** 381; **5.** 321.
"The Posthumous Notes of the Elder Fedor Kuzmich." **5.** 321.
"Sevastopol in August." **3 ed.** 737.
"Sevastopol in December, 1854." **3 ed.** 737; **4.** 277.
"Sevastopol in May." **3 ed.** 737; **4.** 277.
"The Snowstorm." **3.** 381; **4.** 277; **5.** 321.
"Three Arshins of Land." **3 ed.** 737.
"Three Deaths." **3 ed.** 737; **1.** 207; **2.** 278; **3.** 381; **5.** 321.
"The Three Hermits." **3 ed.** 737.
"Two Hussars." **3 ed.** 737; **4.** 277.
"Two Old Men." **5.** 321.
"The Wood-felling." **3 ed.** 737.

TOMIOKA TAEKO

"Family in Hell." **5.** 322.

FEREYDOUN TONKABONI

"The Sultan's Six Sons." **3.** 381.

JEAN TOOMER

"Avey. **3 ed.** 738; **2.** 278; **3.** 381; **5.** 322.
"Becky." **3 ed.** 738; **3.** 381; **5.** 322.
"Blood-Burning Moon." **3 ed.** 738; **1.** 207; **2.** 278; **3.** 381; **4.** 277; **5.** 322.
"Bona and Paul." **3 ed.** 738; **2.** 278; **3.** 381; **5.** 322.
"Box Seat." **3 ed.** 738–39; **1.** 207; **2.** 278; **3.** 382; **5.** 322–23.
"Calling Jesus." **3 ed.** 739; **5.** 323.
"Carma." **3 ed.** 739; **3.** 382; **5.** 323.
"Drackman." **3 ed.** 739.
"Easter." **3.** 382.
"Esther." **3 ed.** 739; **1.** 207; **2.** 278; **3.** 382; **5.** 323.
"Fern." **3 ed.** 739; **1.** 207–08; **2.** 278; **3.** 382; **5.** 323.
"Fire and Cloud." **3.** 382.
"Kabnis." **3 ed.** 739–40; **1.** 208; **2.** 279; **3.** 382; **5.** 323.
"Karintha." **3 ed.** 740; **1.** 208; **3.** 382; **5.** 323–24.
"Love on a Train." **3 ed.** 740.
"Mr. Costyve Duditch." **3 ed.** 740; **2.** 279; **3.** 382.
"Monrovia." **2.** 279.
"Theater." **3 ed.** 740; **1.** 208; **2.** 279; **3.** 382; **5.** 324.
"Winter on Earth." **3 ed.** 740; **2.** 279.
"York Beach." **4.** 278.

GONZALO TORRENTE BALLESTER

"The Bastard Farruco." **3.** 383.
"The Inn of the Amiable Deities." **3.** 383.
"The Tale of the Siren." **3.** 383.

JAIME TORRES BODET

"Venus Rising from the Sea." **3.** 383.

MICHEL TOURNIER

"L'Aire du Muguet." **4.** 278.
"Le Coq de bruyère." **4.** 278; **5.** 324.
"La Famille Adam." **5.** 324.
"La Fugue du Poucet." **4.** 278.
"La Jeune Fille et la mort." **5.** 324.
"La Mère Noël." **4.** 278.
"La Reine blonde." **5.** 324.
"Tristan Vox." **4.** 278.

CATHERINE WEBB TOWLES

"The Orphan's Miniature." **4.** 278.

CATHERINE PARR TRAILL

"The Settlers Settled; or, Pat Connor and His Two Masters." **5.** 324.

BRUNO TRAVEN [RET MARUT?]

"Assembly Line." **2.** 279.
"Death Songs of Hyotamore of Kyoena." **5.** 324.
"Effective Medicine." **3 ed.** 740.
"Godfather Death." **3 ed.** 740.
"Khundar." **5.** 324.
"Macario." **3 ed.** 740.
"Midnight Call." **3 ed.** 740.
"The Night Visitor." **3 ed.** 741; **1.** 208; **3.** 383.

OWEN C. TRELEAVEN

"Poison Jim Chinaman." **2.** 280.

F. ORLIN TREMAINE

"The Escape." **3 ed.** 741.
"The Upper-Level Road." **3.** 383.

NELSON TREMAINE

"Vibratory." **3.** 383.

MICHEL TREMBLAY

"Gentle Warmth." **4.** 278.
"Lady Barbara's Last Outing." **4.** 278.
"The Thirteenth Wife of Baron Klugg." **4.** 278.

DALTON TREVISAN

"Train." **3.** 383.

WILLIAM TREVOR [TREVOR COX]

"Another Christmas." **3.** 383.
"Attracta." **3.** 384.
"Autumn Sunshine." **3.** 384.
"Beyond the Pale." **5.** 324.
"A Complicated Nature." **5.** 324.
"The Distant Past." **3.** 384.
"An Evening with John Joe Dempsey." **4.** 278.
"The Paradise Lounge." **4.** 278.
"The Raising of Elvira Tremlett." **3.** 384.
"Saints." **3.** 384.
"Teresa's Wedding." **4.** 279.

IURII TRIFONOV

"Another Life." **3.** 384.
"The Exchange." **3.** 384.
"The House on the Embankment." **2.** 280; **4.** 279.
"The Long Goodbye." **2.** 280.
"Preliminary Results." **2.** 280.

LIONEL TRILLING

"Impediments." **5.** 325.
"The Lesson and the Secret." **5.** 325.
"Notes on Departure." **5.** 325.
"Of This Time, Of That Place." **3 ed.** 741; **1.** 208; **3.** 384; **5.** 325.
"The Other Margaret." **3 ed.** 741; **5.** 325.

ANTHONY TROLLOPE

"Aaron Trow." **1.** 208.
"Malachi's Cove." **1.** 208.
"Mrs. General Talboys." **3.** 384.
"The Panjandrum." **4.** 279.
"The Spotted Dog." **1.** 209; **4.** 279.

HENRI TROYAT

"La Clef de voûte." **3.** 384.
"Erratum." **3.** 384.
"The Guinea-Pig." **3.** 384.
"The Judgment of God." **3.** 385.
"The Lady in Black." **3.** 385.
"The Marvellous Journey of Jacques Mazeyrat." **3.** 385.
"Mr. Breadborough." **3.** 385.

"Monsieur Citrine." **3.** 385.
"The Murderer." **3.** 385.
"The Portrait." **3.** 385.
"Le Puy Saint-Clair." **3.** 385.
"Le Ratuset." **3.** 385.
"The Son of Heaven." **3.** 385.
"The Tandem." **3.** 385.
"The Undertow." **3.** 385.
"Vertigo." **3.** 385.

CARLOS ARTURO TRUQUE

"Because People Were This Way." **5.** 325.
"Blood on the Plains." **5.** 325.
"The Dark Sunglasses." **5.** 325.
"The Day Summer Ended." **5.** 325.
"Death Had a Face and Seal." **5.** 325.
"The Encounter." **5.** 325.
"Flight." **5.** 325.
"Fucú." **5.** 325.
"Hailstorm." **5.** 325.
"Martin Finds Two Reasons." **5.** 325.
"The Mystery." **5.** 326.
"The Night of San Silvestre." **5.** 326.
"Reveille." **5.** 326.
"The Sadness of Living This Way." **5.** 326.
"Sonata for Two Dreams." **5.** 326.

KONSTANTIN TSIOLKOVSKY

"Island of Ether." **3.** 385.

TSUBOUCHI SHŌVŌ

"The New Year Season." **5.** 326.
"The Wife." **3.** 385; **5.** 326.

TSUCHIMA YŪKO

"A Bed of Grass." **5.** 326.

TSUMURA SETSUKO

"Luminous Watch." **5.** 326.

KURT TUCHOLSKY

"Die Laternenanzünder." **3 ed.** 741.

FRANZ TUMLER

"The Coat." **1.** 209.

FRANK TUOHY

"The Admiral and the Nuns." **4.** 279.
"Two Private Lives." **4.** 279.

IVAN SERGEEVICH TURGENEV

"Asya." **3.** 386; **5.** 326.
"Bezhin Meadow" [same as "Bezhin Prairie"]. **3 ed.** 742; **1.** 209; **3.** 386.
"Biryuk." **3 ed.** 742.
"The Brigadier." **3 ed.** 742; **1.** 209; **4.** 279.
"A Correspondence." **3 ed.** 742.
"The Country Doctor" [same as "The District Doctor"]. **3 ed.** 742; **2.** 280.
"Death." **3.** 386.
"The Diary of a Superfluous Man." **3 ed.** 742; **3.** 386.
"Faust." **4.** 279.
"First Love." **3 ed.** 742; **1.** 209; **3.** 386; **5.** 326.
"The History of Lieutenant Ergunov" [same as "The Story of . . ."]. **3 ed.** 742; **1.** 209.
"Khor and Kalinitch" [same as "Kor and Kalinch"]. **3 ed.** 742; **3.** 386.
"Klara Milich." **3.** 386.
"A Lear of the Steppes" [same as "King Lear . . ."]. **3 ed.** 742; **1.** 209; **3.** 386.
"Living Relics." **3.** 386; **5.** 326.
"Mumu." **5.** 327.
"Old Portraits." **3 ed.** 742.
"Punin and Baburin." **3 ed.** 742.
"The Singers." **3 ed.** 742; **1.** 209.
"The Song of Triumphant Love." **3.** 386.
"Spring Torrents." **3 ed.** 743.
"Three Meetings." **3 ed.** 743.
"A Tour of the Forest." **3 ed.** 743.
"The Tryst." **2.** 280; **3.** 386; **4.** 279.
"The Unfortunate Girl." **4.** 279.
"The Watch." **3 ed.** 743.
"Yermolai and the Miller's Wife." **3 ed.** 743; **1.** 209; **3.** 386.

HENRY GILES TURNER

"The Confessions of a Loafer." **4.** 279.

ESTHER TUSQUETS

"La casa oscura." **5.** 327.
"En la ciudad sin mar." **5.** 327.
"Exiliados." **5.** 327.
"Giselle." **5.** 327.
"He besado tu boca, Yokanaán." **5.** 327.
"Orquesta de verano." **5.** 327.
"Los primos." **5.** 327.

LISA TUTTLE

"The Hollow Man." **5.** 327.
"The Horse Lord." **5.** 327.
"Wives." **5.** 327.

AMOS TUTUOLA

"The Complete Gentleman." **3 ed.** 743.
"The Wild Hunter in the Bush of the Ghosts." **3.** 386.

MARK TWAIN [SAMUEL L. CLEMENS]

"Baker's Blue-Jay Yarn." **3 ed.** 743; **1.** 209; **3.** 387; **5.** 328.
"The Belated Russian Passport." **5.** 328.
"Buck Fanshaw's Funeral." **5.** 328.
"The Burning Brand." **5.** 328.
"The California Tale." **5.** 328.
"Cannibalism in the Cars." **5.** 328.
"The Canvasser's Tale." **5.** 328.
"Captain Stormfield's Visit to Heaven." **3 ed.** 743; **1.** 209; **2.** 280; **3.** 387; **5.** 328.
"Cecil Rhodes and the Shark." **5.** 328.
"The Celebrated Jumping Frog of Calaveras County" [same as "The Notorious Jumping Frog . . . "]. **3 ed.** 743–44; **1.** 210; **2.** 280; **3.** 387; **4.** 280; **5.** 328.
"A Curious Dream." **5.** 328.
"A Curious Experience." **5.** 328.
"The Dandy Frightening the Squatter." **3 ed.** 744.
"A Day at Niagara." **5.** 328.
"The Death Disk." **5.** 328.
"A Dog's Tale." **5.** 328.
"A Double-Barrelled Detective Story." **3 ed.** 744; **5.** 328.
"A Dying Man's Confession." **5.** 329.
"Edward Mills and George Benton: A Tale." **5.** 329.
"The Esquimau Maiden's Romance." **5.** 329.
"Extracts from Adam's Diary." **5.** 329.
"A Fable." **1.** 209; **5.** 329.
"Facts Concerning the Recent Carnival of Crime in Connecticut." **2.** 281; **3.** 387; **4.** 280; **5.** 329.
"Facts in the Great Beef Contract." **5.** 329.
"Facts in the Great Landslide Case." **5.** 329.
"The Five Boons of Life." **5.** 329.
"A Ghost Story." **5.** 329.
"The Golden Arm." **4.** 280.
"Grandfather's Ram." **2.** 281.
"The Great Dark." **3 ed.** 744; **2.** 281; **3.** 387; **4.** 280; **5.** 329.
"The Holy Children." **3.** 387.
"A Horse's Tale." **5.** 329.
"How I Edited an Agricultural Paper Once." **5.** 329.
"The International Lightning Trust." **5.** 329.
"The Invalid's Story." **3 ed.** 744; **5.** 329.
"Is He Living or Is He Dead?" **5.** 329.
"The Joke That Made Ed's Fortune." **5.** 329.
"Journalism in Tennessee." **5.** 330.
"The Legend of Dilsberg Castle." **5.** 330.
"The Legend of the Capitoline Venus." **5.** 330.
"Luck." **5.** 330.
"The McWilliamses and the Burglar Alarm." **5.** 330.
"The Man That Corrupted Hadleyburg." **3 ed.** 744–45; **1.** 209–10; **2.** 281; **3.** 387; **5.** 330.
"Mrs. McWilliams and the Lightning." **5.** 330.
"A Murder, a Mystery, and a Marriage." **3.** 387.
"The Mysterious Stranger." **3 ed.** 745–46; **1.** 210; **2.** 281; **3.** 387; **4.** 280; **5.** 330.
"The £1,000,000 Bank Note." **2.** 281; **5.** 330.
"Political Economy." **5.** 330.
"Randall's Jew Story." **5.** 330.
"The Second Advent." **5.** 330.
"Some Learned Fables for Good Old Boys and Girls." **5.** 330.
"The Stolen White Elephant." **4.** 280; **5.** 330.
"The Story of the Good Little Boy." **3 ed.** 746.
"The Story of the Old Ram." **3 ed.** 746.
"A Story Without an End." **3.** 387; **5.** 330.
"The $30,000 Bequest." **2.** 281–82; **3.** 388; **5.** 330.
"Three Thousand Years Among the Microbes." **5.** 331.
"A True Story, Repeated Word for Word as I Heard It." **1.** 210; **2.** 282; **4.** 280; **5.** 331.
"Two Little Tales." **5.** 331.

UCHIDA ROAN

"Broken Fence." **3.** 388.

UEDA AKINARI

"The Bloodstained Robe." **3.** 388.
"The Cauldron of Kibitsu." **3.** 388.
"The Celestial Maidens." **3.** 388.
"The Chrysanthemum Pledge." **3.** 388.
"The Destiny That Spanned Two Lifetimes." **3.** 388.
"The Grave of Miyagi." **3.** 388.
"Hankai." **3.** 388.
"The Lust of the White Serpent." **3.** 388.
"The One-Eyed God." **3.** 388.
"The Pirate." **3.** 388.
"The Smiling Death's-Head." **3.** 388.

BECHAN SARMA UGRA

"Ganga Gandatta and Gangi." **3.** 388.

SABINE ULLIBARÍ

"Brujerías o tonterías." **4.** 280.
"Mi abuela fumaba puros." **4.** 280.
"My Magic Horse." **4.** 280.
"Sábelo." **4.** 280.

MIGUEL DE UNAMUNO

"El abejorro—." **3 ed.** 746.
"Abel Sánchez." **3 ed.** 746–47; **1.** 210; **2.** 282; **4.** 280; **5.** 331.
"Artemio, heautontimoroumenos." **3 ed.** 747.
"As the Years Go By." **3 ed.** 747.
"Aunt Tula." **3 ed.** 747; **1.** 210; **2.** 282; **4.** 281; **5.** 331.
"La Beca." **3 ed.** 747.
"Bonifacio." **3 ed.** 747.
"El canto de la aguas eternas." **3 ed.** 747.
"Caridad bien ordenada." **3 ed.** 747.
"Un caso de longevidad." **3 ed.** 747.
"Children of the Mind." **3 ed.** 747.
"El dioa Pavor." **3 ed.** 747.
"Don Bernardino y Dona Etelvina." **3 ed.** 747.
"Don Catalino, hombre sabio." **3 ed.** 747.
"Don Martín, o de la gloria." **3 ed.** 747.
"Don Sivestre Carrasco, hombre efectivo." **3 ed.** 748.
"En manos de una cocinera." **3 ed.** 748.
"Juan Manso, cuento de muertos." **3 ed.** 748.
"El lego Juan." **3 ed.** 748.
"La locura del doctor Montarco." **3 ed.** 748.
"The Man Who Buried Himself." **3 ed.** 748; **2.** 282.
"La manchita de la uña." **3 ed.** 748.
"The Marquis of Lumbria." **3 ed.** 748.
"El misterio de la iniquidad." **3 ed.** 748.
"Nothing Less Than a Man." **3 ed.** 748; **5.** 331.
"El padrino Antonio." **3 ed.** 748.
"El poema vivo de amor." **3 ed.** 748.
"Robleda, el actor." **3 ed.** 748.
"Saint Manuel the Good, Martyr." **3 ed.** 748–49; **1.** 210; **2.** 282; **3.** 389; **4.** 281; **5.** 331.
"El semejante." **3 ed.** 749.
"El sencillo Don Rafael." **3 ed.** 749.
"Soledad." **3 ed.** 749.
"Solitaña." **3 ed.** 749.
"Two Mothers." **3 ed.** 749.
"La venda." **3 ed.** 749.
"Ver con los ojos." **3 ed.** 749.
"Una visita al viejo poeta." **3 ed.** 749.

FRIEDRICH FRANZ VON UNRUH

"Die jüngste Nacht." **3 ed.** 749.

JOHN UPDIKE

"A & P." **3 ed.** 749–50; **1.** 210; **2.** 283; **3.** 389; **4.** 281; **5.** 331.
"Ace in the Hole." **3 ed.** 750; **2.** 283; **3.** 389; **4.** 281.
"The Archangel." **3 ed.** 750.
"The Astronomer." **3 ed.** 750; **1.** 210; **2.** 283; **3.** 389.
"At a Bar in Charlotte Amalie." **3.** 389.
"Australia and Canada." **3.** 389.
"Avec la Bébé-sitter." **3.** 389.
"Bech in Rumania." **3.** 389.
"Bech Panics." **3.** 389.
"Bech Third-Worlds It." **3.** 389.
"Bech Wed." **3.** 389.
"The Blessed Man of Boston, My Grandmother's Thimble, Fanning Island." **3 ed.** 750; **3.** 389; **5.** 331.
"The Bulgarian Poetess." **3 ed.** 750; **2.** 283; **3.** 390.

"The Christian Roommates." **2.** 283; **3.** 390.
"Churchgoing." **3 ed.** 750.
"Couples." **3.** 390.
"The Crow in the Woods." **3 ed.** 750; **3.** 390.
"The Dark." **3 ed.** 750.
"The Day of the Dying Rabbit." **3 ed.** 750; **2.** 283; **3.** 390.
"Dear Alexandros." **3 ed.** 750; **3.** 390.
"Dentistry and Doubt." **3 ed.** 750; **3.** 390.
"The Doctor's Wife." **3 ed.** 750; **1.** 210.
"Domestic Life in America." **4.** 281.
"A Dying Cat." **3 ed.** 750.
"Eros Rampant." **3 ed.** 751.
"The Faint." **3.** 390.
"The Family Meadow." **3 ed.** 751; **2.** 283.
"Flight." **3 ed.** 751; **1.** 211; **2.** 283; **3.** 390; **5.** 331.
"Football Season." **5.** 332.
"Four Sides of One Story." **1.** 211; **2.** 283; **3.** 390.
"Friends from Philadelphia." **3 ed.** 751; **3.** 390.
"A Gift from the City." **3 ed.** 751; **3.** 390.
"Giving Blood." **3 ed.** 751; **3.** 390; **5.** 332.
"The Happiest I've Been." **3 ed.** 751; **2.** 283; **3.** 390; **5.** 332.
"Harv Is Plowing Now." **3 ed.** 751; **3.** 390.
"Here Come the Maples." **2.** 283; **3.** 391; **5.** 332.
"The Hermit." **3 ed.** 751; **3.** 391.
"The Hillies." **3.** 391.
"His Finest Hour." **3 ed.** 751; **3.** 391.
"Home." **3 ed.** 751; **3.** 391.
"I Am Dying, Egypt, Dying." **3.** 391.
"I Will Not Let Thee Go, Except Thou Bless Me." **3.** 391.
"In Football Season." **3 ed.** 751; **3.** 391.
"Incest." **3.** 391.
"The Indian." **3.** 391.
"The Kid's Whistling." **3.** 391.
"Leaves." **3 ed.** 751; **2.** 283; **3.** 391.
"Lifeguard." **3 ed.** 752; **3.** 391.
"A Madman." **3.** 392.
"Marching Through Boston." **3 ed.** 752; **3.** 392.
"The Morning." **3 ed.** 752; **3.** 392.
"Museums and Women." **3 ed.** 752; **2.** 284; **3.** 392.
"The Music School." **3 ed.** 752; **2.** 284; **3.** 392; **4.** 281.
"My Lover Has Dirty Fingernails." **3 ed.** 752; **3.** 392.
"On the Way to School." **3 ed.** 752.
"The Orphaned Swimming Pool." **3.** 392.
"The Other." **5.** 332.
"Other Modes." **3.** 392.
"Packed Dirt, Churchgoing, A Dying Cat, A Traded Car." **3 ed.** 752; **2.** 284; **3.** 392; **4.** 281; **5.** 332.
"The Persistence of Desire." **3 ed.** 752; **2.** 284; **3.** 392; **5.** 332.
"The Peruvian in the Heart of Lake Winnipesaukee." **3 ed.** 752.
"Pigeon Feathers." **3 ed.** 752; **1.** 211; **2.** 284; **3.** 392; **4.** 282; **5.** 332.
"Plumbing." **3.** 392.
"The Pro." **3.** 392.
"The Rescue." **3 ed.** 753; **3.** 392.
"The Sea's Green Sameness." **3 ed.** 753; **3.** 392.
"A Sense of Shelter." **3 ed.** 753; **2.** 284; **3.** 393.
"Should Wizard Hit Mommy?" **3 ed.** 753; **3.** 393.
"The Slump." **3.** 393.
"Snowing in Greenwich Village." **3 ed.** 753; **2.** 284; **3.** 393; **5.** 332.
"Solitaire." **3.** 393.
"Son." **5.** 332.
"Spring Comes to Cambridge." **3 ed.** 753.
"The Stare." **3.** 393.
"Still Life." **3 ed.** 753; **3.** 393.
"Sublimation." **3.** 393.
"Sunday Teasing." **3.** 393.
"The Sunshine Poet." **3 ed.** 753.
"The Taste of Metal." **3 ed.** 753; **3.** 393.
"Tomorrow and Tomorrow and So Forth." **3 ed.** 753; **1.** 211; **2.** 284; **3.** 393.
"Toward Evening." **3 ed.** 753–54; **4.** 282.
"Twin Beds in Rome." **3 ed.** 754; **3.** 393.
"Walter Briggs." **3 ed.** 754; **3.** 393.
"When Everyone Was Pregnant." **3 ed.** 754; **3.** 393.
"Who Made Yellow Roses Yellow?" **3 ed.** 754; **2.** 284; **3.** 394.
"Wife-Wooing." **3 ed.** 754; **2.** 284; **3.** 394; **4.** 282.
"The Witnesses." **3 ed.** 754; **3.** 394.
"You'll Never Know, Dear, How Much I Love You." **3 ed.** 754; **5.** 332.
"Your Lover Just Called." **3 ed.** 754.

EDWARD UPWARD

"The Railway Accident." **1.** 211.
"Sunday." **3 ed.** 754.

VICTORIA URBANO

"Avery Island." **5.** 332.

PEDRO HENRÍQUEZ UREÑA

"En Jauja." **4.** 282.

FRED URQUHART

"Alicky's Watch." **4.** 282.
"Maggie Logie and the National Health." **4.** 282.
"Once a Schoolmissy." **4.** 282.

ARTURO USLAR PIETRI

"The Jack-o'-Lantern." **4.** 282; **5.** 333.
"Rain." **3.** 394; **5.** 333.

GLEB USPENSKY

"The Blind Singer." **5.** 333.
"Coachman with a Device." **3.** 394.
"He Got Angry!" **3.** 394.
"Incubator Chick." **3.** 394.
"The Intelligentsia of the People." **4.** 282.
"Paramon the Holy Fool." **5.** 333.
"Rodion the Concerned." **5.** 333.
"A Sensitive Heart." **5.** 333.
"Sentry Box." **3.** 394.
"Something Went to His Head." **3.** 394.

BORIS BORISOVICH VAKHTIN

"The Sheepskin Coat." **5.** 333.

ABRAHAM VALDELOMAR

"El caballero Carmelo." **3 ed.** 754.
"El vuelo de cóndores." **3 ed.** 754.

GINA VALDÉS

"This Is a Story." **4.** 282.

GUADALUPE VALDÉS-FALLIS

"Recuerdo." **2.** 284.

LUISA VALENZUELA

"Change of Guard." **5.** 333.
"He Who Searches." **4.** 283.
"Neither the Most Terrifying Nor the Least Memorable." **4.** 283.
"Other Weapons." **4.** 283.
"Rituals of Rejection." **4.** 283.
"Unlimited Rapes United, Argentina." **4.** 283.
"The Verb to Kill." **4.** 283; **5.** 333.
"Where the Eagles Dwell." **4.** 283.

JUAN VALERA

"The Double Sacrifice." **3 ed.** 754.
"The Elf-Kiss." **3 ed.** 754.
"Garuda or the White Stork." **3 ed.** 755.
"Good Reputation." **3 ed.** 755.
"The Green Bird." **3 ed.** 755.
"The Knight of the Falcon." **3 ed.** 755.
"Let Him Who Does Not Know You Buy You." **3 ed.** 755.
"The Little Doll." **3 ed.** 755.
"The Magician." **3 ed.** 755.
"Morsanor." **3 ed.** 755.
"Parsondes." **3 ed.** 755.
"The Prehistoric *Bermejino* or the Blue Salamander." **3 ed.** 755.
"The Prisoner of Doña Mencia." **3 ed.** 755.

RIMA VALLBONA

"Chumico Tree." **5.** 333.
"Parable of the Impossible Eden." **5.** 334.
"Penelope." **5.** 334.

RAMÓN DEL VALLE-INCLÁN

"Beatriz." **3 ed.** 755.
"Eulalia." **4.** 283; **5.** 334.
"La generala." **5.** 334.
"Rosarito." **3 ed.** 755; **5.** 334.

JACK VANCE [JOHN HOLBROOK VANCE]

"Abercrombie Station." **3.** 394.
"Cholwell's Chickens." **3.** 394.
"Coup de Grâce." **3.** 394.
"Dodkin's Job." **3.** 395.
"The Five Gold Bands." **3.** 395.
"Guyal of Sfere." **3.** 395; **4.** 283.
"Hard-Luck Diggings." **3.** 395.

"The House of Iszm." **3.** 395.
"The Howling Bounders." **3.** 395.
"I'll Build Your Dream Castle." **3.** 395.
"The King of Thieves." **3.** 395.
"Liane the Wayfarer." **3.** 395; **4.** 283.
"The Men Return." **3.** 395.
"The Miracle Workers." **3.** 395.
"The Moon Moth." **3.** 395; **5.** 334.
"New Bodies for Old." **3.** 395.
"Parapsyche." **3.** 395.
"Phalid's Fate." **3.** 395.
"Planet of the Black Dust." **3.** 395.
"The Potter of Firsk." **3.** 396.
"Sanatoris Short-Cut." **3.** 396.
"Son of the Tree." **3.** 396.
"The Substandard Sardines." **3.** 396.
"T'sais." **3.** 396.
"Ulan Dhor Ends a Dream." **3.** 396.
"Ullward's Retreat." **3.** 396.
"Ultimate Quest." **3.** 396.
"The Unspeakable McInch." **3.** 396.
"The World-Thinker." **3.** 396.

C. M. VAN DEN HEEVER

"Daiel's Farewell." **5.** 334.

GUY VANDERHAEGHE

"Going to Russia." **5.** 334.

MONA VAN DUYN

"The Bell." **3 ed.** 755.

CHARLES E. VAN LOAN

"Easy Picking." **3.** 396.
"Excess Baggage." **3.** 396.

SYDNEY J[OYCE] VAN SCYOC

"When Petals Fall." **3.** 396.

A. E. VAN VOGT

"Black Destroyer." **1.** 211; **3.** 397; **5.** 334.
"Discord in Scarlet." **3.** 397.
"Fulfillment." **3 ed.** 756.
"Resurrection." **3.** 397.
"The Rulers." **3.** 397.
"Vault of the Beast." **3.** 397.
"The World of Null-A." **5.** 335.

MARIO VARGAS LLOSA

"The Challenge." **4.** 284.
"The Cubs." **3.** 397; **4.** 284; **5.** 335.
"The Grandfather." **4.** 284.
"The Leaders." **4.** 284.
"On Sunday." **4.** 284.
"A Visitor." **4.** 284.
"The Younger Brother." **4.** 284.

ELEODORO VARGAS VICUÑA

"Taita Cristo." **2.** 285.

JOHN VARLEY

"The Persistence of Vision." **3.** 397.
"The Phantom of Kansas." **3.** 397.

NIRMAL VARMA

"The Burning Bush." **2.** 285.

JOSÉ VASCONCELOS

"The Boar Hunt." **3 ed.** 756.

M. G. VASSANJI

"Waiting for the Goddess." **4.** 284.

ANA LYDIA VEGA

"Pollito chicken." **3.** 397; **4.** 284.
"Salsa Rhymes and Three Short-Order Tunes." **3.** 397; **5.** 335.

FRANCISCO VEGAS SEMINARIO

"El primogénito de los Godos." **3 ed.** 756.

JOSÉ J. VEIGA

"The Misplaced Machine." **3.** 398.

ALEXANDER VELTMAN

"Erotica." **3.** 398; **4.** 284.

ELIAS VENEZIS [E. MELLOS]

"Akif." **3 ed.** 756.
"The Bandit Pancho Villa." **3 ed.** 756.
"The Broken Branch." **3 ed.** 756.
"The Caique of the Theseion." **3 ed.** 756.
"Death." **3 ed.** 756.
"The Final Hour." **3 ed.** 756.

"A Finn in Algiers." **3 ed.** 756.
"The Home of the Lost Angels." **3 ed.** 756.
"The Immigrant of Grand Canyon." **3 ed.** 756.
"The Knight of Bataan and the Verses." **3 ed.** 756.
"Lios." **3 ed.** 756.
"Moment on the Saroniko." **3 ed.** 757.
"Mycenae." **3 ed.** 757.
"Night of Asklepios." **3 ed.** 757.
"No Passage." **3 ed.** 757.
"The Old Woman of Lamia." **3 ed.** 757.
"On the Kimindeia." **3 ed.** 757.
"The Roar." **3 ed.** 757.
"The Seagulls." **3 ed.** 757.
"The State of Virginia." **3 ed.** 757.
"Tale of the Aegean." **3 ed.** 757.
"Theonichos and Mnisarete." **3 ed.** 757.
"Tourkolimano." **3 ed.** 757.
"The Two Women and the Tower." **3 ed.** 757.

CÉSAR VERDUGUES

"Hay un grito en tu silencio." **4.** 284.

GIOVANNI VERGA

"Black Bread." **1.** 211; **3.** 398.
"The Canary of No. 15." **1.** 211.
"Cavalleria rusticana." **1.** 211.
"Consolation." **3 ed.** 757.
"Cos'è il re." **3.** 398.
"Freedom" [same as "Liberty"]. **3 ed.** 758; **1.** 211; **3.** 398.
"The Ghosts of Trazza Castle." **1.** 211.
"Gramigna's Lover." **1.** 211; **2.** 285.
"The How, the When and the Wherefore." **1.** 211.
"Ieli the Shepherd." **1.** 212.
"Images." **1.** 212.
"In Piazza della Scala." **3 ed.** 757.
"The Last Day." **3 ed.** 757.
"Liberty" [same as "Freedom"]. **3 ed.** 758; **1.** 211; **3.** 398.
"Malaria." **1.** 212; **3.** 398.
"The Mystery." **3.** 398.
"Nanni Volpe." **1.** 212.
"Nedda." **1.** 212.
"The Orphans." **3.** 398.
"Property." **1.** 212.
"Rosso Malpelo." **1.** 212; **4.** 285.
"The She-Wolf." **1.** 212; **2.** 285; **3.** 398.
"A Simple Tale." **1.** 212.
"Stinkpot." **1.** 212.
"The Story of St. Joseph's Donkey." **1.** 212; **3.** 398.
"Temptation." **3 ed.** 758.
"Via Crucis." **3 ed.** 758.
"The Wolf Hunt." **1.** 212.

JULES VERNE

"The Eternal Adam." **3.** 399.

TARJEI VESAAS

"The Adventure." **3 ed.** 758.
"Blue Button Lost." **3 ed.** 758.
"Bread." **3 ed.** 758.
"A Daring Ant." **3 ed.** 758.
"The Gingerbread Man." **3 ed.** 758.
"Grain Across the Sea." **3 ed.** 758.
"The Half-wit" [originally "The Stunted Spruce"]. **3 ed.** 758.
"The Horse from Hogget." **3 ed.** 758.
"In the Fish's Golden Youth." **3 ed.** 758.
"Last Man Home." **3 ed.** 758.
"The Little Tyke." **3 ed.** 758.
"Mist Rain." **3 ed.** 758.
"Naked." **3 ed.** 758.
"Signe Tone." **3 ed.** 758.
"Snow." **3 ed.** 759.
"Three Quiet Men." **3 ed.** 759.
"Twenty-One." **3 ed.** 759.
"The Vision." **3 ed.** 759.

ENDRE VÉSZI

"Chapter from the Life of Vera Angi." **5.** 335.

BORIS VIAN

"Les Fourmis." **3 ed.** 759; **1.** 212.
"Le Rappel." **3 ed.** 759; **1.** 212.

JAVIER DE VIANA

"Andean Legend." **3.** 399.
"Bitter Triumph." **3.** 399.
"Black Abdón's Raffle." **3.** 399.

"The Black Man's Way of Doing Things." **3.** 399.
"Brothers." **3.** 399.
"Chaqueña." **3.** 399.
"The Consumptive." **3.** 399.
"Contradiction." **3.** 399.
"The Crow's Nest." **3.** 399.
"The Cure." **3.** 399.
"Do You Understand?" **3.** 399.
"Don Liborio's Tale." **3.** 399.
"Doña Melitona." **3.** 399.
"The Duty to Live." **3.** 399.
"End of a Dream." **3.** 400.
"Facundo Imperial." **3.** 400.
"The Farmhands." **3.** 400.
"The Gaucho's Bible." **3.** 400.
"The Girl from the Chaco." **3.** 400.
"Give Me Time, Brother!" **3.** 400.
"The Glory of Work." **3.** 400.
"The God Tree." **3.** 400.
"Golden Vision." **3.** 400.
"The Grandmother." **3.** 400.
"The Guaraní from Corrientes." **3.** 400.
"Having Made It." **3.** 400.
"How and Why God Created the República Oriental." **3.** 400.
"In the Family." **3.** 400.
"In Time of War." **3.** 400.
"Juan Pedro." **3.** 400.
"Just Because I Forgot" [same as "It Was Just a Slip"]. **3.** 400.
"Just for Killing the Bird." **3.** 401.
"The Land Is Small." **3.** 401.
"The Last Campaign." **3.** 401.
"Leopoldo Almeida." **2.** 285; **3.** 401.
"Like Real Folks." **3.** 401.
"Like the Good Old Times." **3.** 401.
"The Loves of Bentos Sagrera." **3.** 401; **5.** 335.
"The Making of a Caudillo." **3.** 401.
"Manduca's Place." **3.** 401.
"The Pair from Urubolí." **3.** 401.
"Pals and Godfathers." **3.** 401.
"Persecution." **3.** 401.
"Playing Wolf." **3.** 401.
"The Rascal Ant." **3.** 401.
"The Recalcitrant Dead Man." **3.** 401.
"The Return to the Village." **3.** 401.
"Rounding-Up Calves." **3.** 401.
"The Rustic." **3.** 402; **5.** 335.
"The Shame of the Family." **3.** 402.
"A Static Life." **3.** 402.
"The Storm." **3.** 402.
"The Thistle." **3.** 402.
"Through the Land of Arachanes." **3.** 402.
"A Tie." **3.** 402.
"Tiger vs. Tiger." **3.** 402.
"The Useless Ones." **3.** 402.
"A Useless Trip." **3.** 402.
"Yellow Field." **3.** 402.

GORE VIDAL

"Erlinda and Mrs. Coffin." **3 ed.** 759.
"The Ladies in the Library." **3 ed.** 759; **3.** 402.
"A Moment of Green Laurel." **3 ed.** 759; **3.** 402.
"Pages from an Abandoned Journal." **3 ed.** 759.
"The Robin." **3 ed.** 759.
"Three Stratagems." **3.** 402.
"The Zenner Trophy." **3 ed.** 759.

LUANDINGO VIEIRA

"Grandmother Xixi and Her Grandson Zeca Santos." **2.** 285.
"The Story of the Chicken and the Egg." **2.** 285.
"The Thief and the Parrot." **2.** 285.

ALFRED DE VIGNY

"La Canne de jonc." **3 ed.** 759.
"Laurette." **3 ed.** 759.
"La Veillée de Vincennes." **3 ed.** 760.

VICKI VIIDIKAS

"The Silk Trousers." **4.** 285.

BJØRG VIK

"They Come in Small Groups." **1.** 212.

[COUNT] VILLIERS DE L'ISLE-ADAM [JEAN MARIE MATTHIAS PHILIPPE AUGUSTE]

"A s'y méprendre." **3 ed.** 760.
"Les Demoiselles de Bienfilâtre." **5.** 335.
"The Desire to Be a Man." **2.** 286.
"L'Intersigne." **5.** 335.
"Sombre récit, conteur plus sombre." **5.** 335.

"A Tale of Love." **2.** 286.
"Véra." **2.** 286; **3.** 403.

HARL VINCENT

"Rex." **3.** 403.

JOAN D. VINGE

"The Crystal Ship." **3.** 403; **4.** 285.
"Exorcycle." **4.** 285.
"Eyes of Amber." **3.** 403; **4.** 285; **5.** 336.
"The Hunt of the Unicorn." **4.** 285.
"Legacy." **3.** 403; **4.** 285.
"Mother and Child." **3.** 403; **4.** 285.
"Phoenix in the Ashes." **3.** 403; **4.** 285.
"Psiren." **4.** 285.
"The Storm King." **4.** 285.
"Tin Soldier." **4.** 285; **5.** 336.
"To Bell the Cat." **4.** 285.
"View from the Height." **4.** 285.
"Voices from the Dust." **4.** 286.

JOAN D. VINGE and VERNON VINGE

"The Peddler's Apprentice." **4.** 286.

HELENA MARÍA VIRAMONTES

"Growing." **5.** 336.
"Snapshots." **5.** 336.

KULWANT SINGH VIRK

"The Bull Beneath the Earth." **3 ed.** 760.

ELIO VITTORINI

"Erica e i suoi fratelli." **2.** 286.
"La Garibaldina" [originally "Il soldato e la garibaldina"]. **2.** 286.
"Giochi di ragazzi." **2.** 286.
"The Lady of the Station." **3 ed.** 760.
"My War." **3 ed.** 760.
"Portrait of King Giampiero." **2.** 286.

JOSÉ LUIS VIVAS MALDONADO

"El de los cabos blancos." **5.** 336.
"El héroe." **5.** 336.
"Interludio." **5.** 336.

RENÉE VIVIEN [PAULINE MARY TARN]

"The Crocodile Lady." **5.** 336.
"The Death of Psappha." **5.** 336.
"Mute Siren." **5.** 336.
"The Nut-Brown Maid." **5.** 336.
"Prince Charming." **5.** 336.
"The Veil of Vashti." **5.** 337.
"White as Foam." **5.** 337.
"The Woman of the West." **5.** 337.

GERALD VIZENOS

"Episode in Mystic Verism from Monsignor Missalwait's Interstate." **5.** 337.
"Marleen American Horse." **5.** 337.

GEORGE VIZYINÒS

"The Consequences of an Old Story." **5.** 337.
"Moskóv-Selím." **5.** 337.
"My Mother." **3 ed.** 760.
"The Only Journey of His Life." **5.** 337.

GEORGIĬ NIKOLAEVICH VLADIMOV

"Pay No Attention, Maestro." **5.** 337.

VLADIMIR VOINOVICH

"I Want to Be Honest." **3.** 403.
"Two Comrades." **2.** 286.
"We Live Here." **2.** 286; **3.** 403.

ILIYA VOLEN

"Groundka." **3 ed.** 760.

KURT VONNEGUT

"All the King's Horses." **1.** 213.
"The Ambitious Sophomore." **1.** 213.
"Deer in the Works." **5.** 337.
"EPICAC." **3 ed.** 760; **1.** 213; **5.** 337.
"The Euphio Question." **5.** 338.
"The Foster Portfolio." **1.** 213; **3.** 403.
"Harrison Bergeron." **2.** 286; **3.** 403; **5.** 338.
"The Hyannis Port Story." **3.** 404.
"The Manned Missiles." **1.** 213; **5.** 338.
"Next Door." **1.** 213; **2.** 286.
"The Powder Blue Dragon." **1.** 213.

"Report on the Barnhouse Effect." **1.** 213; **5.** 338.
"Runaways." **1.** 213.
"Tomorrow and Tomorrow and Tomorrow." **1.** 213; **3.** 404; **5.** 338.
"Unready to Wear." **1.** 213; **3.** 404.
"Welcome to the Monkey House." **1.** 213; **5.** 338.
"Who Am I This Time?" [originally "My Name Is Everyone"]. **1.** 213; **3.** 404.

BEB VUYK

"The Last House in the World." **3.** 404.
"A Spectator's Story." **3.** 404.
"Villa Sonja." **3.** 404.

M. S. WADDELL

"The Pale Boy." **5.** 338.

OLIVE WADSWORTH

"Our Phil." **3.** 404.

KARL EDWARD WAGNER

"The River of Night's Dreaming." **4.** 286.
"220 Swift." **4.** 286.
"Where the Summer Ends." **4.** 286.

RICHARD WAGNER

"An End in Paris." **1.** 213.
"A Happy Evening." **1.** 214.
"A Pilgrimage to Beethoven." **1.** 214.

DAVID WAGONER

"The Spinning Ladies." **3 ed.** 761.

JOHN WAIN

"Master Richard." **2.** 287.
"A Message from the Pig-Man." **3 ed.** 761.
"Nuncle." **2.** 287.

H[ERBERT] RUSSELL WAKEFIELD

"Damp Sheets." **4.** 286.
"The First Sheaf." **4.** 286.
"The Gorge of the Churels." **4.** 286.
"He Cometh and He Passeth By!" **4.** 286.
"Jay Walkers." **4.** 286.
"The Red Lodge." **4.** 286.
"That Dieth Not." **4.** 286.
"The Triumph of Death." **4.** 286.

F. N. WALDROP and POUL ANDERSON

"Tomorrow's Children." **3.** 404.

ALICE WALKER

"The Abortion." **3.** 404.
"The Child Who Favored Daughter." **2.** 287; **3.** 404; **4.** 287.
"Elethia." **3.** 404.
"Everyday Use." **2.** 287; **3.** 405; **4.** 287; **5.** 338.
"Her Sweet Jerome." **2.** 287.
"Luna Advancing." **3.** 405; **4.** 287.
"1955." **4.** 287.
"Petunias." **3.** 405.
"Really, Doesn't Crime Pay?" **2.** 287; **4.** 287; **5.** 338.
"The Revenge of Hannah Kemhuff." **4.** 287.
"Roselily." **2.** 287; **4.** 287; **5.** 338.
"Strong Horse Tea." **2.** 287; **4.** 287.
"A Sudden Trip Home in the Spring." **4.** 287.
"To Hell with Dying." **2.** 287; **3.** 405; **4.** 287.
"The Welcome Table." **4.** 287; **5.** 338.

MERVYN WALL

"The Garden of Echoes." **4.** 287.

E. G. WALLACE

"Big Ancestor." **3 ed.** 761.

EDWARD LEWIS WALLANT

"The Days to Come." **2.** 287.
"Fathers." **2.** 287.
"Fight Night." **2.** 287.
"I Held Back My Hand." **2.** 287.
"Life Is a Fountain." **2.** 287.
"The Man Who Made a Nice Appearance." **2.** 288.
"Robert." **2.** 288.

HUGH WALPOLE

"The Clock." **3 ed.** 761.

ERIC D. WALROND

"The Black Pin." **3 ed.** 761.
"A Cholo Romance." **3 ed.** 761.
"City Love." **3 ed.** 761.
"Drought." **3 ed.** 761.
"Miss Kenny's Marriage." **3 ed.** 761.
"Panama Gold." **3.** 405; **4.** 288.
"Tropic Death." **3 ed.** 761; **4.** 288.
"The Vampire Bat." **3.** 405.
"The Voodoo's Revenge." **3 ed.** 761.
"The Wharf Rats." **3.** 405.
"The White Snake." **3 ed.** 761; **4.** 288.
"The Yellow One." **3 ed.** 762.

MARTIN WALSER

"Die Gallistl'sche Krankheit." **5.** 338.
"A Runaway Horse." **5.** 339.

ROBERT WALSER

"The Battle of Sempach." **3 ed.** 762.
"Tobold." **3 ed.** 762.
"A Young Girl from Berlin." **3 ed.** 762.

JOHN H. WALSH

"Mr. Poudicherry and the Smugglers." **2.** 288.

WAN ZHI [CHEN MAIPING]

"Open Terrain." **4.** 288.

WANG CHEN-HO

"Hsiao Lin in Taipei." **2.** 288.
"An Oxcart for Dowry." **2.** 288.
"A Story of Three Marriages." **2.** 288.
"That Year, That Winter." **2.** 288.

WANG T'O

"Aunt Chin-shui." **2.** 288.

EUNICE WARD

"Ah Gin." **2.** 288; **3.** 405.

SYLVIA TOWNSEND WARNER

"But at the Stroke of Midnight." **2.** 288.
"A Dressmaker." **5.** 339.
"A Kitchen Knife." **4.** 288.
"The Mother." **5.** 339.
"The Mother Tongue." **5.** 339.
"On Living for Others." **5.** 339.
"The One and the Other." **4.** 288.
"Poor Mary." **4.** 288.
"The Three Cats." **5.** 339.
"Total Loss." **5.** 339.
"A View of Exmoor." **2.** 289.
"Winter in the Air." **5.** 339.

ROBERT PENN WARREN

"Blackberry Winter." **3 ed.** 762; **1.** 214; **2.** 289; **3.** 405; **4.** 288.
"A Christian Education." **3 ed.** 762.
"Christmas Gift." **2.** 289.
"The Circus in the Attic." **3 ed.** 762–63; **2.** 289; **4.** 288.
"Goodwood Comes Back." **3.** 405.
"Her Own People." **3 ed.** 763; **2.** 289.
"The Life and Work of Professor Roy Millen." **3 ed.** 763.
"The Patented Gate and the Mean Hamburger." **3 ed.** 763; **2.** 289; **3.** 405; **4.** 288.
"Prime Leaf." **3 ed.** 763; **2.** 289; **4.** 289.
"Testament of Flood." **2.** 289.
"The Unvexed Isles." **3 ed.** 763; **4.** 289.
"When the Light Gets Green." **3 ed.** 763; **1.** 214; **2.** 289.

PRICE WARUNG [WILLIAM ASTLEY]

"The Bullet of the Fated Ten." **1.** 214.
"Captain Maconochie's 'Bounty for Crime.'" **1.** 214.
"The Consequences of Cunliffe's Crime." **1.** 214.
"Dictionary Ned." **1.** 214.
"Parson Ford's Confession." **1.** 214.
"The Pure Merinoes' Ball." **1.** 214.

FRANK WATERS

"Easy Meat." **3 ed.** 763.

GRANT WATSON

"Man and Brute." **3.** 406.
"Out There." **3.** 406.

SHEILA WATSON

"Antigone." **5.** 339.

EVELYN WAUGH

"The Balance." **3.** 406.
"Bella Fleace Gave a Party." **1.** 214.
"Compassion." **3 ed.** 763.
"Incident in Azamia." **5.** 339.
"Love Among the Ruins." **4.** 289.
"Mr. Loveday's Little Outing." **3 ed.** 763.
"Out of Depth." **5.** 339.
"Ryder by Gaslight." **4.** 289.
"Scott-King's Modern Europe." **2.** 289.
"The Tutor's Tale." **3.** 406.
"Work Suspended." **2.** 289.

GORDON WEAVER

"The Parts of Speech." **5.** 340.

BEATRICE POTTER WEBB

"Pages from a Work-Girl's Diary." **1.** 214.

FRANK WEDEKIND

"The Burning of Egliswyl." **3 ed.** 764.
"The Hoary Suitor." **3 ed.** 764.
"Princess Russalka." **3 ed.** 764.
"The Scapegoat." **3 ed.** 764.

MASON LOCKE WEEMS

"Good News for the Devil." **3.** 406.

JEROME WEIDMAN

"The Horse That Could Whistle Dixie." **3 ed.** 764.

STANLEY G. WEINBAUM

"The Black Flame." **5.** 340.
"Dawn of Flame." **3.** 406; **5.** 340.
"Flight on Titan." **3.** 406.
"A Martian Odyssey." **3.** 406.
"Parasite Planet." **3.** 406.
"Pygmalion's Spectacles." **3.** 406.

STANLEY G. WEINBAUM and RALPH MILNE FARLEY

"Smothered Seas." **3.** 406.

GÜNTHER WEISENBORN

"Two Men." **3 ed.** 764.

DENTON WELCH

"At Sea." **3 ed.** 764.
"The Barn." **3 ed.** 764.
"Brave and Cruel." **3 ed.** 764.
"The Coffin on the Hill." **3 ed.** 764.
"The Diamond Badge." **3 ed.** 764.
"The Earth's Crust." **3 ed.** 764.
"Evergreen Seaton-Leverett." **3 ed.** 765.
"The Fire in the Wood." **3 ed.** 765.
"A Fragment of a Life Story." **3 ed.** 765.
"The Hateful Word." **3 ed.** 765.
"The Judas Tree." **3 ed.** 765.
"Leaves from a Young Person's Notebook." **3 ed.** 765.
"Memories of a Vanished Period." **3 ed.** 765.
"Narcissus Bay." **3 ed.** 765.
"A Party." **3 ed.** 765.
"A Picture in the Snow." **3 ed.** 765.
"Sickert at St. Peter's." **3 ed.** 765.
"The Trout Stream." **3 ed.** 765.
"When I Was Thirteen." **3 ed.** 765.

H. G. WELLS

"Aepyornis Island." **2.** 290; **3.** 407.
"The Beautiful Suit." **3 ed.** 765; **4.** 289.
"Chronic Argonauts." **3 ed.** 766.
"The Cone." **2.** 290; **3.** 407.
"The Country of the Blind." **3 ed.** 766; **2.** 290; **3.** 407; **4.** 289.
"The Crystal Egg." **2.** 290.
"A Deal in Ostriches." **2.** 290; **3.** 407.
"The Desert Daisy." **3 ed.** 766; **4.** 289.
"The Diamond Maker." **2.** 290.
"The Door in the Wall." **3 ed.** 766; **2.** 290; **4.** 289; **5.** 340.
"A Dream of Armageddon." **4.** 289.
"The Empire of Ants." **3 ed.** 766.
"The Flowering of the Strange Orchid." **3 ed.** 766; **2.** 290; **3.** 407.
"The Flying Man." **2.** 290; **3.** 407.
"The Grisly Folks." **4.** 289.
"In the Abyss." **5.** 340.
"In the Avu Observatory." **3.** 407.
"The Inexperienced Ghost." **4.** 289.
"The Lord of the Dynamos." **3 ed.** 766; **2.** 290; **3.** 407; **4.** 289.
"The Man Who Could Work Miracles." **3 ed.** 766; **2.** 290; **4.** 289.
"Miss Winchelsea's Heart." **2.** 290.
"Mr. Skelmersdale in Fairyland." **2.** 290.

"The New Accelerator." **2.** 290; **4.** 290.
"The Plattner Story." **3 ed.** 766; **4.** 290.
"The Purple Pileus." **2.** 291.
"The Rajah's Treasure." **5.** 340.
"The Remarkable Case of Davidson's Eyes." **3 ed.** 766; **2.** 291; **4.** 290.
"A Slip Under the Microscope." **3 ed.** 766.
"The Spoils of Mr. Blandish." **5.** 340.
"The Star." **3 ed.** 766; **1.** 215; **2.** 291; **3.** 407; **4.** 290.
"The Stolen Bacillus." **3 ed.** 767; **2.** 291; **3.** 407; **4.** 290.
"The Stolen Body." **3 ed.** 767.
"A Story of the Days to Come." **3 ed.** 767; **2.** 291; **3.** 407; **4.** 290; **5.** 340.
"The Story of the Last Trump." **2.** 291; **5.** 340.
"A Story of the Stone Age." **3 ed.** 767; **4.** 290.
"Through a Window." **5.** 340.
"The Time Machine." **3 ed.** 767; **1.** 215; **2.** 291–92; **3.** 407; **4.** 290; **5.** 340.
"The Triumph of a Taxidermist." **3 ed.** 767; **2.** 292; **3.** 408.
"Under the Knife." **3 ed.** 767.
"The Wild Asses of the Devil." **2.** 292; **5.** 341.

EUDORA WELTY

"Asphodel." **3 ed.** 767; **2.** 292; **3.** 408; **4.** 290; **5.** 341.
"At the Landing." **3 ed.** 767–68; **2.** 292; **3.** 408; **4.** 290; **5.** 341.
"The Bride of Innisfallen." **3 ed.** 768; **2.** 292; **3.** 408; **4.** 290.
"The Burning." **3 ed.** 768; **2.** 292; **4.** 291; **5.** 341.
"Circe." **3 ed.** 768; **1.** 215; **2.** 292; **4.** 291.
"Clytie." **3 ed.** 768–69; **1.** 215; **3.** 408; **4.** 291.
"A Curtain of Green." **3 ed.** 769; **1.** 215; **2.** 292; **3.** 408; **4.** 291.
"Death of a Traveling Salesman." **3 ed.** 769; **1.** 215; **2.** 292–93; **3.** 408; **4.** 291; **5.** 341.
"The Delta Cousins." **2.** 293.
"The Demonstrators." **3 ed.** 769; **2.** 293.
"First Love." **3 ed.** 769–70; **1.** 215; **2.** 293; **3.** 408; **5.** 341.
"Flowers for Marjorie." **3 ed.** 770; **2.** 293; **3.** 408; **4.** 291.
"Going to Naples." **3 ed.** 770; **2.** 293.
"Hello and Goodbye." **2.** 293.
"The Hitch-Hikers." **3 ed.** 770; **3.** 408; **4.** 291.
"Ida M'Toy." **3 ed.** 770.
"June Recital." **3 ed.** 770; **1.** 215; **2.** 293; **3.** 409; **4.** 291; **5.** 341.
"Keela, the Outcast Indian Maiden." **3 ed.** 770–71; **1.** 215; **2.** 293; **3.** 409; **4.** 291.
"The Key." **3 ed.** 771; **1.** 215; **2.** 293; **3.** 409; **4.** 291.
"Kin." **3 ed.** 771; **2.** 293; **4.** 291; **5.** 341.
"Ladies in Spring." **3 ed.** 771; **2.** 293.
"Lily Daw and the Three Ladies." **3 ed.** 771; **2.** 294; **3.** 409; **5.** 341.
"Livvie." **3 ed.** 771; **1.** 216; **2.** 294; **3.** 409; **4.** 291; **5.** 341.
"The Lucky Stone." **2.** 294.
"A Memory." **3 ed.** 772; **1.** 216; **2.** 294; **3.** 409.
"Moon Lake." **3 ed.** 772; **1.** 216; **2.** 294; **3.** 409; **4.** 291; **5.** 341.
"Music from Spain." **3 ed.** 772; **1.** 216; **2.** 294; **3.** 409.
"No Place for You, My Love." **3 ed.** 772; **2.** 294; **3.** 409.
"Old Mr. Marblehall." **3 ed.** 772; **1.** 216; **5.** 341.
"Petrified Man." **3 ed.** 773; **1.** 216; **2.** 294; **3.** 409; **4.** 291.
"A Piece of News." **3 ed.** 773; **1.** 216; **2.** 294.
"Powerhouse." **3 ed.** 773–74; **1.** 216; **2.** 294; **3.** 410; **5.** 342.
"The Purple Hat." **3 ed.** 774; **2.** 295; **5.** 342.
"Shower of Gold." **3 ed.** 774; **1.** 216; **2.** 295; **4.** 292.
"Sir Rabbit." **3 ed.** 774; **1.** 216; **2.** 295; **3.** 410; **4.** 292; **5.** 342.
"A Sketching Trip." **5.** 342.
"A Still Moment." **3 ed.** 774–75; **2.** 295; **3.** 410; **4.** 292; **5.** 342.
"A Visit of Charity." **3 ed.** 775; **3.** 410.
"The Wanderers." **3 ed.** 775; **1.** 216; **2.** 295; **3.** 410; **4.** 292.
"Where Is the Voice Coming From?" **3 ed.** 775; **4.** 292.
"The Whistle." **3 ed.** 775.
"The Whole World Knows." **3 ed.** 775; **1.** 217; **2.** 295; **3.** 410.

"Why I Live at the P.O." **3 ed.** 775–76; **1.** 217; **3.** 410; **4.** 292.
"The Wide Net." **3 ed.** 776; **1.** 217; **2.** 295; **3.** 410; **4.** 292; **5.** 342.
"The Winds." **3 ed.** 776; **2.** 295; **5.** 342.
"A Worn Path." **3 ed.** 776–77; **1.** 217; **2.** 295; **3.** 410; **4.** 292; **5.** 342.

ALBERT WENDT

"The Pint-Sized Devil on a Thoroughbred." **4.** 292.
"A Resurrection." **4.** 292.

FRANZ WERFEL

"Not the Murderer but the Murdered Is Guilty." **3 ed.** 777.

GLENWAY WESCOTT

"Adolescence." **3 ed.** 777.
"The Babe's Bed." **3 ed.** 777.
"The Dove Came Down." **3 ed.** 777.
"The Dream of Audubon." **3 ed.** 777.
"The Frenchman Six Feet Three." **3 ed.** 777.
"A Guilty Woman." **3 ed.** 777.
"Hurt Feelings." **3 ed.** 777.
"In a Thicket." **3 ed.** 777.
"Like a Lover." **3 ed.** 777.
"The Pilgrim Hawk." **3 ed.** 778; **5.** 342.
"Prohibition." **3 ed.** 778.
"The Rescuer." **3 ed.** 778.
"The Runaway." **3 ed.** 778.
"The Sailor." **3 ed.** 778.
"The Sight of a Dead Body." **3 ed.** 778.
"The Wedding March." **3 ed.** 778.
"The Whistling Swan." **3 ed.** 778.

ANTHONY C. WEST

"Narcissus unto Echo." **4.** 292.

DOROTHY WEST

"The Typewriter." **2.** 296.
"An Unimportant Man." **2.** 296.

JESSAMYN WEST

"Horace Chooney, M.D." **3 ed.** 778.
"Love, Death, and the Ladies' Drill Team." **3 ed.** 778.
"Mr. Cornelius, I Love You." **3 ed.** 779.
"Shivaree Before Breakfast." **3 ed.** 779.
"Sixteen." **3 ed.** 779.

NATHANAEL WEST

"Business Deal." **3 ed.** 779.
"A Cool Million." **3 ed.** 779–80; **1.** 217; **2.** 296; **3.** 411; **4.** 293; **5.** 342.
"The Dream Life of Balso Snell." **3 ed.** 780; **1.** 217; **2.** 296; **3.** 411; **4.** 293; **5.** 343.
"Miss Lonelyhearts." **3 ed.** 781–82; **1.** 217; **2.** 296; **3.** 411; **4.** 293; **5.** 343.
"The Sun, the Lady, and the Gas Station." **4.** 293.

REBECCA WEST

"The Abiding Vision." **4.** 293.
"Life Sentence." **4.** 293.
"The Salt of the Earth." **3.** 411; **4.** 293.
"There Is No Conversation." **4.** 293.

WALLACE WEST

"The Last Man." **1.** 217.
"The Phantom Dictator." **1.** 217.
"Sculptors of Life." **3.** 411.

A. B. WESTLAND

"A Chinese Misalliance." **2.** 296.

JOZEF WEYSSENHOFF

"Under the Thunderbolts." **3 ed.** 782.

EDITH WHARTON

"After Holbein." **3 ed.** 783; **1.** 218.
"Afterward." **2.** 296; **4.** 293.
"All Souls." **3 ed.** 783; **2.** 296.
"The Angel at the Grave." **5.** 343.
"Autre Temps." **3 ed.** 783; **1.** 218; **3.** 411.
"Beatrice Palmato." **1.** 218; **2.** 296.
"Bewitched." **3 ed.** 783; **1.** 218; **2.** 296.
"The Blond Beast." **3 ed.** 783; **1.** 218.
"Bunner Sisters." **3 ed.** 783; **1.** 218; **2.** 296.
"The Choice." **1.** 218.
"Cold Green-house." **1.** 218.
"Ethan Frome." **3 ed.** 783–84; **1.** 218; **2.** 297; **3.** 411.
"Expiation." **4.** 293.
"The Eyes." **3 ed.** 784; **1.** 218; **2.** 297; **3.** 411; **4.** 293.

"False Dawn." **3 ed.** 784.
"The Fullness of Life." **3 ed.** 784; **1.** 218; **3.** 412; **4.** 294.
"Her Son." **3 ed.** 784.
"The Hermit and the Wild Woman." **3.** 412.
"His Father's Son." **3 ed.** 784; **1.** 218.
"Joy in the House." **3.** 412.
"Kerfol." **3 ed.** 784; **4.** 294.
"The Lady's Maid's Bell." **4.** 294.
"The Lamp of Psyche." **3.** 412.
"The Last Asset." **1.** 219.
"The Legend." **1.** 219.
"The Letters." **3 ed.** 785; **1.** 219; **3.** 412.
"Life and I." **3 ed.** 785.
"The Line of Least Resistance." **3.** 412.
"The Long Run." **3 ed.** 785; **3.** 412.
"Madame de Treymes." **1.** 219.
"Miss Mary Pask." **3 ed.** 785; **2.** 297; **4.** 294.
"The Mission of Jane." **3 ed.** 785; **2.** 297; **3.** 412.
"Mr. Jones." **2.** 297.
"Mrs. Manstey's View." **3 ed.** 785; **1.** 219.
"The Moving Finger." **2.** 297.
"The Muse's Tragedy." **1.** 219.
"New Year's Day." **2.** 297.
"The Other Two." **3 ed.** 785; **1.** 219; **3.** 412.
"The Pelican." **4.** 294.
"Pomegranate Seeds." **3 ed.** 785; **3.** 412.
"The Pot-Boiler." **3 ed.** 785.
"The Pretext." **3 ed.** 785.
"The Quicksand." **3.** 412.
"The Reckoning." **3 ed.** 785; **3.** 412.
"The Recovery." **3 ed.** 785.
"Roman Fever." **3 ed.** 785; **2.** 297; **3.** 412; **4.** 294; **5.** 343.
"Souls Belated." **3.** 412.
"Summer." **3 ed.** 786; **1.** 219.
"The Triumph of Night." **3 ed.** 786; **2.** 297.
"Twilight Sleep." **5.** 343.
"The Valley of Childish Things, and Other Emblems." **1.** 219; **2.** 297; **3.** 413.
"Xingu." **3 ed.** 786; **1.** 219; **3.** 413.

J. D. WHELPLEY

"The Atoms of Chladni." **3 ed.** 786.

CECIL B. WHITE

"The Retreat to Mars." **3.** 413.

E. B. WHITE

"Child's Play." **3.** 413.
"The Decline of Sport." **3 ed.** 786.
"The Door." **3 ed.** 786.
"The Hotel of the Total Stranger." **3 ed.** 786.
"The Morning of the Day They Did It." **3 ed.** 786; **3.** 413.
"The Second Tree from the Corner." **3 ed.** 786; **1.** 219; **3.** 413.

J. C. WHITE

"The Miracle of the Thunder God." **2.** 297.

PATRICK WHITE

"Being Kind to Titina." **3 ed.** 786; **1.** 219; **2.** 297; **3.** 413.
"A Cheery Soul." **3 ed.** 787; **1.** 219; **2.** 297; **3.** 413.
"Clay." **3 ed.** 787; **1.** 219; **2.** 297; **5.** 343.
"The Cockatoos." **3 ed.** 787; **2.** 298; **3.** 413.
"Cocotte." **1.** 220.
"Dead Roses." **3 ed.** 787; **1.** 220; **2.** 298; **3.** 413; **5.** 343.
"Down at the Dump." **3 ed.** 787; **1.** 220; **2.** 298; **3.** 413.
"The Evening at Sissy Kamara's." **3 ed.** 787; **1.** 220; **2.** 298; **3.** 413.
"Fête Galante." **2.** 298.
"Five-Twenty." **3 ed.** 787; **3.** 414.
"The Full Belly." **3 ed.** 787; **2.** 298; **3.** 414.
"A Glass of Tea." **1.** 220; **2.** 298.
"The Letters." **3 ed.** 787; **1.** 220; **2.** 298.
"Miss Slattery and Her Demon Lover." **3 ed.** 787; **1.** 220; **2.** 298.
"The Night the Prowler." **3 ed.** 787; **2.** 298; **3.** 414.
"Sicilian Vespers." **3 ed.** 787; **2.** 298; **3.** 414.
"The Twitching Colonel." **1.** 220; **3.** 414.
"Willy-Wagtail by Moonlight." **3 ed.** 788; **1.** 220; **2.** 298.
"The Woman Who Wasn't Allowed to Keep Cats." **3 ed.** 788; **1.** 220; **2.** 298; **3.** 414.

"A Woman's Hand." **3 ed.** 788; **2.** 298; **3.** 414; **5.** 343.

WILLIAM ALLEN WHITE

"The Mercy of Death." **3.** 414.
"A Most Lamentable Comedy." **3.** 414.
"The Real Issue." **1.** 220.
"A Social Rectangle." **3.** 414.
"The Story of Aqua Pura." **1.** 220.
"The Story of the Highlands." **1.** 220.
"The Tremolo Stop." **3.** 414.
"A Victory of the People." **3.** 414.

ROBERT WHITEHAND

"American Nocturne." **3 ed.** 788.

WALT[ER] WHITMAN

"The Half-Breed" [originally "Arrow-Tip"]. **2.** 298.

RUDY WIEBE

"Bluecoats on the Sacred Hill of the Wild Peas." **3.** 414.
"The Naming of Albert Johnson." **3.** 414.
"Where Is the Voice Coming From?" **2.** 299; **3.** 415; **4.** 294; **5.** 343.

ERNST WIECHERT

"Der Hauptmann von Kapernaum." **3 ed.** 788.
"Der Todeskandidat." **3 ed.** 788.

ALLEN WIER

"Things About to Disappear." **2.** 299; **3.** 415.

KAZIMIERZ WIERZYNSKI

"Patrol." **3 ed.** 788.
"World Frontiers." **3 ed.** 788.

ELIE WIESEL

"The Wandering Jew." **3.** 415.

MARÍA WIESSE

"El forastero." **3 ed.** 788.

L. WARREN WIGMORE

"The Revenge of Chin Chow." **2.** 299.

ELLEN WILBUR

"Wind and Birds and Human Voices." **4.** 294.

RICHARD WILBUR

"A Game of Catch." **1.** 220.

OSCAR WILDE

"The Birthday of the Infanta." **1.** 220–21; **4.** 294; **5.** 344.
"The Canterville Ghost." **3 ed.** 788; **1.** 221; **4.** 294; **5.** 344.
"The Devoted Friend." **3 ed.** 788; **1.** 221; **5.** 344.
"The Fisherman and His Soul." **3 ed.** 788; **1.** 221.
"The Happy Prince." **3 ed.** 789; **1.** 221; **2.** 299; **5.** 344.
"A House of Pomegranates." **1.** 221.
"Lord Arthur Savile's Crime." **3 ed.** 789; **1.** 221; **3.** 415; **4.** 294; **5.** 344.
"The Model Millionaires." **1.** 221; **4.** 294.
"The Nightingale and the Rose." **3 ed.** 789; **1.** 221.
"The Portrait of Mr. W. H." **3 ed.** 789; **1.** 221; **4.** 295; **5.** 344.
"The Remarkable Rocket." **1.** 221–22.
"The Selfish Giant." **3 ed.** 789; **1.** 222; **2.** 299.
"The Sphinx Without a Secret" [originally "Lady Alroy"]. **1.** 222.
"The Star-Child." **3 ed.** 789; **1.** 222; **5.** 344.
"The Young King." **3 ed.** 789; **1.** 222.

MICHAEL WILDING

"Hector and Freddie." **2.** 299; **3.** 415.
"The Phallic Forest." **3.** 415.
"The Sybarites." **1.** 222.

HUGH WILEY

"In Chinatown." **3.** 415.

KATE WILHELM

"April Fools' Day Forever." **3.** 415.
"The Funeral." **2.** 299.

CHARLES WILLARD

"The Power and the Glory." **5.** 344.

HELEN MARIA WILLIAMS

"The History of Perourou; or, The Bellows-Maker." **1.** 222.

JESSE LYNCH WILLIAMS

"The New Reporter." **5.** 344.
"The Old Reporter." **5.** 344.

JOHN A. WILLIAMS

"Son in the Afternoon." **1.** 222; **3.** 415.

JOY WILLIAMS

"Taking Care." **1.** 222; **5.** 344.

TENNESSEE WILLIAMS [THOMAS LANIER WILLIAMS]

"The Accent of a Coming Foot." **5.** 344.
"The Angel in the Alcove." **3 ed.** 789; **2.** 299; **5.** 345.
"Big Black: A Mississippi Idyll." **5.** 345.
"The Coming of Something to the Widow Holly." **5.** 345.
"Completed." **5.** 345.
"The Dark Room." **5.** 345.
"Desire and the Black Masseur." **3 ed.** 789; **1.** 223; **2.** 300; **5.** 345.
"The Field of Blue Children." **3 ed.** 789; **5.** 345.
"The Gift of an Apple." **5.** 345.
"Hard Candy." **2.** 300; **5.** 345.
"The Important Thing." **3 ed.** 789; **5.** 345.
"In Memory of an Aristocrat." **5.** 345.
"The Kingdom of Earth." **3 ed.** 790; **5.** 345.
"Knight's Quest." **3 ed.** 790; **2.** 300.
"A Lady's Beaded Bag." **5.** 345.
"The Malediction." **3 ed.** 790; **5.** 345.
"Mama's Old Stucco House." **2.** 300.
"Man Bring This Up Road." **3 ed.** 790.
"Miss Coynte of Greene." **5.** 345.
"The Mysteries of Joy Rio." **3 ed.** 790; **2.** 300; **5.** 345.
"Night of the Iguana." **3 ed.** 790; **2.** 300.
"One Arm." **3 ed.** 790; **2.** 300; **5.** 345.
"Oriflamme." **5.** 345.
"Portrait of a Girl in Glass." **3 ed.** 790; **5.** 346.
"The Resemblance Between a Violin Case and a Coffin." **3 ed.** 790; **2.** 300; **5.** 346.
"The Roman Spring of Mrs. Stone." **2.** 300.
"Rubio y Morena." **3 ed.** 790; **2.** 300.
"Sabbatha and Solitude." **5.** 346.
"Something by Tolstoi." **5.** 346.
"Ten Minute Stop." **5.** 346.
"Three Players of a Summer Game." **3 ed.** 790; **5.** 346.
"Twenty-Seven Wagons Full of Cotton." **5.** 346.
"Two on a Party." **3 ed.** 790; **2.** 300; **5.** 346.
"The Vengeance of Nitocris." **5.** 346.
"The Vine." **3 ed.** 790; **5.** 346.
"The Yellow Bird." **3 ed.** 790–91; **2.** 300.

THOMAS WILLIAMS

"Goose Pond." **3 ed.** 791.

WILLIAM CARLOS WILLIAMS

"The Accident." **3 ed.** 791; **2.** 300.
"The Burden of Loveliness." **3 ed.** 791.
"The Cold World." **3 ed.** 791.
"Comedy Entombed: 1930." **3 ed.** 791.
"Country Rain." **4.** 295.
"Danse Pseudomacabre." **3 ed.** 791.
"The Dawn of Another Day." **3 ed.** 791.
"The Descendant of Kings." **3 ed.** 791.
"A Face of Stone." **3 ed.** 791; **3.** 416.
"The Farmers' Daughters." **3 ed.** 791; **2.** 300.
"The Girl with a Pimply Face." **3 ed.** 792; **2.** 300.
"The Great American Novel." **3 ed.** 792.
"Jean Beicke." **3 ed.** 792; **3.** 416; **5.** 346.
"The Knife of the Times." **3 ed.** 792; **3.** 416.
"Life Along the Passaic River." **3 ed.** 792.
"Mind and Body." **3 ed.** 792; **4.** 295.
"A Night in June." **3 ed.** 792; **2.** 301; **3.** 416; **5.** 346.
"Old Doc Rivers." **3 ed.** 792.
"Pink and Blue." **3 ed.** 792.
"The Three Letters." **3 ed.** 792.
"The Use of Force." **3 ed.** 792–93; **1.** 223; **2.** 301; **3.** 416; **4.** 295; **5.** 346.
"The Venus." **3 ed.** 793; **2.** 301.

JACK WILLIAMSON

"Backlash." **5.** 346.
"Breakdown." **1.** 223; **3.** 416.
"Guinevere for Everybody." **3.** 416.
"Jamboree." **3.** 416.
"Non-Stop to Mars." **1.** 223.
"Star Bright." **1.** 223.
"With Folded Hands." **2.** 301; **4.** 295.

N[ATHANIEL] P[ARKER] WILLIS

"Kate Crediford." **4.** 295.
"Mabel Wynne." **4.** 295.

ANGUS WILSON

"A Bit Off the Map." **2.** 301; **4.** 295.
"Et Dona Ferentes." **3 ed.** 793; **4.** 295.
"Fresh-Air Fiend." **3 ed.** 793; **3.** 416; **4.** 295.
"Higher Standards." **2.** 301.
"A Little Companion." **2.** 301.
"More Friend Than Lodger." **4.** 295.
"Raspberry Jam." **3 ed.** 793; **3.** 416; **4.** 295; **5.** 347.
"Realpolitik." **3 ed.** 793; **3.** 417.
"Rex Imperator." **4.** 296.
"A Sad Fall." **4.** 296.
"Saturnalia." **4.** 296.
"A Story of Historical Interest." **4.** 296.
"Such Darling Dodos." **4.** 296.
"Ten Minutes to Twelve." **2.** 301; **4.** 296.
"Totentanz." **4.** 296.
"A Visit in Bad Taste." **4.** 296.
"What Do Hippos Eat?" **4.** 296.
"The Wrong Set." **4.** 296.

EDMUND WILSON

"After the Game." **3 ed.** 793.
"The Death of a Soldier." **3 ed.** 793.
"Ellen Terhune." **3 ed.** 794; **3.** 417; **4.** 296.
"Emily in Hades." **3 ed.** 794.
"Galahad." **3 ed.** 794.
"Glimpses of Wilbur Flick." **3 ed.** 794; **3.** 417; **4.** 296.
"Lieutenant Franklin." **3 ed.** 794.
"The Man in the Mirror." **3 ed.** 794.
"The Man Who Shot Snapping Turtles." **3 ed.** 794; **3.** 417; **4.** 296.
"The Men from Rumpelmayer's." **3 ed.** 794; **4.** 296.
"The Messiah at the Seder." **3 ed.** 794.
"The Millhollands and Their Damned Soul." **3 ed.** 794.
"Mr. and Mrs. Blackburn at Home." **3 ed.** 794; **3.** 417; **4.** 296.
"The Oppressor." **3 ed.** 794.
"The Princess with the Golden Hair." **3 ed.** 794; **3.** 417; **4.** 296.
"Reunion." **3 ed.** 794.
"Through the Abruzzi with Mattie and Harriet." **3 ed.** 794.

ETHEL WILSON

"God Helps the Young Fisherman." **3 ed.** 795.
"Haply the Soul of My Grandmother." **5.** 347.
"Hurry, Hurry." **3 ed.** 795.
"Lilly's Story." **5.** 347.
"Mrs. Golightly and the First Convention." **3 ed.** 795.
"On Nimpish Lake." **3 ed.** 795.
"Reflections in a Pool." **5.** 347.
"Tuesday and Wednesday." **5.** 347.
"We Have to Sit Opposite." **5.** 347.
"Winter." **5.** 347.

PHILLIP WILSON

"One World." **3 ed.** 795.

RICHARD WILSON

"The Eight Billion." **4.** 297.

ROBLEY WILSON

"The Apple." **3 ed.** 795; **4.** 297.
"Business. 1947." **4.** 297.
"Loving a Fat Girl." **4.** 297.
"Paint." **4.** 297.
"Saying Goodbye to the President." **4.** 297.
"Thief." **4.** 297.

SLOAN WILSON

"A Letter of Admonition." **3 ed.** 795.

THOMAS WILSON

"The Face of the Enemy." **5.** 347.

ANNE GOODWIN WINSLOW

"Allan Percy's Son." **3 ed.** 795.
"Count Robert's Folly." **3 ed.** 795.
"A Winter in Geneva." **3 ed.** 795.

YVOR WINTERS

"The Brink of Darkness." **3 ed.** 796; **2.** 301.

THEODORE WINTHROP

"Saccharissa Mellasys." **3 ed.** 796.

OWEN WISTER

"Absalom and Moulting Pelican." **3.** 417.
"Bad Medicine." **3.** 417.
"Balaam and Pedro." **3.** 417; **4.** 297.
"Captain Quid." **3.** 417.
"The Drake Who Had Means of His Own." **3.** 417.
"Extra Dry." **3.** 417.
"The General's Bluff." **3.** 417.
"The Gift Horse." **3 ed.** 796.
"Hank's Woman." **3 ed.** 796; **3.** 417; **4.** 297.
"Happy-Teeth." **3.** 417.
"The Jimmy-John Boss." **3.** 418.
"Little Big Horn Medicine." **3.** 418.
"Lone Fountain." **3.** 418.
"Once Round the Clock." **3.** 418.
"Philosophy Four." **3 ed.** 796.
"A Pilgrim on the Gila." **3.** 418.
"The Promised Land." **3.** 418.
"The Right Honorable the Strawberries." **3.** 418; **4.** 297.
"Salvation Gap." **3.** 418.
"The Second Missouri Compromise." **3.** 418.
"Sharon's Choice." **3.** 418.
"Skip to My Lou." **3.** 418.
"Specimen Jones." **3.** 418.
"Spit-Cat Creek." **3.** 418.
"La Tinaja Bonita." **3.** 418.
"Where It Was." **3.** 418.

PUNYAKANTE WIZENAIKE

"My Daughter's Wedding." **1.** 223.

P. G. WODEHOUSE

"Bill the Bloodhound." **3.** 419.
"Chester Forgets Himself." **3.** 419.
"Extricating Young Gussie." **3.** 419.
"It's a Long Way Back to Mother's Knee." **3.** 419.
"The Nodder." **4.** 297.
"Rodney Has a Relapse." **3.** 419.

GABRIELE WOHMANN

"The Boxing Match." **1.** 223.
"Hamster, Hamster!" **1.** 223.
"Internal Excuse." **1.** 223.
"The Sailing Regatta." **1.** 224.
"A Scandal for the Park." **1.** 224.
"Seaway." **1.** 224.
"Sunday at the Kreisands'." **1.** 224.
"The Truth About Us." **1.** 224.

CHRISTA WOLF

"Change of Perspective." **5.** 347.
"New Memoirs of a Tomcat." **5.** 347.
"Selbstversuch." **3.** 419.
"Unter den Linden." **3.** 419; **5.** 347.

GENE WOLFE

"Alien Stones." **4.** 297.
"Beautyland." **4.** 297.
"The Changeling." **4.** 298.
"The Doctor of Death Island." **4.** 298.
"The Eyeflash Murders." **4.** 298.
"The Fifth Head of Cerberus." **4.** 298.
"Forlessen." **4.** 298.
"How I Lost the Second World War and Turned Back the German Invasion." **4.** 298.
"Seven American Nights." **4.** 298.
"A Story." **5.** 347.
"'A Story' by John V. Marsch." **4.** 298.
"Three Fingers." **4.** 298.
"Tracking Song." **4.** 298.
"V. R. T." **4.** 298.

THOMAS WOLFE

"An Angel on the Porch." **3.** 419.
"Boom Town." **3 ed.** 796.
"The Bums at Sunset." **3.** 419.
"Chickamauga." **3 ed.** 796; **3.** 419.
"Child by Tiger." **3 ed.** 796; **1.** 224; **4.** 298; **5.** 348.
"Circus at Dawn." **3 ed.** 796.
"The Company." **3 ed.** 796.
"Death, the Proud Brother." **3.** 419; **4.** 298.
"The Face of War." **3.** 419.
"The Far and the Near." **2.** 301.
"God's Lonely Man." **3 ed.** 796–97.
"In the Park." **3 ed.** 797.
"The Lion at Morning." **3 ed.** 797.

"The Lost Boy." **3 ed.** 797; **2.** 301; **3.** 419; **4.** 298.
"No Cure for It." **3 ed.** 797.
"No Door." **3 ed.** 797; **3.** 419; **4.** 299.
"A Note on Experts." **3 ed.** 797.
"Only the Dead Know Brooklyn." **3 ed.** 797; **4.** 299.
"The Party at Jack's." **3.** 420; **4.** 299.
"A Portrait of Bascom Hawke." **3 ed.** 797; **2.** 301.
"The Return of the Prodigal." **3 ed.** 797.
"The Sun and the Rain." **3.** 420.
"The Train and the City." **4.** 299.
"The Web of Earth." **3 ed.** 797–98; **1.** 224.

TOBIAS WOLFF

"In the Garden of the North American Martyrs." **5.** 348.

MRS. HENRY WOOD [ELLEN PRICE WOOD]

"A Curious Experience." **4.** 299.
"David Garth's Ghost." **4.** 299.
"David Garth's Night-Watch." **4.** 299.
"Reality or Delusion?" **4.** 299.
"The Surgeon's Daughter." **4.** 299.

BARBARA WOODS

"The Final Supper." **3.** 420.

DOUGLAS WOOLF

"Bank Day." **3.** 420; **5.** 348.

LEONARD WOOLF

"Pearls and Swine." **1.** 224.
"A Tale Told by Moonlight." **1.** 224.
"Three Jews." **1.** 224.
"The Two Brahmans." **1.** 224.

VIRGINIA WOOLF

"The Duchess and the Jeweller." **3 ed.** 798; **2.** 302.
"The Haunted House." **3 ed.** 798; **2.** 302.
"The Introduction." **2.** 302.
"Kew Gardens." **3 ed.** 798; **1.** 224; **3.** 420; **4.** 299; **5.** 348.
"The Lady in the Looking Glass." **3 ed.** 798; **2.** 302; **5.** 348.
"Lappin and Lapinova." **3 ed.** 798; **2.** 302; **4.** 299.
"The Legacy." **3 ed.** 798; **2.** 302.
"The Man Who Loved His Kind." **3 ed.** 798; **2.** 302.
"The Mark on the Wall." **3 ed.** 799; **2.** 302; **4.** 299; **5.** 348.
"Mrs. Dalloway in Bond Street." **1.** 224.
"Moments of Being." **3 ed.** 799; **2.** 302; **3.** 420; **4.** 299; **5.** 348.
"Monday or Tuesday." **3 ed.** 799; **3.** 420; **4.** 300.
"The New Dress." **3 ed.** 799; **1.** 224; **2.** 302; **3.** 420.
"The Searchlight." **2.** 302; **4.** 300.
"The Shooting Party." **3 ed.** 799; **2.** 302.
"A Society." **3 ed.** 799; **5.** 348.
"Solid Objects." **3 ed.** 799–800; **2.** 302.
"The String Quartet." **3 ed.** 800; **2.** 302.
"A Summing Up." **3 ed.** 800.
"Together and Apart." **2.** 303; **4.** 300.
"An Unwritten Novel." **3 ed.** 800; **4.** 300; **5.** 348.

CORNELL WOOLRICH [CORNELL GEORGE HOPLEY-WOOLRICH]

"The Light in the Window." **4.** 300.

CONSTANCE FENIMORE WOOLSON

"At the Château of Corinne." **3 ed.** 800; **5.** 348.
"Bro." **3 ed.** 800; **5.** 349.
"Castle Nowhere." **3 ed.** 800; **5.** 349.
"A Christmas Party." **3 ed.** 800.
"Dorothy." **3 ed.** 800.
"Felipa." **3 ed.** 800; **4.** 300; **5.** 349.
"A Florentine Experiment." **3 ed.** 800.
"The Front Yard." **3 ed.** 800.
"In the Cotton Country." **5.** 349.
"In Venice." **3 ed.** 800.
"Jeannette." **3 ed.** 800; **5.** 349.
"King David." **3 ed.** 801; **4.** 300.
"The Lady of Little Fishing." **3 ed.** 801; **5.** 349.
"Misery Landing." **3 ed.** 801.
"Miss Elisabetha." **3 ed.** 801; **5.** 349.
"Miss Grief." **5.** 349.
"Neptune's Shore." **3 ed.** 801.
"The Old Agency." **3 ed.** 801.
"Old Gardiston." **3 ed.** 801; **4.** 300; **5.** 349.
"Peter the Parson." **3 ed.** 801.

"The Pink Villa." **3 ed.** 801.
"Rodman the Keeper." **3 ed.** 801.
"St. Clair Flats." **3 ed.** 801; **5.** 349.
"Sister St. Luke." **3 ed.** 801; **5.** 349.
"The South Devil." **3 ed.** 801.
"The Street of the Hyacinth." **3 ed.** 801; **4.** 300; **5.** 349.
"A Transplanted Boy." **3 ed.** 801.
"Up in the Blue Ridge." **3 ed.** 801; **5.** 349.
"A Waitress." **3 ed.** 801.

EVERIL WORRELL

"The Canal." **5.** 349.

LAN WRIGHT

"And Earthly Power . . .." **3.** 420.

MARGARET WRIGHT

"Happy New Year." **3 ed.** 802.

RICHARD WRIGHT

"Big Black Good Man." **3 ed.** 802; **2.** 303.
"Big Boy Leaves Home." **3 ed.** 802; **1.** 225; **2.** 303; **3.** 420–21; **4.** 300; **5.** 350.
"Bright and Morning Star." **3 ed.** 802; **1.** 225; **2.** 303; **3.** 421; **4.** 300; **5.** 350.
"Down by the Riverside." **3 ed.** 802–03; **1.** 225; **2.** 303; **3.** 421; **5.** 350.
"Fire and Cloud." **3 ed.** 803; **1.** 225; **2.** 303; **3.** 421; **5.** 350.
"Long Black Song." **3 ed.** 803; **1.** 225; **2.** 303; **3.** 421; **4.** 300; **5.** 350.
"Man, God Ain't Like That." **3 ed.** 803; **2.** 303; **3.** 421.
"Man of All Work." **3 ed.** 803; **3.** 421.
"The Man Who Killed a Shadow." **3 ed.** 803; **2.** 303; **3.** 421.
"The Man Who Lived Underground." **3 ed.** 803–04; **1.** 225; **2.** 303; **3.** 421–22; **4.** 301; **5.** 350.
"The Man Who Was Almost a Man" [originally "Almos' a Man"]. **3 ed.** 804; **1.** 225; **2.** 303; **3.** 422; **4.** 301; **5.** 350.
"The Man Who Went to Chicago." **3.** 422.
"Silt." **3 ed.** 804.

S[YDNEY] FOWLER WRIGHT

"Automata." **3.** 422.
"The Choice." **3.** 422; **4.** 301.
"The Rat." **3.** 422.
"Rule." **3.** 422.

WU ZUXIANG [WU TSU-HSIANG]

"Fan Village." **1.** 225.
"Young Master Gets His Tonic." **4.** 301.

ELINOR WYLIE

"Venetian Glass Nephew." **3 ed.** 804.

IDA A. WYLIE

"Witches' Sabbath." **5.** 350.

JOHN WYNDHAM [JOHN BEYNON HARRIS]

"Consider Her Ways." **1.** 225; **3.** 422.
"The Lost Machine." **2.** 304.

XI RONG

"An Unexceptional Post." **5.** 350–51.

VELIMIR XLEBNIKOV

"Ka." **2.** 304.

YEHUDAH YAARI

"Between the Dog and the Shepherd." **3 ed.** 804.

YAMADA BIMYŌ

"The Butterfly." **3.** 422; **5.** 351.

HISAYE YAMAMOTO

"The Legend of Miss Sasagawara." **5.** 351.
"Seventeen Syllables." **5.** 351.
"Yoneko's Earthquake." **3.** 422.

YAMAMOTO MICHIKO

"The Man Who Cut the Grass." **5.** 351.

AUGUSTÍN YÁÑEZ

"Aserrín de muñecos." **5.** 351.
"Las avispas." **5.** 351.
"Baralipton." **3.** 423.
"Gota serena." **5.** 351.
"Música celestial." **5.** 351.
"Pasión y convalecencia." **5.** 351.

YAO XUEYIN

"Fuss over Forts." **5.** 351.
"Story of the Red Lantern." **5.** 352.

CHELSEA QUINN YARBRO

"False Dawn." **3.** 423.

ALEXANDR YASHIN

"Levers." **5.** 352.

YASHPAL [entire name]

"One Cigarette." **3.** 423.

RICHARD YATES

"B. A. R. Man." **4.** 301.
"The Best of Everything." **4.** 301.
"Doctor Jack-o-Lantern." **4.** 301.
"A Glutton for Punishment." **4.** 301.
"Jody Rolled the Bones." **4.** 301.
"Liars in Love." **4.** 301.
"No Pain Whatsoever." **4.** 301.
"Oh, Joseph, I'm So Tired." **4.** 302.
"A Really Good Jazz Piano." **1.** 225.
"A Wrestler with Sharks." **4.** 302.

WILLIAM BUTLER YEATS

"The Adoration of the Magi." **3.** 423.
"The Binding of the Hair." **3.** 423.
"Costello the Proud." **3.** 423.
"The Cradles of Gold." **3.** 423.
"The Crucifixion of the Outcast." **3.** 423.
"The Curse of the Fires and the Shadows." **3.** 423.
"The Death of Hanrahan." **3.** 423.
"Dhoya." **3.** 423.
"Hanrahan and Cathleen, the Daughter of Houlihan" [originally "Kathleen-ny-Hoolihan"]. **3.** 423.
"Hanrahan's Vision." **3.** 424.
"The Heart of Spring." **3.** 424.
"Michael Clancy, the Great Dhoul, and Death." **3.** 424.
"The Old Men of the Twilight" [originally "St. Patrick and the Pedants"]. **3.** 424.
"Out of the Rose." **3.** 424.
"Red Hanrahan's Curse." **3.** 424.
"Rosa Alchemica." **3.** 424.
"The Rose of Shadows" [originally "Those Who Live in the Storm"]. **3.** 424.
"Stories of Michael Robartes and His Friends." **3.** 424.
"The Tables of the Law." **3.** 424.
"The Twisting of the Rope." **3.** 424.
"Where There Is Nothing, There Is God." **3.** 424.
"The Wisdom of the King." **3.** 424.

YEH SHAO-CHUN [same as YE SHAOJUN or YE SHENGTAO]

"Autumn." **1.** 226.
"The English Professor." **1.** 226.
"Rice." **1.** 226.

ABRAHAM B. YEHOSHUA

"Continuing Silence of the Poet." **3 ed.** 804.
"The Day's Sleep." **5.** 352.
"Early in the Summer of 1970." **3.** 424.
"The Evening Voyage of Yatir." **5.** 352.
"Facing the Forest." **3 ed.** 804.
"Flood Tide." **3.** 424.
"Galia's Wedding." **5.** 352.
"A Long Summer's Day, His Despair, His Wife and His Daughter." **3 ed.** 804; **5.** 352.
"Missile Base 612." **5.** 352.
"Three Days and a Child." **3 ed.** 804.

ANZIA YEZIERSKA

"A Bed for the Night." **3.** 425.
"A Chair in Heaven." **3.** 425.
"Children of Loneliness." **3.** 425.
"Dreams and Dollars." **3.** 425.
"The Fat of the Land." **3.** 425.
"The Free Vacation House." **3.** 425.
"How I Found America." **3.** 425.
"Hunger." **3.** 425.
"The Lord Giveth." **3.** 425.
"Lost Beauty" [same as "Lost Beautifulness"]. **3 ed.** 804; **5.** 425.
"The Lower Depths of Upper Broadway." **3.** 425.
"The Miracle." **3.** 425.
"Mostly About Myself." **3.** 425.
"My Own People." **3.** 425.
"The Open Cage." **3.** 425.
"Soap and Water." **3.** 425.
"Take Up Your Bed and Walk." **3.** 425.
"To the Stars." **3.** 426.
"Where Lovers Dream." **3.** 426.
"Wings." **3.** 426.
"Wings and Hunger." **3 ed.** 804.

S. YIZHAR [YIZHAR SMILANSKY]

"Before Leaving." **3 ed.** 805.
"Ephraim Returns to the Lucerne." **3 ed.** 805.
"Habakuk." **5.** 352.
"Ha-Shabui." **3 ed.** 805.
"The Prisoner." **3 ed.** 805.
"The Runaway." **3 ed.** 805.

YOKOMITSU RIICHI

"After Picking Up a Blue Stone." **5.** 352.
"The Bird." **5.** 352.
"The Bridegroom's Reflections, or The Man Who Pursued Current Fashions." **3.** 426.
"The Child Who Was Laughed At." **5.** 352.
"The Defeated Husband" [originally "The Scroll of Love"]. **5.** 352.
"The Expressionist Actor." **5.** 352.
"A Face to Sorrow Over." **5.** 353.
"The Fly." **3.** 426.
"Ginseng and Sky." **5.** 353.
"Heads and Bellies." **5.** 353.
"Ideas of a Flower Garden." **5.** 353.
"The Machine." **2.** 304; **3.** 426; **5.** 353.
"The Pale Captain." **5.** 353.
"Smile." **5.** 353.
"Spring Riding in a Carriage." **5.** 353.
"Time." **5.** 353.

STARK YOUNG

"The Land of Juan de Dios." **4.** 302.
"The Light on the Hills." **4.** 302.
"Ora Pro Nobis." **4.** 302.
"The Passionate Road." **4.** 302.

MARGUERITE YOURCENAR

"Achilles." **4.** 302.
"Clytemnestra." **4.** 302.
"Lena." **4.** 302.
"Mary Magdalene." **4.** 302.
"Patroclus." **4.** 302.
"Sappho." **4.** 302.

YORDAN YOVKOV

"Shibil." **3 ed.** 805.

YU DAFU [YÜ TA-FU or CHAO LIEN]

"Late-Blooming Osmanthus." **1.** 226.
"The Past." **1.** 226.
"Silver-grey Death." **3 ed.** 101.
"Sinking." **3 ed.** 101; **1.** 226.
"Ts'ia Shih Chi." **1.** 226.

MATILDA YUFIT

"Husband and Wife." **3.** 426.

YUN T'ICH-CH'IAO

"The Story of a Laborer." **2.** 304.

AMADO YUZON

"Riddle." **5.** 353.

SAMUEL ARYEH ZAHLEN

"Salmah Mul 'Eder." **2.** 304.

SERGEI ZALYGIN

"By the Irtysh." **2.** 304.
"Witnesses." **2.** 304.

DUILIU ZAMFIRESCU

"To Coteşti." **4.** 302.

EVGENIZ ZAMJATIN [same as EVGENIĬ or EVGENIJ ZAMJATIN]

"Africa." **3.** 426.
"Alatyr." **3.** 426.
"The Cave." **1.** 226; **3.** 426.
"Comrade Čurygin Has the Floor." **3.** 426.
"The Eyes." **3.** 426.
"The Fisher of Men." **3.** 426.
"God." **3.** 427.
"The Islanders." **3.** 427.
"Mamaj." **3.** 427.
"The Nursery." **3.** 427.
"Old Russia." **3.** 427.
"Out in the Sticks." **3.** 427.
"The Provinces." **3.** 427.
"Scythians?" **3.** 427.
"A Story About the Most Important Thing." **3.** 427.
"X." **3.** 427.

ISRAEL ZANGWILL

"Anglicization." **3 ed.** 805.
"The Bearer of Burdens." **3 ed.** 805.
"The Big Bow Mystery." **3 ed.** 805.
"Chad Gadya." **3 ed.** 805.
"Cheating the Gallows." **3 ed.** 805.
"The Converts." **3 ed.** 805.
"The Diary of a *Meshummad*." **3 ed.** 805.
"A Double-Barrelled Ghost." **3 ed.** 805.
"Elijah's Goblet." **3 ed.** 805.
"The Gray Wig." **3 ed.** 806.
"The Hirelings." **3 ed.** 806.
"Holy Wedlock." **3 ed.** 806.
"I Become a Sorter." **3 ed.** 806.
"The Jewish Trinity." **3 ed.** 806.
"The Keeper of Conscience." **3 ed.** 806.
"The King of Schnorrers." **3 ed.** 806.
"The Land of Promise." **3 ed.** 806.
"The Memory Clearing House." **3 ed.** 806.
"Merely Mary Ann." **3 ed.** 806.
"Messiah and Miracle." **3 ed.** 806.
"The Model of Sorrow." **3 ed.** 806.
"Noah's Ark." **3 ed.** 806.
"An Odd Life." **3 ed.** 806.
"The Red Mark." **3 ed.** 807.
"The Sabbath Question in Sudminster." **3 ed.** 807.
"Samooborona." **3 ed.** 807.
"Satan Mekatrig." **3 ed.** 807.
"The Serio-Comic Governess." **3 ed.** 807.
"They That Walk in Darkness." **3 ed.** 807.
"To Die in Jerusalem." **3 ed.** 807.
"Transitional." **3 ed.** 807.
"A Yiddish 'Hamlet.'" **3 ed.** 807.

GABRIELA ZAPOLSKA

"The Cuckoo." **3 ed.** 807.
"Little Kitten." **3 ed.** 807.
"The Victim." **3 ed.** 807.

ROGER ZELAZNY

"And Call Me Conrad." **3.** 427.
"Divine Madness." **2.** 304.
"The Doors of His Face, The Lamps of His Mouth." **2.** 304; **3.** 427.
"The Engine at Heartspring's Center." **3.** 427; **4.** 303.
"The Eve of RUMOKO." **3.** 427.
"For a Breath I Tarry." **2.** 305; **3.** 428; **4.** 303.
"The Graveyard Heart." **3 ed.** 807.
"Home Is the Hangman." **3.** 428; **4.** 303.
"The Keys to December." **2.** 305.
"Kjwall'Kje'k'koothaill'kje'k." **3.** 428.
"Love Is an Imaginary Number." **2.** 305.
"The Man Who Loved the Faioli." **2.** 305; **3.** 428; **4.** 303.
"Passion Play." **2.** 305.
"A Rose for Ecclesiastes." **3 ed.** 807; **2.** 305; **3.** 428; **4.** 303.
"This Moment of the Storm." **3.** 428.

PAUL ZELEZA

"The Married Woman." **2.** 305.

ERACLIO ZEPEDA

"Benzulul." **1.** 226; **5.** 353.
"El Caguamo." **1.** 226.

R. ZERNOVA

"The Sunny Side." **3.** 428.

STEFAN ZEROMSKI

"The Crows." **3 ed.** 808.
"Doctor Piotr." **3 ed.** 808.
"Dusk." **3 ed.** 808.
"The Strong One." **3 ed.** 808.
"Whatever Happens, May It Strike Me." **3 ed.** 808.

ZHANG TIANYI

"A Subject Matter." **4.** 303.

ZHU LIN

"The Web." **4.** 303.

MARIYA ZHUKOVA

"Judgment of the Heart." **3.** 428.
"Self-Sacrifice." **3.** 428.

HEINRICH ZILLICH

"Der baltische Graf." **3 ed.** 808.

ÉMILE ÉDOUARD CHARLES ANTOINE ZOLA

"Adventures of Big Sidoine and Little Médéric." **2.** 305; **4.** 303.
"The Blacksmith." **4.** 303.

"Les coquillages de M. Chabre." **3 ed.** 808.
"A Puff of Wind." **4.** 303.

PAMELA ZOLINE

"The Heat Death of the Universe." **2.** 305; **3.** 428.

MIKHAIL MIKHAĬLOVICH ZOSHCHENKO

"Adventures of a Monkey." **3 ed.** 808.
"An Amusing Adventure." **3 ed.** 808.
"The Bathhouse." **5.** 353.
"Healing and Psychics." **3 ed.** 808.
"Kocherga." **3 ed.** 808.

HEINRICH ZSCHOKKE

"Das Abenteuer der Neujahrsnacht." **3 ed.** 808.
"The Dead Guest." **3 ed.** 809.
"Jonathan Frock." **3 ed.** 809.

CARL ZUCKMAYER

"The Walking Huts." **2.** 305.

ARNOLD ZWEIG

"The Beast." **3 ed.** 809.
"Coffee." **3 ed.** 809.
"The Crow." **3 ed.** 809.
"Departure." **3 ed.** 809.
"Early Spring." **3 ed.** 809.
"The Enemy." **3 ed.** 809.
"Episode." **3 ed.** 809.
"The Firing Range." **3 ed.** 809.
"Glance at Germany." **3 ed.** 809.
"Helbret Friedenbringer" [originally "Man of Peace"]. **3 ed.** 809.
"Little Hero." **3 ed.** 809.
"The Louse." **3 ed.** 809.
"Notes About a Family Named Klopfer." **3 ed.** 809.
"The Receipt." **3 ed.** 809.
"Revenge." **3 ed.** 809.
"Schönberg Quartet." **3 ed.** 810.
"A Spot in the Eye." **3 ed.** 810.
"Wasps." **3 ed.** 810.

STEFAN ZWEIG

"Die Augen des ewigen Bruders." **3 ed.** 810.
"Brennendes Geheimnis." **3 ed.** 810.
"Leporella." **3 ed.** 810; **1.** 226.
"Letter from an Unknown Woman." **3 ed.** 810; **1.** 226.
"Schachnovelle" [same as "The Royal Game" or "The Chess Game"]. **3 ed.** 810; **1.** 226.
"Twenty-Four Hours in a Woman's Life." **3 ed.** 810.
"Verwirrung des Gefühle." **3 ed.** 810.